Francis A. Drexel
LIBRARY

Books For College Libraries
Third Edition

Core Collection

THE ORGANIZATION AND ROLE OF

THE ARMY SERVICE FORCES

GENERAL BREHON B. SOMERVELL

UNITED STATES ARMY IN WORLD WAR II

The Army Service Forces

THE ORGANIZATION AND ROLE OF
THE ARMY SERVICE FORCES

by

John D. Millett

MILITARY INSTRVCTION

OFFICE OF THE CHIEF OF MILITARY HISTORY

DEPARTMENT OF THE ARMY

WASHINGTON, D. C., 1954

For sale by the Superintendent of Documents, U. S. Government Printing Office
Washington 25, D. C. - Price $4.25 (Cloth)

UNITED STATES ARMY IN WORLD WAR II
Kent Roberts Greenfield, General Editor

Advisory Committee
(As of 1 May 1953)

James P. Baxter
President, Williams College

Brig. Gen. Verdi B. Barnes
Army War College

John D. Hicks
University of California

Brig. Gen. Leonard J. Greeley
Industrial College of the Armed Forces

William T. Hutchinson
University of Chicago

Brig. Gen. Elwyn D. Post
Army Field Forces

S. L. A. Marshall
Detroit News

Col. Thomas D. Stamps
United States Military Academy

Charles S. Sydnor
Duke University

Col. C. E. Beauchamp
Command and General Staff College

Charles H. Taylor
Harvard University

Office of the Chief of Military History
Maj. Gen. Albert C. Smith, Chief*

Chief Historian	Kent Roberts Greenfield
Chief, War Histories Division	Col. G. G. O'Connor
Chief, Editorial and Publication Division	Col. B. A. Day
Chief, Editorial Branch	Joseph R. Friedman
Chief, Cartographic Branch	Wsevolod Aglaimoff
Chief, Photographic Branch	Maj. Arthur T. Lawry

*Maj. Gen. Orlando Ward was succeeded by General Smith on 1 February 1953.

. . . to Those Who Served

Foreword

If a reader expects to find a uniform pattern of treatment in the similarly upholstered volumes of this series, he will soon discover his error on reading this one. The author has chosen to relate the story of the Army Service Forces by concentrating on the activities of its organizer and commander, Lt. Gen. Brehon B. Somervell. As a staff officer to General Somervell during the war and one who was personally acquainted with his views, particularly on matters of organization, Professor Millett is exceptionally well qualified to deal with his subject in the manner he has chosen.

Some may complain that the biographical approach, with all the advantages it has in enabling an author to bring life and action into a narrative, has serious limitations when used in dealing with the history of an institution, such as the Army Service Forces. Others, familiar with the atmosphere in which the agency operated, may differ with the emphasis on this or that episode or problem that resulted from seeing its history mainly through the eyes of its wartime chief. Yet it must be recognized that the huge conglomeration of activities that constituted Army Service Forces had its chief element of unity, its one common denominator, in the driving energy and aggressive personality of its commander. This infused his organization with a sense of common purpose that many a smaller and functionally better integrated organization lacked. Necessarily General Somervell's impact on the various components of the Army Service Forces was uneven and certain problems received more of his attention than others. This was particularly true of organizational matters which General Somervell considered the key to operational success. The changes he sought to introduce were many and basic. As was to be expected, they often met with opposition, especially from some of the technical services which resisted the bridle the more because of their traditional freedom of action.

The perspective of the author is that of the "top side" rather than of the official at the operational level. Little attempt has been made to go into detail on the many activities and responsibilities of the Army Service Forces. For more complete information concerning them, the reader can look to other volumes of UNITED STATES ARMY IN WORLD WAR II.

ORLANDO WARD
Maj. Gen., U.S.A.
Chief of Military History

Washington, D. C.
15 January 1953

The Author

John David Millett, Ph.D., LL.D., President of Miami University, earned his doctorate in political science at Columbia University where for a number of years he also served on the faculty. His experience as an adviser and administrator in government agencies and in the field of higher education has been extensive. Among these may be mentioned service on the National Resources Planning Board, the Committee on Organization of the Executive Branch of the Government, The President's Committee on Administrative Management, and the Commission on Financing Higher Education. For the last-named organization, he served as Executive Director. During World War II he was commissioned and brought to Washington to serve on General Somervell's staff as an expert adviser on organizing the newly created Army Service Forces. He also acted as the wartime historian for that command. Through both training and personal experience he was the logical person to prepare this particular volume.

Washington, D. C.
15 April 1953

LEO J. MEYER
Colonel, Reserve Corps
Deputy Chief Historian

Preface

This account of the Army Service Forces in World War II had its origin in the general effort of the Federal Government to record wartime administrative experiences. On 4 March 1942 President Roosevelt wrote to the director of the Bureau of the Budget expressing his interest in the steps taken to keep a "current record of war administration" and urged their extension wherever possible.[1]

The War Department in turn issued instructions on 15 July 1942 for the commanding general of the Army Service Forces to appoint an historical officer and to arrange for an historical program. This communication was addressed also to the commanding generals of the Army Ground Forces and of the Army Air Forces. I was initially appointed historical officer of the Army Service Forces by General Somervell. As a member of the Administrative Management Branch in the Control Division of Army Service Forces headquarters, I participated actively in many organizational studies and in time, assumed other current staff responsibilities within the Army Service Forces. Thus, from the beginning, I had an opportunity to observe organizational experiences at close range.

In the two months preceding my departure from the Army in January 1946, I dictated a draft account of the major organizational events in the history of the Army Service Forces from 9 March 1942 to the end of 1945. This account was deposited in an historical file along with various historical records prepared within the Army Service Forces during the war. Subsequently, the Office of the Chief of Military History invited me to revise and extend the original draft, and this volume for the series UNITED STATES ARMY IN WORLD WAR II is the result.

The present volume is based on the earlier draft and on other materials which were not then readily available. In addition, it relies heavily on the complete personal files of General Somervell which have been preserved intact and which for the first time are here used as the basis for a published work. But this account has not been prepared solely from official documents and other papers. I was present at meetings and conferences of which no records were ever kept, and have tried to convey the impression left by these discussions in various generalizations and observations. In such instances the reader will of course find no footnote references.

---

[1] This letter and others on the subject will be found in the preface to The United States at War, prepared by the Bureau of the Budget, and published by the U.S. Government Printing Office in 1946.

In addition, I have had the active assistance of General Somervell, the commanding general of the Army Service Forces in World War II. I first became acquainted with General Somervell in New York City in September 1936. It was my privilege to be associated in a small way with his work as head of the Army Service Forces in World War II. His aid in providing me with his personal recollections of persons and events is gratefully acknowledged. The assistance of a personal friend, Maj. Gen. Clinton F. Robinson (USA retired), has been equally invaluable.

In my conversations with the chief historian of the Office of the Chief of Military History, it was agreed that any organizational account of the Army Service Forces would be inadequate which did not give proper emphasis to the personality of its commanding general. This story of the Army Service Forces, then, has been told from the point of view of its commanding general. At the same time, this is not meant to obscure the fact that the work of the Army Service Forces was accomplished by thousands of persons in and out of uniform scattered throughout the world. I would not belittle the contribution of any one of them.

The focus of attention throughout this volume has been the *organizational* experience of the Army Service Forces. It was impossible here to tell the full story of the many vital problems of the ASF. These accounts will be found in other volumes dealing with the production, supply, and administrative activities of the Army.

I have been conscious of the very different audiences who might be interested in this record. This is not a "popular" history. Its primary purpose is to provide a record of events which would be available to and could be used by others who, in subsequent years, might have related responsibilities. In other words, the primary audience would be future administrative officers, plus a few others interested in comparable administration experiences. This concept has provided me with a general frame of reference.

Yet in endeavoring to tell a complete story about the Army Service Forces' organizational experience, it was necessary to discuss many of the substantive problems and major issues confronting agencies of the War Department. These are matters which are probably of much more general interest than administrative history. For example, the three chapters dealing with the relations of the Army Service Forces to the War Production Board are in many ways a separate episode which may be of more extensive interest than other chapters dealing with the internal organization of the Army Service Forces. But in thus weaving together many different events and circumstances, the effort was made to retain a central thread of unity. It was simply this: what was the Army Service Forces, how did it come to be, what was it supposed to do, and how did it do it?

It was perhaps inevitable in writing this account to tell primarily the story of controversies. The Army Service Forces was a controversial administrative experiment. There are some in the Army and elsewhere today who would ban all discussion of the Army Service Forces and who wish never again to see anything resembling an offspring. This attitude may disappear with time, but it has been one of my chief aims to explore the many controversies and differences of opinion which arose so that others may more accurately assess the basis of the hostile reactions. General Somervell too was a controversial figure. If he is to be known solely by what his critics have said about him, then a most distorted picture of an able officer and administrator will be perpetuated. I have endeavored to place this picture back in proper focus. I cannot satisfy the partisans of General Somervell, and there are many. Nor can I expect to soothe the ruffled feelings of all those who think they were harshly treated by General Somervell. This account is friendly but at the same time, it is hoped, balanced.

It has not been my purpose here to chronicle all the activities and achievements of the Army Service Forces. Any such attempt of necessity would have been an almost endless one. Nor has it been my purpose, as easy as such an effort would have been, to stress only the accomplishments, the satisfactory relationships of so many individuals in the Army Service Forces, both with one another and with members of other military and civilian agencies. My purpose rather has been to help clarify the misunderstanding that now exists, and that otherwise might well continue to exist, with regard to the real nature of the Army Service Forces.

After completion of the original draft of this volume, other responsibilities prevented me from giving full personal attention to revision of the manuscript. The Office of the Chief of Military History made available the services of Dr. Jonathan Grossman who checked references, investigated other sources of materials, and edited sections of the manuscript. His assistance was both thorough and sympathetic. Much of whatever merit the present volume may have belongs to Dr. Grossman's generous assistance. I have also had the help of many other persons in reviewing the manuscript and checking its facts. These are too numerous to mention in full, but I wish to acknowledge my indebtedness to Dr. Kent Roberts Greenfield, Chief Historian; Lt. Col. Leo J. Meyer, Deputy Chief Historian; Dr. Richard M. Leighton, Chief of the Logistics Section; and Dr. Stetson Conn, Chief of the Western Hemisphere Section. In addition, I appreciate greatly the careful reading of the entire manuscript by Lt. Gen. LeRoy Lutes, who succeeded General Somervell in command of the Army Service Forces. Mr. David Jaffé was editor of the volume, Miss Nancy L. Easterling did the copy editing, Mrs. Pauline Dodd prepared the index, and Miss Margaret E. Tackley was the photographic editor.

It should be remembered that I alone stand responsible for the statements of fact and opinion expressed. The Office of the Chief of Military History has not censored my observations in any way, even though it has been critical of certain points of view contained in the manuscript. Despite what the term "official history" may imply to many, this volume represents personal judgments, which, it is hoped, few will consider unreasonable on the basis of the evidence presented.

JOHN D. MILLETT

Columbia University
15 April 1953

Contents

PART ONE

The Creation of the Army Service Forces

PART TWO

The Role of the ASF in the War Department

PART THREE

The Role of the ASF in Industrial Mobilization

Tables

Charts

Illustrations

The illustrations are from the files
of the Department of Defense.

Introduction

On 9 March 1942 the Army Service Forces (ASF), the Army Ground Forces (AGF), and the Army Air Forces (AAF) came into being as the three major commands within the United States to do the work of the War Department.[1] The Army Service Forces was a unique organization, although it was in part modeled after the Services of Supply (SOS) that had been set up in France as a separate command within the American Expeditionary Forces (AEF) of Gen. John J. Pershing.[2] There was no exact counterpart to it within the United States during World War I. When General Pershing became Chief of Staff of the Army in 1921 and reconstructed the War Department General Staff (WDGS), he did not provide for a Services of Supply. It was not until two months after the Japanese attack on Pearl Harbor that Gen. George C. Marshall, Chief of Staff, and Secretary of War Henry L. Stimson decided on a new organization for the War Department and the Army.

Without direct precedent, the Army Service Forces was unusual likewise in the variety of tasks entrusted to it. In truth, it was a hodgepodge of agencies with many and varied functions. From 9 March 1942 until its official termination in 1946 the ASF struggled constantly to build a common unity of purpose and organization.

The Army Service Forces took over certain basic tasks which had to be performed for the support of military operations. It was a procurement and supply agency for the Army both in the United States and abroad, and during both combat and training operations. This was its central purpose. But there were other tasks as well, many tasks that had to be done to keep a gigantic army in existence and effective in combat. Some of this work involved the handling of men—induction, classification, assignment, maintenance of central personnel records, and eventually separation. In addition there was a world-wide communications service to provide, ports, and land and sea carriers to operate. There were hospitals to be built, staffed, and operated to care for the sick and for both training and combat casualties. There were individual soldiers of service troops to be given technical training, and service units to be organized and trained. There were morale and recreational services to devise and make effective. There were such tasks as military justice to supervise, military prisons to run, military textbooks to print and distribute, and depend-

---

[1] Initially called the Services of Supply, the name of the command was changed to Army Service Forces by War Department General Orders 14, 12 March 1943. It is best known by this designation, which was used from 1943 to 1946. Accordingly, "Army Service Forces" will be used in the narrative of events of 1942 from 9 March 1942 onward.

[2] Accounts of the work of the Services of Supply of the AEF were provided by its commanding general and chief of staff. See James G. Harbord, *The American Army in France* (Boston, Little, Brown and Company, 1936), and Johnson Hagood, *The Services of Supply* (Boston, Houghton Mifflin Company, 1927). See also *Organization of the Services of Supply*, Monograph 7 prepared in the Historical Branch, War Plans Division, General Staff (Washington, U.S. Government Printing Office, 1921).

ents' allowances to pay while the soldier was overseas. There was a world-wide system of mail delivery to maintain. There was the spiritual welfare of soldiers to provide for. There were training films to prepare and a pictorial record of the entire Army to make. There were official orders of the War Department to issue, and official records to keep.

The Army Service Forces was big, sprawling, vital. An Army was inducted, armed, transported, supplied, and brought back again when the fighting was finished. As was to be expected, ASF performance varied in quality from time to time and in different fields. Perhaps the simplest verdict on the Army Service Forces was "It worked, didn't it?"

General Marshall summed up its achievements thus:

The tasks of the Army Service Forces have been difficult and complex beyond description. . . .

The Service Forces have accomplished a prodigious task during the past two years in the supply of food, clothing, munitions, transportation, including the operation of a fleet of 1,537 ships; in the handling of pay and allowances amounting to 22.4 billion dollars; in the processing of approximately 75 billion dollars in contracts; in the management of 3,700 post or cantonment installations in continental United States; in the operation of great base port organizations centered in Boston, New York, Hampton Roads, New Orleans, Los Angeles, San Francisco, and Seattle; in handling 7,370,000 men and 101,750,000 measurement tons of cargo; in the administration of the medical service which has treated 9,083,000 hospital cases and operated 791,000 hospital beds; in the direction of post exchanges now doing a monthly business of 90 million dollars and the organization and management of entertainment and educational opportunities; in the conduct of the administration of the Army and finally in the enormous tasks of redeployment and demobilization.[3]

The Choice of General Somervell To Command the ASF

No introduction to the Army Service Forces would be complete without a brief sketch of its commander, Gen. Brehon B. Somervell. So much of the history of the ASF, its achievements and its difficulties, revolved around his personality that some knowledge of the man is essential. To a greater degree than most organizations, the Army Service Forces reflected the force of a single man.[4] No one who knew the ASF ever doubted that the Army Service Forces and the name of its commanding general were synomomous. Credit, however, for the success of his organization, as General Somervell himself would be the first to point out, must of course go to its hundreds of thousands of loyal workers, military and civilian. The work was done by thousands of contractors and employees, laboring long hours to turn out the necessary supplies. The work was done by the railroad managers and trainmen who moved millions of tons to the seaports. The work was done by the shipping companies, the stevedores, and the seamen. The work was done by the different organizational units which directed the various parts of a vast enterprise. Yet presiding over all of this, holding it together by the sheer force of his own determination, constantly demanding greater performance, was General Somervell. For his many achievements Secretary of War Robert P. Patterson voiced warm appreciation when on 12 October 1945 he awarded to Somer-

---

[3] *Biennial Report of the Chief of Staff of the United States Army July 1, 1943 to June 30, 1945 to the Secretary of War* (Washington, U.S. Government Printing Office, 1945), p. 114.

[4] Interv, Frederick S. Haydon with Gen Joseph T. McNarney, 4 Aug 49, OCMH.

vell an oak leaf cluster to the Distinguished Service Medal.[5]

When General Somervell once briefly enumerated the work which his command had to perform before the subcommittee of the House Committee on Appropriations, which handled the War Department budget, the chairman of the subcommittee laconically remarked, "It would seem that you are kept pretty busy." The commanding general replied: "There are a great many duties there, sir." [6] This was understatement.

Brehon B. Somervell was born in Little Rock, Arkansas, on 9 May 1892. His father was a doctor and his mother a former school teacher. In 1910 he received an appointment to the U.S. Military Academy, was graduated four years later sixth in a group of 106 cadets, and was commissioned a second lieutenant in the Corps of Engineers.

Lieutenant Somervell happened to be in Paris on two months' graduation leave when World War I began. As an assistant to the military attaché in Paris, he helped get Americans in France back to the United States. Returning home in September 1914 he served in various capacities customary to junior officers in the Corps of Engineers. In the spring of 1916, he joined General Pershing's expedition to punish the Mexican raider Pancho Villa.

Promoted to the rank of captain on 15 May 1917, Somervell helped recruit and organize the 15th Engineer Regiment, a railroad outfit which was the first engineer regiment sent abroad. It arrived in England in July 1917 and left for France soon after. Somervell was adjutant of the regiment. Its commanding officer, Col. Edgar Jadwin, later a lieutenant general and a Chief of Engineers, impressed him deeply and was a model for many of Somervell's subsequent ideas and activities. In France the regiment worked on a number of large construction projects, including a great munitions dump at Mehun-sur-Yèvre and the advanced depot and regulating station of Is-sur-Tille. For these activities he subsequently received the Distinguished Service Medal. While the work was exacting and strenuous, it was scarcely exciting.

He visited the front lines in 1918 and volunteered for service on the staff of the 89th Division. For successfully leading a patrol to inspect the damage of a bridge some six hundred yards in front of the American outposts, he was later awarded the Distinguished Service Cross.

With the temporary rank of lieutenant colonel, Somervell in October 1918 joined the 89th Division and became Assistant Chief of Staff, G–3, in charge of operations. After the Armistice he became Assistant Chief of Staff, G–4, in charge of both personnel and supply. When the division was shipped back to the United States in May 1919, Somervell remained overseas as G–4 of the Third Army, the force assigned to occupy the U.S. zone in Germany.

It was as supply officer for the Army of Occupation that Somervell first met Walker D. Hines, who had just become arbitrator of shipping on the Rhine River, and who turned to him for help in preparing a report on Rhine shipping. This association began a friendship which was to have far-reaching influence on Somervell's subsequent career. With the reorganization of the Army on a peacetime basis, Somervell reverted to the permanent rank of major in July 1920.

---

[5] WD press release, BPR, 12 Oct 45 (mimeographed).

[6] *Hearings before the Subcommittee of the Committee on Appropriations*, H. R., 78th Cong, 2d Sess, on Military Establishment Appropriation Bill for 1945, p. 64.

LT. GEN. WILHELM D. STYER.
(Photograph taken 1944.)

In the mid-twenties he again assisted Mr. Hines with surveys and reports dealing with navigation conditions on the Rhine and Danube Rivers. In 1933 and 1934 he worked with Mr. Hines on an economic survey of Turkey to be used as the basis for a five-year plan of industrialization. Somervell covered most of the country by automobile in order to observe conditions for himself. Mr. Hines was succeeded after his death in the autumn of 1933 by his law partner, Goldthwaite H. Dorr. With the help of a small staff, Somervell finished a seven-volume report in three months, worked with Mr. Dorr on the final recommendations, and returned to the United States in April 1934 for duty with the Chief of Engineers.

In 1935, after the passage of the Emergency Relief Appropriation Act, Somer-

vell became executive officer of the newly created Division of Applications and Information. He quickly saw that it would be impossible for this office to review projects, since the final decision in any event had to be made by the operating units, the most important of which soon became the Works Progress Administration (WPA) under Harry L. Hopkins. He joined in recommending that the office be liquidated. In the meantime, on 1 August 1935, Somervell received his first promotion in fifteen years. Now a lieutenant colonel, he was sent to work on the Florida ship canal.

When the New York City WPA, the largest single operating unit of the nationwide program, found itself in need of an administrator who would be acceptable to Mayor Fiorello H. La Guardia as well as to Washington, both Hopkins and the mayor agreed that an Army Engineer officer would be suitable. The choice was Somervell, who served as administrator from 1 August 1936 until November 1940. His handling of relief workers was firm but conciliatory. Furthermore, Somervell succeeded in staying out of newspaper battles between Mayor La Guardia and Commissioner Robert Moses on the problem of park development. Somervell built a disintegrating organization into a tightly knit, loyal, and hard-working enterprise. There was general agreement that the New York City WPA was well run.[7]

When the United States began active preparation for its own defense in 1940, Somervell was eager to return to military duty. He hoped he might be assigned to

[7] See John D. Millett, *The Works Progress Administration in New York City* (Chicago, Public Administration Service, 1938), and Arthur W. Macmahon, John D. Millett, and Gladys Ogden, *The Administration of Federal Work Relief* (Chicago, Public Administration Service, 1941).

duty with troops. Through an intermediary he sought an interview with General Marshall, who had become Chief of Staff on 1 September 1939. Somervell had a brief conversation with General Marshall in the early autumn of 1940. He reminded the Chief of Staff of his service in World War I and of his subsequent staff training. He added that in spite of his varied assignments he still looked upon himself as a field soldier, and asked to be kept in mind for a field command. General Marshall was noncommittal.

Somervell first learned in November 1940, through a personal friend of Robert P. Patterson, the newly appointed Assistant Secretary of War, that he was being considered for a War Department position. He was told that the War Department was concerned about delays in constructing Army camps. Because of the existing emergency, the Department had received a large appropriation for construction. The National Guard had been called into service in August 1940 and the Selective Service Act, passed by Congress in September, provided for 600,000 additional soldiers. It was imperative that the rapidly expanding Army be sheltered before winter set in. Somervell was asked if he thought he could speed up this construction job. He was willing to try.

In November 1940 he was first detailed to The Inspector General's office of the War Department to examine the construction program, preliminary to his assignment as head of the Construction Division in the Office of The Quartermaster General. On 11 December 1940 Somervell took charge of the Construction Division. He was promoted to the temporary rank of brigadier general in the Army of the United States on 29 January 1941. He went to work with enthusiasm, putting many of the individuals who had worked with him in New York City into key places. As his chief assistant he picked an old Corps of Engineers' friend whom he accidently encountered in Washington, Col. Wilhelm D. Styer. Almost at once Somervell was required to testify before several Congressional committees about delays in the cantonment construction program. He pointed to the magnitude of the job and to the evidence of progress in its performance.[8] Before the heavy February rains began in the south, most of the newly inducted soldiers were under some kind of shelter. Everywhere Somervell put emphasis on speed. He accepted no excuses, and economy was secondary to action. While admitting that speed increased the cost at least $100,000,000, he claimed that time was more important than money. By February 1941 more than 485,000 persons were employed on the Army's construction work. At the same time, the building of new powder and ammunition loading plants was hastened. *Time* magazine advised its readers to "watch Somervell."

Toward the end of October 1941 the post of Assistant Chief of Staff, G–4, in the War Department General Staff, became vacant. Apparently the selection of a successor fell to the Deputy Chief of Staff for Supply, Maj. Gen. Richard C. Moore. General Moore picked Somervell and told him of his forthcoming assignment. He was officially appointed on 25 November 1941. This was the first time Somervell had served on the WDGS. On 28 January

---

[8] *Hearings before the Subcommittee of the Committee on Appropriations*, H.R., 77th Cong, 1st Sess, on Fourth Supplemental National Defense Appropriations Bill, 12 Feb, 8 Mar 41, pp. 12–126, 131–51; *Hearings before the Subcommittee of the Committee on Appropriations*, Senate, 77th Cong, 1st Sess, on H.R. 3617, 3 Mar 41, pp. 1–37, and on H.R. 4124, 27 Mar 41, pp. 147–58.

LT. GEN. LEROY LUTES. *(Photograph taken 1945.)*

1942 he was promoted to the temporary rank of major general.

On the same day that the Army Service Forces was officially activated, General Somervell received his third star. (He was to become a full general on 6 March 1945.) The new command was not the field command which he had wanted in the autumn of 1940, and which he still wanted. Instead, he had been given "the biggest headache" in the War Department.

Characteristics of the Choice

The selection of General Somervell to command the Army Service Forces was notable in several respects. He was relatively young and unknown in Army circles. At the time of his appointment he was just two months short of his fiftieth birth-day. There were many officers in active service who were better known, and who held higher permanent rank (on the Regular Army list Somervell was still only a lieutenant colonel). Many of these were now placed under his command.

This situation inevitably meant that General Somervell would encounter resentment from some officers who felt their own military careers entitled them to more consideration than that received as a result of the reorganization. Like others such as Eisenhower and Bradley in Europe, Somervell faced the constant problem of building loyal and co-operative relationships among men who were his seniors in age and in rank.

In the second place, he had had anything but an orthodox military career. An article which appeared in *Fortune* magazine commented: "Somervell is every inch an Army man—but an Army man with a difference. The difference is that he has mixed in civilian affairs too."[9] Somervell had had several lengthy assignments outside the customary Army pattern, including his work abroad with Walker D. Hines and his more than four years as WPA administrator in New York City, as already indicated. To the ordinary Regular Army officer this was an unorthodox military career and was not to be compared with the long drudgery, patience, and even frustration that had been the lot of so many officers between 1919 and 1940.

In the third place, General Somervell's best known characteristics were his energy and his drive. In many of his assignments between the two wars, and particularly after 1935, he had worked in the midst of crisis conditions. He was often asked to do the work of months in a matter of days.

---

[9] "The SOS," *Fortune* (September 1942), p. 68.

He drove himself as hard as he drove his subordinates, perhaps even harder. He was not afraid of responsibility, he was not loath to cut red tape, and he rode roughshod over opposition. The very language of War Department Circular 59 suggested that these qualities were urgently desired in 1942. Each of the three major commanders was instructed in the circular to make use of "judicious shortcuts in procedure to expedite operations." There were probably few officers in the Army in 1942 better prepared psychologically to carry out this injunction to the full. Somervell's energy and determination to overcome obstacles regardless of cost alienated some and occasionally disturbed others, but he did get things done. Senator Harry S. Truman once commented to his colleagues on the Senate Committee on Military Affairs: "I will say this for General Somervell, he will get the stuff, but it is going to be hell on the taxpayer. He has a WPA attitude on the expenditure of money." [10]

With Somervell's sense of urgency and drive went also a quick temper. No one knew this limitation better than did Somervell himself. Because of it there were some misgivings at the time he was being considered to head the ASF.[11] Intellectually alert, he was inclined to be impatient with persons who were slower than himself in reaching a decision and in taking action. Continued indecisiveness aroused his anger, as did a failure to carry out instructions or a surrender to what seemed to him to be surmountable difficulties.

Early in the war a journalist described Somervell in these words:

. . . he is out of the tradition of the Elizabethan Englishman, all lace and velvet and courtliness outside, fury and purposefulness within.

"Dynamite in a Tiffany box" is the impression Somervell left with one WPB industrialist. The General has never found it necessary to invite journalists in to hear him deliver a fierce ultimatum to himself to get tough. While the bureaucrats in mufti are conscientiously trying to transform themselves into fire-eaters and nail-chewers, "Bill" Somervell is working just as conscientiously to water down his own triple-distilled potion of the grapes of wrath. His problem is not to work up a temper but to control one . . . . When goaded beyond endurance, rather than trust himself to act, he will shut himself up in the office until a judicial calm descends.[12]

General Somervell was also well known as an Army officer with an unusually good sense of organization. He had a number of definite ideas about how an organization should be set up and how it should work. Many of these details will be discussed later. But it was typical of his brief career as G–4 of the War Department that he raised fundamental organizational questions and sought consideration of vital relationships between his own office and that of the Under Secretary of War. He was not willing to accept an arrangement just because it happened to be in force, particularly when he saw it as an obstacle to the performance of a basic task. He had revealed his organizational sense further as a participant in the discussions during February 1942 of War Department reorganization. As head of the Army Service Forces it was to be expected that he would always take a keen interest in such matters as they applied to the work of his command.

---

[10] *Hearings before the Committee on Military Affairs,* Senate, 77th Cong, 2d Sess, on Department of Defense Co-ordination and Control Bill, 6 Mar 42, p. 7.

[11] See below, pp. 35–36.

[12] Charles J. V. Murphy, "Somervell of the SOS," *Life,* (March 8, 1943), p. 86.

One other factor should be mentioned. The people who knew Somervell seldom felt neutral toward him. They reacted with either intense like or dislike. There were those to whom the very mention of the name of Somervell was like waving a red flag in front of a bull. They thought him a power-hungry officer, a "man on horseback." [13]

On the other hand, General Somervell aroused sentiments of great loyalty among the people closely associated with him. Within the WPA in New York City, he had found several persons whose work habits suited him and whose performance was so satisfactory that he brought them into the Construction Division of the Office of The Quartermaster General and later into the Army Service Forces. In the short time in which he was in G–4, he spotted two officers, one of whom in particular, Brig. Gen. LeRoy Lutes, was to become his close associate in the ASF and was to be described by him later as the "perfect" staff officer. Yet before 25 November 1941, he had never met this man who was to remain with him throughout the entire history of the Army Service Forces and who was to succeed him in 1945 for the brief remaining period of the ASF's existence. The loyalty of the men around Somervell and his support of them were indispensable for the effective operation of the Army Service Forces.

---

[13] *Hearings before a Special Committee Investigating the National Defense Program* [The Truman Committee], Senate, 77th Cong, 2d Sess, 16 Dec 42, Pt. 16, p. 6676; Lewis Douglas, memo to file, about 30 Dec 42, WSA files, Douglas personal.

PART ONE

THE CREATION OF
THE ARMY SERVICE FORCES

CHAPTER I

The War Department and Army Organization at the Beginning of World War II

When the Japanese dropped their bombs at Pearl Harbor, War Department organization still reflected the basic thinking developed from America's experience in World War I. United States participation in that war had produced its share of organizational conflicts. The most important of these involved the relation between the Chief of Staff and the commanding general of the American Expeditionary Forces, General Pershing. General Pershing had been highly critical of the operation of the War Department General Staff. In his eyes the Chief of Staff in Washington "erroneously assumed the role of Commanding General of the Army."[1] He was convinced that strategic and tactical direction in the field belonged solely to him and that his only superior was the Commander in Chief, the President of the United States. He saw the job of the Chief of Staff in the War Department mainly in terms of providing him with the troops and supplies he requested.

Just how much authority the Chief of Staff had to direct the war effort was not clearly defined until three months before the end of the war.[2] By general order it was then declared that the Chief of Staff

by law took rank and precedence over *all* officers of the Army and had authority in the name of the Secretary of War to issue orders throughout the Military Establishment. This provision was distasteful not only to General Pershing, but also to many of the Army bureau chiefs.

As Chief of Staff after March 1918, Gen. Peyton C. March was confronted with many difficulties other than those arising from General Pershing's concept of his office. The general staff system, established in 1903, had been disliked by many Army officials through the intervening years. World War I provided its first real test. Faced with the necessity of proving itself, it sought to meet the challenge by more effective organization, particularly by bringing the administrative and supply bureaus of the department under close supervision.

The supply responsibilities of the War Department General Staff were exercised from August 1918 and thereafter through a Purchase, Storage, and Traffic Division.

---

[1] John J. Pershing, *My Experiences in the World War* (New York, Frederick A. Stokes Company, 1931), I, 17.

[2] WD GO 80, 26 Aug 18.

This division was scarcely a "staff agency" as most Army officers understood that term. The director of the division, Maj. Gen. George Goethals, was determined to bring all supply activities of the Army into one integrated organization, based on functional specialization. In July 1918 he had developed a plan for centralizing procurement of all but a few items—notably aircraft and heavy guns and ammunition—under The Quartermaster General. The Purchase, Storage, and Traffic Division also took over direct operation of the Army Transportation Service and created a central storage agency to handle all military supplies before they were issued to troops in training in the United States or shipped overseas. On 28 July 1918, Secretary of War Newton D. Baker in a letter to General Pershing proposed that General Goethals' authority be extended to include the Services of Supply of the AEF. General Pershing firmly and successfully opposed this idea, and he immediately strengthened his SOS by placing his intimate associate, Maj. Gen. James G. Harbord, in command.[3]

Much pent-up hostility to WDGS control, especially as exercised by the Purchase, Storage, and Traffic Division, was released by the Armistice. General March defended its actions at some length in his report at the end of the war.[4] He pointed to the earlier tendency of each bureau to purchase supplies without concern for the procurement activities of other bureaus. He mentioned that there had been nine different methods for estimating supply requirements, five different agencies storing and issuing supplies, and ten different agencies handling finances. This had been so confusing that the War Industries Board could not obtain "adequate information" about the supply needs of the

War Department as a whole. Under the circumstances, General March said, "a consolidation of procurement, . . . of storage, of finance, and of transportation, together with a positive central control of these activities by the General Staff, was essential . . . to the rapid, efficient, and economical utilization of the resources of the country for the development of the Army program as a whole."[5] He admitted that the General Staff, forced by circumstances, had extended its control at the expense of the supply bureaus. But in any future war, he continued, it would again be necessary to have a top staff to direct the many agencies of the War Department. "It can be stated without qualification that the success of an army in modern war is impossible without such a general staff."[6]

The bureau chiefs of the War Department were not convinced by such views. When Congress began hearings on War Department proposals for new defense legislation, they directed many criticisms against the General Staff itself. The Chief of Ordnance, Maj. Gen. Clarence C. Williams, told a House committee: "I think I may say, so far as the Ordnance Department is concerned, that not one single constructive thing has come out of the Purchase, Storage, and Traffic Division."[7] The Chief of Engineers, Maj. Gen. William M. Black, was equally vigorous in his statement.[8] The director of the Chemical

---

[3] Pershing, *My Experiences in the World War*, II, 185–86.

[4] Annual *Report of the Chief of Staff to the Secretary of War, 1919* (Washington, U.S. Government Printing Office, 1919), pp. 15ff.

[5] *Ibid.*, p. 20.

[6] *Ibid.*, p. 241.

[7] *Hearings before the Committee on Military Affairs*, H.R., 66th Cong, 1st Sess, on Army Reorganization 1919, p. 493.

[8] *Ibid.*, p. 765.

Warfare Service, Maj. Gen. William L. Sibert, said that the "attempt of the General Staff, through the Purchase, Storage, and Traffic Division, to interfere with or take over largely the administration of the bureaus, is due to a misconception of the real supply problem." He complained that the creation of the "P.S. and T." had led to a "duplication of work" and had tended to cut the bureau chief out of "control of his own bureau."[9]

Aside from such criticism the reorganization of the War Department General Staff proposed after World War I faced another obstacle. Secretary Baker during the war had held that his own office should exercise close supervision over all procurement operations through civilian personnel. With that in mind one of his first steps had been to enlist the assistance of Edward R. Stettinius, who in January 1918 was given the title of Surveyor-General of Supplies and after April became Second Assistant Secretary of War. In the meantime Mr. Baker had asked his assistant secretary and fellow citizen of Cleveland, Benedict Crowell, to supervise War Department procurement activities. Mr. Crowell was given the additional title of Director of Munitions.[10]

Mr. Crowell was deeply perturbed by America's production performance during World War I. Almost no preparation had been made before April 1917 for large-scale output of munitions. It took time to convert industrial resources to actual production of guns, airplanes, and tanks. Then too, the military handling of overseas transportation was faulty so that much of what was produced never reached its destination. American manpower in the AEF was effective in a military sense largely because of the great quantities of armaments provided by the British and French. While the United States supplied most of the food, clothing, and motor transport for the AEF, it produced a mere 160 of the 2,000 75-mm. field guns used by American troops overseas. All 1,000 of the 155-mm. howitzers came from the British and French. The infant air force used 1,000 pursuit planes provided by the French.[11] This experience made a lasting impression on Crowell. It confirmed his opinion that close civilian supervision of procurement operations was necessary in wartime. It also led him to the conviction that henceforth the War Department should include plans for industrial mobilization in its defense preparations.

Changes in the National Defense Act

In August 1919 the Secretary of War presented proposals to Congress for the postwar organization of the War Department. These proposals had been developed by the General Staff under General March's leadership. The suggested legislation provided for a General Staff Corps with a total strength of 230 officers, to be headed by a Chief of Staff with the rank of general. The Chief of Staff was to exercise "supervision of all agencies and functions of the Military Establishment" under the direction of the President and the Secretary of War. The bill further provided that "the Chief of Staff shall be the immediate adviser of the Secretary of War" on military matters. He was to plan, develop, and

[9] *Ibid.*, pp. 557–59.

[10] An interpretation of these events is available in a lecture by Goldthwaite Dorr, Assistant Director of Munitions under Crowell, to the Army Industrial College in 1945. See Goldthwaite H. Dorr, The Reorganization of the War Department of 9 March 1942, 14 Jun 45 (mimeographed).

[11] See Some Accomplishments of the Services of Supply, 2d ed., revised to 1 May 19, mimeographed rpt prepared by Stat Br, SOS, AEF, p. 42.

execute the war program and issue orders to insure the efficient and harmonious execution of policies by the various corps, bureaus, and other agencies of the Military Establishment. The obvious intention was to strengthen the General Staff as the top management organization for the War Department.

Much of the subsequent legislative discussion therefore centered upon the question of the role of the General Staff in the War Department. During the hearings, Assistant Secretary of War Crowell injected a new issue for consideration by Congress when he proposed to the House Committee on Military Affairs that the functions of the War Department be divided into two principal elements, a military function and a procurement function. Although the Secretary of War would be the top civilian administrator over both, Mr. Crowell proposed separate assistants for each activity. The Chief of Staff, as head of the Military Establishment, would advise the Secretary of War on military matters; the head of a Munitions Department would advise him on procurement problems. Yet Crowell did not suggest that the supply bureaus should be placed exclusively under the Munitions Department. The General Staff would give orders to the bureaus on supply requirements, troop training, and distribution of supplies, while the Munitions Department would give orders to the same supply bureaus on the purchase and manufacture of munitions. Mr. Crowell's proposal reflected in part an effort to strengthen civilian control over business matters, in part his belief that it would rarely be possible to find an Army officer with the experience and skill necessary for supervising the procurement and production of war materials. He hoped that an industrialist

with ability and background would head a Munitions Department.[12]

In submitting his proposal, Mr. Crowell omitted any account of his wartime relation to General Goethals, director of the Purchase, Storage, and Traffic Division. His conception of his job then had been to throw "full immediate operational responsibility" on General Goethals. Mr. Crowell did not customarily give orders directly to the supply bureaus; instead he worked through General Goethals. He concerned himself primarily with general supervision and specific trouble spots. As an industrialist, he was especially interested in the production problems of the Ordnance Department. He also maintained close relationships with the War Industries Board, which mobilized the general economic resources of the nation.[13] Thus, in practice, as Director of Munitions, he had actually worked through a General Staff division headed by an Army officer. The House Committee on Military Affairs apparently was unaware that Mr. Crowell's proposal was in contradiction to his own administrative experience in World War I.

Secretary Baker disagreed with Crowell and opposed his recommendation before the House committee. The Secretary told the committee that he doubted that a man of wide business experience could be found, particularly in peacetime, to fill the position of Assistant Secretary of War to head a Munitions Department. In addition, the Secretary disapproved of the proposal to give a statutory assignment to an Assistant Secretary of War because

_____

[12] *Hearings before the Committee on Military Affairs,* H.R., 66th Cong, 1st Sess, on Army Reorganization 1919, II, 1803–04.

[13] Dorr lecture, p. 8, cited in n. 10.

this would interfere with the freedom of the Secretary to assign responsibilities to his principal associates as he saw fit. A future Secretary of War might be an industrialist who would take more interest in the procurement operations of the War Department than in its other work. Under these circumstances he might want an Assistant Secretary who would give principal attention to the nonprocurement activities.[14]

The National Defense Act of 4 June 1920 continued the General Staff organization and the position of Chief of Staff as created in 1903. Under the direction of the President and the Secretary of War, the Chief of Staff was to see that the General Staff made plans for recruiting, organizing, supplying, equipping, mobilizing, training, and demobilizing the Army of the United States. Other functions of the General Staff were to include authority to investigate and report on the efficiency of the Army and its state of preparation for military operations, to develop plans for the mobilization of civilian manpower for war, and to render professional aid and assistance to the Secretary of War. The War Department General Staff was limited to the Chief of Staff, four assistant chiefs of staff, and eighty-eight other officers, a group about one third the size recommended by General March.

Congress adopted in part the recommendation put forward by Mr. Crowell. Section 5a of the law provided that the Assistant Secretary of War would supervise the procurement of all military supplies and plan economic mobilization for war. But Section 5a offered no solution to the basic issue of military versus civilian control of procurement. It did not establish a civilian-dominated Munitions Department; the Assistant Secretary, who was to supervise military procurement, was given no operating staff.

War Department orders issued in August 1920 implied that the Assistant Secretary would look for staff assistance to the Supply Division of the General Staff.[15] Policy control without a staff organization was only the shadow, not the substance, of authority. Unless future Assistant Secretaries were willing to depend upon what help the General Staff could provide them, they would have no alternative but to create their own organization.

There was a curious anomaly in the Assistant Secretary's position. With his responsibility to plan economic mobilization for the government as a whole, he was required to think far beyond the War Department. It seems reasonable to assume that the legislation did not intend to give him supervision of wartime industrial organization; during World War I, the War Industries Board had been a separate agency reporting directly to the President. In the event of another war, it was then probably contemplated that a similar agency would be created. Nevertheless, the Assistant Secretary's responsibility for economic planning made him potentially more important than many cabinet members, possibly even more important than his chief. At the same time he was a subordinate official in his own Department. And as though to heap confusion upon confusion, Section 5 of the National Defense Act gave to the General Staff powers which could easily be interpreted as overlapping those of the Assistant Secretary;

---

[14] *Hearings before the Committee on Military Affairs,* H.R., 66th Cong, 1st Sess, on Army Reorganization 1919, II, 2016.
[15] WD GO 48, 12 Aug 20.

it charged the Staff with the "mobilization of the manhood of the nation and its material resources in an emergency." Section 5 and 5a of the act of 1920 thus constituted a compromise compounded of ambiguity, confusion, and the raw material of future jurisdictional disputes.

The Pershing Reorganization

When General Pershing became Chief of Staff on 1 July 1921, one of his first acts was to create a board of seven officers to study the organization of the War Department General Staff.[16] Its chairman was Maj. Gen. James G. Harbord, who had been General Pershing's first chief of staff in France, and later commanding general of his Services of Supply.

General Pershing's thought was to create a general staff system in the War Department which would closely parallel the staff he had developed for the AEF in France. After arriving in France in 1917, he had at once begun to study the organization of the British and French armies in the field in order to decide on arrangements for his own command. As General Pershing remarked in his memoirs: "It required no genius to see that the coördination and direction of the combat branches and the numerous services of large forces could be secured only through the medium of a well-constituted general staff, and I determined to construct it on the sound basis of actual experience in war of our own and other armies." [17]

The actual experience of AEF headquarters in organizing its activities is not relevant here.[18] Suffice it to say that this experience provided a major field of study for the Harbord Board. Yet curiously enough, the precedent of a Services of Supply as part of the AEF organization was nowhere reflected in the report of the Har-

bord Board. Rather, the board directed its attention primarily to the problem of the position of the Assistant Secretary of War under the National Defense Act of 1920 and to the question of his relations with the WDGS. Implicit in this problem was the delicate policy question of military versus civilian control of the Department. General Harbord appointed a subcommittee of three to inquire into this issue. Two of the three members of this subcommittee were General Staff officers,[19] which may account for the fact that it tended to build up the role of the General Staff and to play down the independence of the Assistant Secretary.

In its report to the board, the subcommittee identified seven essential stages in military supply:

1. Preparation of specifications and drawings.

2. Testing of pilot models.

3. Inspection of facilities to determine their productive capacity.

4. Acquisition of necessary matériel through purchase, lease, or other business or legal arrangements.

5. Production, including those activities necessary to insure the systematic and orderly flow of component parts.

6. Inspection, test, and acceptance.

7. Storage and issue, including all questions of transportation.

By asserting that the Assistant Secretary of War was properly concerned with the

[16] WD GO 155, 7 Jul 21. See also Troyer Anderson, Introduction to the History of the Under Secretary of War's Office, MS, OCMH, Ch. III, pp. 12–17.

[17] Pershing, *My Experiences in the World War*, I, 103.

[18] The author has sketched the story in "The Direction of Supply Activities in the War Department: an Administrative Survey," *American Political Science Review*, XXXVIII (April, June 1944), 249, 475.

[19] *Hearings before the Committee on Military Affairs: Historical Documents Relating to the Reorganization Plans of the War Department and to the Present National Defense Act*, H.R., 69th Cong, 2d Sess, 3 Mar 27, Pt. 1, pp. 580–83.

third through the sixth steps in this process, the subcommittee attempted to guard against the possibility of that official reaching over into the functions of specifying requirements and disposing of matériel after procurement. The Assistant Secretary, the subcommittee held, should supervise the work of the supply bureaus so far as purchasing, production, and inspection were concerned, while the General Staff should supervise the remaining phases of supply. The subcommittee expressed the belief that a formula for coordinating military and economic policy could be easily devised. The General Staff would determine the military requirements for defense and war, and would present these to the "business side" of the War Department, that is, to the Assistant Secretary of War. Where disagreement occurred between the General Staff and the Assistant Secretary, the Secretary of War would have to resolve the difference. The subcommittee further proposed to strengthen General Staff influence by detailing one or more General Staff officers to work for the Assistant Secretary. In general these recommendations were in line with the principle, upheld by the subcommittee, that military efficiency required the subordination of administration and "business" activities to strategic and tactical command.

The report of the subcommittee further stated that the Assistant Secretary had concurred in its proposals. It should have added, though, that this concurrence was won only after the subcommittee had yielded to at least three vital modifications affecting the special status of the Assistant Secretary. The phrase "for the approval of the Secretary of War" was stricken out of the provision charging the Assistant Secretary with responsibility for directing procurement and industrial planning. If

this phrase had been retained, the War Department General Staff would have had a basis for acting on behalf of the Secretary. The subcommittee failed also in its effort to perpetuate the ambiguity of the act of 1920, which had given the Supply Division of the General Staff a toehold in the planning of economic mobilization. The modified version left the General Staff out of the general planning picture and ordered that the various branches of the Army request decision on *military* phases of procurement from G–4, and "decisions on business or industrial questions from the Assistant Secretary of War." Finally, General Harbord withdrew the subcommittee's recommendation for attaching General Staff officers to the Office of the Assistant Secretary.[20]

Other recommendations of the Harbord Board dealt with the organization of the War Department General Staff into five divisions instead of four—Personnel (G–1), Military Intelligence (G–2), Operations and Training (G–3), Supply (G–4), and War Plans (WPD). The Supply Division was to direct the calculation of Military supply requirements and the distribution of supplies. In addition, the Supply Division was to supervise the construction and maintenance of buildings for War Department activities, the hospitalization of troops, and the preparation of the War Department budget. The recommendations of the Harbord Board, as modified, were accepted by the Chief of Staff and the Secretary of War, and duly put into effect.[21]

Perhaps the most important single consequence of the Harbord Board's work was the creation of a strong general staff sys-

---

[20] *Ibid.*, pp. 597, 618, 626, 638, 645, 648; Anderson, Introduction to the History of the Under Secretary of War's Office, MS, OCMH, Ch. III, pp. 18–23.

[21] WD GO 41, 16 Aug 21.

tem in the War Department. General Pershing himself was largely responsible for this development. While his General Staff was limited in size, it was the top management agency of the Military Establishment. Many different commands, supply bureaus, administrative bureaus, and other agencies might function as part of the War Department, but all received top direction from the General Staff. In the second place, the Harbord Board recommendations suggested the desirability, when war seemed imminent, of creating a General Headquarters (GHQ) which would become a field command and eventually move overseas. This recommendation was to be partially put into effect in July 1940. In the third place, the Harbord Board paved the way for a new top office in the War Department, the Office of the Assistant Secretary of War. This acted to some extent as a brake on the authority of the General Staff. Although War Department orders of August 1920 had implied that the Assistant Secretary would carry out his responsibilities through the Supply Division of the General Staff, the orders of August 1921 suggested an independent supervisory responsibility. Henceforth, on procurement matters, the supply bureaus of the War Department were to work under the direction and control of the Assistant Secretary. The bureaus having supply responsibilities at this time were the Coast Artillery Corps, the Air Service, the Ordnance Department, the Quartermaster Corps, the Medical Corps, the Corps of Engineers, the Signal Corps, and the Chemical Warfare Service. Thus, on procurement and economic planning, the authority of the Assistant Secretary of War was established. The jurisdiction of the General Staff no longer embraced all phases of military supply, as it had before

and during World War I. The supply bureaus now had two superiors, the War Department General Staff and the Office of the Assistant Secretary of War.[22] Except for this limitation in the economic field, the influence of the WDGS grew steadily from 1921 to 1940. Assignment to the General Staff Corps became a high military honor with a promise of later field command for most of those selected.

Developments Between 1921–1941

While no major peacetime modifications were made in War Department and Army organization after the report of the Harbord Board, the military organization nevertheless showed signs of stress and strain which indicated that it might not be able to withstand another major war without change. The single greatest problem was the relation of the air arm to the ground arm. Essentially the issue was whether the strategic and tactical mission of the air forces should be considered as being different and separate from that of the ground forces.[23] The establishment of

[22] Various orders and documents on the organization of the WDGS, the AEF in France, and on the history of War Department organization were collected and published by the House Committee on Military Affairs. See *House Hearing . . . Historical Documents*, cited in n. 19. A briefer account of these developments may be found in Otto L. Nelson, Jr., *National Security and the General Staff* (Washington, Infantry Journal Press, 1946), Chs. V–VI. See also Kent R. Greenfield, Robert R. Palmer, and Bell I. Wiley, *The Organization of Ground Combat Troops*, UNITED STATES ARMY IN WORLD WAR II (Washington, U.S. Government Printing Office, 1947), and Ray S. Cline, *Washington Command Post: The Operations Division*, UNITED STATES ARMY IN WORLD WAR II (Washington, U.S. Government Printing Office, 1951).

[23] Wesley F. Craven and James L. Cate, eds., *The Army Air Forces in World War II: I, Plans and Early Operations, January 1939 to August 1942* (Chicago, University of Chicago Press, 1948), pp. 24–29. (Hereafter cited as Craven and Cate, *AAF I*.)

the Air Corps in 1926, and the segregation of combat air units as the General Headquarters Air Force in 1935, were steps toward a greater degree of autonomy for the Army's air component.

Another problem was the organization of the Army on a geographical basis. The establishment of nine corps areas in 1920 proved to be unsatisfactory for the tactical training of ground combat units. Finally in 1932 the corps areas were ,grouped together under four armies for this purpose, and the senior corps area commander in the army area became the army commander.

Throughout this period much attention was paid to the planning of economic mobilization policies for a future war. In fact, this planning became the chief interest of the Office of the Assistant Secretary of War. In June 1922 the Secretary of War and the Secretary of the Navy joined in creating the Army and Navy Munitions Board (ANMB) to provide a common meeting ground for the discussion of procurement planning problems and for the development of joint policies. The Army members generally tended to take more interest in these matters than did those of the Navy. The board itself, made up of the Assistant Secretary of War and the Assistant Secretary of the Navy, was never very active. In February 1924 the War Department also established the Army Industrial College, where primary attention was given to procurement problems of World War I and their implications for a future war emergency.[24] The staff of the Office of the Assistant Secretary of War not only cooperated closely with the staff of the Industrial College, but also after 1926 engaged in the preparation and revision of industrial mobilization plans, the latest revised plan being that of 1939.

Congress also began to take an interest in various aspects of the problem. A War Policies Commission, recommended by President Hoover and set up by legislative action, noted the importance of procurement planning in its report on 3 March 1932. This commission, consisting of six cabinet officers, four Senators, and four members of the House of Representatives, recommended that Congressional committees review procurement plans every two years. In 1933 the Senate special committee inquiring into the munitions industry, under the chairmanship of Senator Gerald P. Nye, extended the scope of its investigation to take into account the current industrial mobilization plans.

In spite of the increased interest of the Office of the Assistant Secretary of War in procurement planning, there was little friction between it and the Supply Division of the General Staff at this time. The volume of military purchasing was too small to raise serious jurisdictional problems. The average annual sum available for augmentation and replacement of arms and equipment in tne fiscal years 1926 through 1933 amounted to $25,500,-000, and but $91,000,000 in the fiscal years 1934 through 1940.[25]

Nevertheless, one incident in the 1930's revealed that conflict between the Office of the Assistant Secretary of War and the War Department General Staff was more than a possibility. Harry H. Woodring, Assistant Secretary of War from 1933 to 1936, was convinced that the so-called protective mobilization plan of the General Staff was unrealistic in its scheduling of Army strength at various periods after

---

[24] WD GO 7, 25 Feb 24.

[25] These data are taken from charts prepared in 1941 by Brig. Gen. Leonard P. Ayres which were filed in the Control Division, ASF.

mobilization. He felt that it would be impossible to provide the necessary equipment for the contemplated force within the time period stated in the plan and so he requested the WDGS to revise its schedule for mobilizing troop strength. This the General Staff was reluctant to do. After the death of George Dern, Woodring became Secretary of War, and the conflict flared out into the open. In an attempt to settle the issue, he directed the General Staff to revise its time schedule.[26]

Several changes in Army organization followed the beginnings of American mobilization in the summer of 1940. As proposed by the Harbord Board in 1921, a General Headquarters was activated on 26 July 1940. In October a second change was made when the command of the four armies and the corps areas was separated. Shortly afterward, on 19 November, the General Headquarters Air Force was taken from the chief of the Air Corps and assigned to the recently activated General Headquarters. Since GHQ was expected to command overseas operations in the event of war, this move failed to please most airmen.

The proponents of an independent air force had long been dissatisfied with War Department organization as it pertained to the air arm. European war experience reinforced their claims that the plane had its own distinct strategic and tactical mission. This was partly recognized by Secretary of War Stimson, who stated in his first report: "The functions of modern air power which have been developed and demonstrated during this war have vitally affected previously approved methods of warfare. They have been carefully studied by our own Army and have powerfully affected our plans and organization." [27] On 20 June 1941 the War Department

created the Army Air Forces which absorbed both the Air Corps and the GHQ Air Force. At the same time, all airfields within the United States were brought under the jurisdiction of the AAF. Combat planes of all kinds were now separated from Army ground troops. A separate air force within the Army had finally come into being. This change in the status of the air arm was the most important alteration in Army organization between 1918 and Pearl Harbor. By comparison, even the creation of General Headquarters was of secondary importance.

The organization for the direction of supply and procurement activities was modified only in a minor particular after the European war began. On 16 December 1940 Congress authorized the President to appoint, with confirmation by the Senate, an Under Secretary of War. In addition, Section 5a of the National Defense Act of 1920 was amended to give the Secretary of War power to assign procurement supervision to any of his staff members. To fill the position of Under Secretary, the then Assistant Secretary of War, Robert Patterson, was nominated and confirmed, and on 28 April 1941 the Secretary of War delegated his procurement supervisory duties to the Under Secretary. Meanwhile, as Army procurement operations expanded during 1940 and 1941, the Office of the Under Secretary of War (OUSW) grew in personnel strength. Whereas on 1 July 1939 the Office of the Assistant Secretary of War had a total strength of only 78 officers and civilians, on 1 November 1941 the Office of the

[26] Annual *Report of the Secretary of War to the President, 1938* (Washington, U.S. Government Printing Office, 1938), p. 1.

[27] Annual *Report of the Secretary of War to the President, 1941* (Washington, U.S. Government Printing Office, 1941), p. 7.

Under Secretary of War numbered 1,136 persons, of whom 257 were officers and 879 were civilians.[28] Supply activity in the General Staff was likewise growing, and at the time of Pearl Harbor it required a G–4 staff of about 250 persons, of whom 100 were officers.

At the outbreak of the war with Japan, the military organization within the United States under the Secretary of War consisted of five major elements:

First, the top direction of military activities was vested in the Chief of Staff, assisted by the General Staff. The volume of General Staff activity had become such that in addition to the five divisions, each headed by an assistant chief of staff, there were three deputy chiefs of staff: one for supply, one for administration, and one for air matters. This last position was held concurrently by the chief of the Air Forces.

Secondly, there were two major commands, the Army Air Forces and General Headquarters. The AAF was responsible for the development and procurement of air supplies, the training and control of air combat units, and the planning of air operations. GHQ was responsible for the tactical training of ground combat units, combined air-ground training, and overall planning for the defense of the continental United States. Four territorial defense commands, created in the spring of 1941, provided a skeleton organization for conducting defense operations.

In the third place, the War Department in Washington contained the offices of a number of combat arms, service arms, supply services, and administrative bureaus. The chiefs of the combat arms—Infantry, Field Artillery, Coast Artillery, and Cavalry—were responsible for the operation of training schools and for developing tactical doctrine for their individual arms. One, the Chief of the Coast Artillery Corps, also had procurement responsibility for certain coastal defense equipment and ammunition. The service arms and supply services were headed respectively by the Chief of Engineers, the Chief Signal Officer, the Chief of Ordnance, The Quartermaster General, The Surgeon General, and the Chief of the Chemical Warfare Service. The Adjutant General's Department, The Inspector General's Department, the Judge Advocate General's Department, and the Finance Department were the War Department's administrative bureaus.

In the fourth place, there were the four armies and the nine corps areas. The armies commanded most of the ground combat forces within the United States, and the corps areas supplied and managed most of the military posts. The corps areas were also responsible for performing much of the work of mobilizing a civilian army in case of an emergency, as they had been doing under the Selective Training and Service Act of 1940.

Finally, there were a number of miscellaneous installations reporting directly to the Chief of Staff in Washington. These included ports of embarkation, certain schools such as the Command and General Staff School and the United States Military Academy, disciplinary barracks, and general depots.

Prior to the outbreak of war the proper role of the Air Forces, the ambiguous position of General Headquarters in relation to the General Staff and to field com-

---

[28] These figures are taken from a report to the Under Secretary of War by the management engineering company of Booz, Frey, Allen, and Hamilton, entitled Survey of the Office of the Under Secretary of War, dated 20 December 1941, and filed in the Under Secretary's office. This report will hereafter be cited as the Booz report.

mand, and the uncertain relationship of the General Staff to the Under Secretary of War in supply matters remained unsolved problems. These accumulated problems brought about a re-examination of War Department organization soon after the United States plunged into the war. From this study emerged the reorganized Army which was to fight World War II.

CHAPTER II

The Reorganization of the War Department

Several different forces produced the extensive reorganization of the War Department which was officially announced by Secretary of War Stimson on 2 March 1942. During the latter half of 1941, demands for changes in the existing organization had come from various sources and were strangely interwoven. The result in 1942 was an attempt to meet existing dissatisfaction and at the same time to construct a workable Army high-command structure to direct the conduct of the war.

The historians of the Army Ground Forces have observed that the Army Air Forces "took the lead and supplied the drive" for reorganization.[1] The motivation was simple enough. One of the paramount aims of many air leaders between the two wars had been the establishment of an independent air force.[2] Although substantial progress toward this objective was made with the creation of the AAF in June 1941, the air leadership in the Army was still not content with its status. By late 1941, many persons within the Army Air Forces had become convinced "that the most successful solution would involve a radical reorganization of the military establishment, with the AAF enjoying virtual autonomy within the War Department."[3]

Though the Air Forces supplied the drive for reorganization, the initial impetus came from Lt. Gen. Lesley J. McNair, the chief of staff of GHQ, who from the beginning had experienced difficulty with the uncertainty of his assigned mission and the relation of his command to the air arm and to the War Department General Staff. Originally General Headquarters was viewed as the body that, when mobilized, would draft war plans and conduct actual operations. Largely based upon World War I experience, the early assumption had been that in the event of another war the United States would again send an expeditionary force to Europe. Just as General Pershing had determined the conduct of military operations without guidance from the General Staff in Washington, so, it was assumed, General Headquarters would move overseas to plan and direct operations of the new expeditionary force. Yet when GHQ was established in July 1940, it did not include the War Plans Division, which continued to be the main center of strategic planning in the War Department. Unlike

---

[1] Greenfield, Palmer, and Wiley, *The Organization of Ground Combat Troops*, p. 153.

[2] Craven and Cate, *AAF I*, p. 17.

[3] *Ibid.*, p. 115. On the Air Forces' drive for autonomy, see also Mark S. Watson, *Chief of Staff: Prewar Plans and Preparations*, UNITED STATES ARMY IN WORLD WAR II (Washington, U.S. Government Printing Office, 1950), Ch. IX.

the situation in World War I, it seemed that military activity in a new conflict would take place on many fronts. It was therefore not practical to send War Department planners to any single theater because of the necessity of having a central headquarters for world-wide over-all planning.

Although General Marshall was both chief of the WDGS and commanding general of GHQ, the staffs of the two organizations had a separate identity and tended to move in somewhat different and even competitive paths. Moreover, when General Headquarters was originally set up, it was assigned a training mission rather than an operational one.[4] Even in this function of training, GHQ's responsibilities came into conflict with those of the chiefs of combat arms. The chiefs of arms propounded doctrine and trained individual officers and men. GHQ supervised the training of tactical units and developed the doctrine for their employment. There remained ample room for conflict between the chiefs of arms and General Headquarters over the development of training doctrine.

The functions of GHQ, aside from training, remained ill-defined. On 3 July 1941 a directive to General McNair gave him wide potential authority over the planning and control of military operations in various fields. On the surface, this seemed to strengthen GHQ, but the authority was more nominal than actual.[5] Hedged by many limitations, General McNair lacked sufficient control over supply to carry out his enlarged responsibility; furthermore other agencies had partial control in other respects over overseas garrisons placed under his supervision. It was not long before General McNair determined to have this anomalous situation remedied. On 25 July 1941 he sent a memorandum to the Chief of Staff of the War Department requesting, simply enough, that overseas bases be grouped into defense commands and that General Headquarters be made responsible for directing all activities of these bases.[6] This memorandum precipitated a fundamental examination of the existing War Department and Army command organization.

In the discussions that followed, the problem of procurement and supply had to be faced. The planners seemed to feel that this problem was incidental to and dependent on the resolution of the larger general problems of command. But General McNair appreciated the fact that a tactical mission without control of supply support created complications. He had encountered that problem in several Atlantic bases. He therefore tended to favor the creation of a Services of Supply, modeled after Pershing's organization in France in 1918, but applied to the zone of interior. The question of supply and procurement thus crept in through the back door, but nonetheless it remained an important consideration in the effort to find an adequate solution to the problem of organization.[7]

In mid-August 1941 Lt. Col. William K. Harrison, Jr., a WPD officer long interested in War Department organization,

[4] Ltr, TAG to CG's of Corps Areas, Armies and Depts, Chiefs SAS and CO's exempted stas, 26 Jul 40, sub: GHQ, AG 320.2 (7–25–42) M (Ret) M–OCS.

[5] Ltr, TAG to CofS GHQ, 3 Jul 41, sub: Enlargement of the Functions of GHQ, AG 320.2 (6–19–41) MC–E–W.

[6] Memo, CofS GHQ for CofS, 25 Jul 41, sub: Defense Comds, WPD 4558, Tab 1.

[7] Memo, McNair for Gen William Bryden, 21 Oct 41, sub: Functions, Responsibilities and Authority of GHQ, and accompanying memos, 15 Aug 41, 2 Sep 41, filed together in WPD 4558 under Tab 12; Greenfield, Palmer, and Wiley, *The Organization of Ground Combat Troops*, p. 148.

presented the first clear-cut description of the principles of the plan which was later adopted. It included a sketch of the functions of a separate service force.[8] The War Plans Division, knowing that General Marshall still hoped to retain the framework of the existing organization, temporarily shelved Harrison's plans, but the seed thus planted shortly took root.[9]

At this point, the Air Forces became the dominant factor in the drive toward reorganization. The idea of a service command fitted in particularly well with its aims. When, toward the end of October, writing for General Arnold, Brig. Gen. Carl Spaatz recommended the abolition of GHQ and the formation under the Chief of Staff of a small General Staff and autonomous air and ground forces, also he recommended a service force.[10] Like the Harrison proposal, this recommendation was at the moment unacceptable. The War Plans Division continued to wrestle with the problem.[11]

General Arnold broke the log jam in mid-November 1941. Emphasizing the importance of air power in modern war, he wrote directly to General Marshall and asked for a complete reorganization that would allow the air force to play its proper role. The Air Forces supported a plan providing for three separate commands—air, ground, and service—with a Chief of Staff and a small General Staff in top control. The War Plans division received the Arnold memorandum for comment and concurred with it in principle.[12] General Marshall was "favorably impressed" and directed that the WPD develop the proposal in sufficient detail to determine its practicability.[13]

Thus the Army Air Forces became the champion of a thorough War Department reorganization which would include the creation of a Services of Supply. Remaining within the existing military framework meant it would need to work with the War Department supply bureaus. Since General McNair had already suggested that his own General Headquarters could not function effectively unless it were given greater control of supply matters, and since the Air Forces was unwilling to see supply activities turned over to GHQ, it could logically support a plan to establish a separate supply command for ground and air forces under War Department direction.

Another strong reason for reorganization, and one tied in with Air Forces' pressure for change, was the fact that the administrative burden of the Chief of Staff was becoming increasingly heavy. This was a difficulty that had plagued generals and statesmen throughout history, and one that had become more and more burdensome with the growing complexity of modern armies. Brig. Gen. Robert L. Bullard during World War I had expressed the fear that the general staff system would break down because no one man could handle the details heaped on the Chief of Staff and still direct a war.[14]

---

[8] Memo for CofS, sub: Org of the Army High Comd, WPD 4618.

[9] Col Frederick S. Haydon, War Department Reorganization, August 1941–March 1942, MS, OCMH. This monograph discusses the reorganization exhaustively from the point of view of the Chief of Staff, but without examining in detail the problem of supply organization. See also Cline, *Washington Command Post*, pp. 70–74, 90–93.

[10] Memo, Spaatz for ACofS WPD, 24 Oct 41, sub: Functions, Responsibilities, and Authority of GHQ, WPD 4558, Tab 11.

[11] Haydon MS, cited in n. 9.

[12] Memo, Arnold for CofS, atchd to chart dated 14 Nov 41, sub: Reorg of the WD, WPD 4614.

[13] Memo, CofS for ACofS WPD, 25 Nov 41, WPD 4614.

[14] O. L. Nelson, *National Security and the General Staff*, p. 225.

On the eve of World War II, in spite of specific orders to bring to his attention only those matters that could be handled by no one else, General Marshall was swamped by the demands on his time to decide relatively unimportant questions. No less than sixty-one officers and agencies, some with overlapping authority, had direct access to him. About fifty staff studies were given to him each day, leaving him time for little else.[15] With the creation of three large commands to which administration in the zone of interior would be delegated, Marshall and the General Staff could concentrate on planning and policy making. Among other things, it was hoped that this easing of the administrative burden would contribute toward a solution of the problem of organizational relationships between air and ground forces. Although in sympathy with the desire of Air officers for a major role in the planning and direction of air operations, General Marshall was determined to keep the Army Air Forces at least nominally in the existing military structure in order to promote collaboration between ground and air operations. He felt that this could be achieved more easily if he personally gave greater attention to the Air Forces. He was firmly convinced that he could do this and attend to general strategic planning and direction of operations only if the War Department were so organized that the work of raising, training, supplying, and servicing the Army in the United States was concentrated in the hands of the fewest possible persons reporting directly to him.

Toward the end of November 1941, General Marshall was thus persuaded to proceed with a study of War Department reorganization. A committee of three was created to undertake this investigation. To serve as chairman of the committee, Marshall brought back Brig. Gen. Joseph T. McNarney from England where he had been serving as an observer. The other two members were Colonel Harrison of WPD and Lt. Col. Laurence S. Kuter of the Office of the Secretary of the General Staff. The work on reorganization was suspended shortly after the Japanese attack on Pearl Harbor when General McNarney was dispatched to Hawaii with the Roberts Board to investigate that military disaster. For the moment, reorganization had to wait, even though the advent of war had given a new urgency to the problem.

Reorganization of the OUSW

The various reorganization plans circulating before December 1941 failed to take into account the vital role of the Under Secretary of War. As noted earlier, his office had grown into a sizable staff supervising War Department activities in the field of procurement and general economic mobilization. A reorganization which affected supply operations would probably necessitate a reorganization of Under Secretary Patterson's office.[16]

Prior to his appointment in 1940 as Assistant Secretary of War, Mr. Patterson had had little experience in procurement or other industrial affairs, nor had he even read Section 5a of the National Defense Act of 1920 which outlined the responsi-

---

[15] Haydon MS, cited in n. 9.

[16] Mr. Patterson had had a distinguished career. His record as an officer in World War I had been exceptional. In the 1920's he had been a successful lawyer in New York City, and in 1930 President Herbert Hoover had appointed him a judge of the United States District Court. Nine years later, President Roosevelt promoted him to the Circuit Court of Appeals. During this period he had kept alive his interest in the Army as a Reserve officer.

bilities of his new position. But, working in close harmony with Secretary of War Stimson, Patterson soon showed in high degree all the qualities that make a successful administrator. Though inexperienced as a business executive, he was an indefatigable worker, co-operative, modest, and willing to take advice. He often conferred with Bernard Baruch, for many years highly regarded as an expert on government problems.[17]

Mr. Patterson took office coincidentally with the launching of a huge mobilization program in the summer of 1940. A major difficulty for him was the relatively indifferent caliber and low rank of the military personnel attached to his organization. Rebuffed in the attempt to gain control over procurement activities after World War I, the General Staff had seemingly acquiesced in civilian domination over the business side of the War Department. One result was that the Assistant Secretary's organization was removed from the main stream of military interest and activity. The officers assigned to it sometimes felt that they had reached a blind alley in their careers. Often their military rank was too low to permit effective performance of duties.[18] But the difficulty was not only one of caliber and rank. The civilian and military personnel were too few in number to take care of the growing responsibilities of their rapidly expanding office. In the first year of Mr. Patterson's incumbency, personnel multiplied about fivefold and new organizational arrangements were improvised in an effort to cope with the situation.

Mr. Patterson set about to remedy matters after his appointment as Under Secretary. In the summer of 1941 he employed a private firm, Booz, Frey, Allen, and Hamilton, management consultants, to make a study of the organization of his office. This firm, which had just completed a survey in the Navy Department, began its work on 5 August and finished the task two weeks after Pearl Harbor.[19]

Before submitting their report, the management consultants made a number of interim recommendations—such as one for the creation of a separate administrative branch. Some of these, the Under Secretary adopted. The final report, given to Mr. Patterson on 20 December 1941, described the organizational structure of the office and listed six major problems. In the first place, it pointed out that neither the personnel in the office nor those in the supply arms and services subject to the Under Secretary's supervision understood clearly the purpose of the office. In the second place, it noted that duplication and overlapping of functions reduced the effectiveness of supervision. Third, the Booz report expressed the opinion that the military personnel often lacked sufficient rank, training, and general ability to perform their assigned duties. Fourth, the report harshly criticised current methods of statistical reporting. Fifth, it also pointed to the difficult problems in the relationship of the office to other units of the War Department and to the civilian defense agencies of the Government. Finally, the report declared that the administrative services of the office needed improvement.[20]

---

[17] Interv, Anderson with Patterson, 22 Sep 44; Anderson, Introduction to the History of the Under Secretary of War's Office, MS, OCMH, Ch. VI.

[18] Booz Rpt; Goldthwaite H. Dorr, Memorandum Notes on the Activities of an Informal Group in Connection with Supply Reorganization in the War Department, January–May 1942, prepared about 1 March 1946, filed in OCMH. (Hereafter cited as Dorr, Memorandum Notes.)

[19] Corresp, 26 Jun 41–9 Mar 42, 310 Business Methods, OUSW, AG Recs.

[20] Booz Rpt.

The management experts were especially concerned about the relationship between the Under Secretary's office and the General Staff Supply Division (G–4). Where did the responsibility of the Supply Division end and that of the OUSW begin? On this question, the Booz report proposed the dividing line suggested twenty years earlier by the Harbord Board. The Supply Division should transmit supply requirements to the Office of the Under Secretary, whose responsibilities would begin at this point. The Under Secretary would then approve the procurement estimates made by the supply arms and services, and determine the industrial facilities, raw material requirements, and manpower needed to provide supplies within the requested time period. The Booz report suggested various techniques for insuring fulfillment of this responsibility. But, significantly, it did not consider whether this separation of supervisory responsibility between the Supply Division of the General Staff and the OUSW was workable. It said nothing about actual methods of obtaining closer working relationships with the Supply Division in the determination of supply requirements or in expediting procurement.

The most important change recommended in the Booz report was the proposal that the Under Secretary appoint a single executive, an Army officer, with the title of Procurement General, to direct the work of the office and to supervise the supply arms and services. This executive should be given the rank of lieutenant general in the Army in order that he might have a military status superior to that of the chiefs of the supply arms and services, all of whom then held the rank of major general. This "improved military leadership" proposal was directly counter to the recommendations put forward in 1920 by Benedict Crowell. Mr. Crowell, it will be recalled, had wanted an industrialist to direct the procurement work of the War Department. With the position of Under Secretary now filled by a man who was not an industrialist, the Booz consultants evidently felt the office needed strengthened contacts with the military procurement agencies. Indeed, in the procurement field it was conceivable that such a post might acquire status and authority comparable to that of the Chief of Staff in the whole Military Establishment.

The system of internal organization proposed by the Booz report for the Office of the Under Secretary was adopted with one glaring omission. The Under Secretary did not take steps to create the position of Procurement General. But the mere fact that such a post was recommended throws a revealing light upon what seemed, to outside observers, the basic weakness of the War Department's supply organization.

Reorganization of G–4

The Booz report, in recommending a clarification of the relationship of the Under Secretary to the Assistant Chief of Staff (G–4) was soon upheld by the march of events. On 25 November 1941 a new and forceful personality, Brig. Gen. Brehon B. Somervell, became G–4, WDGS. Two weeks later the United States was at war. Now, more than ever before, the supply of military forces was of critical importance. The training program had lagged in large part because there was not enough combat equipment. Shortages had slowed the strengthening of overseas garrisons, especially in the Pacific. Necessarily, some supplies had gone overseas under lend-lease. If training were to be speeded up, our allies aided, and military operations undertaken with hope of success, then supplies had to be provided from current industrial production at an ever increasing rate, and at the earliest possible moment. This meant that G–4 had to put all possible pressure upon the supply arms and services to speed up their procurement programs. Yet G–4 was not authorized to issue any orders on production matters, for production was the bailiwick of the Under Secretary of War. Here was an impossible situation, especially in the light of General Somervell's determination to fulfill his supply responsibilities as competently as possible. Being a man of action, he soon went to General Marshall with his views of the existing organizational set up.[21]

General Somervell, as he sized up his mission, realized that he could fulfill his duties and overcome organizational defects only by the closest possible co-operation with the OUSW. He stated this conviction directly to both Secretary Stimson and Under Secretary Patterson, and reiterated it on several subsequent occasions.[22] On 6 January 1942 he telephoned Mr. Goldthwaite Dorr, an attorney in New York City, and asked him to come to Washington to study the problem of supply organization in the War Department.[23] According to both General Somervell and Mr. Dorr, the request was made with the approval of Secretary Stimson and Under Secretary Patterson.[24]

Mr. Dorr arrived in Washington on 7 January 1942. General Somervell requested him to examine the problem of supply organization, particularly the relation of the Supply Division of the General Staff to the Office of the Under Secretary of War and the supervisory relationships

of both to the supply arms and services. Although Mr. Dorr was asked to serve as a consultant to the Secretary of War, he did not obtain an official appointment, received no compensation, and paid his own expenses.[25]

Mr. Dorr became chairman of an informal group which at first consisted of Mr. Robert R. West, director of the Bureau of Industrial Research at the University of Virginia, and Dr. Luther Gulick, who had served on the President's Committee on Administrative Management in 1936 and was then a consultant to the National Resources Planning Board. Subsequently, the group included Brig. Gen. Arthur H. Carter, previously a senior partner in the accounting firm of Haskens

---

[21] Interv, Anderson with Col James H. Graham, probably 1945, OCMH.

[22] Memo, 24 Jan 42, sub: WD Sup System—Preliminary Memo, DAD Misc Corresp; Memo, Somervell for OUSW, 20 Jan 42, Hq ASF, OUSW (1) 1941–42 (1); Memo, Somervell for OUSW, 3 Feb 42, Hq ASF, OUSW (1) 1941–42 (1).

[23] Mr. Dorr was a personal friend of Secretary Stimson and had known General Somervell for at least eight years. In 1906 he had joined Mr. Stimson's staff when the latter was United States Attorney for the Southern District, New York. During World War I he was Assistant Director of Munitions under Benedict Crowell, and had become familiar with the procurement operations of that period. At the end of the war, Mr. Dorr returned to a legal practice in New York City where he was a member of the firm of Hines, Rearick, Dorr, and Hammond.

[24] In an interview with Troyer Anderson, his historian, Patterson said he had no recollection of talking to General Somervell about the Dorr study. It is probable that General Somervell told Patterson that he was planning to study supply and Patterson approved in a general way. But while Patterson may have approved in theory, it is doubtful that he approved or even knew about the specific lines along which the survey developed.

[25] This account is based on the personal memorandum of Mr. Dorr, cited in n. 18. This memorandum was written by Mr. Dorr after the end of the war. A copy was provided the author, who served on the staff of the informal group, by Mr. Dorr from his own personal files.

and Sells and then director of the Administrative Branch in the Office of the Under Secretary, and James H. Graham, dean of the Engineering School of the University of Kentucky, who had been associated with General Somervell during World War I. An officer of General Somervell's staff, Lt. Col. Clinton F. Robinson, was the principal assistant to the informal group.

It is an amazing circumstance that those interested in the reorganization, including Mr. Dorr and General Somervell, were seemingly unaware of the more comprehensive plans then being discussed in the General Staff, while those planning the larger reorganization apparently did not appreciate the full effect of their plans on supply. Two streams could hardly flow very long in the same valley without merging; but during January 1942 they followed independent channels.[26]

The problem which the Dorr group was tackling was by no means novel; nor was the solution at which it arrived altogether original. The then director of defense aid in the War Department, Col. Henry S. Aurand had earlier remarked in an informal memorandum, "the crying need for reorganization of the War Department to put all supply in the hands of one man has been apparent since the time I joined the General Staff in May 1940." Colonel Aurand had consistently advocated unification of the supply system.[27] The organization finally accepted may have differed in structure and detail from the proposal of Colonel Aurand, but it was founded on the same basic principle. Another advocate of this proposal, Col. Ralph H. Tate, in the office of Assistant Secretary of War John J. McCloy, also drew up an organizational scheme centralizing the control of supply activities. Other

individuals in G–4 and in the War Production Board (WPB) had ideas on the subject. Mr. Dorr was familiar with most of these proposals.[28] Indeed, Colonel Aurand was frequently consulted by Mr. Dorr and freely assisted in the informal group.

The work of the Dorr group was, as its designation indicated, most informal. It kept no records. Its members worked individually on various assignments, and met in a "hush-hush" atmosphere after regular working hours. The discussions were kept secret. In the course of its work the group explored a wide variety of subjects, the most important of which, as already noted, was the relation between G–4 and the Under Secretary of War.[29]

Mr. Dorr decided that there were three principal objectives: to develop a War Department supply program stating military supply needs by time periods; to make more effective the powers of the Under Secretary of War in supervising military procurement; and to persuade the WPB

---

[26] On 1 December 1941 the War Plans Division had asked each of the General Staff divisions to comment on the proposed War Department and Army reorganization; this memorandum spoke of a "Commanding General, Service Command." O. L. Nelson, *National Security and the General Staff*, pp. 342–45. General Somervell has stated to the author that he has no recollection of this memorandum. General Harrison remembers discussing this proposal with Somervell and with his branch chiefs shortly after Somervell became G–4. Ltr, W. K. Harrison to Col Thomas J. Sands, OCMH, 7 Jul 50. In any event, before February 1942 there was no attempt to correlate the projected G–4 reorganization with the larger War Department reorganization plan.

[27] Interv, Maj Gen James H. Burns, Ret, with Jonathan Grossman, 9 Feb 50; Informal memo, Aurand for Moore, 24 Nov 41, sub: Necessity for Immediate Action on Certain Projects, DAD Misc Corresp LL. Interestingly enough, a copy of a preliminary memorandum by Mr. Dorr is filed with the correspondence of Colonel Aurand's office.

[28] Dorr, Memorandum Notes, pp. 6–7.

[29] Interv, cited in n. 21.

to give its attention primarily to increasing the production of raw materials and to allocating available supplies, leaving military procurement in the hands of the military agencies.[30] Only the second of these objectives specifically concerned War Department organization. Mr. Dorr favored an arrangement similar to that in force during World War I whereby General Goethals had reported to the Assistant Secretary on the business end of his job and to the Chief of Staff on the military. In other words, Mr. Dorr, as he himself acknowledged, wanted to violate the dictum, "No man can serve two masters." He reasoned that he was dealing with a unique difficulty. Those responsible for military procurement had to know supply requirements as soon as possible in order to shape production plans and schedules. Those responsible for strategic plans wanted to delay committing themselves to specific requirements lest strategy became a "prisoner" of rigid logistical arrangements. The officers in G–4 who translated strategic objectives into specific requirements of men and material were, in effect, in the middle, caught between these opposing pressures. At the same time they alone were in a position to reconcile them. But under the existing arrangement, the determination of requirements was done not only in G–4 but also by a unit in the Office of the Under Secretary of War. Mr. Dorr concluded that it was essential to bring together under one individual the determination of requirements and the control of procurement operations which fulfilled them.[31] Undoubtedly these conclusions of Mr. Dorr were also those which General Somervell had reached in his view of the work of G–4.

Mr. Dorr learned from Assistant Secretary McCloy that this possibility of a unified supply and procurement organization had been canvassed, but that no man had been found for the post who was mutually acceptable to the Chief of Staff and the Under Secretary of War. Apparently, several names were mentioned but none was acceptable to both parties. Mr. Dorr therefore turned his attention to developing a plan for closer relationships between the officers in the Supply Division concerned with requirements and the persons supervising procurement operations in the OUSW. The crucial question of a unified top organization was left unanswered for the time being.[32]

Meanwhile, the Under Secretary was trying to achieve better control over the production operations of the supply arms and services. To assist him, Mr. William S. Knudsen, formerly director general of the Office of Production Management (OPM), was commissioned a lieutenant general and assigned to the Under Secretary's office as Director of Production. General Knudsen turned at once to production trouble-shooting. During the war he visited many plants and helped solve many production problems. Vital as this work was to prove—and Under Secretary Patterson once said that it was the equivalent of "10 percent in war production"— General Knudsen still provided no solution to the problem of top level supply organization in the War Department.[33]

Early in February 1942 General Somervell learned for the first time that a general reorganization of the War Department was in the offing. During much of December and January following Pearl

---

[30] Dorr, Memorandum Notes, pp. 7–9.
[31] Ibid., pp. 11–12.
[32] Ibid., pp. 10–12.
[33] Ibid., pp. 12–13.

Harbor, General McNarney, who had been charged with planning it by Marshall, had been absent from Washington. When he returned on 23 January, the final touches were put on the War Department reorganization and on 31 January his recommendations were submitted to the Chief of Staff and given tentative approval.[34]

General Marshall called his staff together on 5 February and explained briefly the reorganization plan he was considering. He gave the staff forty-eight hours to review the proposal and to make suggestions.[35] General Somervell, acting on the realization that a far-reaching change in the structure of the War Department was being undertaken, consulted Mr. Dorr and his group at once. Both agreed that the proposal for a service command did not go far enough. In their opinion, General McNarney and his planners apparently did not understand the necessity of close interrelationships between the Supply Division and the Under Secretary of War, or the role of the Under Secretary in the procurement activities of the War Department. The fact that the Office of the Under Secretary in June 1941 had been moved into the so-called New War Department Building, a block away from the Munitions Building where the General Staff was located, may have contributed to this lack of understanding. The planners also did not seem to realize the extent to which supply operations at this time were dependent upon current production.[36]

Despite these shortcomings, Mr. Dorr saw in the reorganization plan an opportunity for recreating the kind of arrangement with which he had been familiar during World War I. He recognized that the General Staff apparently was now willing to put its supply responsibilities into a single command. This was one hurdle passed. Two more remained: to combine the large staff in the OUSW with the new supply command, and to find a chief for this command who would be acceptable to both the Chief of Staff and the Under Secretary.

Meanwhile, General McNarney told Somervell to draw up a supply organization which would meet the War Department's needs. Since the Chief of Staff was determined to announce a reorganization during the month of February, Somervell had to act quickly. This meant that only a few far-reaching changes could be introduced; there was no time to plan a thorough-going alteration of the existing system.[37] Assisted by two staff officers—Col. W. D. Styer and Lt. Col. C. F. Robinson—General Somervell prepared a plan for a unified organization to be known as the Services of Supply and commanded by an Army officer. This was very different from an enlarged G–4 type organization such as the Purchase, Storage, and Traffic Division of World War I.

General Somervell accepted the existence of the supply arms and services as then constituted with their combined procurement and distribution responsibilities divided on a broad commodity basis. The only change was the creation of a transportation organization in the headquarters of the new command which would remove transportation from the Office of The Quartermaster General.

The question was raised as to whether there should be a Director of Procurement

---

[34] General McNarney's reorganization recommendations are reproduced in O. L. Nelson, *National Security and the General Staff*, p. 349.

[35] Ltr, W. K. Harrison to Sands, cited in n. 26.

[36] Dorr, Memorandum Notes, pp. 14–15.

[37] *Ibid.*, pp. 15–16.

under the commanding general of the SOS. A plan had been considered for a Director of Procurement and a Director of Distribution or Storage with important supervisory responsibilities. But the decision to retain the supply arms and services made such a scheme unworkable. A compromise was reached with the creation of a Director of Procurement and Distribution who was in a sense a deputy to the commanding general for these functions. At the same time, the new supply command was to become the budget and financial office of the War Department. There was precedent for this step in General Goethals' authority in 1918, but another reason of current importance was the fact that since most of the appropriations to the War Department were for procurement, this arrangement would simplify the appropriation and accounting system for war purposes.[38]

There were many other points to consider. Was the Services of Supply also to be a personnel agency? Just before the armistice of 1918, Secretary of War Baker had favored the creation of a new personnel organization in the War Department, but the war ended before the decision could be effected. There was now a disposition to revive the plan and separate personnel administration from the supply operations of the new command. This immediately raised another question. What should be done with the administrative bureaus of the War Department such as the Judge Advocate General's office, the Chief of Chaplains, the National Guard Bureau, and the Post Exchange Service? Mr. Dorr believed that it would be undesirable to load up the SOS with a wide assortment of organizations functioning under its command. At one time he considered the possibility of placing these various services

under Assistant Secretary of War McCloy. Mr. Dorr discussed the matter with him, but Mr. McCloy was reluctant to take over these diverse responsibilities. Then, the Chief of Staff made it clear that he did not wish to have a fourth command in the United States; since the SOS was expected to handle the common supply problems of the Department, it seemed the appropriate agency also to handle common administrative problems.[39] In the end, it was decided to create a position of Chief of Administrative Services and group the various administrative bureaus under him.

In the second week of February, after several adjustments, General Somervell submitted an acceptable plan for a unified supply and service command to General McNarney. The work on this, like the work of McNarney's committee, had been done in secret so as not to give anticipated opposition a chance to organize before the plan was complete. General Marshall had directed that even Under Secretary Patterson be kept in ignorance of developments.[40] It was Mr. Dorr's belief that, though the reorganization plan "ignored the functions of the Under Secretary of War under the National Defense Act of 1920," particularly in the bald form in which it was presented by General McNarney to Somervell, this was not because of an "intentional design" to change the fundamental structure of the War Department. Rather it was because of "the inadvertence of a group of officers who did not know much about the supply side of the Army."[41]

---

[38] *Ibid.*, pp. 16–18.

[39] *Ibid.*, pp. 19–20.

[40] Notes on Conf in ODCofS, 5 Feb 42, DCofS Recs, Notes on Conf and other Info, Feb 42, Binder 32.

[41] Dorr, Memorandum Notes, pp. 14–15.

Thus General Somervell, with the help of Mr. Dorr, modified the McNarney plan as it affected procurement operations and the Office of the Under Secretary. In working out last minute details, they restated the powers of the Under Secretary in order to conform, at least in part, to the original intention of the National Defense Act of 1920.

Toward the end of February, Assistant Secretary McCloy who was handling reorganization details for Secretary Stimson asked General McNarney, General Somervell, Brig. Gen. Bennett E. Meyers, who was in charge of procurement for the Army Air Forces, and Mr. Dorr, to take up the proposal with Under Secretary Patterson. The latter was practically faced with a choice between accepting a *fait accompli,* or delaying the much needed reorganization. He might still influence details, but the broad outline of the plan was probably already fixed. Mr. Patterson studied the plan. One of the first features on which he commented was the removal of procurement of Air Forces supplies from the jurisdiction of the SOS. Under the plan, the Under Secretary would still supervise air force procurement but not through the Services of Supply. The arrangement was defended by General Meyers on the ground that, because of the legislative interest in a completely autonomous air force, it was essential at this time to keep air procurement separate from the common supply organization of the War Department.[42]

The Under Secretary was still not satisfied with this arrangement. His staff had been supervising air matériel operations along with those of the other arms and services. Now, practically all of his staff was to be placed under the commanding general of the SOS, yet he personally was still expected to supervise the procurement operations of the Air Forces. In the end, the only solution was a dotted line on the organization chart of the proposed Services of Supply which indicated that on procurement and related functions, the matériel command of the AAF would be subject to the supervision of the SOS Director of Procurement and Distribution in the name of the Under Secretary.[43]

The Under Secretary reserved decision on the plan as a whole in order to discuss the details with his own staff. The inclusion of Mr. Dorr in these subsequent discussions did much to clarify the purpose of the reorganization. Indeed, it had been Mr. Dorr's influence which had resulted in the inclusion of words ordering the commanding general of the Services of Supply to act "under the direction of the Under Secretary of War" on "procurement and related matters." The Under Secretary raised the question whether the interposition of a SOS between himself and the supply arms and services would create obstacles to the performance of his basic responsibilities. Mr. Dorr argued that the position of the commanding general of the SOS on procurement matters would be comparable to that of an executive vice-president or a general manager in a large corporation. The staff organization of the SOS would be available to the Under Secretary for his use, and Mr. Dorr saw no reason why he should not be able to deal with the chiefs of the supply arms and services whenever he felt the need to do so. Furthermore, Mr. Dorr expressed the opinion that the Under Secretary would retain his own personal assistants, whom he had previously recruited and who were now associated with him, in his own office. He could devote himself to policy decisions and tough problems while

[42] *Ibid.,* pp. 21–22.
[43] *Ibid.,* p. 22.

the commanding general of the SOS would relieve him of a multitude of burdensome details.[44]

Some of Mr. Patterson's assistants did not agree with Mr. Dorr's arguments. They believed that since the loyalty of the commanding general of the SOS under the proposed plan would be to the Chief of Staff first, the Under Secretary would play a much reduced role. The director of the Bureau of the Budget, who was much concerned, asked that the President protect the Under Secretary by defining his powers. Otherwise he believed, "the proposed arrangement could easily result in purchase and procurement work being insulated from the top civilian side of the Department."[45]

Mr. Patterson himself seemed disposed to follow the general outline of reorganization. He rejected the advice of one of his most trusted assistants who prepared a directive to be included in the plan which would require that important changes in the supply organization be reviewed for final approval by the Under Secretary of War. Mr. Patterson opposed such a measure because he believed that in time he could work out problems with the supply head on an informal basis.[46]

The Under Secretary, on the other hand, did require certain changes in the plan for amalgamating his staff with that of G–4. Initially, the plan had contemplated combining the supervision of requirements and production in a single unit. At the Under Secretary's insistence, the separate identity of the two offices concerned with these activities was preserved, though both were placed under a Deputy Chief of Staff for Requirements and Resources.[47]

Mr. Dorr had several times pointed out that the central problem was to find a head for the new command who would be suitable to both Chief of Staff Marshall and Under Secretary Patterson. Toward the end of February, Mr. Patterson learned that General Somervell was being considered by the Chief of Staff for the job. He had already had some contact with General Somervell. He had admired the vigor with which Somervell as chief of the Construction Division in the Office of The Quartermaster General had pushed the building of Army camps, and had recommended him for an award of an oak leaf cluster to his Distinguished Service Medal.[48] On the other hand, he had experienced at first hand General Somervell's brusqueness which could and did antagonize people. Late in 1941, in order to speed production, Mr. Patterson had approved the construction of an arsenal near the coast at Houston, Texas. Somervell curtly wrote him that the only other similar plant was also near the coast, and he hoped that it "will not be put out of production by enemy action. It is likewise hoped that, with thousands of square miles and almost unlimited facilities . . . no more production facilities will be located outside the strategic area."[49] General Somervell was quick to apologize for the tone of his letter; the very next day, he

[44] Ibid., pp. 23–27.

[45] Memo, Dir Bureau of the Budget, 25 Feb 42, quoted in O. L. Nelson, National Security and the General Staff, p. 351.

[46] Intervs, Anderson with Patterson, Col Gerson K. Heiss, Miles Knowles, H. C. Petersen, and Brig Gen Edward Greenbaum, 1944–45; Interv, Burns with Grossman, 9 Feb 50. Summaries of all intervs are in OCMH files.

[47] Upon General Somervell's recommendation the Under Secretary accepted Brig. Gen. Lucius D. Clay for this latter position.

[48] Memo, USW for SW, 22 Dec 41; Memo, Patterson for Somervell, 27 Nov 41. Both in OUSW file, Personal Folders, Gen Somervell.

[49] Memo, Somervell for USW, 31 Dec 41, Somervell Files, Hq ASF, USW (1) 1941–42 (1).

wrote a "please-do-not-bother-to-answer-this" note saying he held Mr. Patterson in the highest personal and professional esteem and that he was greatly distressed to learn that his memorandum had given offense.[50] The letter and issue were trivial, but they were characteristic of the Somervell drive. Mr. Patterson admired General Somervell's dynamic personality but was somewhat worried about future relations with him. He mentioned it not only to Mr. Dorr, but to many others including the new chairman of the War Production Board, Donald M. Nelson. Mr. Nelson, who shortly thereafter became involved in a hot dispute with General Somervell, at this time recommended him as a good man to occupy this important military position dealing with supply. Mr. Dorr also spoke highly of General Somervell but tactfully added that in a question of personality, Mr. Patterson should use his own judgment. Patterson then acquiesced in both the reorganization and the appointment of General Somervell.[51]

The completed reorganization plan was ordered into effect by the President on 28 February 1942,[52] and on 2 March 1942 Secretary Stimson announced the reorganization in a press release. In a brief memorandum to those members of his staff transferred to the new command, asking that they share their loyalty to him with the new commanding general, Under Secretary Patterson declared that the unification of supply "under the vigorous leadership of General Somervell, will enable us to perform our huge task with greater dispatch and better coordination."[53] On 9 March 1942 General Somervell assumed his new responsibilities as commanding general of the Services of Supply, or, as it will be called hereafter, the Army Service Forces.[54]

The Reorganization of 9 March 1942

The President's executive order directing the reorganization of March 1942 attracted relatively little public attention. It was practically swept off the front pages of the newspapers by the dramatic Japanese push into Java and by British commando raids on the German-held French coast. Nevertheless this brief and prosaic order, in the words of one commentator, directed "the most drastic and fundamental change which the War Department had experienced since the establishment of the General Staff by Elihu Root in 1903."[55]

The President's order authorized the Secretary of War to prescribe the functions and duties of the new commands. As Commander in Chief, the President specifically reserved the authority to deal directly with the Chief of Staff on matters concerning military strategy and tactics.

[50] Memo, Somervell for USW, 1 Jan 42, Somervell Files, Hq ASF, USW (1) 1941–42 (1).

[51] Dorr, Memorandum Notes, pp. 26–27. Somervell had indirectly learned early in February that he was General Marshall's choice for the job. In Somervell's mind there was never any doubt that the crucial factor in his appointment was General Marshall's own decision. He always assumed not only that the new supply command was General Marshall's own creation, but also that whoever headed it was General Marshall's man. It was primarily the Chief of Staff, he believed, who had to be satisfied with the performance of the Services of Supply.

[52] EO 9028, 28 Feb 42.

[53] Memo, USW for Staff, 10 Mar 42, OUSW, misc under sub, SOS Cirs and Memos.

[54] As already noted, the designation Army Service Forces did not come into official use until March 1943. General McNarney's papers generally spoke of a "service command." The old AEF term Services of Supply began to appear in General Somervell's papers about 16 February 1942 and was used in the executive order of 28 February and in War Department Circular 59, 2 March 1942.

[55] O. L. Nelson, *National Security and the General Staff*, p. 335.

The executive order became effective on 9 March 1942, and was to remain in force during the war and for six months thereafter. Detailed War Department instructions with respect to the reorganization were issued in War Department Circular 59, dated 2 March 1942. Simultaneously, the War Department in a press release explained to the public that the creation of three separate commands under the Chief of Staff—ground, air, and service—was needed in order to get away from the existing cumbersome staff structure. The redistribution of duties was expected to streamline the Department and gear it to world-wide operations. Through reorganization, it was hoped to obtain better control over important matters, to delegate details, and to achieve greater co-operation between air and ground forces.[56]

Under the new concept, the War Department General Staff would be composed of a small number of officers who would assist the Chief of Staff "in strategic planning and direction, and in coordinating the activities of the three great commands in order to provide theater commanders with the broad directives and with the means for conducting the actual war operations."[57]

The new Commanding General, Army Air Forces, succeeded to most of the duties previously allocated to the chief of the Army Air Forces, together with some new ones. The air command was to have its own general and administrative staffs. It would train and equip air units for both "independent air striking and for combined combat operations with the ground forces."[58] The Air Forces would also be responsible for the research, design, development, and procurement of all items peculiar to air operations.

The new Commanding General, Army Ground Forces, took over responsibility for organizing and training ground combat troops. The functions of the semiautonomous chiefs of the combat arms of infantry, cavalry, field artillery, and coast artillery were, for the most part, absorbed by the Commanding General, Army Ground Forces, and the arms thereby lost their independent status. In consequence, they could now be better trained as a balanced combat team.

To the Commanding General, Army Service Forces, fell the task of relieving the fighting arms, air and ground, of the "distraction and effort required by supply, procurement, and general housekeeping duties, except for experimental development and procurement peculiar to the Air Forces."[59] He was also expected to relieve the Chief of Staff of details of administration, including budgets, induction of personnel, the maintenance of records, and similar matters.

War Department Circular 59 described the organizational structure of the ASF and set forth the duties assigned to the new command. These duties covered a wide field. The Chief of Staff was determined that there would be no more than three commands in the United States reporting to him. Therefore, all responsibilities which did not fit into the Ground or Air Forces were dumped into the Service Forces. The ASF thus became a catch-all command, as already indicated. Some of the duties logically belonged in it; others were put there because they could not logically be placed anywhere else.

The hard core of the Army Service Forces was the procurement and supply

---

[56] WD press release, BPR, "Reorganization of the War Department," 2 Mar 42.

[57] *Ibid.*

[58] *Ibid.*

[59] *Ibid.*

function. The bulk of the Office of the Under Secretary of War, because it was concerned with procurement and industrial mobilization, along with most of the personnel of G–4 of the General Staff, became part of the new organization. The chiefs of the six supply arms and services, who formerly reported directly to the Chief of Staff, now reported to the Commanding General, ASF. These arms and services were the Quartermaster Corps, the Ordnance Department, the Corps of Engineers, the Medical Department, the Signal Corps, and the Chemical Warfare Service. In addition, the procurement and supply duties of the Coast Artillery Corps were transferred to the Ordnance Department.

The new setup of 9 March 1942 recognized an organizational need which had been evident in the top command of the Army, both overseas and in the United States, since World War I. This need was to handle all procurement and all supply operations as one integrated activity. No supply arm or service could do the job by itself. An army in combat had to have all its supplies, from weapons and ammunition to gasoline, food, and clothing, on a schedule which brought all of these items together in the right place at the right time. The ASF was the War Department's answer to this vital need in World War II.

The "mission" of the ASF "to provide services and supplies to meet military requirements" imposed upon it duties in addition to its functions of procurement and supply, as already stated. These duties were not precisely defined, several overlapped, and some were susceptible of elastic interpretation. Among them were included the direction of research, storage, and distribution of supplies; purchasing and contractual procedures; construction

for the Army; consolidation of supply programs and requirements procured for the Army, Navy, and defense aid; fiscal administration; direction of certain Army-wide functions such as premilitary training, manpower mobilization, and labor relations; operation of reception centers, replacement training centers, and training schools for the supply arms and services; technical training of individuals, basic training of service troops, and technical training of service units; the furnishing of ASF personnel to the Army Air and Ground Forces, theaters of operations, and overseas forces; and a large number of other duties.[60]

Many organizations were made part of the ASF to assist in its "mission" to "provide services and supplies to meet military requirements." Among these were the various administrative bureaus of the War Department. These included the offices of the Judge Advocate General, The Adjutant General, the Provost Marshal General, the Chief of Special Services, the Chief of Chaplains, and the Chief of Finance. Various regional organizations and installations also performed duties which might be classified as supply and administrative duties. Corps area commanders, general depots, regulating and reconsignment stations for overseas shipments, and ports of embarkation were all placed under the Army Service Forces.[61] The commanding general of the new ASF was given the functions, responsibilities, and authority of command which by law, regulation, or custom had been formerly vested in the heads of the units assigned to him.[62] He could also consolidate these

---

[60] WD Cir 59, 2 Mar 42, Sec. 7e.

[61] Ibid., Sec. 2e.

[62] Ibid., Sec. 7b.

units and make "such amalgamation, re-allocation of duties, and reorganization as is necessary or advisable." [63]

Circular 59 expressly noted the dual responsibility of the commanding general of the Army Service Forces; on business matters he reported to the Under Secretary of War and on military matters to the Chief of Staff.[64] No attempt was made to delimit the two spheres of activity. When General McNarney testified before the Senate Committee on Military Affairs on 6 March 1942, he admitted that this was an arrangement "which you might say violates good organization." He added that while the commanding general of the ASF would have two bosses, they were "for two different purposes, but the purposes are somewhat interrelated." McNarney declared that the two functions of procurement and supply had to be merged. Under this arrangement, they were joined at the highest practical level and this was the "best practical solution" to the problem.[65]

Circular 59 also stated, at the insistence of Under Secretary Patterson, that the responsibilities placed on the Secretary of War in Section 5a of the National Defense Act "shall continue to be performed by the Under Secretary of War."[66] But with most of his staff transferred to the Army Service Forces there was some question as to how the Under Secretary would do this work. Theoretically, he would function on a policy level, the ASF on an operating level. The reorganization did provide the Under Secretary with a solid basis of formal and statutory authority to determine policy. It remained to be seen whether with a small personal staff and with General Somervell in a position of dual responsibility, he could make this authority effective.

Some Problems of the Reorganization

The War Department reorganization brought with it serious problems of status and jurisdiction. From the beginning there was much antagonism toward the ASF. A Senator on the Military Affairs Committee commented, "I don't see what use there is in this setup of a commanding general in charge of services and supply." [67] Many men of high military rank also disagreed with the plan. From the moment it went into effect, there were various efforts to upset it. After the war, the structure set up in March 1942 was swept away and replaced by one not unlike the prewar arrangement.

The housekeeping function in an organization can be interpreted both broadly and strictly. Those who perform such duties, especially if they are strong and vigorous personalities, sometimes tend to absorb the powers of those whom they are supposed to serve. The Mayors of the Palace in France during the early Middle Ages, though originally only housekeeping officials, gradually extended their service functions until they replaced their royal masters. The organization of 1942 had endowed General Somervell with a good deal of administrative power and many feared he would build an "empire."

On the other hand, if the Army Service Forces was to have any practical value, it had to relieve the Chief of Staff and the

[63] *Ibid.*, Sec. 7d.
[64] *Ibid.*, Sec. 7b.
[65] *Hearings before the Committee on Military Affairs,* Senate, 77th Cong, 2d Sess, on Department of Defense Co-ordination and Control Bill, 6 Mar 42, pp. 6–7.
[66] WD Cir 59, 2 Mar 42, Sec. 7a; Dorr, Memorandum Notes, pp. 24–25.
[67] *Hearings before the Committee on Military Affairs,* Senate, 77th Cong, 2d Sess, on Department of Defense Co-ordination and Control Bill, 6 Mar 42, p. 5.

General Staff of operating and administrative functions so that the staff could devote itself to planning and strategy. The fact that the ASF took over many functions which previously had been performed on a higher rung of the ladder of the military hierarchy did not mean that the functions themselves were less important. The creation of the ASF did not relegate supply matters to a corner where no one need worry further about them. It simply made one man the key figure in handling these problems and that man had to act with authority. By the nature of his responsibilities, the commanding general of the Army Service Forces could scarcely hope to please everyone. If he interpreted his function strictly and acted with deference to those who had been reduced in the organizational hierarchy, he could not rise to the urgency of the situation; if he acted with vigor and efficiency, he was an "empire builder."

To make a difficult situation even more difficult, the ASF was not a well-integrated organization, and its commanding general, though vested with wide jurisdiction, was not fully the master in his own house. In contrast, the Army Air Forces and the Army Ground Forces were far better unified.

The AAF, since its creation in June 1941, had been composed of two major parts, the Air Force Combat Command and the Office of the Chief of the Air Corps. These two component parts were now abolished and their responsibilities vested in the commanding general of the Army Air Forces. The position of a Deputy Chief of Staff for Air in the War Department was also abolished. All this meant simply that General Arnold, by virtue of one title, would perform all of the duties which he had previously performed

with two or three titles. He was now able to create such subordinate commands and staffs as he thought desirable. Moreover, for several years the component parts of the AAF had developed a common loyalty to the concept of the air mission in combat operations. There was thus a unity of purpose and of tradition within the AAF.

In the case of the Army Ground Forces, the executive order of 28 February 1942 transferred the functions and authority of the chiefs of Infantry, Cavalry, Field Artillery, and Coast Artillery to the commanding general of the AGF, Lt. Gen. L. J. McNair. The new command headquarters of the AGF was the already existing General Headquarters which had first been formed in 1940. Thus, out of the reorganization, General McNair received a mission which was somewhat more limited in scope than that originally envisaged for GHQ, but he retained an existing staff intact. In addition, by absorbing the duties of the four chiefs of combat arms, much of the friction which he had experienced in the past was eliminated.

The commanding general of the Army Service Forces inherited no such unified organization. He simply received command authority over various agencies, each of which retained its separate identity and many of which retained a degree of autonomy. True, with the creation of the ASF, the chiefs of supply and administrative services had been moved down a peg in the hierarchy, for the major organizational change introduced by the establishment of the ASF was to interpose a new level of command into the War Department between the chiefs of supply and administrative services and the Chief of Staff. Whereas each of these chiefs previously had reported directly to the Chief of Staff, they now reported to the commanding general of the Army Service Forces. Nevertheless, the various heads of bureaus still retained a good deal of authority and responsibility. They were not an easy group to transform into a tight-knit, unified organization.

Another difficulty lay in the wide range of separate functions performed by the ASF. It was more than a procurement and supply agency of the War Department. Actually, all the many miscellaneous activities which had grown up within the War Department over a long period of time were simply assigned *en bloc* to the Army Service Forces. In consequence, the ASF was expected, among other things, to relieve the Chief of Staff and the War Department General Staff of housekeeping burdens. The ASF thus became a command of "things in general." This variety of duties was to create one of the major internal organizational problems for the ASF in the years ahead.

A feature that many people failed to understand was that the Army Service Forces was a very different command from either the AAF or the AGF. The latter two were expected primarily to train combat units for military operations against the enemy. The mission of the ASF was to provide services for the other two forces and for overseas commands.

The role of the ASF as a common agency for War Department research and development, and for procurement and supply, was far less important with respect to the Air Forces than with respect to the Ground Forces. This arose from the fact that the AAF did its own research and development work. Although the Army Ground Forces shared responsibility with the ASF for development activities and testing military equipment, and although it decided the quantities of equipment de-

sirable for various types of ground combat units, the really extensive research on ground equipment was done by the technical services within the Army Service Forces. The ASF also determined requirements and made arrangements for production, delivery, storage, and issue of ground equipment. Its procurement and supply activities for the AGF therefore surpassed those for the AAF. The Air Forces procured its own aircraft and related items. It had to turn to the ASF for such supplies as food, clothing, and other items which it used in common with the AGF. In the procurement and supply of such items, the ASF was recognized as a common agency for the War Department. But the largest part of the supply work of the ASF was performed for ground troops, both in the United States and overseas.

The Army Service Forces was unique in other respects than in being a common supply agency for the two commands in the United States and for the various theaters of operations overseas. For one thing, it was initially designated to be the budget agency of the War Department. It became responsible for the induction, initial classification, and the assignment of personnel for the Army as a whole. It also provided common medical, communication, and transportation services for the Army. Thus the ASF was by no means a "co-ordinate" command with the Air Forces and the Ground Forces. Rather, it was a command set up to assist these two commands and to handle overseas service and supply needs. The essence of its special character could be found in its description as the "common supply and service agency" of the War Department.

An important problem for the future was to arise from those provisions of Circular 59 which assigned to the Army Air

Forces the "command and control" of its own air bases in the continental United States. This command included *all* personnel of units and installations located at the air base "including station complement personnel and activities." In practice, the assignment of command authority at air bases to the Army Air Forces meant that the AAF itself retained responsibility for the performance of medical services, utility services, recreational activities, chaplain services, and many other administrative or housekeeping duties at these bases. On the other hand, no such duties were vested in the commanding general of the Ground Forces. The AGF occupied its training stations on a kind of "user" or "lessee" basis. The actual operation of the ground posts which housed troops in training, fell to the ASF.

No one, of course, expected the reorganization of 9 March 1942 to be perfect. Indeed Circular 59 itself stated that "experience of the first three months" would probably indicate the desirability of "minor modifications" in the proposed organization. Yet, at the same time, it was equally clear that no fundamental changes in the 9 March pattern of organization were expected for the duration of World War II. The War Department had decided upon the general scheme of organization for the conduct of its part of the war effort. The Secretary of War and the Chief of Staff expected the arrangement to prove both workable and helpful.

PART TWO

THE ROLE OF THE ASF
IN THE WAR DEPARTMENT

CHAPTER III

The Procurement and
Supply Activities of the ASF

The Army Service Forces came into being during a crucial period. The defenders of Bataan were trading their lives for time. To reinforce them had proved impossible; their battle was but a delaying action to permit the establishment of defense lines to the South and Southeast. Elsewhere in the Pacific the Japanese moved almost at will. In western Europe German forces were unchallenged, and England awaited the long-delayed invasion from across the Channel. If German armies were momentarily stalled in Russia, most observers credited this to the winter weather, and expected Germany to resume her march in the spring.

On the economic front, too, the Allies were still being worsted. In modern warfare, matériel has an unprecedented importance. Leadership, loyalty, courage, and other military virtues are not the monopoly of any one nation. It is no derogation of the quality of American soldiers to say that German and Japanese troops were as patriotic and brave as our own. The difference in the fighting ability of armies is often the difference in the quantity and quality of their weapons. Wars are won and lost partly on the production line. Because of an early start, Germany and Japan were well ahead of the Allies in production at the outbreak of war. But

that lead was overcome during 1941 and for a while, Allied production forged head. Then Germany and Japan began to develop their newly conquered resources and made a new bid for industrial supremacy. During 1942 and 1943 the Axis outproduced Great Britain and Russia. The outlook for United States war production, eventually to be the deciding factor, was still uncertain in March 1942.[1]

Military procurement and supply were only one part of the struggle of economic resources, and the ASF was responsible for only a part of the total American economic effort. Nevertheless it was still faced with a huge task. A few statistics will perhaps indicate how huge. When the United States became involved actively in the war in December 1941, the Army had reached a strength of nearly 1.7 million men. Only 192,663 of these were stationed outside the United States. At that time a total of thirty-seven divisions had been created, but only three of these plus a few nondivisional units were overseas. In terms of training, another seventeen were ready for combat; in terms of supply, there was little

---

[1] Troyer Anderson, Munitions for the Army, A Five Year Report on the Procurement of Munitions by the War Department under the Direction of the Under Secretary of War, 9 Apr 46, OCMH, pp. 20–22.

equipment for them. If all the critical items of military equipment had been pooled, five infantry· and two armored divisions of the thirty-four in the United States could have been prepared for combat soon after Pearl Harbor.

At the end of 1941 the United States Army had 1,100 antiaircraft guns in the hands of troops or delivered to depots. There were 9,000 field guns, 78,000 machine guns, 2,000,000 rifles, 4,000 tanks, and 200,000 trucks. There was sufficient clothing for a million more men than were in the Army, although 300,000 of them would have lacked overcoats. There were no crawler tractors, or airplane landing mats. There were some 10,000 radio sets for ground communication, less than 6,000 radio sets for aircraft, and about 500 radar sets. There was practically no transportation equipment, almost no chemical warfare equipment, and little in the way of medical supplies. In December 1941 the Army provided ground equipment worth $13,500,000 for lend-lease. In the same month procurement deliveries of all kinds, exclusive of aircraft, came to $360,000,-000.[2]

From these meager beginnings the Army Service Forces swiftly moved forward until, in the single month of March 1945, procurement deliveries reached a total of more than two billion dollars. In three-and-one-half years the ASF obtained 96,000 tanks, 61,000 field guns and 7,000,000 rifles. It bought over 2,300,000 trucks. Clothing of all kinds was obtained in large quantities, including 80,000,000 pairs of shoes, 505,000,000 pairs of socks, and 143,000,000 cotton khaki and flannel shirts. The ASF bought 78,000 crawler tractors, 15,000 cranes and shovels, and over 800,000,000 square feet of airplane landing mats. The Army was provided

with more than 1,200,000 radio sets and 20,000 radar sets. For transportation purposes overseas, the ASF bought 98,000 railway cars, 7,000 steam locomotives, and 6,000 barges. In the field of chemical warfare, nearly 2 billion pounds of incendiary bombs were procured, along with 11 million mortar shells, and nearly 41,000 flame throwers. Medical deliveries included 9,000 X-ray machines, 10,000,000 surgical instruments, and 31.5 million first-aid packets. ASF purchases included also such diverse items as 1,000 Diesel locomotives and 136,000,000 pairs of trousers.[3]

There is sharp difference of opinion over whether the ASF paid too much for what it procured. Cost, though a vital consideration in so vast a procurement program, and the subject of constant concern, was secondary to speed and results. Somervell, while still chief of army construction, had expressed his philosophy on expenditures: he tried to save money wherever he could, but in war, speed and results were more important than cost. Spending might be saving in the long run. He told the Truman Committee investigating the defense program that it often took more courage to pay a high price than to pay a low price. With "parachute jumpers" and "bloodhounds," (as he dubbed the inspectors and auditors who

---

[2] These figures have been taken from *Logistics in World War II, Final Report of the Army Service Forces*, A Report to the Under Secretary of War and the Chief of Staff by the Director of the Service, Supply, and Procurement Division of the War Department General Staff, 1947 (Washington, U.S. Government Printing Office, 1948), Chart 2, pp. 16–18. (Hereafter cited as *Logistics in World War II*.) See also Procurement section of the volume, Statistics, now in preparation for the series UNITED STATES ARMY IN WORLD WAR II.

[3] *Ibid.*, pp. 25–27.

turned up at the jobs), always ready to criticize extravagance, many men played it safe.[4] General Somervell looked for and found many ways to save money, but always within the limits of military urgency.[5]

Because production experience with most military items was so limited, prices on initial orders were often little more than the best guess of the producer and the contracting officer. In time, the ASF acquired a body of cost data and obtained reductions in unit prices. And as output increased, it was possible to take advantage of mass production economies. Thus, in the year ending 30 June 1944, the average price on guns, tanks, and ammunition declined 8 percent, the price for radio equipment more than 7 percent.[6]

Storage was another greatly expanded function of the ASF. At the time of its creation, the Army Service Forces operated 55 depots; by the end of the war this number had risen to 127. These storage plants contained nearly 145,000,000 square feet. At the beginning of 1942, depots shipped 1,000,000 tons per month; at the end of 1944, shipments rose to nearly 2,500,000 tons a month. Tonnages received ran somewhat higher.[7]

Some of the most impressive figures were in the field of transportation. Between 1942 and 1945 the Army Service Forces transported 6.9 million soldiers overseas, as well as 250,000 navy personnel, 110,000 civilians, plus 30,000 others. Of the total passengers carried, 4.6 million men went to Atlantic theaters and 2.7 million men went to the Pacific. From a half a million measurement tons of cargo shipped overseas in the first month of 1942, the ASF attained a peak rate of 5.9 million tons in one month in the early part of 1945. Whereas the Army had 154 ships

in operation in January 1942, the ASF was operating 1,765 ships in December 1944.[8]

Perhaps the single ASF undertaking dwarfing all others was the MANHATTAN DISTRICT, which produced the atomic bomb. The Office of Scientific Research and Development (OSRD) requested the Army to take over the active operation of this project in June 1942. The Chief of Engineers officially established a special unit, the so-called MANHATTAN DISTRICT, on 13 August of that year. The Army was asked to be the administrative agency for the project because it alone could obtain the funds and administer so large an undertaking and still preserve secrecy. The very size of the Army Service Forces itself is best indicated by the fact that it absorbed a project which spent 2 billion dollars, built 2 large manufacturing plants, one of which housed 75,000 persons, and employed a peak of 80,000 individuals.[9] Yet all of this was done without attracting undue attention and without arousing any strong suspicions that the Army was engaged in anything other than normal operations in support of the war effort.

---

[4] *Hearings before a Special Committee Investigating the National Defense Program*, Senate, 77th Cong, 1st Sess, 25 Apr 41, Pt. 1, p. 346.

[5] T. B. Worsley, *Wartime Economic Stabilization and the Efficiency of Government Procurement* (Washington, National Security Resources Board, 1949), Chs. XVII, XIX–XXIII.

[6] Annual *Report of the Army Service Forces, 1944* (Washington, U.S. Government Printing Office, 1945), p. 119. (Hereafter cited as Annual Rpt of ASF, 1944.)

[7] CD, ASF, *Statistical Review, World War II* (Washington, U.S. Government Printing Office, 1946), pp. 23, 25.

[8] *Ibid.*, pp. 35, 37.

[9] Annual *Report of the Army Service Forces, 1945* (Washington, U.S. Government Printing Office, 1946), pp. 15, 20. (Hereafter cited as Annual Rpt of ASF, 1945.)

These achievements were attained in the face of great difficulties. In March 1942, the major problem of the ASF was procurement. Production and more production was the overwhelmingly urgent need. As time went on, increasing attention had to be given also to quality, as in the constant improvement of the tank, the development of the recoilless gun and variable time (proximity) fuze, and the many advances in electronics equipment.

As the American production effort began to turn out military supplies in overwhelming quantities, transportation became the great bottleneck. It remained a limiting factor in war operations until the surrender of the Japanese.[10] But even when the supplies arrived overseas, there was not always assurance that they would be properly handled and distributed. The ASF had technical responsibility for overseas supply performance. But it was never very happy about either the organization which was developed to do the task or the character of the supply operations overseas.[11]

In 1944 the most important shortage confronting the Army Service Forces was manpower. While raw material shortages had largely been overcome or brought into balance, there was no corresponding administrative system for directing the best use of the nation's manpower. Partly, industrial manpower shortages reflected the growing need for military personnel.[12] Partly, they arose from lack of efficient methods of manpower control. Labor shortages were all the more vexatious because the ASF itself could do little about the problem. Control of manpower was properly a civilian responsibility which had to be undertaken on a nationwide basis. The ASF managed to reduce its own personnel requirements by improving its

operating efficiency; it encouraged individual contractors to avoid waste of labor; and it proposed production priorities to civilian agencies directing labor assignment. But there was no over-all program of control to insure effective civilian direction of manpower. These problems became acute in the autumn of 1944 and the spring of 1945.[13] They were beyond the control of the Army; the ASF itself could resort only to palliatives.

From the very outset, the ASF emphasized the need for careful planning of procurement needs. When General Somervell was G–4, he had pushed the preparation of a complete and unified Army Supply Program. With the creation of the Army Service Forces, its staff took over active direction of this work.

Procurement was inextricably linked with distribution. Military supplies produced in America's industrial plants were useless unless delivered where and when demanded for military operations. No matter how ample the production, the entire effort was wasted unless the supplies could be delivered to their destination for use as intended. After 1942 the ASF had to give increasing attention to all phases of supply distribution.

In the spring of 1944 the ASF instituted a new procedure which attempted to relate procurement requirements to actual distribution experience. At the beginning of the war future needs could only be roughly estimated. By 1944 figures based on distribution experience made it possible to compare estimates of requirements

---

[10] Annual Rpt of ASF, 1945, p. 21.
[11] *Logistics in World War II*, pp. 158–59.
[12] Greenfield, Palmer, and Wiley, *The Organization of Ground Combat Troops*, pp. 207, 214, 412.
[13] Annual Rpt of ASF, 1945, pp. 205–07.

with actual consumption. This brought into existence the supply control system which, by 30 June 1945, covered 1,887 major items making up about 75 percent of the total dollar volume of all ASF procurement.[14]

In addition to other problems, wartime supply faced a difficulty in the time lag from requisition of an item to delivery at the point of use overseas. To be sure, this time factor varied from item to item. Studies made in early 1945 indicated that eighty-seven days were normally required from the receipt of a requisition at the New York Port of Embarkation until arrival overseas of ships bearing the necessary supplies. But such a time period assumed that the supplies needed were already available in storage in the United States.[15] At one time, the Army Service Forces set up a timetable to serve as an ideal for the supply aspects of overseas operations. As a minimum, it contemplated that six months would intervene between the final decision to undertake a large military operation and the delivery of the necessary supplies overseas. And of course the scale of operations had a further impact upon the timetable. The ASF found that it not only had to anticipate specific operations and their supply needs but also that it had to be prepared for almost any conceivable sudden demand.[16]

The commanding general of the ASF, his staff associates, and the heads of ASF operating units were not under the illusion that supplies alone were winning the war. Perhaps the proper place was indicated in a brief comment which General Somervell made to the Academy of Political Science in January 1943. In his prepared paper for that assembly he remarked: "Good logistics alone cannot win a war. Bad logistics alone can lose it."[17]

Lend-lease

An essential part of American military supply operations after April 1941 was to make available under lend-lease, war matériel to the Allies fighting Germany, Italy, and Japan. Between the passage of the Lend-Lease Act and the end of the war, the War Department provided nearly fifteen billion dollars worth of equipment and supplies for other nations. Of this, the United Kingdom received about 56 percent, Russia 25 percent, France 10 percent, China 5 percent, and other nations the remainder. Included in these supplies were 26,000 medium tanks, nearly 800,000 trucks (including 188,000 "jeeps"), and 3,400 locomotives.[18]

In lend-lease matters, the ASF was fundamentally an operating organization. Policy was determined either on a high political level or by the Combined Chiefs of Staff. Nevertheless, the ASF did influence policy through membership on various policy committees and through exercise of its operational responsibilities. First, the Office of Lend-Lease Administration (OLLA), and later, the Foreign Economic Administration (FEA), was the control agency for civilian type supplies, but for military lend-lease these offices served

[14] Annual Rpt of ASF, 1945, pp. 179–80. See also Richard M. Leighton and Robert W. Coakley, Logistics of Global Warfare, 1941–1943, a volume in preparation for the series UNITED STATES ARMY IN WORLD WAR II.

[15] Annual Rpt of ASF, 1945, pp. 179–80.

[16] Annual Report of the Army Service Forces, 1943 (Washington, U.S. Government Printing Office, 1944), p. 97. (Hereafter cited as Annual Rpt of ASF, 1943.)

[17] Proceedings of the Academy of Political Science, January 1943, p. 61.

[18] These figures are based on the Lend-Lease section of the volume, Statistics, now in preparation for the series UNITED STATES ARMY IN WORLD WAR II.

only an accounting purpose. After Pearl Harbor appropriations for military lend-lease supplies were made directly to the War Department. The ASF procured military supplies for the U.S. Army and for lend-lease in a single unified production program.[19]

American munitions production along with that of the British Empire theoretically was placed in a "common pool" to be distributed according to strategic need. To decide the problem of strategic distribution, two Munitions Assignments Boards, one in Washington and one in London, were set up as a part of the Combined Chiefs of Staff machinery. The Washington Board, responsible for allocation of American production, was composed of equal representation of the British and American Chiefs of Staff with Harry Hopkins, the President's *alter ego*, as chairman. The board was directly responsible to the Combined Chiefs of Staff, and made its decisions in accordance with strategic guidance received from them.

Three subcommittees—Ground, Navy, and Air—prepared allocation for thousands of different items. Each of these subcommittees had one British representative. The chairmanship and secretariat of the Ground Committee were vested in the International Division, ASF, and the spadework for all transfer schedules was largely done by members of that division. Although these schedules had to be approved by the board, only when there was some disagreement in the Ground Committee was this approval anything but automatic. Once transfers were approved, the ASF was responsible for moving the supplies to port.[20]

General Somervell constantly pressed for careful forecasting of the supply requirements of Allied nations in order to prevent undue interference of their demands with the process of equipping U.S. divisions. Lend-lease supply requirements were included in the Army Supply Program alongside those of the United States. General Somervell argued that the Munitions Assignments Board (MAB) should not allocate materials unless a procurement requirement, generally controlled by the ASF, had been presented for it. He felt that U.S. Army needs should get first consideration, and usually he won his point.[21]

Great Britain was the only full partner of the United States in the assignments machinery. These two major powers allocated supplies to the other Allies normally on a strategic, though sometimes on a diplomatic basis. The Russians received lend-lease aid according to a definite protocol drawn up through diplomatic negotiations.

Generally, the Anglo-American supply partnership functioned smoothly, but there were some conflicts. Actually, only the Americans had any real stock of supplies to distribute. The British contended that allocation from American production should be made to the British in one block for their Empire (except Canada), for the European refugee governments under their sponsorship, and for the small nations of the Middle East. General Somer-

[19] *Message from the President of the United States Transmitting a Report on the First Year of Lend-Lease Operations.* (March 11, 1942) (Washington, U. S. Government Printing Office, 1942), pp 36–38.

[20] Intn Div, ASF, Lend-Lease as of September 30, 1945, MS, OCMH, I, 147–66; Robert E. Sherwood, *Roosevelt and Hopkins: An Intimate History* (New York, Harper & Brothers, 1948), pp. 470–73.

[21] Memo, Somervell for Clay, 27 Jul 42, Hq ASF, LL File; Memo, Somervell for Burns, 15 Aug 42, sub: Relationship of WD to MAB and CPRB, Hq ASF, MAB File; Min #766, 64th Mtg, MAC (G), 7 Dec 42.

vell opposed this principle of "proteges," and the MAB eventually ruled against it.[22]

Somervell tried to keep British requirements within reasonable limits, and to reduce to a minimum emergency demands outside the Army Supply Program. He instituted a rigid review of British requirements to prevent use of lend-lease supplies for postwar economic recovery, for nonessential civilian purposes, and for accumulating excessive reserves. When the Middle East ceased to be an active theater, the use of British surplus there for civilian purposes became a serious issue. On one occasion, the Americans learned of large supplies of rubber tires stored in Egypt, and forced the British to restate their tire requirements.[23] In the Far East, where British and American political, economic, and military interests often diverged, Somervell, over British protest, approved a procedure for review of British requirements by the U.S. theater headquarters.[24] In the case of tanks, heavy trucks, and tractors, the United States was virtually the sole source of supply for the British. As a result, negotiations over requirement and assignment programs of these articles were always long and difficult.[25]

In practice, though it was never officially stated, the ASF and other U.S. staff agencies concerned evolved the "residual" theory to replace that of the "common pool." Simply stated, this principle assumed that each country had primary responsibility to produce all munitions required for itself, and that each country had first call on its own productive capacity.[26] For obvious reasons, the British clung to the theory of the "common pool."

Just as the British were dependent on supplies from the United States, the Americans sometimes were dependent on British shipping to transport their troops and supplies. Though there were usually no overt attempts to swap British shipping for American supplies, some of General Somervell's negotiations with the British were essentially horse trading.

The British maintained a full military and civilian staff in Washington to look after their interests. General Somervell had his principal contacts with Sir Walter Venning, head of the military section of the British Supply Council in North America, and his assistant, Lt. Gen. George N. Macready. Sir Walter Venning was a pleasant gentleman with whom it was easy to get along, and Somervell became quite fond of him. General Macready, on the other hand, while an able and intelligent officer, was difficult for Somervell to work with. He forcefully presented the British position on every issue and stuck to it until compelled to retreat. General Somervell clung just as tenaciously to the American position. Venning often smoothed matters over when tempers were ruffled. General Somervell came to the conclusion that Venning and Macready made a happy combination. Macready was the tough man who presented unacceptable demands; Sir Walter then

---

[22] Memo, Somervell for Burns, 5 Jul 43, sub: Munitions Assignments Procedure, Hq ASF, MAB File; MBW 67/8, 18 Nov 43, sub: Retransfer of Munitions under the Lend-Lease Act; Sherwood, *Roosevelt and Hopkins*, p. 473.

[23] See papers relative to this in G–4 File 400.3295, Feb–Mar 44.

[24] Ltrs, Somervell to Lt Gen George N. Macready, 31 Aug 44, and Macready to Somervell, 2 Sep 44, Intn Div, ASF, Lend-Lease, Documentary Supplement, OCMH, Vol. VIII.

[25] Memo, Maj Gen Thomas T. Handy, OPD for ASW, 26 Feb 44, sub: Lend-Lease, OPD 400.3295, Sec. 3, Case 47; Min, MAC(G) & MAB, *passim*.

[26] Intn Div, ASF, Lend-Lease as of September 30, 1945, MS, OCMH, I, 243.

stepped in and agreed to a compromise. In the process, the British usually got as much as they originally expected.

The Russian protocols were worked out on a yearly basis and constituted an iron-clad promise of delivery by the United States to Russia. With rare exceptions, the Munitions Assignments Board in making allocations conformed to protocol commitments. General Somervell was the War Department representative on the President's Soviet Protocol Committee. This was an interdepartmental group under the chairmanship of Harry Hopkins, which advised the President on the offerings in the protocol and determined policy on carrying out commitments. The ASF commander and his staff worked to keep the offerings under the protocol within the limits imposed by shipping and other logistical considerations. Once accepted, the President himself exerted heavy pressure to see that commitments were fulfilled. In consequence the ASF staff had to give priority to meeting them, sometimes even at the expense of supply or transportation for U.S. troops. One whole overseas command, that in the Persian Gulf, was devoted exclusively to the job of getting supplies to Russia.[27]

French rearmament became a major concern after the Casablanca Conference. It was more expedient to supply French troops already in the theater, assuming of course that they were experienced and reliable, than it was to transport U.S. troops there. The size of the French forces to be rearmed was determined in a general way at Casablanca by the President's promises to General Giraud, later augmented by decisions of the Combined Chiefs of Staff. The ASF staff had little to do with these decisions. They were made largely on the advice of General Eisenhower in the thea-ter. Eisenhower also dictated priorities on shipping, for French rearmament was more frequently a problem of shipping than of the availability of supplies. In July 1943 General Somervell did negotiate further understandings with General Giraud at a series of meetings in Washington, but these agreements for the most part reflected requests which had already been submitted by General Eisenhower.[28] On the other hand, ASF responsibilities for delivery to French troops were considerable, since supplies to the theater commander for the French were shipped with supplies for American forces.[29]

Despite the fact that Chinese lend-lease constituted only 5 percent of the total, it presented some of the most difficult of all logistical problems. Supplies for Chinese forces were limited to driblets because of the lack of transportation facilities. Interested in seeing what could be done to remedy this situation, Somervell personally visited the area. He resisted Chinese pressure for more supplies than could be transported into China, and guided himself by the advice of the American commander in the theater.

There was never any particular difficulty in handling lend-lease in the Southwest Pacific because of the harmonious relations between General MacArthur and the Australian Government. For a time,

[27] *Ibid.*, II, 1001–97; T. H. Vail Motter, *The Persian Corridor and Aid to Russia,* UNITED STATES ARMY IN WORLD WAR II (Washington, U.S. Government Printing Office, 1952).

[28] Memo, Marshall for Gens Arnold, Somervell, McNarney, Handy, and Raymond G. Moses, 12 Jul 43, w/incl memo from Giraud, Intn Div, ASF, File 475, Equip of Troops, France, Vol. II.

[29] Marcel Vigneras, The Rearmament of the French Forces in World War II, a monograph in preparation for the series UNITED STATES ARMY IN WORLD WAR II.

shipments were made to General Mac-Arthur for division among the national forces under his command, but this system was abandoned by mutual agreement since the Australian Government had better facilities for receiving and distributing supplies. MacArthur retained the power to divert military supplies where necessary from one national force to another.[30]

Although the procurement of military supplies for lend-lease was entirely under Army control, except in limited instances, the War Shipping Administration (WSA) took over when the supplies arrived in port. Nevertheless, the ASF had to give careful attention to co-ordinating supplies with shipping. Otherwise, large backlogs might clog depots and ports. Also, supplies would be lying idle when they could be used for other purposes. The ASF advocated that after forty-five days, the U.S. Army should repossess supplies assigned to, but unshipped by, a foreign government. The Munitions Assignments Board modified the proposal by requiring that such material should be reported to it for assignment at its discretion.[31] Actual repossessions were infrequent, but the procedure checked additional assignments of material of which there was a backlog.

The complicated international machinery for lend-lease worked with surprising smoothness. No doubt General Somervell's past association with Harry Hopkins and their friendship during the war years had much to do with this happy situation for, until ill health removed him from the scene, Hopkins was the real lend-lease policy maker. Lend-lease was a part of the supply strategy of World War II, and proved an admirable instrument of coalition warfare. In utilizing it, the Army Service Forces had the major operational role.

The Relation Between Strategy and Supply

It was inevitable that the ASF should show a special concern for the supply phases of military operations. What, precisely, were these "supply phases?"[32] According to the official definition of its mission, the ASF was to provide "services and supplies to meet military requirements." Among the seventeen duties specifically assigned to the ASF, there were only two references to supply. One was an omnibus statement covering research, development, procurement, storage, and distribution of supplies and equipment. The other was "transportation and traffic control." These terse phrases embraced an enormous complex of interrelated activities.[33]

---

[30] Cable C-520, CINC SWPA to AGWAR, 18 Sep 42, CM-IN-8399 (9-19-42), Intn Div Cables, Aus LL Procedure; Memo, Hq SOS for Chiefs Svs, 25 Sep 42, sub: Shipmt of LL Goods to Australia, SPLLA 020 Shipping, ID .008, Shipmts, Vol. I.

[31] Ltr, Aurand to Chm British Supply Council, 12 Jun 42, ID 319.1, Rpts–Storage, Vol. I; Min #462, 34th Mtg, MAC(G), 15 Jun 42.

[32] WD Cir 59, 2 Mar 42.

[33] The term "logistics" was used widely during the war and earlier by the Navy and in the high command, i. e. in the WDGS and in the joint and combined committees. It appears somewhat less frequently in the records of the ASF. "Logistics" seems to have been a useful and meaningful word when used to refer, in general terms, to the various material and quantitative limitations considered in strategic planning. But whenever it has become necessary to define in detail the specific factors covered by the term, disagreement has usually arisen. The official wartime dictionaries of the Army defined logistics in terms mainly of supply and transport, and field service regulations did not even recognize the term until after the war. Agencies concerned with supply, services, and transport often tended to identify logistics with their own range of activities—e. g., the Joint Logistics Committee, created in 1943, and the Logistics Division of the postwar War Department General Staff (at first named the Supply, Service, and Procurement Division). General Somervell in 1942 created on his own staff a Strategic Logistics Division which made long-range studies showing the impact of almost any kind of physical limitation upon strategy and op-

All these functions were related, directly or indirectly, to the provision of military matériel for combat operations overseas. (For purposes of the present discussion, "services" are eliminated from consideration.) To provide this matériel and make it available to the troops overseas involved an unbroken chain of activity extending back to the design and development of individual items of equipment and supplies. The close interrelation among all the links of this chain presented constant organizational difficulties which had ramifications beyond the confines of the War Department. It constituted a continuing problem during the war—that of defining the relationship of the ASF to the War Department General Staff and to overseas theaters. This problem will be examined in subsequent chapters.[34] Finally, the close connection between military procurement and control of all the nation's economic resources complicated the relations of the ASF and of the War Department, for which

it was the agent, with the War Production Board as the principal civilian agency concerned with mobilization of the nation's economic resources. These relations will be treated in Part Three of the present volume.[35]

It was the vital relationship between procurement and the employment of military matériel which made the ASF so important a factor in the conduct of military operations.[36] It prevented the ASF from being simply an operating agent for executing War Department instructions, and gave it instead a vital role in the determination of military strategy.

Looking back at four years of supply operations of the most varied kinds, Somervell's planning officers attempted at the end of the war to analyze the influence of logistics on strategy.[37] They conceived the major elements to be four:

1. "Practicabilities" (i. e., the supply of military matériel actually available in the United States during the time of any projected military operation).

2. Shipping and other necessary transport capacity in the United States.

3. Discharge and handling capacity of ports and beaches overseas, and the overland transport capacity to the combat areas.

4. The enemy's ability to interfere with logistical preparations and support.

It was the function of logistical planners, in so far as they could forecast these ele-

---

erations. By the end of the war Somervell's staff had become accustomed to think of logistics as embracing virtually all the activities of the ASF. The official report of the ASF, *Logistics in World War II* (p. vii), asserted that the term referred to all activities not included in "strategy" and "tactics"; it is clear that the authors of the publication had in mind all those material factors which impose limitations upon strategy and tactics—e. g., procurement, storage, distribution of material; transport, construction, maintenance, communications, medical care, personnel administration and services. "Logistics"—both the word and the thing itself—is obviously in a process of evolution under the influence of changing developments in the techniques, instruments, and organization of war. In recent U.S. Army and Joint Army-Navy-Air Forces official usage, as defined by the latest dictionaries, it is significant that the term is now given essentially the meaning contained in the ASF report mentioned above, i. e., as covering all military activities not included in strategy and tactics. In the present discussion, the term "supply" is used to refer to a more restricted field—the procurement, storage, distribution, maintenance and transportation of military matériel. "Logistics," when it is used, may be assumed to have substantially the same meaning.

[34] See below, Ch. VII.

[35] See below, Chs. XIII–XIX.

[36] In a letter to Senator Claude Pepper in December 1942, Somervell expounded at some length on the interrelationship between procurement and military operations. Ltr, Somervell to Pepper, 5 Dec 42, CG ASF files. This letter is discussed at length on pp. 285–86.

[37] *Logistics in World War II*, pp. 32–34.

ments and reduce them to quantitative terms, to determine the bottlenecks which stood in the way of projected military operations. Having done so, they then had to find means of removing these obstacles or, if this were not practicable, to lay down the alternatives open to the strategic and operational planners under irreducible physical limitations. On this basis, military objectives could then be redesigned to fit these limitations. This, in simple terms, was the pattern of "logistical planning," as it was usually referred to, for military operations. It meant, in essence, determining in advance what could and could not be done to put in the hands of troops the military matériel they needed to accomplish stated ends.

The process of actually providing the support estimated to be logistically possible involved four general types of supply operations. In the first place, troops being trained in the United States had to be given training equipment, clothing, ammunition, and many other kinds of supplies. In the second place, as military units went overseas, last-minute efforts were necessary to insure that their equipment was complete and in workable condition. Third, once the troops were overseas, they constantly had to be supplied with fresh stocks of replacement equipment and all types of expendable items. Wear and tear, loss, and battle destruction ate continually into the supply of guns, tanks, communication facilities, trucks, and other military equipment which troops had on hand. Without new stocks to replace these losses, the battle strength of overseas troops would steadily decline the longer they remained overseas. Supplies like ammunition, gasoline, food, and even clothing had to be provided on a continuing basis, since these were expendable. By the beginning

of 1944, more than half of all ASF procurement was designed to provide replacement equipment and expendable supplies for troops already overseas.[38] In the fourth place, each major area of overseas operations had its own special needs for supplies with which to maintain its military operations. It had to have port facilities for unloading supplies shipped from the United States. If these facilities were not available, or if they were inadequate, port equipment of all kinds would have to be shipped from the United States. After supplies were unloaded, they had to be warehoused until required. Depots had to be constructed to handle the steady flow of material from the United States. As troops moved farther and farther forward, supply stocks also had to be moved up into intermediate and advance depots. This meant that trucks and sometimes railroad rolling stock had to be sent from the United States. Each overseas area required communications facilities to ensure that commanders would have rapid and dependable contact with their subordinates. Swift intercommunication between all parts of a vast military organization was indispensable. Hospital facilities, troop accommodations, airfields, depots, and roads had to be built. This required the shipment of bulldozers, caterpillar tractors, lumber, steel, prefabricated hutments, portable bridges, cranes, graders, coal, asphalt, cement. Specially trained troop units also had to be sent to operate and use all this material. In certain areas, the Army had responsibility for supplying the basic needs of the civilian population: food, clothing, and fuel for utilities.

These needs naturally varied from one area to another, and from one phase of

---

[38] Annual Rpt of ASF, 1944, p. 99.

operations to the next. At one end of the scale was the European Theater of Operations (ETO), with a troop population running into millions, complicated rear area activities, and combat operations gigantic in scope and intensity. At the other end was a tiny garrison of an outpost like Ascension Island in the South Atlantic. Each presented special problems of supply. As the war progressed, the WDGS and the ASF worked out separate supply procedures appropriate to the support of the various types of overseas theaters—those in the initial stage of operations; those in which American forces had become fairly well organized, particularly with respect to supply operations; and finally those which had become inactive after the attainment of major objectives.

Of the four general types of supply operations, the first two—supplying troops training in the United States, and checking equipment of units going overseas—absorbed the main efforts of the ASF during the first two years of the war, while the Army was being deployed overseas. The fourth category—supplying major areas of overseas operations by constructing adequate port and other necessary facilities—became increasingly important as American forces in the British Isles in 1943 built a large base establishment launching the European invasion at the same time that large reserves were being assembled in the Pacific. From the middle of 1943 on, the third category—continuing supply of forces already overseas—steadily overshadowed the job of equipping troops in the United States and in process of deployment. Finally, in the spring of 1945, the ASF plunged into the huge undertaking of redeploying troops and supplies from Europe to the Pacific for the assault upon Japan. Seriously complicating this task was the job of returning to the United States troops and enormous stocks of munitions from all the areas where military operations had ceased. Starting as a thin trickle comparatively early in the war, this countermovement increasingly competed with the supply of overseas operations until, with victory over Japan won in August 1945, it became the final supply job of the Army Service Forces in World War II.

CHAPTER IV

Strategy and Supply: Early Phases

The most important strategic decision of World War II was that which made Germany and the Axis in Europe, rather than Japan in the Pacific, the number one enemy. This decision was tentatively made prior to Pearl Harbor and it is evident that supply considerations were less important than other factors in the determination.[1]

The attack on Pearl Harbor and the repeated setbacks of the Allied powers in the Pacific severely jolted this tentative agreement between the United States and Great Britain. In addition to the problem of how to get at Germany, the United States now had to reckon with the difficulty of containing the Japanese. When the Army Service Forces came into existence in March 1942, the War Department was already at work on studies of strategy, utilizing the United Kingdom as a major base. President Roosevelt and Prime Minister Churchill soon endorsed this idea as a basis of combined planning.

As the war progressed, the wisdom of the decision, from a logistic point of view, was shown again and again. General Eisenhower, as head of the War Plans Division, reported to General Marshall that "logistic reasons . . . substantiate the soundness of the decision to concentrate against the European Axis." [2] Great Britain proved an ideal overseas base for the preparation of future military operations. True, it was separated at the narrowest point by a mere twenty miles of water from land dominated by the Germans. The ports and great cities of England were ever subject to the menace of air attack. On the other hand, the supremacy of the Royal Air Force over the Germans in the skies above Britain itself had already been demonstrated. The American Army, in building up its own military forces to participate in an offensive against the Axis, could look forward with some assurance to the use of the British ports, the British rail network, and the many other facilities of

---

[1] Sherwood, *Roosevelt and Hopkins*, pp. 271–74, 415, 519, 536–37; Henry L. Stimson and McGeorge Bundy, *On Active Service in Peace and War* (New York, Harper & Brothers, 1948), p. 415; John J. McCloy, "The Great Military Decisions," *Foreign Affairs*, XXVI (October 1947), 52; *Biennial Report of the Chief of Staff of the United States Army, July 1, 1943 to June 30, 1945, to the Secretary of War*, p. 8; Maurice Matloff and Edwin M. Snell, *Strategic Planning for Coalition Warfare: 1941-1942*, UNITED STATES ARMY IN WORLD WAR II (Washington, U.S. Government Printing Office, 1953); Gordon A. Harrison, *Cross-Channel Attack*, UNITED STATES ARMY IN WORLD WAR II (Washington, U.S. Government Printing Office, 1951). This strategic concept was set forth in the early RAINBOW plans and in the so-called Victory Supply Program of 11 September 1941. See Watson, *Chief of Staff: Prewar Plans and Preparations*.

[2] Memo, WPD for CofS, 28 Feb 42, sub: Strategic Conceptions and Their Application to the Southwest Pacific, Env 35, Exec 4.

a highly industrialized nation. Then too, since the British Isles would have to be made secure in any case, the troops assembled there would serve a double purpose: they would be a defense force for the United Kingdom as well as an eventual offensive army for a cross-Channel invasion.

The fact that the trip across the Atlantic was so much shorter than that across the Pacific, and the fact that most of our port and rail facilities were located on the east coast added even more to the desirability of making Great Britain the major overseas base for our military operations. It took only half as long in 1942 for a ship to carry a load of supplies from the Atlantic seaboard to a British port and return to the United States as it did to carry supplies from the Pacific coast to New Guinea or Australia. Furthermore, not only were our most highly developed ports on the Atlantic coast, but our industrial resources were concentrated in the northeastern part of the United States; and our own rail network was oriented to the movement of goods within this area. The bottlenecks on the transcontinental railways and the congestion of Pacific ports, particularly in the first half of 1945 when supply attention began to concentrate upon the Pacific, helped demonstrate the soundness of the original military plans.

As already noted, by March 1942 the strategy of continental invasion from the British Isles was already taking shape. As approved in mid-April by the two governments, this strategy envisaged both the assembly of ground forces for an eventual cross-Channel operation and the launching of an aerial offensive from United Kingdom bases sometime in 1942. By contrast, the Pacific area, except for the Southwest Pacific, was a Navy "show,"

and the Navy, rather than the Army, ultimately assumed the basic responsibility.[3]

The Army Service Forces was a zone of interior command. Its commander had no direct authority overseas. Yet the basic aim of the ASF was the support of overseas operations. The final test of the supply system was in the theater of operations; the measure of ASF success was the effectiveness of its supplies and services in helping combat troops win battles. The need for close ties between the zone of interior and the overseas theaters therefore was obvious. One of the means adopted to strengthen these ties was by sending key people on his staff to overseas areas, and on occasion General Somervell himself became a globetrotting trouble-shooter.

As commanding general of a large and complex organization, Somervell necessarily personified the supply activities of the Army. He had to represent the command as a whole to the Chief of Staff and to officials outside the War Department. He was the spokesman for his associates in stating what was logistically feasible and what was not. Within his command, General Somervell had to give his personal attention to the major difficulties which arose. In both capacities, as representative of the Army Service Forces in its external relationships and as a final arbiter of matters within the organization, he naturally depended on numerous associates for assistance and advice. To focus attention upon the commanding general's personal participation in the activities of overseas

[3] Marshall to Roosevelt, about 1 Apr 42, quoted Sherwood, *Roosevelt and Hopkins,* pp. 549–50. This point is also discussed in several volumes of the series UNITED STATES ARMY IN WORLD WAR II: G. A. Harrison, *Cross-Channel Attack*; Cline, *Washington Command Post*; and Matloff and Snell, *Strategic Planning for Coalition Warfare.* See also Leighton and Coakley, Logistics of Global Warfare, 1941–1943.

supply, therefore, serves the useful purpose of simplifying a consideration of the more important problems which confronted the ASF.

BOLERO

Support of BOLERO (the build-up of troops and supplies in Great Britain for the cross-Channel operation) early became the most important single supply job of the ASF. To look into preparations for this operation, Somervell, accompanied by Lutes, his chief planner, made his first overseas inspection trip. He was primarily interested in the extent to which British port, rail, and storage facilities could be made available for the build-up of American military strength. He also wanted firsthand information on the numerous organizational problems involved in setting up a new supply command in the United Kingdom and getting it under way.

Somervell and Lutes returned to the United States with a greater awareness of the tremendous job facing the supply command in England, and with the strengthened conviction that not enough supply troops were being made available to Maj. Gen. John C. H. Lee, an Engineer officer who soon was to head the Services of Supply in the United Kingdom. Somervell had first protested the inadequate number of supply troops in the Army troop plans while still G–4. At the time, no service troops had been included above the level of a field army. On the basis of his staff estimates, Somervell urged the addition of 625,000 service troops in General Staff plans. Since the size of the Army for 1942 had already been fixed by the President, General Marshall was reluctant to press for such a large increase. Here the matter rested until June 1942. Then Somervell

and Lutes, impelled by their observations in England, pressed their case with renewed conviction. The War Department General Staff authorized about one third of the ASF recommendation. The necessary training program was started at once, but the time was too short to provide the fully trained troops needed to mount and support the North African invasion of November.[4]

The problem of supply troops for overseas military operations remained a perplexing issue throughout World War II. The Army Ground Forces, naturally enough, pressed constantly for more combat troops and pointedly criticized the large number of men needed for rear area duties. The General Staff was inclined to agree with the Ground Forces. Yet if Army commanders and their troops were to have all the supplies they needed, someone had to discharge, sort, transport, and issue what they demanded. General Somervell was convinced that overseas commanders seldom had enough service troop units to do an efficient supply and distribution job. Events were to substantiate this conviction on numerous occasions.[5]

In the spring of 1942, Somervell also had to begin worrying about the transportation capabilities of the United States. With the assistance of Maj. Gen. Charles P. Gross, his chief transportation adviser, Somervell went to work on the problem. Its solution involved many agencies. New ship construction was the province of the U.S. Maritime Commission; utilization of American ship resources was the responsibility of the War Shipping Administration; use of British vessels involved lengthy negotiation with British officials in Wash-

---

[4] Ltr, Lutes to author, 28 Mar 51.
[5] Leighton and Coakley, Logistics of Global Warfare, 1941–1943.

ington and London; the protection of convoys was the concern of both the Navy
and the Air Forces. With responsibility thus divided and out of his hands,
Somervell could only argue vehemently
for action and more action. This he seldom
failed to do at any and every opportunity.
Frequently, shipping problems ended up
with a White House conference where Mr.
Harry Hopkins helped to adjust the basic
differences.[6]

In late summer of 1942, Somervell sent
General Lutes to the South and Southwest
Pacific Areas with two purposes in mind.
The first was to investigate a shipping jam
which had developed in the harbor of
Noumea, New Caledonia. This base was
then supporting American operations on
Guadalcanal and a build-up on Espiritu
Santo. The second purpose was to inform
General MacArthur in Australia of the
secondary supply priority given his theater
and to encourage him to undertake long-
range planning of his supply needs. To
MacArthur's fears of a Japanese invasion
of the Australian east coast, Lutes responded that he was certain the Japanese
had overextended their supply facilities
and were incapable of mounting an invasion. Although alarmed by what he felt
was an undue lack of concern with his
military position in the Southwest Pacific,
MacArthur had no alternative but to plan
to make the best possible use of whatever
supply resources the ASF would be able to
provide.

Somervell also had Lutes tackle another
problem—that of closer co-operation between the services in matters of supply.
Lutes succeeded in getting a Joint Army-
Navy Logistical Staff started under Admiral William E. Halsey. Also, Admiral
Chester Nimitz, after discussing the desirability of such a staff with Lutes, requested

Navy Department approval of a joint
Army-Navy staff, with an Army officer in
charge of logistics. The necessary authority
was delayed nearly eight months.[7]

North Africa

The planned orderly build-up of a military base in the British Isles for an assault
on the Continent was interrupted by several developments. Submarines took a
large toll of ships and supplies; the over-all
lend-lease program involving the supply
of Russia, China, and other Allies, consumed a large part of American production; and the support of American outposts
became a serious matter. For example, as
a result of the Japanese occupation of the
western tip of the Aleutian Islands, defense
of Alaska became urgent, and Somervell
in August 1942 made a hasty trip to observe progress of the Alaska Highway and
to discuss the supply aspects of Alaska's
defense. But by far the greatest diversion
from the cross-Channel build-up came as
a result of the invasion of North Africa
(Operation TORCH).

The outline of the plan was drawn up at
the end of July but the final pattern of a
two-coast three-pronged invasion with one
Atlantic and two Mediterranean task
forces was not fixed until September.[8] The
involved nature of the plan, and the short-
ness of time for preparation placed a severe
strain upon the Army Service Forces.[9]

---

[6] Chester Wardlow, *The Transportation Corps: Re-
sponsibilities, Organization, and Operations,* UNITED
STATES ARMY IN WORLD WAR II (Washington,
U.S. Government Printing Office, 1951).

[7] Ltr, cited in n. 4.

[8] Sherwood, *Roosevelt and Hopkins,* pp. 611–12;
George F. Howe, Operations in Northwest Africa,
1942–1943, a volume in preparation for the series
UNITED STATES ARMY IN WORLD WAR II.

[9] Leighton and Coakley, Logistics of Global Warfare, 1941–1943.

Providing equipment for both the Western Task Force and the Mediterranean Task Forces was increasingly troublesome. An added burden in the already complicated supply preparations for North Africa at this time resulted from the fact that the American forces in England were unable to provide for their requirements from quantities already delivered or being delivered to the European Theater of Operations. Most of what was needed was unquestionably on hand, but so scattered among various newly set-up depots that its actual location was unknown. There were not enough service troops on hand to go through all the equipment, find the necessary items, and deliver them to combat troops within the available time period.

On 8 September 1942 the ASF was given a long list of essential equipment required by the assault forces sailing for North Africa from the United Kingdom.[10] A total of 131,000 ship tons of cargo was delivered at United Kingdom ports between 16 and 25 October to be placed on the assault convoys. Another eight fully loaded cargo ships were sent from the United States to join the convoys as they left England for the Mediterranean.[11] All this meant extra shifts in American plants, express railway shipments on American railways, and special handling in ports—thus adding to the cost, and waste, of war.

Further complications arose when the Navy indicated that it could not provide escorts for all the convoys which were intended to move the initial assault forces. On 27 September 1942, the ASF informed the commanding general of the ETO that he would have to make a choice: reduce the size of the Western Task Force from 167,000 men to 100,000 men and provide the full equipment and reserve supplies for

the entire force, or land the original number of men with only about 50 percent of their equipment. The second alternative was selected; the chief consequence was a substantial cut in the number of trucks moved with the landing troops.[12]

Still another problem of the operation was the responsibility placed upon the ASF to supply, load, and move the so-called Western Task Force—the assault force which was to land at Casablanca and other sites on the Atlantic coast of North Africa. Hampton Roads was selected as the embarkation port loading point. The combat troops had to be equipped almost completely since such training items as they had were largely worn out. This was the Army's first experience in large-scale "combat loading"—the loading of men and supplies so that both could be discharged in the order in which they would be needed once the assault began. Maj. Gen. George S. Patton's staff had to be initiated in the mysteries of code marking for outloading, and the delay in completing assault plans prevented a full-scale rehearsal of loading and disembarking. And at the same time the loading of men and supplies had to be done in the greatest secrecy. But it was done, and the troops made their landings on 8 November.[13]

During the preparations for loading the Western Task Force, General Somervell invited General Patton to observe a dem-

---

[10] Cable 1949, London to AGWAR, 8 Sep 42, Folder TORCH, Tab Rads, Lutes File.

[11] *Logistics in World War II,* p. 37.

[12] Memo, Lutes for Maj Gen Mark W. Clark, 28 Sep 42, sub: Maint of U.S. Troops in Center and Eastern Task Forces, ASF Plan Div #18, Shipping, Vol. I, A46–371, Drawer 10.

[13] For a graphic description of the work of the ASF in this operation, see Don Wharton, "How the North African Campaign was Organized," *Reader's Digest,* XLII (February 1943), 95.

onstration of the latest ordnance equipment, including the new "bazooka." Patton was so much impressed by the defensive possibilities of the weapon in the hands of infantry troops that he immediately asked for a large number to be provided his task force.

In fact, General Patton was pleased with the whole North African supply effort. "The Services of Supply," he wrote to Somervell, "performed magnificently. . . . Without your help this operation could never have started, nor could it have operated successfully upon its arrival here." [14]

Operations in Europe, 1943

The first overseas conference of the Combined Chiefs of Staff with the President and Prime Minister was held at Casablanca in January 1943. The President insisted on a small American delegation. It included General Marshall; General Arnold of the AAF, a member of the U.S. Joint Chiefs of Staff (JCS); three officers from the Operations Division (OPD) of the War Department General Staff; and General Somervell as supply adviser. Though Somervell lacked a staff to assist him with the logistical problems which occupied an important place on the conference agenda, he fortunately was able to press into service two of his former supply officers then serving on General Eisenhower's staff.

At the conference the Combined Chiefs of Staff again decided to defer a cross-Channel attack. The American representatives reluctantly yielded to the British and substituted for a genuine "second front" the invasion of Sicily, to take place at the conclusion of the pending Tunisian campaign. The preparations for the opera-

tion, as well as for the Battle of Tunisia, were left in the hand of the theater commander. [15]

The most important logistical problem at Casablanca was that of shipping losses due to German submarine and air action. The ability to support the North African theater and to continue the preparation for an invasion of the European Continent now depended more than ever upon the success of antisubmarine measures. Even though new vessels were being constructed with unprecedented speed, continued loss at the existing rate would cripple the entire overseas effort. Here was a problem over which supply officers had no control. General Somervell could only point to the seriousness of the situation and urge renewed efforts by both the Navy and the Air Forces to reduce, if not eliminate, the submarine menace. Somervell found his chief support on antisubmarine measures among the British.

Another important problem was that of equipping French units for participation in future African and European operations. General Somervell was asked how much matériel could be made available to the French, and a program for equipping eleven French divisions was agreed upon as a general objective. Because of the shipping shortage and political and manpower uncertainties, this project was given a low priority. [16]

At Casablanca the Combined Chiefs of

---

[14] Patton to Somervell, 22 Nov 42, Hq ASF, North African Theater.

[15] Cline, *Washington Command Post*, Ch. XII, pp. 215ff.

[16] Min, 58th Mtg, CCS, 6 Jan 43, Official Casablanca Conference Book; James D. T. Hamilton, Southern France-Alsace, a volume in preparation for the series UNITED STATES ARMY IN WORLD WAR II; Vigneras, The Rearmament of French Forces.

Staff also began to consider which of several possible Allied operations in the Mediterranean area should follow the occupation of Sicily. An operation in Greece could have been supported as long as the objectives were strictly limited. Army Service Forces planners pointed out, however, that only in southern France would the port capacities and the inland lines of communication permit the buildup of a large force for a decisive campaign against the Germans. At the same time they warned that as long as the eventual major cross-Channel operation for which BOLERO was preparing remained the primary operation against Germany, any other campaign must necessarily interfere with its accomplishment. With supply factors in mind Somervell recommended that all available resources after the occupation of Sicily be devoted to preparation for the cross-Channel invasion, with southern France as the only subsidiary operation. Against the advisability of an Italian campaign, the ASF presented the argument that Italy could not be self-supporting in supplies at any time under an Allied occupation. Large-scale shipments of coal, food, clothing, and medical supplies would be required for the civilian population.[17]

All of these arguments illustrated the bearing of logistical factors upon the determination of strategic objectives. Somervell did not propose that supply considerations alone should govern wartime strategy; he did ask that the strategic planners give full and realistic consideration to the logistical factors in deciding on possible campaigns. It was not easy to reconcile political objectives with the military objective of engaging the enemy on terrain where his forces could be successfully overcome with the least cost. Somervell constantly pressed for military objectives where supply superi-

ority could be effectively realized.

Despite such counsel, the Combined Chiefs of Staff, with the approval of the President and Prime Minister, decided that an invasion of Italy should follow quickly upon the conclusion of the Sicilian operation.[18]

The Post-Casablanca Trip

Immediately after the Casablanca Conference, General Somervell inspected various ports and installations in North Africa and the Near East. While thus engaged, he learned a dramatic lesson on the importance of personal contact in determining the most urgent overseas supply requirements. In Algiers on 25 January, he reported to General Eisenhower at his headquarters at the Hotel St. George.[19] At a meeting that afternoon, with Generals Marshall and Eisenhower attending, Somervell was informed that the greatest single supply obstacle in the forthcoming Tunisian campaign was the absence of adequate transportation in North Africa. There was an urgent need for both truck and rail equipment. The shortage had in part arisen from the fact that General Eisenhower's forces had not yet received all the trucks left behind in November. In addition, the Algerian railways were in a poor state of repair and were inefficiently operated. Although knowledge of this situation had been conveyed to them in general

---

[17] CCS 172, 22 Jan 43, sub: Shipping Capabilities for BOLERO Build-up, Official Casablanca Conference Book.

[18] CCS 242/6, 25 May 43, sub: Final Report to the President and Prime Minister, Official TRIDENT Conference Book.

[19] Log, Somervell's Party, 24–29 Jan 43, Hq ASF, Casablanca Conf, 1943 (Jan–Feb); Min of conf at Hotel St. George, 25 Jan 43, Hq ASF, North African Theater.

terms, few people in the War Department had realized its seriousness.[20]

General Somervell at once began to see what could be done to improve the situation. It developed that if some 5,000 additional 2½-ton trucks, 100 locomotive engines, and other rolling stock for the railways could be immediately provided, preparations for the Tunisian campaign would be greatly accelerated. Somervell assured General Eisenhower that these items could be shipped from the United States if the Navy would provide the necessary protection for the cargo ships. At Somervell's suggestion, Eisenhower asked Admiral Ernest J. King, who had not yet departed from North Africa, for Navy protection. Admiral King promised the necessary convoy assistance, whereupon General Somervell sent a direct radio message on 26 January to his own chief of staff in Washington to arrange for immediate shipment of trucks and railway equipment. Within two and a half weeks, a special convoy of 21 ships carrying over 200,000 measurement tons of material was on its way to North Africa. The difficulties involved in making such emergency shipments prompted General Styer to conclude his response to Somervell's message with the words: "We will not let you down. However, if you want the Pentagon Building shipped, please allow more time."[21]

From Algiers, General Somervell went to Cairo.[22] After the great British victory at El Alamein the preceding October, this area was no longer close to the fighting front. The American supply operation here, undertaken in the summer of 1942 to assist the British, was now largely completed. Aside from the need of continued support of the Air Forces still located in Egypt, the problem now rather was one of cleaning out American supplies and service troops.

General Somervell went on to visit the Persian Gulf Service Command, which had begun large-scale unloading of supplies for the Russians in December 1942. In that desolate area of seasonal torrential rains, high humidities, and summer temperatures which reached 125 degrees in the shade, there was still much to do to prevent the supply lines to the Soviet from choking up. Any one of more than a dozen factors could (and some temporarily did) cause supplies to back up at various stations all the way from Soviet receiving points to the original ports of shipment in North America. A partial list of potential bottlenecks included inadequacy in any of the following: ship's gear, dockside equipment such as cranes and fork lifts, berthing space, labor supply, sorting sheds, dock storage space, trucks, barges, lighters, railroad track and equipment, and highway facilities. General Somervell inspected many key points in the area and spoke to a number of people in an effort to learn at firsthand as much as possible about this complicated situation.[23]

General Somervell found even more difficult problems in the China-Burma-India theater. Upon arriving at Karachi, he received an urgent message to go at

---

[20] Joseph Bykofsky and Harold Larson, The Transportation Corps: Activities in the Oversea Commands, III, a volume in preparation for the series UNITED STATES ARMY IN WORLD WAR II.

[21] Msgs, 26, 29 Jan 43, Hq ASF. See also Dwight D. Eisenhower, *Crusade in Europe* (New York, Doubleday & Company, Inc., 1948), pp. 148–49.

[22] Memo for Somervell's Party, 27 Jan 43, Hq ASF, Middle East Theater.

[23] Motter, *The Persian Corridor and Aid to Russia*, Ch. XVIII; Bykofsky and Larson, Activities in the Oversea Commands; Ltr, Maj Gen Donald H. Connoly to Somervell, 1 Dec 42, OCT, HB. See also 29–31 Jan 43, Hq ASF, T of Opns, Persian Gulf (12), 1942–43.

once to Delhi to join General Arnold and Field Marshal Sir John Dill, both of whom bore messages for Field Marshal Sir Archibald P. Wavell and Chiang Kai-shek about the decisions of the Casablanca Conference. Arnold and Dill had flown to Chungking to get the Generalissimo's consent for an operation in Burma during the 1943–44 dry season. Somervell was told that increased operations by the Air Forces, accelerated road building, and the provisioning of the Chinese troops who would participate in the campaign to open a land route to China—all depended on an enlarged movement of supplies from Calcutta to Assam. Somervell began to investigate the transportation situation at once. He learned that while port facilities at Calcutta were adequate, the Bengal-Assam railway could not support the projected needs. He decided that with efficient management, the Assam line of communications could carry a far greater tonnage than it was then doing. Later, on his return to the United States, Somervell urged, among other specific improvements, U.S. Army operation of the heavily-congested meter-gauge portion of the Bengal-Assam railway, the inauguration of an American barge line on the Brahmaputra River, and the construction of pipelines from Calcutta to Assam.[24]

While in India, General Somervell also visited Assam and rode with Field Marshal Wavell to inspect the construction of the Ledo Road in northeast Assam. He then traveled south to Imphal on the Indo-Burmese border and witnessed the launching of a unique type of warfare. The initial success of this experiment in operating behind the Japanese lines on air supply, under the leadership of the man who conceived it, Maj. Gen. O. Charles Wingate of the British Army, helped as-

sure Somervell that the Ledo Road could be completed and protected from the Japanese and that land communication could be reopened with China.[25]

Back in the United States, after a trip of 32,000 miles, he called together his principal staff officers to give them instructions based on the information he had acquired abroad. Two lengthy memoranda, dictated on 22 February 1943, reveal the problems which loomed large in the mind of the ASF at this time. One memorandum was directed to General Lutes, the supply planner of the ASF, and the other to Maj. Gen. Lucius D. Clay, the staff head for all procurement operations.

In his memorandum to General Lutes, Somervell made a number of observations and recommendations on several matters. He expressed the opinion that the Persian Gulf Service Command should be separated from the Middle East Command, and that the latter's mission should be redefined in the light of changed circumstances. Since there was some possibility that if Turkey entered the war in 1943, Allied forces would be moved into the northeast to support that government, General Somervell wished to obtain information from the Operations Division of the WDGS about intentions in the Near East. He suggested that American service troops should be used to support American combat units and should not be given a

---

[24] Charles F. Romanus and Riley Sunderland, *The China-Burma-India Theater: Stilwell's Mission to China*, I, UNITED STATES ARMY IN WORLD WAR II (Washington, U.S. Government Printing Office, 1953); Bykofsky and Larson, Activities in the Oversea Commands; COS Com, India Comd, USB/7, 9, 15, 19, 24, and Decisions USB/22, History of CBI, Sec. 3, Ch. VII, Arnold-Somervell-Dill Mission, OPD 314.7; Somervell to CofS, sub: Bengal-Assam Railroad.

[25] Log, Somervell's Party, 2–6 Feb 43, Hq ASF, Casablanca Conf, 1943 (Jan–Feb).

general assignment of helping the British Middle East Command. He asked for a study and recommendation on this subject. Somervell also mentioned that it might be possible to use the Levant ports for forwarding supplies to Russia and he asked that the ASF planners explore this possibility. He called attention to the fact that the supply officer of the Middle East Command was forming an engineer regiment from contractors' personnel in the area and from such American citizens as he could find in Palestine. This would mean necessary replacements and supplies from time to time.

As a result of his observations in Algiers, General Somervell expressed the belief that it was "essential that we have a foolproof method of keeping in touch with developments in North Africa and those connected with HUSKY." The ammunition situation for HUSKY, the Sicilian invasion, was of particular concern: "As long as we insist on reports from Eisenhower rather than his bases," Somervell wrote, "we should be able to meet requirements." He had discussed the possibility of a "proper G–4" report with General Eisenhower and asked what had or should be done on this score. He added that reports alone would not do the job and proposed that there should be one visit a month by ASF personnel to the North African theater. Somervell then took up the complaints made to him about the arrival of troops without individual and organizational equipment. He asked that General Lutes and the Chief of Transportation, General Gross, iron this out.

Somervell's next concern, as expressed in the memorandum, was to make certain that equipment required for HUSKY should be sent to North Africa as far in advance of the actual movement of troops as possible. He asked General Lutes to obtain troop requirements for the operation at once from the OPD of the WDGS, to calculate the equipment required in tonnages, and to arrange a schedule of movement with the Chief of Transportation. He did not want it to be said later that a supply breakdown had interfered with the operation. Somervell also directed that the automatic supply system for North Africa be checked and that any imbalances in particular items be rectified.

General Somervell listed three needs of the Persian Gulf Service Command: food rations for native laborers; accountants to record the receipt of goods consigned to the Russians; and Military Police (MP) battalions for traffic control and reduction of pilferage. Not only native laborers, but some of the soldiers of the American port battalions as well, were stealing supplies. While the British reluctantly accepted pilferage up to 5 percent of total supplies landed and forwarded, Somervell pointed out that such a rate meant the loss of one ship out of every twenty. "This is higher than our losses from the German submarines and cannot be tolerated." It seemed ridiculous to ship goods at great sacrifice 15,000 miles and then have them stolen. Somervell asked Lutes to arrange to ship additional MP personnel to the Persian Gulf. While some increase in strength was forthcoming, the Persian Gulf Service Command was never satisfied with its MP allotment, and pilferage remained to the end an unsolved problem.

Among other items in his memorandum to General Lutes, Somervell mentioned special rations for flight crews and urged that the experimental work in this field be expedited. There was particular need for smaller cans of fruit juices in hot climates. He also noted that the Air Forces needed additional landing mats in India and asked that these be supplied.[26]

In his memorandum to General Clay, Somervell made a number of observations about lend-lease. He insisted that there must be "no confusion" about the handling of supplies for the French troops in North Africa. The shipments should be made promptly and be clearly indicated for French use. Pointing out that he had been told in North Africa that the question of importing coal was still unsettled, he instructed General Clay to make sure that it was clearly understood that all coal would be provided by the British. Supplies for the Russians should be consigned directly to the commanding general of the Persian Gulf Service Command, rather than to the British, in order to prevent any delay in delivering supplies to the Russians. Lend-lease supplies consigned to the British for distribution to a third party might be diverted to the British Army, although the British had promised to inform the United States of any diversions. Somervell also pointed out that he had seen large numbers of trucks still standing on the docks at Calcutta. This led him to order that no supplies should be shipped overseas that were not immediately needed.

Somervell observed that Brig. Gen. Raymond A. Wheeler, handling supply operations for General Joseph W. Stilwell in China-Burma-India, did not have a general purchasing agent and directed that the officer who had just installed the purchasing system in Australia should now be sent to India. The purchasing system in North Africa should also be checked. Somervell recommended that the officer assigned to handle the shipment of Russian lend-lease supplies should keep well informed about available routes, shipping schedules, stocks of supplies in the United States, and all other aspects of the operation. He also noted that American lend-lease representatives abroad seemed to be less well informed than the British about shipments of lend-lease supplies and requested that this situation be rectified.[27]

The TRIDENT Conference

In May 1943 the TRIDENT Conference of the Combined Chiefs of Staff was held in Washington. The decision with regard to the cross-Channel invasion was reaffirmed with a target date of spring 1944, and the command in the Mediterranean was directed to keep seven divisions available for transfer to the British Isles. In addition, the cargo shipping requirements for the build-up were discussed and tentative schedules drawn up. For General Somervell, however, the most important problem of the conference was future military operations in China, Burma, and India. The Army Air Forces, at the urging of Maj. Gen. Claire L. Chennault, desired to step up air operations in China against Japanese forces. But any such effort meant more supplies from Calcutta to Assam and over the Hump. At the same time, Somervell, in accord with General Stilwell, was convinced that expanded air operations, with or without corresponding ground operations, would be possible only if land communication with China was restored. He believed that construction of the Ledo Road should be pushed more vigorously,

---

[26] Memo, Somervell for Lutes, 22 Feb 43, Hq ASF; Motter, *The Persian Corridor and Aid to Russia,* Ch. IV; Rpt of MP Activities, Persian Gulf Comd, U.S. Army, Persian Gulf File 130, p. 62.

[27] Memo, Somervell for Clay, 22 Feb 43, Hq ASF; Bykofsky and Larson, Activities in the Oversea Commands.

which meant that it would be necessary to clean the Japanese out of this part of Burma. The chief of the Imperial General Staff of the British Government insisted that no campaigns could be fought during the monsoon periods. Relying on his observations, Somervell expressed doubt about this opinion. The discussion was inconclusive. However, later experience was to demonstrate that the monsoon was no insuperable hindrance to determined military operations.[28]

In the meantime the ASF was giving current attention to the supply support of the forthcoming invasions of Sicily and Italy. After the Battle of Tunisia, the North African theater found itself unable to equip all the troops to be used in the Sicilian invasion. As a result, one of the major units, the 45th Infantry Division, reinforced, was combat-loaded in the United States and transported directly, with a short stop along the Algerian coast, to the point of attack on Sicily. In addition, the ASF had to provide all replacement equipment and expendable supplies for HUSKY directly from the United States. Even before the operation began, the ASF started to ship the supplies which it calculated would be needed to support the troops in Sicily. The spectacular progress of this invasion without major loss of equipment left large excess stocks of matériel on hand, both in North Africa and Sicily. The ASF exerted unremitting pressure in the months following to have these residual supplies sorted out, repaired where needed, and reissued for later military campaigns in the Mediterranean.[29]

As the time for the invasion of Italy grew nearer, the Army Service Forces was once again called upon to ship supplies directly to the Salerno beachhead and later to Naples for the support of military operations. It was easier to find the supplies in the United States and ship them directly to Italy than it was to find the same supplies in Sicily or North Africa and move them across the Mediterranean.

Both manpower and supply limitations prevented the concentration of a decisive force on the Italian peninsula, even had the terrain permitted military operations on a large scale. In the meantime, heavy shipments continued to be necessary in preparation for the cross-Channel operation which had not been abandoned. There were still minimum supply needs to be met in the Pacific. By the spring of 1944, some troops had to be removed from the Mediteranean theater in preparation for the cross-Channel operation.

The Build-up for OVERLORD

BOLERO had envisaged the massing of over a million troops in Great Britain by the spring of 1943. ASF logistical planners from the outset were doubtful whether so large a force, with all its necessary supplies, could be transported and discharged in such a short period of time. British ports did not have sufficient reserve capacity to handle a sudden influx of large proportion, and the British manpower situation was too tight to permit any large diversion of labor to construct depots and camps in a two or three months period. Moreover, there was some British and American shipping capacity which would be underutilized during the summer and autumn of 1942 if BOLERO were concentrated in the early months of 1943.

[28] Papers & Min, Mtgs 84–90, 93–96, CCS, May 43, Official TRIDENT Conference Book; Romanus and Sunderland, *Stilwell's Mission to China.*

[29] Memo, Col Carter B. Magruder to Lutes, 15 Oct 43, Lutes File.

Accordingly, ASF planners suggested that at least the supply build-up should proceed steadily throughout 1942, thus avoiding the prospect of so large a shipping peak in 1943. The major drawback to this plan was the inadequate number and poor training of American service troops in Britain who were to care for supplies shipped well in advance of their actual need.[30] The ASF pressed its plan nonetheless, although it was behind schedule by August 1942 when the North African campaign intervened. But it was not long before the build-up for the cross-Channel operation had to be suspended temporarily while supply attention was focused on the new theater.

In the spring of 1943 the BOLERO program was revived, looking to a European invasion in 1944. The ASF suggested once more that the port capacity of the United Kingdom might be utilized more efficiently by the shipment of military material in advance of troops. The situation in brief was this: the combat troops to be provided by the United States for the cross-Channel invasion, because of their training schedules, could not be moved from the United States until late in 1943 and early in 1944. Up to this time it had been customary to move troop units and their equipment at approximately the same time from the United States to an overseas base. If this practice were continued throughout 1943 and early 1944, the port capacity of the United Kingdom would not be fully utilized during most of the summer and autumn of 1943; after that time the pressure of discharging men and supplies in the United Kingdom would create unmanageable congestion. Accordingly, the ASF wanted to begin to ship supplies to England in advance of troops. The commanding general of Amer-

ican forces in England at this time, Lt. Gen. Frank W. Andrews, seconded this recommendation, observing that under existing arrangements, equipment was arriving as much as 80 to 100 days after the troops for whom intended.

The War Department General Staff gave approval in principle to the "preshipment" recommendations of the ASF in March 1943. Detailed plans and procedures were drawn up in May. Of the total supplies shipped to the United Kingdom between January 1943 and September 1944, about 26 percent represented material thus shipped in advance of troops. In the month of November 1943 alone, 54 percent of the cargo unloaded in the United Kingdom was equipment for troops scheduled for later arrival.[31]

The Early Campaigns in the Pacific

The Japanese march southward in the Pacific was not halted until the summer of 1942 when, after the naval victories of the *Coral Sea* and *Midway,* Allied forces were able to undertake limited offensives against the Japanese in the lower Solomon Islands and New Guinea. These critical and bitterly contested campaigns came to a successful conclusion in the early months of 1943 when the Japanese advance was stopped. Thereafter, one by one, different operations in the Central Pacific, the South Pacific, and the Southwest Pacific began to drive the Japanese steadily back toward their home lands.[32]

---

[30] See above, p. 59.

[31] For a more detailed account of this program, see Richard M. Leighton, "Preparation for Invasion," *Military Affairs,* X (Spring 1946), p. 3. For General Somervell's views see Memo, Somervell to Handy, 10 Jul 43, sub: Preshipmt, Hq ASF, ACofS OPD, 1942–44.

[32] Matloff and Snell, *Strategic Planning for Coalition Warfare.*

The supply problems of the Pacific were tremendous. The whole area was dependent on shipping not only for delivery of supplies from the United States but also for their distribution within the three Pacific theaters. Since there was an acute shortage of shipping, with first priority given to operations in North Africa and Europe, a relatively small amount of cargo lift was available to the Pacific. Even these ships could not be used effectively in the South and Southwest Pacific because of the almost complete absence of adequate base and ports facilities, and because the average turnaround time that had to be allowed for shipments to these two theaters was half again as long as that for European cargo movements. The lack of storage facilities at terminal points in the Pacific contributed to serious port congestion at a number of key bases.[33]

During the summer of 1942 the ASF began long-range planning for the support of the Pacific campaigns. Equipment for amphibious warfare and operations in difficult jungle terrain had to be produced and delivered in great quantities. Special methods of packaging had to be devised to protect supplies from the effects of the tropical climate. Warehousing, harbor, and other equipment for the establishment of bases at key forward points, had to be assembled and shipped. The need for an extensive communications network covering thousands of miles had to be met. Above all, logistical plans had to be carefully co-ordinated with the Navy and a program of joint supply to the Pacific theaters developed.[34]

The build-up of supplies in the Pacific continued slowly, while preparations were being made for a new kind of strategy. The occupation of key points, the construction of airfields for defense and eventual assault, the build-up of port facilities for later operations to seize other key points, domination of the seas, and steady advance toward the Philippines and to Japan itself, where the enemy might be decisively engaged—these became the key elements of Pacific strategy. Supply support was crucial to these efforts. In the last half of 1943, the offensive in the Pacific began to get under way. The ASF worked continually with the Navy in the preparation of arrangements for logistical support.

The QUADRANT Conference

In August 1943 the Combined Chiefs of Staff met once more, this time in Quebec. The most important single supply issue discussed was the division of shipping resources between the Atlantic and Pacific theaters. The British were eager to obtain more tanks in North Africa for use in the forthcoming invasion of Italy. Since United States Army and Navy officials usually agreed among themselves before such a conference on the allocation of shipping for the two theaters, there was little disposition to accede to British requests.

At the conference General Somervell

---

[33] (1) Detailed accounts of supply problems in the Pacific are given in the following theater histories: History of the United States Army Forces in the South Pacific Area during World War II, 30 Mar 42–1 Aug 44, MS, OCMH; History of United States Army Services of Supply and United States Army Forces Western Pacific, MS, OCMH; History of United States Army Forces Middle Pacific and Predecessor Commands during World War II, 7 Dec 41–2 Sep 45, MS, OCMH. (2) ASF Man M–409, Logistic Data for Staff Planners, 1 Jul 44. (3) Bykofsky and Larson, Activities in the Oversea Commands. (4) James R. Masterson, U.S. Army Transportation in the Southwest Pacific Area, 1941–1947 (Monograph), OCT, HB.

[34] History of Planning Division, ASF, OCMH, Vol. I, Pt. 3.

pushed his recommendation for American operation of the Bengal-Assam railway. At the same time, the two governments decided to enlarge the airlift of supplies across the Hump as well as to hasten the construction of the Ledo Road. Somervell had sent General Styer to the area in July 1943, and Styer's report on Ledo Road progress strengthened Somervell's disposition to push construction of the overland route to China.[35]

Along with Gen. Sir Thomas Riddell-Webster, his counterpart in the British War Office, Somervell submitted to the QUADRANT Conference a joint memorandum on supply routes in northeast India. This paper emphasized the urgent need for opening an overland route to China at the earliest possible date. The Assam line of communications as then set up was expected to haul no more than 102,000 tons a month, including petroleum products by 1 November 1943. This quantity would be sufficient only to provide minimum maintenance of essential ground and air forces in the area and about 10,000 tons a month for delivery to China. An additional 118,-000 tons a month could be realized when the overland route was opened. Accordingly, the memorandum recommended that the Combined Chiefs of Staff approve in principle the use of a ground supply route to China from Assam through Burma and that a directive be issued with the target dates as set forth in the memorandum for increasing the capacity of the Assam line of communications. The memorandum said further that the United States Joint Chiefs of Staff had agreed to provide the special personnel, equipment, and supplies to construct and operate the road from Ledo to Kunming, and also, to make available the personnel to achieve the increased tonnage for the Assam line of communications.[36]

The Combined Chiefs of Staff referred the question of rehabilitation of occupied and liberated territories to an *ad hoc* committee made up of General Riddell-Webster, General Somervell, and Rear Adm. O. C. Badger. The committee's problem was to determine the basic policy with regard to such territories, and to agree on a division of responsibility between the United Kingdom and the United States in providing supplies for initial phases of relief and rehabilitation of reoccupied countries. The committee's report recognized that minimum economic relief would be necessary during the period of military operations and for some time thereafter until civilian administration could be restored. The paper also pointed out that since the War Department used military priorities for securing civilian supplies, it was necessary that this procurement be limited to basic food, medical supplies, fuel, and other items essential for the preservation of civilian well-being during military operations. It was not the Army's task to provide a more generous standard of assistance or to promote rehabilitation.[37]

The Combined Chiefs of Staff accepted the recommendations of Somervell and Riddell-Webster. But the increased supply operations of the Assam line of communications depended upon steps taken in India, and some of the recommendations, such as American Army operation of part

[35] Styer, Notes on Ledo Road . . . Based on Inspection by Maj Gen Styer, 2–3 Jul 43, Hq ASF, Ledo Road.

[36] Memo, Somervell for JCS, 19 Aug 43, w/incl Memo, Somervell and Riddell-Webster for CCS, Hq ASF.

[37] Memo for CCS, 22 Aug 43, Hq ASF.

of the Bengal-Assam railroad, had to have the prior approval of the Indian Government. Somervell planned to go personally to India in an effort to speed up the supply program approved at Quebec.

When the QUADRANT Conference of the Combined Chiefs of Staff came to an end, Allied forces were ready to increase the tempo of military operations all over the world. American production was now providing the means on an increasingly large scale.

CHAPTER V

Strategy and Supply: Final Phases

As soon as the QUADRANT Conference was concluded, General Somervell and a number of his staff officers departed on an extended trip to the Pacific theater, returning to the United States by way of India and the Mediterranean. He was eager for an on-the-spot survey of conditions in the Pacific, and for another look at how things were progressing in some of the theaters that he had visited earlier in the year. Both General Marshall and Admiral King sent letters to Army and Navy commanders in the Pacific informing them of General Somervell's trip and requesting full assistance to the party in its effort to obtain information on supply problems.

Somervell took with him General Clay, ASF director of matériel, General Gross, Chief of Transportation, General C. F. Robinson, director of the Control Division, and two of General Lutes' principal assistants. At the last minute Maj. Gen. Oliver P. Echols, the director of matériel for the Army Air Forces, and two of his assistants were included in the party. Careful preparations were made for the trip. Each technical service was asked to submit questions about matters on which it would like to be informed. On the basis of their responses and known problems, a detailed questionnaire was prepared before the group left the United States, and each member of the party was assigned certain questions to which he was to secure answers.[1]

The group left Washington on 7 September 1943, on a trip that was to cover 42,188 miles in 231 hours of flying time.[2] As on General Somervell's earlier trip in 1943, a list of immediate supply needs uncovered during the course of the inspection was radioed to the United States for prompt action. In informal letters to General Marshall, written from various points throughout the journey, Somervell commented in a general way on some of the more serious conditions that he had come across. In letters to the ASF chief of staff, General Styer, he added more detailed information.

The first stop was Hawaii, where he met Under Secretary of War Patterson, who, with General Lutes, was on his way back to Washington after a visit to the Pacific theaters.[3] Here Somervell was primarily

---

[1] Questionnaire, Pers of Trip, 6 Sep 43; Rad, Marshall to Lt Gen Robert C. Richardson, Jr., Lt Gen Millard F. Harmon, Gen Douglas MacArthur, 6 Sep 43. Both in Hq ASF, Trips, Somervell–Round the World Trip, 1943.

[2] WD press release, 25 Sep 43; Memo, Col Paul E. Ruestow for Somervell, 4 Nov 43, sub: Around the World Flights. Both in Hq ASF, Trips, Somervell–Round the World Trip, 1943.

[3] Rad, Somervell to Patterson, 7 Sep 43, Hq ASF, Trips, Somervell–Round the World Trip, 1943.

interested in learning about the progress of joint Army-Navy supply planning for offensive operations. At the moment, the Central Pacific theater was moving from defensive into offensive operations. The attack on the Gilbert Islands was projected for November. The change in mission meant new supply demands for which the ASF must be fully prepared. This joint Army-Navy supply planning staff had finally been approved and an Army officer placed in charge—Maj. Gen. Edmond H. Leavey, who had been recommended for Admiral Nimitz' staff by Somervell. General Leavey's task was to plan joint Army-Navy supply operations in the Central Pacific. There was a good deal of disagreement about how this should be done. The eventual solution worked out was that there should be a formal agreement in advance of each operation, specifying just what supply and service activities would be provided individually by the Army and the Navy for the use of both. Somervell spent a good deal of time conferring with the Army commander, General Richardson, on joint supply as well as other problems.

From Hawaii General Somervell and his party traveled to the South Pacific theater, then commanded by Admiral Halsey. At this time the campaign in the Solomons was moving toward an end. In July landings had been made at New Georgia. Munda airfield had been captured on 5 August. The immediate problem for the theater was one of consolidating positions and preparing for advances toward the North in conjunction with the Central Pacific theater.

From Port Moresby, New Guinea, on 27 September, Somervell wrote General Marshall in detail about his observations. He mentioned that he had talked with all of the division commanders in the South Pacific. He expressed his belief that the Army people had done an impressive job in spite of being low on the supply priority list. His only criticism was a feeling that they had not been sufficiently aggressive in making demands upon the resources of the War Department. General Somervell expressed concern that nonessential construction was being undertaken at many rear bases. He felt that forward bases should be selected in advance and that construction in all rear areas should be limited to essential requirements. He also urged that service units be moved in closely upon the heels of the combat troops and that rear areas be cleaned out as soon as they no longer were needed to support immediate and projected combat areas. Indeed, the problem of "mopping up the rear" became a continuing concern of General Somervell's from this time on. Many supplies were being unnecessarily stock-piled and wasted in rear areas, and service troops were needlessly spending much energy on the care of supplies for which there no longer was a need in the area. This situation had arisen because those responsible for logistical planning in the Pacific areas believed the local build-up of supply was necessary for the conduct of military operations. Somervell and his staff persuaded them that such operations could more efficiently be supported by direct shipment from west coast ports in the United States.

Much of Somervell's letter to General Marshall dealt with the problem of rotation of troops and the incidence of malaria. Better sanitation discipline had improved the situation, but General Somervell nonetheless urged the War Department to review the problem of rotation and to formulate some policy on it before the spring of 1944. The remainder of the letter dealt with lack of enough service troops in the South Pacific. Combat troops were being extensively used to unload supplies and to perform other service duties. General Somervell stated that division commanders were properly concerned about the need for additional medical, engineer, quartermaster, and transportation units. He recommended that the theater commander be given authority to form provisional service units or to break up and reassign existing service units. "It should be realized, in connection with the need for service troops in this area, that the Army is really fighting two battles: one against the enemy and the other against the jungle." The islands of the South Pacific lacked roads, water supply, and docks. The Japanese had made no particular effort to remedy these shortcomings, while the Americans were molding the jungle to their own type of operation, an undertaking which was a major factor in American success.[4]

From the Solomons and the Central Pacific theater, General Somervell and his party moved to the Southwest Pacific. The fighting here was on New Guinea, with Allied troops based on Australia. Just before his arrival, Lae had been captured and the attack upon Finschhafen launched by the U.S. Army, while Australian troops had succeeded in an overland advance upon Salamaua. Preparations were going forward for a series of "leap frog" operations along the New Guinea coast in preparation for the attack on the Philippines nearly a year later. Here, too, commanders, with an insufficient number of service troops for the job, were struggling both to build bases for future operations and to move supplies forward for current needs.

In Australia Somervell had a long talk with General MacArthur. The general wished to have a more definite idea regarding what supply resources he could expect in the next year to support his advance toward the Philippines. Somervell did his best to provide at least some satisfaction on this score.

From Australia, General Somervell and his party flew across the Indian Ocean to Ceylon and then to New Delhi to confer with Admiral Mountbatten, who had been appointed Supreme Commander of the South-East Asia theater at the Quebec Conference. Lord Mountbatten requested that General Wheeler, who had been supply commander under General Stilwell, should now be made his deputy. This was done and General Somervell had to recommend a new American supply commander.[5]

In India Somervell had two definite tasks to accomplish; both were major reasons for his overseas trip at this time. The first was to impress upon the supply organization in India the importance of the Quebec decisions to increase the flow of supplies into Burma and India. The second was to press personally his offer to the Indian Government of American troops to operate the Assam railroad, an offer which the Indian Government seemed hesitant to accept. Lord Mountbatten's intervention helped to persuade the government to turn the railroad over to American operation. Somervell also endeavored to encourage all commanders along the Assam line of communications to new efforts, from the unloading zone in Calcutta to

[4] Memo, Somervell for Marshall, 27 Sep 43, Hq ASF.

[5] Rad, TIGARGW-877 to AGWAR, 10 Oct 43, Hq ASF, Wires, Somervell–Round the World Trip, 1943.

the advanced depots in Assam. Both the pipeline construction and the operation of the barge line on the Brahmaputra also needed additional pushing. At the same time, Somervell acquired further firsthand acquaintance with some of the problems of Army operations in India: problems which he identified as difficult terrain, limited transportation facilities, an Indian bureaucracy which feared change and blocked efficiency, a clash of strong personalities, and a record of vacillation which he suspected was unequaled in any other theater of operations.

In New Delhi General Somervell also encountered an unexpected problem, one scarcely within the scope of his responsibility.[6] T. V. Soong, then Chinese Minister of Foreign Affairs, informed Somervell that Generalissimo Chiang Kai-shek would have nothing more to do with General Stilwell and would demand his relief when Somervell arrived in Chungking. The news upset Somervell very much. Lord Mountbatten was likewise greatly disturbed by this information. Having just assumed command in Southeast Asia, Mountbatten was reluctant to have so drastic a change. On the other hand, he feared that if he became a partisan of Stilwell, he would bring down the wrath of the Generalissimo upon himself and jeopardize the position of his command. Also, if the Generalissimo's attitude remained one of unalloyed hostility to General Stilwell, he expressed himself as believing it would be better to have a change immediately rather than in the middle of projected military operations. General Somervell immediately sent a radio message, through British channels (the only ones available), informing General Marshall about the situation.

General Somervell arrived in Chung-king on the afternoon of 15 October. He immediately arranged to see Generalissimo Chiang Kai-shek the following morning. Officially, General Somervell was no more than an American Army officer visiting the Chinese wartime capital to inquire into supply matters for approved Burma operations. He had come with no letters of introduction from either the President of the United States or the Chief of Staff. Yet General Somervell was regarded as something more than a mere military messenger or investigator. And he himself never doubted that, confronted with top command bickering, he should do all he possibly could while on the scene to adjust the difficulties. General Somervell was not the kind of person to plead either nonjurisdiction or embarrassment.

On the morning of 16 October, Somervell paid a courtesy call on the Generalissimo during which he was informed that Stilwell was no longer *persona grata* to him. General Somervell could do no more than express astonishment and concern and ask to confer with the Generalissimo at greater length later. Upon his return to his quarters, Somervell got in touch with General Stilwell and informed him about what had taken place. He told Stilwell that he planned to request Generalissimo Chiang Kai-shek to reconsider his demand the following day and asked for arguments with which to arm himself. In addition, General Somervell found unexpected support from within the Chinese military

---

[6] This account of the episode which follows is based, in addition to Somervell's own personal recollections, upon a lengthy personal letter from Somervell to General Marshall, 24 Oct 43, Hq ASF, CofS, 1943. The essential outlines of the episode were contained in a radio, Somervell to Marshall, 24 Oct 43, Hq ASF, Wires, Somervell–Round the World Trip, 1943. Both messages were transmitted from New Delhi after Somervell had returned from Chungking.

itself. Both the War Minister and the officer who had been present at Somervell's conference with the Generalissimo expressed their disagreement with Chiang Kai-shek's action and promised that they would attempt to talk with him.

The next day Somervell officially requested Chiang Kai-shek to reconsider his demand for General Stilwell's relief. He pointed out the unfortunate effect which such action would have on American public opinion. He emphasized America's determination to continue to help the Chinese, but at the same time, implied that Chinese-American differences might result in a reconsideration of American policy. He stressed the importance of forthcoming operations intended to open a new land route to China and hinted that General Stilwell's departure might delay the re-establishment of land communication. He added that there was no senior officer in the American Army with the personal background, the command of the Chinese language, and the other qualifications which General Stilwell possessed for his present assignment. Somervell left with at least the promise that the Generalissimo would reconsider the matter. At noon this same day and far into the afternoon, the Generalissimo conferred with Lord Mountbatten, who had arrived to discuss his new command.

In the meantime, Madame Chiang Kai-shek sent for General Stilwell and arranged for the Generalissimo to see him. That evening the Chinese War Minister, General Ho Ying-chin, gave a party for Lord Mountbatten. In the middle of the evening General Ho departed for a conference with Chiang Kai-shek. When he returned, he told Somervell that the Generalissimo would reverse his position at another interview which he would grant

the following day. Somervell then sought out General Stilwell and told him what he had just learned. Stilwell himself had just returned from seeing Chiang Kai-shek. He reported that the Generalissimo had asked him if he had any complaint to make about Chinese pledges and performances. To this General Stilwell had replied in the negative, going on to say that he himself had probably made a great many mistakes and that, if he had, they were not intentional but were the result of the fact that he did not fully understand Chinese psychology. This had apparently mollified the Chinese leader.

The next day, Chiang Kai-shek informed Somervell that General Stilwell had fully satisfied him about his objections. These objections appeared to Somervell to consist primarily of alleged petty slights to the Chinese and charges of arrogance. From his conversation, Somervell understood the Generalissimo to desire certain conditions which Stilwell should observe, but these were left for future adjustment. For the time being the controversy about General Stilwell's position was settled.[7]

Part of the hostility to Stilwell seemed to arise from inside the Chinese official family. Indeed it was General Somervell's distinct impression that T. V. Soong himself had done much to stir up difficulty and had probably urged Chiang Kai-shek to demand Stilwell's relief. On the other hand, Stilwell was frequently less than diplomatic in his expression of opinion about Chinese officials. But Somervell felt that General Stilwell had by no means exhausted his usefulness in China. More

---

[7] For an account of these developments from the point of view of the China-Burma-India Theater of Operations, see Romanus and Sunderland, *Stilwell's Mission to China.*

than this, Somervell received a radio message from General Styer, while in Chungking, which suggested that if Stilwell were relieved, he, Somervell, would be appointed to take his place. He was ordered not to leave the area until he heard from General Marshall.[8] Though Somervell had twice asked General Marshall for an overseas command, he had no desire to relieve Stilwell. The mere prospect of such a change gave him an added incentive to arrange an amicable settlement which would keep Stilwell in his position. The result of his efforts was that the climax to irreconcilable conflict between Chiang Kai-shek and General Stilwell was postponed until a year later, when Stilwell was finally recalled.

While Somervell's mediation of the Stilwell-Chiang Kai-shek controversy had little to do with supply problems directly, this episode was to have far-reaching repercussions for the Army Service Forces. Somervell had displayed again his characteristic initiative and drive in handling a difficult situation. The controversy had been settled much to General Marshall's satisfaction. At the very time when certain newspapers were attacking Somervell because of his plans for internal reorganization of the ASF, he himself succeeded in handling a delicate mission with finesse and without the benefit of instructions from above. There is reason to believe that the episode made a very favorable impression upon General Marshall, just as it had on Secretary Stimson, and that from this time on Somervell's position in Marshall's estimation was secure.[9] This meant too that the Army Service Forces was to endure throughout World War II, no matter what hostile criticism might gather around it.

A minor problem which confronted General Somervell in Chungking was disagreement about the boundaries of the Southeast Asia Command. Lord Mountbatten wished to include Thailand and Indochina in the area of his military operations. Chiang Kai-shek was opposed, saying in part that if such action was taken it would be interpreted throughout Asia as a reassertion of British imperialism. In joint discussions, Chiang Kai-shek, Lord Mountbatten, and Somervell found a satisfactory solution. For the time being, no change would be made in the boundaries of the China theater of which the Generalissimo was supreme commander. When Lord Mountbatten was ready for active operations in the area, the boundary lines would be adjusted.[10]

While in China, Somervell received a radio message from General Marshall stating that President Roosevelt was disturbed by the inefficiency of the airlift operation over the Hump. Evidently, part of the trouble lay in the morale of the personnel.[11] Somervell explored the situation as carefully as he could under the pressure of time and discussed it with Maj. Gen. George E. Stratemeyer and General Wheeler. He reported to Marshall that the causes of inefficiency were weather conditions, lack of runways, the distrust

[8] Rad, AGWAR to TIGAR, 18 Oct 43; AGWAR to TIGAR, 22 Oct 43. Both in Hq ASF, Wires, Somervell–Round the World Trip, 1943.

[9] Stimson's impression was that Somervell was the only wartime emissary to Chungking whose work had been "truly helpful." Stimson and Bundy, *On Active Service in Peace and War,* p. 536.

[10] Memo, Somervell to Dill, 3 Nov 43; Rad, Somervell to Marshall, 21 Oct 43. Both in Hq ASF, Wires, Somervell–Round the World Trip, 1943.

[11] This was not surprising to the crew of Somervell's plane, who found the living quarters at the base "miserable." The floor of their tent was a "mud hole," the food was terrible, and recreational facilities were nearly nonexistent.

felt by the men for the untried C–46 planes, lack of spare parts, poor organization, inexperienced personnel, and bad management. As a result of a shakeup in officer personnel, accompanied by recommendations for demotions, and through the introduction of various measures to improve conditions and morale, a marked increase in tonnages carried was soon to take place.[12]

From India, Somervell flew on to the Persian Gulf Service Command. There had been unfavorable reports about this command—drunkenness among the troops, poor discipline as compared with the Russians, an unhealthy attitude of men toward their officers, and other discouraging information. Somervell on personal inspection found conditions more satisfactory than these reports indicated. American operation of the Iranian railroad to Tehran was proceeding well and road travel had been greatly improved. New port facilities were largely installed and the command was pushing supplies in steadily increasing volume up the Persian Corridor for delivery to the Russians. Somervell was particularly pleased with the high tonnages moved and with the excellent relations with the Russians. Very shortly after his return to the United States, he passed on to Marshall a scribbled note from the American Ambassador to the USSR, W. Averell Harriman, commending the *great* job in getting on a frank and friendly basis with Russians in Iran." [13]

The Cairo and Tehran Conferences

In November 1943 the Combined Chiefs of Staff met in Cairo for their fifth conference since Pearl Harbor. A conference so soon after the August meeting in Quebec was unexpected and produced some suspicions among Americans that the cross-Channel invasion was once more to be questioned by the British. "The logistic problem was whether we could retain OVERLORD in all its integrity and, at the same time, keep the Mediterranean ablaze." [14] But the build-up in England was now well under way, and the discussions at Cairo once more affirmed OVERLORD.

The conference was interrupted by a trip to Tehran where President Roosevelt, Prime Minister Churchill, and Marshal Stalin came together for the first time. At Tehran, General Marshall asked for a plan for an attack on the south of France. Somervell had such a combined strategic and logistics plan with him, one prepared by his own supply planners, along with plans for other hypothetical operations. Generals Marshall and Handy used Somervell's plan in the discussions with both the British and the Russians.

The strategy decided upon was to launch OVERLORD in May 1944, in conjunction with a supporting operation in the south of France on the largest scale permitted by the landing craft available at that time. Projected operations in Southeast Asia were accordingly reduced

[12] Rad, Marshall to Somervell, 17 Oct 43; Rad, Somervell to Marshall, 20 Oct 43; Rad, Somervell to Marshall, 23 Oct 43; Rad, Col Frederick C. Kelly to CG Air Transport Comd, 6 Nov 43, sub: Narrative Rpt. All in Hq ASF, Wires, Somervell–Round the World Trip, 1943.

[13] Rad, Kelly to CG Air Transport Comd, 6 Nov 43; Memo, Somervell to CG Persian Gulf Service Comd, 29 Jul 43, sub: Rpt of Dr. Elgin Groseclose on Certain Activities of the Persian Gulf Comd; Ltr, Somervell to Connolly, 30 Oct 43; Handwritten note, Harriman to Somervell, probably Nov 43. All in Hq ASF, T of Opns, Persian Gulf Comd, 1942–44 (13).

[14] Roosevelt at Cairo Conf; Min, 2d Plenary Sess, EUREKA Conf [Tehran], 29 Nov 43, Official SEXTANT Conference Book.

in scope. Marshal Stalin's insistence on a second front, coupled with the hope that Russia would go to war against Japan once Germany was defeated, were decisive factors in the formulation of this plan.[15] From Tehran, the Combined Chiefs of Staff returned to Cairo to resume their own meeting.

As far as Somervell was concerned, the high spot of the Cairo-Tehran Conferences was the decision to launch an invasion of southern France timed to coincide with OVERLORD. Somervell had pressed for such a commitment because he was convinced of its strategic soundness and because he was very anxious to make the best available use of the supplies which had been accumulated in the Mediterranean. At Tehran Somervell learned directly from Marshal Stalin that he was generally satisfied with the work of the Persian Gulf Service Command in delivering supplies to the Russians. This was of course welcome news. When possible, during the Cairo Conference of the Combined Chiefs of Staff, Somervell reminded the strategic planners of the supply needs of MacArthur's theater.

Before returning to Cairo, Somervell dispatched General Lutes to North Africa and India. Some complaints had been voiced about supply support of the American Fifth Army in Italy. Lutes found that the major shortages in Italy resulted from faulty manifesting of cargoes shipped out of Oran. Thus the difficulty was not ASF performance in the United States but supply work in the theater. It was vital for the ASF to know this. In India Lutes followed up the arrangements made by Somervell for increasing the supply capacity of the Assam line of communications. He recommended that one supply officer be replaced, a move which was promptly

carried out. He also found that the absence of an adequate priority system over the Hump was creating supply conflict between air and ground units in China. By the time he left this situation had been corrected.

Preparations for OVERLORD

Throughout the first half of 1944, General Somervell's main worry was the preparations for OVERLORD. There must be no repetition of the unfortunate experience in England in the summer of 1942 when supplies could not be used for the North African invasion because they could not be unearthed in British warehouses. The United States had long been advocating the cross-Channel invasion. It would be the largest Allied military operation of World War II and the first time in the war that the full might of American manpower and matériel would be thrown against the enemy. None of the preparations for North Africa, Sicily, Italy, or the Pacific was an adequate guide to the present undertaking.

Early in April therefore, General Lutes was sent to England to review the logistical preparations for the Normandy invasion. General Lee, the SOS commander in the theater, quite naturally was not happy about this apparent overseeing of his operations.[16] While Lutes found the theater supply situation satisfactory in general, he also noted that it contained grave weaknesses which boded ill for the future. He advised General Lee to strengthen his staff organization, to establish a definite program of advance plan-

---

[15] Min, cited in n. 14.
[16] Memo, Lutes for Somervell, 11 May 44, Hq ASF, T of Opns (5), European 1944.

ning, to improve the methods for computing supply needs, to institute better stock control, to expedite the delivery of critical supply items, and to develop better relations with General Eisenhower's headquarters. Lutes explained to Somervell that he had not taken up all these matters with General Eisenhower because Lee was Somervell's nominee; in Lutes' eyes loyalty to Somervell demanded that he refrain from "exciting Eisenhower on any deficiencies." [17]

Moreover, General Lutes believed that in spite of weaknesses, it was too late to make serious staff changes. He contented himself with plugging loopholes. When he was ready to leave he informed General Eisenhower that the assault forces were sufficiently equipped, that plans for maintenance up to forty-one days after landing were satisfactory, that new plans would probably insure supplies up to ninety days, and that while Lee's staff was "not the tops," it was "learning" and there was time to remedy weaknesses. [18]

In April 1944 Somervell invited the key supply officers of the European theater to bring a statement of their last-minute needs to the United States in person on 1 May. A series of conferences was held in Somervell's office, in which technical service chiefs met with their ETO counterparts and discussed both the existing supply situation and the manner of meeting the inevitable problems that would arise. By 15 May the European supply officers had returned to the United Kingdom, and the ASF was sending the last-minute cargoes overseas. By the first of June, General Somervell felt that he had done practically everything within his power to insure against a supply failure in the Army's greatest military operation in American history. [19]

Italy and France

At the end of the first week in August 1944, General Somervell accompanied Under Secretary Patterson on a trip of more than 14,000 miles to North Africa, Italy, and the French areas under Allied control.

One of the early stops was at the port of Naples which was found to be bristling with activity, and congested. Here they met and talked to Marshal Tito, leader of the Yugoslav resistance movement. The Germans in that area were pictured as being on a "front window" basis—everything in front and almost nothing behind. After inspecting various installations in the vicinity of Naples, the group went on to Rome, observing battlefields along the way.

The Under Secretary had taken more than a casual interest in the preparations for the invasion of southern France, now scheduled for 15 August. Following a brief visit to the fighting front in Italy, which had moved north of Rome to the valley of the Arno River, the Under Secretary and the commanding general of the ASF crossed to Corsica to watch the launching of the invasion of southern France. Prime Minister Churchill, who was also on hand for the event, invited the two Americans to accompany him to watch the actual landings. Then, a day or two later,

---

[17] Memo, Lutes for Somervell, 29 Apr 44, sub: Rpt on ETO; Ltr, Somervell to Lutes, 4 May 44; Memo, Lutes for Somervell, 8 May 44, sub: Personal Rpt. All in Hq ASF, T of Opns (5), European 1944.

[18] Memo, Lutes for Somervell, 9 May 44, Hq ASF, T of Opns (5), European 1944.

[19] The preparations for OVERLORD are described in detail in Roland G. Ruppenthal, *The European Theater of Operations: Logistical Support of the Armies*, I, UNITED STATES ARMY IN WORLD WAR II (Washington, U.S. Government Printing Office, 1953).

Mr. Patterson and General Somervell sailed for the French coast in an American destroyer and landed on the beachhead. Somervell took great pride in the way in which the supply operation was being handled by Generals Larkin and Wilson and in the strategic success which the entire campaign was achieving. Though the date of the operation had been postponed because of a shortage of landing craft, the campaign when launched was highly successful. Indeed throughout the whole winter of 1944–45, the supply system up the Rhone Valley helped reduce the supply pressures in western and northern France and the Low Countries. Once again, supply planning had had a direct effect upon military operations.

The Under Secretary's party then flew to England for a short stay. On 21 and 22 August they visited the U.S. forces in France which had broken through enemy resistance at St. Lo and were racing for the German border, putting General Eisenhower's supply organization to a supreme test. While Somervell was gratified to see that the rear areas were not seriously clogged, he saw great potential danger in relying long on the beaches to handle all the supplies required to maintain the offensive. Only by getting ports into full operation before the arrival of the autumnal storms could a steady and sufficient flow of supplies be assured.[20]

On 27 August Somervell was once more back in the United States, greatly concerned about two situations. The rapidity with which the Germans were driven out of France had brought a great wave of optimism in the United States and a conviction that the war in Europe would be over within a month. Having just seen Allied forces stalled in northern Italy, and suspecting that the Siegfried Line would prove a greater barrier than popularly believed, General Somervell was worried about the prevailing optimism. He feared that it might have the effect of slowing down the output of munitions in the United States.[21] In the second place, Somervell was gravely concerned about supply in the European theater. General Patton had been halted in front of Metz and Verdun by enemy resistance and by overextended supply lines. There was still no port with adequate facilities for unloading supplies from England and the United States. The Germans held the Breton ports and there was little prospect of using Bordeaux. Drastic action of some sort was needed. The original plans for the invasion of France had called for the prompt capture of the French western ports, especially Cherbourg, and, if possible, Brest, in order to provide unloading capacity for continued support of military operations. Thereafter, additional troops and supplies were to be shipped to them directly from the United States to strengthen the invasion operation. Estimates of the equipment needed for reconstruction of the ports were submitted to the Army Service Forces in the summer of 1943, and the supplies were in England before the actual assault upon the Normandy beaches on 6 June 1944. But execution of these plans was hampered by the delay of the Allied forces in breaking out of the Normandy peninsula, the slowness in restoring the port of Cherbourg, and the failure of our forces to capture any other Atlantic port on the coast of France.

The progress of the antisubmarine cam-

[20] Memo, E. Martin Jr., Aide-de-camp, to CG, Aug 44, sub: Informal Recs of Trip, 8–27 Aug 44; USW Patterson, Log of Trip, Aug 44. Both in Hq ASF, Trips (10), Somervell's Trip, 1944.

[21] See below, pp. 385–86.

paign in the Atlantic by the end of 1943 had led the ASF to recommend a reduction in the supplies stored temporarily in England for the use of the invasion forces in France. Thus, in the period between 6 June and 30 September 1944, one million long tons of supplies and equipment were discharged in France directly from the United States, while another 1.7 million long tons were transshipped from the United Kingdom. But in September when the Allied forces pushed all the way to the German border, more than half of all supplies sent to France were still being discharged over the Normandy beaches. Ships were crowded in the English Channel awaiting discharge.[22] Shipping schedules were being disrupted by these delays, and military operations were being stymied by the slowness with which supplies reached the front lines.

The Combined Chiefs of Staff met again in September 1944 at Quebec. With the end of the war against the Nazis seemingly so close at hand, the most important single issue confronting President Roosevelt and Prime Minister Churchill was the occupation policy for Germany. Somervell's interest still centered on shipping capacities, and on the arrangements for shifting Allied military weight to the Pacific. Great Britain, with the postwar world in mind, was deeply concerned about supply and lend-lease, and Churchill was willing to make many concessions on other matters in order to bolster Britain's future economic position. General Somervell, who had always been opposed to the idea of letting England calculate future political and economic advantages as part of its war plans, favored a policy by which all lend-lease materials left after the defeat of Germany and not used against Japan would be returned to the

United States. His point of view did not prevail.[23]

Disagreement between the British and Americans about inventories of petroleum supplies in Europe was evident at Quebec, but this difference was finally settled after some negotiations in November. In essence, the problem was one of the amount of petroleum reserves to be maintained in the United Kingdom. The British wanted to hold on to these reserves and to supply operational needs in France from other sources, largely American. On the other hand, there were few facilities on the Continent in which to store petroleum reserves. In the end, a single inventory level was agreed upon for both England and the Continent. As storage facilities were provided in France, the share of the reserves carried there would go up. Even so, the inventory level was high enough to permit maintenance of sizable petroleum supplies in the United Kingdom.[24]

Supply Crisis in the European Theater

Shortly after the second Quebec Conference, General Somervell again sent General Lutes to the European Theater of Operations to see what could be done to improve the situation there. By this time it was apparent that there would be no quick victory against the Germans in western Europe. Enemy withdrawal to the German border had shortened their supply lines and greatly extended our

---

[22] *Logistics in World War II*, p. 43.

[23] Memo, Somervell for CofS, 11 Sep 42, sub: Policy Concerning Disposal of LL Material Following the Defeat of Germany, Hq ASF, Quebec Conf; Henry Morgenthau, Jr., "The Morgenthau Diaries," *Colliers*, (October 18, 1947), p. 16.

[24] Memo, Somervell to CofS, 4 Nov 44, sub: Levels of Sup of All Petroleum Products in All Theaters, Hq ASF.

own. The stiff defense of Aachen, which was reduced only after a heavy siege, revealed the quality of opposition which the Germans could still offer. To cope with the situation, General Eisenhower now wanted more ammunition and more big guns.[25]

As General Lutes analyzed the supply crisis in October and November, he came to the conclusion that the greatest single difficulty arose from the absence of an adequate system of supporting depots. From the time of the invasion until early August, the beaches and ports in Normandy served both as base depots and as depots issuing directly to units in the field. When the break-through came, the supply organization had no choice but to haul supplies all the way from the Normandy dumps to the combat troops. There was neither time nor personnel for moving supplies to intermediate or advance depots where they could be sorted and then issued to the combat commands only a short distance away.[26] The famous Red Ball Express and other devices simply hauled the most urgently needed supplies, especially food, gasoline, and ammunition, all the way from Normandy to the French border for immediate pickup by supply units of the combat commands. Sometimes, when certain specific replacement supplies were needed, combat supply troops went all the way back to Normandy to find what they wanted. With the front lines stabilized in September, General Lutes joined with the staff of the Communications Zone in arranging a program for building up advance depots close to the combat zone. This meant that the combat commands would look to the advance depots for all their supply needs, while the advance depots would in turn be assured of a constant flow from Normandy.[27]

The inadequate depot situation on land was matched by a serious breakdown in ship discharge. The ASF earlier had consented to selective discharge, which resulted in ships becoming "floating warehouses." This consent had been reluctantly given to the theater and with the understanding that it was to be a temporary expedient. But more and more throughout August and September, ships remained tied up in Channel waters still fully or partially loaded, upsetting the whole world-wide shipping program.

Another problem was direct shipment. While the ASF was willing to ship supplies directly to France from the United States to support the large numbers of additional troops which were sent to the Continent after 15 August, it was not prepared to meet all Allied supply needs solely from the United States. General Somervell was convinced, for instance, that much of the ammunition which Eisenhower's headquarters was now requisitioning was actually on hand in England.[28] ETO supply officers were so harassed in trying to get matériel from the Normandy peninsula to the German border that they had practically forgotten about the supplies which remained in England.

In October General Somervell decided to send General Clay to Europe to look into these vexing matters.[29] In a memorandum to General Clay upon the eve of

[25] Ltr, Lutes to Somervell, 7 Dec 44; Memo, Lutes to Somervell, 20 Dec 44. Both in Hq ASF, T of Opns (7), European Theater.

[26] For a fuller account see Ruppenthal, *Logistical Support of the Armies*.

[27] Ltr, Brig Gen Royal B. Lord to Lutes, 27 Sep 44, Hq ASF, T of Opns (10), European Theater.

[28] Ltr, Lutes to Lee, 11 Aug 44; Memo, Lutes to Clay and Gen Wood, 10 Aug 44. Both in Hq ASF, Trips (10), Somervell's Trip, 1944.

[29] Rad, Somervell to Eisenhower, Personal from Marshall, 18 Oct 44, Hq ASF, T of Opns (7), European Theater.

his departure, Somervell specified two subjects for his primary consideration. One was the ammunition situation, particularly the possibility of unearthing an unused ammunition supply in England. The second was the delay in discharging ships. In the first fifteen days of October, the European theater had indicated that it would be able to unload seventy-five ships, whereas actually it had discharged but fifteen.[30] General Clay gave special attention to the reconstruction of the port of Cherbourg in order to increase discharge capacity and speed the turnaround of vessels. Somervell then sent his chief of transportation, General Gross, to France in November to check on shipping problems.[31] A big step toward the solution of the transportation log jam proved to be the acquisition of the port of Antwerp, which fortunately had fallen almost intact into Allied hands in September. The Germans had withdrawn so precipitately that they had had no opportunity to destroy the extensive facilities of one of the largest ports in northwestern Europe. The enemy still controlled the estuary of the Scheldt, however, so no Allied shipping could gain access to the port. Not until November, after General Eisenhower had brought the urgency of the situation directly to Field Marshal Montgomery's attention, did the 21st Army Group succeed in clearing the way to the port. But the opening of Antwerp alone was not enough. Twenty-seven piers were of little use unless ships were discharged promptly and the supplies quickly moved from portside to distribution depots beyond the port area. At the end of November both General Lutes and General Gross were pressing for prompt release of ships from Antwerp piers. Some of the officers on General Lee's Communications Zone staff believed supplies should be held in Antwerp until the Rhine was crossed before the setting-up of sorting and distribution depots. Lutes insisted upon immediate action.

In the middle of December General Somervell himself once more went to France, this time upon the direct personal insistence of Under Secretary Patterson, who was concerned about the capacity of the supply organization to meet the needs of the winter offensive.[32]

General Somervell arrived just about the time the Germans launched their big counteroffensive in the Ardennes. The immediate problem of Supreme Headquarters, Allied Expeditionary Force, was to halt it. With the passing of the initial crisis, attention once more was directed to reorganizing the supply needs of the theater. After careful consideration Somervell embodied his recommendations in a memorandum for General Lee which was personally approved by Eisenhower. One proposal was to consolidate the supply organization in northern France and southern France. Up to this time, the southern line of communication, based upon Marseilles, had continued its separate operation in support of the 6th Army Group under Lt. Gen. Jacob L. Devers. Between the two ports of Antwerp and Marseilles, Somervell felt that the combined supply needs of General Eisenhower could be adequately met. The Communications Zone of the European theater now took over the southern France supply organization, with Maj. Gen. Thomas B. Larkin, the commanding general of the latter becoming chief of staff under Gen-

---

[30] Memo, Somervell for Clay, 21 Oct 44, Hq ASF.

[31] Ltr, Col L. W. Finlay, OCT, to CG NYPE, 14 Dec 44, OCT, HB, Gross Day File.

[32] Ltr, Somervell to Eisenhower, 12 Dec 44, Hq ASF, T of Opns (7), European Theater.

eral Lee. Somervell also recommended several steps to strengthen the staff of the Communications Zone of the ETO. For example, he urged the creation of a Control Division in the Communications Zone headquarters, and sent General Robinson from Washington to organize the unit.

The confusion that had developed in the supply system in the theater had led several field commanders to look upon the system as at best mediocre. This led to a movement for the reorganization of the Communications Zone command and staff which General Lutes seemed to favor. General Eisenhower, although aware of the existing conditions, hesitated to relieve a lieutenant general unless it became necessary to avoid a complete breakdown. There was no such clear-cut breakdown— the best way to put it, according to General Lutes after he talked with Eisenhower, was "that the machine does not move smoothly, but it does run."[33]

Malta and Yalta

In January 1945 General Somervell went to Marseilles to join General Marshall. They spent a few days at Cap d'Antibes reviewing the situation in the European theater. Somervell reported on his own activities and gave assurances that the supply should now be adequate to meet the needs of the planned operations.[34]

From southern France, General Somervell accompanied the Chief of Staff to Malta for a meeting of the Combined Chiefs of Staff. The main supply problems that came under consideration dealt with steps necessary for the successful conclusion of the campaign in the Pacific.[35] General Somervell was called upon to present the Combined Chiefs with timetables and

estimates of the volume of supplies available for the war against Japan. Also an agreement was reached with the British whereby the Americans would have Bremen as a port to supply our occupation forces in Germany.[36]

From Malta, Somervell accompanied the Combined Chiefs of Staff, the President, and the Prime Minister to Yalta for the second conference with the Russians. Once again, political problems were of primary importance, but also discussed as incidental matters were problems of supply and of cargo shipping.[37]

The War in the Pacific

In the meantime, events were proceeding rapidly in the Pacific. By the summer of 1944 the Central Pacific forces under Admiral Nimitz had reached Saipan and Guam. In the Southwest Pacific, General MacArthur had reached the northwest tip of New Guinea and was poised for an attack upon the island of Morotai in September.

One of the most interesting episodes in ASF supply planning occurred about this time. Among the different Pacific studies started by the ASF in 1942, there was one

---

[33] Memo, Lutes for Somervell, 17 Dec 44, sub: Preliminary Rpt; Memo, Lutes for Somervell, 31 Dec 44. Both in Hq ASF, T of Opns, European Theater, 31 Dec 44.

[34] Ltr, Somervell to Styer, 11 Jan 45, Hq ASF, CofS ASF, 1945.

[35] Earlier, while in Paris, Somervell had talked at length with General Lee and his principal assistants about arrangements to be set up for shipping men and supplies to the Pacific. See Min, Comd and Staff Conf, Hq Communications Zone, ETO, Hq ASF, T of Opns, European Theater, 1945.

[36] Min, 185th Mtg, CCS, 2 Feb 45, ARGONAUT Conf [Malta], Official ARGONAUT Conference Book.

[37] Min, 186th–87th Mtgs, CCS, 6, 8 Feb 45, ARGONAUT Conf [Russia], Official ARGONAUT Conference Book.

which looked forward to the eventual re-
capture of the Philippines. These studies
were based on an assumption that the
island of Mindanao would be occupied
first and used as a base of operations for
an assault on Luzon.[38] It was on this
strategic concept that ASF procurement
and distribution plans and operations for
the Pacific had been undertaken. All previous planning had to be reconsidered
when, at the SEXTANT Conference in November 1943, the Combined Chiefs of
Staff suggested dropping plans for an attack on Luzon alone in favor of an operation against Luzon, Formosa, and the
China coast. This they believed would
open the way for an earlier attack on the
Japanese home islands.[39] It soon became
apparent however that a simultaneous operation of this sort presented great difficulties and unjustified risks, and so no final
decision was made on strategy to be followed in defeating Japan.

In May 1944 the Joint Strategic Survey
Committee of the JCS considered a proposal for an operation against Formosa
alone. The ASF representative on the
Joint Logistics Committee (JLC), Maj.
Gen. Walter A. Wood, Jr., supported instead the plan for a Philippine campaign
as more feasible than a direct attack on
Formosa. Although Formosa was farther
to the north than the Island of Luzon and
somewhat closer to Japan itself, it was a
great distance from any of the existing or
planned supply bases in the Pacific. In
addition, Formosa as a base would place
U.S. forces in constant danger of both
aerial and naval attack, particularly if the
Philippines remained in Japanese hands.
Formosan ports were small and might
easily be blocked. Luzon, on the other
hand, not only was a much larger island
which might more easily be defended, but

it had larger airfield capacity, a better
road network, and the great harbor of
Manila Bay. Moreover, the friendly Philippine population could be counted upon
to do much of the work in developing airfields and supply facilities for the later assault upon the home islands of Japan
itself.[40]

Meanwhile the Joint Chiefs of Staff
asked MacArthur to plan for an invasion
of Luzon with a target date of 15 February 1945, while Admiral Nimitz was to
prepare a plan for the attack on Formosa
with the same target date. Neither plan
was definitely approved at the time.[41] The
ASF representative on the JLC continued
to press his argument that the supply aspects of a Formosa operation made it
definitely inferior to the Philippines as an
objective. While a decision was pending,
the ASF pushed its own supply preparations for an operation based on the seizure
of the Philippines.

A decision was eventually forced by circumstances. The sequence of dramatic
events has been told by General Marshall
in his final report. The JCS on 13 September 1944, were meeting with the British at
the OCTAGON Conference in Quebec when
they received a copy of a communication
from Admiral Halsey to Admiral Nimitz.
As a result of his naval operations in and
around the Philippines, Admiral Halsey
recommended that projected operations
against Mindanao and other islands to the
south should be canceled, and that American forces occupy Leyte in the central

---

[38] Planning Div, ASF, Job A47-147.
[39] CCS Papers 397, 417, 426, Dec 43, Official SEX-
TANT Conference Book.
[40] Logistics Study of Proposed Plan for Invasion of
Formosa, 15 Mar 44; Logistical Capabilities of Formosa in a Limited Operation, 24 Aug 44. Both in
Planning Div, ASF, Job A47-147.
[41] JCS 713/4, 12 Mar 44.

Philippines as rapidly as possible. On this same day, Admiral Nimitz informed the JCS that he could place certain forces, then loading in Hawaii, at General MacArthur's disposal. MacArthur's views were requested by the JCS. Two days later he advised them that he would be able to land on Leyte on 20 October. This message from General MacArthur arrived at Quebec when the four members of the United States Joint Chiefs of Staff were being entertained at a formal dinner. Within ninety minutes of the time that the message was received, orders were issued to Admiral Nimitz and General MacArthur to abandon the previously approved intermediary landings, and to carry out the Leyte operation on 20 October. MacArthur's acknowledgement of his new instructions reached General Marshall while he was returning to his quarters from the dinner.[42]

After the successful occupation of Leyte, the JCS, in October 1944, ordered the seizure of Luzon, an operation which began in January 1945. The continued support of General MacArthur's operations by the new overwhelming naval power in the Pacific made his land achievements possible. In the meantime, the Navy, with the Tenth Army under its command, began the Okinawa campaign on 1 April 1945.

After his return from Yalta, General Somervell was preoccupied with a twofold problem: the demobilization of part of the Army after the defeat of Germany, and the transfer of another part of the Army and its supplies from Europe to the Pacific. Even though Luzon was not entirely in American hands until April 1945, plans had already been made to use the island as the principal base for the attack on the Japanese home islands. Added to Somer-

vell's concern over the immediate ASF performance of redeployment and demobilization were his apprehensions regarding the quality of the supply job to be done in the Philippines.

Tentative supply plans for the operations against Japan were proposed as early as December 1944. These plans in turn were used by General MacArthur's command as a guide in its own planning. The target date for the first operation, an attack on the southernmost island of Kyushu, depended upon the redeployment of troops from Europe and the assembly of the necessary shipping. The main island of Honshu was to be attacked four months later.[43]

In April 1945, Somervell sent General Styer to the Philippines to observe the preparations that were being made in building up the great base for future military operations.[44] General Styer, shortly after his arrival, sent word back that MacArthur wished him to become the supply commander for future operations. Somervell was happy to release General Styer, believing that he would bring to the task an intimate knowledge of the difficulties which had been encountered in Europe as well as a complete understanding of ASF thinking about supply organization and operation. Here seemed to be the solution to the problem of maintaining close working relationships between an overseas supply command and the ASF in the United States.

General Styer returned to the United

---

[42] *Biennial Report of the Chief of Staff of the United States Army, July 1, 1943 to June 30, 1945 to the Secretary of War*, p. 71.

[43] Logistics Studies for Projected Operations, ASF-P-SL-1, 28 Nov, 11 Dec 44, Planning Div, ASF, Job A47-147.

[44] Ltr, Styer to Somervell, 6 Apr 45, Hq ASF, CofS ASF, 1945.

States in May and made arrangements to take back with him many of the key officers of the ASF. But when he got back to the Pacific, the command which awaited him was not the one he had originally accepted. Instead of becoming supply commander for all of the Army in the Pacific, he was appointed Commanding General, Army Forces, Western Pacific, with headquarters in Manila. Lt. Gen. Robert C. Richardson, Jr., commanding at Hawaii since 1943, had become the commander of Army Forces, Middle Pacific in mid-1944. Both were subordinate to General MacArthur as Commander in Chief. Styer's responsibilities included supply installations in the Philippine Islands. But all combat troops in the area were also under his command until their departure for the scene of the actual invasion. The basic planning and control of supply operations as a whole remained in MacArthur's own headquarters. Thus General Somervell's hopes for a unified supply command of high efficiency throughout the entire Pacific area were not realized.[45]

When the war ended in Europe in May, transportation within the United States became the redeployment bottleneck which the ASF had anticipated. At first General Somervell and General Gross, the Chief of Transportation, had opposed the idea of returning to the United States troop units destined for use in the Pacific. Their opposition was based upon the logistical factors in the situation. It would take more ships to move men across the Atlantic to the United States and then from the west coast across the Pacific, than to move them directly from Europe to Pacific bases by way of either the Suez or the Panama Canals. Moreover, railroad transportation within the United States was scarcely adequate to handle the load.

Transcontinental rail facilities were limited, as was the capacity of west coast ports. But ASF objections were overruled by the Chief of Staff and the Secretary of War on the grounds of soldier morale. They decided that the men who had served in Europe were entitled to a brief visit in the United States before being shipped to the Pacific.[46]

In compliance with this decision, Somervell pressed the Office of Defense Transportation (ODT) for more and more restrictions on civilian travel by rail. Many Pullman cars previously had been made available to the Army, but were now, for the first time during the war, removed from all civilian passenger runs of less than four hundred miles. Other restrictions on civilian traffic were under consideration but never had to be introduced.[47]

Potsdam

In July 1945 General Somervell returned to Europe to attend the Potsdam Conference. The problems under discussion involved only a few matters of direct concern to him. He was deeply worried about the disposition of the vast stores of military supplies in Europe, but a large part of these was scheduled for shipment

---

[45] USASOS GO 166, 30 May 45, sub: Assumption of Comd; "MacArthur Sets Up Supply Command," *The New York Times*, June 24, 1945; History of United States Army Forces Middle Pacific and Predecessor Commands during World War II, MS, OCMH, III, 436–48.

[46] There is a series of reports and studies of various dates on the subject, redeployment of U.S. forces after the fall of Germany, in Planning Div, ASF, Job A47-147.

[47] Wardlow, *The Transportation Corps: Responsibilities, Organization, and Operations*, Ch. IX; Min, ASF Staff Conf, 14 Aug 45, OCT, HB, ASF Weekly Confs, p. 7. See also Gross to Johnson, 30 May 45; USW to Johnson, 9 Jul 45. Both in OCT, HB, Gross, ODT.

directly to the Pacific area or to the United States for repair before subsequent military use.[48]

While the Potsdam Conference was in session, word came that the atomic bomb had been successfully tested in New Mexico. The development of this new weapon had been one of the tasks of the ASF. Somervell shared the general satisfaction brought about by the knowledge that this great effort had not been in vain. It seemed likely that the war in the Pacific might be over earlier than expected.

After the Potsdam Conference, General Somervell began an extensive tour of the facilities being used for sending American soldiers back home. He was especially concerned that the unfortunate experience at the end of World War I should not be repeated. At that time American soldiers had been moved rapidly into the vicinity of Brest only to camp under tents in the mud for weeks, and even months, awaiting transportation home. This time troops were to be moved into the port area only as ships were available to return them to the United States. Great recreational and educational programs were already under way to keep soldiers occupied.[49] The American troops, scattered all over France, the Low Countries, and western Germany, were gradually being concentrated in a few locations. The vast amount of supplies to be inventoried, cared for, and either shipped to the United States or moved into Germany for the occupation forces, gave American soldiers a good deal to do. It looked as if redeployment and demobilization would proceed on an orderly basis.

General Somervell returned to the United States the first week in August. The first atomic bomb was dropped upon Hiroshima on 5 August and the second

was dropped upon Nagasaki three days later. On the morning of 14 August the Japanese decided to surrender. The war was over. But the job of the ASF was far from finished. There were contracts to cancel, surplus property to be identified and disposed of, troops to be brought home and discharged, and the transition from a wartime to a peacetime military command to be arranged. Many of the problems accompanying demobilization had been anticipated and detailed plans had been prepared. The job now was to carry them out.

Other Overseas Operations

The Persian Gulf Command was altogether a supply operation. Until September 1942, American responsibilities in the area were in the field of construction and assembly of motor vehicles and aircraft. By directive of the Combined Chiefs of Staff in that month, the mission was extended to the field of transport. Soon thereafter, American troops began to arrive in Iran to take over the operation of port facilities and the state railway, and to establish an auxiliary motor transport system. New docks and warehouses and new plane and truck assembly plants had to be constructed. Rail transport was augmented by improving the highways and organizing a motor transport service. Eventually, nearly 30,000 supply troops of various kinds were located in the command. During the period of active Anglo-American transport operations (1942–45) more than 5.1 million long tons of cargo

---

[48] Min, 193d–200th Mtgs, CCS, 16–24 Jul 45, TERMINAL Conf [Potsdam], Official TERMINAL Conference Book.

[49] Memo, CofS, 10 May 45, Hq ASF, CofS USA, 1945.

moved through the Persian Corridor en route to Russia.[50]

Except for the activities of the Air Forces, including the later operations of the Twentieth Bomber Command from Chinese bases, Army duties in China, Burma, and India also were largely of a supply nature. In order to keep China actively engaged in the war, it was essential to keep up a steady flow of military supply to her armies. The only available avenue of communication after the summer of 1942 was by air over the Himalaya Mountains from Assam in northeast India. But airlift could scarcely deliver heavy construction equipment, machinery, tanks, and artillery in sizable quantities for Chinese troops. Therefore the opening of an overland line of communications was indispensable to success. The primary task assigned to the China-Burma-India theater in 1942 and 1943 was to increase the airlift over the Hump and to begin the construction of a new land route into China, the so-called Ledo Road. This could be completed only with the successful elimination of the Japanese from North Burma. But military operations largely depended upon the rate of construction of the road. In the autumn of 1943, when the airlift operation was being expanded, the American Army organized a combat team, popularly known as Merrill's Marauders, to assist Chinese, British and Indian forces opening the way for the construction of the road. Air operations in support of ground attack also played a major role. Eventually, the combined Ledo and Burma Roads, renamed the Stilwell Road, were reopened in January 1945. A pipeline to Kunming, China, was completed by July.

Necessarily the ASF maintained close contact at all times with the military activity in India, Burma, and China. Although it was never possible to undertake large-scale efforts here when the main military force was employed against Germany, almost no part of the world presented more challenging supply difficulties than Southeast Asia.

Immediately after the American naval victory of Midway in 1942, Japanese troops landed and occupied three westerly islands at the end of the Aleutian chain of Alaska. The elimination of these Japanese forces was entrusted to the Western Defense Command in the United States supported by the Alaskan Department. Only a few military supplies of a special kind could be provided by the ASF for this undertaking. American forces landed at Attu Island on 11 May 1943, and annihilated the Japanese by 31 May. When forces landed on Kiska on 15 August, they found that the Japanese had evacuated the island. For the ASF, this campaign demonstrated two lessons: the importance of protective clothing and materials in harsh climates, and the importance of service troops in bringing an amphibious campaign to a successful conclusion.

The variety of matters which directly or indirectly affected supply factors in World War II are evident from this cursory review of military events. Yet at the time, because of the pressure of circumstances, the importance of these factors was sometimes overlooked. The Army Service Forces constantly reminded operational planners of the vital interrelationship between strategy and supply. And it was this interrelationship which defined the role of the Army Service Forces in the strategic planning of World War II.

---

[50] Motter, *The Persian Corridor and Aid to Russia*, p. 6.

On 9 March 1945 General Somervell told a group of some three hundred key officers of the ASF that this war, more than any other, had demonstrated the importance of supply. "The difference in supply superiority and in mobility between the Germans and the Americans is the contribution that we in the Army Service Forces are making to this war." [51]

[51] Third ASF Anniversary Talk, distributed to all key pers of the ASF (mimeographed).

CHAPTER VI

Services[1] for the Army

Procurement and supply were not the only activities of the Army Service Forces; a wide variety of other duties were also assigned to it. Before the reorganization of 9 March 1942, most of these duties had been performed by a heterogeneous group of administrative agencies. With the creation of the ASF, these agencies were brought together under one superior other than the Chief of Staff.

Medical Service [2]

Some idea of the size of Medical Department operations in World War II can be obtained from a few statistics. During the years 1942–45, the number of admissions to Army hospitals from the Army alone was 14,700,000. This does not include thousands of other patients who received treatment in these hospitals—certain personnel of the Navy and Coast Guard, members of Allied forces, prisoners of war, and civilians. From November 1942 to the end of 1946, the Army moved more than 660,000 patients from overseas areas to the United States; of these, 533,-000 returned by water and 127,000 by air. The movement reached a peak in May 1945 when a total of 60,000 patients were returned to this country.

The Surgeon General of the Army, who became a part of the Army Service Forces on 9 March 1942, was the chief of all Army medical activities. His status as such

was not altered by the War Department reorganization. While he had certain procurement and supply responsibilities, these were incidental to his larger task: the direction and supervision of professional medical service throughout the Army.

In the strictly technical field, the Medical Department made valuable contributions to the fields of medical research, preventive medicine, and therapy. It worked in close collaboration with governmental and private agencies, both in the United States and in Allied countries. From this collaboration resulted such spectacular achievements as the successful use of Atabrine as a malarial suppressive and of penicillin in the treatment of a wide range of wounds and general infec-

---

[1] The term "services" is used in this chapter to cover the major tasks performed by the ASF not directly a part of supply operations. In order to clarify the discussion of organizational relationships treated in later chapters, a description of the nature of these tasks and in some cases a discussion of the organizational problems they created is considered desirable.

[2] The following account is based mainly on data furnished by the Historical Division of the Army Medical Library, which is preparing a detailed history of the Army Medical Department in World War II. For a fuller discussion of some of the points mentioned here, see "Developments in Military Medicine during the Administration of Surgeon General Norman T. Kirk," *Bulletin of the U.S. Army Medical Department*, VII (Jun 47), 520–62, (Jul 47), 594–646. The death and disease rates given are those most recently established by the Medical Statistics Division of the Surgeon General's office.

tions, and further progress in the use of the sulfonamide compounds. Even more noteworthy was the development of new insecticides, especially DDT, which proved so effective in the control of such diseases as louse-borne typhus, one of the scourges of armies from the earliest times.

The use of Atabrine was only one, though a highly important, item in the Army's program of preventive medicine. The policy of immunizing every soldier against typhoid and paratyphoid fevers, smallpox, and tetanus kept the incidence of these diseases so low as to be almost insignificant. With a better vaccine available, the incidence of typhoid dropped from 0.37 in World War I, to 0.03 in World War II, and that of paratyphoid from 0.05 to 0.03. (These figures represent the number of cases per 1000 of Army strength per annum.) Only 12 cases of tetanus occurred during 1942–1945, a rate of 0.44 per 100,000 wounds and injuries as compared with 13.4 in World War I, during which a policy of universal immunization against tetanus was not adopted. The number of smallpox cases declined from 853 in World War I to 116 in World War II, a noteworthy result in view of the larger forces engaged and the difficulty of maintaining the effectiveness of a highly sensitive vaccine under extreme climatic conditions. Immunization against other diseases was limited to troops serving in regions where these diseases were a hazard, as for example, in the case of troops serving in areas where there was yellow fever. In spite of the fact that troops were exposed to it in these areas, there were no cases of the disease. Unfortunately 50,000 cases of jaundice were traced to the use of certain faulty lots of yellow-fever vaccine before these could be eliminated.

In the field of curative medicine, a notable example of the military importance of improved methods of treatment was the decline in noneffective rates for venereal disease. The average number of men absent from duty each day on account of this disease (or group of diseases) in World War I was 45 per 100,000; in World War II the number had dropped to 13. Another advance resulted from the growing reliance on plasma, later supplanted in large part by whole blood, especially for the treatment of shock as an incident to wounds or surgery. Surgery also profited from the practice of "phasing," which consisted of treating severe wounds by a series of predetermined procedures taking place at the points where each could be most efficiently performed. This reduced the gap in space and time between disablement and expert attention. Aiding in this reduction was the revival of mobile surgical units, a form of which had been used in World War I; these enabled highly skilled surgeons to be rapidly concentrated very near the front at points of greatest need. Improved means of transport served the same purpose, and the rapid movement of patients by air to centers of definitive treatment became a factor of increasing value in promoting recovery. Another important factor enabling World War II surgeons to keep the mortality rate low among the wounded was the use of improved agents and equipment for inducing anesthesia.

Neuropsychiatric disorders constituted a major problem for both preventive and curative medicine throughout the war; no less than 18.7 percent of all patients evacuated to the United States during 1942–45 were returned for this cause. At first much stress was placed on the screening process—"diagnosis and disposal"—

as a preventive. The great loss of man-power through this process and the grow-ing evidence that anyone could develop a psychoneurosis under certain conditions caused a shift of emphasis to the preven-tion of mental casualties by alleviating the circumstances which helped to create them: among other things, excessive length of combat, misassignment, poor leadership, and lack of personal convic-tion about the necessity of the war. With this approach went a more determined ef-fort to improve psychiatric treatment so that as many of the mentally ill as possible would be fit for at least a limited kind of military service. Part of this program was carried out through an elaborate system of rehabilitation which developed gradu-ally during the war and which was de-signed not only for psychoneurotics but for the physically disabled in the final stages of their treatment.

The extensive use of "consultants"—highly trained experts from civilian life—to supervise the professional and in some cases the administrative activities of the Medical Department was an important development of World War II, although it had its precedent in World War I. These experts were armed with authority to work out policies and standards of practice which would give the Army the highest type of service in every branch of medicine.

Professional decisions about medical care, so far as they could be separated from administrative action, remained the exclusive province of the Medical Depart-ment throughout the war. General Somer-vell followed clinical developments with interest and tried to keep himself in-formed, but he never bypassed The Surgeon General in seeking advice on such matters.[3] The administrative prob-lems to which ASF headquarters gave some attention during the war included such subjects as the procurement and use of personnel, the number and administra-tion of hospitals, the procurement and distribution of medical supplies, and the organizational structure of the Medical Department. Since decisions in these fields often had an important effect on the standards of professional care, and since the Medical Department rightly consid-ered itself the proper guardian of those standards, it was not always easy to recon-cile the viewpoints of ASF headquarters and The Surgeon General's office. As a result, one or the other sometimes acqui-esced in a particular line of action with considerable reluctance.

The Surgeon General reported short-ages of medical personnel throughout the war. Most constant and most serious was the shortage of physicians—particularly the various categories of specialists—but periodically there was also a shortage of nurses, dentists, veterinarians, and other types of medical personnel. The ASF in-sisted that the Medical Department economize in the use of doctors and other members of the medical profession, and it was largely in response to the urging of ASF headquarters that members of the Medical Administrative Corps, composed of nonmedical officers, were increasingly used for administrative duties instead of doctors, dentists, and veterinarians. The Medical Department also found it possible

---

[3] Somervell's refusal to interfere with professional Army policy on the cure of syphilis, in spite of his in-terest in the "five-day treatment," is a good example of his attitude. See Ltr, Dr. H. T. Hyman to Somer-vell, 22 Mar 43; Memo, Acting SG to CG ASF, 25 Mar 43, sub: Short Intensive Treatment for Syphilis; Ltr, Somervell to Hyman, 29 Mar 43. All in Hq ASF, SG, 1943.

TABLE 1—COMPARISON OF MEDICAL SERVICE, WORLD WAR I AND WORLD WAR II

	Admissions for disease	Death from disease	Death from wounds	Death from injuries
World War I . . . . (Apr 17–Dec 18)	*946. 8	*16. 5	4. 4	1. 4
World War II . . . . (Jan 42–Dec 45)	580. 4	0. 6	1. 1	2. 3

*These figures were swelled by the incidence of influenza, which reached epidemic proportions in late 1918.   Excluding influenza, disease admission and disease death rates for World War I would be 715.0 and 9.1 respectively; for World War II they would be 573.1 and 0.6.

to turn over a sizable portion of the Army nurse's duties to civilian graduate nurses who could not meet the requirements for a commission, and to cadet nurses, nurses' aides, and male and female enlisted technicians. Nevertheless, at no time during the war was The Surgeon General's demand for medical personnel fully met; nor was the problem of efficient and full-time use of this personnel ever solved to the satisfaction of all parties.

The construction and maintenance of hospitals in the zone of interior was a joint responsibility of The Surgeon General and the Chief of Engineers. ASF headquarters took a hand in negotiations between them not only as a superior authority but as a controlling force in the distribution of materials and supplies among the various branches of the Army. A similar division of authority existed in the movement of patients, which devolved upon the Chief of Transportation as well as The Surgeon General; here, ASF headquarters had to mediate between the services in order to establish proper priorities in transportation and to insure full use of facilities. Medical training and medical supply also were subjects in which ASF headquarters took great interest. Thus, while Army medical service was a responsibility of the Medical Department, its duties were performed as a part of the work of the Army Service Forces.

A rough means of gauging the success of that medical service is to compare World War II with World War I as to rates of admission (to hospital and "quarters") for disease and as to rates of death from disease, wounds, and injuries. These rates as shown in the table on this page represent the number of cases per 1000 of Army strength per annum.

Communications and Photographic Activities

The Chief Signal Officer was more than a buyer of communications equipment. He was also in charge of the Army communications system, a network of radio, teletype, and wire communications linking the War Department with Army installations in the United States and Army commands overseas. This work was highly technical, and had greatly improved through the years with the growth in technological knowledge.[4]

The Army Communications Service was frequently called upon to provide

[4] During the observance of the centennial of the telegraph on 24 May 1944, the Signal Center in Washington sent a message around the world, through five different relay centers, in three-and-one-half minutes. Annual Rpt of ASF, 1944, p. 188.

message facilities on short notice. At the Yalta Conference in January 1945, for example, the meeting between the political heads of the United States, the United Kingdom, and Russia was scheduled at a place lacking communications facilities. Some 250 tons of equipment, including radio transmitters and receivers, teletypewriter apparatus, and a complete telephone system for local use were transported to the Crimea. The telephone network covered an area of 2,376 square miles, with land-line telegraph circuits crossing two mountain ranges. The long-range radio transmitting facilities were installed in a ship anchored sixty-five miles from the conference site—the first use of such a device in American communications history. Yet this complex, extensive installation was completed and placed in operation in nine days.[5]

The work of the Communications Service was of special interest to the Intelligence Division (G–2) of the War Department General Staff for two reasons. In the first place, it was essential to insure the secrecy of messages transmitted to and from overseas. To maintain this secrecy, a variety of technical devices was used, ranging from automatic coders and decoders to "scramblers." [6] Secondly, radio interception of enemy messages became one of the important sources of information about enemy plans and intentions. It was inevitable then that the Communications Service should operate under the closest scrutiny of G–2. This was a relationship with which ASF headquarters was entirely satisfied.[7]

On the other hand, the operation of the Army Pictorial Service was a constant source of concern to General Somervell. Essentially, the Signal Corps had two basic photographic missions. The first was

to prepare training films and film strips for use at Army training posts; the second, to provide pictures of Army activities. These films and pictures might be used for combat analysis, for training purposes, for public relations, or for an historical record.

The production of training films involved close working relationships with the motion picture industry centered in the Los Angeles area. Producers and actors were among the first groups in this country in 1940 to volunteer their services free or on a cost basis to the government. However commendable their actions may have been, motion picture producers and their staffs were difficult to work with. Partly because of this situation, and partly because of the photographic service itself, many of the training films that were produced failed to meet the needs of the Army.[8] After 1942 more and more training films were prepared at the Signal Corps Photographic Center on Long Island.[9] For a time, the Army Pictorial Service was removed from the jurisdiction of the Chief Signal Officer and placed directly under the Commanding General, ASF. This action was shortly reversed when a new Chief Signal Officer, Maj. Gen. Harry C. Ingles, took over on 1 July 1943.[10]

General Somervell was quite unhappy about "this picture business." Shortly after Ingles assumed command of the Signal

---

[5] Annual Rpt of ASF, 1945, pp. 131–32.

[6] Memo, Brig Gen Robert H. Dunlop to Somervell, 27 Jan 44, sub: Overseas Secret Rad Tel, Hq ASF, SigC, 1942–44.

[7] Ltr, Somervell to Maj Gen James A. Code, Jr., 3 Mar 44, Hq ASF, SigC, 1942–44.

[8] CD Rpt 47, Report of Training Film Program, 1943, CD, ASF.

[9] Ibid.

[10] See below, p. 303.

Corps, Somervell sent him an extract from a report he had received which read:

The utter confusion that surrounds the photographic departments in the field, is unbelievable. There are thousands of Signal Corps photographers and they take millions of pictures but what happens to them no one knows. . . . The photographers are encouraged by public relations officers in many cases to bear down hard on pictures of the Commanding General whether or not he is a photogenic type. In one base, out of 4,000 pictures, more than 2,500 were of the commanding general eating lunch, picking roses, riding horses, going to the latrine, what have you. . . .[11]

As a result of such prodding, there was a marked improvement in the management of the Army Pictorial Service, and as time passed Somervell and his assistants gave less and less attention to photographic activities.

Construction

The Office of the Chief of Engineers in December 1941 was the Army agency responsible for the construction of all types of military installations, from Ordnance factories to military posts and airfields. This agency was also responsible for the operation of utility systems and for the maintenance of the structures at army installations both in the United States and overseas.

The work of the Chief of Engineers began with the acquisition of building sites. From 1 July 1940 to the end of the war, the War Department acquired title to about thirty-nine million acres of land, an area larger than the state of Illinois. More than five sixths of this total involved simply the transfer of public land from one custody, primarily that of the Interior Department, to that of the War Department. Much land and many facilities were leased

rather than purchased. Whether wanted or not, real estate problems became a big job for the Army.[12]

The Army's construction program was one of the first and largest phases of defense mobilization to get under way. As of 30 June 1942, the Army's authorized construction program amounted to about 7.5 billion dollars, of which 2.7 billion dollars was for Ordnance plants and depots, 2 billion dollars for air installations, and 1.4 billion dollars for Army camps to train ground troops. The remaining 1.4 billion dollars was divided among a large number of other installations. Only about one half of this total program was then in place.[13]

During the period from July 1942 to June 1943, the construction program expanded in total volume from 7.5 billion dollars to 9.3 billion dollars, of which 95 percent was in place by 30 June 1943. In the following two years only an additional 1.3 billion dollars was spent on new plants inside the United States. Much of the construction in the late war years was for production of the atomic bomb and for air facilities to accommodate large bombers. The construction program during World War II was the largest construction program ever undertaken over a five-year period of time under single direction in American history.[14]

As construction slowed down in 1943 and 1944, maintenance problems increased. By the end of fiscal 1945, the Corps of Engineers was supervising the

[11] Memo, Somervell for Maj Gen Harry C. Ingles, 25 Aug 43, Hq ASF, SigC, 1942–44.

[12] Annual Rpt of ASF, 1943, pp. 187–88; 1944, pp. 183–84; 1945, pp. 293–96; CD, ASF, *Statistical Review, World War II*, p. 13.

[13] Annual *Report of the Services of Supply, 1942* (Washington, U.S. Government Printing Office, 1943), p. 61; CD, ASF, *Statistical Review, World War II*, p. 11.

[14] Annual Rpt of ASF, 1943, p. 181; CD, ASF, *Statistical Review, World War II*, p. 11.

maintenance of 75,000 miles of road, 23,000 miles of electric wire, 13,000 miles of water mains and an almost equal mileage of sewer lines, nearly 3,000 miles of gas mains, and 1,600 miles of steam pipe.[15]

That General Somervell should be interested in the construction work of the Engineers is not surprising. An Engineer officer himself, he had been head of a major part of Army construction work from December 1940 to November 1941. He had a personal knowledge of the whole program. Since certain groups in the War Production Board were critical of the size of Army construction, after 1942 General Somervell tried to make sure that the additional facilities were actually needed and that materials and manpower would be available for their operation.[16] After 1944 the efficient utilization of space in Army posts was a major objective of ASF headquarters. For example, it was more economical to operate a few training posts at or near full capacity than to operate twice as many at 50 percent capacity. But to convince others accustomed to time-honored methods of operation was a difficult chore.

Personnel

Between March 1942, when the Army Service Forces was created, and August 1945, some 6,881,011 men were inducted into the Army. Through The Adjutant General's office the ASF became the operating agency for performing this work.

Induction consisted of four basic procedures: medical examination, formal induction, classification, and initial assignment. An important question in medical examination was setting the physical standard required for Army service. At various times during the war, the actual physical qualifications for "general service" were altered. Medical rejection of men having a venereal disease, for example, decreased during 1943 as the Army found penicillin effective in combating syphilis.

Another problem was "limited service." For a time in 1943, the War Department refused to accept "limited service" men from the Selective Service System because of difficulty in making good use of them. Beginning in November 1943 the War Department tried to assign such men to the type of work for which they were best suited physically. A committee was organized to work out a new physical classification system with the Deputy Chief of Staff for the War Department as its chairman. Part of this burden fell upon the Army Service Forces.

On 18 May 1944, the War Department officially announced a Physical Profile plan. The plan identified six primary physical characteristics: stamina, hearing, eyesight, motion and efficiency of upper and lower extremities, and neuropsychiatric condition. Within each characteristic there were four grades—the first two qualified a man for general service, grade three for limited service, while a person falling predominantly in grade four was rejected for military service. The complexity of the new classification system was troublesome, but at least fuller information about the physical condition of each person became available. With the introduction of this plan, initial assignment

---

[15] Annual Rpt of ASF, 1945, p. 297.
[16] A more detailed history of construction during the war in the zone of interior will appear in Jesse A. Remington, Blanche D. Coll, and Lenure Fine, ZI Construction, II, one of the Engineer volumes in preparation for the series UNITED STATES ARMY IN WORLD WAR II.

tended to be based primarily upon physical condition.[17]

After being inducted, the men were sent to reception stations operated by the ASF where they were issued Army clothes and given a number of tests. The most important of these was the Army General Classification Test which divided men into five grades according to a person's ability to learn. Those in Grades IV and V were "slow learners"—one might say, persons impossible to teach. Other tests were intended to indicate mechanical, technical, and clerical aptitudes. On the basis of these tests and of personal interviews, a provisional classification was made of the kind of military work for which the individual seemed best fitted. Various types of military duties had been classified into a system of "military occupation specialty" numbers.

While this system was useful, the effort to match military assignment with classification was difficult to administer. In a time of mass induction, assignments could not be made on an individual basis. Moreover, personnel demands at a particular moment did not necessarily fit the classification qualifications of the group of men currently being inducted. Classifications did identify those particular specialists who were in "critical supply" at any one time, such as radio operators. These could be individually assigned. But with the specialized manpower needs of war, and with ten times as many different types of occupations in civilian life as in the Army, the classification process could not insure that all inductees would be placed at tasks related to their previous training and experience. It was very important in selecting specialists to fill Army needs to find men who had had equivalent civilian occupations. Encouragingly, a sample survey in 1943 indicated that 78 percent of the men studied were doing military work related to their civilian occupational specialty.[18]

Shortly after it came into existence, the Army Service Forces began to study procedures in commissioning officers from civilian life. The Army had earlier adopted the practice of training young officers for combat assignments in officer candidate schools open to men selected from the ranks. Other combat officers came from National Guard and Reserve Corps rolls. But many noncombat branches and higher headquarters of the Army necessarily recruited officers directly from civil life. This had always been the practice, for example, in the Medical Corps, since the Army never had a school to train doctors. Similarly, the Ordnance Department, the Transportation Corps, the Air Corps, the Quartermaster Corps, the Signal Corps, the Corps of Engineers, The Judge Advocate General's Department, the Chief of Chaplains, and other units, especially in ASF headquarters, needed many officers with special nonmilitary skills. All these agencies separately recruited officers who were subject only to hasty review by a Personnel Board appointed by the Secretary of War.

The commissioning of so many officers in so little time involved many problems, one of the most complicated of which was weeding out incompetents. Time was pressing and officer procurement officials necessarily relied heavily on recommendations. Occasionally this had its humorous side as when one bank executive recom-

<hr>

[17]Annual Rpt of ASF, 1944, pp. 201–02.
[18]Annual Rpt of ASF, 1943, p. 136; WD Pam 12–8, The Evaluation, Classification, and Assignment of Military Personnel, 28 Jul 44.

mended a West Texas county judge in the following terms:

. . . The old gentleman was a pretty good old guy in his day, but he has approached the age of senility, in addition to which he is probably the laziest man in West Texas. Although he is a veteran of the Spanish War, he still has ideas about his prowess, and is continually chasing blondes. He drinks a case of Budweiser every day, and his wife has to put him to bed every night. The least said about his honesty and ability is too much. If the Army can find any use for this old bastard, they are welcome to him. . . .[19]

Very few recommendations were so outspoken. In fact one of the most serious drawbacks to this method of obtaining officers was that too often influential individuals tried to get a job for the man rather than a man for the job. There were many complaints that only people of political or social prominence were eligible for commissions, and that "pull" rather than merit was too often the deciding factor.[20] Such protests were natural in any situation where so many people seeking commissions had to be turned down. Remedial measures were taken when criticism seemed legitimate, but undoubtedly there was much truth in Secretary of War Stimson's jest that to satisfy everybody, the Army would have to abolish the rank of private.[21]

In fact, if it had been left entirely to Secretary Stimson, very few commissions would have been given to civilians. The Secretary believed that the honor of a commission should be reserved for fighting men. In September 1942 he approved the creation of an Army Specialist Corps where men were selected on the basis of nonmilitary skills and wore uniforms different from those of the Army. The experiment was abandoned in November 1942 and the practice of commissioning civilians

in the regular branches of the Army was resumed.[22] This attempt to establish an Army Specialist Corps failed because the Army did not recognize the importance of technicians and other experts in modern war and because such men could be more easily obtained if they were offered commissions in the Army of the United States.

The ASF established an Officer Procurement Service to recruit specialized officer personnel.[23] During the year 1942 approximately 104,000 officers were commissioned from civilian life. Nearly half of these were medical personnel, with most of the remainder about equally divided between special units of the Army Air Forces and of the Army Service Forces.[24] In July 1943 the Acting Secretary of War, Mr. Patterson, directed that, with certain exceptions, officer recruitment from civilian life be discontinued. In the year ending 30 June 1944, only 16,119 persons were commissioned from civilian life, 80 percent of whom were doctors and chaplains.[25]

A major innovation in Army personnel policy came in the summer of 1942 when Congress authorized a Women's Army Auxiliary Corps, renamed in September 1943, the Women's Army Corps (WAC). The ASF supervised the recruitment and training of this corps; by April 1945 its

---

[19] Copy ltr, to San Antonio Offs Procurement Div, 3 Sep 42, Hq ASF, Pers Military, 1942–44.

[20] *Kansas City Star,* May 4, 1942.

[21] Stimson and Bundy, *On Active Service in Peace and War,* p. 350.

[22] *Ibid.,* pp. 456–57. See also EO 9078, 26 Feb 42; Memo, C. F. Robinson for Somervell, 25 Sep 42, sub: Army Specialist Corps. Both in Hq ASF, Army Specialist Corps, 1941–42.

[23] WD Cir 367, 7 Nov 42.

[24] Annual Rpt of ASF, 1943, p. 139.

[25] Annual *Report of the Secretary of War to the President, 1944* (Washington, U.S. Government Printing Office, 1944).

personnel totaled nearly 100,000 women.[26]

After legislation in November 1942, lowering the induction age limit from twenty to eighteen years, the War Department developed the Army Specialized Training Program for assigning some 150,-000 young soldiers to institutions of higher education. The program was administered by the Army Service Forces. The principal fields of study were engineering, medicine, mathematics, and various other branches of science, with a few assigned to personnel psychology and foreign area study. The program served in part to provide uninterrupted training for professional specialties of importance to the Army; it also served to insure continued operation of institutions of higher education, many of which might otherwise have faced financial ruin. Because of Army manpower shortages, the program was almost completely liquidated on 1 April 1944, the medical phase being the major survivor.[27]

The War Department General Staff abolished the limited service classification in July 1943, and directed that all men be discharged who could not meet the current medical definition of "general service." [28] The policies of discharging physically disqualified and overage enlisted personnel, discussed earlier, caused the ASF to separate nearly 70,000 men a month in 1943.[29] The experience brought the realization that existing separation processes were slow and clumsy. The ASF staff then set up new and simplified separation practices. The effectiveness of these changes was evident in the rapidity with which men were able to leave the Army at the end of the war.

In June 1943, the War Department decided upon a policy of rotation in order to return to the United States men with lengthy overseas service. Rotation was a basic morale problem. There was a saying common among battle-weary troops, that "the Army consists of this division and eight million replacements." [30] Such troops needed relief. In September 1943 the ASF set up fourteen stations to receive soldiers returning from overseas and to assign them to new duties in the United States. In the year ending 30 June 1944, some 74,000 men were handled by these reception stations.[31] As more and more overseas personnel became eligible for return to the United States, General Marshall grew concerned about the arrangements for their reception. He talked the matter over with General Somervell and others, and suggested the use of resort hotels to which enlisted men and officers might bring their wives for a period of ten to fourteen days before receiving a new assignment.

In September 1944, the Army Service Forces accordingly opened five so-called redistribution centers at well-known resort hotels located at Lake Placid, Asheville, Miami Beach, Hot Springs, and Santa

---

[26] A detailed study of the WAC will appear in Mattie Treadwell, the Women's Army Corps, a volume in preparation for the series UNITED STATES ARMY IN WORLD WAR II.

[27] Memo, C. F. Robinson to CG ASF, 3 Jul 43, sub: Army Specialized Tng Program; Transcript-tel conversation, Maj Gen Ray E. Porter and Brig Gen O. L. Nelson, Jr., 18 Feb 44. Both in Hq ASF, Army Specialized Tng Div. Annual Rpt of ASF, 1943. See also Robert R. Palmer, Bell I. Wiley, and William R. Keast, The Army Ground Forces: The Procurement and Training of Ground Combat Troops, II, UNITED STATES ARMY IN WORLD WAR II (Washington, U.S. Government Printing Office, 1948).

[28] WD Cir 161, 14 Jul 43.

[29] The total for 1943 of 821,366 is shown in Strength of the Army, prepared for WDGS by Machine Recs Br, AGO, under direction of Stat Br, GS, STM–30, 1 Jul 46, DRB AGO.

[30] Memo, Morale Svs Div, ASF for CofS, 23 Dec 43, sub: Rpt B–81, What the Front-line Infantryman Thinks, Hq ASF, Morale Svs, 1941–44.

[31] Annual Rpt of ASF, 1944, p. 204.

Barbara. A sixth was opened at Atlantic City in December. Two Army posts also became redistribution stations. This arrangement came to an end on 12 May 1945, just after V-E Day. Altogether, more than 130,000 officers and men and 20,000 dependents went through these redistribution stations.[32]

In January 1944 the Personnel Division of the General Staff made new efforts to retain men regarded as essential. Previously, each of the commands in the United States—the Army Air Forces, the Army Ground Forces, and the Army Service Forces—had its own procedures for shifting enlisted personnel from one type of work to another. The ASF created three reassignment centers which received about 23,000 persons between February and June 1944. Reassignments of some kind were found for all but about 1,000 of these. The operation ceased on 1 July 1944.[33]

Two new activities in the personnel field, started by the War Department after 1940, came under the ASF in 1942. One, originally called morale services and later designated information and education activities, involved primarily an effort to maintain morale and to provide useful information. The media of communication ranged from a weekly newsmagazine, *Yank,* to motion pictures (the "Why We Fight" series), radio broadcasts, and booklets about foreign lands.[34] Correspondence courses, discussion materials, and eventually European schools for soldiers awaiting transportation home, were also parts of this program. Much of the material produced in furtherance of this work was imaginative and marked by excellent craftsmanship. How effective it proved was always uncertain. Soldiers' attitudes were ascertained through questionnaires and the results used to determine policies.

For example, the War Department scheme of discharges after V-E Day on a point system was devised after a survey of soldier opinion.

The second activity was recreational, involving organized sports, motion pictures, USO shows for troop entertainment, books (specially printed pocket editions), musical materials and records, handicraft and art materials, and the management of post exchanges (the soldiers' general store).

In February 1944 ASF headquarters established a personal affairs program to provide individual counseling to soldiers. The biggest single task was to make certain that officers and enlisted men fully understood the arrangements for making allotments to dependents. Soldiers or their families also sought advice about insurance and bond matters, employment, housing, maternity and medical care, and death benefits. Personal affairs officers and their assistants not only provided a central source of information for those needing help but were also expected to help make arrangements to insure that the necessary aid was actually provided.[35]

In connection with this program, a Women's Volunteer Committee, national in scope, was established to promote the participation of Army wives and others in Army welfare activities. Women were encouraged to volunteer their services to the American Red Cross and Gray Ladies. Others worked directly with the Army Emergency Relief Fund and with personal affairs officers in visiting the homes of sol-

---

[32]Annual Rpt of ASF, 1945, p. 107.
[33]Annual Rpt of ASF, 1944, p. 203.
[34] Ltr, Brig Gen Frederick H. Osborn to Somervell, 15 Jun 42, Hq ASF, Morale Svs, 1941–44.
[35] There is a collection of interesting letters, mostly by soldiers, in a small file in Hq ASF, Personal Affairs Division, 1944.

diers' families when children were born, when there was an illness or other emergency, and when word of overseas death was received.[36]

ASF Relations With G-1

The Personnel Division of the War Department General Staff, G-1, was responsible for over-all policy, but the actual administration of most War Department central personnel policies was in the hands of the Army Service Forces.[37] It was inevitable, perhaps, that the ASF should regard its personnel responsibilities somewhat differently from its duties with respect to procurement and supply. General Somervell tended to give more attention to procurement and supply matters than to personnel administration, since the former seemed always more crucial. In fact the assignment of extensive personnel operating duties to the ASF had not been a part of the reorganization which Somervell had himself desired. To a real extent, the Personnel Division of the WDGS (G-1) remained the top planning unit on personnel matters, and ASF personnel officials closely consulted G-1 about all personnel policies. The ASF director of personnel, Maj. Gen. Joseph N. Dalton, therefore did not exercise the control over personnel matters that General Clay did over procurement activities or General Lutes over supply matters.

The close relationship between G-1 and ASF was formalized when on 4 April 1945 the Assistant Chief of Staff, G-1, sent a memorandum to the War Department Deputy Chief of Staff entitled "Personnel Operating Responsibilities of Military Personnel Division, Army Service Forces." This memorandum reiterated that the Military Personnel Division, ASF, would be the operating arm for G-1 on all questions involving military personnel throughout the Military Establishment.

In a memorandum on 29 June 1945, the Assistant Chief of Staff, G-1, informed the Commanding General, ASF, of the military functions, Army-wide in scope, which were being delegated to him, subject to WDGS policies. The delegated functions included a wide variety of duties, among which were the preparation of legislation and executive orders affecting military personnel, staff supervision of the naturalization of worthy aliens serving in the armed forces, the operation of War Department personnel centers, the processing of prisoners of war, War Department liaison with the national headquarters of the Selective Service System, and the preparation of recommended changes in personnel policies and procedures.[38]

In effect this memorandum restated the existing operating duties of the ASF. It served primarily as a reminder to both the Army Ground Forces and the Army Air Forces that the ASF was the central personnel agency for the War Department and that as such, it was expected to take the lead in this field. This memorandum was welcome to the ASF. It confirmed that G-1 would confine itself to review of personnel administration by the ASF and would not try to duplicate activities which the ASF was prepared to perform. The ASF felt that this memorandum made for continued harmonious relations with the Personnel Division of the War Department General Staff.

---

[36] Plan of Org for Women's Volunteer Com, probably Apr–May 44, Hq ASF, Personal Affairs Div, 1944.
[37] AR 10–15, 13 Jul 42.
[38] Memo, CG ASF, 29 Jun 45, sub: Delegation of Pers Functions to Military Pers Div, WD GAP 320, MPD.

Police Activities, Internal Security, and Custody
of Military Prisoners

The Provost Marshal General, who became a part of the Army Service Forces in 1942, had three major responsibilities: the organization and training of military police units, the protection of vital military and industrial installations from sabotage, and the custody of prisoners of war. In 1942 the Provost Marshal General also began the task of supervising the recruitment and training of military government teams for service overseas.

Military police personnel guarded military installations, apprehended soldiers "absent without leave," and patrolled trains and major cities to insure the proper behavior of soldiers. In the year ending 30 June 1945, the Provost Marshal General investigated over 47,000 complaints of alleged criminal acts performed by military personnel within the country, about 20 percent involving crimes against other persons, and about 80 percent crimes against property.

Internal security operations were troublesome because the extent of military responsibility was not clearly defined. Of the Army's duty to insure the security of its own installations, there was no doubt. But there was uncertainty about what the Army should do to protect vital industrial properties, especially when local police forces and the Federal Bureau of Investigation were on the job. As the war progressed, the number of industrial plants whose security arrangements were inspected by the ASF declined from a peak of 13,701 in May 1943 until by 30 June 1945, only 698 remained.[39] Fortunately sabotage was never a great problem during World War II, partly because of the relatively small number of people inclined to be disloyal and partly because of the careful antisabotage precautions which were taken.

The training of personnel for military government duties overseas created more than the usual number of difficulties, including controversies with other agencies in Washington. Army doctrine stipulated that military government was primarily responsible for preventing interference with military operations. But in attempting to conform to this doctrine broadly in the Army's training program, Somervell was accused of trying to take over the duties of other American Government agencies. Then on other occasions, the ASF was accused of being indifferent to the need for reconstructing the civilian economy in occupied areas previously devastated by the enemy. The Army doctrine just mentioned in general confined military government to those activities necessary to maintain order and public health.

With mounting victories abroad, the custody of prisoners of war within the United States became a major task. By 30 June 1944 there were about 200,000 German and Italian prisoners of war in the United States, and about 569 Japanese. A year later the number had increased to over 425,000, mostly Germans.[40] General Somervell insisted that these prisoners play a part in easing the manpower shortage, and he took pride in the fact that from 86 to 94 percent of all prisoners of war were usefully employed.[41]

Beginning in the autumn of 1944, the

[39] Annual Rpt of ASF, 1945, p. 273.
[40] Annual Rpt of ASF, 1945, p. 275; CD, ASF, *Statistical Review, World War II,* p. 159.
[41] WD PW Cir 5, 18 Jan 44, DRB AGO, RG 209, Governing PW's Misc; Memo, USW for SW, 26 Sep 44, sub: Importation of Additional PW's, DRB AGO, RG 104, USW 383.6 (9–26–44) (1).

custody of American military prisoners came under the jurisdiction of The Adjutant General, who supervised rehabilitation centers and disciplinary barracks, the two types of Army penal institutions where military prisoners convicted by courts martial served their sentences. The Under Secretary of War named a board of prominent penologists to advise in this work. Any military prisoners not guilty of a capital offense or certain other major crimes might be sent to a rehabilitation center where an effort was made through rigorous training and psychological guidance to restore men to military duty. Of the 34,209 prisoners admitted to rehabilitation centers during the war, about 13,940 were restored to military duty and 10,562 were sent on to disciplinary barracks to serve out their sentences. By the end of the war, the numbers held in disciplinary barracks (penitentiaries) had reached 13,-468.[42]

Legal Activities

The Judge Advocate General was the legal officer of the War Department. Throughout the war his major responsibility was the supervision of the system of military justice. His office received the records of all general courts martial held in the United States—some 18,000 in the year ending 30 June 1945.[43] Boards of review, established overseas, studied the records of general courts in their respective areas. Cases were also reviewed to determine the desirability of clemency. A special effort was made to cut the time lag between the specification of charges against an officer or enlisted man and the conclusion of his trial.[44] Secretary Stimson and Under Secretary Patterson took a great interest in all aspects of military justice, and sought, through review of cases,

to prevent malfunctioning of the system. During the war the Judge Advocate General's office reviewed a total of 67,318 cases.[45]

The Judge Advocate General's office studied all legislation pending in Congress affecting the Army, and prepared written opinions on all legal matters on which the War Department General Staff or any of the three commands sought advice. This office also handled tort claims against the Army, tax problems of Army procurement, land and patent law matters, and a variety of other legal matters. In September 1944 the Judge Advocate General, upon the direction of the Secretary of War, began preparations for the trial of enemy individuals charged with cruelties, atrocities, and acts of oppression against members of the armed forces. Also, the Judge Advocate General took the lead in behalf of the United States Government in preparing evidence on war crimes after the creation of the United Nations War Crimes Commission in London.[46]

Fiscal Activities

The Chief of Finance was the War Department's disbursing and accounting agent, and in addition, was responsible for a number of other financial services which had grown up in the Office of the Under Secretary of War. With the reorganization in 1942, all financial activities were consolidated within the Army Service Forces. An important fiscal problem through-

---

[42] CD, ASF, *Statistical Review, World War II*, pp. 154–55.

[43] Annual Rpt of ASF, 1945, p. 265.

[44] Memo, Maj Gen George Grunert to Somervell, 12 Apr 43, sub: Resume . . . of Military Justice, Hq ASF, JAG, 1942–44.

[45] CD, ASF, *Statistical Review, World War II*, p. 156.

[46] Annual Rpt of ASF, 1945, pp. 265–70.

out the war was to insure that War Department obligations were promptly and accurately paid. In the month of June 1945, for example, the Army paid 940,000 commercial invoices and had only a backlog of seven days' bills at the end of the month. Another 1,100,000 bills for common carriers were paid in that month for the transportation of troops or war supplies. None of the bills unpaid at the end of the month had been on hand for more than twelve days. In one year, the War Department, in paying its various obligations, issued more than 130 million checks.[47]

As troops arrived overseas in increasing numbers, two new problems appeared. One was to devise a method of handling foreign currency that would enable the Army to pay for local purchases. The other was to find a way to discourage individual soldiers from obtaining local currency with American dollars. Troops were urged to send more money home, to save through deposit accounts paying 4 percent interest, or to buy savings bonds. Through these measures, it was estimated that the amount available to military personnel overseas for making local purchases was reduced to about 15 percent of total pay.[48] Moreover, special currency was devised for soldiers to use in post exchanges and in paying military bills. This currency was useless to local inhabitants.

The Office of Dependency Benefits became one of the big operations of the Army Service Forces. This office, located in Newark, New Jersey, kept control records on all family allowances (for the support of dependents of enlisted men going overseas) and family allotments (voluntary assignment of officers' and enlisted men's pay to dependents). Under the family allowance program, the government contributed about two dollars to every one by a soldier up to a maximum of about $60.00 a month. By June 1945 there were 4 million family allowance accounts and 3.8 million family allotment accounts. The speedy payment of these obligations was a vital morale factor, and even at the risk of overpayment and duplication, these checks were mailed promptly.[49]

Payroll deductions from civilian and military payrolls for the purchase of war bonds, adequate banking facilities for civilian and military personnel, the careful examination of all disbursements, the management of nearly 7 billion dollars in advance payments to contractors and of another 7.6 billion dollars in guaranteed loans from banks, the auditing of terminated contracts, property accountability— these were just some of the fiscal problems of the ASF.

Among the deductions from military pay handled by the Army were premium payments for National Service Life Insurance administered by the Veterans Administration. Every officer and enlisted man in the armed forces was entitled to term life insurance up to a total amount of $10,000. The ASF urged every inductee to purchase the full $10,000 policy. General Somervell believed that this insurance should be compulsory, but he was never able to persuade the War Department General Staff to agree.[50]

The ASF Fiscal Director, General Carter, convinced Somervell that since the

[47] *Ibid.*, pp. 259–60.

[48] *Ibid.*, p. 263; Memo, Somervell to SW, 18 Jul 42, sub: Currency for Use in Invaded Countries, Hq ASF, Currency.

[49] Memo, Maj Gen Arthur H. Carter to Somervell, 29 Jan 44, Hq ASF, Fiscal, 1942–44; Annual Rpt of ASF, 1945, p. 261.

[50] Memo, Somervell to CofS, 3 Jul 43, sub: Proposed Revision of National Service Life Insurance Program, Hq ASF, Fiscal 1942–44.

government assumed administrative costs, the rates on National Service Life Insurance were too high. New mortality tables had been adopted by private insurance companies, while the Veterans Administration ignored the new data on the increased life span. General Somervell forwarded this information to the General Staff with a strong recommendation for remedial action which would have reduced the average monthly cost of a $10,000 policy from $6.95 to $2.25. The Personnel Division of the WDGS on 3 February 1944 opposed the recommendation. Finally, Secretary Stimson on 27 April 1944 signed a letter, drafted in the ASF, to the Veterans Administration suggesting the distribution of premium dividends to all policy holders. Administrator Hines replied to the Secretary on 12 May, agreeing that arrangements should be made for dividend payments and outlining the policies his office would follow in making such payments. But the letter said nothing about *when* dividend payments would begin.[51] Somervell thereupon wrote a memorandum for the files—the only time in his nearly four years as commanding general of the ASF that he ever wrote this type of document—stating that the action taken by General Hines did not remove the "abuse of premium rates greatly in excess of those which current actuarial tables provide."[52] Five years later, Somervell's position was substantiated when on 1 January 1950, the Veterans Administration began to pay dividends resulting from insurance premiums paid during World War II.

Postal Service and Publications

The Adjutant General operated the Army Postal Service, whose biggest prob-

lem was the overseas delivery of mail to troops. In the months of March through June 1945, air mail expanded to 2 million pounds, while mail hauled by surface ships reached a peak of 1.7 million pounds in January 1945. Parcel post reached a peak of 1.7 million sacks in October 1944. V-mail, whereby letters were microfilmed and then reproduced at their destination, was especially advantageous in the early years of the war when airlift was scarce, but the volume declined as air-mail service became available. By April 1945 the average time for an air-mail letter to reach the European continent from any part of the United States was 10.2 days; for the South Pacific it was 7.3 days.[53]

The Adjutant General was also the central publications office of the War Department, publishing and distributing all kinds of War Department orders and instructions, as well as Army manuals, the text books of military activities. Each month in the year ending 30 June 1945, the office handled an estimated 6,000 tons of forms and publications. The time required to print and distribute this volume of matter, and the prevention of unduly large stockage at any one point or at any one time were continuing problems.[54]

The Management of Posts, Camps, and Stations

Most of the activities just mentioned, and much supply work in the United States

---

[51] Memo, Carter to Somervell, 23 Dec 43, sub: Proposed Revision of National Service Life Insurance Program; Ltr, Somervell to Brig Gen Frank T. Hines, 6 Feb 44 (ltr not sent—G–1 did not concur); Memo, Somervell to Marshall, 9 Feb 44; Ltr, Gen F. T. Hines to SW, 12 May 44. All in Hq ASF, Fiscal, 1942–44.

[52] Memo, Somervell to file, 16 May 44, Hq ASF, Fiscal, 1942–44.

[53] Annual Rpt of ASF, 1945, p. 281; CD, ASF, *Statistical Review, World War II*, p. 151.

[54] Annual Rpt of ASF, 1945, pp. 285–88.

focused upon the posts, camps, and stations where troops were trained. The management of these posts for the Army Ground Forces, and the supervision of certain functions at air bases, fell to the Army Service Forces. Army posts were areas where transportation, communication, and other facilities had to be provided; hospitals, motion picture theaters, and post exchanges operated; supplies furnished to troops, publications distributed, chapel services conducted, and eventually, troops and trains moved to ports of embarkation for shipment overseas. This housekeeping job in the United States was a major concern.

Training

The Army Service Forces was also, to a limited extent, a training command. The procurement, supply, and service duties of the ASF often obscured the fact that the command also trained individuals and troop units for overseas duties. The component services of the ASF, such as the Quartermaster Corps and the Ordnance Department, trained individual men for assignment to the quartermaster battalions and ordnance companies which were an integral part of a ground combat division. These services also trained individuals for assignment to similar duties for the Army Air Forces. In addition, each higher tactical command, such as a corps or particularly an army, had to have communications, transportation, motor maintenance, medical, construction, and other service units. These units, as well as individuals assigned to them, were trained by the ASF.

More than this, each overseas theater as a whole had ports of debarkation, storage depots, medical facilities, financial

offices, maintenance shops, communications units, and recreational facilities. Theater commands needed units for guarding military prisoners and prisoners of war, units for construction and repair of military installations, units to operate or manage transportation, units to take care of records and general office management, units to handle the legal work of the overseas command, chaplains, and others. Personnel, both officer and enlisted, were trained to meet all of these needs in overseas commands. In other words, the ASF had to train people to do, on a somewhat more limited scale for each overseas command, the same services that the ASF performed within the United States for the War Department itself.

When training statistics were first collected in January 1943, there were 519,000 persons undergoing some form of instruction at ASF installations. This number rose to a total of 700,000 in the month of September 1943 and then declined to a low of 207,000 in March 1945. Altogether, from the beginning of 1942 to the end of the war, some 6,000 troop units with a total personnel of more than 1,000,000 men with more than 300,000 individual replacements were trained and shipped overseas for supply and service activities within theaters of operation.[55] But in spite of this seemingly large total, the role of the ASF in this field was relatively small when compared to that of both the Army Ground Forces and the Army Air Forces.

The Organization and Training Division, G–3 of the WDGS, provided the over-all supervision of training. Apart from General Somervell's constant concern about the insufficient number of sup-

---

[55] CD, ASF, *Statistical Review, World War II*, pp. 219, 221, 223.

ply troops available to perform the overseas support operations, the ASF had few disputes with G–3 of the WDGS. Since a small part of the G–3 personnel had been transferred to the ASF at the time of the War Department reorganization, the ASF had to construct a training staff almost from scratch in 1942. These training responsibilities tended to grow with the course of the war, but the personnel in charge found no difficulty in working closely with G–3. The quality of the training staff within the Army Service Forces was such that General Somervell was content largely to leave training problems to its discretion. This staff in turn, seldom embarked upon any new training policies without prior informal consultation with G–3.

The ASF developed its own schedules for activating and training supply troops, and occasionally disagreed with the AGF about the division of training responsibilities between the two commands for supply troops.[56] The ASF was ready to accept G–3 as arbitrator, and the resulting division of organization and unit training responsibilities between the ASF and AGF was on the whole satisfactory to the ASF.

Occasionally the ASF felt that G–3 was not sufficiently prompt in issuing revised military unit organization programs (the so-called troop basis), but recognized that the fault was not controllable by G–3. Every time a general change was made in the number of divisions, air groups, and nondivisional units to be organized, or in the size and internal organization of troop units, the Army Service Forces had to revise its procurement plans. Therefore, the ASF constantly sought to keep abreast of any changes in the thinking about troop organization and strength. G–3 was dependent in turn upon the strategic and tactical planning of the Operations Division of the War Department General Staff before it could introduce official changes in military organization.

No summary can give adequate attention to the multitude of problems which arose in the service activities of the Army Service Forces. But it is important to understand that the ASF had many responsibilities extending well beyond the procurement and distribution of supplies and the operation of a transportation system. It was a cardinal element of General Somervell's thinking at all times that the ASF was a *service* command of the Army, and that its role had to be understood in terms of the ramifications of its many and widely varied duties.

---

[56] This controversy and its solution is discussed in Palmer, Wiley, and Keast, *The Procurement and Training of Ground Combat Troops,* pp. 504–07.

CHAPTER VII

The ASF and the OPD

The Army Service Forces had many disagreements with the Operations Division of the War Department General Staff. It was in essence a jurisdictional conflict, a type of conflict that commonly serves as the theme of administrative history. Controversy might have been averted had both the OPD and the ASF interpreted their responsibilities narrowly. Theoretically, a jurisdictional boundary might have been drawn between them by distinguishing policy from operation and strategy from logistics. But such a boundary is vague and ill-defined, and since both organizations were aggressively led by men who were determined to do their jobs well, friction was inevitable. Jurisdictional border raiding during a great war may appear unseemly, but in spite of this rivalry, or perhaps because of it, both OPD and ASF met their responsibilities admirably.

Specifically, the principal controversies were (1) over the problem of exchanging information on strategy and logistics, and over the time factor in logistical planning; (2) over the feeling by each organization that the other was assuming responsibilities not properly its own, particularly in handling details of overseas supply; (3) over relative merits and uses of weapons, particularly antiaircraft artillery and heavy guns; and most serious of all (4) over the representation of the ASF in the committee system of the Joint Chiefs of Staff. In order to understand the issues more clearly it is necessary to examine the role of the Chief of Staff and the Operations Division under the War Department reorganization of 9 March 1942. The reorganization was not intended to diminish the essential authority of the General Staff as the top command of the Army. The revised army regulations issued in July 1942 made it clear that the Chief of Staff of the War Department was "the executive" through whom the President in his role as Commander in Chief exercised his responsibilities for deciding basic military issues. In addition, the Chief of Staff was the "immediate adviser" to the Secretary of War and responsible to him for planning and executing the military program.[1] Thus the reorganization had not diminished the importance of the Chief of Staff: he remained the top professional military leader of the Army. The WDGS continued to be his immediate, personal organization.

At the same time, the reorganization had made some change in the scope of work performed by the General Staff. The revised regulation stated that the staff would make "such broad basic plans and policies" as would enable the commanding generals of the Air Forces, the Ground Forces, the Service Forces, and of the theaters of operations to prepare and execute

[1] AR 10–15, 13 Jul 42.

detailed programs. The regulation made the implied limitation even more explicit by saying that while the General Staff would "supervise" the execution of programs, it was not to engage in administrative duties or in operations *"for the performance of which any agency exists."*[2] Accordingly, the General Staff was to remain on a high level of policy making and supervision, while the maximum amount of detailed planning and administration was left to the major commands of the Army, three in the United States and others overseas. It was the interpretation of this division of responsibility that was to become a chief source of dispute.

The most important single unit of the General Staff throughout World War II was the Operations Division. Its function, succinctly described in the official statement of July 1942, was to perform "those duties of the War Department General Staff which relate to the formulation of plans and strategic direction of the military forces in the theater of war." By virtue of this authority, the OPD has been characterized as the command post of the Chief of Staff during World War II. Of the five sections of the General Staff, it was the only one which, after the reorganization, retained a large number of officials on the policy making level. Its staff of more than three hundred civilian and military personnel was twice as large as the total staffs of G–1, G–2, G–3, and G–4 combined. The division was ably led, first by General Dwight D. Eisenhower, and then in turn by Generals Thomas T. Handy and John E. Hull.[3]

The Army Service Forces was supposed to receive from the Operations Division all the information it needed relating to strategic plans. The ASF believed that the Army Supply Program, the basis of all its procurement effort, could be computed accurately only if it knew in advance where and when military operations were to take place. The supply planners of the ASF, moreover, constantly worked with the OPD on preparations for the movement of men and supplies overseas.

This brings us to the first source of friction. Difficulty developed because of the feeling in the ASF that the OPD was not sufficiently aware of the length of time needed for the purchase, delivery, and transportation of military supplies. As already indicated, the ASF either sought to push the OPD into strategic and tactical commitments, or to make its own recommendations for military operations, based on estimated supply capabilities.[4]

The kind of difficulty which arose is illustrated in the preparations for TORCH, the invasion of North Africa. From a supply point of view, the entire operation was a nightmare. A final decision to launch an attack on North Africa was not made until the end of July with a target date less than three months later. Anticipating such an invasion, Generals Somervell and Lutes had begun to prepare for it even before the decision was made. In this the ASF received little guidance from OPD. As late as 6 September 1942, just two months before the invasion force landed, the ASF had still to learn what units were scheduled to sail from the United States and on what dates; whether any units sailing from the United Kingdom were to be supplied from the United States and when; what special equipment and supplies were necessary for the force sailing from the United States, and whether these supplies were to be

---

[2] *Ibid.* The italics are the author's.
[3] Cline, *Washington Command Post*, Ch. XI; Min, WD Gen Council, 19 May 42.
[4] See above, Ch. III.

combat loaded; what the special supply requirements were for the task forces sailing from the United Kingdom; the size of the force which would eventually be moved from the United Kingdom to North Africa; and finally, the objectives to be assigned General Patton's force. The ASF had to know all this in order to estimate shipping requirements for troops and military equipment.[5]

The Army Service Forces did not receive a clear-cut reply to the questions thus posed, simply because at this time there were no answers. President Roosevelt and Prime Minister Churchill had agreed on the North African campaign on 24 July. Planning took place in both Washington and London, and General Handy of the Operations Division had to fly to London in mid-August to keep his own division posted.[6] It was not until early September that even the main outlines of the operation were set; by 6 September OPD was therefore not yet in a position to provide Somervell with the specific information requested by him. TORCH became a kind of symbol to the ASF of the plight it would constantly be finding itself in if strategic decisions were not made well in advance of actual operations, and ample time afforded for logistical preparations.

On 20 July 1943, General Somervell asked the Chief of Staff for guidance on supply questions. Under the heading of current problems he listed frequent shifts in plans involving the transfer of large numbers of men and supplies, uncertainty about the cross-Channel operation, and the advancing tempo of operations in the Pacific. He also inquired whether the build-up of troops and supplies in England was to be continued; whether there was some expectation of moving from Italy into France or Austria; and whether

preparations for military operations in the Pacific should be accelerated.

Next, taking up long-range problems, Somervell argued that the Army Service Forces needed more detailed information about joint strategy, as, for example, the timetable for the redeployment of troops to the Pacific after the defeat of Germany, and the approximate scale of the redeployment. This information was needed in the revision of the Army Supply Program for the calendar year 1944, and for the formulation of at least a part of the production program for 1945. Somervell also pointed out that while, for the remainder of 1943 and all of 1944, shipping capacity was in balance with the procurement program, in 1945 more shipping would be available than military equipment. The question was, should present supply and shipping schedules be reduced accordingly; or should the supply program for 1945 be increased to take care of possible relief demands?

Finally, General Somervell asked for more detailed information about the forthcoming operations against Japan. What would be the character and magnitude of operations on the mainland of China? How large an army would be required in the Pacific? To what extent would supplies still be provided the Russians after the defeat of Germany? In what parts of the Pacific would the major operations take place? And more specifically, was an operation based on Alaska still contemplated?[7]

---

[5] Somervell for Handy, 6 Sep 42, sub: Spec Opn, Hq ASF, Folder ACofS OPD.

[6] Handy (in England) to Marshall, 22 Aug 42, CM–IN–8444.

[7] Memo, Somervell for CofS, 20 Jul 43, sub: Planning, Hq ASF. This memorandum was drafted by the Planning Division under General Lutes, the office most closely and continuously working with the OPD.

This memorandum was one of several similar reminders to the OPD that the Army Service Forces had to have information about military operations in advance if it was to plan its own work with accuracy and with a minimum of expense and waste motion. But again, the OPD was scarcely in a position to respond in detail. Military plans were too uncertain to enable it to supply the definite information he sought. While General Somervell appreciated these difficulties he felt it necessary to impress the needs of the ASF upon OPD, and to point out once more the close relationship between supply activities and strategic planning. The Operations Division, on the other hand, was already familiar with these problems, and Somervell's not-too-gentle reminders had the effect of opening up old wounds.

The claim that procurement and supply activities required a precise and early knowledge of strategy may at times have appeared unwarranted. Divisions were equipped under fairly standardized tables of allowances calculated to meet general rather than specific needs. There was a danger too that early strategic commitments might destroy the element of surprise and might even prevent the full exploitation of unexpected opportunities. No strategic planner could overlook the possibility of a "break," even if he dared not definitely count on one. Nor could he overlook the possibility of unforeseen setbacks. The strategic planners of World War II wanted sufficient supplies of all kinds to meet any strategic change. They were wary of production schedules geared closely to inflexible strategic concepts. Some War Department officers felt that maximum over-all production should be undertaken and that procurement plans should not wait for a fully developed strategic concept with a detailed plan for troop deployment.[8]

The ASF did not share this point of view. For one thing, standardized troop equipment tables were not an adequate guide for procurement. They did not take into sufficient account such variables as where and when the troops would fight, and in what numbers. The kind of clothing provided troops destined for England and northern Europe had to be very different from the clothing for troops fighting in the Pacific. Climatic conditions made substantial differences in the demands for waterproofing and other preservative materials, not to mention medical supplies. Then too, the availability and condition of overseas port facilities, roads, railways, utility systems, and similar considerations made a great deal of difference in the procurement of construction supplies.

Furthermore, in an economy which apparently was straining to meet war production needs and whose civilian administrators were inclined to be critical of "excessive" Army requirements, General Somervell could scarcely accept a concept of "maximum over-all production." This latter idea suggested a vast supply pool on which the strategic planners would draw as the occasion required. General Somervell wanted a procurement program calculated reasonably well to meet specific supply demands. He abhorred the possibility of waste under the other arrangement, knowing full well that criticism growing out of the accumulation of large stores of unused military supplies would eventually be directed at him, not at the strategic planners.

---

[8] Memo, Aurand for Moore, 10 Nov 41, sub: Method of Properly Financing Victory Program, DAD Procedure 1, LL; Memo, Aurand for Clay, 18 Jun 42, sub: Basis for Present Programs, Intn Div 334, MAB, Vol. I.

The North African campaign, begun in November 1942, suffered too well the consequences of tardy preparation. It is illustrated by the story of the 829th Signal Service Company which has been told under the apt title, "Case History in Confusion." The company was made up of carefully selected personnel and, under terrific pressure from the beginning, it was subjected to a confusing volley of contradictory and supplementary orders, that made fulfillment of its mission impossible. Somervell, in explaining the subsequent failure of this as well as other units, attributed it to "the difficulty in obtaining authorization for such units in adequate time to give them the necessary training."[9]

General Somervell wished to be promptly and thoroughly informed about everything that was going on. When he found, for example, that certain memoranda announcing decisions or instructions of the Joint Chiefs of Staff were being withheld, he requested that all secret papers which might require planning or action by the Army Service Forces be sent to him. In the case of the particular memoranda just referred to, he wished to learn the strategic concept for the year of 1943, adding significantly that he believed that nearly all matters of strategy would require action on the part of at least some of the agencies of the ASF.[10]

To this problem of providing early information on strategic plans to the logistical staffs, no clear or wholly satisfactory solution was ever worked out. A great many factors had to be taken into consideration such as, for example, the experience and size of the organizations involved. Unquestionably, the ASF did not get nearly enough time to prepare for the invasion of North Africa or for many other operations.

In those instances when information was provided well in advance, results were gratifying. By being present at the Casablanca Conference, Somervell learned immediately of the decision to undertake the invasion of Sicily, and so was able to advise General Lutes what to expect. Indeed, General Lutes' own diary reveals that by 3 February 1943, long before the Tunisian campaign itself was even well begun, he was estimating the number and capacity of the landing craft and the combat-loaded transports which would have to sail from the United States to land on the shores of Sicily; by the first of March, he had prepared timetables covering a period up to the end of May for convoys carrying necessary supplies.[11] As the war progressed, the Operations Division and the ASF worked together more efficiently, but the dispute over the time factor in logistical planning continued throughout the war. Another source of difference between the ASF and the OPD was the conviction that OPD was encroaching on ASF prerogatives, particularly in the handling of the details of overseas supply. According to the Army Service Forces, the OPD often handled details which bogged it down and created supply bottlenecks. For example, General MacArthur in the summer of 1942 sent a radiogram asking information about certain types of jungle clothing and equipment. Because of the nature of OPD's relationship with the theaters, it was technically within its rights when it decided to handle this matter. But ASF officers felt that this was really a supply problem and that unless the request raised questions of high policy, OPD

---

[9] Cline, *Washington Command Post*, Ch. X, p. 186.

[10] Memo, Somervell for Intn Secretariat of JCS, 24 Dec 42, Lutes File.

[11] Lutes' diary, Lutes File.

should have turned it over to ASF.[12] Service Forces people felt the same resentment when the Operations Division intervened in a routine memo dealing with requirements for automotive spare parts.[13]

The ASF objected on much the same grounds when OPD passed on the qualifications of supply officers selected by the ASF to fill overseas positions. "This office," Somervell tartly asserted, "will not refer the selection of service staff officers to your office for approval in the future." In the same memo he also took issue with OPD action disapproving arrangements to organize an engineer regiment in Egypt. The ASF had recommended that a civilian construction contract be terminated and that its work be done by an engineer regiment to be formed from personnel in the Middle East. The OPD sent out contrary orders. The exchange of messages with the Middle East Command dragged on for over a month, involving, as General Somervell observed, "an inexcusable waste of time." He continued: "I am sure that inefficiency will result in the event that junior officers in OPD continue to interfere with matters of supply."[14]

A few days later, General Somervell wrote another sharp memorandum to the Operations Division on troop requirements for the Northwest Service Command.[15] And after a lapse of three more days, he again took issue with OPD over its disapproval of the assignment of an Army music band to the Persian Gulf Command. In justification of the assignment Somervell remarked, "There is absolutely no form of recreation in the isolated and depressing spots where a great many of this command must work," and concluded that the "band will do no good in the United States and as long as it exists, we might as well put it in a the-

ater where we can get some results from it." On the copy of this memorandum, when it was returned by OPD, was a penciled remark, "Reported band on way. Do you want two?"[16]

These disputes in themselves were trivial. But it was just because they were so trivial that General Somervell objected to OPD's intervention. A basic motive of the reorganization of March 1942 was to relieve the Chief of Staff of unnecessary administrative burdens, and now the Operations Division as the Chief of Staff's own staff seemed to go out of its way to enter into the pettiest kind of detail. Not only the ASF, but the Air Forces as well, complained of this situation.[17]

On the other hand, the OPD had the major responsibility of supporting the theaters of operations. It is a natural tendency for hard-working, energetic individuals to be reluctant to delegate authority because they feel they themselves could do the job better than someone else. OPD, understandably, in carrying out its major responsibility, did not always draw a fine jurisdictional boundary line. In fact, many of the specific interventions into detail about which the ASF grumbled could be justified on the grounds of emergency, or that they were loose ends of a larger transaction handled in OPD, or that they were unique, or that they were

---

[12] Memo, Lutes, 12 Sep 42, Lutes File.

[13] Memo, Lutes for Handy, ACofS OPD, 1 Jul 43, Lutes File.

[14] Memo, Somervell for Handy, 24 Feb 43, Hq ASF, Folder ACofS OPD.

[15] Memo, Somervell to Handy, 26 Feb 43, Hq ASF, Folder ACofS OPD.

[16] Memo, Somervell for Handy, 1 Mar 43, Hq ASF, Folder ACofS OPD. Incidentally, only by strenuous efforts on the part of the officers at the New York Port of Embarkation did the band obtain its instruments before it sailed.

[17] See below, Chs. VIII, XI.

part of OPD's policy-making functions.

Another of the important points of conflict between ASF and the OPD stemmed from a difference of opinion over the best use of certain weapons, particularly antiaircraft artillery and heavy guns.[18] General Somervell belonged to the group that believed in more antiaircraft protection for troops. There was a great deal of support in the War Department for this point of view.[19] General McNair of the Army Ground Forces was one of the leaders of an opposing group. McNair believed that manpower and matériel ought not be diverted into purely defensive operations. He objected to the defensive psychology and the loss of mobility caused by added equipment. Antiaircraft fire was important when the enemy commanded the air, he argued, but since it was expected that Allied planes would dominate the sky, Allied antiaircraft guns would be largely unnecessary.[20] The Operations Division went along with McNair's arguments. In his protest, Somervell wrote to the OPD that "the action taken by the Department in reference to antiaircraft protection is a short-sighted one," and he suggested that "General McNair be directed to spend two weeks at the front under aircraft attack to see if this changes his ideas. If after this stay he is still of the opinion that there should be no antiaircraft weapons as a part of the organic equipment of a division, I will withdraw my position."[21] The course of events, on the whole, seemed to support McNair's stand.[22]

General Somervell took an equally strong stand on the use of heavy artillery. He expressed the opinion that when the time came to crack the defenses of Bizerte and Tunis or any pill box and masonry fortifications, field commanders would be pleased to have weapons of 90-mm. caliber or better. "It seems inexcusable for us," he wrote, "to have in arsenals in this country weapons of heavier caliber which are not being used because of some technical theory or because the theater commander has not thought to ask for them."[23]

As a matter of fact, the calibers and quantities of heavy artillery were a source of disagreement between the ASF and the Army Ground Forces, with OPD incidentally involved. The AGF was reluctant to commit itself to the use of heavy artillery pieces which might delay rapid maneuver of troops. The Ordnance Department, on the other hand, was eager to build heavier calibers in artillery and to provide larger quantities of ammunition than the Ground Forces and even overseas theaters had first recommended. Indeed, requirements for heavy artillery appeared in the Victory Program of 1941 and in later Army Supply Programs. The Ordnance Department was by no means un-

---

[18] On one occasion, Somervell complained that the OPD had not forwarded a message on these subjects to General Eisenhower. This message, prepared in the Ordnance Department, was, in Somervell's opinion, so important that he had presented it personally to General Marshall. He now requested that Eisenhower also be informed of its contents immediately. The implication was that the OPD, in trying to put across its own viewpoint, deliberately withheld opposing arguments from the proper policy-making authorities. Memo, Somervell to Handy, 13 Mar 43, Hq ASF.

[19] Memo, Devers for CofS, 1 Nov 42, sub: Gen McNair's and Col Feller's Comments, AGF 354.218 (Desert); Memo, USW for CG AGF, 18 May 42, sub: AA Protection for Infantry Divs, AGF 321/78.

[20] Memos, McNair for SW, 13 May, 29 Jul 42; Memo, McNair for SW, 17 Feb 43, sub: Gen Dever's Rpt 400/4, AGF 321/78 CAC.

[21] Memo, cited in n. 18.

[22] Somervell later regretted the hasty comment that McNair would change his view if subjected to the perils of combat. McNair was wounded in Tunisia in 1943 and killed in Normandy in 1944 while observing front-line action.

[23] Memo, cited in n. 18.

mindful of the requirements of mobility, but believed that even heavy pieces of artillery could be mounted on self-propelled carriages or tanks or pulled with some rapidity by heavy tractors. First in Italy and later in France and on the German border, the Army was grateful that it had heavier and heavier artillery available.[24] This time events supported Somervell's stand.

Perhaps the principal source of friction between the ASF and OPD was the problem which arose over the representation of the ASF in the committee system of the Joint Chiefs of Staff. As time went on, the JCS became more and more important in the conduct of the war, and its committees and subcommittees tended to be the place where vital issues on military operations were discussed and resolved. During the first year of its existence, the JCS constantly increased the scope of its interests and the size of its machinery. The ASF contributed its share of influence in this direction, particularly in bringing to the attention of the JCS certain procurement and logistical problems. A case in point is when General Somervell in October 1942 recommended that the War Production Board should ask the JCS to fix procurement limits for various military supply programs in the calendar year 1943.[25] In January 1943 he prepared a memorandum for the JCS reviewing the major categories of possible procurement for the year, and requesting a decision on whether these programs were to be considered as of equal priority or whether special emphasis should be given to aircraft procurement, escort vessels, high octane gasoline, and synthetic rubber development. In the latter event, he stated, other military programs, the Russian protocol commitments, and essential civilian supplies, would have

to be carried along at a lower priority rate.[26] Such action on the part of the ASF tended to bring it within the scope of the JCS system.

Although in other respects content with the joint committee system, Somervell felt strongly that the Army Service Forces should have a voice in that system. As G–4, following Pearl Harbor and the early phase of overseas deployment, he had played a prominent role in determining the use of shipping. When he took over command of the ASF, he wished to retain such influence for that agency. In this effort he had a head-on collision with OPD, which wanted the ASF to provide logistical advice, in a technical but not in a policy-making sense. In effect, the ASF was to speak only when spoken to. The nub of the issue was in the overlapping of the task of translating logistical data into strategic decisions with the task of translating strategic decisions in their initial stages into logistical plans for supporting operations.[27]

The most important supporting committee in the JCS system was the Joint Staff Planners (JPS). Its Army representative was Maj. Gen. Albert C. Wedemeyer of the Operations Division. Wedemeyer readily agreed with Somervell that logistics was basic to any plan and went so far as to quote from a British officer in Washington who said that knowledge of logistical possibilities was more important than

---

[24] Rpt of Spec Bd of Offs for CofS, 4 May 44, sub: Adequacy of FA Program and Doctrine, 320.2/12 (Tub 44).

[25] See below, p. 218.

[26] Memo for JCS, 4 Jan 43, sub: Production Priorities, Concurred in by Vice Adm. V. G. Horne, Vice CNO, Hq ASF.

[27] Cline, *Washington Command Post*, Ch. XIII, contains a detailed description of the system for joint strategic and joint logistic planning.

understanding strategic possibilities.[28] But both he and the British members believed that logistical advisers should not be planners as such; rather they ought to be technical experts who would be called upon whenever the planners felt they needed advice.[29] In other words, the Operations Division attitude, as expressed by General Wedemeyer both in OPD and in the JPS, was that ASF technical and logistical data were both proper and desirable. But he believed that it was the business of the planners and not the Army Service Forces to interpret and use that data as they saw fit. Somervell did not accept this position. To him it seemed necessary and wise that the ASF participate in and help determine strategic decisions. In practice the ASF and its commander did influence strategy, largely through its determination of the logistical feasibility of Army plans. Yet General Somervell was never a member of the JCS. Unwilling to accept the position of a mere technical adviser, Somervell in September 1942 recommended the formation of a new joint committee to serve the Joint Chiefs of Staff as specialists in logistical planning. He argued that the Joint Staff Planners were ignorant of procurement and supply problems and their opinions were "predicated neither on knowledge nor experience." The new committee ought to be made up of himself and a Navy officer in a comparable position. Since both men would have large, experienced staffs at their beck and call, the new committee could furnish reliable logistical advice quickly.[30] The experience of 1942, both in the North African campaign and in the build-up of supplies in England for a cross-Channel operation, buttressed Somervell's arguments. The consequences of poor co-ordination in these operations was another grim reminder of the truism that logistics and strategy were inextricably intertwined.

The Operations Division did not dispute Somervell's contention that much closer co-ordination between strategy and logistics must take place; but it did take issue with the manner in which Somervell proposed to bring it about. It opposed setting up a committee which could have direct contact with the Joint Chiefs of Staff and in effect bypass the JPS on many subjects. At that very time, the Joint Chiefs were considering the appointment of requirements representatives from the War and Navy Departments to advise the strategic planners. OPD pushed this proposal as an alternative to Somervell's plan.[31] Four War Department representatives were chosen, one of whom came from OPD and another from ASF. General Marshall asked Somervell whether he thought his proposed committee was still necessary. Somervell wrote his reply on Marshall's memo: "No Sir, not at present anyway." [32]

But the addition of requirements representatives was a makeshift which failed to achieve its purpose. The whole joint staff system was creaking badly, and the JCS was poorly served, particularly at the level of the JPS. The planners were busy men. They tried to do more than they could rea-

[28] Informal British paper, 19 Feb 43, title; Org for Joint Staff Planning, w/Memo for Info 48, ABC 381 United Nations (23 Jan 42), 2.

[29] Paper, A. C. Wedemeyer, title: Comments on Gen Somervell's Memo to CofS Pertaining to Supporting Agencies of JCS (JCS 202/2), filed with JCS 202/3, ABC 381 (1–29–42), 1.

[30] Memo, Somervell for CofS, 9 Sep 42, WDCSA 334 JCS.

[31] Memo, OPD for CofS, 25 Oct 42, sub: Production Requirements Representatives, filed with JCS 98/3/D, ABC 400 (6 Sep 42).

[32] Memo, Marshall for Somervell, 26 Oct 42, WDCSA 334 JCS.

sonably be expected to do, and they made decisions in fields with which they were personally unfamiliar. They attempted to remedy the weakness by adding nonvoting members as in the case of the requirements representatives, and by delegating their work to subordinates.[33] Their efforts failed. The woeful performance of the American joint system was evident at the Casablanca Conference where, in the opinion of many observers, the polished professional performance of the British joint staff made the Americans look like rank amateurs.[34]

In January 1943 the Joint Chiefs of Staff considered revamping their supporting committees. Somervell was attending the Casablanca Conference, and in his absence, General Styer pushed the claim that ASF logistics specialists should have more representatives on the joint system.[35] But the Army and Air Forces planners sought to reduce rather than increase the influence of the ASF. In streamlining the system, the Joint Staff Planners recommended that the Army representatives should come from the Air Forces and the Operations Division solely, and that an ASF representative be invited to attend meetings only when the others wished to get comments on problems with which the ASF might be specially concerned. General Styer dissented sharply from this proposal.[36]

An even more extreme recommendation by OPD involved the creation of a three-man Joint Administrative Committee (JAC) without ASF representation. The word "administration" was used in the sense that the British used the term, as roughly equivalent to logistics. From this special logistics committee, according to the recommendation, the Army Service Forces would be excluded; the Army

representative would come from the Operations Division, which had a small logistics unit of its own. The ASF representation on joint staff committees would be limited to membership on technical committees such as the Military Transportation Committee, the Joint Communications Committee, and others of a similar nature.[37]

On 27 March 1943, Somervell personally addressed a vigorous protest to General Marshall on the proposed reorganization of the supporting agencies of the Joint Chiefs of Staff. He began his memorandum with a first paragraph consisting of ten words: "I must ask your help on this most important matter." He explained that no one in the ASF had been consulted during the preparation of the recommendations and added that the paper was "tragic evidence of the lack of understanding of its framers of logistics, and shows a faulty concept of the elementary principles of sound administration." If the proposals were to be adopted, it would "make it next to impossible to handle the supply and logistics of the Army on an efficient basis." In his opinion the OPD proposal was "highly reactionary and a distinct step backwards."

Somervell then commented upon the importance of logistical factors in determining military strategy: "Owing to our exceptionally long supply lines, the location of our theaters of operations around the entire globe, and critical shortages in shipping, logistics are, in most cases, the

---

[33] Cline, *Washington Command Post*, Ch. XIII.

[34] *Ibid.*, pp. 236–37, quoting ltr, Wedemeyer to Handy, 22 Jan 43.

[35] Memo, Styer for DCofS, 22 Jan 43, sub: War Planning Agencies, WDCSA 334 JCS II.

[36] Memo, Styer for DCofS, sub: War Planning Agencies, Hq ASF.

[37] *Ibid.*

final governing factors in decisions involving action in the field. If this war has demonstrated anything, it has shown that our efforts to launch attacks on the enemy have, in every case, been governed by logistics—transportation and supply. Where these factors have not been given due weight," the result has been "confusion, delay, and disaster."

Somervell based a large part of his case on the unfamiliarity of OPD with the field of logistics; he reminded the Chief of Staff that before the ASF took part in the deliberations of the Joint Staff Planners, many of the papers were "superficial." He cited as examples certain staff papers on production, shipping, and aluminum which had come before the JCS. He added that "it was for this reason that I sought to be present to give you full information on logistics problems and to be represented on lower committees so that papers presented to the Joint Chiefs of Staff would be real staff papers and not so superficially treated as some had been." Somervell insisted that unless General Marshall was officially represented on the JPS by an officer who knew supply requirements, production availability, and transportation capabilities, he would be badly served, and the Army and the war effort would suffer. He agreed that committees could be too large, but the addition of one more member under such circumstances seemed scarcely unreasonable. He also pointed out that the Joint Administrative Committee would have a Navy representative. But, with representation for the Army confined to OPD, there would be no Army representation with the detailed knowledge of administrative problems.

In conclusion, Somervell asked Marshall to request the withdrawal of the JCS

reorganization plan in order to consider further the Army part of the paper. Somervell made many proposals, particularly with regard to representation of the ASF on many JCS subordinate committees. But the heart of his recommendation was that logistics be an integral part of war planning and not introduced condescendingly with the words "when certain service planning remains necessary." He urged that no logistics or procurement questions be referred to the Joint Deputy Chiefs of Staff as set up under the plan, and he asked that the proposed Joint Administrative Committee be reconstituted as a logistics committee on which the ASF would be represented.[38]

The Operations Division argued in reply that logistics was not the exclusive monopoly of the Army Service Forces. OPD people as well as those from other branches of the Army, understood the significance of procurement, supply, and administration, though they did not pretend to be expert in the more technical aspects of logistics. For details and fine points, planners depended on the ASF to serve them in a subordinate technical role, and they were perfectly capable of assimilating for their policy and strategy-making functions the logistical data thus provided. If, in the past, this logistical material was not well prepared, an OPD general noted, it "is unfortunate because the logistic information and data required for such plans was invariably obtained from the ASF."[39]

General Somervell's protest had some

---

[38] Memo, Somervell to CofS, 27 Mar 43, sub: Reorg of Supporting Agencies for JCS, JCS 202/2, Hq ASF; Memo, Somervell to Lt Gen Stanley D. Embick, 7 Apr 43, sub: Reorg of Supporting Agencies for JCS, JCS 202/2, Hq ASF, CofS (Joint and Combined).
[39] Wedemeyer for CofS, 5 Apr 43, sub: Comments on Gen Somervell's Memo to CofS . . ., WDCSA 334 JCS II.

effect. The effort of the planners to eliminate the influence of the Army Service Forces from an important place in the joint system failed. Though the ASF did not get official representation on the JPS, and though even its nonvoting requirements representative was eliminated, it was given one of the four members of the new JAC which specialized in logistics. Originally Brig. Gen. Patrick H. Tansey of the Operations Division had been the Army designee to the committee, but instead, General Styer, Somervell's chief of staff, was appointed.[40]

Unfortunately the struggle did not end there. The JAC represented a revolutionary step in joint organization, and the Army and Air Forces members of the JPS feared that the new committee would formulate conclusions on logistics which might influence basic strategy. The planners feared that if they did not modify strategy to conform to the recommendations of the logisticians, the Joint Administrative Committee would appeal to the JCS. The planners would tolerate no challenge to their primary position, and throughout the war urged that they alone should direct planning activity.[41]

In July of 1943 President Roosevelt directed the JCS to provide for joint planning in logistics to parallel joint strategic planning so that there would be "one unified and balanced supply program consistent with up-to-date strategic concepts." In a memo to General Marshall, Somervell commented, "Evidently the information furnished the President has been neither accurate nor complete," and he enclosed a draft of a proposed reply. The Joint Chiefs relied heavily in their answer on a memorandum by Somervell which stated that the JAC was working to achieve the President's goal.[42] OPD officers, however, took issue with the accuracy of General Somervell's reply, which led the Joint Administrative Committee to draft a new charter. It proposed that it be renamed the Joint Logistics Committee, that membership be increased from four to six, and that two of the three Army members should come from ASF.

The Operations Division opposed this suggestion. Its representative on the JPS, in collaboration with the Air Forces planner, argued effectively that the JLC ought not to be on a par with the planners in the co-ordination of logistics with strategy. As a result, the ASF logisticians suffered a double defeat. First, in the final phraseology adopted, the new committee was to "advise" rather than "act in co-ordination," and the JPS was specifically named as the body which was to integrate logistics with strategy in the preparation of joint war plans. In this way, the logisticians would be checked in attempts to make strategy. Second, the additional member of the new JLC was to come from the Operations Division rather than from the ASF.[43]

With its victory over the ASF on the powers and membership of the new committee, the JPS dropped their opposition to another proposal, that of providing the JLC with a working committee. This unit, called the Joint Logistics Plans Committee, was made up of a control group of six members, one of whom was from the ASF and another from OPD. Besides these,

---

[40] Memo, DCofS for Secretariat, JCS, 5 May 43, sub: Army Representatives on JAC, JCS 202/10/D.

[41] Cline, *Washington Command Post*, Ch. XIII, discusses JPS–JAC relations in greater detail.

[42] Memo, Somervell to CofS, 19 Jul 43; Ltr, Admiral William D. Leahy to President. Both in Hq ASF, CofS (Joint and Combined).

[43] JCS 450/1, 9 Sep 43; JCS 450/3, 14 Sep 43; JCS 202/29/D, 13 Oct 43, Charter JLC.

there were a great many associate members who worked with specific problems. The Army associates came from all parts of the War Department that had logistical problems and staffs. But by far the largest number came from the Army Service Forces. Through their expert knowledge of many of the subjects that came before the committee, they enabled the ASF to make its weight felt on lower levels and to exert a considerable influence.[44]

In summary, it may be said that the Operations Division tended to move into the field of logistics and build its own logistical staff, while the Army Service Forces tended to enter the field of strategy. This tendency to encroach arose naturally because OPD could not determine strategy in a vacuum, while the ASF in working out logistical possibilities was also, in effect, imposing limitations on strategy. Strategic employment of the Army was essentially a problem of movement of men and supplies to where they could be effectively employed against the enemy. *This movement aspect* was the overlapping area of strategy and logistics.

In this zone of overlapping interest, OPD was unhappy about the role played by the ASF in matters of strategy, and the ASF was equally unhappy about the role of OPD in logistics. General Somervell wrote to General Marshall that the Logistics Section in the Operations Division was

"a straight and unnecessary duplication of effort" which ought to be eliminated and its duties "absorbed in the appropriate agencies of the Army Air Forces and the Army Service Forces."[45] On the other hand, OPD tried to cut down the influence of the ASF. It particularly objected to the Strategic Logistics Division in ASF, which prepared long-range operational studies. In an extreme case, an OPD colonel pleaded that certain information be withheld from ASF, because "the Planning Division, ASF, has been notorious for its meddling in strategic planning."[46]

Unfortunately all this had repercussions in personal resentments and animosities. General Somervell never realized the extent of the hostility in the Operations Division against himself, although General Lutes, whose working relations with OPD were closer and on a more continuous basis than those of Somervell, realized what was happening. At the end of the war, the OPD was one of the important advocates of the move to break up the Army Service Forces.

---

[44] JCS 450/7/D, 10 Nov 43, Charter JLPC; JLC, Memo for Info 2, 4 Dec 43, sub: JLPC Associate Members.

[45] Memo, Somervell for CofS, 3 Apr 43, sub: Suggested Changes in Org of the WD, OPD 320 WD 1.

[46] Memo, Col Harvey H. Fischer for Chief Strategy and Policy, 13 Aug 44, sub: ASF Request for Japanese Forces on Hokkaido, with SS 250, ABC 381, Strategy Sec Papers (7 Jan 43).

CHAPTER VIII

The Army Air Forces and the ASF

The War Department reorganization of 9 March 1942 also produced numerous organizational difficulties between the Army Service Forces and the Army Air Forces. The air arm of the Army had finally achieved an autonomous position within the Department. But it still felt the need to gain "adequate" recognition of air power, and this effort brought about many conflicts over the respective responsibilities of the ASF and the AAF.

The reorganization gave the AAF a special position in the War Department. Not only was it left free to develop its own basic doctrine on combat employment of the air arm, but also its commanding general became the strategic and tactical adviser in the War Department on all Air Forces operations. Second, the AAF was made responsible for the procurement of all equipment "peculiar to the Army Air Forces." In the third place, it was given command of "Army Air Forces stations and bases not assigned to defense commands or theater commanders," though as a final exhortation, the AAF was told to minimize its administrative activities by utilizing the services of the ASF. The exhortation was at best a pious wish.[1]

The difficulties between the ASF and the AAF arose mainly in the fields of procurement and of post management. This second difficulty stemmed from the fact that the AAF exercised command over all Air Forces installations located within the United States, while the Army Ground Forces used posts managed by the ASF. The problem here was whether the AAF was to follow practices different from those developed by the ASF, or whether it was to utilize the supervisory services of the ASF to insure the proper management of post operations.

There were other irritations besides these two major ones. The Army Air Forces objected to the budgetary authority of the ASF and repeatedly proposed that the War Department should have a budget division at the General Staff level.[2] Then too the AAF desired to use its own communications system rather than the War Department system built up by the Signal Corps. Eventually the administrative—as contrasted with the tactical—communications system of the AAF was integrated with that for the War Department generally. Occasionally there were differences over accounting matters, although for the most part the Air Forces kept the type of records required by the Fiscal Director, ASF. These were only the pin pricks in ASF–AAF relations, how-

---

[1] WD Cir 59, 2 Mar 42, pars. 6b, 6c (19).
[2] See below, p. 152.

ever; the real difficulties, as already stated, arose over procurement and post management operations.

Procurement and Supply Relationships

The procurement relations of the Army Service Forces and the Army Air Forces were of two kinds. One relationship arose at the policy level; the other in the actual procurement of various types of matériel. Prior to 9 March 1942 the Air Corps, in a sense, had simply been another supply arm of the War Department, subject, like the others, to the procurement supervision of the Under Secretary of War. After 9 March 1942 the supervisory organization of the Under Secretary was transferred to the staff of the Commanding General, ASF.[3] Most of the people who had previously been with the Office of the Under Secretary of War and the G–4 Division of the War Department General Staff were now with the headquarters staff of the Army Service Forces. The ASF was recognized as the principal procurement agency of the War Department. To what extent then was the AAF to follow procurement policies and procedures developed within the ASF? Actually, on a dollar volume basis, the seven technical services of the ASF spent about two thirds of the procurement funds of the War Department and the Army Air Forces about one third. The headquarters staff of the ASF was a supervisory agency setting the procurement policies for the technical services. Somervell thought it desirable that the AAF follow the same standard policies.

The parties concerned resorted to various devices so that the supervisory duties could be performed without lacerating corps consciousness too severely. For example, General Somervell's director of the Purchases Division acted as an ASF officer when dealing with the technical services, but became Director of Purchases for the Under Secretary of War when supervising the Army Air Forces.[4] The purchasing policies and the contract provisions developed in the Purchases Division thus applied equally to the AAF and to the technical services of the ASF. To facilitate co-operation, the Army Air Forces placed a liaison officer in the Purchases Division to keep in touch with purchasing policies and to clear them with the AAF.

The same type of relationship developed in the field of contract renegotiation. The director of the Renegotiation Division in ASF headquarters was also chairman of the War Department Price Adjustment Board. This officer assigned contract renegotiations to the AAF in the name of the Under Secretary. The AAF filled out the same reports as those filled out by the technical services. The Renegotiation Division kept a War Department-wide record of contract renegotiation. In this field too, then, the same standards, the same procedures, and the same policies governed the technical services and the Army Air Forces.

Similarly, the Readjustment Division in ASF headquarters developed policies and procedures for contract termination. This division kept a record of the progress made in settlement of terminations and handled policies on the determination of excess property. The AAF followed the Readjustment Division's instructions in the same way that the technical services did.

Just as in the case of the Purchases Division, whenever the Renegotiation Division or the Readjustment Division were dealing with the AAF, the respective heads of

---

[3] See above, Ch. II.

[4] Dorr, Memorandum Notes, pp. 31–34.

these divisions acted as "special represent-ative" of the Under Secretary of War, thus preserving the fiction that the Under Sec-retary supervised the procurement oper-ations of the AAF. But there was no duplication of staffs between the Office of the Under Secretary and the Command-ing General, ASF. On procurement policy matters the Air Technical Service Com-mand (before 1944 the Air Service and the Air Matériel Commands) was simply an additional technical service. The AAF did not question the need for standard War Department policies on contract clauses, pricing policy, contract renegotia-tions, and contract termination. As long as the provisions were promulgated in the name of the Under Secretary of War and not in the name of the Commanding Gen-eral, ASF, the AAF seemed to be satisfied.

The AAF was also favorably disposed toward the work of the Procurement As-signment Board in the Purchases Division. This board fixed procurement responsibil-ity among the technical services for newly standardized items of equipment and re-assigned responsibility when overlapping in procurement operations became evi-dent. The board sometimes assigned items for procurement by the Army Air Forces, and in one or two instances took procure-ment from the AAF for assignment to a technical service.

The ASF provided similar leadership in handling labor and manpower problems. With the growing shortage of labor, and with the expansion of both War Produc-tion Board and War Manpower Commis-sion (WMC) organizations to handle such shortages, the War Department saw the need of developing field machinery of its own. On 5 November 1943 the Under Secretary pointed out to the ASF and AAF commanding generals that labor re-

lations and labor supply were an essential part of procurement. Accordingly, the AAF was to handle all intraplant labor problems in facilities under its jurisdiction, while the technical services would dis-charge a similar responsibility in plants under their authority. But the "general directing and supervising" of all War De-partment labor activities was to be exer-cised on behalf of the Under Secretary by the Industrial Personnel Division in ASF headquarters. Thus another staff division of the ASF became likewise a staff unit of the Under Secretary when dealing with the labor relations and manpower prob-lems of the Army Air Forces.[5]

But except for labor matters, no such arrangement was worked out in any other "production" field. The AAF developed its own methods of estimating raw mate-rial requirements and presented these sep-arately to the WPB. It had its own pro-cedures for controlling allotments of raw materials, and for maintaining production records. The ASF Production Division was never used by the Under Secretary of War in following the progress of the AAF pro-duction program. Production statistics of the AAF were very different from those of the ASF. Even on matters such as packing and packaging and the conservation of materials, the Army Air Forces followed one program and the Army Service Forces another.

In addition, when the ASF was first set up, Somervell had hoped that the newly developed Army Supply Program would include requirements of the AAF. This hope was short-lived. The AAF followed its own practices in determining its pro-curement needs. Only after long argument was the ASF able to include in its supply

---

[5] WD Cir 317, 7 Dec 42, w/atchd Memo of USW, 5 Nov 43.

program the requirements of the Army Air Forces which were purchased by the technical services of the ASF. These included bombs procured by the Ordnance Department and the Chemical Warfare Service and other specified types of equipment. Items of air matériel "peculiar" to the Air Forces were consolidated in a separate section of the Army Supply Program. Accordingly, in determining supply requirements and directing production, the AAF and the ASF went their own separate ways. No serious disputes resulted from this arrangement, although occasionally there were conflicting points of view.

In specifying that the AAF would procure supplies "peculiar" to its activities, War Department Circular 59 presumably referred primarily to aircraft engines, aircraft frames, and certain equipment which went into aircraft. Other supplies, it was supposed, would be provided by the ASF, as in the case of the food, the hand weapons, the trucks, and the other equipment used by the AAF, even when some of these items were not entirely the same as those used by the Army Ground Forces and the service troops themselves. Actually, there was constant difficulty in drawing a line between items "peculiar" to the AAF and those which were not.

Throughout the war, the Ordnance Department of the ASF provided armament for aircraft. The air-cooled .50-caliber machine gun, the 20-mm. gun, and the 75-mm. cannon were weapons that were used by the Air Forces. The Ordnance Department likewise produced ammunition for aircraft armament, and in co-operation with the AAF developed the high explosive bombs which were dropped by the medium and heavy bombardment groups. From time to time the AAF proposed that it should take over all procurement of ordnance equipment going into aircraft. The proposals were rejected, and until the end of the war, the Ordnance Department continued to be the procurement agency for AAF armament.

Extraordinary progress in the development and procurement of incendiary bombs was made by the Chemical Warfare Service working with the Army Air Forces. Apparently the AAF was satisfied with the arrangement. The only controversies were over the size of AAF requirements for incendiary bombs. The Chemical Warfare Service accepted AAF estimates of requirements, although it believed that the requirements at times were unduly high.

The Quartermaster General was the procurement agency of the Army for foodstuffs and for clothing. The early experience in long-range bomber attacks indicated that some method of special feeding was needed to help combat fatigue on return journeys. At the same time, the food had to be edible at high altitudes. The AAF sought the assistance of the Office of The Quartermaster General and the problem was successfully solved through their joint efforts. On the other hand, air-sea rescue boats and much other equipment carried in airplanes were similar to items purchased by both the Corps of Engineers and the Transportation Corps. But the AAF maintained that the items were "peculiar" to the AAF and insisted upon its own procurement.

Similarly, the Army Air Forces insisted upon procuring all photographic equipment used in aerial photography, even though other photographic equipment was for the most part purchased by the Signal Corps. In addition, AAF was assigned responsibility for procuring all photographic film, including that distributed by the Signal Corps for use by ground cameramen.[6]

The greatest expansion of Army Air Forces procurement during the war occurred in 1944–45 when responsibility for the development, purchase, and storage of all communications and radar equipment used in aircraft was transferred from the Signal Corps to the AAF. Early in 1944 the AAF had recommended to the Chief of Staff that Signal Corps procurement of aircraft communications equipment be transferred to it. The Signal Corps had established a procurement office for this activity at Wright Field, headquarters of the Air Technical Service Command. Eventually all procurement of communications equipment for the AAF was centralized in this office. The AAF maintained that since the office was located at Wright Field and was working with the Army Air Forces, its operations should be transferred to AAF control. The Signal Corps replied that while the office had been placed at Wright Field simply as a matter of convenience to the AAF, the research and development program of the entire Signal Corps was utilized in developing air communications equipment. Moreover, the Wright Field office depended upon other Signal Corps offices for expediting production and other contract services.

On 26 July 1944 General Marshall wrote a memorandum addressed jointly to Generals Arnold and Somervell expressing the opinion that the time had come when airborne radar and radio equipment, guided missiles, ground radar, and radio navigational aids should be considered items of equipment peculiar to the Air Forces. But he indicated his belief that the procurement of all these items should not be transferred at this time from the Signal

Corps to the Army Air Forces. He suggested only that the AAF should now assume full responsibility for research and development, including procurement of experimental items. By implication, but not in so many words, the Chief of Staff invited comment upon this issue.[7]

General Somervell "strongly recommended" to the Chief of Staff that he consider certain factors before issuing the proposed directive. Such a directive would separate radio and radar research and development for aircraft from similar research and development of equipment for ground use. This step would also hamper the growing collaboration of the Signal Corps with the Navy. Moreover, the existing arrangement, with Signal Corps laboratories and procurement located at Wright Field, permitted the closest co-operation and association with the AAF while still retaining the advantage of centralized research and procurement. This was particularly important because about 75 percent of the component parts of Air Forces radio and radar equipment was the same kind as that in the equipment used by the AGF. Furthermore the Signal Corps was about to promote complete standardization of component parts and common types of equipment. Finally, the proposed separation of activities would probably result in competition for limited and essential facilities and equipment. In

---

[6] An account of AAF procurement outside of the airplane itself will be found in Col William H. Draper, Jr., and Capt Lewis L. Strauss, Coordination of Procurement Between the War and Navy Departments: III, Matériel Studies (multilithed by TAGO), Feb 45, pp. 124–57. This is the so-called Draper-Strauss report prepared at the direction of the Secretary of the Navy and the Under Secretary of War. (Hereafter cited as Draper-Strauss Rpt.) See below, p. 270.

[7] Memo, Marshall for Arnold and Somervell, 26 Jul 44, WDCSA 413.44 (26 Jul 44).

conclusion, General Somervell remarked that the AAF had not given any particulars about Signal Corps failure to provide satisfactory service. He suggested that General Arnold and he should examine the situation so that both could develop plans which would remedy any unsatisfactory performance and at the same time avoid the "real and extensive difficulties which the proposed action would entail."[8]

Arnold, in giving his reaction to General Marshall's proposed directive, remarked that the help the Air Forces had received from the ASF had been commendable. Nevertheless, the new policy would enable the Air Forces to synchronize development of vital radio and radar equipment with aircraft development.[9]

After weighing the arguments on both sides, the Chief of Staff decided to transfer development and development procurement of air communications equipment to the AAF.[10] A joint committee of the Signal Corps and the AAF was established to work out details of the transfer,[11] which was effected on 1 April 1945.[12] A total of 600 officers, 390 enlisted men, and 8,245 civilian employees of the Signal Corps were shifted to the Army Air Forces. The total dollar value of the procurement program thus transferred averaged a billion dollars a year during World War II.[13]

The Conflict Over Post and Base Management

More acrimonious than the foregoing dispute over procurement and supply was the controversy between the two commands resulting from divided responsibilities in the management of Army posts in the United States.[14] As will be explained later, the nine service commands of the ASF provided the regional channels through which the ASF managed military

posts where Army Ground Forces and ASF personnel were trained. Post management was a sizable task. Central management of all posts by the ASF would have permitted a single system of supervision as well as uniform methods of supply. But the AAF insisted upon the complete and separate management of its own posts, or air bases.

Originally the AAF argued that bases where its troops were trained were different from posts for ground troops, the more important difference centering mainly in the airfields themselves and the hangars. All characteristics common to post and base management were held to be subordinate to this differentiating feature. The Air Forces belittled the importance of hospital administration, post exchange business, the disbursement of funds, the management of motion picture theaters, the operation of supply warehouses, the provision of utilities, the storage of clothing and other items, and of other activities performed at both types of installations. The features peculiar to an air base, the AAF insisted, made it essentially different from an Army post and therefore justified exclusive management of the base by the Air Forces itself.

Army regulations in August 1942 placed

---

[8] Memo, Somervell for CofS, 31 Jul 44, Hq ASF, CofS, 1944.

[9] Memo, Arnold for Marshall, 28 Jul 44, WDCSA 413.44 (22 Jul 44).

[10] Ltr, McNarney to CG AAF and CG ASF, 26 Aug 44, sub: Trf of Research, Development and Development Procurement of Communications and Radar Equip to AAF from ASF, WDCSA 413.44 (10 Aug 44).

[11] Memo, Lutes and Arnold for CofS, 10 Aug 44, sub: Trf of Research, Development and Development Procurement of Communications and Radar Equip to AAF from ASF, CofS ASF, AAF, 1944.

[12] WD Cir 429, 3 Nov 44.

[13] Annual Rpt of ASF, 1945, p. 191.

[14] See below, p. 163.

all AAF bases in a category labeled Class III, "installations under command of Army Air Forces." [15] At these installations the service commanders of the ASF were directed to supervise fourteen activities which ranged from general courts martial jurisdiction to the operation of laundries. The list was enlarged a little on 24 December 1942, but there were still glaring omissions, notably medical service and supply operations involving common Army items.

The ASF took the initiative in preparing the original Army regulation. The AAF agreed to the list of activities in the performance of which the commanding officer at a Class III installation would come under the supervision of the service command. Within this specified list, air bases and Army posts within the United States operated under a single set of instructions, with uniform standards of service, and subject to the same supervision. With respect to all other activities, however, the base commanding officer was responsible to his designated superior in the organizational hierarchy of the Army Air Forces.

This arrangement for dual supervision of Air Forces bases soon created trouble. Even though the regulations made it clear that the AAF would designate the air base commander and that this commander would report to the Air Forces on Air Forces matters and to the service commander on Service Forces matters, the AAF never liked the arrangement. The issues that arose were in themselves trivial. They became important because they involved the basic question of whether the ASF would provide services to the AAF in the same way as it did for the AGF, or whether the Army air arm would become completely self-contained and duplicate the organization of the ASF.

One conflict developed over the method of supply distribution to air bases. The zone of interior supply distribution system established by the ASF was a relatively simple and direct one. Technical service depots or branches of ASF general depots were designated as distribution depots to fill requisitions from posts in their area. Post supply officers were given a list of the appropriate depots from which they might requisition various types of supplies needed by troops in training at the post. Requisitions flowed from the post to the depot and supplies from the depot to the post. The technical service depots were prepared to render a like service to all air bases.

In May 1943 the War Department issued a technical manual on stock control at posts, camps, and stations. [16] This manual was prepared by the ASF, and the Army Air Forces concurred. But after it became necessary in 1944 to rewrite the manual to incorporate the lessons gained from a year's experience, the AAF proposed a series of changes which would have established supply procedures for air bases entirely different from those for other Army posts. When the ASF objected, the Air Forces proposed publication of its own technical manual governing supply procedures of the Air Forces. ASF headquarters objected to these proposals on the ground that the manual was intended to govern the distribution of ASF supplies wherever needed in the United States, and that a uniform procedure was indispensable in order to keep stocks at a minimum level and so reduce purchases.

Protracted direct negotiation followed between the two commands. On those

[15] AR 170–10, 10 Aug 42.
[16] WD TM 38–220, Stock Control at Posts, Camps, and Stations, 3 May 43.

matters where agreement was not possible, the issues were presented to the War Department General Staff for decision. In the end, the manual was revised and applied to both the ASF and the AAF, but the commanding generals of the various Air Forces commands in the United States were made responsible for carrying out its provisions.[17] Thus the ASF had its own supervisory organization for insuring that stock levels were fixed at posts in accordance with the provisions of the manual, while the AAF, through a number of different commands, had the same supervisory responsibility at all air bases.[18]

The method of handling repairs and utility matters was another sore point with the AAF. From the time that Army regulations governing Air Forces bases were first put into effect in August 1942, the AAF began to recommend other arrangements for dealing with these responsibilities. The Army Service Forces wanted its service commands to handle funds, personnel allotments, and technical instructions for the operation of water, electrical, and sewage systems, and for the maintenance of buildings. Service commands then dealt directly with air bases on these activities. In July 1943 the commanding general of the Eighth Service Command reported that AAF headquarters was allotting personnel for repairs and utilities activities. These allotments not only differed in size from those made by the ASF, but were also subjected to different personnel policies. For example, ASF instructions prohibited the use of enlisted men for repairs and utilities duties at posts, while the AAF made it mandatory that a certain number be used for this activity.[19] There was also disagreement about the position of the post engineer in post organization at air bases. The post engineer at ground

posts reported directly to the post commander, while the Air Forces had introduced an intervening echelon which service commanders felt complicated their relationship with base engineers.

There was little that the ASF could do about these situations. Internal organization of air bases was entirely the responsibility of the AAF. At most, commanding generals of service commands could only press their repairs and utilities responsibilities as best they could at each air base.

On 14 April 1944 the commanding general of the Army Air Forces sent a memorandum to the Chief of Staff (attention: G–4), recommending that all the repairs and utilities responsibilities at air bases be delegated to the AAF. The ASF attitude toward this recommendation was expressed by General Styer who said, on 21 April 1944, that he was "strongly opposed" to such a proposal unless the Army Air Forces became independent of the rest of the Army. By law, the Chief of Engineers was responsible for repair and utility activities, and in the ASF this responsibility was performed through service command engineers. This arrangement provided a simple, direct method for performing the work on a geographic basis throughout the zone of interior. To adopt General Arnold's proposal would mean two separate supervisory organizations for repair and utilities functions. General Styer remarked that there were no difficulties in the present organization which could not be solved by a co-operative relationship between the ASF and the AAF

---

[17] WD TM 38–220, Stock Control at Posts, Camps, and Stations, revised, 9 May 44.

[18] Summarized from a study, E. L. Bland, Army Service Forces–Army Air Forces Relations, prepared by CD, ASF, OCMH.

[19] Min, Conf of CG's Sv Comds, Chicago, 22–24 Jul 43, pp. 252–53.

similar to that which the ASF had worked out with the Army Ground Forces. He recommended that "the principle be adopted and put into effect that the Army Service Forces will supply and service all Air Forces installations in the same manner that the Army Service Forces now supplies and services all installations utilized by the Army Ground Forces." [20]

The recommendation from the commanding general of the AAF was disapproved by the Deputy Chief of Staff of the War Department. But the counterrecommendation of the ASF was also disapproved. The issue, therefore, remained very much alive.

Another controversy concerned hospital administration. To care for AAF personnel at air bases, the AAF had station hospitals which were supervised through various commands terminating in the headquarters of the AAF, where the Air Surgeon was the top medical officer. The Surgeon General of the Army, who was a part of the ASF, had almost no authority over AAF hospital facilities. On 30 April 1943 General Somervell requested the Chief of Staff to reaffirm that the Surgeon General was the chief medical officer of the entire Army.[21] The Deputy Chief of Staff replied that existing regulations adequately prescribed the functions of The Surgeon General, who had "over-all responsibility of providing adequate medical service for the entire Army." At the same time, he advised, there must be "sufficient decentralization" to insure that "policies" in practice met the needs of overseas theaters and the three major commands within the United States.

The Deputy Chief of Staff set forth three "principles" for the guidance of The Surgeon General and the Air Surgeon. First, the procurement of all medical personnel was a responsibility of The Surgeon General. Second, station hospitals at Air Forces bases were under the command of the AAF. Third, aviation medicine and medical treatment of combat crews were responsibilities of the AAF, under the direction of the Air Surgeon. General hospitals to meet this need would be assigned to the AAF by the Chief of Staff.[22]

This statement of responsibilities was by no means satisfactory to The Surgeon General. On 30 June 1943 General Somervell wrote to the Chief of Staff, forwarding a memorandum which he had received from The Surgeon General. At the outset, Somervell expressed his belief that it was not the intention of the Chief of Staff to have two medical departments in the Army, one for the Air Forces and one for ground troops. It was true that airmen were subject to certain maladies and injuries which would require specialized treatment. The same was true of tank crews. Yet this did not justify a separate medical service for the armored forces. The Surgeon General desired to develop in his office a group of specialists in diseases and ailments peculiar to aviation and also to have these specialists in general hospitals. General Somervell particularly objected to the assertion that the Air Corps medical service operated more efficiently and more economically and therefore the Air Corps ought not be deprived of superior medical care. Such an assertion, Somervell said, rested on "no foundation in fact." The "intransigent at-

[20] Ist Ind, CofS ASF, signed W. D. Styer, to ACofS (G-4), 21 Apr 44, CG ASF.
[21] Memo, Somervell for CofS, 30 Apr 43, sub: Unification of Med Sv of the Army by SG, Hq ASF, SG, 1943.
[22] Memo, O. L. Nelson, Asst to DCofS, for CG AAF, CG AGF, and CG ASF, 20 Jun 43, sub: Med Sv of the Army, WDCSAL 320 (5–26–43).

titude of the Air Surgeon must be overcome," he added, and proposed that the Air Surgeon should be made a Deputy Surgeon General for Aviation Medicine and placed in The Surgeon General's office. General Somervell objected that the instructions of the Deputy Chief of Staff were not conducive to the development of a unified medical service for the Army as a whole.[23] But Somervell's recommendation was not accepted, and for the time being the situation remained as first outlined by the Deputy Chief of Staff.

As a result of the growing shortage of doctors in 1944, a study was made of ASF and AAF hospital facilities in the zone of interior and recommendations made for conserving medical facilities and personnel. The Deputy Chief of Staff approved these recommendations and directed the commanding generals of the ASF and the AAF to work out a mutually satisfactory hospital system, whereby facilities would be utilized by military personnel on a basis other than that of command jurisdiction. In a conference on 30 March 1944, substantial agreement was reached by the two commands. As a result, an arrangement was put into effect in April which provided that military personnel would be treated at the nearest adequately staffed and equipped Army dispensary or Army hospital regardless of command jurisdiction. A station hospital was ordinarily expected to serve an area within a radius of approximately twenty-five miles. In addition, the circular provided for a new type of hospital, the regional station hospital. Regional station hospitals for all practical purposes replaced the general hospitals as the medical facility providing definitive surgical and hospital care within the United States. The War Department was to determine the location of regional station hospitals upon the recommendation of the Commanding General, ASF and the Commanding General, AAF. The Surgeon General was to be professionally responsible for medical service throughout the zone of interior. One of his responsibilities was to inspect the quality of medical treatment in the Army.[24] The Surgeon General and the Air Surgeon agreed upon the designation of regional station hospitals to provide area coverage throughout the United States. These were to be adjusted from time to time when necessary.[25]

Thus the problem of hospital jurisdiction was solved for the remainder of the war. Service command medical consultants inspected AAF hospital facilities and reported on them through AAF channels to The Surgeon General of the Army. Service commands and the field commands of the AAF arranged the geographical structure whereby regional station hospitals were designated and duplication of medical facilities and personnel was avoided. The AAF retained control over its post hospitals and its regional station hospitals. But some degree of co-operative relationship had been achieved. The solution was not entirely satisfactory to either party but it was at least a working arrangement which prevented a flagrant duplication of medical facilities and personnel.

---

[23] Memo, Somervell for CofS, 30 Jun 43; Memo, SG for CofS (through ASF), 29 Jun 43; Memo, The G–4 to CofS, 15 Jun 43, sub: Med Sv of the Army. All in Hq ASF, SG, 1943.

[24] WD Cir 140, 11 Apr 44.

[25] By 30 June 1945, the ASF was operating twenty-six regional hospitals which were located at large military posts and were enlarged station hospitals. The more serious medical and surgical patients who were formerly transferred from station to general hospitals were now sent to regional station hospitals. The general hospitals were reserved for the care of sick and wounded from overseas. Annual Rpt of ASF, 1945, p. 79.

The Controversy Over Allotment of Funds

In the spring of 1944 the Army Air Forces charged the ASF with "interference" in the management of air bases. Service commands were violating command channels, it complained, by allotting funds to Class III installations for repairs and utilities and a number of other activities. The AAF argued that these funds should be allotted directly to the Commanding General, AAF, who in turn would allot them to various air bases and other installations. Furthermore, the AAF refused to acknowledge that the chain of command on these particular responsibilities could be from the Commanding General, ASF, to the commanding general of a service command, to the commanding officer of an air base.

On 10 May 1944 the Secretary of War intervened and suggested a survey of the problems causing dispute.[26] About a month later, the Deputy Chief of Staff, General McNarney, submitted a formal proposal for a study, and shortly thereafter the Secretary appointed Under Secretary Robert P. Patterson; Assistant Secretary for Air Robert A. Lovett; Mr. George L. Harrison, Special Consultant to the Secretary of War; Maj. Gen. Lorenzo D. Gasser; and Brig. Gen. O. L. Nelson as an *ad hoc* committee to survey the War Department fiscal and budgetary organization and to submit recommendations for improvement. This committee in turn, appointed a working group which eventually was made up of four persons, one each from the Office of The Inspector General, the Budget Division of the War Department Special Staff, the Army Air Forces, and the Army Service Forces.[27]

The *ad hoc* committee had before it various suggestions, including one by the

AAF that the Chief of Finance be separated from the ASF Fiscal Director and be set up parallel to The Adjutant General and the Judge Advocate General.[28] Somervell replied that such confusion about fiscal organization as existed could be attributed primarily to the transfer of War Department budget activity from the Army Service Forces to the War Department Special Staff. The original concept of the ASF set forth in the reorganization of March 1942 was "sound." Three alternatives were now available. Each major command might have its separate fiscal organization; responsibility for fiscal policy and procedure might be returned to the Army Service Forces; or the existing arrangement which gave central budgetary duties to the War Department Special Staff and central accounting to the ASF might remain unchanged. General Somervell recommended either the second or third alternative.[29]

The real issue before the *ad hoc* committee was the fiscal position of the AAF. Under existing arrangements, the bulk of War Department appropriations was given to the technical services and the

---

[26] This memorandum on fiscal organization and functions of the War Department, together with all papers on this subject were collected and reproduced by the Deputy Chief of Staff of the War Department under the title: Fiscal Organization and Functions of the War Department (1944). A copy of this publication is in the files of the Control Division, ASF. A copy may also be found in the files of the Deputy Chief of Staff.

[27] *Ibid.*

[28] *Ibid.* This memorandum of 20 May 1944 was addressed to the Deputy Chief of Staff and signed by Brig. Gen. Patrick W. Timberlake, Deputy Chief of Air Staff. It mentioned a memorandum as early as 27 June 1942 in which General Arnold had recommended that the Chief of Staff remove the budget office from the ASF and attach it to his own office. Various comments are attached.

[29] *Ibid.*

Chief of Finance, Army Service Forces. Part of these funds was being allotted to AAF fields and bases through the field organization of the ASF. This was the aspect of fiscal organization which the *ad hoc* committee proposed to change at this time.

On 7 September 1944 the Deputy Chief of Staff of the War Department informed General Somervell that the Secretary of War had approved the recommendation of the *ad hoc* committee:

That Army Service Forces funds for the operation of Class III installations be allotted . . . in a lump sum by appropriation and project direct to the Commanding General, Army Air Forces, for his distribution to Class III installations, with full responsibility placed on him for furnishing appropriate reports on the use and status of such funds.[30]

This recommendation was to go into effect on 1 October 1944.

This recommendation represented a victory for the Army Air Forces. Shortly before it took effect, General Styer asked that the matter be reconsidered. He said that the working group of the *ad hoc* committee was revising Army regulations in a way which, in effect, would remove many ASF supervisory responsibilities at Air Forces posts. This was a major organizational change in the structure of the War Department rather than a mere shift in the system of allotting funds. General Styer questioned whether the steering group in making this recommendation was aware of the organizational implications. In reply, the Deputy Chief of Staff stated that by direct appeal to the Under Secretary of War the ASF had already obtained a reconsideration. Both the Under Secretary of War and the steering group of the *ad hoc* committee had declined to alter their previous recommendations. Accord-

ingly, the request for new action was not "favorably considered." [31]

Army regulations were shortly afterward modified in accordance with the recommendation.[32] The statement of mission of service commands was revised so that their responsibilities were enumerated as in force "except at Class III installations." The responsibilities of ASF service commands at Air Forces installations were specifically limited. The supervisory duties removed from ASF jurisdiction were fixed signal communications, ordnance maintenance, special service (recreational) activities, repairs and utilities, operation of laundries, and salvage activities.

The changes in jurisdiction produced considerable confusion throughout the Army Service Forces. The Chief Signal Officer pointed out that about 30 percent of fixed signal installations in the continental United States were located at approximately six hundred Class III installations previously receiving allotments from service commands. With the change in allotment of funds, he declared, the whole existing system for co-ordination and integration of fixed signal communications would be "seriously impaired."

The director of the Special Services Division asked whether the commanding general of the Army Air Forces would now take over responsibility for selecting entertainers for soldier shows and for films to be sent overseas. Would the Army Motion Picture Service be barred from relations with the Air Forces and would service commanders be permitted to inspect athletic and recreation programs at

---

[30] Memo, McNarney for CG ASF, 7 Sep 44, sub: Fiscal and Budgetary Functions of the WD, CG ASF.
[31] 1st Ind, Styer to CofS, 12 Sep 44; 2d Ind, McNarney to CofS. Both in Hq ASF.
[32] Changes 13 to AR 170–10, 11 Sep 44.

Class III installations? The Quartermaster General noted that there would now be a duplication of technical staffs inspecting laundry operations and that the AAF would have to acquire its own technical supervisory personnel. He also pointed out that of thirty-three laundries then located at Class III installations, fifteen were performing laundry service for nearby ASF installations. Another sixty located at ASF installations in turn provided laundry service to Class III installations. Were these arrangements to be abolished in favor of a self-sufficient laundry service for Class III installations? Similarly the Chief of Engineers pointed out that Public Law 326 of the 77th Congress would have to be amended in order to remove from the Chief of Engineers his responsibility for *direction* of repairs and utilities work at Class III installations. Furthermore, he added, the Army Air Forces would find it difficult to acquire proper supervisory personnel, since only 12 percent of the personnel engaged in the supervision of repairs and utilities operations could be released by the Engineers with the transfer of Class III responsibility.[33]

These questions were brought to the attention of the Deputy Chief of Staff. He directed the AAF and the ASF to agree upon clarifying instructions which would remove the confusion and prevent any expansion of existing facilities for post operations. Intensive negotiation resulted in a new agreement, embodied in a War Department directive in September 1944.[34] This circular enumerated the activities at Class III installations which were no longer under the supervision of generals heading ASF service commands. The list concluded with a clause, which while uncertain in meaning, suggested that whereever funds for activity at an Air Forces base no longer came through an ASF service command, service command supervision was to cease.

The circular drew a new jurisdictional boundary line between the ASF and the AAF. While it increased the authority of the Air Forces, it made it clear that the principal change involved was one in the flow of funds. Technical supervision by the ASF was reaffirmed and a duplication of facilities was prohibited. Close working relations between the ASF and the AAF therefore remained necessary. If the Army Air Forces had hoped for a complete escape from ASF supervision under the new arrangement, its expectations were not realized.

These and other controversies between the AAF and the ASF during World War II grew out of opposing views of the mission of the two commands as well as from clashes of personality and an aggressive *esprit de corps.*[35] In each dispute all these elements were inextricably mingled.

General Arnold and his associates had some justification for their attitude. The airmen of the Army still suffered from the psychological consequences of twenty years of what they considered "suppression" at the hands of unimaginative "ground" officers. General Somervell in World War II just happened to be in the spot where he could reap some of the harvest of distrust sowed for him by the top officials of the War Department from 1919 to 1939. Army air officers would not be

---

[33] All of the memoranda of 18 Sep 44 were replies to an inquiry from the Chief of Staff, ASF, and are filed in Hq ASF.

[34] WD Cir 388, 27 Sep 44, also preliminary draft in CofS AAF, 1944.

[35] See below, Ch. XI.

satisfied until their corps had become an autonomous air force, and they were suspicious of all arrangements which tended to make them merely a part of a larger entity, the Army of the United States.

There were considerations of prestige at stake, too, something not easy to measure but always important. On the one hand, the AAF disliked the suggestion that its status as a "command" did not confer complete control over every phase of its work. Since the commanding officer of an air base was an Air Forces officer, it seemed inconsistent that he should receive some of his instructions from a headquarters outside the Army Air Forces. On the other hand, the ASF, while seeking a uniform standard of service throughout the Army and a single supervisory arrangement for identical activities on the grounds of efficient, economical administration, was also concerned about its own prestige and preservation.

Personalities and attitudes of mind came into play, as well. General Arnold was determined to be both "staff and line" on Air Forces matters within the War Department. On the other hand he seemed unwilling for General Somervell to be "staff and line" on supply and service matters. Arnold's closest wartime associate told General Somervell in 1945 that the AAF might have turned aircraft procurement over to the Army Service Forces in 1942, but decided "he has enough to do" and that "he just shouldn't have this too." Whether the statement was made jokingly or seriously, it indicated an attitude that played a part in determining organizational decisions. The War Department in the middle of a war was still an organization of men.

In any event, the controversy helped precipitate the reconsideration of the role of the ASF in the War Department, to be dealt with in a later chapter.

CHAPTER IX

The Somervell Proposals for War Department Reorganization

Although the provisions of the reorganization of 9 March 1942 contained many seeds of conflict, as already described, the chief reason that Somervell suggested a further change in the logistics organization was the continuing uncertainty about the division of responsibility between the ASF and the Supply Division (G–4), the Personnel Division (G–1), and the Operations Division, all of the WDGS.[1]

In regard to ASF and G–4 difficulties, it appeared at first that a division of responsibility existed between the ASF and the Supply Division of G–4. At the time of the reorganization, Army regulations indicated that basic supply planning would be carried out by the Supply Division of G–4. Indeed these regulations specified that G–4 would prepare "broad basic supply plans" to carry out mobilization and strategic plans while the commanding general of the ASF would "prepare detailed programs and plans." Such a statement would seem to imply that the commanding general of the ASF was expected to receive his general instructions from the War Department General Staff through its supply division, and that the Assistant Chief of Staff, G–4, would continue to be the top supply planner for the Army.[2]

Actually, as already noted, the arrangement was not followed during World War II. In practice the "top supply planner" of the War Department was not the Assistant Chief of Staff, G–4, but the commanding general of the Army Service Forces. General Marshall continually looked to General Somervell rather than to the Assistant Chief of Staff, G–4, for advice and guidance on logistical matters. At such conferences as Casablanca, Quebec, Teheran, and other important meetings, the Chief of Staff used Somervell and the staff of the ASF as his staff on supply, in much the same way as he used OPD on strategy.[3]

Moreover, there were organizational factors which contributed to the special status of the ASF. In the first place, on 9 March 1942 the Army Service Forces absorbed almost all of the key personnel previously associated with G–4. This required the new G–4, Brig. Gen. R. G. Moses, to

---

[1] See above, p. 118, for a discussion of ASF relations with OPD Logistics Group.

[2] AR 10–15, 13 Jul 42.

[3] Dorr, Memorandum Notes. See above, Chs. IV–V.

rebuild his staff out of other officers, few of whom could match the experience of men like Brig. Gen. LeRoy Lutes, Col. W. A. Wood, Jr., Col. F. A. Heileman, and Lt. Col. C. B. Magruder—to mention only a few of those who moved from G–4 to important jobs in the ASF on 9 March 1942. Even if General Moses had been able to find people of the highest caliber, the cut in staff from 149 officers shortly before the reorganization to 11 shortly after made it difficult to assume a great deal of responsibility.[4]

In addition, ASF headquarters was in close daily touch with the actual procurement and storage operations performed by the seven technical services. The Supply Division of the General Staff was a step removed, and could not expect to be as intimately or as expertly informed. Then too, there was the accidental fact that the Chief of Transportation, Maj. Gen. C. P. Gross, was a classmate and friend of General Somervell. Accordingly, the closest relation existed between the Chief of Transportation and the commanding general of the Army Service Forces, and transportation was the key to overseas supply operations throughout the entire war. If the G–4 of the General Staff had tried to go directly to the technical services for information, then it could have been accused of attempting to short circuit the headquarters of the ASF. If, on the other hand, it sought constant and detailed information from ASF headquarters, then it opened itself to charges of interfering with and hampering the work of that headquarters.

On the whole, the Supply Division of the WDGS played only a minor part in the supply phases of World War II. That conflict inherent in this situation did not break out earlier is due to the fact that General Moses, while G–4 in 1942 and 1943, continually subordinated himself to ASF supply planners. Under him, the Supply Division was never disposed to engage in controversy. General Moses seemed to realize that G–4 was a sort of fifth wheel, and acted accordingly. Besides, he was a personal friend of General Somervell.[5] However, as might well have been expected, the duplication of functions concealed in this relationship caused trouble when a new G–4 took over.

Another potential source of conflict between ASF and a WDGS agency lay in the overlapping of functions in the field of personnel. The reorganization of March 1942 assigned to the Army Service Forces the "administration of all functions which are Army-wide in scope and which pertain to personnel as individuals, both military and civilian. . . ."[6] This sweeping power seemed to open the way for a central direction of the whole personnel function. While The Adjutant General's office became a part of the ASF, and a large segment of G–1 was also transferred to it, the reorganization left responsibility split, for G–1 was endowed with personnel authority similar to that of the ASF.[7]

The existence of a Logistics Group in the Operations Division of the WDGS was also a constant challenge to the ASF, as previously noted.[8] Just as OPD looked upon a strategic logistics planning unit in ASF as a threat to its top position in strategic planning, so ASF regarded a logistics unit in OPD as a thorn in its side.

As General Somervell contemplated this situation in 1943, his sense of organizational nicety was disturbed. He could

[4] Min, WD Gen Council, 19 May 42.
[5] Dorr, Memorandum Notes, pp. 37–38.
[6] WD Cir 59, Sec. 7.
[7] Dorr, Memorandum Notes, pp. 38–40.
[8] See above, Ch. VII.

not help but believe that the formal organizational structure in the War Department should reflect the realities of informal relationships, and he felt that the Chief of Staff should complete the reorganizational steps begun in 1942. A year's experience seemed to suggest the basis for final solution of War Department structure.

Accordingly, Somervell took a somewhat drastic step. On 3 April 1943 he wrote to the Chief of Staff proposing further changes in the War Department organization. He insisted that these changes were in line with the purposes behind the organization of 9 March 1942. The basic concept upon which that organization was founded, Somervell noted, was to create a fighting power which would consist of a directing head with a small staff, an Army ground force, an Army air force, and an Army service force. The service force would handle supply, administrative details, and otherwise support the combat forces by relieving the other services of many housekeeping burdens. The Army Service Forces, Somervell said, is "therefore, quite properly and by design a catch-all for a large variety of functions."

In commenting on the organization of the War Department General Staff, Somervell remarked that the need for OPD and an Intelligence Division (G-2) was apparent. He was not so certain about the Training Division (G-3) and thought it might be more effective as part of OPD. But, he insisted, there was no doubt that G-1 and G-4 "duplicate largely the work which must perforce be carried out by the Army Service Forces" and by the supply units of the AAF. Somervell added that in matters of supply and administration, it was often impracticable to separate policy from operations because "the enforcement

of the policy inevitably tends to become the actual operation of that policy with all of the extra administrative detail and personnel required for an additional agency to do the work of another." General Somervell further pointed out that broad operational plans originated with the Operations Division of the War Department General Staff, but that detailed planning necessarily had to be performed by the staffs of the three major commands. He "seriously doubted" whether G-1 and G-4 were generally consulted about operational plans. If they were consulted, they did little except perhaps to delay and confuse the final decisions. The only possible justification for G-1 and G-4 was to render "decisions on controversial matters which might arise between the Army Air Forces, the Army Ground Forces, and the Army Service Forces. . . ." But there should be no fear that the ASF in acting for the War Department would be inclined to make decisions favoring itself above the AAF and the AGF, because the only reason for the existence of the Army Service Forces was to serve the combat forces and all decisions would have to be made in their favor. As between the two, the ASF was as disinterested as the War Department General Staff.

Somervell then observed that there appeared to be "some duplication of effort" between the Logistics Section in the OPD of the WDGS and the staff of the ASF and the AAF. The planners of the Army Service Forces were in "close and daily contact" with the OPD, they attended General Handy's daily conferences, and they had more detailed and more up-to-date logistical information than the OPD itself. Indeed, one purpose of the supply planners of the ASF was "to serve the Operations Division."

General Somervell therefore recommended that G–1 and G–4 Divisions of the WDGS be abolished, that the Logistics Group in the OPD be eliminated, and that the Deputy Chief of Staff be assigned the function of deciding "controversial questions" which might arise between the three commands. These changes were "in the interest of efficient conservation of personnel, and in conservation of effort." If the changes were approved, the ASF would absorb the personnel thus released in appropriate assignments in the Army Service Forces.[9]

General Somervell's memorandum came as a bombshell to the War Department. It was referred to all of the staff divisions of the General Staff for comment. The very fact that General Marshall turned the memorandum over to these divisions indicated that he was not inclined to accept the changes suggested. As should have been expected, the recommendations were strongly opposed by the staff divisions.[10]

The objections to his recommendations did not discourage Somervell. On 1 June 1943 he submitted another proposal, through the medium of an ASF paper attached to a memorandum to Marshall, dealing with the organization of service activities in overseas theaters. In this paper he once more suggested that the G–1 and G–4 Divisions of the General Staff be abolished because their activities largely duplicated work done by the ASF and the AAF. It again expressed the opinion that G–3 would probably be more effective as a part of the Operations Division of the General Staff. Much of the reasoning previously put forth in Somervell's other memorandum to the Chief of Staff was repeated. The paper mentioned again that there was little need for either G–1 or G–4

to serve as an umpire between the three major commands. It added that if the suggested elimination of G–1 and G–4 should prove in practice to be undesirable, it would be relatively simple to re-establish them.[11]

The opposition to General Somervell's proposals was again almost unanimous. This is understandable because basically the proposal would make the Army Service Forces a logistics command post of the War Department in much the same manner as the Operations Division was the strategic command post. If adopted, the commanding general of the ASF would be both a staff and command officer. In short, the General Staff would be abolished and OPD and ASF would dominate the field.

As already indicated, OPD's opposition to the proposal probably stemmed from the fear that it would not be able to hold its own against the ASF. Operational plans depended so heavily on logistics that in time OPD might have become subordinate to the Army Service Forces. Particularly in a postwar period, experience had shown that service elements increased their power at the expense of other elements. Through the control of allotments, funds, and personnel, a service commander could practically run the Army. The bugaboo of the old "bureaus" and their struggle against the General Staff idea was recalled, and an OPD study pointed to the possibility that the Chief of Staff might lose control of the Army. General Handy of the Operations Division strongly supported the staff concept, opposed what he called Somervell's attempt

---

[9] Memo, Somervell for CofS, 3 Apr 43, sub: Suggested Changes in Org of the WD, Hq ASF.

[10] G–4 files, Hist Recs Sec, AGO.

[11] Memo for CofS, 1 Jun 43, sub: Reorg of Sv Activities, Hq ASF, CofS.

to abolish the staff, and endorsed the strengthening of G–1 and G–4 by returning many of the functions they had lost. At the same time, OPD vigorously defended its own Logistics Group and felt that its abolition would be a step backward.[12] Even General Moses, the G–4, who usually supported Somervell's program, went along with the opposition on this issue. In a memorandum to Somervell on 3 June, he noted that he approved the "basic thought" of a service commander for all operating ground forces, but expressed the belief that the Service Forces commander should not also be a "staff officer." He objected emphatically to the elimination of the "staff system taught to all of us before the war and in common use everywhere now." He added that the memorandum discussing this subject was "too one-sided" for presentation to the Chief of Staff and that it contained "erroneous statements."[13] In particular, G–4 felt it had an essential role to play as an arbitrator between the Ground Forces, the Air Forces, and the Service Forces, and in overseeing the operations of the ASF itself.

General McNair, the commanding general of the Army Ground Forces, also opposed the ASF proposal. In a memorandum to Somervell, he pointed out that the ASF staff "aggregates over 20,000, while G–1 and G–4 of the War Department aggregates 90. If there is duplication of personnel and effort, it is in your house. In general, the modern headquarters is a fearful and wonderful thing." Nor was McNair impressed by the argument that General Staff divisions tended to interfere in operations. No one could delineate between policy making and operations and the whole question was "quite irrelevant." There could be only one kind of command of combat forces or of theaters of operations, "over-all command," and there was

no "such animal as administrative command." Somervell's proposals tended to disrupt the "unity of over-all command." McNair concluded:

I believe in your ASF because you are essentially the commander of the zone of interior. . . . But I do not admit that you are responsible for the logistic operations in the War Department or in overseas theaters. G–4 is the proper adviser of the Chief of Staff on logistic policies, even though such is not the case today due to the force of your personality.[14]

It is doubtful whether McNair clearly understood Somervell's proposals. Certainly the concept of a service commander was not intended by any means to impair the responsibility of the corps, the Army, or the theater commander for service activities. Rather the proposal was only expected to give a combat commander what the ASF thought would be a more adequate organizational arrangement for performing his supply and service activities. The crux of the situation was acknowledged by McNair in his admission that Somervell was, in fact, the G–4 of the War Department as well as the commanding general of the Army Service Forces. The question was whether a subordinate commander should also be a major staff adviser to the Chief of Staff.

In addition to reflecting the realities of War Department organization as it operated during the war, Somervell's recommendations further evidenced the peculiar composition of the ASF itself. Before 9 March 1942, as noted earlier, G–4 of the

---

[12] Memo, Handy to Somervell, 6 Apr 43, OPD 320, WD 1; Draft Study, 26 Jun 43, title: Notes on Proposed Org of Sv Activities, OPD 320, 53.

[13] Memo, Moses for Somervell, 3 Jun 43, sub: Reorg of Sv Activities, WD G–4 020, Vol. I.

[14] Memo, McNair for Somervell, 24 Jun 43, sub: Reorg of Sv Activities, Hq ASF, AGF (1943–44). The memo was signed by the AGF chief of staff with the place for McNair's signature vacant.

War Department General Staff and the Office of the Under Secretary of War had jointly supervised the procurement and supply operations of those large War Department units which were now called technical services. Instead of serving as a staff officer supervising these technical services, however, Somervell had become a commander with direct authority to issue orders to these agencies. Yet Somervell still looked upon himself as the G–4 of the War Department and, in fact, he had become General Marshall's principal adviser on all supply and movement matters.

The kind of formal relationship Somervell envisaged did in fact exist between General Marshall and General Arnold. As the commander of the AAF, Arnold was far more than the head of a training and supply command within the United States. He and his staff were the principal War Department agents directing air operations in overseas theaters. This special status of the commanding general of the Army Air Forces during the war has been recognized in the official history of the AAF. ". . . Regardless of the legal position of the AAF as a service and training organization without combat functions, its chief was in fact a most powerful agent in the conduct of war in the several theaters." [15] In overseas commands, the head of the Air Forces was also the chief air planner for the commanding general. In a letter to General Spaatz on 30 July 1942, Arnold clearly indicated his idea of desirable organization for air activities: "In connection with planning," he wrote, "I would like to have you see Eisenhower and get him to accept your headquarters as his air planning unit. Get him to use you in that way as he is the head of the United States Armed Forces in Europe. I want him to recognize you as the top air man in all Europe." [16]

The organizational difficulty within the War Department was simply that the concept of staff organization, as advanced by the Harbord Board in its recommendations of 1921, had apparently been frozen in the minds of most Army officers. Confronted with a situation involving numerous separate operating units, the War Department had developed the concept of a general staff which enabled a commander to deal effectively with all of these agencies. Few seemed to realize that when the number of subordinate operating units was reduced, one of two situations could result: the prior staff organization might become unnecessarily elaborate, or the subordinate commanders would now have a much larger point of view and accordingly be prepared to present plans which previously had depended on staff endeavor.

Following the rejection of Somervell's reorganization proposals, the General Staff assumed the offensive and sought to reestablish its position. The subsequent history of the relations between G–4 and the Army Service Forces is a case in point.

On 2 July 1943, the Secretary of War created a War Department Procurement Review Board with instructions to examine procurement plans and machinery of the ASF and the AAF. [17] From a technical point of view, the recommendations of the board were important, for they brought

---

[15] Craven and Cate, *AAF I,* p. 576.

[16] *Ibid.*, pp. 590–91.

[17] WD SO 183, 2 Jul 43. Director of War Mobilization James F. Byrnes wrote to Secretary Stimson on 24 June 1943 repeating in part a suggestion by the Bureau of the Budget to the War Department on 8 May 1943. Secretary Stimson's reply to Justice Byrnes, and General Marshall's instructions to the chairman of the War Department Procurement Review Board were drafted by General Clay of Somervell's staff. In turn, Somervell on 1 July 1943 instructed Generals Clay, Lutes, Gross, and C. F. Robinson to furnish the board with "full information." This correspondence is in Hq ASF, Procurement Review Board.

about changes in the calculation of the Army Supply Program.[18] But these technical changes are not of major interest here. The board commented several times that G–4 should check the methods used to calculate the Army Supply Program or otherwise exercise supervision over the ASF. Thereafter, the influence of G–4 was greater, or at least ASF found it expedient to keep G–4 fully informed about what it was doing.

This development did not substantially change ASF relations with G–4 although two conflicts, one toward the close of 1944 and the other in 1945, did take place. On 24 September 1944 ASF requested the War Department for permission to disregard computed requirements for a two-front war in 1945 when those requirements exceeded production capacity as of December 1944. This request was contrary to a memorandum from G–4. Early in October the Deputy Chief of Staff told General Somervell that his proposal was generally acceptable. He indicated that G–4 would gradually adjust total requirements for all supplies downward. But since G–4 did not wish to make revisions until 1 July 1945, Somervell, on 13 October again wrote the Chief of Staff. He argued that the progress of the war to date was such that the War Department could afford to take the risk of not building additional production facilities for items of equipment whose demand would increase in 1945. The Army Service Forces had prepared a separate procurement program for the war against Japan, and contractors had already been informed of the expected changes in production schedules occasioned by the shift from a two-front to a one-front war.[19]

This time Somervell's recommendation was officially accepted, and the ASF was instructed not to attempt to procure sup-plies in the first half of 1945 in excess of existing production capacity. Thus the reluctance of the Supply Division to approve a reduction of supply requirements as of 1 January 1945 was overruled.

Another conflict between ASF and G–4 arose after V-J Day over the subject of reserve supplies to be kept by the Army. The Army Service Forces suggested that items such as guns, tanks, and ammunition, which would continue to be of use to the Army, should be retained, while other items of general supplies, such as tents, axes, clothing, building equipment, trucks, and railroad rolling stock, should be released. Somervell believed that such a policy would make a substantial contribution toward easing civilian shortages. G–4 objected to the ASF proposal because it feared that the War Department might have difficulty in the postwar years in obtaining appropriations to purchase new supplies.[20] Confronted by conflicting recommendations, the Secretary of War (now Mr. Patterson, the former Under Secretary) in November 1945 appointed a board of officers to review both proposals. Eventually, a compromise was effected.

That such difficulties arising from the anomalous relationship of the ASF and G–4 did not become more formidable was largely the result of Somervell's own aggressive behavior in pushing the work of

---

[18] The report of the Procurement Review Board and other documents arising out of the board's work were collected in two volumes which were multilithed and distributed by the Office of the Deputy Chief of Staff under the title, Levels of Supply and Supply Procedures, 1 January 1944. The report of the Procurement Review Board was Appendix B; See also Annual Rpt of ASF, 1944, pp. 101–04.

[19] Memo, Somervell for CofS, 23 Oct 44, sub: The Army Sup Program, Hq ASF, CofS.

[20] This account is based upon a discussion summarized in the staff conference minutes of the ASF for 30 November 1945.

the ASF. On supply matters in particular there was no one in the War Department General Staff, especially in G–4, who felt it necessary to question the performance of the ASF. Had that performance ever been less than exemplary, the record of ASF-General Staff relationships might well have been very different.

In the spring of 1943 Somervell was interested not only in a reorganization of the WDGS but also in setting up a standard organization for supply and service activities performed within large combat units and in overseas theaters. The "basic idea" for the memorandum on organization of service activities in theaters of operations, signed by Somervell on 1 June 1943, was "to effect unity of command—of linking responsibility and authority—over-all supply and administrative matters in each theater and in each tactical unit through one individual responsible to the commander both as a staff officer and as the commander of service troops." One purpose of the proposal was "to eliminate the present duplications between the administrative side of the General Staff (G–1 and G–4), the special staff, and the commanders of certain supply and administrative areas, units, and installations by bringing them under a single logistical control at both the staff and line levels." A second purpose was to reduce the number of special staff officers reporting directly to a military commander.

In essence, Somervell's suggestion amounted to this. A military commander, whether of a division, an army, an army group, or of a theater of operations, should have a small staff made up of two units, one on intelligence and the other on operations. He would then have such subordinate combat commanders as might be assigned to his command, plus a single individual commanding all services, supply, and administrative activities. This supply commander would advise the operations staff on the administrative and supply aspects of all proposed military operations and would similarly advise the commanding general himself. He would then be responsible for executing supply and service aspects of the proposed military operations. In a sense, these recommendations did no more than suggest a standard organization for large combat commands and overseas theaters similar to the arrangement which in reality already existed for the War Department in the United States.[21]

In October 1943 the War Department did suggest a standard organization for overseas theaters and published instructions "for the information and guidance of all concerned."[22] One part of the circular dealt with the organization of large combat units, such as corps and armies; another with the organization of a "communications zone." The circular suggested that, in the interests of economy and efficiency, unnecessary decentralization and dispersion of supply activities should be avoided. Consolidated supply and repair depots were more efficient than small establishments and the storage of theater supplies in a few rather than many places would simplify inventory control and reduce inventory levels. The recommendations also emphasized that it was essential to clear ports of debarkation rapidly. A general concept was set forth that the hospitals, the signal service, the engineer construction service, and the transportation service of the communications zone should serve the entire theater.

---

[21] Memo, ASF for CofS, 1 Jun 43, sub: Reorg of Sv Comds, w/incl on theater sv orgs, G–4 020, Vol. I.

[22] WD Cir 256, 16 Oct 43.

Organization charts attached to the circular sketched a desirable organization for a theater of operations. Under the headquarters of the theater, there were four component commands: two armies, an air force, and a communications zone. This same chart indicated the component parts of the suggested communications zone. These were six in number, consisting of a Base Section, an Intermediate Section, an Advanced Section, a Transportation Service, a Communications Service, and a Construction Service. Four supporting charts suggested desirable organization for a section (whether base, intermediate or advanced), a port, and a depot.

The War Department circular, however, said nothing about the relationships which should exist between the commanding general of the communications zone and the commanding general of the theater of operations. It was apparently assumed that there would still be a G–4 on the staff of the theater commander and that there might even be such "special staff officers" as the commander desired.

Thus, in the European Theater of Operations for the invasion of France, there was a communications zone with a commanding general. There was also a G–4 section in Supreme Headquarters, Allied Expeditionary Forces, which also served as the G–4 of the American commanding general (Eisenhower). There was a medical officer for the commanding general of the theater, separate from the medical officer in the communications zone. For the most part, however, the chief engineer, the chief quartermaster, signal officer, and other such officers in the communications zone also served as the chief of the service for the theater as a whole. This arrangement caused considerable confusion.

Not all overseas theaters adopted the pattern suggested by War Department Circular 256. Many variations continued to exist, in part because General Marshall believed that the overseas commander should make such organizational arrangements as he thought desirable. At the same time he encouraged Somervell to develop close and direct communication between ASF headquarters and supply officers in the field through overseas visits. This was as far as the Chief of Staff would go.[23]

General Somervell never succeeded in obtaining a revision of the War Department General Staff that reflected the actual situation which made him in fact the Chief of Staff's principal adviser on supply matters. Potentially, he might have occupied a similar status on all personnel matters. But he was never to have this status formalized in official orders.

Somervell conceived of the ASF as a supply and service command which was prepared to do for the War Department Chief of Staff everything that before 1942 had been performed by G–1, G–4, all the units of the so-called special staff, and the OUSW. He felt that this role should be formalized in the War Department structure and in overseas commands. He was in effect the advocate of a wholly new concept of staff and command for the Army.

Never at any time did he question the command role of the Chief of Staff of the Army. Nor did he question the need for a "general staff." He said only that formally the Chief of Staff should organize his staff into two units—an intelligence unit and an operations unit. Somervell recognized also that the operations unit would necessarily have to be large; it probably would

---

[23] The Control Division, ASF, collected charts of overseas supply organizations which were analyzed at the end of the war in a staff paper. This paper was never used outside the division.

require personnel and troop organization groups as well as a logistics group within it. But Somervell thought the real planning should be carried on in the headquarters of the Army Air Forces, the Army Ground Forces, and the Army Service Forces.

General Marshall's attitude toward the Somervell proposals can only be deduced from the events. There is no evidence that he discouraged Somervell from submitting his suggestions. But neither did he push them after he received them. Marshall probably regarded the whole issue as theoretical, or perhaps as relatively unimportant. He was undoubtedly fairly well satisfied with War Department organization as it was functioning in 1943. The proposed changes would not have made any real change in Somervell's status, and Marshall was presumably more interested in the realities than in the formalities of individual position and authority. With his well-known belief that "details" should be left to the overseas commanders, Marshall was also satisfied to let personalities and performance in the theaters of operations determine the desirable and workable organizational arrangements. He could see no real reason for making a change in 1943, and so he let his staff argue as they wished the niceties of organizational structure. For the duration of the war nothing came of the whole discussion. Somervell's authority remained as before. In fact he was still the *supply staff* and the *supply command* of the War Department when the war ended.

CHAPTER X

The Transfer of ASF Activities to the War Department Staff

The place of the Army Service Forces in the structure of the War Department was never clearly understood or defined during the course of World War II. Was the ASF simply a new, consolidated command with certain operating responsibilities but subordinate to the broad planning duties of the War Department General Staff? Or was it a kind of consolidated staff and central service agency for the War Department, essentially different from the Army Ground Forces and the Army Air Forces?

Within the structure of the War Department, the position of the ASF had to be determined in practice by groups other than General Somervell and his staff. The relations which were crucial in this determination were those between the ASF and the WDGS, the Air Forces, and the Army Ground Forces. The controversies with the Air Forces and G–4, WDGS, have already been noted. The first resulted in some curtailment of the role of the ASF. In its contest with OPD of the War Department General Staff, the ASF fared somewhat better. To be sure, Somervell's position as logistical planner for the Chief of Staff was never officially recognized, at least not in the manner he desired, but on the other hand, the Operations Division of the WDGS did not succeed in having the

function of the ASF limited to an "operating" supply agency subordinate to its own logistical and operational planning. Yet while the ASF remained throughout the war as the "supply planner" of the Chief of Staff, some other staff functions exercised by the ASF were transferred to units officially designated as War Department General or Special Staff Divisions. Before reviewing further the basic issues involving ASF status in the War Department it will be necessary to enumerate the changes which were made in the duties of the ASF as a central staff agency.

Public Relations

When the Army Service Forces was set up in March 1942, General Somervell created a public relations unit in his headquarters. The personnel and activities of this unit were brought into the ASF from the Office of the Under Secretary of War, who had had an Industrial Information Division primarily concerned with publicizing the procurement problems of the War Department. Actually many of the employees of this unit had been recruited by the Bureau of Public Relations (BPR) of the War Department and were carried on the bureau's pay roll, although physically located in the Under Secretary's office.[1]

In the summer of 1942 Secretary Stimson sponsored a study of public relations organization and activities in the War Department. As a result, he directed that all public relations work was to be concentrated in the BPR which reported directly to him. At the same time, the Secretary indicated that the commanding generals of each of the three commands within the United States, and other organizations such as those of the chiefs of technical services, might maintain offices of technical information. Such offices, however, would release no information directly to the press or to any other medium of communication. They would simply assist the Bureau of Public Relations by providing it with requested data and by submitting publicity suggestions for bureau approval.[2]

In accord with Stimson's directive, the Public Relations Division in ASF headquarters was abolished and a greatly reduced Office of Technical Information was set up.[3] Most of the personnel of the division were transferred to the BPR. Somervell retained a single officer in his own office who helped him prepare speeches, answer inquiries, and who kept a watchful eye over public relations matters affecting the commanding general and the ASF as a whole.

In 1943 the procurement activities of the War Department were so important and so pressing that special instructions were issued defining public relations responsibilities in this field.[4] Three different parts of the Department were vitally concerned: the Under Secretary of War as the civilian chief supervising procurement, the BPR as the official agency for handling the details of public relations, and the ASF as the agency immediately concerned with

actual procurement. Accordingly, the Bureau of Public Relations created as part of its organization an Industrial Services Division which was responsible for formulating and executing a public relations program that would result in favorable attitudes toward war output by management and labor alike. In carrying out its mission, the division was to receive all policy direction from the Under Secretary of War. In guiding its activities, Under Secretary Patterson in turn depended upon the labor adviser to the Secretary of War, Mr. Edward F. McGrady (whose office was actually adjacent to that of the Under Secretary), and upon the Industrial Personnel Division of ASF headquarters. A major activity of the BPR was the awarding of the Army-Navy "E" to industrial plants achieving outstanding war production records.[5] The bureau also co-operated on specific projects with the Office of War Information, the labor division of the War Production Board, the War Manpower Commission, and other government agencies. An aggressive public relations program was an important phase of War Department procurement efforts.

The Army Service Forces was, of necessity, vitally interested in the activities of the Industrial Services Division of the War Department Bureau of Public Relations. The association between the two agencies was very close and friendly. In 1944 the head of the Industrial Services of BPR was transferred, becoming director of the Industrial Personnel Division in ASF headquarters. BPR also assigned an officer to

---

[1] Booz Rpt, Vol. I.
[2] Memo, SW, 14 Aug 42, sub: Reorg of Public Relations Agencies, AG 020.4 (8–13–42) MB-F-PS-M.
[3] SOS Cir 54, 29 Aug 42.
[4] WD Cir 251, 14 Oct 43.
[5] Ibid.

the staff of each service command to carry on its work at industrial plants within the geographical area of the service command. Direct communication was authorized between these service command officers and the BPR.[6]

This organization of public relations activities proved satisfactory in every way. General Somervell clearly understood that public relations was a basic responsibility for the War Department as a whole and should be performed under the personal direction of the Secretary of War. He had no occasion to protest the arrangement because it never slighted or interfered with the ASF's role within the Department's organization. In the specialized field of industrial public relations, for example, the Secretary delegated his responsibility to the Under Secretary. Since Somervell was the principal adviser to the Under Secretary on procurement matters, he and his staff had ample opportunity to make such suggestions, especially through the Industrial Personnel Division, which worked directly with the BPR on details of procurement public relations.

Budgeting

War Department Circular 59 of 1942—the reorganization "bible"—specified that the Army Service Forces would be responsible for preparing War Department budget estimates, for defending them before the Bureau of the Budget and Congress, and for controlling fiscal policy. There were several reasons for this arrangement. In the past, the Assistant Chief of Staff, G–4, had been designated as the aide to the Secretary of War and the Chief of Staff on budget matters. As G–4 Somervell had performed this function, and he continued to do so as commanding general

of the Army Service Forces. In addition, budgeting depended heavily upon the accounting records of the Chief of Finance, who was now under the supervision of the Commanding General, ASF. Then too, the peculiarities of War Department appropriation practice resulted in most Congressional appropriations being made formally to the chiefs of technical services and the Chief of Finance, all of whom were under the ASF. The only important exceptions were the appropriation to the Air Corps for the procurement and maintenance of aircraft, and to the Department as a whole for expediting production. Finally, since the Army Service Forces was created to be the administrative agency of the War Department as a whole, budgeting was logically one of the tasks assigned to it.

Wartime budget practices did not actually provide the occasion for review of or decision on fundamental military policies. The basic plans of the War Department for the size, composition, and deployment of the Army were determined within the General Staff. The limitations to these plans were not a matter of finances but of resources: the manpower, industrial, and technological strength of the nation. The Army Supply Program was adjusted primarily to fit the natural resources and the industrial facilities that the War Production Board decided were available to the Army. The budget merely reflected these basic decisions. After Pearl Harbor the general temper of the House Appropriations Committee and of the entire Congress was simply that, in terms of money, the War Department could have whatever it asked for. In the first seven months after Pearl Harbor, Congress appropriated 104

---

[6] *Ibid.*

billion dollars to the War Department.[7] Thereafter, the War Department each year for the remainder of the war simply requested sums as needed to supplement this overwhelming amount voted at the beginning of the war.

At the conclusion of the budget hearing before the House Appropriations Subcommittee in June 1943, the chairman of the subcommittee passed along a word of advice to the Under Secretary of War. Mr. J. Buell Snyder remarked that it had been his observation during the course of the hearings that the War Department General Staff was "getting out of touch, in a sense, with department administration." He noted that some branch chiefs did not seem to be closely in touch with activities at home or in theaters of operations. This was apparently a criticism of the ASF, and of the subordination of chiefs of technical services. Mr. Snyder went on to say he thought "that a mistake was made in taking the budget function out of the War Department General Staff." While he acknowledged that the ASF was doing a good job, he expressed his belief that "money runs the Army and controls every phase of its activity and that the control of the purse should be a General Staff function. . . ." He felt that the ASF should continue in an accounting capacity, but believed there would be greater co-ordination and economy "if there were a budget desk re-established in the General Staff. . . ." Mr. Snyder suggested, and Mr. Patterson agreed, that the subject would be brought to the attention of the Secretary of War and the Chief of Staff.[8] In making his observations Mr. Snyder gave no detailed argument to support his views. He asked merely that the position of the budget officer in War Department organization be reconsidered.

Since the suggestion of a chairman of a House appropriations subcommittee is one to be taken seriously by the department concerned, the Fiscal Director of the ASF, Maj. Gen. A. H. Carter, immediately prepared a memorandum on the subject for Judge Patterson. He recommended a prompt reply by the Under Secretary to Chairman Snyder defending the existing organization of the War Department. His action, General Carter thought, might persuade the chairman to withdraw his comment before the hearings were finally printed. Somervell approved of this recommendation, and a copy of it was sent to General McNarney, the Deputy Chief of Staff. Under Secretary Patterson agreed with General Carter and signed a letter drafted for him. But the letter was withdrawn at McNarney's request before it reached the chairman of the House subcommittee.

Somervell then wrote to General Marshall and summarized this sequence of events. He noted that one way to carry out Mr. Snyder's desire would be to re-establish general budget responsibility along the lines of the former Legislative and Planning Branch of the War Department General Staff. He doubted whether this would be as effective as the present arrangement and asserted that "the broad budgetary policy of the War Department is now and should be under the complete control of the Chief of Staff." General Somervell added that if the existing "organizational set-up" implied otherwise, he would recommend that the Deputy Chief

---

[7] Annual Rpt of ASF, 1943, p. 193.

[8] *Hearings before the Subcommittee of the Committee on Appropriations*, H. R., 78th Cong, 1st Sess, on Military Establishment Appropriation Bill for 1944, pp. 588–89.

of Staff deal directly with the budget officer on all matters of policy "without reference through the Army Service Forces." General Somervell went on to point out that of the 120 billion dollars appropriated to the War Department from 1 July 1941 to 1 July 1943, about 104 billion dollars was for equipment and supplies whose procurement was supervised by the Under Secretary. Furthermore, the ASF, under the War Deparement reorganization, had "just completed the assembly of all budgetary and fiscal functions under one head," the new organization was "functioning efficiently," and it would be a "backward step to dismember it by pulling from it the budget operations which are inextricably tied in with the proper administration of the over-all fiscal operations of the War Department." General Somervell presented three recommendations: one, that the present organization be maintained; two, that the present budget officer continue to act under the policy direction of the Under Secretary of War and the Deputy Chief of Staff; and three, that the Chief of Staff concur in the Under Secretary's letter for Mr. Snyder, signed on 15 June 1943. "These recommendations would place in the General Staff satisfactory control of the War Department budget policy, and, at the same time, preserve the present well-integrated functions of budget and fiscal operations in one organization." [9]

General Somervell's memorandum apparently was unconvincing for in July 1943, the War Department issued orders removing the War Department budget office "from the jurisdiction of the Fiscal Division, Army Service Forces," and redesignating it the Budget Division, War Department Special Staff.[10] The immediate consequence was to transfer an officer with a small staff from General Carter's office in the ASF to the War Department Special Staff. This new Budget Division necessarily had to rely upon the Fiscal Director of the ASF for information and even advice. No fundamental change in either budgeting or accounting practices followed. But at least the appearance was now created that the War Department Special Staff, and not a subordinate command, was in charge of budgeting.

The change provided some satisfaction to the Army Air Forces, which as early as 27 June 1942 had suggested that the War Department staff rather than the ASF should exercise the budget function.[11] In 1944 the Air Forces and the budget officer of the War Department suggested that the Chief of Finance should be transferred from the Army Service Forces to a separate status under the budget officer; the position of Fiscal Director in the ASF would then be abolished. This proposal must have been unacceptable to both the Chief of Staff and the Secretary of War as well as to the ASF, since no such order was issued.

One consequence of the transfer of the budget function from the ASF to the War Department Special Staff was to encourage the further growth of this part of War Department organization. Another result, at least, in the budget field, was to draw a sharp distinction between the War Department General Staff proper as the top policy-determining level and the Army Service Forces as an operating agency. The accounting work remained in the

---

[9] Memo, Somervell for CofS, 19 Jun 43, sub: Org and Functions of WD Budget Office, Hq ASF, Fiscal 1942–44.
[10] WD GO 37, 7 Jul 43.
[11] See above, p. 124.

ASF; top budget policy direction as a staff activity did not.[12]

The Civil Affairs Division

Shortly after the Army Service Forces was created, the War Department began preparations for the military government of occupied areas taken over from the Axis powers. Proposals for training personnel were developed within the Provost Marshal General's office, and led to the establishment of a School of Military Government at the University of Virginia in May 1942.[13] The Provost Marshal General also set up a small unit in Washington to plan general policies for military government. Actual experience in military government in World War II began in November 1942 with operations in North Africa. One of the first questions that arose to complicate policy was whether French Morocco and Algeria should be regarded as conquered enemy territory or as that of an ally to be used as a base for further military operations.[14] But in preparing for the invasion of Sicily, there was no question about the need for or the status of military government since the area was unmistakably enemy territory.

Toward the end of 1942, President Roosevelt had created an Office of Foreign Relief and Rehabilitation Operations within the State Department under the direction of former governor Herbert H. Lehman of New York. This office was assigned general responsibility for planning relief in areas liberated from Axis control. Necessarily, its interests and those of the ASF were closely related. In the spring of 1943 Lehman called upon Stimson and pointed out that the Secretary's organization had failed to provide him with adequate means and powers to carry out his assignment. Governor Lehman drew attention to the fact that the operating agency in military government, the Provost Marshal General's office, was many echelons removed from the Secretary of War's office. This seemed to him to be too low an echelon to represent the Secretary of War in negotiations with the Department of State on vital matters pertaining to occupied and liberated areas.[15]

Shortly thereafter, the War Department issued a memorandum creating the Civil Affairs Division in the War Department Special Staff.[16] While the Provost Marshal General continued to conduct training programs for military government officials under policies prescribed by the Civil Affairs Division, this division became the center of all War Department planning on military government policies. The International Division in ASF headquarters in time also played a major role in military government planning, since its function was to supervise arrangements for War Department's purchase and distribution of civilian supplies in occupied areas. The ASF Industrial Personnel Division handled many personnel and labor matters for overseas commanders of occupied areas, while the ASF Fiscal Director han-

[12] Goldthwaite Dorr records that General Orders 37 was issued from the Chief of Staff's office by General McNarney without Judge Patterson's knowledge. Secretary Stimson was preparing for a trip overseas at the moment and apparently approved the order without discussing it or without realizing that his Under Secretary disapproved of it. When Secretary Stimson returned, neither General Somervell nor Under Secretary Patterson were then disposed to raise the issue again. Dorr, Memorandum Notes, pp. 48–49.

[13] Annual *Report of the Services of Supply, 1942,* p. 90.

[14] Memo, Styer to Somervell, 25 Feb 43, Hq ASF, Civil Affairs Div 1943–44.

[15] This is the story told the writer by one of Governor Lehman's staff assistants, Dr. Luther H. Gulick.

[16] WD Memo 10–1–43, 4 May 43.

dled currency matters. The work of all these units was performed under general policies officially emanating from the Civil Affairs Division.

Research and Development

Within the Army Service Forces the basic responsibility for research and development of new weapons remained with the seven technical services. A small ASF headquarters unit kept itself informed in a general way on research and development matters, attempted to prevent obvious duplication of effort, and helped the technical services whenever they encountered difficulties in obtaining raw materials or facilities for research purposes. The actual initiative in research matters, however, remained largely in the hands or the technical services, working closely with the using arms.

Secretary Stimson was especially interested in research and development matters, and one of his purposes, as he himself has pointed out, was to make clear to the Department and to scientific leaders that it was the policy of the War Department to make use of scientific help in every part of the Army's work.[17] Soon after assuming office he asked one of his associates, Mr. Harvey H. Bundy, to follow scientific matters for him. Mr. Bundy was aided by Dr. Edward L. Bowles.

A former Chief of Ordnance, Maj. Gen. C. C. Williams, was recalled to active duty to handle ASF headquarters' interests in research. This arrangement was not very satisfactory to Dr. Bowles. As early as November 1942, a special section on new weapons had been created under the Assistant Chief of Staff, G-4, of the War Department General Staff. In September 1943 Mr. Bundy and Dr. Vannevar Bush

of the Office of Scientific Research and Development suggested to Secretary Stimson that a new weapons unit should be set up as a separate part of the War Department Special Staff.[18] A New Developments Division was proposed and Somervell's opinion requested. Somervell referred the matter to General Clay, ASF director of matériel, who protested vigorously that there would be little purpose in adding a staff at War Department level to supervise staff responsibilities already exercised at ASF level. Stimson nevertheless decided in favor of the recommendations of Mr. Bundy and Dr. Bush,[19] and in October a War Department circular was issued setting up the New Developments Division.[20] This division, initially under the direction of Maj. Gen. Stephen G. Henry, formerly head of the Armored Forces School at Fort Knox, gave primary attention to the problem of demonstrating new weapons and equipment to overseas commanders. In addition, it followed many phases of research work within the United States. The New Developments Division tended to duplicate some of the work of the Research and Development Division of the ASF staff. In a special report submitted to General Somervell in January 1945 the ASF staff division pointed to much overlapping and duplication of activities.[21] But since

---

[17] Stimson and Bundy, *On Active Service in Peace and War*, p. 465.

[18] *Ibid.*, p. 466.

[19] Goldthwaite Dorr subsequently observed about the New Developments Division: "So far as I had an impression, it was that the main value of the Division lay in making more effective Ed Bowles' exceptional technical ability, imagination, and drive. Like most organizational matters it reduced itself in the last analysis primarily to a question of personnel." Memorandum Notes, p. 56.

[20] WD Cir 267, 25 Oct 43.

[21] This report was forwarded to the CG ASF with an accompanying memo by the director of the Control Division on 5 January 1945. Files, CG ASF.

it was at a higher level, the new division was able to gain from other branches of the Military Establishment the co-operation that an ASF agency probably could not have obtained. It did not actually take any staff responsibility away from the Army Service Forces but simply added a new agency in the War Department Special Staff to give greater impetus to research and development activities.

The New Developments Division was generally successful in the work it undertook. Because of the quality of its leadership and personnel, the New Developments Division not only made important contributions of its own but also probably stimulated ASF headquarters to greater interest in research and development matters.

National Guard and Executive for Reserve and Reserve Officers' Training Corps Affairs

In May 1945, just after V-E Day, the War Department issued orders transferring the National Guard Bureau and the Executive for Reserve and Reserve Officers' Training Corps Affairs from General Somervell's staff to the War Department Special Staff.[22] This action was intended to suggest that concern for National Guard and Reserve matters would now become especially important in War Department planning and that these agencies could better deal with the Army Ground Forces and the Army Air Forces if they were parts of the War Department Special Staff. During the war neither of these two offices was of great importance—there was no Army Reserve Corps in wartime, and the National Guard had been incorporated into the Army of the United States before Pearl Harbor. This transfer after V-E Day forecast that it

would be military policy to recreate the Reserve Corps and the National Guard following the defeat of Japan.

Postwar Planning

In May 1943 General Somervell received secret instructions from the Chief of Staff to set up a small unit in his office to begin planning for demobilization of the Army. Personnel for this task was quickly assembled and tentative planning programs laid out. In July 1943 Secretary Stimson and General Marshall decided that this activity should not be left in the ASF. Accordingly, a Special Planning Division was created as a new unit in the War Department Special Staff.[23]

Counterintelligence

One activity transferred to the Army Service Forces from the WDGS during the war was supervision of counterintelligence functions within the United States. Before 9 March 1942 most Army counterintelligence activity within the United States had been performed through the corps area commands under the direction and supervision of the Intelligence Division (G–2) of the WDGS. When the corps areas came under the ASF and were transformed into service commands, counterintelligence personnel remained attached to them but operated under the supervision of G–2. ASF headquarters had no responsibility for this phase of service command work. Finally in December 1943, this arrangement was terminated. In the meantime, the ASF had created its own small intelligence office, and G–2 was now

[22] WD GO 39, 17 May 45.
[23] History of Planning Division, ASF, ASF Planning Div, II, 280.

willing that it should take over such security activity as the Army had to perform within the United States.[24]

There was a continuing, if not extensive, trend during World War II to move certain activities performed by the Army Service Forces headquarters into new units making up the War Department Special Staff. When the ASF was created, it was Somervell's understanding that the ASF was in itself a kind of consolidated "special staff" for the War Department. On logistical matters he conceived of the ASF as part of the WDGS. As noted earlier, this concept endured throughout the war, even if never formally embodied in official instructions other than the original reorganization directive of 9 March 1942. But the concept of the ASF as a special kind of "special staff" for the War Department as a whole gradually changed. More and more policy-making responsibilities were transferred from the ASF to direct War Department staff status. It appeared that the original role of the ASF, at least as Somervell understood it, was no longer binding in War Department organizational practice. By the autumn of 1944 General Somervell felt that developments had gone so far that it was time to raise formally the question with the Chief of Staff of the future role of the Army Service Forces within the War Department.

---

[24] WD Cir 324, 14 Dec 43.

CHAPTER XI

Further Reconsideration of the Role of the ASF

General Somervell was not disposed to treat lightly the gradual, continuing alteration of the role of the Army Service Forces. As he understood it, the War Department reorganization of 1942 was predicated upon two or three basic ideas. First of all, the elaborate War Department General Staff system built up between World War I and World War II was to be radically altered. Second, the many special staff units subject only to general direction by the WDGS were to be reduced. Third, the combat training work in the United States was to be concentrated in two commands: the Army Air Forces and the Army Ground Forces. The third command, the ASF, was to take over the supply and service duties, including WDGS supervision of these activities. As far as the ASF was concerned, the General Staff was to remain in full control of strategic direction of the war.

As already noted, various pressures resulted in a transfer of some ASF activities to new special staff units under the direction of the Chief of Staff. Most of these activities were of minor importance to the ASF and their transfer caused little disturbance. It was the constant attack of the AAF upon the role of the Army Service Forces which caused the greatest concern in ASF headquarters. If these attacks continued and were as successful as before (see Chapter VIII), it was reasonable to believe the very concept of the ASF was threatened.

In the background of the conflict was the long-standing ambition of the Air Forces to become a separate service enjoying equal status with the Army and the Navy. General Marshall and General Arnold had tacitly agreed that for the duration of World War II, Air Forces aspirations for such a status were to be shelved. Because of this agreement, General Somervell held that the ASF should perform supply and service duties for the AAF just as it was doing for the AGF and the overseas theaters of operations. To General Arnold and his colleagues this kind of arrangement probably appeared too "compromising." They did not desire to become too deeply tied in with War Department organization because it might make eventual separation more difficult.

Conflict was more or less inevitable under such circumstances. It was brought to a head when Somervell in 1944 raised with General Marshall the whole question of the proper role of the Army Service Forces in the War Department. In order to understand better the whole review of ASF responsibilities that followed, it is necessary first to examine briefly the relations that existed between the AGF and the ASF. It was to these relations that the ASF constantly referred as the desirable model, and it was just such relations that the Army Air Forces did not want.

The AGF and the ASF

The relations between the Army Ground Forces and the Army Service Forces rested upon a basic principle embodied in the War Department reorganization of 1942: namely that command of combat troops in training, including the supply and service units organic to combat commands, could and should be separated from the command of service agencies which rendered supply and service support to the Army as a whole. The relations between AGF and ASF as prescribed in Circular 59 differed on two essential points from those laid down for the AAF and the ASF.[1] The AAF was explicitly authorized to supply the matériel peculiar to the Air Forces, and to control all Air Forces installations. No such prerogatives had been granted to the Army Ground Forces. The AGF was merely given the right to "review" the matériel requirements of the combat forces. It was assigned no control over installations even when used by ground force units.[2] Even had the opportunity to extend its authority into the areas assigned to the ASF existed, it is doubtful that it would have been done. Its commander, General Mc-Nair, held firmly to the conviction that the mission of the AGF was to provide trained combat units for the overseas theaters. He held with equal firmness the view that this mission could be most effectively performed by a small operating headquarters which would concentrate on

the training and organization of ground combat troops, leaving all other tasks to other War Department agencies. General McNair's views continued throughout the war, at the level of general policy, to control the relations between the AGF and ASF.

Although the AGF and ASF did not engage in any serious rivalry, there were occasional differences. These were perhaps inevitable since the War Department reorganization of 1942, while clear in general about the separation of functions between the two commands, left certain marginal areas in which lines of authority were ambiguous. The progress of the war, moreover, created problems which had not been anticipated in the initial organization of the War Department. Some adjustments of the original formula therefore had to follow. Furthermore, co-operative effort by large organizations of markedly different types, engaged in highly diverse activities, is naturally subject to misunderstanding and confusion. And finally, the personal attitudes and habits of the two commanders were responsible for at least some of the difficulties that arose.

Certain agencies, subordinated to ASF in the 1942 reorganization, formulated policies and executed programs affecting, in the name of the War Department, all three commands alike. One such agency was the Office of The Adjutant General which, although under the ASF, was the War Department agency for the Army-wide initial classification and assignment of personnel. In this duty The Adjutant General had the delicate task of adjudicating, in the best interests of the Army as a whole, the rival claims of the three com-

[1] See above, p. 37.
[2] WD Cir 59, 9 Mar 42, par 5c (1).

mands—and eventually of the theaters as well—on a precious and limited commodity wanted by all—men. Provided the War Department General Staff was strong enough to enforce impartiality in the operation of an agency like The Adjutant General's office, this arrangement was not likely to produce insuperable difficulties. But McNair believed the General Staff lacked the necessary strength, and he thought that The Adjutant General functioned too often not as an impartial instrument of the War Department policy, but as an interested element of the ASF. This belief undoubtedly underlay General McNair's refusal to support Somervell's plan to combine the functions of ASF commander and Assistant Chiefs of Staff, G–1 and G–4 and it continually conditioned the approach of AGF to the problem of personnel.[3]

Disagreements between the AGF and ASF concerning the recruitment and assignment of personnel, although they did not attain major proportions, began early in the mobilization period and continued throughout the war. From the beginning of selective service, AGF was convinced that it was not receiving a proportionate share of high-quality men. Men of the highest intelligence, whose capacities for leadership and combat effectiveness AGF believed would be high, tended to be men having some identifiable civilian trade or profession. These fell within the occupational specialties for which AGF units, by their nature, provided few openings, but which abounded in the more technical units of the ASF and AAF.[4]

General McNair criticized the ASF again and again for the Army's classification and assignment policy, especially during 1942 and 1943. He complained that large numbers of men originally as-

signed to the Ground Forces were permitted to go to officer candidate and specialist schools of the technical services, from which they often did not return to AGF.[5] The Army Specialized Training Program was a major point of controversy. This program, managed by the ASF, contemplated sending some 150,000 enlisted men to college for special training in science, engineering, and languages. The AGF opposed the project vigorously, largely on the grounds that the training to be given was unnecessary to the prosecution of the war and that it would withdraw from positions of leadership in the combat forces a large number of the best inductees. Eventually the replacement crisis in early 1944 forced the dissolution of the program and the assignment of Army Specialized Training Program trainees to replacement centers and units, chiefly of the ground arms.[6]

The continuing struggle for high-quality personnel culminated in 1943 and 1944 in the discussion of the Physical Profile System, in which the AGF and ASF were again ranged on opposite sides. The AGF, convinced after two years of mobilization experience that assignment of inductees by specialty—especially when classification and assignment procedures were under the control of the ASF—could lead only to the receipt by the ASF and AAF of a disproportionate share of high-quality men, undertook to obtain a radical change in the basis for Army classification. It wished to substitute a physical basis for the current mental and technical criteria for classification. Under such a scheme,

[3] See above, p. 142.

[4] Greenfield, Palmer, and Wiley, *The Organization of Ground Combat Troops.*

[5] Palmer, Wiley, and Keast, *The Procurement and Training of Ground Combat Troops,* pp. 4–13.

[6] *Ibid.*, pp. 28–39.

the Ground Forces would have no difficulty demonstrating its superior need for
men in prime physical condition, and so
would get a larger proportion of well-
qualified individuals. The ASF repeatedly
objected to the institution of a physical
basis for classification. But the demand
for combat replacements became so acute
in late 1943 and 1944 that the Physical
Profile Plan was adopted over the objections of the ASF in the spring of 1944.[7]

Closely related to these controversies
over the quality of personnel were certain
problems of utilization of personnel which
disturbed the relations of ASF and AGF,
especially in 1942 and 1943. Throughout
the mobilization period it was the view of
the AGF that too large a proportion of the
national manpower was being invested in
service functions and too little in combat
forces. The rate of growth of service elements was dramatic: constituting but 26.3
percent of the strength of the Army at the
end of 1941, they comprised 36.5 percent
at the end of 1943.   In the same period,
the strength of the combat arms declined
from 52.4 percent to 32.8 percent of the
total.[8] The rapid expansion of the ASF
was in large measure a result of the effort
to build up supply installations, both in
the zone of interior and in overseas theaters. The AGF, while conceding the necessity for some reapportionment of Army
strength for this and other purposes, nonetheless believed the situation was getting
out of hand and repeatedly urged the
need for the strongest possible combat
force.[9] The Army Service Forces, McNair
told General Gasser, president of the War
Department manpower board, was "very,
very fat, particularly in headquarters,"
and he strongly affirmed his belief that
"radical corrective action" was required
"to effect the assignment of a much

greater proportion of the manpower to
units designed for offensive combat."[10]

The AGF felt that the ASF was wasting
manpower and thereby threatening not
only the formation of a powerful combat
force, but also interfering with AGF's primary mission of training. The relative
decline in AGF strength and the rise in
ASF strength resulted only in part from
the assignment of new inductees to ASF in
large numbers. It resulted also from the
cancellation of planned AGF units from
the Troop Basis, and, far more serious in
their effects on orderly training, from the
depletion of ground units already
formed—as well as the diversion of men
from ground units in the process of formation—to fill new service units. These
policies had disastrous effects on the training of ground units. Training either was
interrupted, had to be repeated, or had to
be carried on at two or three levels simultaneously. Until 1944 the most important
influences on organization and training in
AGF were shortages of men and changes
in Troop Basis plans. AGF believed that
unessential and overstaffed ASF units
were in large measure responsible for both
of these circumstances.[11]

Training problems presented other difficulties for the AGF and ASF. Initially the
responsibility for training service units was
not clearly defined. The AGF and ASF
were each responsible for training service
units—the AGF trained those service units
which became an integral part of a combat command and the ASF trained units

---

[7] *Ibid.*, pp. 64–69: See above, p. 99.

[8] *Ibid.*, p. 203.

[9] Greenfield, Palmer, and Wiley, *The Organization
of Ground Combat Troops*, pp. 198–230.

[10] AGF Memo slip, CG to Plans, 23 Feb 43.

[11] Palmer, Wiley, and Keast, *The Procurement and
Training of Ground Combat Troops*, pp. 457–58, 466–69,
546–55.

to be used by the communications zone of an overseas theater. But the ultimate use of a service unit was not always clearly forecast. During 1942 and 1943 several schemes for compromising the conflict between ASF and AGF were tried without success. Finally, in January 1944 the War Department adopted the policy of specifically designating in the Troop Basis those service units which were to be activated and trained by each command.[12]

The controversy over responsibility for training service units was intensified by two circumstances, both arising out of the differing conceptions in AGF and ASF of their primary missions. During 1942 and most of 1943 the emphasis in AGF was on the organization and training of large combat elements, particularly divisions. While AGF recognized its responsibility for training service units organic to ground combat forces, it was very slow to provide plans for the organization and training of such units. Not until May 1943 did it prepare a systematic activation schedule for building service units and arrange for effective supervision of their training. In part this neglect of AGF service units resulted from the graver problems surrounding the training of divisions. In part it resulted from the continued existence of the chiefs of technical services, which had first directed the training programs. But the effect was to make these service units the "forgotten men" of the AGF, and undoubtedly to bolster the conviction in the ASF that it should seek control over the training of as many service units as possible.

In their conception of the best type of training to be given service units, moreover, the two commands differed radically. In accordance with its mission of preparing ground combat forces, the AGF insisted that each man, whether an ordnance repairman or a rifleman, be trained primarily as a soldier and secondarily as a specialist. In the ASF, on the other hand, primary emphasis was given to technical and specialist training. It was believed, both in the ASF and among the technical service staff officers of the AGF, that the training of service units of the Ground Forces had suffered because of an overemphasis on military training. The AGF, taking an opposite view, was convinced that the ASF would concentrate too heavily on technical duties, if it obtained wider authority over the training of service units. This conviction doubtless stimulated it to insist on its responsibility for training all service personnel who would function in direct support of ground combat elements.[13]

Training did not stop when a unit or an individual replacement was ordered to a staging area or replacement depot for shipment overseas. Troops were given physical examinations, final training tests, and often a certain amount of training in these installations. When units or individuals trained by the AGF passed through staging areas and replacement depots, they came under the command of port commanders. In 1943, as a result of criticisms of the state of training of combat troops arriving in the theaters, the AGF sought to extend its control over ground units and replacements up to the moment of embarkation. Units, many of which arrived at staging areas inadequately trained to begin with, often remained for extended periods, during which their training deteriorated further. While under the control of ASF staging area commanders,

---

[12] *Ibid.*, pp. 505–06.
[13] *Ibid.*, pp. 558–60.

these units could be given suitable training by the AGF only with difficulty.

Training facilities in the staging areas were practically nonexistent because no training activity during the process of moving troops overseas had been contemplated when training facilities were being constructed elsewhere. It was expected at the time that only fully prepared troops would be ordered overseas. Since this was not so, the AGF sought to continue training until the last moment. That meant moving troops from staging areas to posts where facilities existed, disrupting final processing for overseas shipment, and causing no end of confusion in the staging areas. The AGF, more concerned with its responsibilities for training than those of port commanders for efficient final processing, attempted to obtain War Department permission to retain command of ground units in staging areas and to conduct such training and administrative preparations for overseas movement as seemed necessary. The ASF strongly opposed this move as impractical and inconsistent with the principle of command. The War Department directed a number of measures to permit the AGF to supervise training in staging areas without depriving port commanders of command of units while in the staging areas. None of the measures were completely successful. The improvement in the shipping situation in late 1943 and 1944 eased the problem somewhat by making extended delays in staging areas unnecessary, but a solution satisfactory to all concerned was never found.[14]

In like manner in 1943, when the replacement crisis began, the processing of combat replacements through replacement depots controlled by the ASF revealed grave deficiencies in accounting,

administration, and training. Although in 1942 the AGF had been unwilling to seek authority over personnel depots for ground arms replacements, in 1943 it changed its position. Separate personnel depots were set up for AGF and ASF replacements, under the separate control of the two commands.[15]

In addition to problems pertaining to personnel and training, problems involving the supply of equipment arose between the AGF and the ASF. During 1942 and 1943 combat equipment for AGF units was severely limited, creating great training difficulties. The AGF repeatedly attempted to obtain equipment allowances from the ASF and the War Department, but world-wide requirements were so enormous, that the ASF seldom found it possible to meet these demands. Other differences between the two commands aggravated the supply situation. Faced with the need to move combat forces overseas on limited shipping, the ASF in 1943 adopted the policy of preshipping equipment. The AGF was concerned lest this stock-piling produce even graver shortages of equipment for training in the United States. But although temporary shortages did develop, the net result in the long-run was beneficial in conserving shipping space and in permitting the re-use of equipment left behind in the zone of interior.[16]

Difficulties with the AGF also arose over the development and procurement of equipment for combat troops and units. Under the March 1942 reorganization di-

---

[14] *Ibid.*, pp. 573–77, 585. See also Chester Wardlow, The Transportation Corps: Movements, Training, and Supply, a volume in preparation for the series UNITED STATES ARMY IN WORLD WAR II.

[15] *Ibid.*, 179, 185–87.

[16] *Ibid.*, pp. 456–57, 464–66, 555–58.

rective, a Requirements Division was set up in AGF to establish military characteristics of weapons and equipment. This division was responsible for co-ordinating the design and procurement of matériel with the technical services under ASF command. Through its Development Section, the Requirements Division attempted to satisfy and balance the demands of the combat arms for matériel. The technical services, for their part, had to translate requirement into designs and into plans for industrial production, often in the face of shortages of raw material, labor, and plant facilities. The elaborate machinery for developing, testing, and purchasing equipment revealed numerous small points of friction, but all were adjusted in one way or another.

Somervell Raises a Basic Issue

In comparison with the dispute between the ASF and the Air Forces, these conflicts of the ASF with the Army Ground Forces were unimportant. The fact that the AGF and the ASF were in agreement on the economy and viability of the 1942 reorganization enabled them to avoid serious rifts in their relationships. Actual co-operation between the two organizations was close, continuous, and on the whole, effective throughout the war. The Ground and Service Forces worked together with good results at camps, posts and stations. The conflicts treated above did not raise basic questions of military organization or of the responsibilities and authorities of the two commands. The problems were operational, involving specific issues, and for the most part were handled successfully, unembarrassed by debates over higher staff and command policy.

On the other hand, disputes over seemingly technical matters between the Air Forces and the Service Forces had a way of becoming vital issues which threatened to undermine the organizational integrity of the ASF.[17] Every Air Forces gain provided a fulcrum for more and more leverage in a jurisdictional offensive. Thus General Somervell became convinced that the change in the method of allotting War Department funds was a dangerous step toward stripping the ASF of some of the authority necessary for carrying out its basic supply and service responsibilities.

With this issue as a starting point, Somervell decided to bring up again the whole question of ASF–AAF relationships. In a memorandum for the Chief of Staff in September 1944 he called attention to the broad implications of the action taken in changing the method of allotting money. He listed six functions which had now been transferred from Service Forces supervision at air bases to Air Forces supervision and ten functions which still remained. He concluded that "in short, the action removes, for all practical purposes, the control of the Commanding General, Army Service Forces, and the chiefs of technical services over the major activities for which they are responsible insofar as the Air Forces is concerned." This development went a long way toward dividing the Army into two parts—the Air Forces and the Ground Forces—with chiefs of technical services limited to Ground Forces functions except as the AAF might request their assistance. Somervell then turned to the basic issue. The relation of the ASF to the Ground Forces was clear, he declared, but the relation to the Air Forces had been uncertain ever

---

[17] See above, Ch. VIII.

since the reorganization of March 1942, and was now made more complex by this recent action.[18]

Since the War Department reorganization, Somervell asserted, the ASF had tried to carry out "the letter and spirit of the orders by rendering all possible service to the Army Air Forces and the Army Ground Forces." In general, there had been no difficulty with the AGF, and, Somervell noted, the AGF apparently did not feel any lack of adequate control over the services rendered its troops. The AGF had never asked that the military posts it used be transferred to its command. "On the other hand there has been a continuous trend and agitation towards transferring to the Army Air Forces the supply and service functions being performed by the Army Service Forces at Air Forces stations." Somervell then explained that the ASF had resisted these proposed changes in the belief "that they were not in accordance with the concept of the reorganization plan; that they would lead to a duplication of effort, to adoption of nonuniform standards and procedures, and to an uneconomical utilization of manpower, supplies, and facilities." He added that the ASF had usually been supported in its opposition by the War Department General Staff.

Next in his memorandum Somervell was careful to insist that he had no wish to prejudice postwar military organization. The form this organization would take was still unknown and the organization for another war could not be predicted. "The extent to which air and other developments may bring about an almost complete change in the method of utilization of air and other arms may be far more spectacular than the mingling of all arms in this war." But in any event, service functions would always be necessary. What was needed was "a clean-cut division of responsibility but nevertheless one which will not unduly prejudice freedom of action in the future."

Somervell discussed several ways of meeting the existing situation and pointed out advantages and disadvantages of each possible course of action. A return to the pre-March 1942 organization, he felt, was impractical. One solution was to place the AAF in the same relation to the Service Forces as the Ground Forces. This meant that supply and service activities at air bases would be performed by station complements under the command of the ASF. If all airfields were thus made comparable to installations used by the AGF, the Air Forces could devote its time entirely to its tactical mission and a single standard of supply and service activity would obtain in the zone of interior. On the other hand, this action would place certain restrictions on the freedom of the Air Forces, although the Ground Forces had not found such restrictions a vital disadvantage.

Another alternative was to make the Air Forces completely self-contained with its own separate service force consisting of medical, engineer, ordnance, and other components responsible only to the chief of the Air Forces. Such an arrangement would provide the advantage of complete independence for the AAF which would thereafter be only vaguely tied into the War Department at the top echelon. The disadvantage would be the creation of two separate organizations within the War Department with resulting waste of personnel, equipment, and facilities. It would also mean the end of the conception of the

[18] Memo, Somervell for CofS, 27 Sep 44, sub: Recent Changes in Responsibilities of the ASF, Hq ASF, U.S. Army, 1944.

ASF as a common supply and service agency for the War Department as a whole and would place a larger co-ordinating burden upon the Chief of Staff.

A fourth possibility was to return to the original conception of the reorganization as defined by Army Regulations 170–10, 10 August 1942, which made the post commander at Air Forces installations responsible to the commanding general of the service command for specified service and supply activities. This would avoid duplication of organization and supervisory personnel in the War Department but would mean that the Air Forces post commander would have two channels of command and would probably lead to the same objections which the Air Forces had raised ever since 1942. Finally, if the ASF were abolished, the chiefs of technical services could supervise their activities throughout the Air Forces, but the Chief of Staff would again find himself with the large overhead organization which he had found so burdensome before.

General Somervell pointed out other possibilities, but thought they had too many drawbacks. The most clean-cut decision, he believed, would be either to place the Air Forces in the same relation to the Service Forces as the Ground Forces or to establish a completely self-contained air force. The next best solution was to revert to the original arrangement decided upon in 1942. He asked General Marshall to settle the issue.

Somervell brought up this problem at a time when the War Department was studying the idea of a single department of national defense and when the General Staff wanted to avoid jurisdictional flare-ups.[19] On 26 October 1944 General Marshall took up this perplexing problem by means of a memorandum to the commanding generals of the AAF, the AGF, and the ASF. The Chief of Staff doubted "the advisability of initiating any substantial organizational changes at the present time." The entire question of War Department and Army organization would have to be considered at the end of the war when the comments of overseas commanders would carry great weight. If the War Department was to obtain acceptance of the idea of a single department of national defense it would first have to demonstrate within the Army a satisfactory relation of service agencies to the combat forces. The Chief of Staff then asked the commanding generals of the three commands to resolve among themselves "the over-all question of service and supply functions and responsibilities and their relation to command." He hoped that they would be able to settle minor differences which might arise from time to time without appealing to him for a decision. Where differences could not be resolved, they should be presented to him as issues for decision. He then requested a statement giving the combined views of the three generals on how common supply and service activities should operate.[20]

The Effort To Resolve the Issue

General Arnold of the AAF, Lt. Gen. Ben Lear, commanding the AGF at the time, and General Somervell, held a series of meetings in an effort to reach an agreement about the role of the Service Forces. Toward the end of November 1944 they

---

[19] See Memo, Gen W. A. Wood, Jr., for Somervell, 29 Apr 44, sub: Reorg of National Defense (JCS 749/4), Hq ASF, CofS (Joint and Combined) 1942–44.

[20] Memo, CofS for CG AAF, CG AGF, and CG ASF, 26 Oct 44, sub: ASF Responsibilities, WDCSA 321 ASF (26 Oct 44).

sent General Marshall a report.[21] The three generals recognized that unity of purpose within the Army and a satisfactory relation of service to combat forces were indispensable prerequisites to obtaining a single department of national defense. Nevertheless they found it impossible to reconcile their differences.

General Arnold held that the basic mission of his command was to dominate the air and that to accomplish this overriding purpose, "administrative, supply, and service functions related to maintenance of air superiority" had to be integrated under his control. The intercession of a service command in these fields created "fatal divided responsibility."

General Lear of the Ground Forces and Somervell, on the other hand, looked at the War Department mission from an Army-wide point of view rather than that of a single command. A supply and service organization should "promote the maximum combat effectiveness . . . of the Army as a whole, as distinguished from that of an individual component," such as the Air Forces. A single agency to provide supplies and render common services was in the interest of economy. The relations between the Ground and Service Forces and between the Air and Service Forces should be uniform. Combat forces ought to devote themselves to training and combat and perform only those functions which are organic to their combat mission. All other service and supply responsibilities should be left to a common service agency.

The opposing views on details were presented to the Chief of Staff in parallel columns, one column stating the views of Ground and Service Forces, the other of the Air Forces.[22] The case for the Air Forces seemed to lie in the oft repeated

phrase "peculiar to the AAF." Air warfare, according to this approach, had its own special supply and service problems which were different from those of other combat forces, and should therefore be administered by the Air Forces. The ASF, while recognizing certain exceptions, believed that by and large the supply, administrative, and other service functions of the Air Forces did not possess inherent characteristics which distinguished them from the same functions of the Ground Forces.

The Air Forces protested in particular against a combination of command and staff functions in an independent service agency. This was an important point of the conflict and was expressed in Item 8 of the detailed list of differences:

AGF and ASF are of the opinion that . . .

8. ASF should act as the staff agency of the Chief of Staff and the Under Secretary of War for supply and service activities throughout the entire Army; i. e., there should be only one Surgeon General who should act as *The* Surgeon General of the Army.

AAF is of the opinion that . . .

8. The AAF believes that all of the activities of the ASF should be subject to general policies laid down by the General Staff as now constituted, that the requirements of the combat forces should be determined and adjudicated by a General Staff in no respect subject to one of the major commands, and further that many staff functions now performed for the Army by ASF should be restored to General Staff level, ASF to retain necessary operating functions subject to General Staff direction. The AAF disagrees with

---

[21] Memo, Arnold, Lear and Somervell to CofS, 27 Nov 44, sub: Relation of Sup and Sv Agencies to Combat Forces, Hq ASF, CofS, 1944.
[22] Tab A to Memo, cited in n. 21.

the view that a service agency under independent command should act as a staff agency for the Chief of Staff and the Under Secretary of War for administrative, supply or service activities.

General Arnold further maintained that, if the position of the Ground Forces and Service Forces was adopted, vital functions would be placed under the authority of a service agency independent of a combat force. A service agency by definition was only a means of assistance to a combat force. If a combat force did not include "certain essential functions" under its own control, its effectiveness would be crippled. Under the conception advanced by the ASF, the AGF and the AAF would exist as "tenants of the service agency" without any control of their stations and facilities. This concept ignored "the obvious fact" that the direction of a great combat force like the AAF was necessarily the management of a huge business which could not be farmed out to "an independent contractor." In the words of General Arnold: "Administrative control is an essential of command control." He then outlined the many different functions of the Air Forces and declared that these were interrelated and indispensable to the tactical mission of the AAF.[23]

The position of the commanding general of the Army Air Forces was obviously diametrically opposed to that of the commanding generals of the Army Ground Forces and the Army Service Forces. General Arnold saw the management of a combat force in terms of a widespread control over all of the activities contributing to operational effectiveness. The other two commanding generals saw the command of a combat force in terms of maximum possible dependency upon a separate service force operating behind the front lines overseas and extensively throughout the United States. There was little hope of reconciling these different conceptions of command responsibility within the Army.

General T. T. Handy, Deputy Chief of Staff of the War Department, tried to find a solution to this seemingly unsolvable conflict. Accompanied by Maj. Gen. C. F. Robinson, director of the Control Division in Somervell's office, he visited both a large post operated by the ASF where troops of the Army Ground Forces were in training, and a large training base of the AAF. Upon their return, Robinson wrote to Handy stating the conclusions which their inspection trip seemed to justify. As far as internal post and base operations were concerned, the system in use for supply and services at both seemed to be functioning satisfactorily. The AAF base had received satisfactory assistance from ASF agencies. Regardless of War Department organization, in practice the air base was relying for many services upon service commands. The AGF–ASF relationship could be applied, with minor modifications, to an air base without much difficulty.

General Robinson argued that the major difficulty in existing organization for supply and service activities did not "lie at the post level but in higher echelons." The AGF–ASF system provided for supervision of these activities through a single geographical organization, which he believed was the more effective and efficient method. Under the AAF system, supervision of service activities was divided among a number of different tactical commands, resulting in "unnecessary duplication" and uneconomical "use of

---

[23] Tab B to Memo, cited in n. 21.

personnel." Finally, under a dual system of supervision as at present, the chiefs of technical services could not adequately supervise the supply and service activities for which they had technical responsibility.[24]

The War Department Decision

On 28 December 1944 General Handy transmitted a memorandum to all three commanding generals outlining the principles which were to govern relationships between their commands.[25] First, the War Department General Staff was the "overall policy and co-ordinating staff for the War Department and the Army," while the three commands were primarily "operating agencies." Second, military personnel of the three major commands should receive "equal consideration and enjoy equivalent facilities." Third, commanders should concentrate upon their "primary responsibilities" and delegate "to a common supply service such duties as are not essential to their exercise of the command prerogative." The common supply service was to emphasize service, not command. Fourth, a supply service organization was essential for procurement and "wholesale" distribution of common articles of Army supply and for common administrative service. The fifth principle recognized a twilight zone in which the wishes of the commander would govern. For example, there was no question but that procurement of common articles of clothing was a responsibility of the Army Service Forces; there was no question but that the procurement of aircraft was a function of the Army Air Forces. But the procurement and distribution of high altitude flying clothing was in the indeterminate area and therefore the wishes

of the Army Air Forces would govern.

The essence of the position of the Deputy Chief of Staff was summarized in his final point that "no major change in present procedures and organization is contemplated." The AAF retained command control over all but a relatively few responsibilities performed at its air bases. The ASF, through its service commands, still exercised supervision of Army exchanges, disbursement offices, and hospitals at air bases. In effect the December 1944 decision reaffirmed the status quo.

But the difficulties between the AAF and the ASF continued even after they had been supposedly settled by a War Department circular.[26] When a change was ordered there were controversies over interpretation and procedure. Agreements between the two commands became increasingly difficult to achieve.

The Relations of the ASF and the AAF to the Technical Services

The attack of the Air Forces on the so-called Somervell empire not only had the effect of removing some supply, service, and administrative functions from the jurisdiction of the ASF, but even more damaging, it threatened to undermine the internal structure of the ASF. The reorganization of 1942 brought many technical and administrative services, previously almost autonomous units of the War Department, under the command authority of General Somervell. These technical and administrative services at best tended to be somewhat restive under ASF juris-

---

[24] Memo, C. F. Robinson for Handy, 16 Dec 44, CD, ASF.
[25] Memo, Handy for CG ASF, 28 Dec 44, sub: Sup and Sv Responsibilities, Hq ASF.
[26] WD Cir 388, 27 Sep 44.

diction. The AAF attack had the effect of encouraging internal dissatisfaction. The ASF suffered damage not only in that some of its functions were assigned elsewhere, but also in that the chiefs of the technical services gained a greater independence from ASF headquarters.

For example, in the dispute between The Surgeon General of the Army and the Air Surgeon, the final compromise provided that The Surgeon General would forward "through" the ASF his communications to the Chief of Staff. This meant that while the Commanding General, ASF, might comment, he could no longer exercise command authority over all the activities of The Surgeon General.[27]

The same type of situation evolved from the controversy with the Air Forces over the maintenance of real property and the operation of utilities. ASF internal organization provided that division engineers, the head of geographic areas within the United States under the Chief of Engineers, should also serve as a service command engineer in supervising property repairs and utility operations. In practice, most division engineers appointed a deputy who was in effect the engineer in charge of repairs and utility operations of a service command. While repair and utility funds to Air Forces installations no longer went from service commands directly to the air base, the Army Service Forces saw no reason to change its existing organization for supervising repair and utilities activities. Accordingly, service command engineers were directed to inspect repair and utility work at Air Forces installations in the same manner as at other installations under service commands. After the change in methods of allotting funds went into effect, the Army Air Forces objected to this arrangement.

It was opposed to inspection of its air bases by an individual designated "service command engineer." It was willing to recognize the authority of the Chief of Engineers, but objected to service command engineers. On the other hand, the ASF maintained that its internal inspection organization was something it should determine for itself; its authority to inspect was specifically stated in War Department Circular 388; and it already had a large inspection staff which it proposed to use for inspection at Air Forces installations.

The dispute went to the Assistant Chief of Staff, G–4, who stated that Circular 388 distinguished between the *command* function of the AAF and the *service* function exercised by the ASF at Air Forces installations. The service function was defined to include technical assistance, review, inspection, and supply. G–4 declared: "It is not to the best interest of the War Department to require a change in the ASF regional organization at this time for service to Class III [Air Forces] installations."[28]

This rebuff did not prevent the AAF from submitting a staff study arguing that War Department Circular 388 was intended to be only temporary in nature. The AAF therefore requested a transfer of authority from the ASF to the AAF to make all technical inspections at Class III installations. G–4 replied that it opposed the "elimination of technical inspections at Class III installations. . . . It is the policy of the War Department that the chiefs of technical services, in addition to their other duties, will act as chief technical advisers to the Chief of Staff and the

---

[27] See above, p. 133.

[28] G–4 Disposition form, addressed to CG ASF, 24 Apr 45, sub: Relation of Sv Comdrs and Class III Installations, WDGDS 12275.

War Department." [29] Thus the position of chiefs of technical services was reaffirmed, although nothing was said about the authority of the Commanding General, ASF, as the superior of these chiefs.

The Deputy Chief of Staff reiterated this policy. He added that as technical advisers to the Chief of Staff, chiefs of technical services or their designated representatives were authorized to make technical inspections at Class I, II, III, and IV installations,[30] to establish budgetary standards for expenditure of funds. Communications on all matters pertaining to technical activities of the War Department would be forwarded to the Chief of Staff through the Commanding General, ASF. The statement further provided that the commanding general might make such additional remarks and recommendations as he deemed appropriate, but implied that he could not refuse to forward recommendations of chiefs of technical services.[31]

The existing inspection system on repairs and utilities operations was not disturbed. The effort of the Army Air Forces to escape from supervision by chiefs of technical services or from service commands was thus forestalled. But at the same time the authority of the Commanding General, ASF, was weakened by the provision that chiefs of technical services could prepare recommendations for the War Department General Staff on which the commanding general could only comment. Nothing was said about the authority of the Commanding General, ASF, to prescribe such organizational arrangements as he deemed desirable. Not only was the supervisory authority of the ASF undermined with respect to the Engineers; the WDGS took a similar position on the responsibilities of the Chief Signal Officer.

In fact, on 23 July 1945 the War Department General Council provided that all the chiefs of technical services would act as "chief technical advisers to the Chief of Staff and the War Department." [32]

The War Department position was based on a distinction it drew between technical and service responsibilities of the chiefs of technical services. Under this interpretation the technical services would deal directly with the War Department General Staff on technical matters, while on other matters they would still be under General Somervell's jurisdiction.

Somervell protested against these developments vehemently and at length. The distinction between technical and service activities, he said, was meaningless in practical application. The changes threatened the stability of the ASF because they challenged its authority both over its Army-wide supply and service activities and over its own subordinate units. This tendency, General Somervell charged, "can only result in three independent self-sufficient commands—each with its own supply and service functions, each duplicating the overhead of the other." [33]

Somervell then drew up a statement which clarified the organizational position of the ASF. He sought his authority in the principles of the War Department reorganization of March 1942, which among other things had affirmed that "the mission of the Services of Supply is to provide services and supplies to meet military requirements except those peculiar to the

[29] G-4 Disposition form, addressed to CG AAF, 17 Jul 45, sub: Elimination of ASF Tech Inspections at Class III Installations, WDGDS 15173.

[30] See below, pp. 314–15.

[31] Min, WD Gen Council, 23 Jul 45.

[32] Ibid.

[33] Memo, Somervell to CofS, 6 Aug 45, sub: Position of the ASF in the WD, Hq ASF, CofS.

AAF," and that "supply arms and services and War Department offices and agencies will come under the direct command of the Commanding General, SOS. . . ." Somervell spelled out specifically what in his mind seemed the proper way in which these principles ought to be applied to the problems that had since arisen. He recommended that this statement be sent to the three major commands, and that it be inserted in the minutes of the War Department General Council.[34]

This memorandum and statement by General Somervell was to prove a final statement of his organizational thinking about the Army Service Forces. One week after it was sent to the Chief of Staff, the Japanese Government announced its surrender. World War II was over. Somervell's proposals were not considered.

The basic problem of the role of the Army Service Forces in the War Department thus remained unsolved. At most, Somervell's effort to bring about a solution served only as an opportunity for a restatement of the opposing points of view.

The ASF insisted on its position as an Army-wide service agency. Throughout, it adhered to the view that it was not a coordinate command, but an administrative arm of the War Department. More than this, it considered itself a planning agency for the Chief of Staff in the logistics field as well as in various technical operations.

In support of this broad conception of its role, the Army Service Forces could point, among other things, to the fact that it was often called upon to defend decisions on behalf of the War Department as a whole. For example, in early 1943 it bore the brunt of the defense for the Army decision, in the face of manpower stringencies, to raise a force of 8.2 million men.

Again when the Army argued for national universal service, the ASF carried the burden of the case. National universal service was intended to provide manpower for industry and agriculture rather than manpower for the Army itself. Since the ASF was concerned with the procurement of military supplies, it was perfectly natural that it should be the best prepared of all War Department agencies to present the Army argument for such legislation. The ASF also performed the bulk of the work in preparing the War Department's advocacy of universal training and for similar matters which transcended the fields of individual organizations within the War Department.

The basic doctrine of the Army Ground Forces was defined at the time of the reorganization of the War Department in 1942. Though occasionally objecting to Somervell's jurisdictional claims, the AGF was a consistent supporter of the need for an Army Service Forces as a common War Department supply and administrative agency.

The Army Air Forces did not share this view. Its hostility to the ASF position transcended specific issues, but stemmed rather from its basic desire for complete separation from the other major components of the Army. In view of this attitude, efforts toward a better understanding were well-nigh hopeless. At one time, Somervell and his immediate advisers thought relations might improve if the AAF would place a high-ranking officer in ASF headquarters to serve as liaison on post management, which would be an arrangement similar to that in force on purchasing matters. General Arnold agreed and on 19 August 1943 named a liaison officer with

---

[34] Tab H to Memo, cited in n. 32.

Headquarters, ASF.[35] Other AAF liaison officers were stationed in the headquarters of each service commander. But this arrangement brought no real improvement in relations between the ASF and the AAF.

It was necessary for the ASF to reaffirm its role constantly in order to maintain its position in the War Department as originally intended. The alternative was to devise some new type of organization. The wartime solution to problems were compromises which outwardly preserved most of the original structure and functions of the ASF. But the opposition encountered by the ASF in the effort to meet its responsibilities reflected subsurface currents of thinking within the Army which, if allowed to develop to their logical conclusion, threatened to undermine the whole theory of an Army-wide service agency.

[35] ASF Cir 64, 19 Aug 43.

CHAPTER XII

Somervell's Relationship With Patterson and Marshall

In the final analysis much of the wartime role of the Army Service Forces depended upon personalities, specifically upon the relations of its commanding general to the Under Secretary of War and to the Chief of Staff. The existence of a satisfactory personal relationship between these three men was a major factor in the ability of the ASF to perform its responsibilities and to survive as the War Department's command organization for supply and service activities.

Somervell's position in the top organization of the War Department was, for such a high-ranking official, unique. He had not one but two bosses: the Under Secretary and the Chief of Staff. It was a peculiar kind of arrangement in the light of Army doctrine pertaining to "unity of command," but one made necessary by War Department organizational experience after 1920. On the whole, it turned out to be a workable arrangement, at least insofar as relations between the three individuals involved were concerned.

General Marshall respected the Under Secretary's position; he was too good an Army officer imbued with the doctrine of the subordination of military to civilian authority to behave otherwise. He never encouraged Somervell to bring procurement problems to him. There is no indication in the record of any instructions from Marshall to Somervell on purchasing or production matters. He expected Somervell to obtain necessary policy direction on these matters from the Under Secretary. In turn the Under Secretary seemed to have great respect for the military judgment of General Marshall, and accepted as proper the fact that on strategic matters Marshall dealt with Secretary Stimson and the President. Patterson had no apparent disposition to enlarge his authority unduly.

Somervell for his part, conscientious in his observation of organizational arrangements, encountered no difficulty in working for two masters. Nor did he yield to the temptation, inherent in all such situations, of trying to play one superior against the other. He realized General Marshall was not interested in any excuse such as "the Under Secretary wants it this way." It was Somervell's duty to present the professional military judgment to the Under Secretary and then follow such civilian modification as might be expressed.

The Under Secretary

Perhaps no top individual in the War Department had more reason to be concerned about the creation of the Army Service Forces than the Under Secretary of War. He lost a large supervisory organization which had previously enabled him to fulfill the responsibility, delegated to him by the Secretary of War, of directing the Department's procurement and related business activities. All the staff units which had been a part of the Office of the Under Secretary of War became, on 9 March 1942, staff units of the commanding general of the ASF. But while the Under Secretary lost an organization, he gained an executive officer of high rank and great drive. It was up to Somervell to demonstrate that in the reorganization the Under Secretary had gained in personal influence and that civilian control had not been weakened by the change.

Mr. Goldthwaite H. Dorr suggested one arrangement to demonstrate the close relationship which was expected to exist in fact between the commanding general of the ASF and the Under Secretary of War. One factor creating a gulf between the Supply Division of the War Department General Staff and the OUSW after June 1941 had been the physical separation of the two offices. The Under Secretary of War and his staff had moved into the so-called New War Department Building which had just been finished at 21st Street and Virginia Avenue, two blocks away from the old Munitions Building. This modern, air-conditioned, government office building had been intended as the headquarters for the War Department to replace the old Munitions Building which had been constructed during World War I. By the time the new building was completed, however, the War Department had expanded so greatly that it was adequate to house only the Office of the Under Secretary and the Office of the Chief of

Engineers. All of the War Department General Staff remained in the Munitions Building. Recalling that the offices for Assistant Secretary Benedict Crowell and General Goethals during World War I were adjacent, Mr. Dorr proposed that Patterson and Somervell should likewise have adjoining offices with no secretaries or assistants between them.

After 9 March 1942, General Somervell insisted upon moving most of the units in the Office of the Under Secretary of War into the Munitions Building. The Under Secretary then gave up his new, modern office in order to return to the old building. There he and the commanding general of the ASF occupied adjoining offices immediately above those of the Secretary of War and the Chief of Staff. By the end of 1942 it was possible to move both offices into the new Pentagon Building. Here, General Somervell had a specially designed section on the third floor over the Mall entrance to the building which gave the Under Secretary and the commanding general of the ASF adjoining offices with a connecting door. The Secretary of War and the Chief of Staff had a similar arrangement on another side of the building.

Undoubtedly the proximity of these offices had much to do with promoting close-working relationships between Mr. Patterson and General Somervell. Tempermentally, the two men were very different. Mr. Patterson was usually calm, cautious, and inclined to look at all sides of most issues. General Somervell was impatient, tense, and decisive. Both men probably went through a somewhat trying period of mutual adjustment. It was a tribute to the integrity and determination of both men that they rose above personal differences and that they should have found a way to work together. Indeed, before the end of the war each had come to have real respect for the other. On the one hand, Mr. Patterson realized that Somervell's energy and willingness to make decisions were vital to the procurement and supply support of military operations. On the other hand, General Somervell appreciated that civilian control of military operations was a vital part of the American political tradition and that many decisions had to be approved by a politically responsible official of the War Department.

After 9 March 1942, the Under Secretary's immediate office was quite small. In March 1943, for example, the office consisted of Mr. Patterson, Lt. Gen. W. S. Knudsen as director of production, an executive officer, an administrative officer, an executive assistant, and seven special assistants. In addition, there were one or two personal assistants to some of these individuals and the usual secretarial and clerical personnel. A few more personal assistants were appointed during the course of the war, but the OUSW remained a small group at all times. When any continuing administrative duty was to be started in which the Under Secretary was interested, General Somervell insisted that the unit should be located in the Army Service Forces although the director of the work then might have such personal relations with the Under Secretary as Mr. Patterson desired.

When Congress in 1942 authorized the renegotiation of contracts, for instance, General Somervell established a Renegotiations Division as a staff unit under the director of matériel in headquarters of the ASF. At the same time, the director of the Renegotiations Division became the chairman of the War Department Price Adjust-ment Board. Renegotiation of contract prices was an activity in which the Under Secretary took very much interest. At one time, indeed, without consulting General Somervell, he directed that the War Department Price Adjustment Board should be a part of his own office rather than attached to the ASF. After General Somervell protested, both men agreed that the Renegotiations Division should be located within the ASF but that the director of the division should be appointed only with the approval of the Under Secretary. They also agreed that when the board gave final official approval to a renegotiation agreement, it should act in the name of the Under Secretary.

In 1944 General Somervell established a Correction Division in the Office of The Adjutant General to supervise rehabilitation centers and disciplinary barracks where military prisoners were held. The Under Secretary exercised the power of clemency, delegated to him by the Secretary of War, over military prisoners convicted by courts martial. As a result of his review of such cases, the Under Secretary became more and more interested in the whole penology program of the Department. The actual penal institutions of the Army were under the ASF. When the number of prisoners confined in these institutions became sizable—the number of men in disciplinary barracks increased from 5,300 to 8,600 between July and December 1944—the Under Secretary was more concerned than ever that the penal practices of the Department should be above reproach.[1] A solution was sought in the creation of the Correction Division in the ASF headquarters under the direction of an officer in the Under Secretary's

---

[1] CD, ASF, *Statistical Review, World War II*, p. 151.

office who had previously assisted the Under Secretary in clemency matters. In addition, the Under Secretary created a Board of Consultants composed of the country's leading penologists and prison administrators to advise him. The chairman of the board, Mr. Austin MacCormick, became a personal assistant to the Under Secretary. This administrative arrangement proved entirely workable in practice.

From the very beginning of the Army Service Forces, General Somervell always invited the Under Secretary to attend ASF staff conferences. These conferences were held regularly twice a month. Attending whenever he was in town, the Under Secretary sat at the right of the commanding general. In his absence, his executive officer usually was present. This gave the Under Secretary an opportunity to participate in the discussion and to express his opinion regarding any matter which might arise. On both purchasing and production matters General Somervell always requested the Under Secretary's opinion. In addition, the Under Secretary or his executive officer usually attended the semiannual conferences of the commanders of the service commands which were begun in June 1942 as a means of maintaining close personal contact between the headquarters of the ASF and the headquarters of the nine service commands. Here again, the Under Secretary had an opportunity to learn exactly what was happening in the ASF, the problems which were arising, and the policies and programs which were being followed. The regular monthly reports prepared within the ASF for the guidance of the commanding general and his staff divisions were also given to the Under Secretary for such use as he might wish to make of them.

In one respect, the Under Secretary necessarily developed a peculiar relationship to the ASF. As mentioned earlier, the commanding general of the Army Air Forces exercised important procurement responsibilities. Like the commanding general of the ASF, he operated under the supervision of the Under Secretary of War. The ASF staff became the Under Secretary's staff when dealing with the AAF. This arrangement applied primarily to two and later three staff divisions of the ASF: the Purchases Division, the Renegotiations Division, and, after November 1943, the Readjustment Division (particularly concerned with contract terminations). Actually, the Under Secretary was probably more interested in the work of these three staff divisions of the ASF than in any other. In any event, General Somervell was only too glad to defer to Judge Patterson's judgment on all legal and price policy matters affecting procurement.

The directors of these staff divisions saw the Under Secretary frequently. For example, they consulted him often with regard to contract termination policies, the development of which he followed very closely. While General Somervell was likewise deeply interested in these developments, War Department points of view were determined by discussions held in the Under Secretary's office. The director of matériel of the ASF, first General Clay and later Mr. Howard Bruce, also saw the Under Secretary frequently, as did the legal adviser on procurement matters, Mr. William C. Marbury. General Somervell encouraged these individuals to consult freely with the Under Secretary, and the Under Secretary in turn called upon them directly whenever some matter arose in which he was interested.

The wide range of the Under Secretary's interests and activities was well indicated in a report to the Secretary of War which was prepared in the Under Secretary's office in the autumn of 1944. This was the first such report prepared in the Under Secretary's office after the reorganization of 1942.

The Under Secretary was the official representative of the War Department on the War Production Board, the War Manpower Commission, and the Committee for Congested Production Areas. In addition, the Under Secretary took an active role in labor relations, in public relations involving procurement matters (including the award of the Army-Navy "E" for outstanding industrial achievement in war production), and in industrial safety and protection. In September 1943, he sponsored a meeting in Washington of two hundred industrialists and labor leaders to hear confidential information about the status of war production. A similar meeting was held at Ft. Knox, Kentucky, in October 1943 and at Los Angeles in January 1944. The basic work for this conference was prepared jointly by personnel from the ASF and from the Industrial Services Division of the Bureau of Public Relations.

The Under Secretary was also much interested in so-called economic warfare, and matters involving relations with the Foreign Economic Administration were usually taken up with him. For example, on 19 September 1944, General Somervell sent a memorandum to the Under Secretary on the disposal of surplus property overseas. Somervell was opposed to the performance of this work by the FEA on the grounds that that administration would be unlikely to push rapid liquidation of military property overseas, which would in turn require the continued presence of thousands of troops overseas to guard and care for such property. The

War Department, in General Somervell's eyes, should seek "prompt, clean-cut and definitive settlements" for the disposition of overseas property.[2] Earlier in the year, when the Army Industrial College was reopened under the nominal supervision of the Under Secretary of War, one of its immediate purposes was to train officer and civilian personnel in contract termination and property disposal procedure. Thus the college became an important part of the War Department's preparations for procurement demobilization after V-E and V-J Days. Its instructors were drawn almost entirely from the Readjustment Division of the ASF.

Under Secretary Patterson was a loyal, consistent supporter of the Army Service Forces throughout the war. His satisfaction with the organizational arrangement was evidenced by his failure to make any effort to reconstitute the OUSW along prewar lines in the reorganization of the War Department in 1946. If he had been even slightly dissatisfied, he would probably have followed a different course. In turn, General Somervell found the Under Secretary's counsel and assistance constantly helpful and reassuring. The Under Secretary had learned that he could control activities in which he was interested by working through the commanding general of the ASF. General Somervell, on the other hand, had learned that an Under Secretary of War sympathetic to Army needs and of unquestioned integrity was a real asset in guiding procurement operations.

The Chief of Staff

Somervell's personal relations with General Marshall were direct but formal.

[2] Memo, Somervell for USW, 10 Sep 44, sub: Disposal of Surplus Property Overseas, CG ASF.

Although he saw the Chief of Staff almost daily, it was invariably on matters of business. The Chief of Staff had a rigorous code of what he regarded as appropriate conduct in officers. In turn, General Somervell never presumed on his relationship to the Chief of Staff. He always acted with the understanding that he was Marshall's subordinate whose responsibility was to carry out the Chief of Staff's desires to the very fullest extent possible.

Indeed, it was this latter attitude which explained Somervell's continuance in the position of commanding general of the Army Service Forces throughout the war. Had Somervell ever failed in either loyalty or performance of duty, he would probably have been relieved. No matter how much controversy might rage around General Somervell, the Chief of Staff gave no evidence of being displeased as long as he felt that essential work for the Army was being performed with maximum possible vigor. At times there were efforts to stir the Chief of Staff to dissatisfaction with his commanding general of the ASF. These efforts failed. In this connection, there is a revealing comment about General Marshall's attitude in an account written by his wife. Without indicating either the individual or issues involved, Mrs. Marshall records:

A group of Congressmen were much perturbed over rumors that were afloat in Washington concerning one of George's most trusted Staff officers who was carrying a tremendous load and doing it magnificently. In fact, he was handling his job with such authority and skill that the rumor-mongers said he had his eye on the job of the Chief of Staff. This rumor was fanned into a flame by those who had fallen afoul of him because of their failure to live up to his high standards of efficiency. The group of Congressmen came to warn George. He listened to what they had to say, then smiled and said,

"Thank you, gentlemen. I have heard these rumors. You do not have to worry about me. If I can't control my own Staff, I would not be here." [3]

It seems most likely that this comment was occasioned by the controversy involving General Somervell in the autumn of 1943.[4] But whether Somervell was the officer whom the Chief of Staff had in mind upon this particular occasion is not important. The attitude expressed did characterize the relationship between the Chief of Staff of the War Department and the commanding general of the Army Service Forces.

Somervell always looked upon the ASF as peculiarly the creation of the Chief of Staff. What it was and what it did was primarily the result of General Marshall's desire. It has already been noted that, had Somervell been the architect of the ASF, the command might well have been solely a procurement and supply command without the administrative service work which was included in it. He never questioned the addition of the administrative services simply because it was the arrangement which General Marshall had put into effect. In explaining the Army Service Forces on one occasion, General Somervell revealed his attitude in these words. He said that the ASF "handles logistics and administration. Its purpose was to take these loads as far as possible off the mind of the Chief of Staff." [5]

Somervell made it a regular practice to keep the Chief of Staff fully informed

---

[3] From *Together: Annals of an Army Wife,* by Katherine Tupper Marshall, copyright 1946, 1947, by Katherine Tupper Marshall by permission of Tupper and Love, Inc., publishers, pp. 108–09.

[4] See below, Ch. XXIV.

[5] Brehon B. Somervell, "The United States Army Services of Supply," *Proceedings of the Academy of Political Science,* XX (January 1943), 67.

about what he was doing. He constantly sent papers to Marshall intended to indicate what was being accomplished. Somervell asked the Chief of Staff to attend the ceremonies observing the first anniversary of the Army Service Forces on 9 March 1943. General Marshall did so, and subsequently requested a copy of the talk Somervell made reviewing the accomplishments of the ASF in its first year. He sent the talk to the editor of the *Reader's Digest* with the suggestion that the publication might be interested in preparing an article on this subject. The result was the first of two or three articles about the ASF which appeared in that magazine during the war.

On another occasion, General Somervell, taking note of the fact that both the Navy and the Air Forces had gone to considerable effort to provide popular reading matter about their operations, arranged, with the Chief of Staff's approval, for one of his officers to prepare a booklet which would deal with the Army as a whole. This was published in early 1945 as *The Mightiest Army.*[6]

Communications which Somervell received from either subordinates or from overseas commands, summarizing problems or accomplishments, were frequently sent to the Chief of Staff's desk. Most of these the Chief of Staff personally reviewed. For example, General Somervell received a letter from the director of the Military Railway Service in the China-Burma-India theater, shortly after the Transportation Corps took over the operation of the Bengal-Assam railway on 1 March 1944. The director reported that in the first eighteen days of American operation, the military tonnage hauled had increased 36.4 percent over the same period in the preceding month. The improve-

ment had been realized without any increase in yard expansion or trackage. Somervell forwarded the letter to General Marshall with the hand-written comment: "You will note our organization has done a lot *in a few days.* Have urged the British to do this for over a year." The letter was returned with the notation: "Fine business—GCM."

On his overseas inspection trips, General Somervell invariably wrote fairly long accounts of his observations in personal letters to the Chief of Staff. Some of these comments have already been quoted. No replies were expected and none were received. Indeed there is almost no indication in the files of the commanding general of the ASF that General Marshall ever communicated instructions to Somervell in writing. As a general rule, the Chief of Staff issued orders and communications orally. Written communications from his office came from the Deputy Chief of Staff or the assistant chiefs of staff.[7]

On the subject of organization and management, Somervell never succeeded in obtaining an expression of marked interest from the Chief of Staff. Deeply concerned with this matter himself, Somervell was proud of the achievements of the ASF in building an integrated organization with some degree of unity and common purpose out of the many diverse elements inherited on 9 March 1942. In addition,

---

[6] The book, written by Karl W. Detzer, formerly a roving editor of the *Reader's Digest,* was published without profit by the Readers' Digest Association and distributed at cost by the S-M News Company. All profits from the enterprise were contributed to the Army Emergency Relief Fund. More than 300,000 copies were sold.

[7] There are a few minor exceptions, such as a note to General Somervell from the Chief of Staff, dated 18 December 1944, expressing dissatisfaction with the ASF post commander at Camp McClellan. Files, CG ASF.

the ASF placed constant emphasis upon improved methods of performance which would reduce the cost of operations. On one occasion, General Somervell did persuade the Chief of Staff to come to his own office and look over the record of management improvements achieved by the ASF. General Marshall gave no indication that he was particularly impressed.

Marshall usually referred Somervell's various protests about the changing status of the Army Service Forces to General McNarney, the deputy chief of staff. The most serious protest, that of 27 September 1944, resulted in a memorandum from the Chief of Staff to the commanding generals of the three commands, already described. While General Marshall asked for a clear-cut statement of the differences, the whole problem was then turned over to the Deputy Chief of Staff.[8]

The Chief of Staff generally allowed his subordinate commanders the greatest latitude in working out their problems. He was not one to interfere with minor details or to attempt to follow every development. His practice was to provide general instructions and then to expect intelligent, prompt action in fulfilling them. There seems little doubt but that the Chief of Staff wanted and appreciated the kind of subordinate commander General Somervell proved to be. The Chief of Staff wanted action, and vigorously. He was not tolerant of failures or of constant requests for additional instructions.

Although General Somervell indicated on two or three occasions that he would be happy to have a different assignment, General Marshall showed no disposition to make a change. Once in an extemporaneous talk to some three hundred key officers of the Army Service Forces, including the chiefs of technical services, the

Chief of Staff indicated that he had been dissatisfied with the supply organization of the War Department as it existed before 9 March 1942, principally because responsibility had been too diffused. He emphasized that he wanted only one man reporting to him on supply and transportation matters. He had insisted upon such an arrangement, and he made it clear that he would not tolerate any different arrangement for the conduct of the war. He then went farther and voiced his approval of the manner in which the ASF had been functioning under the leadership of its commanding general.[9]

In his work for the Joint and Combined Chiefs of Staff, General Somervell was at all times the agent of the Chief of Staff. His role was one of defining the Chief of Staff's desires and putting them into execution. As a subordinate of the Chief of Staff, General Somervell had almost no relations with the President. ASF matters of concern to the Chief Executive were handled through General Marshall. But on one or two occasions Somervell saw the President personally and, when he did so, it was upon instructions from the Chief of Staff. Because of his past association with him in the WPA, General Somervell occasionally had access to Harry Hopkins. During the heated controversy with the WPB, Somervell kept Mr. Hopkins informed of developments and the Army's point of view.[10] Since Mr. Hopkins was the chairman of the Munitions Assign-

---

[8] See above, p. 165.

[9] These remarks were made in the Pentagon auditorium on 9 March 1945, the occasion of the celebration of the third anniversary of the creation of the ASF. No record was made of General Marshall's comments and the above account reflects the author's recollection of what was said.

[10] See below, p. 222.

ments Board, Somervell also had considerable correspondence with him on the matter of supplies to the British and to the Russians. Somervell wanted Mr. Hopkins to know about all lend-lease matters involving the Army. Like General Marshall, Somervell enjoyed Mr. Hopkins constant support.

General Somervell had little contact with the Secretary of War, but there were some occasions when the latter official turned to him for help. On the occasion when the President requested the Secretary of War and the Secretary of the Navy to compose their differences with Mr. Nelson over the duties of the Production Vice-Chairman in the WPB, General Somervell was necessarily called upon to provide Secretary Stimson with full information about the origin of the difficulty and the argument which had led to the existing impasse. On another occasion when a strike threatened to halt all railroad operations within the United States, the Secretary of War called upon General Somervell to prepare a plan for Army operation of the nation's railways. Army control was actually ordered on 27 December 1943 by the Secretary in accordance with the terms of an executive order of the President, and continued until 18 January 1944 when the railways were returned to their owners after settlement of the dispute between management and labor. The Secretary was deeply interested in this entire activity. On Army operation of industrial establishments taken over in order to insure uninterrupted production, the Under Secretary was the top War Department official fixing policy and practice.

The importance which General Marshall attached to Somervell's position was clearly indicated by his action in taking Somervell to all the international conferences. When the Casablanca Conference was held in January 1943, Somervell was one of the few officers accompanying the Chief of Staff. He attended all subsequent conferences and remained Marshall's logistics planner and commander to the very end of the war.

The Army Service Forces was set up to meet a War Department organization need which General Marshall saw as a vital factor in the conduct of the war. In order to overcome the fatal bifurcation which had developed between procurement and distribution activities in the top War Department organization, the Under Secretary consented to a single supply command. The ASF was both logistics staff and command for the Chief of Staff. On industrial relations matters, the Under Secretary initiated or approved basic policies. General Marshall seemed to be less concerned with the work of the ASF in the service field than he was with its work in the supply field. Eventually the War Department General or Special Staff came to be the policy-fixing echelon on service or administrative duties.

The role of the ASF in the War Department in World War II was not determined simply by General Somervell's conception of it. In the last analysis it depended primarily upon what Judge Patterson as Under Secretary and General Marshall as Chief of Staff wanted. Theirs were the crucial attitudes in determining what the Army Service Forces was and how it was to operate.

PART THREE

THE ROLE OF THE ASF
IN INDUSTRIAL MOBILIZATION

CHAPTER XIII

The ASF and the WPB: Early Attempts To Define Responsibilities

The Army Service Forces during World War II never experienced budgetary stringencies. From 1 July 1940 through 31 December 1941, Congress appropriated some twenty-five billion dollars to the War Department for the procurement of war supplies other than aircraft. About three billion dollars had also been allotted for lend-lease purchases. Between 1 January and 30 June 1942, Congress appropriated another 23.5 billion dollars for military procurement by agencies of the newly announced Army Service Forces. Appropriations for the fiscal years 1943 and 1944 added another fifty billion dollars.[1]

But funds to purchase supplies were very different from the delivery of completed articles for Army use. In the whole calendar year 1941 the procurement agencies which later made up the Army Service Forces received actual deliveries of supplies amounting to 3.5 billion dollars. Of this amount, food stuffs were a major item.[2] From 1 July 1940 through December 1941 the total production of American industry for Army and Navy use included merely 65 heavy guns, 4,705 light field and antitank guns, 6,787 tank guns and howitzers, 9,518 mortars, 87,172 machine guns, 4,203 tanks (almost all light), 7,833 scout cars, and 208,034 trucks.[3] This was a start, but only a start toward the output of the tremendous quantities of military matériel required to win World War II.

Military procurement involved a whole complex of economic relationships—the necessary production plants, specialized machine tools and the "know-how" to make them effective, raw materials and component parts, adequate labor force, and on top of all these, a "civilian" (i. e., essential but not directly military) production adequate to support military output. Military procurement could not operate in a vacuum; it had to be part of a highly planned and highly organized total war production effort. As an agency of the War Department, therefore, the Army Service Forces was only one element of an intricate governmental machine for industrial mobilization.

---

[1] Annual *Report of the Services of Supply*, 1942, pp. 1–2; Annual Rpt of ASF, 1943, p. 193.

[2] CD, ASF, *Statistical Review, World War II*, p. 2.

[3] Civilian Production Administration, *Industrial Mobilization for War: History of the War Production Board and Predecessor Agencies 1940–1945*, I (Washington, U.S. Government Printing Office, 1947), p. 170. This volume is the official, published history of the WPB. (Hereafter cited as *Industrial Mobilization for War*.)

This lesson had been taught in World War I.[4] The need for general industrial preparedness had been acknowledged by Congress in amending the National Defense Act of 4 June 1920. Among the provisions of the legislation was Section 5*a* which said that the Assistant Secretary of War would supervise War Department procurement and should make *"adequate provision for the mobilization of matériel and industrial organizations essential to wartime needs."* [5] Upon the basis of this somewhat ambiguous language grew the industrial mobilization planning of the War Department from 1920 to 1940. The Navy Department was associated, in name at least, with this effort through the device of the Army and Navy Munitions Board.

The Industrial Mobilization Plan

Although it had borne the responsibility for industrial mobilization planning for the federal government between the two wars, the War Department never had any doubts about the necessity for separate and distinct administrative machinery to direct industrial mobilization. The 1939 revision of the so-called Industrial Mobilization Plan was the last one prepared and published by the ANMB before World War II.[6] Actually, the document was a "plan" only in a limited sense. It was not a *substantive* program dealing with details of operations or with estimates of magnitude; rather it set forth a proposed organizational plan for agencies to be set up in order to accomplish industrial mobilization.

The Industrial Mobilization Plan briefly sketched the reasons for government control of industrial resources in wartime and outlined the broad elements involved in such control. The plan then presented positive organizational proposals. When war became imminent, the President, "under the authority accorded him by the Constitution and by the Congress," was to supervise industrial mobilization before serious economic problems developed. But the magnitude and emergency nature of the task required an "adequate organizational set-up to which this responsibility may be delegated. It is contemplated that such a *set-up will be manned by qualified civilians chosen by the President.* Appropriate representatives of the military services will advise and assist in the accomplishment of the task involved." [7] The plan then gave suggestions for the internal organization and the responsibilities of a proposed War Resources Administration, together with brief statements about other needed emergency agencies, such as a War Finance Administration, a War Labor Administration, and a Price Control Authority.

There are three features of the Industrial Mobilization Plan which deserve particular notice. First, the plan contemplated a civilian agency to direct industrial mobilization as a whole. The plan specifically declared that in wartime the operation of the various emergency agencies would be undertaken by civilian administrators selected by the President.[8] Second, the Army and Navy would continue to be

---

[4] See Bernard M. Baruch, *American Industry in the War* (New York, Prentice-Hall, Inc., 1941), principally a reprint of the 1921 report of the War Industries Board; *America's Munitions* (Washington, U.S. Government Printing Office, 1919), a report of Benedict Crowell, the Assistant Secretary of War and Director of Munitions.

[5] 41 Statute 764, Sec. 5*a*. Italics are the author's.

[6] *Industrial Mobilization Plan, Revision of 1939*, approved jointly by the acting Secretaries of the War and Navy Departments, Senate Doc. 134, 76th Cong, 2d Sess.

[7] *Ibid.*, p. 4. Italics are the author's.

[8] *Ibid.*, p. 13.

responsible for determining direct military supply requirements and for actually placing orders and expediting the production of war equipment. The plan recognized that in war, the "actual procurement of the munitions needed by the services" should continue to be performed by military officials. In the third place, the role of the War Resources Administration was one of "wartime industrial coordination": it was to adjust military requirements for productive resources with other essential needs. The extent and nature of the measures necessary to this task would be determined by the civilian agency.

Thus there was nothing in the prewar thinking of the War Department which suggested any belief that the Army or the Navy or the ANMB could or should "control the civilian economy." Indeed, in response to the criticism that industrial leaders themselves had played no part in creating the Industrial Mobilization Plan, the War Department in July 1939 set up a Committee of Review, composed of prominent business men, to make suggestions about industrial mobilization.[9] The War Resources Board, established with President Roosevelt's approval on 9 August 1939, criticized the centralization of economic controls in a proposed War Resources Administration and suggested that the seven agencies contemplated by the plan function directly under the President. But the board said nothing to indicate that the Army and Navy should not be responsible for the procurement of end-items of military equipment.

Industrial Preparation for War

From the time that President Roosevelt set up the Advisory Commission to the Council of National Defense (NDAC) on 28 May 1940 until the creation of the War Production Board on 7 January 1942, a number of different agencies and a variety of methods were employed by the federal government to mobilize the industrial resources of the nation.[10] Two general aspects of this development are pertinent here. At first the central civilian agency gave most of its attention to assisting the armed forces in expanding their organization and in improving their procedures for large-scale procurement. This phase had practically been completed at the time of Pearl Harbor. Thereafter, the principal task was to control the use of the nation's productive resources for military output and essential civilian needs. This was increasingly necessary after Pearl Harbor.

When the NDAC began to operate, the procurement bureaus of the War Department were just beginning to recover from twenty years of limited personnel and meager operations. Under the circumstances the Advisory Commission saw as its first task the job of helping the armed forces, both in finding the necessary productive facilities and in letting contracts for the rapidly increasing volume of desired supplies. This assistance was provided mainly through two units, a Purchases Division and a Production Division, as they were identified in the Office of Production Management after January 1941. The Purchases Division helped the Office of The Quartermaster General in the purchase of food stuffs, clothing, and general Army supplies (including trucks). Mr. Douglas C. MacKeachie of this division was instrumental in persuading The Quartermaster General to set up regional market centers for the purchase of produce to be supplied Army posts and air

---

[9] *Ibid.*, pp. 6–7.
[10] *Industrial Mobilization for War*, pp. 17–197 *passim*.

bases. This system was retained throughout the war and proved highly satisfactory.
The Production Division worked closely
with the Office of the Chief of Ordnance
in finding contractors for tanks, guns, and
ammunition. During 1941 when the OPM
took over the Social Security Building for
its work, the Chief of Ordnance moved his
Washington office into the building in
order to work even more closely with
OPM. At this early stage there was little
for a civilian agency to do in "controlling"
the economy since there were great unused
resources in materials, manpower, and
facilities to be absorbed by the defense
effort.

A priorities system on a very simple
basis was begun as early as August 1940.
The Army and Navy agreed on the preferences to be assigned some two hundred
primary items of equipment, and priorities were accordingly assigned by military
procurement offices. While the NDAC
gave its consent to the arrangement, the
operation remained entirely in the hands
of Army and Navy purchasing officials.
Then in October 1940, the President officially created a Priorities Board, and a
further extension of preference ratings to
military procurement items was arranged
in December.[11]

While there were occasional disagreements over priorities between the OPM
and Army and Navy officials, the pattern
begun in 1940 was retained throughout
1941. Army and Navy purchasing officers
assigned preference ratings to their procurement contracts according to a scheme
jointly worked out through the Army and
Navy Munitions Board and approved by
OPM. These preference ratings might be
handed to a first subcontractor by the
prime contractor, and to all subcontractors
for military items placed on a "critical

list." The official history of the War Production Board comments that "the inadequacy of the OPM staff, and its complete
lack of a field organization, were the primary reasons why so much of the priorities
power was thus surrendered to the Armed
Services."[12]

During the second half of 1941 the
Ordnance Department began to take over
from OPM the personnel who had been
helping to find production facilities and to
let contracts. By the time the Army Service
Forces was created this process of absorp-
tion was practically completed. This
change, described as "one of the significant developments of 1941," has been
lamented in the official history of the
WPB. "These transfers marked the end of
any effective civilian influence over the
production or scheduling of direct military
items or components."[13]

In the second half of 1941 there was a
policy conflict within the government over
the curtailment of civilian production of
items consuming large quantities of metals,
such as automobiles and refrigerators. Indeed, the basic issues confronting OPM
just before Pearl Harbor were how far to
curtail civilian production and consumption, how fast to convert from industrial to
war output, and how most effectively to
exercise central control over the distribution of basic metals production. The armed
services contributed to, but certainly did
not dominate, these discussions.

According to the official history of the
War Production Board, three basic developments in military procurement and industrial mobilization had taken place by
the time of Pearl Harbor. First, the armed
forces continued to let contracts for all

[11] *Ibid.*, pp. 61, 64–67.
[12] *Ibid.*, pp. 117–18.
[13] *Ibid.*, p. 119.

end-items of military equipment. Their procurement officers issued preference ratings to their own contractors to help them obtain necessary raw materials and component parts. Second, civilian-managed agencies reporting directly to the President had been created. At first these agencies had worked with the military procurement agencies to improve purchasing operations, but gradually the OPM became more and more of a central control agency, directing the utilization of national productive resources. Third, close relationships between military procurement agencies and the central control agency became increasingly essential. Naturally, Army and Navy officers asked for a voice in formulating economic mobilization policy. But the Office of Production Management had begun to object on the ground that this would give the military too much power over predominantly civilian interests.[14]

On the other hand, civilian leaders never questioned the advisability of having the military direct its own procurement activities. Mr. Bernard Baruch, who headed the War Industries Board in World War I, advised that a civilian agency should never sign Army contracts. Mr. Donald M. Nelson, Baruch's counterpart in World War II, noted: "This advice sank into and anchored itself into my mind, and I never deviated from it."[15]

The Creation of the WPB

A month after Pearl Harbor the President created a new general policy body, the War Production Board. In contrast to its predecessors—the Supply Priorities and Allocation Board (SPAB)[16] and the Office of Production Management[17] which lacked the authority to meet the rising emergency—the new board had wide, though somewhat ill-defined, powers.[18]

In addition to absorbing the authority vested in OPM and SPAB, the War Production Board was to "exercise general direction" over wartime procurement and production. Specifically, this included the power to determine basic policies, plans, procedures, and methods for guiding federal agencies in the matter of purchasing, contracting, specifications, construction, conversion, requisitioning, and plant expansion. The chairman of the WPB would issue whatever directives were necessary; he would report from time to time to the President; and, of course, he would perform any other duties that the President desired. Moreover, federal departments and agencies were to comply with the policies and procedures on war procurement and production as determined by the WPB chairman, as well as to provide him with necessary information. The chairman was to exercise his powers through such officials or agencies as he might determine, and his decisions were to be final. As chairman, President Roosevelt appointed Mr. Donald M. Nelson.

The authority conferred upon the chairman of the War Production Board was broad indeed. But it was also vague. What constituted "general direction" over war procurement? Did the authority "to determine policies, plans, procedures, and methods" of federal departments and agencies purchasing war supplies imply the power to transfer procurement activities from one agency to another—specifically from the Army to the WPB?

---

[14] *Ibid.*

[15] Donald M. Nelson, *Arsenal of Democracy* (New York, Harcourt, Brace and Company, 1946), p. 103.

[16] EO 8875, 28 Aug 41.

[17] EO 8629, 7 Jan 41.

[18] EO 9024, 16 Jan 42.

Mr. Nelson later recorded that at one time he did consider the possibility of transferring all military procurement to the WPB. It was his belief that the President would have approved and supported such a decision on his part. But after thinking the problem through, he "decided against such action in the interest of more rapid production." He added that "if I had the same decision to make over again I would do exactly the same thing." [19] Mr. Nelson gave several reasons for his decision: the time needed to build a new organization, the recollection of Mr. Baruch's advice against a civilian agency signing munitions contracts, the disruption of the military services if procurement officers were all transferred to a civilian agency, the confusion that might result over specifications and inspection responsibilities, and the legal obstacles including appropriation practices. [20]

Whatever Nelson's reasons for not taking this step, one may entertain at least a grave doubt that the authority conferred upon the chairman of the WPB conveyed the power to transfer procurement operations away from the Army and Navy. By long-standing legislation the purchase of military equipment had been vested in various parts of the War and Navy Departments. Under the First War Powers Act of 1941, the President might have transferred this authority to another agency, but he did not actually do so in Executive Order 9024. While the language of the order was very broad, it seems unlikely that the President was delegating to Mr. Nelson his statutory authority to determine needed wartime administrative organization. The understanding which had begun to develop between the procurement offices of the Army and OPM during 1941 suggested a work-

able relationship. The language of the executive order seemed to say only that the WPB was still to be a central agency with general authority over industrial mobilization as a whole, rather than the actual procurement agency for all war supplies.

The Army-WPB Agreement

Nonetheless, the meaning of Executive Order 9024, and Mr. Nelson's intent thereunder, became immediate and vital concerns to the War Department. Before 9 March 1942 the Office of the Under Secretary of War was responsible for War Department relations with the War Production Board. The Army half of the ANMB was a part of the Under Secretary's office. Moreover, General Somervell as G–4 had taken steps in January 1942 to build closer working relations with Mr. Nelson. The informal group working on supply reorganization of the War Department requested Mr. Nelson to assign someone to participate in this activity. Both Mr. A. C. C. Hill, Jr., and Mr. E. A. Locke, Jr., personal assistants to Mr. Nelson, sat with the group in February. Mr. Nelson, it will be recalled, was consulted about the pending reorganization of the War Department, and in fact had expressed the opinion that General Somervell would be a good man to command the new Army Service Forces. [21]

On 12 March 1942, just three days after the ASF came into being, Under Secretary Patterson and Mr. Nelson signed a joint agreement defining the respective functions of the War Department and the WPB in military procurement and indus-

---

[19] D. M. Nelson, *Arsenal of Democracy*, p. 198.
[20] *Ibid.*, pp. 198–200.
[21] See above, p. 36.

trial mobilization. In an account of his wartime experiences, Mr. Nelson reproduces this agreement in full and then comments:

I have never felt any reason to regret the arrangement made that spring with the fighting services, for I am convinced of the soundness of the pattern we set: the Armed Forces undertook to assume full responsibility for all phases of the job which they were best qualified to handle, while the civilian agency became accountable for the maximum use of the Nation's economic resources, doing for the common benefit the tasks which, if left to themselves, the Armed Forces could not possibly have performed.[22]

No one in the Army Service Forces of the War Department at any time would have dissented from any part of this statement by Mr. Nelson.

The impetus for the 1942 agreement came from the same informal group under Mr. Goldthwaite Dorr which worked on internal War Department reorganization. The relations of the procurement agencies of the Army to the War Production Board in 1942 were at a crucial stage. Though the Army had been neither too well prepared nor too aggressive in pushing military procurement before Pearl Harbor, the situation had definitely changed thereafter. Yet it was quite apparent that great confusion surrounded Army-WPB relations after the 16 January executive order. If the collaboration of the two, so vital to the success of the war effort, was to go forward effectively, fear and suspicion had to be allayed. Unless this was done, there was danger that persons within the WPB might charge that the Army was trying to "take over the civilian economy." On the other hand, early in 1942 the Army was definitely worried about the WPB taking over direct military procurement. Whereupon Mr. Dorr, joined by Mr. Robert R.

West and Colonel C. F. Robinson of General Somervell's staff, approached Nelson's assistants, Mr. Hill and Mr. Locke, about setting forth a joint agreement on mutual responsibilities. Nelson's assistants acknowledged the need for such an agreement, and accordingly the 12 March document was worked out.[23]

The 12 March agreement was vitally important.[24] True, it did not prevent subsequent conflict between the ASF and the WPB, but it did indicate General Somervell's belief in the importance of maintaining desirable relationships between the two agencies. During all major disputes that later arose, Under Secretary Patterson, General Somervell, and other ASF representatives came back to this agreement as the "magna charta" defining relationships with the WPB. Their attitude was that all difficulties could be settled by using this agreement as the basic formula.

The agreement of 12 March stated that the War Production Board had certain over-all functions in controlling the resources of the American economy, including the production and distribution of raw materials. Under it the War Department would present its supply requirements to the WPB and would procure end-items of munitions. More specifically, the WPB was charged with making the basic decisions about the allocation of economic resources in accordance with strategic plans; with providing the means—i. e. materials, services, tools, and facilities—needed to

---

[22] D. M. Nelson, *Arsenal of Democracy*, p. 376.

[23] Dorr, Memorandum Notes, p. 64.

[24] Memo, Chm WPB and USW to offs and employees of SOS and Matériel Comd, AAF WD, and WPB, 12 Mar 42, sub: Relationships Between the WPB and the WD, Hq ASF, WPB (3) 1942. (Reproduced in Appendix D.)

carry out the total war effort; and with organizing industry for war production. To carry out these duties most effectively, it would be necessary for the WPB to co-operate with the War Department in the review of supply programs, and, in the light of military necessities, to adjust civilian programs within the limitation of total resources. Besides integrating and adjusting military and civilian requirements, the WPB would supervise the total utilization of the economic resources of the nation; develop sources and production of raw materials as well as services (including transportation, power, and communications); stock-pile raw materials and those end products which were likely to be in short supply at some future date; expedite the production of raw materials, machine tools, and industrial supplies, or any items where the War Department could not do so without conflicting with other agencies; curtail nonessential uses of materials, facilities, services and manpower indispensable to the accomplishment of the munitions program; expand available skilled manpower (through training, transfer, and reduction in man-hours); direct the provision of facilities needed to produce raw materials, equipment, tools and services; determine the plants or industries which should be converted to the production of supplies for the War Department and help the War Department to carry out that conversion; assure the production of necessary facilities auxiliary to the production and distribution of military supplies; organize industrial co-operation with government agencies; maintain a virile civilian economy consistent with war necessity; distribute the available supply of raw materials and industrial equipment with particular reference to the major using agencies; and finally,

make decisions, legal or otherwise, which had to do with priorities, allocations, and requisitions, and placement of orders in existing facilities.

On the other hand, the War Department would continue its traditional interests in supply matters. Through the Army Service Forces and through the newly created Matériel Command of the Army Air Forces the War Department would, in compliance with WPB directives, carry on the research, design, development, programming, purchase, production, storage, distribution, issue, maintenance, and salvage of military equipment. To carry out this mission, the War Department would determine military needs and translate them into a statement of requirements for raw materials, machine tools, and labor; convert available plants and industries to war production (assisted by WPB); negotiate the purchase of military supplies by the placement and administration of contracts; produce, inspect and accept military goods; issue shipping instructions and plan for distribution; construct and expand plants for the production of end-items; expedite production of finished items where there was no conflict with other agencies; conserve raw materials insofar as possible by the elimination of nonessential items and by the simplification and standardization of others. Finally, the WPB and the War Department were to develop close organizational relationships by direct contact between officials in both agencies who were concerned with common problems.

Even before this agreement was made, Under Secretary Patterson had begun to arrange for the transfer of key personnel from the WPB to the Army. One of the phases of military procurement specified in the statement was: "purchase, including the negotiation, placement, and administration of contracts." As previously noted, the predecessor agencies of the War Production Board at first had done much to assist Army procurement bureaus in placing contracts. Mr. Patterson, and then General Somervell, had asked that key WPB personnel performing this work be transferred to the military staff where these individuals could use direct command authority to continue their work. The two most prominent persons transferred shortly thereafter were Mr. D. C. MacKeachie, formerly of the Great Atlantic and Pacific Tea Company, and Mr. Albert J. Browning, formerly president of the United Wall Paper Factories, Inc. Both men were commissioned as colonels and given the responsibility of directing the Purchases Division in ASF headquarters. Though the action was criticized within the WPB and elsewhere as an abdication to the armed forces, Mr. Nelson apparently believed this to be a wise policy.[25]

Trouble Starts

In March 1942 the prospects of friendly and effective co-operation between the WPB and the ASF looked bright indeed. But there were portents of trouble ahead, portents of which leading officials in the ASF, including General Somervell himself, unfortunately were unaware.

According to the official history of the WPB, hostility within that agency toward the Army Service Forces began to brew within a month. In the process of working out the supervision of the seven technical services, which were the procurement agencies of the War Department, General Somervell's office continued to discuss his problems with the WPB. In amalgamating the Supply Division of the War Department General Staff and the Office of the Under Secretary of War, Somervell had created a Resources Division in ASF headquarters.[26] None of the duties assigned this office were any different from those for which the Under Secretary had been responsible since 1920. There were units to supervise machine tools, raw materials, power, product standardization, facilities, and manpower problems within the ASF. The Resources Division was to follow these aspects of procurement operations by the seven technical services, make adjustments among them, and present consolidated requirements to the WPB. There was no implication in this arrangement that the ASF could settle all these problems, but only that the ASF as a unit would deal directly with the WPB on these matters. But the duties of the Resources Division in ASF headquarters were regarded inside the WPB as a "duplication of functions," as threatening to diminish and even to eliminate WPB controls.[27] In the past the WPB and its predecessors had dealt directly with the heads of technical services. Now it was expected to deal primarily with ASF headquarters, rather than with each technical service individually. Key personnel in WPB apparently believed that this development would impede their operations. Mr. Nelson has written that "our relations with the Quartermaster Corps, the Ordnance Department, the Signal Corps, the Medical Corps, and the Corps of Engineers, which were the chief procurement agencies, were always splendid. But above this level we always had trouble." [28]

---

[25] D. M. Nelson, *Arsenal of Democracy*, p. 370.
[26] See below, p. 339.
[27] *Industrial Mobilization for War*, p. 215.
[28] D. M. Nelson, *Arsenal of Democracy*, p. 358.

The reason for this "trouble," according to Mr. Nelson, was a fundamental difference in viewpoint between General Somervell and himself. Nelson believed that Somervell was opposed to making raw materials available for even the most essential civilian needs. Actually Somervell took no such position. The determination of "essential civilian requirements" for wartime production planning and control was so complex that the WPB itself was never able to solve this problem satisfactorily.[29] Because essential civilian production requirements limited military procurement, it was natural that the Army Service Forces should ask about and examine estimates of civilian supply just as WPB officials reviewed and revised military estimates to make them conform to production possibilities. General Somervell and his aides disagreed with the WPB on details and specific figures, but they never took the position that there was no such thing as essential civilian requirements nor did they ever question the fact that the final decision on these requirements rested with Mr. Nelson, and after May 1943, with Justice James F. Byrnes.

The controversy over essential civilian needs raged ceaselessly. On the one hand, the ASF could quote Mr. Julius A. Krug, Nelson's successor as chairman of the War Production Board. His final report to the President at the end of the war pointed out that as great as our war effort was, it never absorbed more than two fifths of our national output. Because of their higher and steadier income, civilians during World War II consumed more than they did in the best prewar years. "Throughout the war," Mr. Krug said, "the people at home were subjected to inconvenience, rather than sacrifice." [30] On the other hand, Mr. Nelson argued that the ASF

was unreasonable on the question of providing essential civilian goods. Asserting that a healthy civilian economy was a prerequisite of maximum war production, he observed that General Somervell objected even to such items as new replacements for farm machinery and for repairs to coal mining equipment. Certainly the WPB was subjected to intense pressure not only from Somervell, but from Secretary of War Stimson, Secretary of the Navy Knox, Under Secretary of War Patterson and other top military officials. Nelson grimly stuck to his guns in defending his position.

Even though there was disagreement over what constituted essential civilian requirements, there was little doubt that as national production reached its maximum, military needs could be met only by cutting allocations to the civilian economy. In order to reconcile civilian and military claims with the nation's economic resources, it was necessary for representatives of the WPB and the armed forces to work closely together. Within a month of his appointment as commanding general of the ASF, Somervell asked his Control Division, working with representatives from Mr. Nelson's office, to explore this problem in organizational terms and to recommend a desirable solution. The result was a study which General Somervell transmitted to Mr. Nelson on 15 May 1942. Because of the cover in which it was bound, this study came to be known as "the black book." [31] In his letter of trans-

---

[29] *Industrial Mobilization for War*, p. 216.

[30] *Wartime Production Achievements and the Reconversion Outlook: Report of the Chairman, War Production Board, October 9, 1945* (Washington, U.S. Government Printing Office, 1945), p. 1.

[31] Somervell to D. M. Nelson, 15 May 42, Hq ASF, WPB.

mittal, General Somervell pointed out that the proposals contained in the study had already been informally discussed with the chairman of the WPB and that they were designed to streamline procedure. The organizational arrangements, he stated, seemed to be inadequate and remedial measures were essential. The proposed changes, he added, could be carried out easily within the existing framework of war organization and without destroying public confidence in the War Production Board.

The study which Somervell forwarded for Mr. Nelson's consideration was entitled *Report on Certain Features of the Organizational Problems Involved in Developing Resources to Meet Strategic Requirements.*[32] The report was predicated on a general proposition which was already being much discussed within the ASF; namely, that the military operations of the war would be greatly influenced, if not dominated, by the limitations of industrial output. For example, the supply of copper was insufficient to meet all requirements. Accordingly, it was essential for strategic decisions to be adjusted in the light of available supplies of raw materials and the resulting military equipment provided from current war production. The principal defect of the present organization for industrial mobilization was, the report declared, an inadequate arrangement for correlating strategy, logistics requirements, and productive resources. The report also pointed out the need for more systematic procedures in the WPB for controlling the distribution of available raw materials. To meet the need, it recommended a system of formal committees to promote closer collaboration between the WPB and the War and Navy Departments. Most important of all, it suggested

new machinery to tie together the Combined Chiefs of Staff, the War Production Board, and the procurement agencies of the armed forces.

The ASF report acknowledged the generally accepted fact that existing procedures for controlling the distribution of raw materials were unsatisfactory. Although the Army point of view on a "satisfactory" method of control was in process of development, it was not presented in the report. The report did propose certain changes in internal WPB organization, on the assumption that control of raw materials production, conservation, and distribution had become the central tasks of the WPB. It suggested that the WPB Requirements Committee, which had been officially created on 20 January 1942 by Mr. Nelson, and which included representatives of the Army and Navy, become the center of WPB decision making on raw materials questions and that subordinate committees for each essential raw material be created, each with Army, Navy, and other appropriate representation.[33] Once more the ASF report contemplated that decisive authority would remain in the WPB; it was simply recommending what it thought was stronger machinery for collaborative relationships.

The ASF report further dealt with a suggested over-all arrangement for the correlation of production and strategy. The period immediately after Pearl Harbor brought a number of efforts to develop close military co-operation between the United States and the United Kingdom. One of these was the creation of a Com-

---

[32] A copy of the report may be found in the files of the Control Division, ASF.

[33] *Ibid.,* pp. 29ff.

bined Raw Materials Board,[34] announced by the President and the Prime Minister on 26 January 1942.[35] On the assumption that the Combined Raw Materials Board might become a major factor in determining the use of American raw materials, the ASF proposed that the board be set up as an agency of the Combined Chiefs of Staff, just as the Munitions Assignments Board was. This would acknowledge that raw material resources and their use in war production were intimately related to military strategy. In addition, the membership of the board should be reconstituted, although the chairman should be a civilian. By proposing that the chairman of this board should be the same person who was chairman of the MAB, the ASF was nominating Mr. Harry Hopkins for the position. It was also suggested that the American membership on the board should be increased to include representatives of the Army, Navy, and Air Forces.

This recommendation was not intended to suggest that military officers would outvote the WPB on the Combined Raw Materials Board. Rather, the civilian chairman was expected to have the same power of decision as that vested in the chairman of the WPB, who while he might seek advice from the military, had final and complete authority. The Army did not want power, it wanted an opportunity formally to know what was happening and to present its case. And it wanted to make sure that American raw materials were used in substantial proportion for American war needs rather than for United Kingdom production.

It should be emphasized once more that the ASF report was for discussion only; that it was transmitted to Mr. Nelson for his "consideration." It was by no means a carefully worked out, detailed organization plan. Moreover, the report had been shown beforehand to persons in Mr. Nelson's office, and none of them advised General Somervell not to transmit the ASF report to Mr. Nelson. Rather, they indicated that the report would be helpful in the internal reorganization of the WPB which was pending and which was eventually announced by Mr. Nelson on 8 July 1942.[36] To make matters worse, General Somervell's trip overseas at this time prevented a personal meeting to iron out difficulties, and the subsequent "leaking" of the story to the press aggravated the situation. By June when General Somervell returned, it was too late. The sparks had been fanned into a flame.

Mr. Nelson's reply to the Somervell letter came as a bombshell.[37] From a later vantage point, to be sure, much of it seems reasonable. But in the atmosphere of the war production crisis of 1942 the letter crystallized a disagreement on fundamentals. In a sense it was an open challenge to the Army Service Forces. Apparently in fear of military encroachment, important figures in the WPB had persuaded Mr.

---

[34] In spite of the fact that the American representative on the board, Mr. William L. Batt, was a high official of WPB, others in the War Production Board feared that the combined agency might duplicate their own work. In May 1942 General Somervell and his advisers made the mistake of believing that this Combined Raw Materials Board might become an important international agency. They did not foresee that the board would play only a minor role throughout the war. See *Industrial Mobilization for War*, pp. 222–24, 628–29. Cf. S. McKee Rosen, *The Combined Boards of the Second World War* (New York, Columbia University Press, 1951), pp. 1–70.

[35] Joint Declaration, Churchill-Roosevelt, 26 Jan 42, ABC 334.8 MAB (1–31–42) Sec. 1.

[36] According to Mr. Dorr, when Somervell's letter transmitting the "black book" reached Mr. Nelson's office, it was not routed to the people who had been informed of its contents, but went instead to other individuals who were already alarmed by what they regarded as ASF encroachment upon the WPB. See Dorr, Memorandum Notes, p. 74.

[37] Ltr, D. M. Nelson to Somervell, 21 May 42, Hq ASF, WPB.

Nelson to fight for his authority. To them it involved the fundamental issue of civilian control over the nation's economy.

The charge that the Army was trying to take over the civilian economy had been made before and was to be repeated over and over in subsequent disputes. The difficulty seems to have been a lack of mutual understanding. Not only Somervell, but Under Secretary Patterson, and even General Marshall himself, expressed their concern over the impact of civilian consumption on Army supply.[38] Shortly before Mr. Nelson's answer to Somervell, the WPB had become involved over a similar issue with the Army and Navy Munitions Board.[39] To many sensitive civilians, raising the question of military interest in economic matters seemed a threat to civilian rights. Statements by a man as forthright as General Somervell, driving relentlessly to achieve the goals of the Army Supply Program, could easily be interpreted as an effort by the military to sit in judgment upon essential civilian requirements. Actually Somervell had no such idea and he believed that Mr. Nelson's remark that "it would be a fundamental mistake to put the apportionment of materials for the essential civilian economy under the military"—was as irrelevant as it was unfounded.

Mr. Nelson in his reply also discussed three other elements of the ASF proposal. He agreed that the existing machinery for controlling the distribution of raw materials was inadequate but held that this was largely because of the loose manner in which Army and Navy procurement officers issued preference ratings, and because of "the failure of the services to present accurate statements of their requirements." For example, on a common nonmilitary item such as typewriters, the Army's originally stated requirement for 1942 was more than double the amount calculated to be adequate for the entire civilian economy in the same year.

Mr. Nelson noted the ASF proposal for reorganization within the War Production Board and observed that the WPB was already studying desirable changes. The ASF suggestions concerning the Requirements Committee and subordinate commodity committees were helpful, Mr. Nelson remarked, and he suggested further conversations on this matter.

To Mr. Nelson the most far-reaching ASF suggestion was the one proposing a new over-all arrangement for co-ordinating strategy and production. He agreed "emphatically" that this was necessary, but declared that the ASF method was "basically in error." The ASF misconceived the nature of the materials problem on two scores. First, the management of raw and basic materials could not be "ripped out of the process of managing production, segregated, and handled separately." The attempt to draw a parallel between the work of the Combined Raw Materials Board which dealt with the "whole vast process of production" and the Munitions Assignments Board, which was merely a scheduling agency, missed the point, Mr. Nelson asserted. Second, it was strategy and production goals of end-items and not strategy and the distribution of raw materials which had to be correlated. Moreover, he argued, the success of the program rested "not with the Chiefs of Staff, but with the chiefs of production. . . . The battle of production is the primary responsibility of the chairman of the WPB in much the

[38] Min, 5th Mtg, CCS, 17 Feb 42, Item 3.

[39] Memo, Roosevelt to D. M. Nelson, 1 May 42, included in Memo, Roosevelt to JCS, 1 May 42, sub: Recommendations . . . for Priority of Production of War Munitions, CCS 400.17 (2–20–42) Sec. 1.

same sense that military battles are the primary responsibility of the military chiefs." The solution to the problem of co-ordination of strategy and production was a continuous and harmonious co-opera-tion between the Combined Chiefs of Staff and the War Production Board.

Mr. Nelson's heated reply to the ASF "black book" opened "a breach which was never closed," to use Nelson's own words.[40] The WPB chairman used the in-cident as the occasion to assert that the WPB could control the economic re-sources of the nation without organiza-tional advice or assistance from the ASF. Instead of simply thanking General Som-ervell for his interest and then overlooking the matter, Mr. Nelson retorted in what appeared at the time to be some heat, re-futing the ASF ideas and putting forth other propositions. The WPB reaction was all the more disconcerting because it was unexpected. The close co-operation be-tween Nelson and Somervell which seemed in prospect in early 1942 had thus evaporated by the end of May.

The Agreement on Field Offices

Yet the ASF and the WPB had to work together, whether they liked it or not. And out of this early attempt at organizing re-lationships to mutual advantage, at least something was salvaged. The 12 March agreement recommended that there be a "continuous survey of working relation-ships between the two agencies." As a first step in this direction, the ASF Control Division embarked upon two so-called field surveys. Colonel Robinson, director of the Control Division, invited leading personnel from WPB to participate in these surveys. On the first survey, five per-sons from the WPB worked closely with

eight persons from the ASF. On the sec-ond, six WPB men collaborated with ten persons from the ASF.

These field surveys made a general study of local Army procurement office operations, relations with contractors, and relations with regional offices of the WPB. The purpose was to obtain information which would be useful in organizing ASF headquarters and in determining which problems most needed attention. For ex-ample, from these surveys came warnings of growing raw materials shortages which were hampering military deliveries, and of prospective manpower stringencies.[41] This WPB–ASF collaboration was cordial and helpful. Out of it came the Office of Organization Planning in the WPB, with the ASF consultant who had directed the field surveys as its head, Dr. Luther Gu-lick. Out of it too, came an agreement on WPB–ASF field relationships. The field surveys called attention to confusion in the relationships between the regional offices of the War Production Board and the local procurement offices of the ASF technical services.

After preliminary discussions between Control Division personnel and field op-erations officials of the WPB, General Somervell sent a letter to Mr. Nelson on 29 June 1942, setting forth the ASF posi-tion on field relations. Finally, on 11 Sep-tember Nelson replied in a fourteen-page letter which was distributed throughout the ASF on 22 September 1942.[42] Nelson began by observing that he believed "a

[40] D. M. Nelson, *Arsenal of Democracy*, p. 359.

[41] See Cincinnati Field Survey, Apr 42; New York Field Survey, Contl Br, SOS, May 42 (mimeo-graphed), CD, ASF.

[42] SOS Cir 67, 22 Sep 42, w/2 incls. Same corresp distributed within WPB as Field Sv Co-ordinating Bull 105, 21 Sep 42, w/Ltr, Somervell to D. M. Nelson, 17 Sep 42.

pattern has been set for continuing under-standing of our respective field organiza-tions." He agreed that the proposals were based upon the 12 March agreement and upon the principle that "functions now be-ing performed satisfactorily by either of our agencies should not be disturbed re-gardless of how logical it may seem to do so from an organizational or jurisdictional standpoint." Then Mr. Nelson reproduced Somervell's letter paragraph by paragraph and added his own comments.

Somervell had noted that, in general, the technical service procurement district offices "need no asistance in the produc-tion expediting and engineering field for end-items." WPB personnel performing useful services of this nature ought to be transferred to appropriate ASF offices and WPB units should then withdraw from this work. Mr. Nelson assented but added that where substantial delays in delivery performance arose, procurement district offices might request WPB regional offices to investigate the reason. He likewise agreed that except where required by the law setting up the Smaller War Plants Corporation, the WPB had no responsi-bility for placing contracts for military equipment. This "routine day-by-day matter" was a function of the procurement district office, although WPB regional or-ganizations might help in locating con-tractors or subcontractors for either a procurement district office or a military prime contractor.

In a long paragraph General Somervell had set forth his concept of how WPB re-gional offices could render "a much needed and useful service, by expediting and increasing the supply of raw materials, semifinished items, and certain compo-nents." They could increase the supply by encouraging additional shifts; by opening closed mines and plants; by urging full utilization of refining or smelting capacity, by locating hidden, frozen or excess inven-tories; and by expediting the production of component parts such as boilers, pumps, and valves which were being produced by the same manufacturer for the armed services and the Maritime Commission. To this Mr. Nelson replied simply that the ASF should look to the WPB for the "de-velopment of programs for the increased production of raw materials, semifinished items, and certain components."

In the next place, General Somervell had expressed his belief that design, speci-fications, and the use of substitutes were "so intimately connected with the prob-lem of the usefulness of finished munitions for the purpose intended" that these must be left to the Army procurement agencies. Mr. Nelson assented. In other paragraphs of his letter, Somervell had noted duplica-tion and lack of uniformity in surveys of both production facilities and machine tools. He proposed that WPB adopt and administer standard systems and make its information available to Army procure-ment offices. Nelson agreed and added that regional WPB offices would collect and provide information and report on unused capacity. The procurement dis-tricts would then be asked to indicate whether any of this capacity could be used.[43]

General Somervell had further asked that the WPB act as a "screen" and a "wailing wall" for manufacturers seeking

[43] SOS Cir 88, 25 Nov 42, officially announced that WPB regional offices would be "solely responsible for all future general facility surveys," and directed pro-curement districts to co-operate with regional offices and to make "the fullest use of this new service." The WPB developed a standard "Plant Facilities Record" for the joint use of the armed services and WPB. (Form WPB–1546, 12 Nov 42.)

war work. It should also provide information about WPB regulations and about procedures in obtaining raw materials. On this point Mr. Nelson commented that the regional offices would be advised to continue valuable work of this sort which they were already performing. He asked that procurement districts notify the proper regional office from sixty to ninety days in advance of the expiration of any contract which would make a plant available for other work. Subsequent paragraphs in Somervell's letter had dealt with WPB's role in working with federal, state, and local agencies on community problems arising out of war production, such as local transportation and housing for workers; and in working with the War Manpower Commission on the use of skilled and semi-skilled labor for war production. Mr. Nelson agreed substantially with them and indicated how much of this work was already being done.

On the problem of regional boundaries Somervell had said only that there appeared to be "no fully satisfactory solution." Nelson referred to the "problem of co-ordinate regional boundaries" as "almost insurmountable," but added that he would have his staff continue to study it in collaboration with the ASF Control Division. The remaining paragraphs were mostly of a general nature. Somervell had expressed the hope that ASF procurement districts might call upon the WPB regional offices for assistance in cases of difficulties. He had also expressed the opinion that appropriate instructions should be issued embodying this agreement. This was done by distribution of the correspondence within the ASF and WPB.

This 11 September 1942 letter of Mr. Nelson was important for two reasons. First, it indicated that WPB officials at the working level could sit down with ASF officers and adjust their differences satisfactorily. Specific issues had been involved in these discussions, and presumably the final result was as satisfactory to the WPB as to the ASF. No "ideological" disputes about civilian-military relationships were permitted to intrude, and no newspaper fanfare accompanied or complicated the discussions.[44] Second, the Somervell-Nelson correspondence of September 1942 reaffirmed understandings first put forth in the 12 March agreement. Obviously the ASF regarded full responsibility for letting contracts for direct military items and for expediting the production of such items as essential to its war supply mission. But there was still a big job for the WPB to do in allocating raw material and other industrial resources among various wartime needs, and in expediting the production of raw materials, component parts, and general supplies.

The ASF never suggested that the WPB was unnecessary or that it could do the WPB job better. Rather, the ASF concept was that the two should work together, complementing each other in the task of supporting the armed forces in their quest for military victory over the Axis.

---

[44] Certainly the WPB had great difficulty in deciding just what its field offices were to do and how their functions were to fit in with Washington operations. See Caroll K. Shaw, Field Organization and Administration of the War Production Board and Predecessor Agencies (mimeographed), Spec Study 25, WPB hist rpt on war adm, released by the Civilian Production Adm.

CHAPTER XIV

The ASF and the WPB: The Control of Raw Materials

It is impossible to examine here all of the working relationships of the Army Service Forces and the War Production Board. They were many and varied. But all ASF thinking and actions were based upon the clear recognition that the military procurement program of World War II could not be accomplished without the work of the WPB.

As already indicated, relationships between the civilian industrial mobilization agency and the military procurement services changed with changing circumstances. Thus the Office of Production Management reviewed all war contracts for more than $500,000 during 1941; in 1942 the figure was raised to $5,000,000, but contract clearance became a mere formality and soon practically disappeared. In 1942 a Plant Site Board was very active in OPM giving final approval to the selection of locations for large-scale new plant construction. By the end of 1942 this work had virtually ceased to have any importance. There was some controversy about whether the Army was trying to build more plants than could be operated with the prospective supply of raw materials. This issue simmered throughout 1942 and was more or less settled by the final determination of 1943 military production requirements.[1]

If output of munitions was the Army's number one supply problem in 1942, the control of the distribution of raw materials was the number one problem of production management. It has already been pointed out that a priorities system had been introduced as early as the autumn of 1940 and had been considerably extended in February 1941. The early priorities system was relatively simple. When letting a contract for ammunition, tanks, guns, radios, or any other military supply item, the procurement district offices of the technical services assigned a "preference" rating to the contract. This rating was then used by the contractor in ordering raw materials and component parts for the end-item he had agreed to make. Suppliers were supposed to be guided by these preference ratings in distributing materials to various industrial users. In addition to the military preference ratings, there were also ratings for essential civilian production. These were granted directly by the OPM and later the WPB, usually on an individual basis.

The local Army procurement offices assigned preference ratings in accordance with a general pattern of priorities approved before March 1942 by the Office of the Under Secretary of War, which also

---

[1] *Industrial Mobilization for War*, pp. 389–95.

endeavored to get agreement from the Navy to follow the same or similar scheme of preferences. The Army would then not assign higher or lower ratings to tents, or clothing, or medical equipment than the Navy, or vice versa. The organizational device for negotiating these agreements was the ANMB. This board was composed of two persons, the Under Secretary of War and the Under Secretary of the Navy. In December 1941 Mr. Patterson and Mr. James V. Forrestal persuaded Mr. Ferdinand Eberstadt, a New York financier, to join them as chairman of the board.[2]

A priorities system for guiding the distribution of raw materials and component parts worked satisfactorily as long as the supply exceeded demand. When demand began to catch up with and outstrip supply, the establishment of priorities alone was inadequate. As early as February 1941, OPM began to experiment with a new process of allocating aluminum deliveries. This was the first, and for a long time the only, metal whose military and other essential demand outran supply. Gradually however, in 1941, civilian demands for raw materials and industrial supplies expanded as the entire economy operated at increased levels of output. As long as priorities insured adequate deliveries to military contractors, the War Department was not directly concerned about this situation. It recognized that the problem of insuring essential civilian production belonged to the OPM, not to the War or Navy Departments.

Shortly after Pearl Harbor, however, it became evident that the priorities system was collapsing. As large new sums of money were appropriated for military supplies, Army and Navy procurement officers raced one another in letting new contracts. On each they assigned the pre-vailing preference rating for the item or items involved. In a short time, contractors found that preference ratings were simply licenses to hunt raw materials; they were no guarantee of delivery. The whole system was being used for a purpose it had never been designed to serve and it broke down badly.

Because manufacturers failed to get materials with the preference ratings that had been assigned to them, procurement officers began to upgrade ratings. As a result, the differentiation in ratings upon which the Army and Navy had agreed and which the OPM had approved in 1941 gradually became meaningless. Within the preference rating A–1 there were subdivisions ranking from A–1–a to A–1–j. Supposedly, in the name of the ANMB, the officers supervising procurement operations in the Army and Navy Departments had agreed upon types of equipment for each rating and even upon quantitative limitations. But these agreements meant nothing in the face of existing supply demands and in the absence of any means for enforcement. A procurement officer under pressure to get delivery of machine guns, for example, increased the preference rating to help the manufacturer. By early 1942, more than 55 percent of the war production program was rated A–1–a by procurement officers.[3] There was another serious defect in the system. With military preference ratings clogging the industrial system, few if any supplies of raw materials were available for essential civilian production such as transportation, and other public utilities,

---

[2] For more details about the ANMB, see below, p. 290.

[3] Memo, ANMB for CCS (American Sec.), 26 Feb 42, sub: Resume of Priorities Situation and Request for Revised Directive, JB 355 Ser. 745, CCS 400.17 (2-20-42) Sec. 1.

and industrial maintenance requirements.

The first reaction of OPM was to set up an allocation system for crucial materials like steel, aluminum, and copper. Processors and fabricators of these materials were required monthly or quarterly to submit a record of their orders on hand, with preference ratings, to the appropriate industry division of WPB (steel, aluminum, and copper). In consultation with Army and Navy officers, the WPB industry division then undertook to tell the processors and fabricators what were the most urgent orders they should fill in the next month or quarter. This was called allocation. But this process was not satisfactory to either the WPB or the armed services since it was not easy to trace orders for raw materials up to end-items of war output. In addition, there was no way of knowing when the contractor with a high priority proposed to use the ordered material in production.

It will be recalled that in his letter of 15 May to Mr. Nelson, General Somervell had spoken of "inadequate control over the supply of critical materials," and the report he had transmitted had mentioned various weaknesses in the existing practices.[4] But Somervell had not proposed a specific means of improving materials controls. These were already being discussed by the representatives of the two agencies. Two issues were involved. One had to do with a revision in the preference rating, or priorities, system. The other had to do with the introduction of a whole new system for controlling the distribution of materials.

Revision of the Priorities System

As early as 21 February 1942 the Army and Navy Munitions Board, which theoretically at least was charged with assigning military priorities, requested the Joint Chiefs of Staff to issue a revised priorities directive.[5] Other agencies also pressed for a change. In the meantime the military procurement officers continued to meet the problem by reshuffling priorities. For example, on 11 March 1942, General Somervell asked for assignment of priorities within the ASF, seeking first priority for about half the Army Supply Program.[6] Meanwhile various committees of the Joint Chiefs of Staff[7] studied the relative urgency of military procurement programs; their suggested amendments were presented to the JCS early in April 1942.[8] The Joint Chiefs accepted these recommendations and submitted them to President Roosevelt.[9]

The President concurred, particularly approving the emphasis given to three classes of equipment: aircraft and related items, shipping, and equipment for a decisive land and air offensive. The President directed the JCS to ask the ANMB to establish priorities within the services,[10] and wrote Donald Nelson a letter in which he enclosed his memorandum to the military chiefs. The President expressed his assurance that the WPB would assist the ANMB in this revision and would approve

---

[4] See above, p. 194.

[5] Memo, ANMB for CCS (American Sec.), 21 Feb 42, sub: Resume of Priorities Situation and Request for Revised Dir, CCS 400.17 (2-20-42) Sec. 1.

[6] Memo, Secy JB for JPC, 26 Mar 42, sub: Priorities for Equip, w/incl, CCS 400.17 (2-20-42) Sec. 1.

[7] JPS 20 (2d draft), 31 Mar 42, sub: Priorities in Production of Munitions Based on Strategic Considerations, CCS 400.17 (2-20-42) Sec. 1.

[8] Min, 10th Mtg, JPS, 4 Apr 42, Item 3, CCS 400.17 (2-20-42).

[9] Memo, JCS to President, 10 Apr 42, CCS 400.17 (2-20-42) Sec. 1.

[10] Memo, President for JCS, 1 May 42, sub: Recommendations to JCS for Priority of Production of War Munitions, CCS 400.17 (2-20-42) Sec. 1.

the necessary changes without delay.[11] On 6 May the Joint Chiefs forwarded their approved proposal to the ANMB and requested the board to prepare new priorities which would insure production of the most urgent Army and Navy needs during the balance of 1942.[12]

Mr. Eberstadt, chairman of the ANMB, had been pressing for this kind of action since January 1942. In addition, he wished to reform the priorities system by adopting new, simplified designations, and by limiting the quantities of end-items for which these ratings would be used to obtain raw materials. The Army and Navy Munitions Board submitted a proposed priorities directive to Mr. Nelson on 20 May. It recommended five new preference ratings. These were AA–1 to AA–4, with an emergency classification of AAA. Second, it proposed that the quantities of end-items of military equipment to be assigned these priority ratings should be definitely limited. For example, the AA–1 preference ratings were to be issued for 60,000 war planes, the Presidential objective, together with critical and essential items of the Army Supply Program necessary to equip these planes. For the Army, the AA–1 rating was to be used for 50 percent of the major items in the revised Presidential objective for the Ground Forces in 1942. This meant 50 percent, for example, of some 25,000 tanks, 10,000 pieces of heavy artillery, 25,000 antitank weapons, and 9,000 armored cars. Also the top rating was to be used for 50 percent of the Maritime Commission's ship construction program of nine million dead-weight tons, and for naval vessels which could be commissioned by 1 March 1943. The AA–2 rating was to be assigned to the remaining items of the 1942 procurement program as approved by the President and to naval

vessels which could be commissioned between 1 April and 31 December 1943. The AA–3 category was to be used for aircraft equipment needed in 1942 to meet the 1943 objectives and to the Army Supply Program on the same basis.[13] The ANMB memorandum made no estimate of the raw material requirements needed to fulfill the program. It did recommend that no priorities be granted for civilian supplies which would compete with the military program, unless the ANMB concurred.

The War Production Board received the proposal with considerable hostility. As with other suggestions of a similar nature, some WPB officials interpreted this as a move by the military to take over control of the economy. On more technical grounds, they also feared that the new priority system would interfere with the Production Requirements Plan which was based on the spread of the old priorities ratings. Because of these factors the WPB delayed approval.[14] On 30 May 1942 Mr. Eberstadt reported to the Under Secretaries of War and the Navy about a meeting which had been held that day in Mr. Nelson's office. The Statistical Division of WPB had made some preliminary calculations about dollar amounts of production required by the proposal and also about raw material requirements. In general, the raw material requirements for the program were within available supplies except possibly for aluminum. Mr.

---

[11] Memo, President for D. M. Nelson, 1 May 42, CCS 400.17 (2-20-42) Sec. 1.

[12] Memo, JCS for ANMB, 6 May 42, sub: Priorities in Production of Munitions Based on Strategic Considerations, CCS 400.17 (2-20-42) Sec. 1.

[13] Memo, ANMB for Chm WPB, 20 May 42, Hq ASF, WPB.

[14] Min, 39th Mtg, Planning Com, WPB, 9 Jun 42, p. 62.

Eberstadt agreed that some effort should be made to set up preference ratings for essential civilian supplies and certain foreign raw material commitments which were not included within the proposal.[15]

Mr. Nelson was inclined to accept the new priorities system over the objections of his staff. After all, the proposed procedure had the tremendous advantage of setting quantitative limits by time periods in the assignment of preference ratings to essential needs. Some of the unbalanced production of the past might thereby be avoided. The new system also provided for a workable relationship between the War Production Board and the Army Service Forces. The WPB would approve the over-all arrangement, and military procurement offices would assign specific ratings to individual contractors within the limits of this approval. The WPB would then police the assignment of ratings. Mr. Nelson discussed the proposed directive with the President and secured his approval of the recommendation that essential civilian needs should get higher priorities.[16] Then on 9 June, Nelson accepted the new priorities directive with certain modifications which added additional merchant shipping and some 1942 production for 1943 end-items. The Joint Chiefs of Staff accepted the modifications on 12 June.[17]

Although the directive was approved, the controversy over the magnitude of civilian production continued unabated. The provision that the War Production Board had to obtain the concurrence of the ANMB for preference ratings for civilian programs was obnoxious to the WPB. Mr. Nelson told his assistants that the maintenance of the civilian economy was their responsibility. They were to consult the ANMB, but if they failed to get

concurrence they were to assign the rating regardless. The ANMB could then take its appeals to him.[18]

Early in July the Under Secretaries of the War and Navy Departments, and Chairman Eberstadt protested that the production goals set forth in the directive would be hampered by failing to allocate raw materials to programs in the stated order of preference. Accordingly, they urged that no additional ratings within the primary categories should be issued without the concurrence of the Army and Navy Munitions Board. The memorandum recognized that "maintenance of a sound economic basis for continuance of the war effort necessitated provision for certain essential services and materials within the framework of the priorities directive." It argued that such essential requirements, however, should not be provided at the expense of the munitions requirements included in the AA–1 and AA–2 categories. The ANMB members asked assurance that no items other than end-items of munitions would be included in AA–1 or put ahead of the AA–3 and AA–4 items without Army and Navy approval "excepting only such as may be specifically directed by you."[19] The ANMB also appealed to the JCS, claiming that Mr. Nelson's action would prejudice the "principle and intent" of the

[15] Memo, ANMB for USW and USN, 30 May 42, sub: ANMB Priorities Dir, Hq ASF, WPB.

[16] Min, 39th Mtg, WPB, 9 Jun 42, p. 62.

[17] ANMB, 12 Jun 42, sub: Priorities in Production of Munitions Based on Strategic Considerations, CCS 400.17 (2-20-42) Sec. 1.

[18] Memo, D. M. Nelson to Batt, J. S. Knowlson, Henderson, Weiner and Matthiessen, 19 Jun 42, sub: Effect of Rerated Military Program on Work of the WPB, CCS 400.17 (2-20-42) Sec. 1.

[19] Memo, ANMB for Chm WPB, 5 Jul 42, sub: Priorities and Allocations, Hq ASF, WPB.

President's directive.[20] At the same time, the Under Secretaries also tried to impress their point of view directly upon members of the War Production Board. In September 1942 the ANMB informed the JCS that the conflict over concurrences had been adjusted. Thereupon the JCS dropped the issue from its agenda, and the WPB added a new preference rating— AA–2X for urgent domestic and foreign nonmilitary items.[21] Eventually, still higher priorities were given to various nonmilitary needs, including use of the AA–1 rating. General Somervell and leading members of his staff often challenged the magnitude of essential civilian requirements as recommended by WPB committees, but there is no indication that they ever took the position that civilian requirements finally determined to be essential should not have a high rating.

The revised priorities directive covered only vital war production for the last six months of 1942. Subsequently, the same type of arrangement was continued for 1943 and 1944 production. The WPB charged that the ASF and other military procurement agencies failed to observe strictly the quantitative limits in assigning preference ratings. The difficulty seemed to grow out of a desire for flexibility in setting anticipated military production requirements, as well as from the complexity of calculating needs in precise detail. Mr. Nelson, dissatisfied with the way the services were handling their priorities function and perhaps goaded by charges within his own agency of "surrender" to the military, informed the Under Secretaries of War and the Navy on 22 August 1942 that the WPB would "immediately undertake supervision over functions now exercised by contracting and procurement officers of the Armed Services with relation to the issuance of priority orders and certifi-

cates." [22] He asserted that a control system "which must often restrict parts of the program for the benefit of the whole," could not be supervised effectively through field officers "whose primary function is expediting the particular parts of the program entrusted to them." Therefore, he requested the co-operation of the Army and Navy in assigning military personnel to the WPB district offices "to advise" on the issuance of preference ratings. The district offices (under the regional offices) would receive proposed priority orders and certificates prepared and forwarded by military procurement officers. The WPB would actually issue rating and certificate. Nelson promised this would be done within twenty-four hours. He ended by saying that he had issued orders to put the new arrangement into effect on 7 September.

The announcement of this basic change without prior consultation, coupled with the fear in military circles that the WPB desired to take over Army procurement, threatened to produce a direct clash. Fortunately, this was avoided in part by the action of Mr. Eberstadt, who immediately began negotiations with WPB officials. Then on 27 August 1942 the armed services assured Nelson of their desire to co-operate "in every way" in realizing his objective, but countered with a suggested modification.[23] Their representatives commented that they were certain Mr. Nelson

---

[20] Memo, ANMB for JCS, 19 Jul 42, sub: WPB–ANMB Conflict with respect to Concurrences, CCS 400.17 (2-20-42) Sec. 1.

[21] Memo, ANMB for JCS, 23 Sep 42, sub: WPB–ANMB Conflict with respect to Concurrences, CCS 400.17 (2-20-42) Sec. 1; *Industrial Mobilization for War*, pp. 298–301.

[22] Ltr, D. M. Nelson to Patterson, Forrestal, and Eberstadt, 22 Aug 42, Hq ASF, WPB.

[23] Ltr, Patterson, Vice Adm Samuel M. Robinson, and Eberstadt to D. M. Nelson, 27 Aug 42, Hq ASF, WPB.

realized the importance of effecting a major change in priority procedure with a minimum of disturbance to production. The limited time available to prepare for "so radical a change" worried them. Accordingly, the services proposed that the WPB should assign its own personnel to Army and Navy procurement offices to approve their issuance of preference ratings. Nelson accepted the counterproposal. The Army and Navy were satisfied with this because it preserved, untouched, their direct relationship with contractors, and the new method of supervising military issuance of preference ratings became effective 10 September 1942. It remained in effect throughout most of the war. The arrangement not only solved the priority issue but worked well, and even provided a mutual protection to the Army and Navy against the other's failing to carry out priorities agreements.

Allocating Raw Materials

The problem of directing the distribution of raw materials was still unresolved. Although the relative importance of military items was now indicated, this alone was not sufficient to insure that raw materials would go primarily to essential production. One group within the Office of Production Management had developed a scheme whereby certain industries might voluntarily submit estimates of their raw materials demands for desired production programs. At first this Production Requirements Plan was used almost exclusively by industries producing nonmilitary items. From the point of view of the industry, the arrangement was advantageous because it presented requirements for a number of different metals needed to meet production schedules. OPM liked the arrangement because it not only re-

lated raw material needs to production plans but also revealed inventories on hand.

As dissatisfaction with existing methods of allocating raw materials grew, both within the War Production Board and the armed services, WPB began to consider the possibility of applying the PRP to all American industry. On 4 March 1942 the director of industry operations in WPB formally proposed to Mr. Nelson that PRP become a mandatory system, covering an estimated 18,000 of the largest consumers of raw materials who accounted for over 90 percent of the basic materials fabricated in the country.[24] The plan would become general on 1 July 1942.

The story of PRP has been adequately told elsewhere,[25] but the reaction of the armed services to it is pertinent here. On 13 May Mr. Nelson informed Under Secretaries Patterson and Forrestal and Chairman Eberstadt that the WPB had decided to apply the Production Requirements Plan to all American manufacturers, including those who produced end-items of munitions. The members of the ANMB replied on 20 May that they were concerned about the possible consequence of such "precipitate adoption" of PRP and expressed the hope that "no such action will be taken without further and more thorough consideration of this matter." They pointed out that there was still no agreement on a plan for the most effective distribution of available raw materials. Patterson, Forrestal, and Eberstadt recommended that a committee be appointed whose members would be relieved of all duties save that of attempting to find

---

[24] *Industrial Mobilization for War*, p. 459.
[25] *Ibid.*, pp. 457–74. See also David Novick, Melvin L. Anshen, and William C. Truppner, *Wartime Production Controls* (New York, Columbia University Press, 1949).

a satisfactory solution to the materials distribution problem.[26]

Mr. Nelson had already created a WPB committee to consider raw materials controls. There was no direct military representation on this committee and Nelson was not disposed to change its composition. In the meantime Army and Navy personnel continued their exploration of the mechanics of the proposed plan. On 28 May Mr. Eberstadt submitted to Patterson and Forrestal a memorandum setting forth his views about PRP, views, he said, which were shared by the principal Army and Navy representatives working with him. He admitted that PRP would produce substantial additional information about production requirements for raw materials as well as much needed data on inventory positions, but he held that it would provide only general information about the ultimate destination of raw materials. While recognizing that there would be some advantages from the system, Mr. Eberstadt expressed the strong opinion that the administration of PRP would be an impossible task. Also he insisted that the contemplated allocations process would still not insure distribution of raw materials to the desired military end-items of production. In conclusion he suggested that the effective date of the plan be postponed and that further efforts be made to find an acceptable modification or substitute. Under Secretaries Patterson and Forrestal forwarded Eberstadt's memorandum to Nelson with the laconic notation: "We concur." [27]

In spite of these protests the WPB announced on 30 May that PRP would be introduced on a compulsory basis. On 8 June 1942 Mr. Eberstadt assured Mr. J. S. Knowlson, WPB director of industry operations, that under the circumstances the Army and Navy would do their best to see that "no harm resulted" from the introduction of PRP.[28] During the next month Army and Navy officers worked closely with WPB officials in an attempt to make the plan effective. But PRP failed. Though it was clearly evident that the Army and Navy were opposed to the arrangement, no charge was made within the WPB that the hostility of the Army and the Navy was a major factor in bringing about its collapse. There may indeed have been some justice in Mr. Knowlson's view that PRP "apparently failed" more because the problem of total military procurement requirements had not been solved than because of inherent defects. The PRP might have been more successful also if there had been more time to put it into operation, and if there had been more thorough administrative preparation. Whatever the actual reason for the failure, military authorities had forecast these difficulties rightly enough.

Army and Navy representatives continued to urge a different procedure. On 1 June 1942 Mr. Eberstadt created an Allocations Steering Committee with personnel drawn out of the ASF, the Navy, the AAF, and the Maritime Commission. Members of this committee were directed to work with WPB personnel in exploring further the problems of materials control. As early as 8 May 1942 Mr. Eberstadt, with a representative from the ASF and one from the Navy Office of Procurement and Material, had explained a so-called warrant plan to a WPB committee. This

---

[26] Ltr, Patterson, Forrestal, and Eberstadt to D. M. Nelson, 20 May 42, Hq ASF, ANMB.

[27] Memo, Patterson and Forrestal for Chm WPB, 28 May 42, sub: PRP, Hq ASF, WPB.

[28] Memo, Eberstadt for USW and USN, 8 Jun 42, sub: Discussion with Knowlson—Revised Priorities Dir and PRP, CG ASF.

plan was further elaborated in other papers which were presented to the War Production Board. For the moment there was no immediate disposition within the WPB to accept the War Department proposal. The failure of PRP, amid general industrial criticism, brought the warrant plan once more to the fore. Large automobile corporations like General Motors, as well as the steel industry, favored an arrangement similar to that urged by the Army and the Navy. Mr. Ernest Kanzler, who became WPB Director General of Operations early in September 1942, was further inclined toward the warrant system. Mr. Eberstadt and Mr. Kanzler together made substantial progress in preparing a new system for controlling materials. Then on 20 September 1942 Nelson announced the appointment of Mr. Eberstadt as a vice-chairman of the WPB in charge of program determination. At the same time, Nelson gave Eberstadt unofficial assurance that he would be free to introduce a new system of materials control.

With Mr. Eberstadt's appointment, an extensive internal reorganization of the WPB was begun, and detailed planning was started on a new system for controlling materials. On 2 November the WPB publicly announced the adoption of a Controlled Materials Plan (CMP), to become fully effective on 1 July 1943 and applying primarily to the allocation of steel, copper, and aluminum.[29] There was a basic difference between the Production Requirements Plan and the Controlled Materials Plan which it is essential to observe. The two systems were sometimes contrasted as "horizontal" as against "vertical" allocation of raw materials. These terms in themselves do not convey a full understanding of Army dissatisfaction with the first and preference for the second. Under a system of horizontal allocation, as in PRP, every important manufacturing concern in the United States was expected individually to indicate its production schedules by quarter, its corresponding needs for major shapes and forms of basic metals, and its raw material inventories. The War Production Board would then receive all of these estimates, consolidate them, compare raw material needs with supplies, and inform each individual company of the quantities of materials which it might obtain in a succeeding quarter. Under the vertical allocation scheme, as in CMP, raw material requirements were presented to the WPB, not by individual industries, but by so-called major claimants. These were the ASF, the Navy, the AAF, the Maritime Commission, and the civilian economy. The WPB was responsible through its industry divisions for determining essential civilian production requirements. The War Production Board then adjusted demands to supply, and informed claimant agencies of the total quantity of various metals which each might consume in a given quarter of a year. The claimant agencies in turn apportioned their allocations to various industries which placed their orders accordingly with raw material suppliers.[30]

Interestingly enough, in one respect the horizontal and vertical systems of allocations had a common meeting ground. There were certain kinds of industrial

---

[29] For a history of the CMP, see *Industrial Mobilization for War*, pp. 485–501; also, Min, WPB, 27 Oct 42, p. 147.

[30] Min, 54th Mtg, Planning Com, WPB, 3 Sep 42, pp. 88–89; Planning Com Recommendation 17 for D. M. Nelson, 5 Sep 42, sub: Contl of the Flow of Materials, WPB Doc Pub 5, Appen. X, p. 158. The WPB, as well as the Army, had come to prefer the vertical CMP system.

products which might be used as component parts or subassemblies of many different items. These products were sometimes called off-the-shelf items, or general industrial supplies. Under the PRP horizontal allocation system, the manufacturers would obtain raw material rights directly for such products. Under the CMP vertical allocation, the manufacturer of general industrial supplies would have to depend upon an eventual "trickling down" of many separate allotments of raw materials from every end-product manufacturer who needed his parts. The Controlled Materials Plan recognized this absurdity in vertical allocation and set up a special category of Class B products. These included such items as bearings, batteries, nuts and screws, steam condensers, containers, electric generators, electric motors, mining machinery, plumbing supplies, pumps, spark plugs, valves, and transformers. Under CMP, manufacturers of Class B products received direct allotments of raw materials from the War Production Board.

The essential difference between horizontal allocation and vertical allocation was this. Under horizontal allocation, the WPB received individual applications for raw materials from 18,000 or more separate industrial establishments. This imposed a terrific operating burden upon a central agency. The WPB could sarcely have acted as a top control agency concerned with broad issues of production balance. It would have been submerged under literally thousands of operating details. Vertical allocation, on the other hand, worked differently. The WPB received its estimates of need from relatively few agencies, and each of these in turn proceeded through successive organizational levels to divide up the job of deter-

mining raw material requirements and controlling the distribution of raw materials. Vertical allocation also preserved intact an intimate association between a military procurement office and its prime contractor. No third party with any authority to give separate instructions intervened in this relationship. Horizontal allocation meant that the military procurement office might let a contract and agree with the contractor upon delivery schedules, but the contractor then had to go to another government agency in order to obtain the raw materials needed to fulfill his contract. Under it, the possibility that the contractor would receive conflicting instructions was real. No one in the Army Service Forces ever maintained that the Army should have an unlimited amount of raw materials. What the ASF did say was: "Tell us how much steel, and copper, and aluminum we may have, and we will then divide it in balanced proportions among our supply programs and inform our contractors what they can have and what they should plan to produce." The ASF was satisfied when a method for controlling the distribution of raw materials had been devised which preserved this fundamental relationship between procurement office and contractor.

On 8 July 1942 Mr. Nelson announced a "realignment" of internal WPB organization which, among other things, was to clear "the decks to make controlling and expediting the flow of materials the board's central effort." [31] All industry divisions were brought under single direction within the WPB. But the ASF request for formal recognition of a working relationship with these industry divisions was rejected. On 10 November 1942, after Mr. Eberstadt

---

[31] WPB press release (WPB–1494), 8 Jul 42, National Archives, WPB papers.

had become a WPB vice-chairman, Mr. Nelson approved organizational changes which did two principal things. The Director General for Operations in charge of industry divisions was put under the Program Vice-Chairman (Mr. Eberstadt), and each industry division was directed to form a division requirements committee on which there was to be an Army and a Navy representative along with representatives of other agencies such as the Maritime Commission and the Board of Economic Warfare.[32] This officially recognized an existing situation, for Army and Navy personnel, in the name of the ANMB, had been physically located in WPB offices for a long time. The job of these Army officers, who were a part of the Production Division in ASF headquarters, was to keep in touch with the production situation in various industries and to inform the industry divisions of ASF military requirements. The Army representatives helped the WPB in fixing production policies, and the WPB in turn helped the ASF greatly in improving its requirements data and in following industrial conditions. At this working level, ASF–WPB relations were cordial and co-operative throughout the war.

The November WPB reorganization realized two major ends which General Somervell had in mind when he gave his "black book" to Mr. Nelson for consideration on 15 May. The internal organization of WPB was now fully oriented to make the distribution of raw materials its major task, and ASF participation had been officially recognized at various working levels within WPB.

By the end of 1942 there was every indication that economic mobilization for vital military needs would go forward unimpeded. But such was not to be the case.

The Army-WPB controversy flared up anew with a bitterness more intense than ever when on 16 February 1943 Mr. Eberstadt was summarily dismissed from the WPB by Mr. Nelson. This, in the words of columnist David Lawrence, was a "solar plexus blow to the Army and Navy." [33] The story is told in Mr. Nelson's memoirs and in the official WPB history.[34] Nelson says that he learned suddenly one night that the Army was determined to have him fired the next day. He does not identify his personal antagonist or antagonists in the War Department. He notes that Secretary Stimson recommended this action to the President, but acknowledges that the Secretary of War had to take responsibility for such recommendation, regardless of who may have instigated it. The WPB history more carefully reports that an internal WPB jurisdictional conflict between Eberstadt and Mr. Charles E. Wilson had reached the point where James F. Byrnes, then director of the Office of Economic Stabilization, joined by the Secretaries of War and the Navy, recommended Mr. Nelson's removal to President Roosevelt. Mr. Baruch was to be appointed in Nelson's place.[35]

General Somervell was at the Casablanca Conference in January 1943 and had no direct part in this effort to replace Nelson with Baruch. But months earlier in the midst of another dispute, when he had charged Nelson with trying to take away Army and Navy control over war material, Somervell had suggested to President Roosevelt's chief of staff, Admiral William D. Leahy, that Nelson

---

[32] WPB Gen Adm O 2–65, 11 Nov 42.
[33] The Evening Star (Washington) February 17, 1943.
[34] D. M. Nelson, Arsenal of Democracy, pp. 388–89; Industrial Mobilization for War, pp. 580–82.
[35] Industrial Mobilization for War, p. 581.

should be replaced by Bernard Baruch.[36]

In any event, Nelson dismissed Mr. Eberstadt and so preserved his position for the time being. Mr. Wilson then emerged as the active head of WPB. He immediately informed General Clay, Somervell's procurement deputy, and later General Somervell, that he contemplated no change in the Controlled Materials Plan or in existing ASF–WPB relationships. This was adequate reassurance, and there was no reason for Somervell to concern himself further with the matter. ASF officials found Mr. Wilson increasingly satisfactory to work with; relationships were cordial and effective.

During 1942 there were vigorous discussions between Army and WPB officials about desirable procedure for the control of raw materials. Once the Controlled Materials Plan had been devised and accepted, previous disagreements subsided. CMP continued to give the WPB effective control over the supply and distribution of raw materials. This was as the ASF wished. General Somervell had never quarreled with WPB authority but constantly urged effective action. Throughout 1943, 1944, and 1945, there were no more serious disagreements about raw material procedures. A satisfactory working arrangement had finally been found.

---

[36] William D. Leahy, *I Was There* (New York, Whittlesey House, 1950), p. 130.

CHAPTER XV

The ASF and the WPB: The Control of Production

From the very beginning of the defense effort in the summer of 1940, the Army and the Navy were asked time and again to lay out in advance a fairly detailed program of production goals for military equipment and supplies. This was attempted with varying results insofar as degree of detail was concerned. Comprehensive procurement planning involved two major difficulties for the Army's supply arms and services. In the first place, there were no well-developed procedures or basic data for translating general military plans into specific quantities of weapons. In the second place, strategic plans, together with lend-lease needs, were constantly changing so that production goals determined at any one time were inadequate a month or two later.

In 1941 the Office of Production Management, with President Roosevelt's approval, began to develop tentative programs listing specific defense requirements. In the process it increased its pressure on the armed forces to prepare better information on production goals by time periods. It also urged the services to set higher goals so that all possible contingencies might be covered. Immediately after the 1942 fiscal year appropriations for the War Department had been passed on 30 June 1941, the President gave instructions for the OPM and the War Department to prepare a requirements program calculated to defeat the enemy in case the United States was attacked. On the basis of a Joint Board (Army-Navy) estimate of military objectives, the War Department revised its manpower program, and this in turn increased the requirements for various kinds of equipment. The War Department General Staff also enlarged the contemplated reserve of critical weapons, especially tanks and guns. This program was known as the Victory Program.[1]

When General Somervell took office as assistant chief of staff, G–4, WDGS, he immediately became interested in improving Army procurement planning. The goal was an Army Supply Program which would set forth desired quantities for some 1,000 major items; requirements for such classes of supplies as food stuffs would be estimated in dollar volume. No such Army supply program existed before he took over as G–4 in December 1941, although preparatory steps had been taken. The first section of the Army Supply Program setting forth procurement goals for ground equipment for the calendar years 1942,

---

[1] See History of the Determination of Supply Requirements, prepared by the Requirements Div, ASF, OCMH.

1943, and the first six months of 1944, appeared in April 1942, just a month after the ASF was created. In July 1942 the Army Supply Program became the official authorization enabling the technical services of the ASF to purchase the quantities of items set forth in the program. In addition, the Army Supply Program became a primary document in determining the budget needs of the Army.[2]

On Christmas Eve, 1941, Mr. Stacy May of the WPB urged General Somervell to raise Army requirements. Two months later, in February 1942, when a tentative supply program was calculated, the Supply Division of the War Department General Staff recognized that the quantities desired were too large for reasonable expectation. It had tentatively projected production goals totaling sixty-three billion dollars for ground equipment through the end of 1943. When the estimates for the Army Supply Program were completed in April 1942, the goal was reduced to about forty-three billion dollars. Another revision in May brought the procurement objective in ground equipment through December 1943 down to thirty-eight billion dollars.[3]

While Mr. Eberstadt was proposing a revised priorities directive, Mr. Stacy May as chief statistician of the WPB suggested that the procurement goals of the armed forces had become too large—in fact, larger than could be produced by the American economy. Whether true or not, the argument was not fully explored at the time. During the summer the planning committee of the War Production Board gave particular attention to the problem of the "feasibility" of military production goals. Instead of pushing the Army to adopt requirements large enough to provide a cushion for any contingency, as

May had done in December 1941, the prime consideration of the WPB had now become the limiting of the ASF to "feasible" requirements. This concept of "feasibility" was a new approach to production goals. It ran contrary to the widely accepted notion of setting high goals as incentives—"something to shoot for." Under prewar conditions of ample raw materials, manpower, and plant facilities, a doctrine of "feasibility" would have been unthinkable. Many practical men both in and out of the Army believed that even under war conditions "feasibility" was simply a high sounding theory.

The proponents of the "feasibility" concept argued that overambitious procurement programs would result in great waste. For example, if a manufacturer was able almost to finish 100,000 trucks but could not get tires, carburetors, or other components, because higher-priority aircraft producers had obtained all these items, the almost finished but still useless trucks would be a wasteful drain on our economic resources. In the same way, industrial facilities might be constructed, but because of the scarcity of machine tools or raw materials they might never get into production. Procurement demands in excess of production capacity would result in unbalanced output, confusion, and chaos.

The War Production Board's method of measuring feasibility was based upon two different approaches. One was to calculate the supply and demand of certain limiting factors such as a particular raw material like copper, available industrial facilities, or labor force. A shortage in supply of any of these would cause the whole production effort to bog down. The second method

[2] Annual Rpt of ASF, 1943, p. 16.
[3] Ibid., pp. 18–19.

was that of employing a statistical technique based upon the concept of the potential gross national product. The economists and statisticians of the WPB planning committee began to estimate the production potential of America's industry by studying both single, basic, limiting factors and the potential gross national product. They had to consider not only military requirements but also those goods required to sustain the American economy.

A determination of feasible military procurement depended also upon how goods were to be divided between military and civilian demands. It was generally assumed that the smaller the share the civilian population received, the larger would be the share of the military. Yet this was an involved issue fraught with political, social, and economic considerations. For example, one of the many complicated questions to consider was just how far civilian transportation or housing or food supplies might be cut before over-all production would suffer. At the beginning of 1942 war supplies consumed about 27 percent of the national output. Many economists believed that not more than 45 to 50 percent of the total production could be devoted to war purposes.

In July 1942 the WPB planning committee estimated that war production objectives for the calendar year of 1942 would total fifty-five billion dollars, while on the basis of past production rates and reasonably expected increases, military production would in fact be only forty-five to forty-seven billion dollars. This would leave a deficit of eight to ten billion dollars. Similarly, in 1943 military requirements totaled 87.4 billion dollars (soon raised to 92 billion dollars) against "feasibility" estimates of 75 to 80 billion dollars.

To the accumulated deficit of 1942 and 1943, nonmunition expenditures for food and military pay would have to be added. To cover all these items, total war expenditures for 1943 would have to reach about 115 billion dollars, or 75 percent of the estimated gross national product.[4]

On 8 August 1942 Mr. Nelson informed the members of the ANMB that he was convinced that the total military procurement objectives for 1942 and 1943 were beyond attainment. He did no more, however, than express a hope for downward adjustment. On 8 September 1942, at the suggestion of Nelson, Mr. Robert R. Nathan, chairman of the WPB planning committee, sent a memorandum to Vice Adm. Samuel M. Robinson, Mr. Harry Hopkins, and General Somervell, asking them to review the latest analysis prepared by the committee's chief statistician, Mr. Simon Kuznets. The analysis was a long and detailed document setting forth the figures which have already been mentioned and pointing out that production goals substantially exceeded production capacities. But the WPB memorandum did not confine itself to recommending "a more feasible set of production goals." It also recommended a more careful system of production scheduling.

The document declared that with proper production scheduling and control the production program could proceed in balance. In a balanced program, where one part of the production effort did not absorb more than its share of resources at the expense of another, excessive production goals would not be harmful and might in fact prove a stimulus to greater production. But in the absence of adequate machinery for scheduling produc-

---

[4] *Industrial Mobilization for War*, pp. 275–85.

tion, it was important to set feasible limits to military output.

To General Somervell, however, the Kuznets' recommendation that was most objectionable had little to do with production scheduling or "feasibility." This was a proposal for relating war production objectives, strategic factors, and social policy considerations through a "supreme war production council." This "supreme" council was to be made up of individuals responsible for military strategy, production strategy, and social or political strategy. The report implied that in dealing with Somervell, the WPB was not receiving adequate guidance or broad strategic factors affecting military procurement.

General Somervell personally wrote out a sharp reply in longhand. It was typed and dispatched on 12 September with a carbon copy for Mr. Nelson. In his memorandum Somervell mentioned that Mr. Kuznets admitted that his data might be "unreliable." He expressed the opinion that procurement goals 10 to 20 percent higher than "feasibility" estimates scarcely seemed large enough to justify any wholesale change in production goals. He noted that only a few months before, WPB statisticians had been urging "this office" to increase military requirements. As for the proposed "supreme war production council," Somervell characterized the whole plan as "an inchoate mass of words." He added that in determining military and production strategy he much preferred the decisions of the President, Mr. Nelson, and existing military personnel to some board of "economists and statisticians." General Somervell ended up with an often quoted sentence: "I am not impressed with either the character or basis of the judgments expressed in the report and recommend that they be carefully hidden from the eyes of thoughtful men." [5]

Mr. Kuznets was an eminent statistician, recognized in his profession as an authority on national income figures. He had confidence in his economic analysis. With Kuznets' assistance Nathan drafted and dispatched an answer marked by such phrases as "I hesitate to take your memorandum seriously"; there is no reason "for now adopting an ostrich-like attitude"; and your conclusion "that these judgments be carefully hidden from the eyes of all thoughtful men is a nonsequitur." The Nathan letter went on: "I am obliged to be frank with you in expressing my disappointment in your reply. The problems discussed are important and their intelligent consideration is urgent." Nathan decried the fact that Somervell overlooked the basic findings of the report "in favor of minutiae" and urged that the main problem was the aggressive mobilizing of national resources for war.

Two issues had become badly confused in the exchange of correspondence between Mr. Nathan and General Somervell. First of all, there was the question of total military production which might reasonably be expected in 1942 and 1943. General Somervell was certainly not prepared to maintain that "unreal" procurement goals should be set up by the armed forces. For the most part, however, the ASF and others had been thinking in terms of physical limits to military production such as available industrial plants, labor supply, and raw materials. An analysis which attempted to summarize all of these limits in terms of the dollar as a common denominator was a new ap-

---

[5] Memo, Somervell for Nathan, Chm Planning Com, WPB, 12 Sep 42, CG ASF.

proach. Somervell feared that the whole technique of such analysis contained sufficient possibility of error to result in an unnecessary cut in production goals.

But along with the problem of determining military production feasibility the Kuznets document had raised the issue of machinery for relating strategy and production. True, General Somervell had raised this very issue himself in May 1942. Then he had been rebuffed by Mr. Nelson largely on the advice of the same persons who were now pressing for somewhat different machinery to accomplish the same purpose. But since May, Somervell had changed his mind. In any event it was this question of top administrative machinery in the Nathan correspondence rather than that of economic analysis which angered him.

The "feasibility" issue came to a head at the meeting of the War Production Board on 6 October. Prior to this meeting Mr. Nathan sought out key individuals to support his position. He spoke to Mr. Leon Henderson, and obtained an interview with Mr. Harry Hopkins and Mr. Isador Lubin who usually represented Hopkins in these matters. For an hour the three men had sat on the back porch of the White House while Nathan argued his case. In the meantime Somervell gained the support of Under Secretary Patterson and Vice Admiral Robinson. Most important of all, he came to the meeting with a letter from General Marshall to Mr. Nelson. General Marshall noted that "effective and elaborate machinery has been established for the guidance of the strategic efforts of the combined armed forces. I do not believe that a joint committee consisting of an economist, a politician, and a person familiar with strategy but not with production, could be an effective means of controlling the war effort." General Marshall also designated Somervell as the "representative of the War Department for the interpretation of strategy to the War Production Board."

The arguments at the meeting ranged over a wide variety of issues related to the "feasibility" question. In spite of the attack on excessive military requirements, it did not seem likely that the armed services would consent to lower goals. Then Leon Henderson, the OPA administrator, entered the argument. Henderson, when aroused, was a fighter. Beginning in a low voice he commented that the ninety billion dollar military program was greater than the value of our entire national output in several prewar years. Then he remarked that if the country couldn't wage war on ninety billions, maybe "we ought to get rid of our present Joint Chiefs, and find some who can." He then made a violent personal attack on Somervell whom he charged with padding and inflating his requirements regardless of the disastrous consequences. He expressed himself as disgusted with Somervell's ignorance of production problems, his overbearing manner, and his obstinacy. When a listener attempted the role of peacemaker by remarking that after all, Somervell did not make the strategy, Henderson referred to Marshall's instructions and sarcastically asked, "Ain't he got a letter." [6] The meeting adjourned without any decision.

The day after the meeting Under Secretary Patterson told General Somervell that at the next session the War Production Board would probably recommend a military production objective for 1943 to-

---

[6] Min, WPB, 6 Oct 42; The Feasibility Dispute: Determination of War Production Objectives for 1942 and 1943, Com on Public Adm Cases, 3 Thomas Circle, Washington 5, D. C., 1950, pp. 90–95.

taling some eighty to eighty-five billion dollars and added his belief that "production objectives ought not to be far in front of estimated maximum production." He then expressed the further thought that if the Army and Navy programs were to be reduced to the limits set by the WPB, such a decision should be made by the Joint Chiefs of Staff with the approval of the President. The reduction would have to be "governed by consideration of military strategy." Patterson ended by expressing his desire to discuss the whole matter at greater length with both Generals Somervell and Clay.[7] In private discussions the Under Secretary stressed his desire to settle the issue amicably.

The next meeting of the WPB took place on 13 October 1942. The meeting of the previous week had been unusually large as the contestants had rallied their supporters for the fight. It was a good omen for peace that, instead of forty participants, only a dozen people were present at the second meeting. Mr. Nelson opened the session by referring to the previous discussion and by stating his belief that the present program for 1943 was impracticable. He indicated that he was not certain whether the "maximum feasible level of munitions production and war construction" was seventy-five or eighty-five billion dollars. But he felt that the total was probably somewhere between the two figures. Mr. Leon Henderson expressed his general agreement, as did Isador Lubin, sitting at the board meeting for Mr. Hopkins. Somervell then expressed agreement with most of the discussion, although he stated that he was more optimistic than the others about the management and control of the production program. He suggested that Nelson should inform the Joint Chiefs of Staff that the

existing military production programs for 1943 were too large to be attained within the established time limits. It would then be the responsibility of the JCS to determine the necessary action "to bring the over-all program within the limits of production feasibility."[8]

This simple solution was immediately accepted by the WPB as official policy. The controversy, according to WPB historians, was stopped "practically in mid-stride."[9] Members of the WPB planning committee looked upon the result as a great victory. Actually, each side won the point that it considered most important. The War Production Board wanted production goals for 1943 reduced to what it called "feasible" objectives, and as a by-product had recommended a production strategy board. Somervell, on the other hand, was more optimistic about what was feasible, but he did not object to some reduction of procurement goals. He was strongly opposed to the "grand super super board." The controversy ended with both sides satisfied when Somervell accepted a limit to production goals and the WPB dropped the organizational proposal.

On 19 October 1942 Mr. Nelson addressed a memorandum to the Joint Chiefs of Staff in which he pointed out that military requirements in the calendar year 1943 for munitions, facilities, and war construction then totaled ninety-two billion dollars. With the carry-over of the incompleted portion of the 1942 program, the procurement goal would become ninety-seven billion dollars. This did not include subsistence, pay of the Army, and

---

[7] Memo, Patterson for Somervell, 7 Oct 42, Hq ASF, USW.

[8] Min, 35th Mtg, WPB, 13 Oct 42.

[9] *Industrial Mobilization for War*, p. 289.

other miscellaneous expenditures. On the basis of the best available evidence on available production facilities and the supply of raw materials and other critical resources, the WPB had concluded that the nation's total capacity to produce munitions, industrial facilities, and military construction could be set roughly at seventy-five billion dollars. The WPB believed, Mr. Nelson said, that unless steps were taken to bring military procurement requirements into line with this production capacity, important parts of the program would not be fully achieved and there would be general confusion and chaos in the entire production effort. The WPB felt that the most satisfactory way to adjust requirements to productive capacity was to extend the date of delivery for some parts of the program into 1944. At the same time, it held that full provision must be made for the "must" programs as established by the President.

Mr. Nelson added that the chairman of the Production Executive Committee of the WPB was being instructed to obtain from the procuring services a monthly schedule to meet the President's "must" programs, and to accomplish the remaining parts of the military production program in 1943 and such part of 1944 as would be necessary. He estimated that about 40 percent of the second part of this program would have to be scheduled for production in 1944. In deciding what part of the program could be extended into 1944 with least damage to the war effort he asked the guidance of the Joint Chiefs of Staff. This he wished to have not later than 15 November. To aid the JCS in making a decision, Nelson enclosed two papers, one summarizing the war production objectives for 1943 in dollar terms, and the other summarizing the estimated

requirements for carbon steel, alloy steel, copper, and aluminum. The "must" programs—aircraft, merchant shipbuilding, escort vessels, the USSR protocol, and raw materials plants—amounted to 48.8 billion dollars. The remaining programs for the Army Ground Forces, the Navy, lend-lease, military and war housing, and industrial facilities totaled 44.1 billion dollars. In both alloy steel and copper, estimated requirements exceeded total supply; the first by 7 percent and the second by nearly 24 percent.[10]

The reply, shaped in large part within the ASF, was delayed nine days beyond the stipulated date. It was given to WPB on 24 November 1942 by Admiral Leahy, acting in behalf of the Joint Chiefs of Staff. He announced that the procurement goals for 1943 had been reduced from ninety-three billion dollars to eighty billion dollars. Leahy added that the JCS believed that the revised 1943 military program had to be met in substance if the war objectives for that year were to be accomplished. Accordingly, the JCS urged an all-out effort to supply the required production facilities and materials. In revising the war production objectives downward, the aircraft program was reduced from 37 billion dollars to a little over 33 billion, the lend-lease program was reduced from 7.8 billion to 5.9 billion dollars (excluding Russian aid), the AGF equipment program from 18.8 billion dollars to 14.8 billion dollars, the Navy program from 10.4 billion to 8.1 billion dollars, command construction (except industrial plants) from 5.5 billion to 4 billion dollars, and industrial facilities construction from 2 billion to 1.65 billion dollars. This brought

---

[10] Memo, D. M. Nelson for JCS, 19 Oct 42, w/incls, Hq ASF, WPB.

about a reduction of nearly thirteen billion dollars in procurement goals.[11]

This story of the adjustment of military procurement requirements in the autumn of 1942 is particularly important for one reason: it illustrated necessary interrelationships between the WPB, the JCS, the War Department, and the ASF. This action had other significance as well. It is probable, for example, that the reduction in procurement goals for 1943 played a very substantial part in guaranteeing the successful operation of the Controlled Materials Plan. Organizationally, moreover, a solution to the problem of relating strategic planning to production goals had now been found. The WPB estimated the total productive capacity of the nation and then fixed what in its judgment constituted the total proportion of productive effort which might be devoted to direct procurement of military supply. The Joint Chiefs of Staff in turn adjusted military procurement programs within the general limits set by the WPB. Strategic decisions were accordingly modified to meet this new situation, an arrangement that functioned throughout the remainder of the war. Productive capacity and military procurement requirements were thus brought into a rough but workable balance.

Production Scheduling

At the time that the issue of feasible military procurement goals was reaching a crisis, a new storm was gathering. On 18 September 1942 Mr. Nelson had announced the appointment of Mr. Charles E. Wilson, president of the General Electric Company, as Production Vice-Chairman of the WPB. At the same time a Production Executive Committee was established with Mr. Wilson as chairman.

The various procurement agencies of the war program were represented on this committee, including the ASF, which was represented by General Somervell himself. The precise functions of the Production Executive Committee and of the Production Vice-Chairman were not immediately determined. In a letter written in October, Somervell indicated the kind of production problem to which he thought Mr. Wilson should turn his attention. Confirming a discussion arising at a meeting of the Production Executive Committee, Somervell informed Wilson that there was an "urgent and immediate need" for one billion rounds of .30-caliber ammunition, but in order to achieve this output, the Ordnance Department would have to have nine thousand tons of copper in November and December each, and ten thousand tons in January. Would Mr. Wilson look into the possibility of increasing copper production sufficiently to achieve this 100 percent increase in ammunition objectives? [12]

The Office of the Production Vice-Chairman seemed disposed to a different concept of its functions and inclined to ride herd on the various military procurement agencies. Indication of this tendency was not long in coming. In the October *Monthly Progress Report* of the WPB, released in the third week of November, the Office of Progress Reports declared that recent increases in deliveries of munitions were disappointing. The report then went on to say that output had not increased commensurately with the availability of raw materials for Army use. This failure it ascribed entirely to faulty production

---

[11] Ltr, Leahy to JCS and D. M. Nelson, 24 Nov 42, CG ASF.

[12] Ltr, Somervell to Wilson, 28 Oct 42, Hq ASF, WPB.

scheduling by the procurement services.[13]

The change was apparently an opening shot in a new campaign to change the relationship of the WPB to the War Department. At a meeting of the Production Executive Committee on 11 November 1942, Mr. Wilson proposed that a director general of production scheduling be set up who would be responsible to him, and that each procurement agency establish its own scheduling unit. Representatives from scheduling units in the armed services would make up a Production Executive Committee Subcommittee on Scheduling, which would establish criteria for scheduling, review production schedules, and adjust schedules to fit available production facilities and competing requirements. Final authority would rest with Mr. Wilson.[14]

The next day General Somervell, joined by Admiral Robinson of the Office of the Secretary of the Navy, Admiral Davison of the Navy Bureau of Aeronautics, and General Echols of the AAF, sharply criticized these proposals. The suggested scheduling plan, their memorandum said, would be "impossible of execution" and was "in direct contravention of the agreements reached between the War Production Board, the Army, and the Navy." The proposed authority would enable the director general of production scheduling "to dictate whether we made cannons, tanks, airplanes, battleships, or other war matériel." Such powers, the military representatives declared, were outside the province of the WPB, and the Army and Navy "would be entirely unwilling to vest them in another agency." They asserted that "the decisions as to the priority in the manufacture of war matériel is closely allied to strategy and tactics and must be made by the Joint Chiefs of Staff." The

memorandum added that though the War and Navy Departments "must insist on the maintenance of the terms of the 12 March agreement," the two departments would be willing "to review with WPB the progress on end-item scheduling." [15]

Nevertheless, Nelson supported Mr. Wilson in his determination to go through with his production scheduling plans. On 21 November Under Secretary Patterson received copies of two draft orders which Nelson indicated he was prepared to issue. Mr. Patterson showed these at once to General Somervell. One glance was enough to tell the worst. The Under Secretary agreed that the armed services should oppose these orders.[16]

The first draft order of one page only, was entitled "Powers of Production Vice-Chairman." Section 2 terminated "those provisions of the agreements with the War and Navy Departments . . . which delegate to the War Department or the Navy Department powers over production. . . ." Section 4 gave the Production Vice-Chairman the responsibility for scheduling out "the entire war production program . . . with the maximum productive possibilities of our economy, in the best possible balance with the requirements of the services under the strategic plans of the Chiefs of Staff." The proposed WPB order did leave one loophole whereby the armed services might retain some power over production. It provided that the Production Vice-Chairman might delegate to various agencies "such portions of his production functions as he finds it will be most efficient for them to perform."

---

[13] Min, 41st Mtg, WPB, 24 Nov 42.

[14] *Industrial Mobilization for War,* pp. 512–13.

[15] Memo, Somervell, S. M. Robinson, and Davison for Wilson, 16 Nov 42, Hq ASF, WPB.

[16] Copies of both draft orders are in Hq ASF, WPB.

The second proposed order established the Office of the Production Vice-Chairman within the War Production Board and prescribed its functions in detail. Among the most important of these was the provision that the Production Vice-Chairman should "direct the formulation of production schedules for all war material, including delivery dates by months, by procuring agencies of the United States Government." He would approve production and delivery schedules of the procuring agencies and would "co-ordinate production and delivery schedules for war materials to assure a balanced program correlated to strategic plans developed by the Chiefs of Staff."

These proposed orders indicated the full extent of WPB intentions. They meant that the 12 March 1942 agreement was to be terminated and that the WPB would now assert authority to fix military production schedules. To General Somervell this was a direct challenge which must be met head-on. He asked his assistant, General Clay, to prepare a critique of the orders. He himself intervened at the White House through Mr. Hopkins. Actually the ASF prepared three different papers. There was a rather thorough analysis by General Clay, a five-page condensation by Clay of his longer paper, and a still briefer summary which reflected General Somervell's own estimate of the situation. Copies of all these papers were given to Under Secretary Patterson, who brought the whole matter to the attention of Secretary of War Stimson.[17]

In these papers Generals Somervell and Clay argued that the WPB orders would abrogate the existing arrangements on production between the WPB and the armed forces, would usurp the powers of the Joint Chiefs of Staff, and would introduce procedures which violated "sound principles of organization and authority." They accused the WPB of failing to meet its responsibilities in several critical fields, and implied that the board was incompetent to handle the job it wished to assume. The WPB proposals, Somervell and Clay said, would create wasteful and divided authority, would interpose an agency which would interfere with the smooth flow of materials, and would destroy the full control that the Joint Chiefs of Staff ought to have over all phases of military supply. Finally, Somervell and Clay asserted that the 12 March agreement was "logical and workable" and recommended that Mr. Nelson be given "explicit instructions" not to issue any orders contrary to it.

At this point Nelson realized that he had a battle on his hands. Although he received an offer of assistance from the President, he expressed confidence that he could negotiate a settlement.[18] By nature he was inclined toward conciliation, a trait that his friends interpreted as democratic. His opponents on the other hand viewed it as an indication of weakness as an administrator. In any event, President Roosevelt called Nelson, Secretary Stimson, and Secretary Knox together and instructed them "to compose their differences." On 26 November 1942, five days after the two draft orders had been circulated, Mr. Nelson addressed a conciliatory letter to Secretary Stimson. He began by

---

[17] The Headquarters, ASF, reading file contains a letter to Mr. Hopkins beginning "Dear Harry" dated 21 November 1942, which indicates that Somervell had talked previously about the issue with him. The papers forwarded with this letter are found in Hq ASF, WPB, with these notations on them: "Somervell Digest of Clay Memo," "Clay Digest of Clay Memo," and "Clay Memo."

[18] *Industrial Mobilization for War*, pp. 514–15.

noting that the executive order creating the WPB gave him responsibility "in connection with procurement and production" and that he had appointed Mr. Wilson his deputy for production. He explained that he had asked Mr. Wilson to do two things: first, to supervise the aircraft program, the radio and radar program, and the escort vessel program in order to achieve the President's goals for 1943; second, to exercise "central control and general supervision," through the Production Executive Committee, over the scheduling of the various production programs of the services. Mr. Nelson insisted that it was not his responsibility to determine what the military services required for strategic purposes, and that he did not want to upset the duties and responsibilities of the production divisions of the services where the programs were going well. He wished only "to investigate and supervise" production programs to insure that they were proceeding satisfactorily and in accordance with the wishes of the chiefs of staff and the government's war program. He noted somewhat plaintively that he would like "the wholehearted co-operation of the armed services in fulfilling this responsibility." In turn he pledged WPB co-operation with the "one aim that we shall get the maximum production of which this country is capable." [19]

Mr. Nelson may have delivered his letter in person. In any event he called upon Secretary Stimson during the morning of 26 November to discuss the Army disagreement. There was no doubt that the letter provided a basis for agreement. Stimson asked Assistant Secretary McCloy and Under Secretary Patterson to participate in discussions with Mr. Nelson to clarify the whole problem. Nelson, in a second letter to Secretary Stimson, sent on the afternoon of 26 November, wrote that "the point at issue seems too essentially simple," and added that he was "disturbed and puzzled by the amount of confusion which seems to have grown up around it." He then explained the situation as he saw it. The Joint Chiefs of Staff were engaged in determining the program of munitions to be produced in 1943, "fixed with due regard to the practicable limits of production as indicated by the chairman of the War Production Board." In order to accomplish this large program, the WPB had to make sure that resources in materials, facilities, management, and labor were efficiently utilized. To do this, Nelson said, there must be a central control agency to prevent competition among the various procurement agencies of the government. This competition, Mr. Nelson declared, extended far beyond raw materials. It included rivalry for common components, such as generators, bearings, valves, compressors, blowers, and fractional horsepower motors as well as a struggle for control of facilities, labor, and management. Since competition became more intense as production requirements became larger, only "effective central direction and control," could stem the rivalry. "It seems to me," Mr. Nelson wrote, "to be my plain duty as chairman of the War Production Board to furnish this central direction and control. I do not see how it can be furnished by any other existing organization." He admitted that the scheduling of end-items of weapons and munitions was a responsibility of the procurement agencies but held that to insure that these schedules were adjusted to the "applicable limiting factors" there

---

[19] Ltr, D. M. Nelson to Stimson, 26 Nov 42, Hq ASF, WPB.

must be some central review and control. This power he desired to vest in Mr. Wilson, guided by the Production Executive Committee. Nelson concluded by saying that "it is my considered opinion that unless such a step is taken, the war production program for 1943 will not be achieved." [20] Even more than the first, this second letter of Mr. Nelson on 26 November indicated a desire for an adjustment of Army-WPB differences.

Secretary Stimson and his aides met Nelson and Wilson again on 27 November. They agreed to prepare a statement which would embody their latest understanding of WPB relations to the armed services. Under Secretary Patterson and Assistant Secretary McCloy then went to Nelson's office and prepared two drafts of a statement for mutual agreement.

On the same day that top Army-WPB officials were meeting, General Somervell requested a special meeting of the WPB so that the Army Service Forces could present its point of view on production scheduling for the information of WPB officials. At this meeting the Ordnance Department, which had the largest proportion of ASF procurement, explained the procedures used for production scheduling and forecasting. Maj. Gen. Levin H. Campbell, Jr., Chief of Ordnance, emphasized the constantly changing needs for end-items of war supply and with the aid of several assistants, related how the Ordnance Department had established industry integration committees bringing together the engineering talents and production skills of the producers of an individual item. Modifications in schedules were recommended to the Ordnance Department by these committees. These schedules had to be altered to meet changes in design, or tardy delivery of

materials and components. This presentation demonstrated that the ASF was concerned with production scheduling, had devised procedures for it, and had made changes to fit available raw material supplies and other factors.[21]

The following day, on 28 November, Secretary Stimson sent Nelson a draft of the new Army-WPB understanding. He explained that this draft, while not substantially different from the one Mr. Nelson had presented to him, "accords most nearly with my own recollection of the course of our united discussions yesterday," and constituted a sort of "bill of rights for the practices of the services." The Secretary concluded by stating that this paper, with Mr. Nelson's two letters, should furnish a "workable understanding for the future" and meet the "President's directive to us to compose our former differences." He then enclosed a copy of his statement signed by Secretary of Navy Knox and promised that if Mr. Wilson encountered any difficulty in accomplishing his objective, "We will all try to meet you again in the same spirit." [22]

On 1 December at the next regular meeting of the War Production Board, General Clay presented a document entitled Production Progress and Scheduling. This paper protested that whatever shortcomings there might be in military production scheduling could be attributed to an inadequate supply of raw materials and to the absence of firm control over their distribution. For example, General Clay mentioned that the failure to forecast accurately the deliveries of medium

---

[20] Ltr, D. M. Nelson to SW, 26 Nov 42, Hq ASF, WPB.

[21] Min, WPB, 27 Nov 42.

[22] Ltr, Stimson to D. M. Nelson, 28 Nov 42, Hq ASF, WPB. See Appen. G for the Stimson-Knox statement.

tanks, as pointed out in the WPB report, was the result of the fact that the WPB had not allocated alloy steel with which to make tank treads.[23] In other words, General Clay implied that failure in production scheduling was the fault not of the armed services but of the WPB.

The final solution to the production scheduling controversy preserved the essentials of the 12 March agreement. If Mr. Nelson had not permitted someone in WPB to draft or to circulate an order which categorically declared that the agreement was terminated, there never would have been such a controversy. But to declare the agreement ended and to assert that the WPB would "direct the formulation of production schedules for all war materials, including delivery dates by months," was simply asking for trouble.[24]

For the record it should be made clear that General Somervell and others in the ASF never at any time opposed WPB scheduling of component parts. The Controlled Materials Plan announced on 2 November 1942, set up a category of Class B products for which the WPB allocated materials directly. No one in ASF objected to that arrangement. What Somervell and his staff in ASF opposed was the WPB effort to terminate the 12 March agreement by unilateral action. They objected also to the WPB insistence upon fixing production schedules for end-items of military equipment. General Somervell felt so strongly on both scores that, as has been noted, he went so far as to suggest that Mr. Baruch should replace Nelson in order to prevent the WPB from taking over Army functions.[25] Only after Mr. Nelson's letters of 26 November, when the WPB chairman made clear that he was *not* trying to take over ASF procurement duties, was the way opened to settling the controversy.

It seems likely that Nelson at the outset didn't know what he wanted his Production Vice-Chairman to do. Mr. Wilson was probably invited to join the WPB as a counterweight to Mr. Eberstadt, whom many persons inside the WPB were reluctant to accept because of his previous vigorous championship of Army and Navy viewpoints. One group in WPB was always fearful that the Army would take over "control" of the economy, and constantly watched for opportunities to restrict the ASF. Furthermore Nelson seems never to have appreciated how much importance General Somervell attached to the 12 March agreement defining WPB-War Department relationships, possibly because he was not particularly sensitive about organizational matters; Somervell was. Under such circumstances it was difficult for the two minds to meet.

Undoubtedly another factor making for complication was the very different relationship which existed between the WPB and the Army Air Forces. There was an elaborate array of joint committees and

[23] Min, WPB, 1 Dec 42. A copy of Production Progress and Scheduling may be found in Hq ASF files.

[24] It is impossible to reconcile Nelson's own account of this controversy with his correspondence to the War Department. He does not mention the draft orders or the intention to abrogate the 12 March agreement. He reports that Mr. Wilson's task was first, to increase the supply of critical components and second, to set up an orderly scheduling program. This intention alone, he suggests, stirred up "the bitterest fight I ever had with the War Department people. The fundamental principles underlying the scheduling and allocation of critical components were involved." He adds that he was convinced that the WPB should take over the allocation of raw materials. Mr. Nelson even says that Secretary Stimson decided that he, Nelson, was right, and directed the Army to "go along." See D. M. Nelson, *Arsenal of Democracy,* pp. 382–85.

[25] Leahy, *I Was There,* pp. 130–31. Admiral Leahy recalls the proposal but entirely misplaces the episode in time. He confuses the issue with the dismissal of Mr. Eberstadt the following February. See p. 211.

boards which linked together the WPB, the AAF, and the Navy Bureau of Aeronautics in the production of aircraft. These included an Aircraft Production Board, an Aircraft Resources Control Office, and an Aircraft Scheduling Unit, the last located at Wright Field. Much of this machinery had been set up as early as the spring of 1941. Under existing arrangements, the AAF and the Navy practically turned production scheduling of aircraft over to WPB officials. In the light of this fact WPB could not see why the same procedures should not apply to the Army. But General Somervell was opposed to such an arrangement. He had an active division in ASF headquarters carefully watching production scheduling by the ASF procurement agencies—the technical services. If the WPB worked directly with these technical services, one reason for the existence of an ASF headquarters would have been removed. But more than this, ASF headquarters wished to be free to shift production schedules as changing overseas combat experience or plans demanded. If the WPB had to be consulted about and approve every shift, delays might result. Somervell was determined to keep supply closely intermeshed with procurement operations, for in that relationship he saw the primary contribution of the ASF to the war effort.

Unfortunately, the WPB–ASF controversy seeped down to the operating levels of both organizations and also became public. After the issues had been adjusted, the War Department, the Navy Department, and the War Production Board tried to pour oil on troubled waters by issuing a joint press release stating that the dispute from the first "had to do with method, never with purpose or principle. To win the war quickly, effectively, and

with the lowest expenditures of life, is everybody's goal." Conversations among officials of the organizations involved had resolved all issues, the release declared, and the new arrangements assured "that the immense production task for 1943 will be carried through to a successful conclusion." [26] A separate statement by Mr. Nelson accompanied the joint release explaining more fully just what Mr. Wilson's duties would be. On 9 December 1942, the WPB issued a series of orders defining Wilson's duties. Then on 17 December, Under Secretary Patterson wrote to Mr. Nelson that it was the Army understanding that the WPB intended through its Production Executive Committee to establish feasible limits of the several military programs; to control the scheduling and allocation of common components; and to review scheduling methods and procedures in the procurement agencies. [27] But it was the Army's distinct understanding that it alone would "be responsible for the establishment and adjustment of end-item schedules as it deems necessary to the war effort. . . ." These press releases, orders, and letters marked the official end of the controversy over production scheduling. No further difficulty on that score arose throughout the rest of the war.

Reconversion

The question of production control raised basic problems of relationship between the WPB and the ASF. The prob-

<hr>

[26] This press release is quoted in full in D. M. Nelson, *Arsenal of Democracy*, pp. 386–87.

[27] Ltr, Patterson to D. M. Nelson, 17 Dec 42. A copy of this letter is in Hq ASF files with the handwritten notation at the bottom: "Delivered in person to Mr. Nelson Dec 17 by the USW, Mr. Nelson agreeing fully to the principles, L.D.C." These are Gen Clay's initials.

lem of feasible military procurement goals was partly one of substance—of economic policy—and partly one of organizational relations, of how to fix total military procurement goals and of how to divide available productive resources among various military procurement programs. The issue of production scheduling had also raised questions as to who should have primary responsibility for fixing production schedules of end-items of military matériel.

In 1944 a different kind of controversy arose between the WPB and the ASF. This time no organizational relationship as such was involved. The issue was entirely a matter of policy on which there was basic disagreement between the War Department and some civilian agencies on the one hand and certain groups within the WPB on the other. In the end, the Executive Office of the President had to intervene and settle the dispute. Here again, the entire controversy was argued not just on its merits but on ideological grounds. The War Department was accused once more of trying to "control the civilian economy." The conflict was also portrayed in the public press as a struggle between "big" and "little" business for postwar markets. The subject of this controversy was the timing of production reconversion from war to peacetime output.

Apparently, Mr. Nelson began to think about industrial reconversion early in 1943. In April of that year he asked Mr. Ernest Kanzler, a former WPB official, to prepare a report for him on reconversion problems.[28] Kanzler reported in June. From then on there was a rising crescendo of interest in the subject. In October President Roosevelt asked the director of the Office of War Mobilization to appoint Mr. Bernard Baruch and Mr. John M. Han-

cock to study industrial demobilization.[29] Three weeks later the Truman Committee issued its report entitled Outline of Problems of Conversion from War Production.[30] Mr. Nelson announced that as manpower, facilities, and materials became available in a given area, and where there was no conflict with programs of a higher urgency, WPB would authorize the production of additional civilian goods.[31]

Under Secretary of War Patterson and General Somervell opposed this reconversion proposal. Both men were alike in their single-minded concentration on meeting Army procurement requirements. They doubted that the "coddling" of civilians by producing additional nonmilitary items could be accomplished without hurting military needs. Both believed that even if the industrial problems could be overcome, reconversion would create a peace psychology with an accompanying letdown in military production effort. They did not object to reconversion planning as such but they did to Nelson's timing and to the publicity given to his program.

The ASF believed that a large part of the evils of reconversion planning could be mitigated if the control of the operation were in suitable hands. Accordingly Somervell's director of matériel, General Clay, asked one of his assistants, J. A. Panuch, to prepare a recommendation that both cutbacks and reconversion be handled by the Production Executive Committee in WPB. In spite of the earlier dispute between ASF and WPB over the Production

[28] D. M. Nelson. *Arsenal of Democracy*, p. 392.

[29] *The New York Times,* October 7, 1943.

[30] *Additional Report of the Special Committee Investigating the National Defense Program,* Senate, 78th Cong, 1st Sess, 5 Nov 43, Senate Rpt 10, Pt. 12.

[31] Min, WPB, 30 Nov 43.

Executive Committee and its powers, the armed forces by this time had a great deal of influence in the committee and worked very well with its chairman, Mr. Charles Wilson. In a sense, Wilson was now being pitted against Nelson, since he favored the Panuch plan. On the other hand Nelson hesitated to accept it, which was interpreted as fear that the plan would give the determination of reconversion policy to the military. Ultimately Nelson agreed to accept it and after long delay both cutbacks and reconversion were put under the jurisdiction of the Production Executive Committee.

Nelson's position was becoming increasingly difficult. By 1944 the status of the WPB had deteriorated and the "center of power" had shifted. Manpower had become the crucial problem, and control over this resource was vested in the War Manpower Commission, not the WPB. Moreover, the Office of War Mobilization, headed by former Justice James F. Byrnes, had been created.[32] Byrnes was on the best of terms with representatives of the armed forces, but there was some doubt about his attitude toward Mr. Nelson. Mr. Byrnes in his new assignment not only had some powers which had formerly been assigned to Nelson, but also the authority to decide conflicts between WPB and other agencies. In short he, rather than Nelson, had become the top policy maker on war production issues.

Nelson faced a dilemma. On the one hand he was anxious to proceed with reconversion planning; on the other hand he had to obtain Mr. Byrnes' approval, overcome Army objections, and find an alternative to the proposals that would put authority into the hands of the Production Executive Committee. On 11 January 1944 he told the War Production Board that cutbacks in the production of military

goods would create pockets of unemployment throughout the country. Reconversion he argued, ought to take up the slack in employment. To this Under Secretary Patterson immediately replied that any talk of reconversion before the European invasion was even launched was premature. He added that relaxation on the home front would damage morale on the military front. As a result of this discussion, the board put off proposals for immediate reconversion.[33]

Interest in reconversion did not cool, however. On 15 February 1944 Baruch and Hancock issued their *Report on War and Post-War Adjustment Policy;*[34] a week later Mr. Byrnes ordered all war agencies to implement the recommendations of the report;[35] and at the beginning of March, the Truman Committee publicly championed Nelson's earlier announced program of gradual reconversion.[36] Then on 22 May 1944, the Navy suddenly announced a cutback of its fighter plane program and the cancellation of a contract with the Brewster Corporation which would result in closing its Long Island plant. Angry workers, with a good deal of public backing, threatened a "stay in" strike until they got work.[37]

These events spurred Mr. Nelson to action. A chief reason for his previous delay was that he still hesitated to place reconversion authority in the Production Executive Committee, which he felt had too many military members to handle an es-

---

[32] *Industrial Mobilization for War,* p. 721.

[33] Min, WPB, 11 Jan 44.

[34] Bernard M. Baruch and John M. Hancock, *Report on War and Post-War Adjustment Policy,* Senate, 78th Cong, 2d Sess, 15 Feb 44, Senate Doc. 154.

[35] *The New York Times,* February 22, 1944.

[36] *Additional Report of the Special Committee Investigating the National Defense Program,* Senate, 78th Cong, 2d Sess, 4 Mar 44, Senate Rpt 10, Pt. 16.

[37] *The New York Times,* May 23, 30, 1944.

sentially civilian problem. But no satisfactory substitute machinery had been developed, and since the pressure was great, Nelson surrendered. On 18 June he announced a program under the control of the Production Executive Committee which among other things made some raw materials immediately available for civilian production.[38]

Nelson's announcement came just twelve days after the invasion of Europe had begun, which led the Army to protest its timing. Patterson wrote to Nelson that while he appreciated the desirability of reconversion planning, he was apprehensive of positive steps at a time when American troops were locked in mortal combat with the enemy. A few days later, the Joint Chiefs of Staff publicly announced that it opposed immediate reconversion. On 4 July in a heavily attended meeting of the War Production Board, the question again came up for discussion. Nelson was not on hand, having been hospitalized with pneumonia. The opposition to reconversion was led by Mr. Patterson who pointed to the very serious "slippage" in war production and stated that if the trend continued, "the ability of our soldiers to pour it on in full measure to the Germans and the Japs is sure to be impaired."[39] On 8 July 1944 a letter of the Joint Chiefs of Staff to Mr. Nelson was made public which stated that the "existing lag in war production . . . may necessitate revision in strategic plans which could prolong the war."[40]

In the meantime General Somervell spear-headed a drive to increase war production. On 4 July he announced that munitions output was behind schedule and urged "stop delaying production. . . . Put off that fishing trip, it can come after the war is won." He told the Indiana Chamber of Commerce: "We must re-

member that our sons are fighting on a twenty-four hour shift in Normandy and there's no double pay for overtime, and no time out for their postwar planning either."[41]

Mr. Nelson was incensed at what he believed were exaggerated and misleading statements. He complained to Mr. Byrnes about the actions of the services. At the same time, Under Secretary Patterson and Somervell were also pleading with Byrnes to help get a "sense of urgency" into the war effort. Again, they pointed to the disastrous psychological effect of immediate reconversion. In effect, Byrnes sided with the services when he gave the War Manpower Commission, whose outlook on reconversion was basically the same as that of the armed services, the authority to review all specific reconversion proposals.[42]

It is important also to note that the War Department was not alone in its opposition to Nelson's reconversion proposals. The staff of the WPB itself was divided. Mr. Wilson was only one of many board officials who were less than enthusiastic. He and many other leaders of industry who had patriotically left their private pursuits to serve within the War Production Board were deeply wounded and indescribably bitter at the smear attack which attributed their opposition to reconversion to fear that small business would get a headstart on big business. The WMC was also opposed to an early resumption of peacetime production, even on a small scale. Again and again Chairman Paul McNutt had asserted that reconversion

---

[38] *Ibid.*, June 18, 1944.
[39] Min, WPB, 4 Jul 44.
[40] *The New York Times,* July 9, 1944.
[41] *The New York Times,* July 5, 1944.
[42] *Industrial Mobilization for War,* p. 808.

would aggravate an already tight man-power situation.

In the face of all this opposition Nelson grimly determined to go through with his plans. He had a good deal of backing from labor, from small business, and from such a powerful Congressional body as the Truman Committee. He tried to soften the impact, however, by instituting his orders gradually. Three were issued between 15 July and 29 July.[43] The fourth and most controversial, the "spot authorization order" provided that a WPB regional director could authorize, under certain circumstances, a small manufacturer to produce civilian goods. This order was put into effect on 15 August.[44]

The long simmering conflict had come to a boil. President Roosevelt was troubled by what had become a public brawl. Consequently, when Chiang Kai-shek requested him to send a personal representative to China, the President saw a possible solution to his problem in offering the assignment to Mr. Nelson. Nelson accepted. In spite of the charge that Nelson was being "exiled" and the statement by a Nelson intimate to Sterling Green of the Associated Press that "Nelson is being kicked right square in the groin," Nelson himself declared that he was going to China willingly because he felt he had an important mission to perform.[45]

Meanwhile, Mr. Wilson had grown more and more bitter over the charges that he represented big business. He believed that they were inspired by Nelson's personal staff and that Nelson had hesitated both in exonerating him and in curbing his opponents. At an eventful meeting on 24 August 1944, Nelson told the WPB staff about his coming trip to China. Trying to avoid an open break, he eulogized Wilson. But Wilson refused to be placated. He told the same meeting

that with Nelson in China, every action he took would be held as a betrayal of his absent chief. Rather than be put in such a situation, he declared, he had sent his resignation to the President. Later, at a press conference Wilson savagely attacked Nelson and his policies. On the same day Mr. J. A. Krug, much to his own amazement, was asked by the President to become acting chairman of the War Production Board.[46]

Subsequently, Mr. Nelson described the conflict over reconversion as "the most severe fight between military and civilian elements which our government ever witnessed."[47] His statement completely overlooked the opposition of Mr. Wilson and other civilian officials within his own agency, the opposition of the chairman and staff of the War Manpower Commission, and the intervention of Byrnes, who decided against the Nelson program. His statement also implied that Under Secretary Patterson had no mind of his own on the issue and was only a mouthpiece for men in uniform. Blind to all these facts, Mr. Nelson then proceeded to level such charges as these: (1) that the Army tried to protect war production "by the simple means of creating pools of unemployment";[48] (2) that the military "mistrusted American management as well as American labor" and did not want them to think about reconversion;[49] and (3) that the armed forces "miscalculated" their military procurement needs in reducing some

[43] *The New York Times,* July 11, 16, 23, 29, 1944.

[44] D. M. Nelson, *Arsenal of Democracy,* pp. 401–02; *The New York Times,* August 15, 1944.

[45] *The New York Times,* August 20, 21, 24, 1944.

[46] *Industrial Mobilization for War,* pp. 731–41; Harold Stein, ed., *Public Administration and Policy Development* (New York, Harcourt, Brace and Company, Inc., 1952), p. 215.

[47] D. M. Nelson, *Arsenal of Democracy,* p. 402.

[48] *Ibid.,* p. 402.

[49] *Ibid.,* p. 407.

schedules and then in increasing them later.[50]

The intemperance of these charges must provide their principal refutation. There need to be added but a few facts for the record. First, it is important to note that during the first seven months of 1944, military procurement deliveries steadily declined in volume. To help remedy this situation which was regarded as a matter of serious concern within the ASF, General Somervell in the summer of 1944 launched a vigorous campaign for increased war output.[51] On 1 July 1944 the WMC announced the extension of its manpower priorities program to three hundred major production areas over the whole country. Labor shortages had become a serious obstacle to military procurement. Previously, Mr. Nelson had said that the military should determine its procurement needs. In 1944 he contended that those needs were unduly high and that complaints of shortages were "phony." He stated that he was prepared to maintain that the war could be won with fewer military supply deliveries than those previously approved and scheduled for delivery during the year but offered no basis for his belief, however.

Second, neither Under Secretary Patterson nor General Somervell at any time expressed opposition to WPB and industrial planning for postwar reconversion to peacetime production. In its relations with its contractors, the ASF was actually encouraging just such planning during 1944 and especially in early 1945. What the Army representatives objected to was a program to start actual reconversion while the war was still on and when neither its outcome nor date of termination could be clearly forecast. They firmly believed that an active reconversion program would encourage management and labor to believe that the war was won, that military pro-

duction was no longer important, and that it was time to scramble for a good competitive position in the postwar production of civilian goods. Patterson and Somervell were both convinced that to encourage attitudes like these, which they believed the Nelson order of 15 August 1944 did, would endanger the successful outcome of the war.

Third, the reconversion controversy, as already noted, was settled by Byrnes, a civilian. As director of the Office of War Mobilization and Reconversion (OWMR), he exercised his authority in the name of the President. His position was one of arbitrator of home-front problems. The War Department was opposed to Nelson's reconversion orders, which was its privilege. It could not prevent the issuance of those orders; indeed, the orders were issued over the protest of War Department representatives, including Mr. Patterson. The War Department then in accord with established procedure appealed its case to the OWMR for decision. Byrnes indicated that he felt the Nelson orders were inadvisable at that time.[52]

On 30 September 1944 Mr. Nelson formally resigned the chairmanship of the War Production Board. In the meantime the military services continued to press

---

[50] *Ibid.*, p. 408.

[51] Annual Rpt of ASF, 1945, p. 192.

[52] The historian of the OWMR, noting Mr. Nelson's reference to his reconversion disagreements with the Army as "the bitterest of all arguments with the Army," remarks that Nelson "might have said with equal accuracy 'the bitterest of arguments with WMC,' or 'the bitterest of arguments with WPB.'" This historian adds later that Mr. Nelson "regarded the entire issue as a 'long and bitter controversy with the military over control of America's civilian economy' rather than a difference over the timing of reconversion steps, and whether such steps would interfere with the war." See Herman M. Somers, Presidential Agency, *The Office of War Mobilization and Reconversion* (Cambridge, Mass., Harvard University Press, 1940), pp. 183, 188.

against "spot authorizations." On 19 November General Eisenhower stated that a lack of ammunition had delayed the capture of Aachen, and Somervell said that shells were in such short supply that they had to be flown to the front. On 23 November 1944 a "memorandum of agreement" was drawn up between Krug and Hiland G. Batcheller of WPB, and General Somervell and Mr. Howard Bruce, civilian successor to General Clay in the ASF in charge of production. The WPB agreed to permit no further relaxation of restrictions on civilian production for the time being and to expand civilian production in the future only after "full consideration" of any military objections.[53] Finally on 1 December, the chairman of the WPB, the chairman of the WMC, Under Secretary of War Patterson, and Under Secretary of the Navy Forrestal agreed to suspend spot authorizations for reconversion in 103 areas where there were serious manpower shortages.[54] Nelson's program had been all but abandoned.

At no time had Somervell been interested in opposing Nelson for personal reasons; to him reconversion was only a small part of the larger danger of complacency, of a slackening in military production. Even after the victory over the Nelson program, he continued his campaign to create a sense of urgency in war production. In Boston on 2 December 1944 he said that the war's end was being delayed because workers were deserting their jobs and in New York he told an audience that workers were worrying about their postwar futures when the postwar future of many of our soldiers would be under six feet of German sod.[55] Such talk naturally aroused a good deal of resentment among business and labor people. They did not dispute the need for greater production but held that the Army itself was responsi-

ble for shortages when it miscalculated requirements and when it ordered cutbacks. By castigating others, they said, the Army was trying to cover its own mistakes. Moreover, actual shortages at the front arose more from logistical difficulties than from production failures.[56]

Such opposition tended to make General Somervell more circumspect. When he appeared before a Congressional committee, he still pleaded the same urgency, but was much more careful than he had been in his public speeches. He pointed out that in spite of the shortage of manpower, no military campaign had yet suffered from shortages. "Our problem," he told the committee, "is to keep us from suffering from a lack of supplies." When Senator James M. Tunnell of Delaware remarked that on the Army Radio Hour he "heard one fellow make the statement that they fired two shots where they could have fired five because of the shortage of ammunition," General Somervell explained, "That's because of the difficulties of getting ammunition from the ships to the gun and not because of any failure of production yet. . . ."[57]

Though Somervell was more careful in his remarks he did not become less forceful. He waged his war against complacency as vigorously as ever. On 6 December 1944 he carried his fight for an appreciation of the need for more war production to the National Association of

---

[53] Memo of Agreement, Conf between Krug and Batcheller, Somervell, Bruce, Col. Frank R. Denton, and Col. Maurice R. Scharff, 23 Nov 44, Hq ASF, WPB.

[54] Industrial Mobilization for War, p. 812.

[55] The New York Times, December 2–4, 1944.

[56] Stein, Public Administration and Policy Development; The Reconversion Controversy, Com on Public Adm Cases, 3 Thomas Circle, Washington 5, D. C., passim.

[57] Hearings before a Special Committee Investigating the National Defense Program, Senate, 78th Cong, 2d Sess, Pt. 26, pp. 11989–93.

Manufacturers. He began his speech there with the words: "This is the most important speech I have ever made." He then said, "Make no mistake about our situation, they have supplies at the front right now. It's the future we must provide for." Greater weight of munitions, he emphasized, could shorten the war and save lives. "This nation," he said, "has committed its troops to fighting the war in one specific fashion—with an overwhelming superiority of material. . . . American industry and American workers must rededicate themselves, here and now, to an upsurge of production on the home front so that our forces on all fronts shall be limited in their use of matériel only by our ability to get it to them and by elbow room on the fighting fronts in which to use it." [58]

The Germans in their counterattack in the Ardennes on 16 December 1944 provided emphasis for this speech. The Battle of the Bulge, creating the necessary sense of urgency on the home production front, completed the demise of the Nelson reconversion proposals. Early in December 1944 General Clay was transferred to become Mr. Byrnes' deputy in the Office of War Mobilization and Reconversion.[59] It is probable that Clay was influential in drawing up the first report of that office under the Reconversion Act. This report placed part of the blame for production shortages on Nelson's "too early start toward reconversion." [60]

Reconversion talk was not renewed until after the defeat of Germany had become almost certain. By that time Nelson's proposals had become only a small part of a much larger program. The battle was renewed on as fierce a scale as ever, and the charges of military dictatorship were again raised. Mr. Byrnes' own advisory committee blasted him for his surrender of home-front control to the Army, castigated

General Clay and demanded his removal. Mr. Byrnes told them, "He's leaving." [61] But this time the end of the war in Europe was in sight. Somervell himself recommended to the Chief of Staff that Clay be transferred to the European Theater of Operations. The ASF was ready now to think more seriously than ever before about reconversion and neither Patterson nor Somervell wished to oppose a positive step looking toward actual reconversion to peacetime production.

Smaller War Plants

Just as the Army and the WPB had to mesh their policies and operations in large-scale undertakings, so did they find it necessary to establish careful and satisfactory working relationships down to the smallest war plant. Public Law 603 of the 77th Congress, approved on 11 June 1942, provided for the chairman of the War Production Board to appoint a deputy specifically assigned to mobilizing the productive capacity of small business concerns. Under the terms of the act, the WPB chairman was to direct the attention of procurement officers of the government to the productive capacity of small plants and to take such action as would result in the granting of government contracts to small businesses. Here again it was left for administrative officers to develop working

---

[58] WD press release, 6 Dec 44, address by Somervell before the NAM.

[59] Ltr, Dir OWMR to Clay, 4 Dec 44, Industrial Rec Div, National Archives.

[60] *Problems of Mobilization and Reconversion: First Report to the President, the Senate, and the House of Rrepresentatives by the Director of War Mobilization and Reconversion, January 1, 1945* (Washington, U.S. Government Printing Office, 1945). See also below, pp. 588–89.

[61] The Reconversion Controversy, *passim.*, cited in n. 56; *The New York Times*, March 29, 1945.

relationships to effect the purpose of the law.

In August 1942 a Small War Plants Branch was established in ASF headquarters to promote as full a utilization of small plants as possible, consistent with quality, quantity, and speed requirements in the delivery of war supplies. A month before, officials of the ASF had begun a series of discussions with the Smaller War Plants Division of the WPB to determine the best methods for carrying out the act. An agreement in principle was reached within a short time, but it was not officially announced until October. The delay was caused by the absence of the chairman of the Smaller War Plants Corporation from the United States and the reluctance of any of his subordinates to give final approval.

On 30 October 1942 the commanding general of the ASF distributed a statement of policy on the use of smaller war plants to the seven technical services. This policy outlined the procedures which had been agreed upon in order to derive maximum benefit from the Smaller War Plants Division. A representative of the War Production Board was assigned to each technical service to work with an officer designated by the service. The two were to review the procurement requirements of the Army Supply Program and select products suitable for manufacture by plants recommended by the WPB. They would then ascertain the total quantities of products which might be provided by small plants and direct contracting officers to place definite orders. In addition, existing prime contracts were to be examined, with representatives of the WPB to determine the possible extent of additional subcontracting. Subcontracting of future contracts was also to be extended. The statement made clear that it was War Department

policy to place contracts with small businesses without the necessity of compulsory certification by the WPB or the actual making of procurement contracts by the Smaller War Plants Corporation. Representatives of the Smaller War Plants Division were also stationed in each of the district procurement offices of the technical services.

Preferential treatment for smaller concerns was provided for in a WPB directive issued on 10 October 1942. Under existing procurement directives a percentage of business was usually earmarked for small companies and forwarded for execution to buying offices in the field. In time, most of the screening took place entirely in the field rather than in Washington, thus avoiding the duplication of work. This program of decentralization was finally formalized on 24 April 1943 in an agreement signed by the Under Secretary of War and the chairman of the Smaller War Plants Corporation. By mid-summer of 1943 the Smaller War Plants Corporation representatives in field offices had familiarized themselves with Army procurement methods to such an extent that few discussions were necessary in Washington. The relationship of the two agencies in the matter of spreading contracts to small plants continued on a very friendly basis to the end of the war.[62]

With the assistance of WPB officials, the ASF in the year of July 1944 to June 1945, awarded 25 percent of all contracts, measured in dollar value, to plants employing fewer than five hundred persons.[63]

---

[62] This section is based largely on the ASF monograph, Purchasing Policies and Practices, prepared by the Purchases Division, ASF, pp. 106–09, Hist Rec, ASF. See also *Hearings before the Special Committee to Study and Survey Problems of Small Business Enterprises*, Senate, 77th Cong, 2d Sess, Testimony of Gen Somervell, 7 Dec 42, Pt. 11, p. 1479.

[63] Annual Rpt of ASF, 1945, p. 216.

The production quarrels between the ASF and the WPB provided a good deal of excitement. In large part the difficulties could be traced to the personalities of Mr. Nelson and General Somervell. In Somervell's eyes Nelson was vacillating, apparently unable to understand the Army's point of view on military procurement, and inclined to listen to certain groups within the WPB staff who seemed sincerely to believe that the Army was politically reactionary and must be kept in its place, war or no war. In Nelson's eyes, Somervell no doubt seemed to be a positive, inflexible, and even presumptuous individual, inclined to tell Nelson how to run his own job. That the difficulties were largely those of personality is supported in part by the fact that neither Somervell nor his associates had any similar clashes with Mr. Wilson or with other high officials in the WPB.

One factor which made these personal relationships even more troublesome was Nelson's unwillingness or inability to keep his associates from reporting every issue to the press, usually in a garbled form. On one occasion, on 13 September 1942, Somervell addressed a memorandum to key ASF personnel deploring the "continual airing in the public prints of the alleged controversy between the War Production Board and the War and Navy Departments." He added that "our personal relations with Mr. Nelson are of the best," and warned against statements that might be "construed as criticism of the WPB. . . ." Somervell ended with the remark that the "battle is being fought abroad and not in Washington" and that "Mr. Goebbels would pay millions of dollars to stir up dissension" among war agencies.[64] One thing Somervell and his staff did not do was to run to newspapermen

with their side of any occasional difference with the WPB. For that very reason the Army point of view was seldom understood by the outside observer.

In Somervell's eyes, moreover, the issues which arose were important, even vital, matters of procedure and policy, but he was not inclined to be personal about them. In fact a criticism which might justifiably have been leveled against Somervell was that he thought too infrequently in personal terms, that he was insensitive to the impression made upon others by his own drive and positive beliefs. Somervell never had an inclination to make his differences with Nelson a purely personal matter; after any conflict he was ready and willing to sit down with him the next day to try and iron out any issue. It was apparently difficult for Mr. Nelson to understand such an attitude. He was certain that Somervell's criticisms were personal. For this reason, after the "feasibility" dispute of October 1942, Somervell endeavored to remain in the background and leave all ASF relations with the WPB to Under Secretary Patterson and General Clay.

In summary, the record of these ASF–WPB relationships seems to suggest first of all that the difficulties arose from fundamental differences between the personalities of Nelson and Somervell. A second factor was the absence of a clear-cut understanding of the respective roles of the military procurement agencies and the central economic control agency. From the ASF point of view it seemed clear that it was the WPB—or certain persons inside the WPB—who could not or would not understand the differences in the responsibility of each agency.

---

[64] Files, CG ASF.

CHAPTER XVI

The ASF and Other Civilian Agencies Controlling Procurement Resources

Throughout World War II differences between the War Department and the War Production Board attracted considerable public attention. Yet the WPB was by no means the only civilian agency controlling vital war production resources. There were several other emergency agencies as well. The Army Service Forces worked closely and amicably with them, avoiding the controversies that attended ASF–WPB collaboration.

As in its attitude toward the WPB, the ASF never suggested that any of these civilian agencies was unnecessary. On the contrary, it depended heavily upon each one for the performance of activities essential to the procurement of war supplies. Naturally there were differences of opinion; but no controversies ever developed over basic issues such as "military control of the economy" or "civilian direction of military strategy." When differences arose, they were adjusted on the merits of the particular issue at hand. The civilian agencies and the ASF found a general formula for successful collaboration. In general, this was the same one which the ASF constantly urged upon the WPB, namely, that the ASF would control the final items of military production, while the civilian agencies would control primary economic resources and direct the distribution of an appropriate portion of these resources to military procurement. These amicable relationships are much less sensational than the storms and crises which marked efforts at collaboration with the WPB. They are none the less important.

Research and Development

On 28 June 1941 the President created the Office of Scientific Research and Development to assure adequate provision for research on scientific and medical problems arising out of the war. This agency absorbed the National Defense Research Committee (NDRC) created by the President in June 1940. It was prepared to undertake any research projects desired by the armed forces as a contribution to the improvement and development of weapons. The committee operated mainly through contracts awarded to research institutions, both university and industrial.[1]

---

[1] EO 8807, 28 Jun 41.

The OSRD frequently suggested new types of military equipment. A case in point is the development of the DUKW, an amphibian 2½-ton truck, adopted by the Army for use in ship-to-shore operations.[2] The variable time (proximity) fuze, which introduced a whole new element into antiaircraft and field artillery ammunition, was another product of research by the OSRD.[3]

When the Office of Scientific Research and Development was created, it also became the parent agency for a Committee on Medical Research. Within the ASF this committee maintained relations almost exclusively with The Surgeon General's office, co-operating on a variety of projects ranging from malaria control to the development of penicillin.[4] In this extensive collaboration the two offices adhered to the pattern of medical research and practice which prevailed generally between doctors, hospitals, and research personnel. The work went on so smoothly that no major problems of medical research arose requiring General Somervell's intervention.

Perhaps the closest working relationship between the ASF and the OSRD grew out of the MANHATTAN project which produced the atomic bomb. The original interest in atomic fission as a possible military weapon came from a group of scientists who were formally organized as a uranium committee under the NDRC in June 1940. In November 1941 uranium research for military purposes was centered in a special section of the Office of Scientific Research and Development. At the same time, Dr. Vannevar Bush of the OSRD recommended that the whole project should be transferred to the Army when the time came for building production plants. This transfer took place in

August 1942 when the MANHATTAN DISTRICT was created by the Chief of Engineers to begin construction activities.[5] General Somervell had already designated his chief of staff, General Styer, to be his representative in the OSRD on atomic research. Thereafter General Styer followed developments of the project for Somervell, working very closely with Dr. Bush.

The MANHATTAN DISTRICT project was unique in that extensive basic research was still being conducted while production plants were being built and a military laboratory was being set up. Key personnel were civilian scientists or engineers, working under the direction of Brig. Gen. Leslie R. Groves. The atomic bomb was eventually constructed at the Los Alamos Laboratory, forty-five miles from Santa Fe, and tested on the night of 16 July 1945 at the Alamogordo Air Base in central New Mexico. An atomic bomb was dropped at Hiroshima on 6 August and another at Nagasaki on 9 August. The two-billion-dollar enterprise representing the joint efforts of scientists, industry, and the Army thus proved itself a great success.

The creation of the National Defense Research Committee was necessary because of the inadequate attention given to research activities by the armed forces between World Wars I and II. At a time when military funds were meager at best, little money was spent on the development of new weapons. When large-scale procurement began in 1940, however, the various supply arms and services of the

---

[2] This story is summarized in James P. Baxter, *Scientists Against Time* (Boston, Little, Brown and Company, 1946), pp. 76–82, 248–51.

[3] *Ibid.*, Ch. XV.

[4] *Ibid.*, Chs. XX–XXIII.

[5] Annual Rpt of ASF, 1945, Ch. I; Henry D. Smyth, *Atomic Energy for Military Purposes* (Princeton, N. J., Princeton University Press, 1946).

Army were suddenly able to spend considerable sums on research projects. The NDRC existed primarily to help these procurement agencies in mobilizing scientific resources.

There were two ways in which the NDRC assisted the technical services of the ASF. In the first place, it called attention to promising work already done or being done in industry and universities in the development of new or improved weapons. In the second place, it made its services available to the procurement agencies requesting scientific assistance in solving technical problems encountered in meeting a military desire for new or improved equipment. Thus, for example, when the Army and the Navy both pointed out the need for better antiaircraft fire control devices, the NDRC led scientists in industry to develop electronic fire control systems.

On occasion the proposal was made by both Army officers and scientists that the military laboratories should concentrate on applied research, that is, the development of new weapons and the improvement of existing weapons. The university laboratories, under guidance of OSRD, on the other hand, should concentrate on basic research for the advancement of scientific knowledge which might have future military usefulness. No such dividing line was ever feasible in practice. In the early period from 1940 to 1942 the procurement agencies, especially those which became the technical services of the ASF, were unable to enlarge their applied research and development activities on a broad scale and so the NDRC had to supplement their development work. Later, as the research and development programs of the technical services expanded, some contracts made by the two operating

units of the OSRD were turned over to them. But the OSRD was always available to help the services on any research or development problem. From the records of the OSRD it seems evident that the closest working relationships with the NDRC, apart from the MANHATTAN project, were maintained by the Signal Corps and the Army Air Forces. The next largest agency of the Army utilizing NDRC assistance was the Ordnance Department.[6] For the most part the technical services maintained direct relations with the NDRC and the Committee on Medical Research of the OSRD.

After the creation of the ASF, an officer in that headquarters was designated War Department liaison officer with the OSRD. Between April 1942 and August 1945 there were five such liaison officers. This was a rapid turnover which some charged hampered efficient collaboration.[7] But it may perhaps be said in Somervell's defense that he had considerable difficulty in finding the right officer for the assignment. The liaison officer was primarily available to adjust any difficulties which might arise in the co-operative effort of the OSRD and the technical services. His assistance might be requested by the OSRD in attempting to overcome indifference or even hostility on the part of a technical service to certain scientific undertakings. Or a technical service might occasionally need assistance in dealing with the OSRD. For the most part, however, the technical services and the OSRD worked together harmoniously. The chief problem was an occasional reluctance within the technical services to consider scientific proposals. Usually this reluc-

[6] Irvin Stewart, *Organizing Scientific Research for War* (Boston, Little, Brown and Company, 1948), p. 323.
[7] *Ibid.*, p. 154.

tance was overcome by pressure from General Somervell's office or from the Office of the Secretary of War, which prevented major conflicts from arising to bedevil their relationships with the OSRD.

The deputy director of the OSRD has commented that in the event of another war "there should be no need for another OSRD," adding that only in the event of a "large deficit of military research such as existed in 1940" would such an office have to be created.[8] Whether true or not, it is beyond question that in World War II the work of the OSRD was essential to the development of new and improved weapons.

Before his departure in 1945 to join General MacArthur's command, General Styer wrote Dr. Bush a letter which revealed the attitude of top personnel in the ASF toward the OSRD. He said, in part: "My wandering through wonderland, while being led by your guiding hand, has been most enjoyable. My rubbing elbows with the men of science . . . has enlarged my realms of thought and keenly whetted my imagination. I hope that the association between science and the military can be continued by men of vision after the war."[9]

Special Handling of Food, Petroleum, Rubber

Three commodities were given an administrative status apart from the War Production Board during World War II. These were food, rubber, and petroleum.

In 1941 there existed a separate Office of Agricultural Defense Relations (later, Office of Agricultural War Relations), which had developed originally under the Advisory Commission to the Council of National Defense. Early in 1942 the WPB set up a Food Division. By a memorandum dated 4 June 1942, the WPB chairman also established a Food Requirements Committee to handle allocations of food to various competing demands. The War Department was represented on this committee. The Office of Agricultural War Relations was transferred to the Department of Agriculture in the summer of 1942. Later, in December 1942 the President concentrated all food and agricultural aspects of the war effort in the Department of Agriculture.[10] This order provided that the Secretary of Agriculture should assume full responsibility for the control of the nation's food resources and directed him to establish an advisory committee composed of representatives of the State, War, and Navy Departments, and other government agencies. He was to obtain estimates of food requirements from the members of this advisory committee and consult with the committee before making food allocations.

The powers conferred upon the Secretary of Agriculture were later concentrated in a War Food Administration established in March 1943.[11] This step, however, did not change the basic powers originally vested in the Secretary of Agriculture nor did it affect the relationships in food administration between the War Department and the central food agency.

The Quartermaster General of the Army Service Forces was appointed the War Department representative on the food advisory committee. Throughout the course of the war the association between him and the War Food Administration was harmonious. Military requirements were presented to the War Food Adminis-

---

[8] *Ibid.*, p. 325.
[9] Ltr, Styer to Bush, 1 May 42, Hq ASF, CofS.
[10] EO 9280, 5 Dec 42.
[11] EO 9322, 26 Mar 43.

tration, which exerted every effort to meet those needs. Set-aside orders and allocation orders were issued requiring canners, meat packers, and other food producers to earmark a certain portion of their output for military and other governmental purchase. Nothing in the arrangement disturbed the existing system of military procurement. Indeed, the War Food Administration encouraged other governmental agencies to make such food purchases as they required through the Subsistence Division of the Quartermaster Corps. The Chicago Quartermaster Depot, primarily responsible for food procurement, became the center for most of the food purchasing operations of the federal government. A local office of the War Food Administration was established there to work closely with Army officials. Since the Navy Department obtained more than 80 percent of its food requirements through the Army, the War Food Administration was eager to consolidate all food procurement through this single channel. Most purchases for the Treasury Procurement Division and certain other government offices were also handled through Army machinery.

No major difficulties arose in defining the respective roles of the two agencies. The War Food Administration recognized that it was the War Department's responsibility to purchase the foodstuffs required by it and to establish the specifications and packaging requirements. In turn, The Quartermaster General followed the recommendations of the War Food Administration in timing food procurement and in spreading contracts among various producers. Food requirements were also modified from time to time to meet supply conditions. In 1944, for example, the Army reduced its allowance of butter by 40 percent because of the shortage in this commodity. In short, it can be said that it would have been difficult, if not impossible, to have arranged for the orderly procurement of food needs without the existence of the War Food Administration.[12]

On 28 May 1941 the President, in a letter to the Secretary of the Interior, announced that he was designating him to be Petroleum Co-ordinator for National Defense. From the outset, Secretary Harold Ickes sought the co-operation of the War Department in discharging his responsibilities. On 12 August 1941 for example, Mr. Ickes wrote to Secretary Stimson suggesting that the Army and Navy Munitions Board should have a permanent liaison officer with his organization, especially to help in pushing projects for the expansion of petroleum production.[13] Subsequently, in December 1942, the President issued an order establishing the Petroleum Administration for War, headed by the Secretary of the Interior serving *ex officio*.[14] The new administration became the center for handling all wartime petroleum problems. Mr. Ickes had earlier created a Petroleum Supply and Distribution Board for reviewing "the world-wide petroleum supply and transportation situation" and for planning "to insure adequate petroleum supplies when and where needed by the military forces and by war industry." Representatives of

---

[12] For a concise, general account of the War Food Administration, see "Food for War" in *The United States at War: Development and Administration of the War Program by the Federal Government,* prepared under the auspices of the Committee on Records of War Administration by the War Records Section, Bureau of the Budget (Washington, U.S. Government Printing Office, 1946), p. 321. (Hereafter cited as *The United States at War.*)

[13] Ltr, Ickes to Stimson, 12 Aug 41, Hq ASF, Petroleum.

[14] EO 9276, 2 Dec 42.

the Army, Navy, and War Shipping Administration were invited to serve on this board.[15]

At the time the ASF was set up, General Somervell had on his staff the officer who had previously been in charge of petroleum matters for the Under Secretary of War. This officer continued to function as before, but the main problems turned out to be not procurement of petroleum but its shipping and distribution. The actual purchases of petroleum products within the Army, except for aviation gasoline, were made by The Quartermaster General's office. An Army-Navy Petroleum Board was first established on 14 July 1942 in a joint announcement signed by General Somervell and the Vice Chief of Naval Operations, Admiral Horne. This board was responsible for effecting close co-operation between the two departments in petroleum procurement, shipment, and distribution. It also maintained close relations with the Petroleum Administration for War. The Army-Navy Petroleum Board became an agency of the Joint Chiefs of Staff and was thereafter the representative of the armed forces on all petroleum matters.

The petroleum industry was so organized in the United States that it was able, through existing storage and distribution channels, to meet all domestic military requirements. The Army-Navy Petroleum Board presented petroleum requirements to the Petroleum Administrator, who then made such adjustments in production and distribution practices as were necessary to meet these requirements. The Petroleum Administrator kept in close touch with the industry and knew at all times the exact status of petroleum stocks throughout the country. Frequently he requested the Army or the Navy to take delivery of petroleum at Galveston or some other point in order to relieve the burden on inland storage and distribution facilities. Had this not been done, refining in the southwestern part of the United States might have outrun storage and distribution capacities and have curtailed production.

At one time Secretary Ickes was alarmed lest a letter of instruction sent out by General Somervell and Admiral Horne on 16 December 1942 implied a desire on the part of the armed forces to ignore the Petroleum Administration for War. In a reply to his protest against the action, Secretary Stimson in February 1943 assured Ickes that the Army-Navy Petroleum Board realized that the Petroleum Administration for War was charged with responsibility for crude oil production and refining, pointed out that representatives of the board had co-operated wholeheartedly with Mr. Ickes' office, and assured him that this would continue. He explained that the December letter was intended to apply only to internal Army and Navy procedures. Secretary Stimson added: "I assure you that Army officers, who have occasion to handle petroleum matters, clearly understand the original order setting up the Army-Navy Petroleum Board, and the letter of 16 December 1942. Therefore, you need have no fear that the prerogatives of your office will be usurped, either by the original directive, or the letter of 16 December 1942." Secretary Stimson concluded by saying that a copy of his letter was being given to the Army-Navy Petroleum Board for its guidance.[16] Stimson's letter, drafted in

---

[15] Ltr, Ickes to Stimson, 4 May 42, Hq ASF, Petroleum.

[16] Ltr, Stimson to Ickes, 3 Feb 43, Hq ASF, Petroleum.

Somervell's office, represented the official ASF point of view on co-operation with the Petroleum Administration for War.

The attitude of the Petroleum Administration at all times favored enabling the Army and Navy to obtain their requirements with the least possible disruption of the industry's extraction, refining, and distribution activities. No serious jurisdictional disputes arose, and whenever a disagreement on policy or procedure arose, it was quickly adjusted between the Petroleum Administrator and the Army-Navy Petroleum Board. The entire operation worked smoothly, and no great difficulties were encountered in obtaining the necessary petroleum supplies. There were some problems in developing refining capacity for aviation gasoline, but these were outside the province of the ASF.

In September 1942 the President ordered new arrangements for the co-ordination and control of the rubber program.[17] The order directed the chairman of the War Production Board to assume full responsibility for all phases of the rubber program including technical research. In addition, it provided for a Rubber Director to be appointed by and to be responsible to the chairman of the WPB. The terms of the order were purposely broad in order to end current controversies over responsibility for developing all phases of the rubber program. One effect of the order was to establish virtually a separate organization, nominally tied to the WPB, but actually in full control of rubber activities. To carry out his mission, the Rubber Director appointed a Requirements Committee on which the ASF was represented and established a separate allocations system whereby the Army Service Forces was permitted to purchase stated quantities of rubber products.

The most important rubber product bought by the ASF was tires. These were purchased directly to replace tires with which all vehicles were originally equipped. Army tire requirements continually exceeded the rubber allocations available to it. Because of the critical nature of the items, the War Department inaugurated a tire conservation program, directed by the Chief of Ordnance, which extended throughout the entire Army both in the United States and overseas.[18] The shortage did not disturb the amicable relationship which at all times existed between the Army Service Forces and the Office of the Rubber Director. The only major difficulty that arose between the War Department and the Office of the Rubber Director concerned the division of equipment and raw materials between the synthetic rubber program and the aviation gasoline program. Under Secretary Patterson personally intervened to insist upon resolving this conflict.

No difficulties were experienced in defining the respective authority of the ASF and the Rubber Director. The ASF recognized the need for an agency to control all phases of the rubber program and to direct the utilization of the limited rubber resources. At the same time, the procurement authority of the War Department was not questioned by the Office of the Rubber Director. Military requirements were carefully scrutinized, frequently questioned, and, as already mentioned, not always met. On the other hand, the Office of the Rubber Director conscientiously endeavored to help the ASF obtain its rubber quotas.

---

[17] EO 9246, 17 Sep 42.
[18] Annual Rpt of ASF, 1944, p. 146; 1945, pp. 198–99.

WMC and Labor Relations [19]

As the armed forces of the United States in the last half of 1943 approached full mobilization, the problem of labor supply became increasingly bothersome to those responsible for military procurement. Originally the War Production Board had been given authority to handle the mobilization of manpower. A Labor Division was established for this purpose. In April 1942, the President established a War Manpower Commission to consist of the Federal Security Administrator as chairman and of representatives from the War, Navy, Agriculture, and Labor Departments, the WPB, the Selective Service System, and the Civil Service Commission.[20] After consultation with members of the commission, the chairman was authorized to formulate plans and policies for the most effective utilization of the nation's manpower. In addition, the chairman was authorized to establish policies for federal agencies governing the recruitment, training, and placement of workers in industry and agriculture, as well as within the federal government itself. At first, Mr. G. H. Dorr, special assistant to the Secretary of War, was designated as War Department representative on the WMC. Subsequently, the Under Secretary became the official War Department representative.

The question of the size of the Army in relation to the total manpower of the country was settled early in 1943 when the Chief of Staff set a ceiling for an Army of 7.7 million men. The peak strength of the Army actually rose to almost 8.3 million men. The recruitment of labor to work in Army arsenals, depots, and ports, and in the plants of prime contractors was also a matter of continuing interest to the ASF. Only one important jurisdictional issue

seems to have arisen between the War Department and the WMC. This involved the authority of the WMC to check actual labor utilization by War Department contractors. The War Department took the position that it should be responsible for the labor utilization of its prime contractors and that it would take whatever steps were necessary to prevent labor hoarding by these manufacturers. The War Manpower Commission at one time contemplated establishing a corps of investigators to check manpower utilization within plants. Following protests from the War Department, the WMC made no such investigations at plants of Army prime contractors.

The problem of labor supply was a many-sided one and at no time did it come solely within the purview of the WMC. The establishment of both WPB production urgency committees and WMC manpower priorities committees in critical labor areas illustrated the overlapping concern. Production urgency was determined by the WPB, and the manpower priorities committees had almost no alternative but to channel labor in accordance with these priorities. There is no need here to go into the question of whether the techniques of labor mobilization were adequate during World War II. The War Department contended that they were not, and while supporting the WMC in all its undertakings, it also pushed for more effective measures, in-

---

[19] This section is based on the annual reports of the ASF together with three statements which were especially prepared by the Industrial Personnel Division of the ASF. These are filed in OCMH. See also Jonathan Grossman, Industrial Manpower Problems and Policies of the War Department, a volume in preparation for the series UNITED STATES ARMY IN WORLD WAR II.

[20] EO 9139, 18 Apr 42.

cluding national service legislation. The ASF found that in attempting to meet labor shortages which adversely affected war procurement, it had to work with a number of different agencies, including the War Production Board, the War Manpower Commission, the National War Labor Board, the Office of Price Administration, the National Housing Agency, the Federal Works Agency, and the Office of Defense Transportation. The large number of agencies involved was partly responsible for the delay in satisfying War Department requirements.

When the War Department developed a team approach to labor problems in such specific industries as cotton duck, cotton tire cord, military tires, and forges and foundries, or in such specific areas as Newark, New Bedford, Seattle, and Los Angeles, the principal objection came from the WPB rather than from the WMC. Subsequently, both the WPB and the WMC favored a much broader program under War Department leadership in order to attack labor supply problems in the many different industries and localities. The War Department insisted that emergency measures should be taken only in a few specific cases and this point of view was eventually accepted as general governmental policy.

One method of meeting the labor supply problem was to avoid, insofar as possible, the letting of contracts in labor shortage areas, in accordance with WPB Directive 2, issued as early as 19 October 1942. This was not an entirely satisfactory device, since the most important consideration in awarding contracts was satisfactory quantitative, qualitative, and time performance in the delivery of war supplies. Moreover, the location of existing facilities determined for the most part where contracts might be let. In December 1942 the War Manpower Commission began to classify labor market areas as I, inadequate labor supply; II, anticipated inadequate labor supply; and III, adequate labor supply. This gave contracting officers a guide in the placement of contracts. Moreover, the ASF authorized procurement offices to pay premiums up to 15 percent in order to place contracts in labor areas with surplus manpower.

In September 1943 WPB Directive 2 was amended to establish new criteria for the placement of contracts. Thereafter, among the other items to be considered were labor cost and efficiency of manufacturers. The Army Service Forces then began to establish techniques for measuring the labor utilization of contractors in an effort to guide both contract terminations and contract placement. As changes in war production occurred and it became possible to cancel certain contracts, an effort was made to cancel first those contracts in labor shortage areas that were held by manufacturers whose relative number of man-hours per unit of output was higher than that of other producers in the same field.

When the west coast manpower program was started in September 1943, the ASF agreed to avoid placing contracts there. In December of the same year the program was extended to include six other areas—Detroit, Akron, Hartford, Buffalo, Chicago, and Cleveland. Procurement regulations were amended so that the placement of additional contracts in these areas was limited. The ASF inspected the practices of the technical services to insure that procurement district offices were avoiding tight labor market areas. In taking these steps the ASF carried out its labor supply responsibilities in accordance with general policies fixed by the WPB and WMC.

Closely related to the question of labor supply was the government's policy on labor relations and wage stabilization. These responsibilities were assigned to the National War Labor Board, created in January 1942.[21] The board considered itself a service agency and accepted War Department opinion on the importance of various kinds of procurement. Minor friction between the board and the Department arose out of certain internal security issues, but these were easily worked out. In one or two cases the War Department pressed for plant seizure when the board thought this unwise. In other cases, as in the Montgomery Ward dispute, the board insisted that the War Department take over even when the Department had no direct interest. Altogether there were twenty-five plant seizures during the war, jointly arranged by the National War Labor Board and the War Department. In thirteen of these cases, seizure resulted from labor's failure to comply with board directives; in twelve, it resulted from management's refusal to comply. There was initial disagreement between the War Department and the board on only four of these seizures.[22]

Since wage questions were most likely to arise in connection with labor disputes, the enforcement of a national wage policy became a function of the National War Labor Board. At the same time, the board adopted the administrative arrangement of designating agents to enforce its broad policies within specific labor fields. Thus the Army Service Forces administered wage policies in construction at Army installations, at government-owned, privately operated (GOPO) plants, and also among maritime workers on transport and cargo vessels operated or chartered by the War Department.

From time to time the National War Labor Board checked with ASF headquarters and installations on the enforcement of these policies. In many cases, the War Department appeared before local panels established by the National War Labor Board or before the board itself to press for exceptions to the wage stabilization policy. At times, the labor members of the board criticized War Department handling of wage matters, principally at GOPO plants, as for instance on the question of whether certain jobs should be paid on the basis of construction or maintenance wages. These issues were amicably settled, and the War Department continued to be the wage administration agency for all its plants and other installations. Altogether the War Department presented about thirty-five cases during the war for unusual wage adjustments, and these were all approved in whole or in part. The War Department (which meant the ASF) and the National War Labor Board co-operated in noteworthy fashion during the entire period of their association.

The ASF also served as War Department liaison with the Selective Service System in handling the problem of the industrial impact of military drafts. The ASF presented deferment policy requests to national headquarters only after the most careful screening. After V-E Day the ASF withdrew many deferment requests, and got out of the field entirely after V-J Day, leaving the matter of deferments for direct negotiation between industry and the Selective Service System. In December 1944 the Office of War Mobilization and

---

[21] EO 9017, 12 Jan 42.

[22] John Ohly, War Plant Seizures, MS, OCMH.

Reconversion asked the War Department to draft men under 38 voluntarily leaving essential industrial employment, and with the help of the Selective Service System, the Army examined about 71,000 such persons, accepting over 12,000 of them.[23] Relations between the ASF and the Selective Service System also were of a friendly co-operative character.

Price Control [24]

In April 1941 the President created the Office of Price Administration and Civilian Supply, combining two of the original divisions established under the Advisory Commission to the Council of National Defense.[25] The name was changed to Office of Price Administration (OPA) in August 1941. Price control was placed on a statutory basis by the passage of a Price Control Act, and approved by the President on 20 January 1942.

During the debates over this legislation, the Secretary of War and the Secretary of the Navy addressed a joint letter to the President dated 19 December 1941 proposing an amendment to the bill about to be passed. The two secretaries pointed out that the Army and the Navy were responsible for the procurement of war supplies and that this obligation could not be discharged unless cases of conflict between combat needs and price considerations were decided by them. Both expressed full appreciation of the need for price stability and pledged the two departments to be "very sparing in negotiations above ceiling prices." The suggested amendment provided that no regulation made under the act would apply to any sale to the War or Navy Department if the Secretary of War or the Secretary of the Navy certified to the Office of Price Control that this exemption was essential to the national defense. The next day the President replied that he could not approve the proposed amendment since it was absolutely imperative that final authority be vested in one person. The Army and Navy would be expected to conform as well as everybody else. He suggested, however, that a permanent liaison officer be assigned to work with the Price Control Administrator and that final appeals be brought to him.

From its creation in April until 11 May 1942, the OPA directed a program of selective price control. Certain designated basic materials were placed under price ceilings in accordance with the theory that by controlling their price the general price level would not rise unduly. The early price schedules affected metals, building materials, industrial chemicals, and textiles. In the autumn of 1941 some additional items were brought under price control, as for example, semifabricated goods and machinery.

On 24 April 1942 the approach changed when the OPA issued the General Maximum Price Regulation covering prices at all levels for every commodity not otherwise covered by a separate OPA regulation. Effective 12 May this general regulation set the highest price charged in March 1942 as the top legal price for every kind of goods. It limited Army control over the prices paid to its contractors at a time when the vast military procurement program was just getting well under

---

[23] For a more detailed study of the relationship of the ASF to Selective Service, see Albert A. Blum, Deferment Problems and Policies of the War Department, MS, Columbia University, 1953.

[24] The material in this section has been condensed from Purchasing Policies and Practices, prepared by Purchases Division, ASF, pp. 194–227.

[25] EO 8734, 11 Apr 41.

way. The new regulation upset the Army considerably. In the absence of any previous manufacturing experience for such items as airplanes, tanks, guns, and ammunition, prices fluctuated greatly. The Army had promised contractors that where unit prices turned out to be too low, it would make adjustments. On 13 May 1942, at the request of the War and Navy Departments, the OPA acknowledged the effects of its regulation by issuing Supplementary Regulation 4 exempting a large number of military items. This supplementary regulation, however, referred only to the General Maximum Price Regulation. It did not affect specific maximum price regulations which might cover materials or supplies of interest to the Army.

Out of the discussions about the General Maximum Price Regulation, a formal liaison arrangement developed between the War Department and the OPA. A Price Administration Branch was established in June 1942 in the Purchases Division, ASF, while the OPA in turn set up a War Goods Office the following October. The primary function assigned to the Price Administration Branch was the handling of all procurement matters involving the OPA. Discussions between the two agencies continued as individual price regulations brought additional items of military interest under price control. Thus the application of Maximum Price Regulation 136, covering gasoline, steam and diesel engines, pumps and compressors, and construction equipment, became a subject of mutual concern.

A little later the OPA, as an anti-inflationary safeguard, indicated a desire to review the various military combat items exempted by Supplementary Regulation 4 to the General Maximum Price Regulation. Deeply concerned over the effect this might have on the procurement program of the armed services, Under Secretary of War Patterson and Under Secretary of the Navy Forrestal addressed a lengthy memorandum to Mr. Henderson, the Price Administrator, on 23 July 1942, objecting to the imposition of price control in the field of military equipment.[26] The two Under Secretaries declared that they were "alive to the serious consequences of inflation" and that they heartily approved of the OPA's efforts to control prices. At the same time, they pointed out, they were responsible for procuring vitally needed military supplies without delay. They then presented a number of reasons why they believed that prices of military goods should not be handled in the same manner as other price controls. In their opinion the prices of equipment for purely military purposes did not contribute directly to inflation, since they did not create corresponding rises in the cost of living. Unduly large profits in any war industry, they argued, could be curtailed by renegotiation and excess profits taxes, and where large corporation incomes contributed to an increase in wages, effective wage stabilization would serve as a counterbalance.

Since prewar production experience was lacking as a basis for determining fair prices, they went on to say, it seemed unlikely that any price formula could be devised which would be adequate under the circumstances. Moreover, to vest price control of military items in the OPA would necessarily supplant the Army and Navy in the negotiation of prices on their contracts. Whenever a potential contractor was unable or unwilling to produce at the maximum price fixed by an OPA formula,

---

[26] Memo, Patterson and Forrestal for Henderson, 23 Jul 42, sub: Maximum Price Regulation of Military Equip, Purchases Div, ASF.

he would have to apply to the OPA for adjustment. In such cases the OPA would have to substitute its judgment for that of the Army or Navy as to whether the production was necessary to the war effort and as to whether the proposed price should be granted. This would produce long delays in the delivery of vital supplies. The two Under Secretaries then repeated an earlier proposal that the OPA exempt any military article from price control upon certification by the Secretary of War or the Secretary of the Navy that the exemption was necessary for the prosecution of the war. If this proposal was not satisfactory, they suggested that the same end would be accomplished by the OPA exemption of specific categories such as aircraft, military vehicles, and ordnance items. A suggested list was attached to the memorandum. They pointed out that the items had been limited to those which under OPA price regulation were impeding or threatening to impede military procurement.

Long discussions between officials of the OPA and the ASF followed this memorandum from the two Under Secretaries. Finally, on 16 September 1942 Mr. Henderson put forth a counterproposal in a letter to the Under Secretary of War. In it he expressed doubt whether the dangers of inflation arising from high war contract prices could be prevented in the absence of strict price control. He feared that contracting officers, more concerned with procurement than prices, would have little incentive to reduce costs. He stated his position in these terms: "Unless prices and profits in the military goods area are controlled effectively, the entire program for avoiding inflation in this country will be threatened and perhaps undermined." He went on to acknowledge, however, that the questions at issue were complex and that there was room for disagreement and added that it made no difference who had the job of preventing inflation in the military goods area as long as it was accomplished. He denied any "desire to engage in a jurisdictional dispute."

Accordingly, the Price Administrator expressed his willingness to refrain from any further extension of maximum price control in the area of strictly military goods, if assured by the two departments that they would use all of their powers as effectively as possible to control both prices and profits in the exempted area. In an attempt to define their respective fields of control, Mr. Henderson said that the OPA would refrain from an extension of price control over the sales of commodities which were in such form that they could be used only for military purposes. The OPA, however, would control the prices of materials and commodities at a stage below the first emergence of an article in military form. To work out such a general line of demarkation, he designated one of his assistants.

Additional conferences were held in an effort to define more precisely the controls to be exercised by each agency. In the case of a tank transmission, for example, the first sale of the rough casting came under OPA control, but subsequent operations were in the area reserved for military control. All existing exemptions were frozen and the armed services agreed to request further exemptions only when actual difficulties arose. The OPA in turn made a similar commitment for military exemptions below the line of demarkation. The final agreement was formalized in a letter from Under Secretary Patterson and Under Secretary Forrestal on 14 October 1942 and on 12 November an official press release was issued announcing the arrangement.

It should be added that the War Department immediately followed up these discussions by holding a series of meetings at Tryon, North Carolina, on 31 October and 1 November 1942. From these meetings came a "statement of purchase policies" dated 19 November 1942, in which the War Department principle was announced that prices and the cost of war equipment should be kept at the lowest possible level as a means of encouraging efficiency in production and of conserving manpower and materials. This general principle was elaborated in other parts of the statement. Special care was taken to impress upon all contracting officers that they were not being exempted from price control, but rather that War Department price control was being substituted for OPA price control. A price index was begun as a means of measuring the effectiveness of each technical service in negotiating close prices in each field of procurement.

From then on, many negotiations took place between the Purchases Division in ASF headquarters and the OPA on individual price problems. The general line of demarcation in price control worked out in September and October 1942 was carefully observed. As of 30 June 1945, it was estimated that approximately 65 percent of the dollar value on all War Department prime contracts was exempted from OPA price control.

The most troublesome price problems developed thereafter in the textile and clothing field. Continued negotiations between the two agencies finally produced a supplementary order on 9 March 1945 which permitted the War Department to pay more than ceiling prices in certain agreed-upon instances. ASF headquarters

kept all price regulations under constant study and reviewed proposed OPA price regulations and changes prior to their issuance. Representatives from ASF headquarters attended meetings of OPA industry advisory committees. While occasional differences of opinion and of policy between the two agencies arose, they were always amicably settled. Beyond question OPA actions had a great effect upon War Department pricing, a fact which the Department readily acknowledged. By and large, however, the agreement contained in Mr. Henderson's letter of 16 September 1942 represented a workable and satisfactory division of authority.

The rationing program of the OPA did not directly concern military supply except once when the OPA gave some consideration to developing a plan whereby the Army's rationed food requirements would be administered by the OPA. This idea was abandoned, however, in favor of exempting the armed forces from OPA food rationing. The Army purchased its foodstuffs through the Quartermaster Corps on an unlimited ration banking account. The Quartermaster General established the necessary controls over organized military messes in order to limit the amount of rationed food served each month. Other feeding facilities such as post exchanges, civilian messes, officers clubs, and service clubs received point allocations from local OPA war price and rationing boards on a civilian point basis. In January 1945 a central procurement officer was established at each post to make all purchases of rationed foods.

The OPA also exempted The Quartermaster General and the Army Exchange Service from the ration controls imposed on manufacturers of candies and soft drinks using sugar. The Quartermaster

General received an unlimited ration bank account while the Army Exchange Service received an over-all allocation of these rationed ingredients in a limited account. Quartermaster purchases were entirely for overseas shipment.

In the sale of shoes the Army Exchange Service was placed in the same category as commercial shoe dealers. The OPA made the Army an issuing agent for shoe purchase certificates after approving the general terms on which the Army agreed to issue them. Voluntarily, the Army agreed to restrict its sale of shoes to officer personnel through Quartermaster outlets. In addition, enlisted personnel, under prescribed conditions, might obtain a certificate for shoes other than those normally issued to them. Only the Army could issue shoe purchase certificates to military personnel, thus preventing any attempt to obtain shoe certificates from local war price and rationing boards.

Since gasoline and fuel oil for use in the United States were purchased through local suppliers, the Army and the OPA established an arrangement whereby the Army issued a special OPA form for buying petroleum products for military use. This entitled the local supplier to replenishment by petroleum companies of his military sales. Some difficulties arose in this procedure and changes had to be made. The sale of gasoline to privately owned vehicles operated by military personnel was placed under the same restrictions as those governing civilians, and the same procedures were employed.

The OPA sanctioned many local arrangements whereby Army installations established their own war price and rationing boards, issuing ration coupons in accordance with the general standards set up by the OPA. This was done not only

for gasoline but also for tires, stoves, and automobiles. These arrangements likewise worked satisfactorily. Necessarily, the War Department and the OPA had to work together closely in administering both price and rationing controls.

Housing and Community Facilities

One major omission of the Industrial Mobilization Plan as published before World War II was any reference to the possibility of labor shortages aggravated by a lack of housing and other community facilities in the vicinity of war plants. There were a number of different federal agencies responsible for handling relations with local governments in this field. Direction of public housing activities early in 1941 was placed under a Division of Defense Housing Co-ordination which was established by the President.[27] This agency gave way to a National Housing Agency in February 1942.[28] An Office of Defense Health and Welfare Services was also established to handle local health and welfare requirements.[29] This office was eventually absorbed by the Federal Security Agency. In addition, the Federal Works Administration was involved in the making of grants for roads and for other public facilities. The Office of Defense Transportation had general supervision of local transportation facilities.

As already mentioned, in 1942 the Army Service Forces pressed the WPB through its regional offices to take the lead in co-ordinating all federal services dealing with community facilities problems. Later the President established a Committee for

---

[27] EO 8632, 11 Jan 41.
[28] EO 9070, 24 Feb 42.
[29] EO 8890, 3 Sep 41.

Congested Production Areas.[30] This committee had as its chairman the director of the Bureau of the Budget, and as members, the Under Secretary of War, the Under Secretary of the Navy, the chairman of the War Production Board, the administrator of the Federal Works Agency, the administrator of the National Housing Agency, and the chairman of the War Manpower Commission. The committee handled the co-ordination of federal activities affecting some eighteen different congested areas in the United States. The principal role of the ASF in the work of this committee was simply to indicate the areas in which war procurement was being seriously hampered by inadequate community facilities and services. Thereafter, the committee made sure that various agencies of the federal government concentrated upon the solution of the problems in these particular areas. The Army also worked with the committee in an effort to relieve its own burden upon the local area as far as possible. It was no part of the job of the ASF or of the War Department to handle the problems of community facilities. Yet it was the impact of war procurement which produced most of the local difficulties. The device of a committee for congested production areas was a necessary expedient in World War II because of the many agencies involved and because of the absence of any integrated government machinery for dealing with local communities.

The Office of War Mobilization

In May 1943 President Roosevelt created one of the most important of the emergency war agencies, the Office of War Mobilization. As has been stated, former Justice James F. Byrnes was appointed as its head.[31] In part the office was created because of a general feeling that too many different agencies existed that were only loosely co-operating in the task of controlling the use of the nation's economic resources. The executive order directed the office "to develop unified programs and to establish policies for the maximum use of the nation's natural and industrial resources for military and civilian needs" and "to unify the activities of federal agencies and departments engaged in or concerned with production, procurement, distribution or transportation of military or civilian supplies, materials, and products, and to resolve and determine controversies between such agencies or departments."

Manpower problems at the time were looming more and more as the chief industrial bottleneck. To break it an attack had to be made on several fronts. At the behest of the Office of War Mobilization, the War Department in July 1943 arranged to release soldiers who had previously worked in the nonferrous metal mining industry. The office also helped the WPB and the War Manpower Commission in setting up a program for fixing labor priorities in congested areas. Later, in October five production urgency committees were set up on the west coast where a labor situation existed in the aircraft industry that was of grave concern to the Army Air Forces.

In the autumn of 1943 the Office of War Mobilization became particularly interested in certain postwar problems, and officers from ASF headquarters contributed substantially to the work which eventuated in the Baruch-Hancock *Report on War and Post-War Adjustment Policy* of 15

---

[30] EO 9326, 7 Apr 43.
[31] EO 9347, 27 May 43.

February 1944. This collaboration con-
tinued until the passage of the Contract
Settlement Act of 1 July 1944 and the
Surplus Property Act of 3 October 1944.

The Contract Settlement Act provided
for a Director of Contract Settlement, who
later became a part of the Office of War
Mobilization and Reconversion. Relations
between the ASF and this office were very
close. As a result, the ASF continued to
play a major part in developing policies
and procedures for contract termination.
Although the Surplus Property Act established broad policies on the disposal of
surplus property, it did not change practices already put into effect by the Office
of War Mobilization. The War Department retained full authority to decide
when property was surplus. The actual
disposition of the property was handled by
the Reconstruction Finance Corporation
(RFC) or the Department of Commerce,
two of the designated disposal agencies.
Later the RFC and then the War Assets
Administration became the sole disposal
agency. The only problem arising in this
relationship was one of storage space for
surplus property. From the War Department's point of view the ideal relationship
would have been one which permitted the
immediate transfer of surplus property to
the physical custody of the disposal agency
until its actual sale. A general shortage of
storage space, however, prevented such
an arrangement. Moreover, the disposal
agencies, for reasons of their own convenience and because of the availability of
Army storage facilities, preferred to leave
surplus property with the Army until actual sale had been arranged. The Army
Service Forces co-operated with the RFC
in setting up storage facilities for surplus
industrial property which was moved out
of plants. The ASF held other property

until the disposal agencies could arrange
for its disposition. Although the ASF at
times felt that the disposal agencies moved
too slowly, it had no desire whatsoever to
take over the function.

It was not until the summer of 1944,
during the controversy over Mr. Nelson's
reconversion program, that the ASF was
disposed to make a definite appeal for intervention by Byrnes in a dispute with a
civilian agency. It was then that Mr.
Byrnes indicated his sympathy with the
ASF point of view. Shortly after this controversy Congress passed legislation giving
Byrnes' office a statutory base and renam-
ing it the Office of War Mobilization and
Reconversion.[32] Byrnes, in need of an expanded staff, asked Somervell to release
General Clay to him. This Somervell did,
but the action was probably a mistake.

General Somervell definitely did not
suggest to Justice Byrnes that he should
use Clay as his principal assistant on production matters. General Clay had represented Somervell in the WPB Production
Executive Committee since early 1943,
and otherwise had carried the main burden of procurement operations while General Somervell was giving his attention to
other ASF problems. Clay's presence in
OWMR was regarded in many places,
certainly by many persons in WPB, as the
final proof of military control of the economy. When General Somervell began to
realize that this was an unfortunate arrangement, he supported Clay's reassignment to the European Theater of
Operations.

The official history of the WPB has
commented: "Clay had been a vigorous
opponent of any substantial reconversion

---

[32] Public Law 458, 78th Cong, 1st Sess, approved
3 Oct 44.

action and his transference to a key role in the administration of occupied Germany was probably not without its effect in lifting the lid from reconversion activity in the United States." [33]

Civil-military relations on production matters were undoubtedly somewhat complicated in the autumn of 1944 and the spring of 1945 by General Clay's participation in OWMR. Had there been any serious controversies between the ASF and WPB in this period, the situation might have proved embarrassing. But Clay's own good sense and Mr. Krug's attitude of co-operation with the armed services prevented any real difficulty.

From the ASF point of view, the OWMR was always helpful, and its activities were considered a necessary part of the government's wartime administrative machinery.

With the many civilian agencies other than the War Production Board, the ASF developed close working relationships without recriminations or ideological controversy. This experience demonstrated that the ASF could co-operate with civilian agencies. Even where responsibilities seemed to overlap, the ASF and the civilian agencies worked out lines of demarcation which apparently were satisfactory to both and conducive to the efficient mobilization of the nation's economic resources.

---

[33] *Industrial Mobilization for War*, p. 863.

CHAPTER XVII

The ASF and Civilian Agencies Concerned With Military Supply and Defense

Among other wartime civilian organizations, the federal government created emergency agencies to handle certain matters closely related to direct military operations. The Army Service Forces worked primarily with four such agencies: the War Shipping Administration, the Office of Defense Transportation, the Office of Lend-Lease Administration (later the Foreign Economic Administration), and the Civilian Defense Administration. The only generalization to be made about ASF relationships with these groups is that they raised few basic questions. Since these civilian agencies were performing duties more closely concerned with military operations, in some ways the collaboration required here was of a more delicate character than that required for procurement matters. But in spite of the fact that problems vital to military strategy were sometimes involved in these relationships, they were satisfactorily worked out.

Ocean Transportation

In 1941 the Atlantic and Pacific Oceans were for America mighty zones of defense. These zones, however, had to be crossed in aiding our allies and in attacking our foes. Naval and aerial domination of the sea lanes became an indispensable element of strategy. Also necessary was the construction and maintenance of sufficient shipping to carry supplies to overseas theaters. Nothing devours as much as global warfare. General Somervell was among the first to impress this point upon military and political leaders. He actively participated in the initial shipping planning.[1] In June 1942 he warned that the submarine menace threatened "failure of our war effort." [2] In March 1943 he reported to General Marshall that the chances for an effective offensive in 1943 and 1944 were "measured almost entirely by the shipping which can be made available for military operations." [3] And in November 1943 Somervell told a Senate subcommit-

---

[1] Ltr, Somervell to Admiral Emory S. Land, 31 Jan 42, G-4/29717-116; Draft of Memo for President for Marshall's signature, Hq ASF, Shipping 1941-43, Somervell file. Material otherwise not documented is taken chiefly from Wardlow, *The Transportation Corps: Responsibilities, Organization, and Operations.*

[2] Memo for CofS, 18 Jun 42, OCT 569.14 Losses.

[3] Memo, 25 Mar 43, sub: Proposed Allocation of U.S. Shipping, Hq ASF, CofS 1942-43.

tee, "We can never have more ships than are needed for all-out offensive warfare." [4]

The solution to the shipping problem was threefold: to build new ships, to curb sinkings, and to use available vessels efficiently. A record-breaking construction program between 1942 and 1945 produced more than five thousand ocean-going vessels totaling fifty-three million dead-weight tons. [5] Building new ships, however, was like pouring water into a leaky barrel unless losses to enemy submarines and planes could be checked. In the early days of the war, sinkings created a critical situation. But antisubmarine measures cut losses from twelve million dead-weight tons in 1942 to two million in 1944. [6] General Somervell, just as interested in the effort to curb submarine losses as in new construction, received regular reports, studied them carefully, and did not hesitate to make suggestions for meeting the menace to the proper agencies. But of more immediate concern to him was the proper use of available shipping space, and its allocation among the various agencies requiring ships.

At the beginning of World War II, both the construction and management of the merchant marine were in the hands of the United States Maritime Commission. In February 1941 the commission set up a Division of Emergency Shipping which planned to control the use of American vessels to meet defense requirements. [7] In this way the United States had made a start in the problem of dealing with the shipping shortage. After 7 December 1941 however, American shipping capacity was squeezed to the limit. As G–4 of the War Department General Staff, Somervell was immediately confronted with the effect of the shortage of ships on Army supply and troop movements. Both he and his adviser

on transportation, Colonel Gross, immediately went to work on the problem. They recognized the urgent need for an agency, under civilian domination, to control the use of all merchant marine resources. Somervell wished, however, to hedge its powers with specific limitations, to insure the primacy of strategic interests. This led him to draft an executive order to create a central agency which he cleared through the War Department and then took to the White House for the attention of Mr. Harry Hopkins. [8]

Of course, there were others besides Somervell who at the same time were urging such an agency. In any event, on 7 February 1942 the President, following the suggestion of his advisers, established a War Shipping Administration. By and large, the limitations with which General Somervell wished to circumscribe the new agency were omitted and broad powers were granted to the administrator. In essence, the civilian WSA held final and exclusive power over shipping allocations, subject to a vague qualification that the administrator would "comply" with strategic and military requirements. [9] Despite the fact that his suggested limitation on the authority of the agency was not adopted, General Somervell achieved his

[4] *War Mobilization,* rpt of Subcom to Com on Military Affairs, Senate, 78th Cong, 1st Sess, 7 Oct 43, Subcom Rpt 3, pp. 3–5.

[5] *United States Maritime Commission Official Construction Record, Vessels Delivered 1939–45* (No. 106) (Washington, U.S. Government Printing Office, 1946).

[6] Wardlow, *The Transportation Corps: Responsibilities, Organization and Operations,* pp. 149–51.

[7] Col Marcus B. Stokes, Jr., Shipping in War, p. 5, Planning Div, OCT, Mar 46.

[8] Leighton and Coakley, Logistics of Global Warfare, 1941–1943, Ch. IX, contains a penetrating analysis of the Gross-Somervell plan.

[9] Memo, Gross for Somervell, Jan 43, Hq ASF, Shipping 1941–43, Somervell File, contains summary of controversy.

main objective, a unified and centrally directed program for the allocation of ships. Admiral Emory S. Land, chairman of the Maritime Commission, was appointed also to be War Shipping Administrator. But the two organizations functioned separately: the Maritime Commission directed shipbuilding, and the WSA assumed operating control over vessels.[10]

The Maritime Commission based its construction program upon estimates presented by interested agencies. The Chief of Transportation in the ASF listed Army needs for a year in advance, the Navy submitted its requirements for merchant-type vessels, the Army-Navy Petroleum Board worked out tanker needs, and the Joint Staff Planners of the JCS decided on the necessary number of combat loaders. Cargo space for lend-lease and commercial uses was determined by the War Shipping Administration. The Maritime Commission took all estimates and adjusted them to fit existing and anticipated shipbuilding facilities. Its plans were then studied by appropriate joint committees and reviewed by the Joint Chiefs of Staff. Unresolved disagreements between the Maritime Commission and the JCS might be decided by the President. Although carried on by a civilian agency, the shipbuilding program was essentially a military program, and the military interest predominated. As needs varied with the fortunes of war, adjustments in the ship construction program were made to meet demands. General Somervell occasionally intervened in the shipbuilding program to urge an increase in production to meet anticipated Army needs.[11]

In the field of small boat construction, the Army, Navy, and Maritime Commission each had its own program. The Army Transportation Corps purchased harbor craft and other vessels under one thousand gross tons or less than two hundred feet in length. It worked out informal agreements with groups interested in small boats on the apportionment of construction facilities among various contractors. By and large the Transportation Corps and the Maritime Commission experienced little difficulty in working together. The commission was usually happy to give the Army the type and tonnage of new construction it desired. Ship utilization, naturally, was closely intertwined with ship construction. Proper use of existing cargo space cut down the need for new ships. Idle tonnage was no more useful than tonnage not built.

The administrator of the WSA directed the operation, purchase, charter, requisition, and use of all American-controlled ocean-going vessels except combat vessels and transports of the Army and Navy, and coastwise traffic under the control of the Office of Defense Transportation. The administrator also allocated United States ships for use by the Army, Navy, other federal agencies, and governments of the United Nations. In addition, he represented the United States in dealing with the British Ministry of War Transport, kept current data on shipping, and informed the President on the shipping situation. He also collaborated with all military and civilian agencies performing wartime functions connected with overseas transport.

After the creation of the War Shipping Administration, Somervell negotiated an understanding with the new agency on operating relationships in the use of ships. The Navy had previously made an agree-

---

[10] EO 9054, 7 Feb 42; EO 9244, 16 Sep 42.

[11] Ltr, Somervell to Land, 5 Aug 42, Hq ASF, Shipping 1941–43, Somervell File.

ment with the WSA, and General Somervell, on behalf of the Army, worked out a similar arrangement with Mr. Lewis W. Douglas, deputy administrator of the shipping agency. A *modus operandi* was signed on 13 June 1942.[12] This agreement provided that the Army Transportation Corps would operate vessels owned by the War Department but would keep the WSA fully informed on the use of this tonnage. Since Army-owned ships would barely begin to meet Army needs, the WSA was to assign to the Army the additional ocean-going vessels it required. These ships would be allotted on a voyage basis, and on the home trip, unless otherwise arranged, they would revert to the control of the WSA. Overseas commanders were permitted to retain cargo vessels in their own service if military emergencies demanded. The Army and the WSA also agreed to exchange information and maintain the closest possible liaison, both in Washington and at ports of embarkation. Each organization would furnish the other full information for planning the best possible use of ships. Finally, the two agencies agreed that each had no desire to absorb or control the functions of the other.

The agreement settled a threatened jurisdictional dispute between the Army Transportation Corps of the ASF and the WSA. In essence, General Somervell, and his chief of transportation, General Gross, accepted civilian control over the United States merchant shipping pool. But once ships had been allocated to it, the Army wished full authority over its share. The ASF accepted the 13 June *modus operandi* and Somervell, in transmitting a copy of the agreement to Mr. Harry Hopkins, wrote that it was "eminently satisfactory."[13] It is doubtful, however, whether

the Transportation Corps was really fully satisfied by the agreement. General Gross, writing on another proposal involving civilian control over Army cargo in a war theater, suggested that Marshall telegraph General Eisenhower: "I cannot endorse your proposal to share responsibility in so important a matter as the control of shipping in an active theater of operation with a cumbersome board operated by a civilian head. . . . I know of no function of your Chief of Transportation more important than those you seek to delegate elsewhere. . . ."[14] Colonel J. H. Graham, a trusted confidant and adviser to Somervell in World War II, in a memo which probably reflected the opinion of a good many transportation officers, wrote candidly of the Somervell-Douglas agreement: "That will serve for a while, two to four months, and will probably be the germ of something better."[15]

But it was the War Shipping Administration which struck the first blow against the *modus operandi*. Mr. Lewis Douglas was even less satisfied with the arrangement that General Somervell's transportation advisers had negotiated. He thought in terms of complete WSA authority over cargo space. True, the WSA had the power to divide shipping among claimant agencies. But after these agencies had received their shares, Mr. Douglas was not inclined to relinquish authority. He

---

[12] Memo, Somervell and Douglas, 13 Jun 42, sub: Memo Covering the Interdepartmental Relations Between the Army and the WSA To Form a Basis for Full and Complete Co-operation in Connection With the Purchase, Charter, Use, and Operation of Vessels and Terminal Facilities, Hq ASF, WSA.

[13] Memo, Somervell for Hopkins, 14 Jun 42, Hq ASF, WSA.

[14] Memo, Gross for Somervell, Hq ASF, Trans SOS 1941–43, Somervell File.

[15] Memo, Graham for Somervell, about 30 Jun 42, Hq ASF, Trans SOS 1941–43, Somervell File.

wished to remodel the WSA along the lines of the British Ministry of War Transport, at least insofar as that organization combined the operation of civilian and military shipping in a single agency.

About six weeks after the signing of the agreement, top level American and British officials, including Prime Minister Winston Churchill, met to discuss shipping for BOLERO. In the course of the discussions Churchill inquired why the American Army in the United Kingdom needed fourteen million tons of shipping while twenty-five million sufficed for the entire British Isles. Of more specific concern to the ASF, however, was the fact that officials of the WSA at the conference challenged General Gross's shipping figures for BOLERO, and someone, possibly Mr. Douglas, stated that the Army was wasting cargo space because of improper loading.[16] Mr. Douglas argued that savings in cargo space could be made by unified planning. "Dear Bill," he wrote to General Somervell on 9 October 1942, "I am enclosing herewith a memorandum on combined planning for cargo ships." He then spelled out proposed savings by combining WSA, Army, and other cargoes, giving specific and detailed examples of waste arising from the absence of such combination.[17] The ASF did not react kindly to the Douglas proposals, and General Gross presented studies refuting the charges of waste.[18]

In the midst of this mild disagreement the War Shipping Administration loosed a torpedo when on 18 December 1942 Admiral Land and Mr. Douglas obtained from President Roosevelt a memorandum saying, in effect, that except for task forces or assault forces, the WSA should load overseas military supplies provided by the Army. Admiral Land enclosed the directive in a letter to Secretary of War Stimson.[19] Secretary Stimson retorted: "I must express my surprise that a matter which so obviously affects the interest of the Army should be initiated without anyone in authority from this Department having an opportunity to state his views either to the Budget or the President. . . ." The battle was joined. Secretary Stimson postponed designating Army representatives to confer with the WSA.[20]

Somervell and General Gross were the driving forces behind the Army opposition. On the day before Christmas, Somervell forwarded, for Admiral Leahy's signature, a memorandum to the President. This memorandum protested the directive of 18 December because it destroyed "the authority of the armed forces over the movement of supplies essential to their success." If Army port facilities were to be used for loading only combat task forces going overseas, these facilities would be only partly and hence wastefully used. The Army moreover, they argued, was better able than commercial loaders to make rapid adjustments in cargo to meet battle needs. Under the proposed arrangement, military cargo might be badly scattered and even lost. The memo implied that the Transportation Corps was the best agency for "marrying" cargo and seeing that it arrived at the correct destination.[21]

---

[16] Memo for Gross, 26 Jul 42, Hq ASF, Shipping 1941–43.

[17] Ltr and Memo, Douglas to Somervell, 9 Oct 42, Hq ASF, Shipping 1941–43.

[18] Memo, Gross for Somervell, 21 Oct 42, Hq ASF, Shipping 1941–43.

[19] Ltr, Land to Stimson, 18 Dec 42; Memo, Roosevelt for Land, 18 Dec 42. Both in OCT, HB, Gross WSA.

[20] Ltr, Stimson to Land, 23 Dec 42, Hq ASF, Shipping 1941–43.

[21] Memo for President, prepared 24 Dec 42, signed by Leahy for JCS on 6 Jan 43, Hq ASF, Somervell File.

On 31 December 1942 Mr. Douglas proposed a compromise whereby military technicians would be on hand whenever WSA operators loaded Army cargo. Admiral Leahy seemed interested in the suggestion, but General Gross bridled at the very thought of divided responsibility. Somervell thereupon explained to Admiral Leahy the need to protest in writing to the President. In a memo he stated that the executive order setting up the WSA provided for "collaboration" with the Army on vessels "for use by the Army." Accordingly, he argued, Mr. Douglas was exceeding the authority of this order. The larger issue, however, General Somervell pointed out, was whether the chiefs of staff "shall determine the strategic employment of shipping in its over-all relation to military operations . . . or whether the War Shipping Administration shall determine the disposal of shipping on the strategic basis and inform the Chiefs of Staff what shipping they may have available for military purposes." [22]

Admiral Leahy signed the memorandum of protest on 6 January. In it the President was requested to rescind his directive and confirm the authority of the Joint Chiefs of Staff over the "means of transporting supplies and troops overseas." Shortly thereafter, General Marshall, who had become interested in the issue, wrote Mr. Douglas a personal letter in which he stated that the WSA was trying to change established procedures, and that the Army had drawn from civilian life a group of shipping experts who were competent to do the work. The Army, he implied, seemed to be doing a good shipping job, and the procedure of the WSA in this case could serve no other purpose than cause difficulty and animosity. [23] At the same time, Secretary of War Stimson

advised Admiral Land that the controversy had been placed in the hands of the President. The opposition to Mr. Douglas' proposal was too formidable. He therefore yielded gracefully, protesting that he had no desire to interfere in strategic matters. While the President did not rescind his directive, it was not enforced, so it can be said that the ASF had won its defensive jurisdictional battle. Both sides thereafter scrupulously observed the *modus operandi* of 13 June 1942.

In a sense the whole affair had been unnecessary. General Gross had always been interested in full loading, and had several pet projects for combining heavy bottom cargo such as steel for Britain with space-consuming balloon cargo such as assembled motor vehicles. Although the Army Transportation Corps made some mistakes, it had usually loaded as efficiently as military exigencies allowed. With the spotlight of controversy on this issue, there was perhaps an even greater effort to balance compact heavy cargo with bulky balloon cargo. Most Army vessels left port, loaded "full and down." [24]

For some time after this conflict all was quiet on the ASF–WSA front. General Somervell and Mr. Douglas continued to write their "Dear Lew" and "Dear Bill" letters, and the agencies worked in harmony. During 1944 a mild flurry broke the calm. In November Admiral Land protested to the Joint Chiefs of Staff that

[22] Memo, Somervell for Leahy, 2 Jan 43, Hq ASF, Somervell File.

[23] Ltr, Marshall to Douglas, 8 Jan 43, AG 334.8, WSA.

[24] Memo for Somervell, 9 Apr 43, sub: Army Shipping Situation, Hq ASF, Shipping 1941–43; Memo, Gross to Somervell, 22 Oct 42, sub: Memo from Douglas, Hq ASF, Shipping, Somervell File; Rpt, about 9 Apr 45, title: Data on Shipping Situation, Hq ASF, Shipping, Somervell File.

the retention of a large number of vessels in the European Theater of Operations if continued would cause a severe shipping shortage. A bad situation had developed slowly, almost imperceptibly. The theater had called for more supplies than could be discharged. Overseas ports were clogged, stevedoring equipment was inadequate, and ships were being held offshore as floating warehouses. The backlog of ships gradually piled up, until by November 1944, nearly four hundred ships were awaiting discharge.[25]

General Somervell reported to the JCS that the existing shortage was partly caused by the failure of the Maritime Commission to meet its construction schedule. But at the same time he recognized the validity of Admiral Land's charge.[26] Indeed, he had been watching the situation develop with increasing misgiving. Now he worked vigorously to rectify matters. His pressure on responsible headquarters in the ETO, plus the opening of the port of Antwerp, soon reduced the number of ships retained to a reasonable number.[27]

In innumerable day to day shipping activities the ASF and WSA worked closely together. At ports, local representatives of the two agencies constantly exchanged cargo in order to attain more efficient loading. The arrangement whereby WSA assigned outgoing cargo ships to the Army, with the vessels returning to WSA authority for the home voyage, proved a workable one. Whenever an overseas command had more than a thousand tons of cargo to return to the United States, the WSA designated a vessel to move it. An Interdepartmental Shipping Priorities Committee under the War Production Board determined the most urgently needed return cargo, and shipping space

on vessels was allotted to carry it. An ASF representative served on the committee and the Chief of Transportation made Army vessels available as needed. Another group, the Joint Military Transportation Committee, prepared long-range plans for the use of shipping capacity.

Usually the ASF presented to the WSA a forecast of its own probable shipping needs for the coming six to eight weeks. This showed where and in what amounts cargo lift would be required. These forecasts, reviewed twice monthly, helped the WSA to plan its deployment of ships. Final allocation of specific ships were worked out at semiweekly meetings between the agencies and by direct telephone wire between the two offices.

Troop ships required a somewhat different arrangement. They remained constantly in the service of the Army. At first, particularly if they had some cargo space, the WSA was interested in their home voyage. In co-operation with the Army, it did utilize some of this space. But with the growing number of troops and casualties to be returned to the United States later in the war, the Army Transportation Corps utilized all space on transports in carrying troops and their baggage for the round trip.

The changing needs of war demanded constant adjustment in shipping plans. When American troops were first sent overseas in large numbers, Army troop ships could not meet the load. The Navy therefore assigned some of its transports to the Army. But the major aid in providing

---

[25] Memo, Land for CofS, 22 Nov 44, sub: Merchant Shipping, Hq ASF, Shipping, Somervell File.
[26] Memo, Somervell to CofS, 23 Nov 44, sub: Memo, Admiral Land on Merchant Shipping, Hq ASF, Shipping, Somervell File.
[27] See above, p. 85.

troop lift came from ships loaned by the British. The *Queen Mary* and the *Queen Elizabeth* were particularly helpful. These two "Queens," equipped with tiered bunks, and with men often sleeping in shifts, carried up to fifteen thousand troops each, the equivalent of an entire American division. Relying for safety on their tremendous speed, they carried without incident from enemy action nearly a million soldiers from the United States to the United Kingdom.[28]

But not even these huge liners could satisfy the increasing requirements for troop lift. When cargo construction was well along on schedule, the Joint Chiefs of Staff approved the conversion of various types of ships to troop transports. Conversion was a useful device in giving the ship program some of the flexibility required by the exigencies of war. Later, after troop lift demands were temporarily met, vessels were converted into hospital ships, repair ships, spare parts ships, and even a news ship. Smaller vessels became floating refrigerators, floating warehouses, and floating service shops of numerous varieties. Conversions were carried out by several agencies and by the armed services.[29]

The Army negotiated directly with the WSA on all matters involving privately operated vessels under WSA control. It dealt with the WSA when it wanted British cargo ships for Army service, but worked directly with the British Ministry of War Transport when it needed British troop ships. The two agencies agreed on regulations for carrying civilian passengers engaged in essential travel. On 28 January and 7 March 1944 the WSA, the Army, and the Navy reached agreements whereby they accepted each other's barges for towing when their tugs had free time. Detailed understandings were also arrived at with regard to financial procedures.

An important field of co-operation was in matters of personnel. The Army Transportation Corps usually followed WSA procedures. It paid the prevailing wage rates including overtime and war bonuses. As far as practicable, it also followed established precedents on war risk insurance. The WSA used the overseas facilities of the War Department when it investigated and processed matters dealing with marine insurance. The Transportation Corps recruited crews for its own transports, but co-operated with the WSA in so doing. It also made its facilities available to the WSA for training officers for merchant crews. The Transportation Corps followed the forms and procedures of the WSA on deferments under the Selective Service Act, and the WSA personnel organization issued necessary re-employment certificates and handled negotiations with local draft boards.

This catalogue of co-operation could be greatly extended. But enough has been said to indicate how extensive were the operating relationships between the ASF and the War Shipping Administration. In short, the WSA controlled the entire pool of cargo vessels coming under the jurisdiction of the United States Government. The Army received most of its cargo ships through the WSA and retained authority to operate them according to its judgment of military needs. Under this arrangement

---

[28] Hillary St. George Saunders, "The Queens," *Life*, July 9, 1945; Harold Larson, Troop Transports in World War II, Monograph 12, pp. 20–24, OCT ASF, Mar 45.

[29] Final Report of Troopship Conversion Program, Sep 43–Jan 46, prepared by Maint and Rep Br, 30 Jan 46, OCT, HB, Water Div, Ship Rep and Conversion; Annual Rpt, Water Div, OCT, Fiscal Year 1945, OCT, HB, Water Div Rpts.

involving numerous points of interagency contact, there occasionally were misunderstandings, but it is noteworthy that these were so few in number.

Rail Transportation

For domestic transportation, the War Department depended primarily upon the services of the American railroad companies.[30] The position of the War Department was in effect that of any other user of transportation facilities. The War Department contracted directly with the railroads for both passenger and freight services, and was subject to all the limitations imposed upon both carrier and user by the Interstate Commerce Commission (ICC). The rail transportation problem of the Army was twofold: to obtain the necessary transportation service, and to avoid traffic congestion at ports engaged in the overseas shipment of Army freight. The essential difference between the Army and other commercial shippers was the military urgency of Army freight and the overseas destination of most of its shipments.

As early as the summer of 1941, the Association of American Railroads voluntarily joined with the Assistant Chief of Staff, G–4, to establish a control system over Army cargo moving into ports. Thereafter, no Army agency in the United States could ship any freight to a port area without a prior permit issued upon the basis of available shipping. A Traffic Control Division, set up as part of the Transportation Corps after it was created, continued to work with the Association of American Railroads in issuing freight permits and in arranging for necessary passenger service.

Earlier, on 18 December 1941, the President had established the Office of Defense Transportation by Executive Order 8989. That agency was an outgrowth of the Transportation Division of the Advisory Commission to the Council of National Defense. The ODT was given authority to co-ordinate transportation policies and activities of federal agencies and private transportation groups in order to insure that the domestic transportation system met war requirements. In carrying out its responsibilities, the ODT was directed to collaborate with existing agencies and to utilize their facilities and services to the maximum. In particular, it was instructed to maintain close liaison with the Maritime Commission, the ICC, and the War and Navy Departments. Several government agencies, including the War Department, were directed to designate a representative to work with the Office of Defense Transportation.

The ODT, shortly after it was set up, took steps to prevent the congestion of freight at port areas. An agreement was reached between the War Department, the ODT, and the WSA in March 1942, whereby a Transportation Control Committee was established, consisting of representatives from these three agencies and the British Ministry of War Transport. The Navy Department was later added to the committee. An assistant chief of transportation from General Gross's office represented the War Department on the committee. The first ODT regulation establishing control machinery was issued on 23 May 1942.

---

[30] The information summarized here has been taken from the study, Operating Relationships of the Office of the Chief of Transportation, Army Service Forces, With Civilian Government Agencies, prepared in the Office of the Chief of Transportation, ASF, ASF Hist files.

The system worked in this manner. The Transportation Control Committee, on the basis of official information about availability of cargo space, established what were known as ODT block releases under which specified quantities of cargo might move to ports during a given month. The Traffic Control Division in the Office of the Chief of Transportation then issued the unit permits within the limits fixed by the Transportation Control Committee for the shipment of all government and lend-lease freight except Navy. Unit permits for Navy freight were issued by the Navy. Those for such commercial freight as was being shipped overseas were issued by the Association of American Railroads. The Army continued to issue its own permits on its.own authority for the shipment of military cargo to.ports for loading in vessels assigned to the Transportation Corps.

The ODT at one time suggested that the entire system of issue of releases for shipment to ports be transferred to its direct operating control. The Army Service Forces opposed this move, maintaining that it was strictly a military responsibility to control the movement of Army freight to ports. This position was eventually accepted. Transportation Corps machinery was utilized for the issuance of other permits in order to avoid the creation of duplicating and confusing administrative machinery.

The ODT exercised general supervision over the utilization of all rail facilities. Its orders affected War Department shipping, unless specifically exempted, in the same way as other freight. At the request of the Transportation Corps the ODT agreed to consult the Army before issuing any specific order. In many cases exemptions were provided for military freight. For example, ODT General Order 1 issued on 1 May 1942 prohibited the railroads from accepting for transportation any closed freight car containing less than ten tons. An amendment to the order issued on the same day prohibited the use of closed cars for moving merchandise within the same city or shipping area. In both instances exemptions were made for specified commodities of an obviously military character. In addition, the Army asked for and obtained an exemption for cars used as storage facilities during military maneuvers. In another case Army-owned tank cars were exempted from the ODT's regulations covering the assignment and routing of loaded tank cars. Since only about one third of the Army's domestic shipments of petroleum products were made by Army-owned cars, the Transportation Corps assigned representatives to work with the ODT in the routing of commercial tank cars. The ODT Tank Car Advisory Committee included a representative of the Chief of Transportation, and at three different shipping points Army representatives worked jointly with the ODT. There were many other orders of a similar nature controlling the use of rail facilities on which the ASF co-operated with the ODT.

The Interstate Commerce Commission, on the other hand, refused to permit the ASF to review its orders prior to issuance. Thus, for example, the ICC, in Service Order 68 on 30 January 1942, required shippers to pay for the minimum weight of the car furnished by the carrier regardless of the size of the car specified by the shipper. This was done to avoid switching delays in providing the exact freight car requested. Such an order necessarily had the effect of increasing freight charges for the Army; thereupon the Transportation Corps sought an exemption. Originally the

ICC offered a limited exemption based upon a permit system, but this was not acceptable to the Army because of the large number of Army installations involved and the delays which would result. No satisfactory solution to this problem was ever devised. By another order issued in February 1943, the ICC vested authority in a joint agency of the ICC and ODT to divert transcontinental carload traffic from congested routes. The Army Service Forces succeeded in obtaining an exemption from this order through the ODT.

The Army dealt directly with the Association of American Railroads in routing military passenger traffic in groups of forty or more persons. The Transportation Corps and the railroads agreed upon the types of accommodations to be provided and upon the rules to be followed in utilizing equipment. The conversion of baggage cars to kitchen cars was one such agreement. The Transportation Corps, working with the railroads, also took steps to reduce military demands, as, for example, by assigning three men to each section of Pullman space. Another expedient was to time military movements in such a manner as to permit the maximum use of a particular assignment of rail equipment. Thus, on one occasion, three long-run hauls of Army personnel were made with the same set of passenger cars. Yet another method used to reduce military demands was to halt the practice of shipping wheeled vehicles with troop units when moving from one part of the United States to another. All of these steps were taken by the ASF without any order from the ODT.

The ODT was kept informed of the general volume of military traffic anticipated by the War Department. On the other hand, the ODT was not consulted about any specific movement of either passenger or freight traffic. These movements were worked out directly between the Transportation Corps and the Association of American Railroads, acting as a central agency for all railroad companies.

The requirements of American railways for new equipment were presented to the War Production Board by the ODT. Before acting on these requirements, the WPB asked the War Department whether the construction program would interfere with the purchase of rail equipment for military use overseas. These questions were handled by ASF headquarters and the Chief of Transportation. The advice of the ASF was also sought by the WPB in granting tax amortization certificates to railroads for new construction or new equipment. The ODT purchased some twelve hundred troop sleeping cars and four hundred troop kitchen cars which it rented to the railroads for troop train service. The safety and convenience features of this equipment were established by the Chief of Transportation.

There were a number of other agencies with which the Army dealt in the domestic transportation field. The ASF was consulted by the Public Roads Administration after 1942, for example, on the question of what state highway projects should receive federal funds. With the co-operation of the ODT, the Army Service Forces worked with state agencies in removing limitations on the truck haul of military freight. In addition, the Transportation Corps worked with the ODT on questions of transporting persons in accordance with Public Law 779 of the 77th Congress, approved 1 December 1942. Under this law, the War Department was empowered to furnish transportation for workers at private plants after the ODT had determined that other private and public facilities could not render adequate service. On behalf of private manufacturers, ASF field installations presented proposals for bus service to the Chief of Transportation. After local investigation and approval, the Chief of Transportation submitted his recommendations to the ODT. As of 30 June 1945 the Army owned some 7,498 buses, of which nearly 5,000 were used for bus service to military installations and over 1,000 for bus service to war plants. The ASF also assisted motor carriers in requesting new or replacement equipment from the ODT and the War Production Board. Army-owned oil barges, when not fully employed in military traffic, were made available to the WPB and the Defense Supplies Corporation for the haul of petroleum products.

In order to prevent congestion at ports—the curse of World War I—the ODT found it necessary to exercise control over shipments to storage points in port areas. These shipments were brought under the same control as shipments to piers, with the result that they were kept in line with available port facilities. The ODT also exercised general supervision over all storage space affecting transportation activities, and at one time, desired to bring army holding and reconsignment points under its supervision. The Army Service Forces objected strongly to this proposal, and an informal understanding was reached which exempted holding and reconsignment points of the Transportation Corps from ODT supervision. However, these facilities were made available by the Transportation Corps to the Treasury Department, the Foreign Economic Administration, and the Department of Agriculture. The ODT sponsored a Federal Emergency Warehouse Association which was helpful in making public warehouse space available to the Army.

As a heavy shipper, the War Department was much concerned with the rates charged for its freight movements. The Chief of Transportation negotiated directly with railways to reduce rates on various classes of military freight, and in cases of an impasse, went to the ICC for a decision. The ODT joined the Chief of Transportation in pressing those cases where governmental agencies generally might benefit from a reduction in freight rates. All other rate cases involving the Army were prosecuted by the Chief of Transportation.

The ASF insisted upon maintaining full control over military traffic within the zone of interior. At the same time, as already indicated, it took necessary steps to reduce its demands as far as possible and to assist the railroads in bearing the burden. During the redeployment period after V-E Day, a 50 percent increase beyond the previous peak in military passenger traffic made it necessary for the ODT under Transportation Corps and ASF pressure to impose a number of restrictions upon civilian passenger traffic. But in spite of these measures, the passenger facilities made available for the Army were in many instances inadequate. These problems were in the process of mutual negotiation and settlement when the surrender of Japan brought about a decrease in the volume of military traffic. Voluntary action was later proposed by the western railroads to meet Army needs for passenger equipment to move men home from the Pacific coast. These various arrangements for mutual action by the Army Service Forces and the other government agencies concerned with domestic transportation provided a satisfactory working relationship throughout World War II.

Lend-lease

From the date of the passage of the Lend-Lease Act in 1941 until the end of the war, a central civilian agency maintained general oversight of foreign aid programs. First, there was the Division of Defense Aid Reports under Maj. Gen. James H. Burns; after 28 October 1941, there was the Office of Lend-Lease Administration under Mr. Edward R. Stettinius; and finally on 25 September 1943, the Foreign Economic Administration was created, headed by Leo Crowley.[31] These central agencies were not strictly speaking operating agencies. Rather they supervised and co-ordinated the procurement and distribution of lend-lease supplies by other departments. Thus the War Department was responsible for procuring all lend-lease supplies for foreign armies. But at first it was dependent upon the OLLA for allocation of funds, and had to follow procedures laid down by that office. During the prewar phase of lend-lease, this division of function led to involved requisitioning procedures which the Army felt seriously hampered its efforts to procure and distribute munitions on a strategic basis. These difficulties were largely resolved after Pearl Harbor by placing the distribution of munitions under the control of the Combined Chiefs of Staff. As a corollary, a consolidated production program was developed by the ASF, combining U.S. Army and lend-lease requirements. To finance this consolidated program, Congress made direct appropriations to the War Department for lend-lease purposes, placing only certain dollar limitations on transfers of military equipment. The Army Supply Program then became the basis of procurement both for the U.S. Army and for military lend-lease;

allocation of the finished product was accomplished by the Munitions Assignments Board in Washington, operating under the directives of the Combined Chiefs of Staff. The administration of this military lend-lease program, nevertheless, remained in the War Department, and in March 1942 was absorbed as one of the functions of the ASF.

This system made lend-lease a basic instrument of military policy and strategy, as noted elsewhere.[32] In March and April 1942 General Somervell was instrumental in the negotiation of agreements whereby the OLLA gave up all authority to influence these decisions. The War Department thus acquired complete autonomy in the operation of its lend-lease program "subject to the policies and directions of the President or the Combined Munitions Assignments Board," and to the establishment of reporting procedures which would permit OLLA to keep accurate record of transfers made.[33] The OLLA (and later the FEA) became an accounting agency insofar as military lend-lease supplies were concerned. The reporting procedures were established by agreement between the International Division, ASF, and the civilian lend-lease authority. The OLLA and FEA retained responsibility for handling civilian lend-lease. Since it was impossible to decide in some cases whether an article was civilian or military, there remained areas of questionable or overlapping jurisdiction. The Army was also interested in the amount and character of civilian lend-

---

[31] EO 8751, 2 May 41; EO 8926, 28 Oct 41; EO 9830, 25 Sep 43.

[32] See above, Ch. III, Lend-Lease Sec.

[33] Ltr, Thomas B. McCabe to Somervell, 12 Mar 42; Ltr, Somervell to McCabe, 13 Mar 42, Both in Hq ASF, LL File. Ltr, McCabe to SW, 9 Apr 42, Intn Div, ASF. File 400.318, Vol. I.

lease provided to other governments. Reciprocal aid (or "reverse lend-lease") and the conditions under which it might assist U.S. military operations were problems of importance to both agencies. It was necessary to delineate responsibility for the supply of the civilian population in occupied areas. Agreements reached in these fields were usually so complicated, and involved so many different government agencies, as to defy simple definition. The International Division, ASF, represented the War Department in these negotiations.

The shipment of lend-lease supplies was also important to the ASF because of its possible interference with the military supply of overseas theaters. By a basic arrangement worked out in late 1942, the War Department was responsible for the movement of military lend-lease supplies to port, but loading and shipment overseas were responsibilities of the War Shipping Administration. This arrangement was never entirely satisfactory to the ASF, which preferred Transportation Corps control of the loading and shipping of military lend-lease, but through close co-operation with WSA it did prove to be at least a workable system. In cases where lend-lease supplies were consigned to U.S. commanders abroad for distribution within a theater of operations, they were moved entirely under Army control.[34]

Since civilian as well as military lend-lease supplies had to be shipped on the same vessels, the co-ordination of storage operations, movement to port, and loading activities required close collaboration between the ASF, OLLA, WSA, and representatives of foreign governments concerned. Through formal and informal conferences and committees, the multiplicity of details inherent in such operations was worked out harmoniously.[35]

Civilian Defense

The President in May 1941 established an Office of Civilian Defense (OCD) as a co-ordinating agency to work with state and local governments in protecting the civilian population and civilian facilities from the possible dangers of enemy action.[36] A board for civilian protection, on which the Secretary of War was represented, was set up within the OCD.

The War Department was obviously vitally concerned with civilian defense. While the Army's role in home defense was primarily to repel any enemy attack, it had already assumed some responsibility for inspecting the precautions taken at vital production facilities to insure uninterrupted operation. The Provost Marshal General in the ASF directed an internal security program which called for plant guards, visitor control, and other safety precautions at vital war installations. A Resources Protection Board in the WPB, composed of representatives of the Army, the Navy, the OCD, and the WPB, indicated specific facilities which were vital to the war effort. These facilities were included on a Master Inspection Responsibility List which guided the ASF in its internal security activities. Later the OCD established, with the approval of the Secretary of War, a Facilities Security

---

[34] Draft ltr, ASW to Douglas, (filed 10 Sep 42), Intn Div, ASF, File 008 Shipmts, Vol. I; WSA Opns Regulation 23, 25 Nov 42; Memo, ASF for Chiefs Sup Svs, 4 Dec 42, sub: Procedure for Shipmts of WD LL Material for Waterborne Export, SPX 400.3295 (11–29–42).

[35] The problems of distribution of lend-lease supplies will be discussed in greater detail in Leighton and Coakley, Logistics of Global Warfare, 1941–1943. This material is based largely on the chapter entitled: Transformation of Lend-Lease into an Instrument of Coalition Warfare.

[36] EO 8751, 20 May 41.

Program designed to assure protection of essential facilities.[37] This program was to be supplementary to the protective programs of the Army, the Navy, and the Federal Power Commission.

There was some difficulty between the OCD and the ASF in drawing a clear distinction in their respective roles. An agreement was negotiated between the two agencies in May 1943 in which the War Department assumed exclusive responsibility for protecting facilities listed on its Master Inspection Responsibility List. The Secretary of War designated a representative to work with the OCD on internal security matters and to prevent any overlapping effort. The whole internal security program was greatly reduced in November 1943 and again in September 1944.[38]

The ASF co-operated in many other phases of the OCD program. The Chief of Chemical Warfare Service provided training in chemical defense for thousands of civilians. The service commands of the ASF worked closely with local OCD offices in calling attention to necessary protection programs by state and local governments. Dangers from possible bomb and gas attack were dramatized by Army personnel in a show which toured principal cities of the country. With allied forces on the offensive all over the world, civilian defense gradually receded in importance, until by 1944, the OCD virtually ceased to exist. It is doubtful if civilian defense experience in World War II was sufficiently extensive or vital to suggest any pattern for future use. Thanks to the fact that all the actual conflict took place at such great distances from the United States itself, the problem of civilian defense actually never became a crucial one.

[37] EO 9165, 19 May 42.
[38] See above, p. 105.

CHAPTER XVIII

Procurement Collaboration With the Navy

The Army Service Forces was by no means the only military procurement agency during World War II. Within the War Department the ASF shared procurement and supply duties with the Army Air Forces, an arrangement that has already been discussed.[1] Within the federal government as a whole the ASF shared war procurement responsibilities with the U.S. Maritime Commission (which contracted for cargo vessels) and with a number of bureaus in the Department of the Navy.

The Navy bureaus—Ordnance, Ships, Supplies and Accounts, Yards and Docks, and Aeronautics—were not organized into a command comparable to that of the ASF. Rather, on procurement activities these bureaus operated under general policies determined by two units of the Secretary's office—the Under Secretary's office (assisted by the General Counsel) and the Office of Procurement and Material.[2] On supply activities the bureaus received instructions from a Vice-Chief of Naval Operations.

Necessarily there were many common interests between the ASF and the Navy. Many of the items purchased and used by the Army and Navy were similar if not identical. Both Army and Navy procurement officers entered into contracts with the same manufacturing companies. Con-

tractors in turn needed the same raw materials and component parts in order to provide Army and Navy supplies. These factors gave the ASF good reason to seek Navy collaboration on procurement and supply activities. Throughout the war, General Somervell was a strong advocate of joint action with the Navy, and after the war he was a firm believer in the unification of the armed forces under single direction. Some of the difficulties that grew out of efforts at voluntary co-operation no doubt helped to produce this attitude.

The Army and Navy Munitions Board might have become a joint agency for promoting co-operative procurement relationships, but it practically went out of existence in 1942.[3] In 1944 the only reminder of the ANMB that remained was a periodically revised statement jointly approved by the Production Division,

---

[1] See above, p. 125.

[2] For a history of Navy procurement organization see Robert H. Connery, *The Navy and the Industrial Mobilization in World War II* (Princeton, N. J., Princeton University Press, 1951).

[3] The historian of Navy procurement reports that there was little for the ANMB to do after Mr. Eberstadt became a vice-chairman of the WPB in September 1942. He then goes on to say that while Mr. Eberstadt wanted to merge the ANMB and the WPB, "it was General Somervell and not the Navy that defeated the plan to merge ANMB and WPB operations. He gradually withdrew the Army officers who

ASF, and the Office of Procurement and Material in the Navy labeled: The Army and Navy Munitions Board List of Prohibited Items for Construction Work. This was first issued in May 1942 and the ANMB designation was continued in the succeeding years, even though meaningless.[4] In December 1945 an official announcement was issued by ASF headquarters saying that "the Army and Navy Munitions Board has been reconstituted."[5] This order implicitly acknowledged that the board had lapsed.

In almost every instance where procurement co-operation eventually developed between the ASF and the Navy, it was only after some difficulty had first begun to hamper operations. In many cases the technicians concerned with a common problem got together and worked out a solution. Sometimes Army or Navy personnel anticipated a problem and sought the co-operation of the other. Most relationships were either informal or were set up to meet a special need. Two examples will illustrate. When the War Department began its Army Specialized Training Program in December 1942, the Navy was already using various university facilities throughout the country for officer and other training programs. For a time, universities and colleges were able to pit Army and Navy needs against each other in obtaining the most favorable contract terms for training facilities. Accordingly, in March 1943 the Under Secretary of War and the Under Secretary of the Navy signed a joint directive creating a Joint Army and Navy Board for Training Unit Contracts and agreed upon a single individual to be chairman and to represent both services. The agreement was revised and extended in August 1943. The second example involved packaging. After long discussions among staff officers, the Under Secretary of War and the Assistant Secretary of the Navy on 10 February 1945 established a Joint Army-Navy Packaging Board to set up uniform procedure in issuing packing and packaging instructions to contractors for various kinds of supplies.[6] These two examples of jointly solving a special problem and setting up a standard practice were not unusual.

Fortunately, a complete and systematic account of Army and Navy procurement relationships was prepared before the end of World War II. This report arose out of peculiar circumstances. When in the autumn of 1943 the War Department began to work closely with the Office of War Mobilization on policies for contract termination, the Navy was invited to participate. A Joint Contract Termination Board was organized in the Office of War Mobilization on 11 November 1943 under the chairmanship of Mr. John M. Hancock. This board consisted of the Secretary of Commerce, the Under Secretaries of War and the Navy, and representatives of other agencies such as the WPB, the FEA, and the Treasury Department. A uniform ter-

had been assigned to ANMB and did not fill the billets left vacant." Connery, *The Navy and the Industrial Mobilization in World War II*, p. 176. There is no record in the files of the commanding general of the ASF to justify this interpretation, nor does it coincide with this author's own recollection of the events. Somervell wanted ASF representation on industry requirements committees in the WPB and kept such representatives to the extent that the WPB was willing and the work of the WPB warranted. Somervell did not withdraw personnel from ANMB because there was no separate agency from which to remove them. The ANMB never had a staff of its own. Somervell in 1942 was not as interested in formal co-operation with the Navy on procurement as in 1944.

[4] This practice is described in the Draper-Strauss Rpt: II, Functional Studies, pp. 196–97.
[5] ASF Cir 441, 11 Dec 45.
[6] WD Cir 80, 13 Mar 45.

mination article to be used in prime contracts having a fixed price was agreed upon and officially promulgated on 8 January 1944. To meet the need of guidance in terminating fixed price subcontracts, the board framed and recommended for use a termination article on 21 May 1944. Then a series of four interpretations of the uniform termination article was agreed upon. Thus, substantially complete understanding was achieved between the War and Navy Departments on termination policies, except for cost-plus-a-fixed-fee contracts. Thereafter, additional negotiations were begun in an effort to achieve procedural uniformity in the termination practices of the two departments. Eventually, on 1 November 1944 a Joint Termination Regulation was issued by the War and Navy Departments. A Joint Termination Accounting Manual accompanied this regulation. Collaboration was extended even to the point where one department arranged to settle the terminated contracts of the other on a company-wide basis. The achievement in the field of contract termination is probably the most outstanding example of success in the effort to unify War and Navy procurement activities during World War II. Within the War Department the entire termination effort was directed by Col. William H. Draper, Jr., of ASF headquarters. His counterpart in the Navy was Capt. Lewis L. Strauss.

With the successful conclusion of Colonel Draper's work, Somervell thought the time propitious for a review of all Army-Navy procurement relationships. In April 1944 both Under Secretary Patterson and General Somervell had appeared before the House Select Committee on Postwar Military Policy to urge unification of the armed forces.[7] Somervell hoped Colonel Draper, by exploring desirable collaborative relations between the Army and Navy, might make a substantial contribution toward better Army-Navy procurement arrangements and at the same time, lay the groundwork for the larger problem of service integration after the war.[8]

A final report was submitted on 8 February 1945 by Colonel Draper and Captain Strauss and was accompanied by two volumes of studies on existing procurement relations.[9] The Functional Studies of the Draper-Strauss Report described the many different relationships which had grown up during the war between ASF headquarters and the Navy. The Matériel Studies presented the various collaborative arrangements existing between the technical services of the ASF, the AAF, and the procurement bureaus of the Navy. The two types of studies together enumerated most of the formal and informal contacts between the War and Navy Departments. The number of these was impressive. Equally noteworthy was the wide variety of measures taken to bring about common action. In general, they fell into one of four broad categories. First, the studies indicated extensive exchange of information on research and development projects and an occasional division of development responsibility between the Army technical services and the Navy bureaus. Second,

---

[7] *Hearings before the Select Committee on Postwar Military Policy*, H.R., 78th Cong, 2d Sess, on Proposal to Establish a Single Department of Armed Forces.

[8] In private life, before World War II, Colonel Draper had been a partner in the New York banking firm of Dillon, Reed and Company. The new Secretary of the Navy, James Forrestal, had also been a member of that firm. Under Secretary Patterson persuaded Secretary Forrestal that Draper should be assigned to this project. The Secretary of the Navy designated Capt. L. L. Strauss of his office to work with Colonel Draper.

[9] Draper-Strauss Rpt: I, Final and Interim Reports; II, Functional Studies; III, Matériel Studies.

for a number of different items, Army technical services procured the requirements as indicated by a Navy bureau, while Navy bureaus procured certain items for Army technical services. In the third place, there were a few instances of joint Army-Navy procurement. Finally, there had been considerable effort to work out joint procurement policies, specifications, and procedures to be followed by the actual procuring agencies. Each of these types of collaborative endeavor can be briefly illustrated.

The technical services of the Army and the procurement bureaus of the Navy exchanged technical information on virtually all research and development projects of any possible common interest. The meetings of technical committees in each technical service were ordinarily attended by Navy representatives, and reports and other development papers were interchanged on a systematic basis. Frequently, co-operation on research matters went much farther than attendance at meetings and exchange of reports. The Ordnance development program is a case in point. The Navy Bureau of Ordnance had for years done much work in the development of armor plate for ships. Tank development in the Army brought many of the same problems into Army research and procurement. The Navy made its heavy armor testing facilities at Dahlgren Proving Ground available to the Army, while the Ordnance Department in turn made experimental facilities at Aberdeen Proving Ground available to the Navy. All information from research in ballistics was likewise exchanged between the two services. The Ordnance Department and the Navy Bureau of Ordnance also divided up much of the work in developing rockets. Facilities were used in common by both

services, and agreements were made whereby each service would tend to specialize in a different field of rocket development.[10] In the field of communications, the Signal Corps of the Army, on the one hand, and the Navy Bureau of Ordnance and the Navy Bureau of Ships, on the other, worked closely together, through the Office of Scientific Research and Development, in using the private research facilities at Westinghouse, General Electric, and Western Electric plants. The Joint Communications Board under the Joint Chiefs of Staff was utilized as the agency for co-operation in the development of radar equipment. This board had nine subcommittees, with representatives from the two departments directing joint work on the design and development of equipment for Army and Navy use.[11] In 1943 a Joint Army-Navy Standardization Committee for Vehicles and Construction Equipment was established which resulted in agreement on standard automotive equipment for the two services. The Navy agreed to use Army specifications for automotive equipment.[12] In 1944 the Chemical Warfare Service was engaged in fourteen research projects set up and financed by Navy funds. In its turn, the Navy Bureau of Ordnance stationed Naval officers at both Edgewood Arsenal and Dugway Proving Ground to keep in touch with the research developments of the Chemical Warfare Service.[13] All of these examples show the procedures used to achieve the maximum benefit for both services in their common interest in research and development.

In the second place, for a number of

[10] Ibid., III, 79, 84.
[11] Ibid., III, 100.
[12] Ibid., III, 109.
[13] Ibid., III, 120–21.

different items the Navy obtained its requirements from the Army, while the Navy in turn purchased some items and delivered them to the Army. Thus the Marine Corps obtained all of its tanks from the Army. The same was true of small arms, machine guns, and ammunition. Marine Corps requirements for these items were incorporated in the ASF Army Supply Program and deliveries were made to the Navy on a reimbursable basis.[14] The Bureau of Ships purchased all landing craft for the Army. Early in 1941 the Office of Production Management designated the Chrysler Corporation to produce 40-mm. antiaircraft guns for both the Army and Navy. In addition, Army arsenals such as Watertown and Watervliet produced heavy guns for the Navy, while the Navy frequently produced large guns and heavy ammunition for the Army.[15] During the calendar year 1944 approximately 46 percent of the Navy's total purchases of motor vehicles were obtained directly from the Army.[16] The Chemical Warfare Service purchased incendiary bombs, gas masks, protective materials, and other items for the Navy Department.[17] A somewhat different arrangement was employed for the procurement of crawler tractors and spare parts. In March 1942 the WPB froze all deliveries of tractors because of competing demands from the military services. Thereafter the WPB agreed to make 85 percent of all crawler tractor deliveries available to the armed forces. This was a lump sum allocation and was not divided between the Army and the Navy. Thereupon the Army Service Forces took the lead in developing a plan whereby the Corps of Engineers purchased and accepted delivery of all tractors under the WPB orders. The distribution of these tractors was then controlled by a War Department Conference Group for Tractors and Cranes. This committee was composed of representatives from three bureaus of the Navy, the Marine Corps, seven ASF representatives, the AAF, and representatives from the War Department General Staff. Working under the aegis of the Munitions Assignments Committee (Ground), this conference group agreed upon the division of total deliveries among all the services.[18] In all these instances the Army or the Navy was completely responsible for all procurement, delivering the desired completed items to the other service on a reimbursable basis.

In the third place, there were a number of examples of joint procurement operations where the ASF and the Navy bureaus worked together in the procurement of common items. The foremost example of joint procurement occurred in the subsistence field. Procurement of all nonperishable foodstuffs for the Army was directed by The Quartermaster General through the Chicago depot. This office also let the contracts for the Navy or assigned portions of contracts to the Navy. The Navy Bureau of Supplies and Accounts then received grade certificates from the War Food Administration and gave its contractors separate shipping instructions. Moreover, the Navy paid all of its food bills directly to contractors. Perishable subsistence items were bought through Quartermaster market centers and buying offices scattered throughout the nation. The Navy maintained offices at fifteen of these market centers and paid

---

[14] *Ibid.*, III, 80, 110.
[15] *Ibid.*, III, 79.
[16] *Ibid.*, III, 109.
[17] *Ibid.*, III, 119.
[18] *Ibid.*, III, 17.

a proportionate share of the salaries of civilian employees. The Navy market offices received requirements from Navy yards and depots for fresh foodstuffs and then turned these over to the Quartermaster officers to be incorporated in the Army's buying program. Delivery instructions to contractors were furnished by Quartermaster officers, but reports of delivery went to the Navy market officer, who prepared the voucher and arranged for payment. About 90 percent of all perishable food supplies for the Navy were thus procured, while 85 percent of Navy nonperishable foodstuffs were purchased through the Chicago Quartermaster Depot.[19]

Another joint procurement operation was established in 1942 for the purchase of lumber for both the Army and Navy. Because of difficulties in obtaining desired lumber supplies, the chairman of the ANMB in August 1942 arranged for the creation of the Central Procuring Agency on Lumber Procurement. The agency was staffed by both Army and Navy officers but operated under the direction of the Army Chief of Engineers. This device permitted one agency to present lumber requirements to the War Production Board and to deal with contractors. The Central Procuring Agency established various field offices, some of which were in charge of Army personnel and others in charge of Navy personnel. In all instances both services had men in each office. Each service paid directly for the lumber delivered to it, but contract letting, production expediting, and production inspection were handled on a joint basis under single direction.[20] Close co-operation in the procurement of petroleum products was obtained through the Army-Navy Petroleum Board, another agency of the Joint

Chiefs of Staff. This board consolidated Army and Navy requirements for petroleum products, presented these requirements to the Petroleum Administration for War, and then designated producers to deliver petroleum products to the Army or Navy. Joint action was also taken in shipping such products overseas.[21] Because of competing demands for diesel engines, a Diesel Engine Subcommittee of the Joint Army-Navy Munitions Assignments Committee was appointed to schedule and allot production deliveries to the armed services.[22] From 1942 to 1943 a Joint Army-Navy Electronics Production Agency expedited deliveries of tubes and other essential radar equipment.[23] In the examples just cited, various co-operative methods were employed by the two departments to bring about close collaboration in the procurement of identical supplies. Each maintained certain phases of the procurement process under its own control, but contracts were let on a joint basis and duplication of facilities and personnel was avoided.

Finally, ASF headquarters worked closely with the Chief of Procurement and Material in the Navy Department in developing joint procurement policies. The outstanding achievement in this field was the issuance by the two departments of the Joint Termination Regulation and the Joint Termination Accounting Manual, as already related. Another important achievement in joint Army-Navy action was realized on 22 December 1942 when the Chief of Procurement and Material of the Navy Department and the command-

---

[19] *Ibid.*, III, 1.
[20] *Ibid.*, III, 17.
[21] *Ibid.*, III, 42.
[22] *Ibid.*, III, 57.
[23] *Ibid.*, III, 99.

ing general of the ASF established a Joint Army-Navy Committee on Specifications. This committee set up various subcommittees to work out common specifications for such items as textiles, chemicals, electronics, engineer equipment, transportation equipment, communications equipment, medical supplies, photographic supplies, and packing and packaging materials. No effort was made to duplicate standard federal specifications. By the end of 1944 there were some 155 joint Army-Navy specifications in use by both agencies.[24] The two departments exchanged considerable information about pricing methods and policies. Some contact was maintained through the WPB Procurement Policy Board, but direct communication between pricing officials of the two departments resulted in the adoption of many identical practices. On the other hand, the two departments used different contract provisions and forms and very different processes in administering contracts.[25]

A Joint Army and Navy Patent Advisory Board advised the U.S. Patent Office on which patent applications should be kept secret for reasons of military security. This was the extent of co-operation in the patent field.[26]

To a considerable degree, through mutual co-operation and discussion, the two departments obtained substantially uniform insurance policies. Thus both departments followed the same practices in insuring government-owned property used by contractors, in using a comprehensive rating plan for workmen's compensation, in providing marine war risk insurance through the War Shipping Administration, and in fixing the insurance provisions for repair time-and-material contracts.[27]

On 31 March 1943 the Under Secretary

of War and the Under Secretary of the Navy adopted a joint statement of principles to govern the renegotiation of contracts. This was worked out in large part by the Renegotiation Division in ASF headquarters. The two departments then voluntarily created a Joint Price Adjustment Board to fix renegotiation policies and procedures on a continuing basis. In February 1944, Congress, by law, directed the establishment of a War Contracts Price Adjustment Board representing all procurement agencies of the government. The Price Adjustment Board of the War Department included a member from the Navy, and the Price Adjustment Board of the Navy Department included a member from ASF headquarters sitting on behalf of the Under Secretary. This brought about a considerable degree of uniformity in renegotiation procedure.[28]

In the course of their studies, Colonel Draper and Captain Strauss found a number of opportunities for further procurement co-operation between the two departments. Interim Report 1 on 21 December 1944, recommended the creation of a Joint Army-Navy Medical Matériel and Specifications Board to design and develop medical equipment, a Joint Purchasing Agency for Medical and Surgical Equipment and Supplies, and a Joint Inspection and Laboratory Service. These recommendations were approved by the Secretary of the Navy and the Under Secretary of War. A second interim report on 28 December recommended that Army and Navy procurement officers be placed

---

[24] *Ibid.*, II, 85.
[25] *Ibid.*, II, 36–49.
[26] *Ibid.*, II, 50.
[27] *Ibid.*, II, 181.
[28] *Ibid.*, II, 69.

in the same office for the procurement of standard stock items, textiles, clothing, and shoes. This also was approved. Interim Report 3 on 8 January 1945 recommended the creation of a centrally located Joint Army and Navy Petroleum Purchase Agency. Interim Report 4 on 11 January recommended the immediate establishment of a Joint Marine Procurement Board as a co-ordinating agency between the Navy's Bureau of Ships and the Army Transportation Corps. Interim Report 5 on 23 January recommended detailed studies of possible further co-ordination in the procurement of various types of ordnance matériel. Interim Report 6 resulted in the creation of a Joint Army-Navy Packaging Board to resolve differences between the Army Packaging Board and the Navy Packaging Board and to insure uniform instructions on packing and packaging. Interim Report 7 on 1 February merely pointed out that further co-operation in procurement of electronics equipment seemed desirable, but it made no recommendations. Interim Report 8 on 5 February pointed to the need for further co-operation in the procurement of construction machinery and mechanical equipment and resulted in instructions from the Under Secretary of War and the Assistant Secretary of the Navy for further effort at realizing common basic specifications and for assignment of procurement to a single agency. Interim Report 10 on 9 February resulted in instructions from the Under Secretary of War and the Assistant Secretary of the Navy for further study of the advisability of unifying the procurement of chemical warfare supplies.[29]

In their final report of 8 February 1945 Colonel Draper and Captain Strauss both agreed that all studies demonstrated "the need for further co-ordination between the two departments in procurement." While in some fields of procurement excellent results had been obtained, in others very little had been accomplished. Moreover, there was serious danger that the benefits of existing co-operation might be lost without additional steps to put all of these arrangements "on a firm and permanent basis." The report stated that the mere creation of many joint committees and boards was not sufficient. Accordingly, it recommended the creation of a staff organization patterned after the Joint Chiefs of Staff to insure uniform policies and procedures and to insist upon further co-operation between the two departments. This joint staff organization was to be known as the Joint Matériel Chiefs and was to function under the direction of the Under Secretary of War and the Assistant Secretary of the Navy. The Joint Matériel Chiefs would consist of the Commanding General, ASF, and the Commanding General, AAF, or a representative designated by him, and two flag officers designated by the Secretary of the Navy. Under the Joint Matériel Chiefs would be a Joint Director of Matériel who would establish general policies and procedures to be followed in some twelve phases of procurement such as purchasing and pricing, contract forms and procedures, financing of production, insurance, renegotiation, contract termination, and the disposal of property. The Joint Director of Matériel would also further co-ordination between the two departments in item identification, inspection, design and specifications, the use of facilities, production scheduling, production controls, and the allocation of materials. He would also supervise co-op-

---

[29] Interim Reports 9 and 11 merely transmitted detailed studies.

erative arrangements between the actual procurement offices.[30]

The recommendation for the creation of the Joint Matériel Chiefs and a Joint Director of Matériel was approved by the Under Secretary of War but was opposed by the Navy Department. At first, in their joint conferences on the report, Secretary Forrestal indicated his approval to Under Secretary Patterson.[31] Then, after long discussion inside the Navy Department, Secretary Forrestal changed his mind and decided against action on any of the Draper-Strauss recommendations. As a result, none of the broad proposals set forth in the report was carried out.

In individual instances, further co-operative action was achieved before the end of the war. The Surgeon General of the Army and the Surgeon General of the Navy established a Joint Medical Matériel and Specification Board with a Joint Catalog Branch and a Joint Specifications Branch in New York City to bring about a greater degree of interchangeability of medical items. The Quartermaster General and the Navy Bureau of Supply and Accounts established a Joint Purchasing Agency for textile procurement in New York City and a Joint Petroleum Purchasing Agency in Washington. The creation of these three boards was the chief accomplishment of the Draper-Strauss report. Little progress was made in attempting to further co-operation between the Corps of Engineers and the Navy Bureau of Yards and Docks; likewise, the Ordnance Department and the Navy Bureau of Ordnance opposed a Joint Procurement Agency for Rockets or the establishment of a co-ordinating board for the two agencies. The Army and Navy Packaging Board made some progress in developing and publishing joint packaging specifica-

tions and instructions for use by all procurement agencies.[32] With the conclusion of hostilities in August 1945 pressure for Joint Army-Navy procurement action came to an end. The whole issue was dwarfed by the larger, more basic question of a single department of national defense.

Thus, under wartime conditions there was a good deal of co-operation between the two military departments on procurement matters. All of this effort was purely voluntary. There were also instances of non-co-operation, as when the Army cut back 40-mm. ammunition production at a plant in Erie, Pennsylvania, at the same time that the Navy was expanding 40-mm. ammunition production at a plant in Elgin, Illinois, and when both bought ten-ton bridge trestles from the same manufacturer in Covington, Kentucky, but set different specifications on the tolerance and spacing of drill holes. During World War II there never existed any systematic, institutional device for promoting and directing procurement co-operation by the two departments. The Draper-Strauss report recommended such machinery but, as already indicated, no action was taken before the end of the war.

Desirable Organization for Army-Navy Collaboration

While the Draper-Strauss report was under consideration General Somervell hoped it would be possible to create joint

---

[30] Draper-Strauss Rpt: I, contains all the interim reports and the final report.

[31] Somervell purposely stayed out of all discussion about the Draper-Strauss report, for he did not want any charge of empire-building against him to arise and complicate the situation.

[32] Memo, Dir of Purchases ASF for USW, 4 Jul 45, sub: Progress Rpt on Joint Navy-Army Procurement Project, Hq ASF, Purchases Files, CG ASF.

Army-Navy machinery in the procurement field comparable to that which had been built up under the Joint Chiefs of Staff. He felt that such an arrangement would be entirely feasible, even though in many respects he was inclined to believe that the JCS machinery was not entirely satisfactory.

The elaborate structure of committees and subcommittees functioning under the JCS were all intended to bring about necessary co-operation between the armed forces in overseas operations. As far as the Army Service Forces was concerned the most important of these committees was the Joint Logistics Committee, which reviewed strategic plans in the light of available supply and transportation resources. Through this and other committees the various agencies of the War and Navy Departments arrived at a common understanding of what was to be done. Each department then proceeded more or less on its own to carry out these agreements. It remained for the single commander in the field to weld the Army, Navy, and Air Forces components assigned to his command into a unified military operation.

Somervell was not always satisfied with these arrangements, as noted earlier. One of the steps he took, through General Lutes, his deputy, was to persuade Admiral Nimitz in the Central Pacific to create a joint Army-Navy staff, with an Army officer in charge of logistics. Somervell even went further on one occasion when he recommended that there be a unified Army-Navy supply and transportation system in the Pacific.[33] The Navy was not enthusiastic about the proposal, since the top operations command of the Navy believed that prospective naval activities in the Pacific would differ too much from those of the Army to permit a single supply and transportation

service. For example, the Navy was already planning the "floating" supply system which in 1944 was to enable combat task forces to remain at sea much longer than previously thought possible.[34] But even so, Somervell was convinced that much waste motion would be avoided by joint action in overseas supply and transportation, especially as the number of common problems increased with the establishment of more and more advance bases in the steady progress across the Pacific.[35]

Many common Army-Navy concerns in supply and in nonprocurement operations began back in the United States. Somervell enumerated some of these when he testified before the House Select Committee on Postwar Military Policy on 26 April 1944.[36] An Ocean Shipping Section of the Army and Navy Munitions Board (it was so designated even though the ANMB had ceased to exist) was a body for bringing together Army and Navy officials concerned with port operations, especially in the San Francisco Bay area. In the early days of the war there was considerable competition between the Army and Navy for piers, warehouses, and other loading facilities. President Roosevelt spoke to Somervell about the situation on one occasion, and Somervell went to work at once to push for Army-Navy collaboration on the

---

[33] CD Rpt 34, Unified Supply Service and Unified Transportation Service for the Army and Navy, Dec 42, CD, ASF.

[34] For an account of these arrangements and the Navy point of view, see Duncan S. Ballantine, *U. S. Naval Logistics in the Second World War* (Princeton, N. J., Princeton University Press, 1947).

[35] For fuller treatment, see Bykofsky and Larson, Activities in the Oversea Commands; Leighton and Coakley, Logistics of Global Warfare, 1941–1943.

[36] *Hearings before the Select Committee on Postwar Military Policy*, H. R., 78th Cong, 2d Sess, on Proposal to Establish a Single Department of Armed Forces, Pt. 1, pp. 96–111.

west coast.[37] A Storage Control Board was set up in 1944 to prevent competition for storage space along the west coast, and some joint use of storage facilities followed. A Joint Military Transportation Committee, on which General Gross represented the Army, studied ocean shipping plans and adjusted various military cargoes to available shipping space. An Army-Navy Allocations Committee worked with the War Shipping Administration in the actual process of allocating cargo vessels to both services. In San Francisco a Pacific Coast Ship Repair and Conversion Committee and a Joint Routing and Scheduling Committee were set up, representing the Army, Navy and WSA. Co-operation was complicated by the existence of varying procedures. The Army exercised a close central control over surface transport while the Navy left most of the control to the commandants of Naval districts or to the chiefs of sea frontiers.

In addition to noting these supply and transportation methods General Somervell called the attention of the House committee to two other arrangements. A Joint Communications Board under the Joint Chiefs of Staff provided a means for common action on some communications problems, although no standardization of engineering and operating practices in this field was ever realized. A Joint Army-Navy Committee on Welfare and Recreation provided a clearinghouse for exchanging information and materials on educational and other services to armed forces personnel.

But in Somervell's eyes all of these arrangements in procurement, in supply, and in other fields, did not seem to go far enough. Too much depended upon voluntary co-operation, leaving many important fields uncovered. Thus, there were separate storage operations in the interior

of the United States, separate maintenance facilities for the repair of automotive and other equipment, separate rail transportation arrangements, separate hospital systems, separate construction activities, separate military police practices, separate fiscal systems, and separate personnel systems.

Like other military officers Somervell was convinced that the JCS machinery had accomplished much, and he hoped that joint procurement machinery would extend co-operative arrangements further in this field. But in the long run, he believed the existing staff structure would prove inadequate. On this point Somervell joined with others in advocating a single department of national defense with a single chief of staff and general staff. He believed that on procurement, supply, and other matters, such a unified staff could and would do much to establish joint procedures and unified operations between the Army, Navy, and Air Forces.

Somervell parted company with other ranking officers of the War Department in his belief that in the future there should be four component branches of the nation's armed forces: an Army (the ground forces), a Navy, an Air Force, and a Service Force (to perform procurement, supply, and many other services for all combat forces).[38] His thinking was based upon

---

[37] In a letter to the President on 10 August 1943, Somervell transmitted information about how the Army and Navy were then working together in the San Francisco area. The President expressed his appreciation on 16 August. This letter is filed in Hq ASF.

[38] Somervell's ideas on this score were briefly outlined in *Hearings before the Select Committee on Postwar Military Policy*, H. R., 78th Cong, 2d Sess, on Proposal to Establish a Single Department of Armed Forces, Pt. 1, p. 111. They were never developed in detail, although Somervell returned to this theme in 1948 when testifying before the Eberstadt task force of the (Hoover) Commission on Organization of the Executive Branch of the Government.

two primary considerations. In the first place, he believed in 1944 and thereafter as he had believed in 1941, that procurement and supply were too inextricably combined to warrant two separate supervisory organizations. He was willing in 1945 to contemplate a Joint Chiefs of Staff and a Joint Matériel Chiefs only because on the Army side he expected to combine procurement and supply in his own person and at the same time be subordinate on all operational matters to the Army Chief of Staff. As a long-term proposition, however, he thought this a faulty concept of organization. Second, he believed that only a single command under one person would be able to achieve maximum economy in the purchase and supply of common items of equipment and in the performance of various services for the three combat forces. In other words, Somervell was so convinced of the usefulness of the

Army Service Forces as a War Department organizational arrangement that he wished to see it applied to all the armed forces in terms of a single service force to procure military supplies and participate in all matters pertaining to national economic mobilization.

Postwar events are not a proper part of this present volume. It may be interesting to glance beyond 1945, however, to note that when the National Security Act of 1947 was passed, it did not provide for a fourth military command, a service force. It did create a Munitions Board under the Secretary of Defense to exercise some supervision over procurement and supply operations of the Army, Navy, and Air Force. While this board had new fields to conquer, it also operated in fields that had already been explored by voluntary Army-Navy collaboration and by the Draper-Strauss report.

CHAPTER XIX

The Procurement Role of the ASF

Out of its experience with civilian agencies, and especially from the controversy with the WPB, the ASF tried to advance a definite opinion regarding the relationships which should exist between key civilian agencies and military procurement agencies during economic mobilization. In a general way such relationships had been more or less assumed in the industrial mobilization plans prepared before World War II. But the war itself was the testing ground where the practicability of those ideas was determined.

It fell to the lot of the Army Service Forces, and particularly to General Somervell, to demonstrate that though both types of agencies, civilian and military, might have different administrative roles to perform, they could nonetheless work together in what was necessarily a joint enterprise.

In attempting to make the fullest use of the nation's resources in carrying on the war, there never was more than one alternative to an organization under which civilian and military agencies worked together. That alternative was to remove all military procurement operations from under the direction of the armed forces and to turn them over to civilian agencies which would be responsible for both general economic mobilization and military procurement. The possibility that economic mobilization might be turned over to the military was never contemplated by the responsible civilian secretaries or military chiefs of the armed forces during World War II. Certainly this writer can assert with absolute assurance that General Somervell never for a moment felt that the military services should assume responsibility for economic mobilization. On the other hand, he was strongly opposed to the idea that military procurement should be turned over to the civilian agencies which were directing economic mobilization.

The essence of Somervell's position, and that of Secretary Stimson and Under Secretary Patterson, and all their principal associates, was simply this: in arming the military forces in a time of all-out war effort, the nation's economic resources had to be called upon to provide in abundance the weapons necessary to defeat the enemy. This meant a large-scale shift of productive resources—manpower, raw materials, and industrial plant—from ordinary consumer goods to military goods. In the process there was bound to be a diminution in the supply of goods and services available for civilian consumption.

The modern concept of war is one of a struggle between national economies. It involves not merely an economic potential to produce great quantities of weapons but a nation's actual output. Only when the economic resources of a nation are readily available for the output of military equipment on a large scale can its armed forces benefit from its productive capacity. And modern strategy of warfare—certainly the American strategy of warfare—has now become based in large part upon the concept of supply superiority—that is, the employment of overwhelming quantities of military equipment against the enemy.[1] Strategy has always depended in some measure upon logistics, but perhaps we are now more dependent upon this factor in our military thinking and action than ever before.[2] Accordingly, economic mobilization is one of the essential elements of total warfare.

In the War Department point of view economic mobilization during World War II had two interrelated but nonetheless separate features. First, there was military procurement: the determination of supply needs, the design and specification of weapons, the contracting with certain industries (those making end-items of equipment) for the delivery of specified quantities of weapons, scheduling and expediting the delivery of weapons, inspection for contract performance, the issuance of delivery instructions, and the payment of contract prices for items delivered. In all these relationships the military procurement agencies should have direct access to contractors unimpeded by intervention of a third party. Second, there was economic mobilization in a more general sense: the central control of the common resources of the nation needed to realize military procurement goals and at the same time to keep the entire national economy functioning. This involved a determination of

total productive resources available for military procurement; necessary action to increase the supply of manpower, raw materials, and productive facilities; production and delivery scheduling of the manufacturers of raw materials, civilian goods (transportation equipment, electric power systems, food distribution facilities, etc.), and common industrial goods used both by the military and civilian producers (ball bearings, motors, copper wiring, etc.); control of the use of transportation facilities; price control; rationing of civilian supplies; war financing; economic warfare and foreign trade; and many other duties. These were responsibilities for civilian agencies in a period of all-out war effort.

Throughout the war the War Department tried to make clear that it was possible and desirable to have military procurement agencies and civilian control agencies working together but with somewhat different responsibilities in effecting economic mobilization for war.

Military Procurement

From the time that the War Department was first set up in 1789, it had enjoyed the statutory authority to purchase military supplies. Under ordinary peacetime conditions military procurement and supply was a problem of internal War Department organization and procedures. These activities raised few questions of broad economic importance. Even during the Civil War the procurement operations of the Union Army apparently proceeded

[1] For an interesting interpretation of this point of view, see Dennis W. Brogan, *The American Character* (New York, Harper & Brothers, 1944), Pt. III.

[2] John D. Millett, "Logistics and Modern War," *Military Affairs,* IX (Fall 1945), 193.

without much concern for their impact upon the economic resources of the nation. It was not until World War I that our government acted on the theory that military procurement must be integrated into the general program for utilization of the nation's total productive resources. Industrial mobilization planning from 1920 to 1940 was based upon this proposition. President Roosevelt acted upon it in May 1940 when he set up the Advisory Commission to the Council of National Defense. There was never any real doubt that military procurement in wartime meant economic mobilization for war. The War Department, however, still retained its responsibility for military procurement. The economic mobilization of national industrial resources, from the Army's point of view, did not involve the removal of procurement responsibilities from the War Department.

As noted above, the NDAC in 1940 and then the Office of Production Management in 1941, gave their primary attention to helping the War and Navy Departments expand and improve their military procurement operations. Between the two wars the procurement bureaus of the War Department were mere skeleton organizations. Even between June 1940 and December 1941 they had been slow in building up their internal operations by commissioning or hiring top-ranking civilians for key positions. The War Department needed and did in fact obtain major assistance from both the NDAC and the OPM.

After mid-1941, however, the War Department felt that some of the persons who had provided this initial help in building up procurement organization and methods should be absorbed within the Department itself. After 9 March 1942, for exam-

ple, General Somervell asked Mr. Nelson to release Mr. William H. Harrison, head of the WPB Production Division and a former vice-president of American Telephone and Telegraph Company. This was done. Harrison was commissioned a brigadier general, and eventually as a major general was placed in charge of the entire procurement program of the Signal Corps. A number of his assistants were likewise brought into the Army.[3]

The shift of key personnel from the central civilian agencies to the military procurement agencies of the Army Service Forces represented, in Army thinking, merely one step toward total wartime economic mobilization. This move was in the accepted tradition which held that in time of national emergency, the military skeleton organization would expand by bringing in civilians to man our defenses in every sphere of activity from procurement to combat. The main impulse for this expansion was supposed to come from within the military agency since military procurement operations could best be handled by the armed forces themselves.

There were some groups in WPB which developed an opposite point of view, a point of view which held that the military procurement power rightly belonged to the WPB under the provisions of Execu-

[3] The accusation has sometimes been made that personnel taken over by the Army from WPB were slighted or ignored. For example, an editor of Harper's writes: "Consequently, he [Nelson] tried to infiltrate his own men into the Army and Navy offices, to 'advise' procurement officers and 'review' contracts. These men were generally ignored, or were taken over by the military. A number were persuaded to accept commissions at high rank and then were tucked out of sight." John Fischer, "The Army Takes Over," Harper's Magazine, 190 (May 1945), 486. This assertion ignores the important and influential roles in the ASF of such persons as Col. D. C. MacKeachie, Brig. Gen. A. J. Browning, Maj. Gen. W. H. Harrison, Col. C. T. Wood, Mr. Robert T. Stevens, and others.

tive Order 9024 which created the WPB, and that those powers were usurped by the military organization. In support of this view the official WPB history states, for example:

Nelson was not aggressive about his jurisdiction and his powers. He allowed ANMB to elude his grasp, although it was subordinate to him, and he permitted the War Department's Services of Supply, over which he said he had no control, to become something decidedly other than what he thought it should be.[4]

And at another point, it adds:

Everything that WPB attempted to do with respect to procurement was conditioned by the primary fact that Nelson had delegated the power of actual procurement to the Services.[5]

The WPB history says in effect that there can be no effective mobilization of the nation's economic resources unless the central civilian direction of economic resources is combined with military procurement under a single administrative agency:

A genuinely effective control of procurement by WPB would have meant that it was in a position effectively to: (1) expedite war procurement; (2) achieve maximum use of existing facilities; (3) conserve critical resources; (4) eliminate competition between the procurement agencies; (5) further the maintenance of a sound national economy by the proper distribution of war contracts; (6) procure at the lowest total expenditure; and (7) develop uniform policies which would guide the procurement agencies in the realization of these goals. To do this it would not be enough merely to enunciate policies; it was necessary to control the actual administration of procurement policies at the point of procurement. WPB would have to insert itself into the flow of procurement plans and orders so that it could clear appropriation requests for noncombat items to determine need and procurement program feasibility; clear purchase programs and schedules for

sufficiency of supplies, timing of orders, and types of purchase transactions; and direct actual placement of orders.[6]

Aside from the jurisdictional issues involved this statement implies that if the War Production Board had been allowed to procure munitions, the over-all war production effort would have been strengthened. The history apparently concludes that (1) there was no effective economic mobilization in World War II and (2) the explanation lies in Nelson's failure to insist upon a transfer of military procurement operations from the armed forces to the WPB. This point of view helps to explain why ASF–WPB relationships were at times bitter. The War Department and the ASF argued throughout the war that organizationally, military procurement had to be integrated with military logistics and strategy. They consistently held that effective economic mobilization could be realized through close collaboration between a central civilian agency and the military procurement agencies. The 12 March 1942 agreement between the War Department and the War Production Board was a statement of respective responsibilities that was entirely workable in practice, and the experience of the war years seemed to confirm this belief.

At the end of 1942 and in early 1943, General Somervell and others in the War Department were alarmed by legislation introduced into Congress calling for the creation of a new "super" economic mobilization agency which would combine the WPB and the procurement activities of the armed forces.[7]

---

[4] *Industrial Mobilization for War,* p. 211.

[5] *Ibid.,* p. 521.

[6] *Ibid.,* p. 524.

[7] S.2871, H.R.7742, 77th Cong, 2d Sess; S.607, 78th Cong, 1st Sess.

Senator Claude Pepper of Florida, one of the sponsors of the proposal, explained his stand in an article in *The New Republic* entitled "To Smash the Final Bottleneck."[8] He argued that the "least proper" agency to be placed in charge of "war production" was the military. He went on to assert that only if the military forces found that they had to depend upon another agency for their supplies would they be "held to a strict accounting, required to present its requirements in terms of a fully developed strategical program." He criticized the military forces for not turning "production" over to "production men from industry."

Somervell was moved by this article to write a lengthy personal letter to Senator Pepper to explain the Army's point of view.[9] In it he expressed surprise and shock because of the Senator's unfriendly tone and apparent "faulty information." Somervell argued first of all that logistics and strategy were inseparable in war and that the armed forces' mission to defeat the nation's enemies could be fulfilled only if they had "complete responsibility and authority in a single chain of command" for the design, procurement, and distribution of weapons. In 1942, when the same kind of relationship was being developed between the War Industries Board and the armed forces that had been worked out in World War I, Somervell had insisted that it was not feasible to try to "rip" military procurement out of the whole process of determining military strategy and providing the logistical resources for its execution. He identified the major steps in the flow of munitions as follows:

a. Strategical and logistical planning.
b. Development of need for all types of supplies and equipment based on that planning.

c. Research to develop new and improved weapons and other matériel.
d. Production and testing of pilot models.
e. Determination of facilities capable of producing the end-items of military supplies and equipment in sufficient quantities at the times required.
f. Construction of production facilities where those existing are inadequate.
g. Placing of contracts.
h. Expediting and following up production.
i. Inspection for quality.
j. Testing and proof firing.
k. Providing shipping orders to the manufacturers.
l. Making transportation arrangements—domestic and overseas.
m. Distribution through bases and intermediate depots, subdepots, holding and reconsignment points, and ports of embarkation to troops either in the United States or overseas.
n. Maintenance of supplies and equipment, including procurement and distribution of spare parts and tools, salvage, and rehabilitation.

These activities did not occur in sequence, Somervell pointed out. *Strategical planning continued throughout,* and production programs were adjusted and readjusted in the light of battle experience. The various proposals for civilian control of purchasing and production would transfer at least those segments of the munitions flow listed in paragraphs *e* to *i.* "*The effect would be to split an integrated process into three parts: The beginning and the end to be under the jurisdiction of the War Department, the middle to be under the jurisdiction of an independent civilian agency.*" With such a plan, it would be difficult to meet emergency needs, virtually impossible to differentiate between the functions of the various agencies, and in case of failure, to determine which was

---

[8] November 30, 1942 issue.
[9] Ltr, Somervell to Pepper, 5 Dec 42, Hq ASF.

to blame. The Army's production achievements had been great. Despite certain specific failures, many of which were not the fault of the services, military specialists and civilian experts, co-operating with committees from industry, had compiled a magnificent record. Germany had begun its all-out war effort in the early 1930's and was devoting 43 percent of its national output to war; the United Kingdom began in 1936 and was concentrating 39 percent of its production on war; the United States, which did not begin its effort until the summer of 1940, was devoting 39 percent of its output to war.

"For more than twenty years the War Department has been designing and developing improved weapons and teaching its officers and industry how they could be best produced," Somervell declared. To supplant these proven men and methods with untried personnel and unproven experiments would be bad enough at any time; in wartime it would be disastrous. In his opinion the Army should control the production of munitions because it was expert in weapons. The civilian agency still had the tremendous job of controlling raw materials, and semifinished products. This meant that War Department supply plans were based upon "an absolute control of the civilian economy in the hands of civilian emergency agencies." To imply that Army control over the production of its own weapons was inefficient or would result in dictatorship, General Somervell concluded, impugned the devotion to duty, the honesty, the loyalty, and the professional competence which had always been the pride of the Regular Army.

The arguments stated in the letter of Senator Pepper were reiterated on many subsequent occasions. When testifying before the Senate Small Business Committee on 7 December 1942, General Somervell put the case more briefly: ". . . it is a cardinal principle of organization and of business administration that you cannot give a man a responsibility without giving him the authority to carry it out. Now, what you are advocating in this bill is to lift out of the middle of the Army's responsibility a piece of it and hand it over to somebody else, and yet hold the Army responsible for winning the war." [10]

On 16 December 1942 Under Secretary Patterson told the Truman Committee that many people incorrectly assumed that the armed forces wanted to take the procurement of weapons away from other agencies and a few people absurdly believed that the Army wanted to regiment the American economy. [11] All that the Army and Navy were defending during World War II was the right they already had of supervising the production of their own weapons. He illustrated dramatically how the flow of munitions from drawing board to battle was indivisible. Bomb fuses used for high altitude or dive-bombing were found to be unsatisfactory for the type of low-level bombing required in the Aleutian campaign. An ordnance officer who participated in the bombing attacks, flew back to Picatinny Arsenal, and designed a new fuse. He supervised production changes, and then rushed back to the Aleutians to teach others how to use the new fuses in battle. Such an accomplishment would have been difficult with "duality of control." The civilian War

---

[10] *Hearings before the Special Committee to Study and Survey Problems of Small Business Enterprises,* Senate, 77th Cong, 2d Sess, on Smaller Concerns in War Production, 7 Dec 42, Pt. 11, p. 1551.

[11] *Hearings before a Special Committee Investigating the National Defense Program,* Senate, 77th Cong, 2d Sess, 16 Dec 42, Pt. 16, p. 6679.

Production Board had a big job to do, Mr. Patterson declared, and was better qualified than the Army to mobilize industry, expand facilities, and distribute raw and semifinished materials. It also had to provide civilian supply necessary to support the war effort. There was "no thought that the military departments should control the American economy." It was essential only that the armed forces procure munitions which they were best able to procure, while civilian agencies directed the economy of the nation in support of the war effort.

In March 1943 Secretary of War Stimson stated the case once again in a long and detailed letter to Senator Robert R. Reynolds, chairman of the Senate Committee on Military Affairs.[12] The Secretary vigorously opposed an Office of War Mobilization with powers over military procurement. The job of providing the Army with munitions was continuous and indivisible. Dual control would hurt military operations. The physical job of transferring organizations and personnel was almost insurmountable. Relieving officers in wartime to serve with the new civilian agency would hurt morale. Above all, turning over a task as important as military procurement to an untried agency which might not be able to do the job was too great a risk to take. The War Department had the primary responsibility of defeating the enemy, and it ought not be deprived of tools necessary to accomplish its mission.

When hearings were finally held on the proposal for an Office of War Mobilization by a subcommittee of the Senate Committee on Military Affairs in May 1943, the War Department simply submitted a brief which was published as Exhibit 6. This brief answered specific questions submitted by the committee about existing organizational arrangements. The brief concluded:

> research, design, engineering, contracting, production, inspection, testing, distribution, and maintenance of military equipment are essentially integral parts of a unified whole, and are necessarily so dependent on each other and on military planning and strategy that no part can be torn loose from the whole without serious injury to the entire operation and to the prosecution of the war. The fact that these operations can be abstracted from the unified whole for the purpose of description must not be permitted to mislead the Committee into thinking that they also can be segregated in their actual performance without disastrous consequences.[13]

Finally, the War Department transmitted to the Senate Committee on Military Affairs a booklet which presented the basic thinking of the War Department about its procurement responsibilities.[14] Again, the arguments were those used before. First of all, in wartime as in peacetime, the Army should fix specifications for military equipment, let contracts for such equipment directly with manufacturers, inspect contract performance, and accept final delivery of completed items for storage or immediate shipment to troops. Research and development, modifications in the light of war experience, and production improvements went along simultaneously with this whole process. Many ideas for change came from manufacturers, but the Army insisted upon final decision on the basis of the specific combat

---

[12] Ltr, Stimson to Reynolds, 3 Mar 43, Hq ASF.

[13] *Hearings before the Committee on Military Affairs,* Senate, 78th Cong, 1st Sess, on S.607, War Mobilization, May 1943, Pt. 1, p. 229.

[14] Robert P. Patterson, Military Responsibility for Equipping the Armed Forces (Printed at Fort Belvoir), 9 Feb 43.

needs to be fulfilled. The Army wanted an unhampered relationship with contractors of end-items weapons so that it could make adjustments in design and production promptly, without seeking the concurrence of another agency. Second, the Army maintained that there was a need for civilian control of economic mobilization generally, and that there were vital tasks to be performed by such agencies as the WPB, the WMC, the OPA, and the National War Labor Board. Military procurement could not take place in wartime without the control over industrial resources exercised by these agencies. Third, there were necessarily vital relationships between military procurement by the Army and the Navy and economic mobilization as controlled by other agencies. The Army, for example, adjusted its supply requirements downward in the light of available raw materials, manpower, and productive plant. The Army recognized that it, plus the Navy and the Maritime Commission, could not claim the entire available supply of raw materials. There were domestic transportation needs, utilities systems, clothing, food, shelter, and many other items essential to keep all industrial production under way. But the Army asked that it be told approximately what it might expect in various resources and that it then be permitted to decide for itself how these might be most advantageously used in fixing and modifying production schedules. The Army thought that the relative spheres of competence between military procurement and economic mobilization could be drawn in general terms and that the necessary collaboration could be realized by mutual adjustment and good will.

This in brief was the War Department's argument for economic mobilization to be accomplished through two separate sets of agencies, one, the military agencies for military procurement, and the other, the civilian agencies for control of basic economic resources. The pattern of relationships which was actually established for the duration of World War II followed the lines indicated by the Army argument.

In any event, Congress in 1943 did not enact the proposed legislation for a super agency combining central economic controls and military procurement. Legislative action perhaps was discouraged or even forestalled by the President's action in May 1943 in creating an Office of War Mobilization in the executive office of the President and in appointing James F. Byrnes to head it. This step added a new organizational entity which had previously been missing in Army thinking. The Byrnes office was not the super agency proposed in the pending legislation. It did not disturb the existing responsibilities of the military procurement agencies and of the central civilian control agencies. It became instead a formalized or institutionalized means whereby the President's top authority could be made effective in settling any controversies which might arise between the military and civilian agencies.

The War Department subsequently never had reason but to welcome the addition of this unit in the Executive Office of the President set up to exercise watchful and friendly oversight of all phases of economic mobilization.

Did the Army Want Control of the Civilian Economy?

The War Department case just summarized should be sufficient to disprove the charge that it wanted control of all machinery and of all policies governing mobilization of the nation's economic resources for war. But this charge was so frequently and irresponsibly made that a few additional words may be warranted.

In his testimony before the Senate Special Committee Investigating the National Defense Program, Under Secretary Patterson had deplored the fact that people were being led to believe that the Army wanted to take over the civilian economy. "How that story got started I do not know," he said at the time.[15] Whatever its source, the story gained credence as it passed from tongue to tongue, and became a favorite topic among journalists.[16] It finally came to be accepted as fact in certain official reports. For example, the report *The United States at War,* prepared in the Bureau of the Budget, states:

> . . . it was the doctrine of the Army that the military should take control of all elements of the economy needed for war, once war was declared. Under "total" war, this would include total control of the Nation, its manpower, its facilities, its economy . . . the Army never gave up the effort to increase its control in these areas. . . . [Military leaders] never abandoned the sincere conviction that they could run things better and more expeditiously than could civilians. This approach was involved, for example, in the transition from the Production Requirements Plan to the Controlled Materials Plan, as is explained below. Similarly, when the WPB, after a bitter struggle in which the President made the decision, reestablished its right to control production schedules, the military promptly reestablished, if it did not actually extend, its influence through the Production Executive Committee and the Staff which surrounded the Executive Vice Chairman.[17]

Similar charges, coupled with direct personal attacks upon General Somervell, are repeated even more extensively in the official history of the War Production Board.[18] This history attributes the inef-

fectiveness of the March 1942 agreement between WPB and the War Department largely to General Somervell's personality and to ASF empire-building. Ignoring Mr. Eberstadt's refutation of the charge, this official history cites as evidence of military desire to control the economy: Somervell's proposal for WPB reorganization, the military attitude on priority ratings, and WPB difficulty in checking on military procurement. Nelson's relations with the Navy, it suggests, were not as stormy as those with the War Department. The implication of the WPB history is that if the WPB had been dealing with almost any individual in the War Department except General Somervell, relations would have been better. A personal attack upon General Somervell fails to take into account the fact that his attitude on economic mobilization reflected the combined thinking of his staff, and that the reasoning on which this attitude was based convinced men like Patterson, Stimson, and later Byrnes, to draw a distinction between direct military procurement and civilian control of economic resources.

Certainly the question whether it is possible to draw a line in wartime between military procurement and control of economic resources is a serious one deserving the most thoughtful, as well as the most unbiased, consideration. War Department statements of its position always assumed that it was possible to draw such a line, and that its attitude was not inconsistent with civilian control of the nation's economy. As stated earlier, there never was any

-----

[15] *Hearings,* cited in n. 11.

[16] See, for example, "The Army Takes Over," cited in n. 3.

[17] Pp. 129, 280–81.

[18] *Industrial Mobilization for War,* pp. 216, 258, 523–24.

attempt by the Army to deny the need for central civilian direction of national resources and there never was any proposal that these functions should be transferred to the Army or Navy.[19] The War Department recognized that "ours is a civilian government"; the War Department itself was headed by civilians. While many top positions in procurement and supply activities were held by professional soldiers, 96 percent of all officers in the ASF and the AAF involved in procurement activities had been recruited from civilian life. "The American military system from the beginning, has been built upon the fundamental distrust of a standing Army. . . . But in time of war, by virtue of our system our Army has always, by necessity, been a citizen Army." [20]

It may well be asked: What basis was there in fact for the accusation of military desire to control the civilian economy? The charges were always vague in nature. For example, the volume published by the Bureau of the Budget reports: "General Somervell found time to prepare an elaborate plan for the organization of WPB which would have placed complete control of WPB and of the economy under the Joint Chiefs of Staff." [21] Similarly, in referring to the same episode, the official history of the WPB argued that General Somervell's plan would have "placed the apportionment of materials for the essential civilian economy under the military," and would have "assigned to the military responsibility for the establishment of policies to govern resources mobilization, use and apportionment." [22] The fact of the matter is that Somervell's suggestions did not put forth what they are thus purported to have said. The organization chart submitted with the text clearly showed the WPB directly under the President and not

under the Combined Chiefs of Staff. General Somervell suggested only that a Combined Resources Board (a new designation for the already existing Combined Raw Materials Board) be placed under the Combined Chiefs of Staff, but with Mr. Harry Hopkins as chairman. Nowhere in the report was it proposed that any military body take over control of the civilian economy.

Undoubtedly the specter of the ANMB greatly confused military relations with the WPB in 1942. It had been the ANMB which officially published the various industrial mobilization plans during the 1930's. The 1939 plan had pointed out that while these plans had been prepared by Army and Navy officers, "Their operation will be undertaken by civilian administrators appointed by the President." [23] Only if there was a delay in creating a central civilian War Resources Administration would the ANMB assume the responsibility for limited guidance of industrial effort.[24] When the WPB was created on 16 January 1942, the executive order provided that "the Army and Navy Munitions Board shall report to the President through the Chairman of the War Production Board."

With Mr. Eberstadt as chairman of the ANMB after December 1941, there were several early attempts to make the board an important means of co-ordinating Army and Navy procurement activities and of "advocating the interests of Army

---

[19] See, for example, Patterson, Military Responsibility for Equipping the Armed Forces, p. 8.

[20] Ibid., pp. 31–33.

[21] The United States at War, p. 129.

[22] Industrial Mobilization for War, p. 258.

[23] Industrial Mobilization Plan, Revision of 1939, Senate Doc. 134, 76th Cong, 2d Sess, p. 13.

[24] Ibid., p. 14.

and Navy" in WPB councils.[25] Subsequently, through June and July 1942 a good deal of confusion existed about what the ANMB was supposed to be, what it was supposed to do, and how it was related to the WPB. Mr. Eberstadt refused to join the WPB staff in July 1942 because the position offered him was to be circumscribed by competing jurisdictions. Then an agreement was made on 25 July which provided for the continuance of the ANMB to "formulate and advocate before WPB the requirements of the Services, to reconcile conflicts arising between the Services with respect to such requirements," and to assign representatives of the services to appropriate divisions of WPB upon WPB approval.[26] Because the discussions in May, June, and July on a revised priorities directive and the relative merits of "horizontal" versus "vertical" allocations of raw materials were conducted in the name of the ANMB, there was still further misunderstanding. Matters improved somewhat when that organization virtually ceased to exist and Mr. Eberstadt joined the WPB in September 1942.

The importance of the ANMB has been greatly exaggerated in the official history of the WPB. A few comments may help to clarify the situation. The Army and Navy Munitions Board, from the date of its creation in 1922 until 1940, was never an important administrative agency. The staff of the Assistant Secretary of War, under the fiction that it was also the staff of the ANMB, carried on economic mobilization planning. Though the Assistant Secretary of the Navy joined in approving industrial mobilization plans, the Navy's participation was limited.

About the time of Pearl Harbor both Under Secretary of War Patterson and

Under Secretary of the Navy Forrestal did have the idea that the ANMB might be built into an important agency for collaboration of the two departments. Mr. Eberstadt had actually been asked to become its chairman in order to achieve that purpose. The idea proved abortive, however, for several reasons. Navy procurement officers were not much interested in collaboration. The WPB questioned the need for the ANMB and looked upon it as a rival. The staff of the OUSW on 9 March 1942 became the staff of the Commanding General, ASF, and was thereafter to become primarily concerned with supervising and expediting the procurement operations of the seven technical services with a command authority never enjoyed as a part of the Under Secretary's office. And then some degree of procurement and supply collaboration between the Army and Navy was worked out under the Joint Chiefs of Staff.

If it hadn't been for Mr. Eberstadt personally, the ANMB would probably have withered away entirely in the spring of 1942. While Mr. Eberstadt became a spokesman on raw materials problems for Under Secretary Patterson and General Somervell of the War Department, and for Under Secretary Forrestal and Vice Admiral S. M. Robinson of the Navy, the real work on these questions was done in Somervell's staff. Actually, the ASF, the AAF, Admiral Robinson's Office of Procurement and Material, and the Navy Bureau of Aeronautics tended to develop their own separate relations with WPB. The relative insignificance of the ANMB

[25] Memo, ANMB to SW and SN, 28 Jan 42, approved by the President 21 Feb 42, cited in *Industrial Mobilization for War*, p. 217.

[26] This story is told in greater detail in *Industrial Mobilization for War*, pp. 219–21.

was revealed as early as June 1942 in a report prepared by an Army and a Navy officer for Mr. Eberstadt. This report made it clear that such procurement co-operation as was then being promoted through the ANMB was confined to priorities, machine tools, and optics matters.[27]

In June 1943 General Clay suggested to Somervell that a memorandum for the President be jointly signed by Under Secretaries Patterson and Forrestal recommending discontinuance of the ANMB for the remainder of the war. The reason for this proposal was that machinery for Army-Navy co-operation already existed, and it was functioning under the Joint Chiefs of Staff.[28] Although the recommendation was not followed, it indicated how unimportant the ANMB had become.

The ANMB was never the rival the WPB sometimes professed it to be. Although, as already indicated, it might have developed into an agency for joint Army-Navy procurement co-operation, neither the Army nor the Navy pushed for such a sphere of operation in 1942 or 1943. Somervell was too busy endeavoring to make the Army Service Forces an effective agency for procurement and supply activities within the War Department. The Navy was never greatly interested in any top machinery to push procurement collaboration between the two departments.

In the light of what actually happened, therefore, it is difficult to understand the fear of the ANMB which is voiced in the official history of the WPB. The Army and Navy Munitions Board for a brief time was a means for War and Navy Department collaboration in a relatively limited sphere—it merely attempted to define and clarify relations between the armed forces and the WPB on control over the distribu-

tion of raw materials. With the adoption of the Controlled Materials Plan these relations were defined to the satisfaction of the Army, at any rate, and the ANMB simply disappeared.

Mr. Nelson's own memoirs may give a basic clue to WPB–ASF difficulties. On the one hand, Mr. Nelson continually asserts that he did not want to calculate military supply requirements or let military contracts. He indicates his general approval of the 12 March 1942 agreement, but never seems to realize that every subsequent quarrel with Somervell and the Army which he records involved some basic modification of that agreement. If the agreement was satisfactory, Mr. Nelson fails to make clear why the Army, and Somervell in particular, should not have objected to its unilateral abrogation. It would seem that Mr. Nelson saw the possibility of a dividing line between military procurement and central control of economic resources but never quite understood it.

Incidentally, it should again be emphasized that it was Nelson, among the top officials of the WPB, who found it most difficult to get along with Somervell. Mr. Wilson, after the initial flurry over the determination of his authority had subsided, developed increasingly co-operative relationships with Army and Navy personnel. The Production Executive Committee became an agency making for harmony between the WPB and the armed forces, as well as an instrument for outstanding production accomplishment. General Somervell felt that Mr. Wilson's

---

[27] CD Rpt 12, Report on the Organization of the Army-Navy Munitions Board, Jun 42, CD, ASF.

[28] Memo, Clay for Somervell, 6 Jun 43, inclosing a draft memo for the President, Hq ASF.

contributions to the war effort were never fully appreciated, and he regretted the interval of WPB feuding which led to Mr. Wilson's resignation in 1944. After J. A. Krug replaced Nelson as chairman of the WPB, relations between the WPB and the ASF continued to be cordial.

All discussion about civilian control of the economy was, as far as the War Department was concerned, completely irrelevant. The real problem was mobilization of the nation's economy through separate, if interrelated, agencies for military procurement and central direction of economic resources. The War Department held that this kind of organizational arrangement was not only feasible but also indispensable in a war where logistics and strategy were so basically intertwined. There is nothing in the report of the Bureau of the Budget or in the history of the WPB which conclusively demonstrates that this position was organizationally unworkable. All the personality conflicts and the disposition of some persons to shift the argument to the ideological level of "civilian versus military" control of the economy should not conceal the real issue: what type of wartime organization will most effectively use the nation's resources in the effort to defeat the enemy?

The War Department's position on effective organization may be summarized as follows:

1. The armed forces should design weapons and other necessary supplies, determine the quantities necessary in the light of the planned size and composition of the armed forces, let the necessary contracts directly with industrial producers, fix delivery schedules, inspect the output, and give the shipping instructions for completed articles.

2. The entire military procurement process could not be divided up into phases since it was vitally interrelated at each step, with numerous changes in design and production made in accordance with tests and battle experience.

3. No third agency should intervene between contracting officers of the armed forces and the contractor, since otherwise the whole vital relationship extending throughout the procurement process would be interrupted.

4. The War Department recognized that its procurement plans during wartime would have to fit within the limitations of other procurement programs and within the limits of the productive resources of the nation.

5. A civilian agency should be responsible for determining the total productive resources of the nation and for deciding the amount of production indispensable to the wartime operation of the entire economy. This was not a job for the War Department. An increase in the output of raw materials; an expansion of fabricating facilities; an expansion of productive facilities for the manufacture of such industrial supply items as wire, generators, electric motors, ball bearings, and other items used in both military articles and other equipment; the control of labor; the control of the use made of raw materials—all these were responsibilities to be exercised by an agency outside the War Department.

6. There must necessarily be close working relationships between the War Department in its procurement operations and a civilian agency directing utilization of the nation's whole resources. These relationships should be based upon a thorough appreciation of the vital role each agency must play in war production. The

agreement of 12 March 1942 between the War Department and the War Production Board was a satisfactory statement of the respective functions and relationships which should exist between the two agencies.

7. If procurement programs exceeded available materials and other resources, thereby raising the question of what should receive priority, the highest military agency, the Joint Chiefs of Staff, should act as umpire determining the relative importance of ships as against aircraft, for example, and tanks as against trucks. Any adjustment in mobilization plans, including the size and composition of the Army, made to conform to production possibilities, should be a military decision.

8. The War Department should learn from the civilian agency the total resources available to it and then be free to use these resources as it saw fit in producing particular types of equipment. Every adjustment in use should not have to clear through a civilian agency.

9. The responsibility of the armed forces for the successful defense of the nation must carry with it responsibility for the means used in achieving the military objective. If a particular tank was faulty or a particular communications set inadequate, or if there was a lack of trucks where they were needed or not enough transport vessels to move the military forces to the desired destination, the fault must clearly be that of the armed forces. There must be no possibility of shifting the blame elsewhere.

10. In wartime all possible resources must be made available to the armed forces in their effort to obtain the matériel to achieve military success.

PART FOUR

INTERNAL ORGANIZATION OF THE ASF

CHAPTER XX

The Technical Services

When the Army Service Forces was created on 9 March 1942, five different elements of War Department organization were brought together. First, there were various parts of the War Department General Staff, especially G–1 and G–4. Second, there was the Office of the Under Secretary of War. Third, there were eight administrative "bureaus." All of these eventually became ASF headquarters, as related below. Fourth, there were nine corps areas, which as service commands were to become the major units of the ASF field organization. Fifth and last, there were six "supply arms and services" of the War Department, later redesignated "technical services." They were the vital operating units performing the supply and certain special activities of the ASF. These supply arms and services were the Offices of the Chief of Ordnance, The Quartermaster General, the Chief of Engineers, The Surgeon General, the Chief Signal Officer, and the Chief of Chemical Warfare Service. Each branch had its own particular history, traditions, and *esprit de corps*. Three of the technical services—Ordnance, Quartermaster, and Engineers—traced their origin back to the Continental Army of General George Washington. As early as 1790 the Congress of the new federal government began to provide for "staff" officers in the War Department, including a quartermaster. In 1792 the positions of surgeon and adju-

tant were added. A separate "corps" of engineers was provided by law in 1802. The Quartermaster "department" and the Ordnance "department" were created on the eve of the War of 1812. In 1860, just before the Civil War, the position of Signal Officer was created, and the Signal Corps was added in 1863. The Chemical Warfare Service was a product of World War I.[1]

Each chief of a supply arm and service headed a large operating organization with a headquarters in Washington and with various field installations scattered throughout the United States under his complete administrative control. Each supply arm and service was a procurement agency of the War Department. This meant that it developed various types of military equipment, bought or manufactured this equipment, stored supplies in large depots, and then distributed these items to posts, camps, and stations in the United States or to ports of embarkation for shipment overseas. The supply arms and services also operated important maintenance facilities for the repair of damaged equipment. Each supply arm and service was a branch of the Army

---

[1] The organizational legislation of the War Department from 1789 to 1920 is traced in Lloyd M. Short, *The Development of National Administrative Organization in the United States* (Baltimore, Md., The Johns Hopkins Press, 1923), Chs. V, XII. See also William A. Ganoe, *The History of the United States Army* (New York, D. Appleton-Century Company, Inc., 1942).

under the National Defense Act. This meant that many officers were commissioned in these services. The chief of the service then watched over the subsequent assignment of these officers and provided continued assistance to them in the performance of their duties. The services trained both officers and enlisted men for assignment to many different commands. Some of the supply arms and services were more than supply and training "bureaus" of the War Department. Three in particular operated essential service activities, the Engineers providing a construction service to the Department, The Surgeon General a medical service, and the Chief Signal Officer a communications service.

The term "supply arm and service" was the common designation, employed in the War Department before 9 March 1942, for the Ordnance Department, Quartermaster Corps, Corps of Engineers, Medical Department, Signal Corps, and Chemical Warfare Service, as well as for the Coast Artillery Corps and the Air Corps. In April 1942 the ASF introduced the designation "supply service" to apply to these agencies under its jurisdiction.[2] A year later the expression "supply service" was officially abandoned in favor of the term "technical service."[3] The first-used label suggested too narrow a scope of responsibility. The operation and supervision of such activities as medical care, communications, construction, and transportation were not readily encompassed by the word "supply." The designation "technical service" better described the work of these agencies, and soon the expression gained widespread and apparently enduring acceptance throughout the Army.

These technical services became a part of the ASF on 9 March 1942 without any change in their previous responsibilities or internal structure. The only alteration was one in organizational status. Whereas previously their superior had been the Secretary of War, speaking through either the Under Secretary on procurement matters or through the Chief of Staff on other matters, he now was the commanding general of the Army Service Forces. This new organizational status created special problems for the technical services, especially in their relationship to the Army Air Forces. As already indicated, the Air Forces had as its long-range goal the attainment of a status separate from and equal to the Army and the Navy. As a step toward it the Air Forces sought to have its own technical service officers. But somehow the technical services couldn't help but believe that their relations with the Air Forces would have been simpler, and their superior technical guidance would have been acknowledged by it, if they had not been under the command of the ASF. To a lesser degree they had the same attitude about their relations with commanding generals of overseas theaters of operations. At best, with the possible exception of the Transportation Corps, the technical services were always restive partners in the common enterprise known as the Army Service Forces.

Creation of the Transportation Corps

In the course of the preliminary planning which preceded the War Department reorganization in 1942, General Somervell decided it would be desirable to add to the original six services a new technical service for transportation. Before 9 March 1942 in the field of military transportation

---

[2] SOS GO 4, 9 Apr 42.
[3] ASF Cir 30, 15 May 43.

there was a Transportation Division under The Quartermaster General and certain separate field installations that reported directly to the Chief of Staff, namely, ports of embarkation, and regulating and reconsignment points (later called holding and reconsignment points) handling domestic and overseas movements of men and supplies. The activities of these different units were closely controlled in practice by the Transportation Branch of G–4. General Somervell determined to merge all of these units into a single operating agency on transportation. Originally, this was designated the Transportation Division.[4] Although called the Transportation Division, the new agency was listed initially as an "operating division" of the ASF, along with the six technical services. The confusion of the label "division," which was also employed for ASF headquarters units, was removed in April 1942 when the designation Transportation Service was introduced.[5]

The creation of the Transportation Service as an operating "service" of the ASF still left a number of loose ends in the organization of transportation activities throughout the Army. Quartermaster officers remained as water transportation officers assigned to various commands. The Corps of Engineers still trained operation and maintenance units for railway transportation activities overseas and exercised supervisory authority over railway transportation activities at posts in the United States. This was an anomalous situation. A chief of transportation in the ASF was operating the transportation system for the War Department as a whole but there was no provision for a similar arrangement in overseas and other commands of the Army. Accordingly, General Somervell recommended that the Trans-

portation Service be recognized by the War Department as a branch of the Army. This recommendation was approved, and in July 1942 the Transportation Corps, under a Chief of Transportation, was created as a recognized specialty in the Army with its own branch insignia.[6] This action was taken under the authority of Executive Order 9082 of 28 February 1942, the same order which authorized the reorganization of the Army. The War Department orders provided that the duties assigned the Transportation Service by ASF orders would be absorbed by the Transportation Corps and that the designation "Transportation Service" would be discontinued. At the same time, the War Department orders transferred four different types of transportation units trained by The Quartermaster General to the Transportation Corps.

A further strengthening of the Transportation Corps followed in November when the War Department transferred from the Corps of Engineers to the new corps the functions of research and development, procurement, and storage and issue of all railway rolling stock and distinctive railway equipment; the operation and maintenance of railways in some overseas areas and at posts in the zone of interior; and the Military Railway Service in its entirety. All officers of the Corps of Engineers on duty with the Military Railway Service and similar units were automatically transferred to the Transportation Corps. In addition, seventeen different types of railway operating and maintenance units organized and trained by the

---

[4] Ltr, CG SOS to Chiefs of all SAS, etc., 9 Mar 42, sub: Initial Dir for the Org of SOS, Ret files ASF, DRB AGO.

[5] SOS GO 4, 9 Apr 42.

[6] WD GO 38, 21 Jul 42.

Corps of Engineers were redesignated Transportation Corps units and assigned to the Transportation Corps for organization and training.[7]

Thus by November 1942 the Transportation Corps had become a full-fledged technical service of the War Department, operating within the Army Service Forces. It had taken over the water transportation responsibilities and troop units of the Quartermaster Corps and the railway troop units and functions previously vested in the Corps of Engineers. It was assigned procurement responsibility for railway equipment and for harbor craft. It arranged all troop movements within the United States for groups of forty or more. It operated ports of embarkation, and performed numerous other duties of an operating, training, and technical nature.[8] As a new technical service, the Transportation Corps became a vital part of the ASF and played a leading role in the war that embraced the globe.

General Depots [9]

In addition to the Transportation Division, the ASF originally established another new operating division alongside the supply arms and services, the General Depots Division. It combined the General Depot Section in the Supply Branch, G–4, with all general depots. Before 9 March 1942 the general depots of the War Department reported directly to the Chief of Staff. The advantages in having a general depot were several. Posts issuing supplies to troops could send requisitions for a variety of items to one place. Shipments could be made in carload lots and many common depot problems could be handled on a unified basis. In practice, the operations of the general depots had been supervised by the Supply Division of the General Staff. The ASF, in creating the General Depots Division, grouped them with a headquarters office in Washington.[10] In April 1942, as in the case of the change in designation of the Transportation Division, the General Depots Division was renamed General Depot Service and its head designated Chief of General Depot Service.[11]

In July 1942 the responsibilities of the General Depot Service were enlarged by giving the ASF staff supervision over all storage and warehousing activities. The General Depot Service was to direct the installation of modern efficient methods of materials handling and space conservation at all warehouses operated by technical services. It was to establish specifications and direct the purchasing of materials handling equipment, to train warehouse personnel, and to co-ordinate the requirements for the construction, leasing, and use of storage facilities.[12] This order was short lived; it was rescinded only five days later, since the functions prescribed for it almost completely overlapped those already being performed by a division in ASF headquarters.[13] Furthermore, its existence was questioned on the grounds that it was a small organization compared with the other technical services. It was these considerations that

---

[7] WD GO 60, 5 Nov 42.

[8] Wardlow, *The Transportation Corps: Responsibilities, Organization, and Operations;* Wardlow, The Transportation Corps: Movements, Training, and Supply, a volume in preparation for the series UNITED STATES ARMY IN WORLD WAR II.

[9] General depots were central warehouses in the United States used to store the supplies of more than one supply arm and service. A service controlled a "section" of a general depot.

[10] Ltr, cited in n. 4.

[11] SOS GO 4, 9 Apr 42.

[12] SOS GO 18, 4 Jul 42.

[13] SOS GO 20, 9 Jul 42.

brought about a comprehensive re-examination of the basic problems of depot operation and the abolition of the General Depot Service.[14] All general depots were designated Army Service Forces general depots.

Since the Quartermaster Corps already operated, on a large scale, depots handling a wide variety of goods and was itself a major user of the general depots, and since The Quartermaster General already had taken a number of steps to improve depot operations, the administration of general depots was turned over to his office. The various sections of general depots allotted to other supply services continued to function under the jurisdiction of those services, but The Quartermaster General was made responsible for the operation of general depots as a whole, including utility services and other common activities.

When The Quartermaster General became the administrative head of the general depots, it meant that an officer designated by him was expected to handle all problems of common concern. What, then, were the common problems? They included hiring civilian personnel, plant maintenance and utilities services, control of incoming and outgoing freight cars, local purchase necessary to the operation of the depot, the keeping of financial records, and the provision of certain administrative services such as arrangements for travel and control of office space. The head of the technical service section of an ASF depot was responsible for the actual storage, stock record keeping, and shipment of the supplies of his service. Some friction was inevitable between an administrative officer responsible for the physical plant and the technical service supply officer responsible for storage and issue of supplies. Altogether there were twelve

ASF general depots in the United States during World War II. The number of technical service sections in these depots varied from six at the Utah general depot to two at the Savannah general depot. An alert administrator would necessarily find many opportunities to achieve management economies in the operation of an ASF general depot. For example, each technical service section of a depot maintained its own stock accounting procedures, usually involving a sizable array of electric accounting machinery. If all of the stock accounting work were combined, substantial economies might be realized. Common direction of warehousing operations might achieve operating economies also. Each technical service section had its own binning procedures and its own open storage areas. It was therefore logical to assume that all supplies which had to be binned could be brought together in one place and all supplies in open storage consolidated by size, some savings might be realized in warehousing costs.

ASF headquarters recognized this fact. In August 1943 it authorized an experiment at the Atlanta general depot in developing an integrated organization. A single stock control division and a single storage division were set up within the depot to perform these functions regardless of the type of supply handled. In January 1944 it was announced that the experiment was being discontinued. Experience had demonstrated that an integrated organization based on function rather than type of supply handled was feasible in practice. The system was recognized as a break in the traditional method of supply whereby each chief of a technical service was responsible for the storage and

---

[14] SOS GO 22, 11 Jul 42.

issue of the commodities purchased by his service. Therefore, despite the advantages in the system each technical service expressed a desire to retain basic control of its responsibility. Consequently, General Somervell decided that no major reorganization of jointly occupied depots would be undertaken. The ASF general depots continued to be operated on an arrangement which assumed that the depot commander was the landlord and that the technical service sections were responsible for the storage and issuance of supplies.[15] The experiment did accomplish one important improvement, however: it increased the number of functions recognized as common to depot operations and placed under the control of the depot commander at an ASF depot.[16] The general depots were thus administered by the chief of one of the technical services, The Quartermaster General.

Adjustments in Responsibilities of Technical Services

Apart from the creation of the Transportation Corps and the transfer of general depot administration to The Quartermaster General, few additional changes were made in technical service responsibilities during World War II. One major change had occurred before the ASF was created when, by legislative act, Congress on 1 December 1941 approved the transfer of construction activities in the United States from The Quartermaster General to the Chief of Engineers. This action, put into effect fifteen days later, was entirely independent of the creation of the ASF. The only other major change in technical service responsibility occurred in July 1942, when the War Department transferred research and development, procurement,

storage, distribution, and maintenance of all general and special purpose motor vehicles from the Quartermaster Corps to the Ordnance Department.[17] This step was taken because of procurement conflicts between the Ordnance Department and the Quartermaster Corps in the automotive field. The Ordnance Department was looking largely to automobile manufacturers for the production of tank engines and tank assembly. Many of the component parts of tanks were common to the automotive industry. After studies by the ASF and the Ordnance Department had suggested the desirability of centralizing all tank and automotive procurement in Detroit, General Somervell asked the General Staff to approve the amalgamation of truck, automobile, and tank procurement. This was done. Immediately thereafter the Tank-Automotive Center of the Ordnance Department was officially established in Detroit. Later this became known as the Office, Chief of Ordnance— Detroit.

There was a constant disposition through the ASF Procurement Assignment Board to centralize the procurement of all common-type items in the Quartermaster Corps. For example, the procurement of all materials handling equipment was assigned to The Quartermaster General. Despite the loss of certain activities to the Transportation Corps, the Corps of Engineers, and the Ordnance Department, the Quartermaster Corps remained, in money volume, second to Ordnance as the most important procurement service of the ASF. It remained responsible for the procurement, storage, and issue of sub-

---

[15] ASF Cir 10, 8 Jan 44.
[16] See ASF Man M–417, Depot Organization, 8 Dec 44.
[17] WD Cir 245, 25 Jul 42.

sistence, petroleum and lubricants, clothing, and all general supplies.

Additional functions were also given to
The Quartermaster General during the
war. For example, in July 1943 The
Quartermaster General was made responsible for developing and supervising a
"food service program" to curtail waste in
foodstuffs at messes on Army posts.[18] Eventually, this program became Army-wide
in scope.[19] In addition, The Quartermaster General was given complete responsibility for the procurement and distribution
of gasoline, fuel oil, and lubricants. At first,
there was a separate staff office in ASF
headquarters on petroleum matters. But
in December 1943 this unit was transferred to the Office of The Quartermaster
General. The purchase and distribution of
petroleum products by the Quartermaster
Corps was subject only to the same general kind of ASF headquarters supervision
which obtained for every other kind of
supply commodity.[20] The Fuels and Lubricants Division in the Office of The Quartermaster General served thereafter as
General Somervell's personal staff on
Army-Navy Petroleum Board matters.

For a time in 1943, when the work of
the Army Pictorial Service in the Signal
Corps caused some difficulty, General
Somervell appointed an independent head
for the service with directions to report to
him personally. Later, when a new Chief
Signal Officer was appointed by the President and confirmed by the Senate to become effective on 1 July 1943, General
Somervell returned the service to the Chief
Signal Officer.[21]

From time to time the commanding
general made minor adjustments in the responsibilities of the technical services or
determined how they were to work together in some common concern. In this

he usually followed the recommendations
of the Procurement Assignment Board in
his headquarters whose job it was to consider any duplications or conflicts in procurement operations of the services. In a
single year at the height of the war, this
board considered as many as 1,428 matters and arranged for one technical service
to purchase such varied items as flags,
public-address systems, interoffice communications systems, dry-cell batteries,
and fire extinguishers.[22] Another time, the
ASF had to prepare a War Department
order for G–4 approval to clarify who
would build laundries and who would
purchase equipment for their operation.[23]
A major jurisdictional problem involved
hospital ships and the evacuation of
wounded and sick personnel from overseas to general hospitals in the United
States. In addition to arranging for the assignment of a medical officer to the Office
of the Chief of Transportation to handle
movements of personnel under medical
care, ASF headquarters had to work out
an elaborate set of instructions on the mutual responsibilities of The Surgeon General and the Chief of Transportation in
evacuating patients from overseas points.[24]
In the course of the war the commanding
general of the Army Service Forces, usually
through his staff, made many such adjustments in the duties of the technical services
in order that they might work more harmoniously with one another.

The creation of service commands as
field installations of the ASF necessitated

[18] ASF Cir 45, 3 Jul 43.
[19] WD Cir 149, 21 May 45.
[20] ASF Cir 151, 15 Dec 43.
[21] ASF Adm Memo G–21, 31 Mar 43; ASF Adm
Memo G–37, 30 Jun 43.
[22] Annual Rpt of ASF, 1944, p. 115.
[23] WD Cir 7, 5 Jan 45.
[24] ASF Cir 36, 31 Jan 45.

further adjustments in technical service operations. These will be described in the next chapter. Actually this reorganization did not affect the specialized responsibilities of technical services. It merely changed their mode of operation from one of complete control of certain field work to one of technical control confined to their particular specialty.

Internal Organization

The internal organization of each technical service was a matter determined by the chief of the service. ASF headquarters never directed a standard organizational pattern for the technical services although plans to do so were considered from time to time. Indirectly, however, ASF headquarters did much to influence the internal organization of the technical services. For one thing, the establishment of an ASF organization manual brought with it certain standardizing tendencies. At the outset, each technical service was asked to label its major units as divisions, a practice reflected in the Services of Supply Organization Manual published in September 1942, and one that was retained until August 1944.[25] Another influence in the direction of a standard pattern was the statement of principles of organization which was first published in an ASF Control Manual and which was later contained in each revision of the Organization Manual. This statement emphasized the importance of keeping the number of units reporting to the chief at a minimum. Also, the grouping of related activities under common supervision below the level of the chief himself became a standard practice in ASF organization.

A third and perhaps the most important influence making for a standard organiza-

tion was the ASF headquarters staff itself. As the headquarters assumed a fairly standard pattern after May 1943, technical services tended in general to parallel this arrangement. Staff divisions in ASF headquarters continually pressed the technical services to create staff counterparts of themselves. The reason was simple; staff officers at the echelon of the commanding general desired counterparts in the office of each chief of a technical service, since this facilitated their own work. Although there never was any official instruction requiring a chief of technical service to follow the ASF organizational pattern, the pressures to do so were quite strong.

On the other hand, there were several factors which militated against a standard organization among the technical services. All but the Transportation Corps had developed over many years their own methods of doing their work. These ingrained practices could not lightly be overcome, even by the centralizing pressures from the ASF. There were also differences in function among the technical services, as between medical work and construction, for example, or as between communications and transportation. These made for organizational differences and variations in procurement, supply, training, and other activities.

To the extent that the ASF—its commanding general and his staff—pressed for standard organizational structure within the technical services, it was pushing the common interests of the ASF as a whole. To the extent that the technical services resisted these pressures and retained or developed their own special organizational practices, they were expressing their individuality and determination

---

[25] ASF Org Man M–301, 15 Aug 44.

not to be absorbed into a completely integrated structure for performing War Department supply and other central services. The result was that the Army Service Forces was never able to achieve the degree of organizational unity which its staff believed desirable. Tradition and pressure for autonomy had to be recognized and accommodated.

Field Installations of Technical Services

Just as each chief of a technical service retained authority to organize his own office in Washington as he pleased, so each was able to have his field installations organized as he saw fit. No standard pattern of organization was ever imposed upon the field operations of technical services. A complete inventory of technical service field installations was made in the spring of 1943. (*Table 2*) [26]

Every technical service had procurement districts and supply depots, although both purchasing and storage operations differed among the services. The number of training establishments depended upon the particular training relationships with the service commands (a subject to be discussed in the next chapter). Only the Ordnance Department operated a large number of manufacturing plants, designated government-owned, government-operated plants (GOGO) to distinguish them from government-owned, privately operated plants. Otherwise, there was a wide variety of field installations under the technical services, such as engineer divisions and districts, transportation ports, storage depots, signal laboratories and repair shops, and general hospitals.

Differences in the field organization of the technical services as a whole may be illustrated by the variety of methods covering the procuring of supplies. Procurement planning during the 1920's had placed considerable emphasis upon regional decentralization. As a result, each technical service had established procurement planning districts. The number of such districts varied from four under The Surgeon General to thirteen under the Chief of Ordnance. With two exceptions— the Office of The Quartermaster General and the Office of the Chief of Engineers— these procurement planning districts became procurement offices after July 1940. As of November 1941, the Chief of Ordnance was purchasing most of his supplies through thirteen district offices, the Chief of Chemical Warfare Service through five district offices, the Chief Signal Officer through three, and the Medical Department through four. The Quartermaster Corps continued its traditional method of procurement. Its ten leading depots were responsible for centralized procurement of different commodities throughout the United States. Thus the Boston depot was the center for shoe procurement, the Chicago depot for food, the Philadelphia depot for clothing, and the Jeffersonville depot for canvas duck and many general supplies. Until November 1941 the Chief of Engineers did all engineer purchasing through a supply section in Washington. Purchasing through district offices began in November and grew only slowly thereafter.

When the ASF was created, its staff gave increased attention to prescribing uniform purchasing policies, standard contract clauses, and close pricing, but it

---

[26] The data in Table 2 are taken from a special table prepared by the Control Division, ASF, entitled "Field Installations of the Army Service Forces," Control Division, ASF. While the table is undated, the figures reflect the 1943 situation.

TABLE 2—TECHNICAL SERVICE FIELD INSTALLATIONS

Ordnance	Total–178
Arsenals	13
Procurement Districts	13
Supply Depots	47
Sections of ASF & Other Depots	9
Sections of H&R Points	8
Tank-Automotive Center	1
Proving Grounds	4
GOGO Plants (total–73)	
TNT & Powder Plants	21
Ammonia & Nitrate Plants	10
Loading Plants	24
Small Arms Plants	12
Other Plants	6
Ordnance School	1
Bomb Disposal School	1
Officer Candidate School	1
Replacement Training Center	1
Miscellaneous Installations	6
Transportation	Total–113
Ports of Embarkation	7
Subports of Embarkation	11
Cargo Ports of Embarkation	2
Staging Areas	22
Unit Training Centers	2
Officer Candidate School	1
Officer Schools	2
Replacement Training Center	1
Transportation Zones	9
District Transportation Offices	13
Port Agencies	14
H&R Points	9
Regulating Stations	6
Army-Navy Consolidating Stations	3
Army-Navy Distributing Agencies	7
Military Railway Service Installations	4
Quartermaster	Total–97
Supply Depots	11
Supply Subdepots	7
ASF Depots	11
Sections of H&R Point	1
Procurement Districts	17
Remount Depots	3
Remount Areas	7
Market Centers	36
Quartermaster Board	1
Quartermaster School	1
Officer Candidate School	1
Replacement Training Center	1
Engineers	Total–92
Engineer Divisions	10
Engineer Districts	55

Engineers—Continued	
Supply Depots	8
Sections of ASF Depots	8
Sections of H&R Points	2
Engineer Board	1
Miscellaneous Installations	5
Officer Candidate School, at Belvoir	1
Replacement Training Centers, Wood and Belvoir	2
Signal Corps	Total–54
Signal Laboratories	6
Photographic Laboratories	2
Procurement Districts	3
ANEPA Regions	6
Inspection Zones	5
Signal Depots	8
Sections of ASF Depots	4
Signal Repair Shops	2
Ground Signal Service	1
Aircraft Signal Service	1
Eastern Signal Service	1
Eastern Signal Training Center	1
Eastern Signal Corps School	1
Officer Candidate School	1
Replacement Training Center	1
Southern Signal Corps School	1
Signal Corps Board	1
Miscellaneous Installations	9
Medical Department	Total–42
Procurement Districts	2
Supply Depots	9
Sections of ASF & Other Depots	11
Sections of H&R Points	5
Sections of Air Depots	3
Field Service School	1
Army Medical Center	1
Dental School	1
Medical School	1
Veterinary School	1
General Hospital	1
Miscellaneous Installations	6
Chemical Warfare	Total–32
Arsenals	4
Procurement Districts	7
Supply Depots	5
Sections of ASF Depots	5
Sections of H&R Points	2
Renovation Plants	3
Proving Ground	1
Chemical Warfare Board	1
Laboratories	2
Chemical Warfare School	1
Officer Candidate School	1

never issued instructions on common procurement organizational arrangements in the field. In practice the various technical services used a wide variety of field offices for procurement operations, changing the arrangements with changing circumstances. The Chief of Ordnance, as noted above, purchased many supplies through thirteen district offices during the war, although automotive procurement was centralized in Detroit. The ordnance manufacturing plants were supervised directly from Washington and not through the district offices. The Quartermaster General continued to channel procurement operations through the depots, although an element of geographical administration was introduced by the creation of zone offices which did some local contracting for a parent depot or inspected and accepted supplies on behalf of a depot. The Signal Corps gradually moved away from a geographical procurement organization until by early 1943 it had developed a commodity procurement organization with three offices in the United States. The Philadelphia district office became the center for procuring all types of radio communications equipment, telephone and telegraph equipment, wire and cable, photographic equipment and other items. The Monmouth procurement district purchased all types of electronics equipment, mainly radar sets, although it also bought telephone and telegraph signaling apparatus. The Wright Field Signal Corps Procurement Office at Dayton purchased all kinds of communications equipment for aircraft. The Medical Department eventually centralized all of its procurement in its New York office. The St. Louis office continued to do a certain amount of procurement as directed from New York. The offices in Chicago and San Francisco were closed out. The Corps of Engineers used both a geographical and a commodity basis for procurement. The New York office was made responsible for the procurement of compressors and certain other types of construction equipment. Designated division engineer officers and district suboffices were also assigned procurement responsibilities. From a total which at one time reached eleven division offices, the Corps of Engineers reduced its procurement district offices to five division offices by the end of the war. The Chemical Warfare Service used six district offices during the war but also tended to concentrate responsibility for certain types of procurement in one of these offices. Its New York office became the center for the purchase of most chemical items manufactured by the chemical industry.[27]

There was a very great variation in the organization of procurement offices during World War II. The primary emphasis was upon obtaining the desired production. Standard purchasing procedures were introduced in December 1944, but organization was not thereby affected.[28] On the other hand, the number and size of technical service depots were carefully controlled by ASF headquarters in order to insure that unnecessary facilities were not constructed. A standard internal organization for depots was prescribed in December 1944.[29] This introduced a common administrative pattern for all depots, regardless of the technical service. This was in fact the highest degree of standardization

_____

[27] See Army Purchase Information Bulletin, 1 Nov 41, issued by OUSW; *Ibid.*, revised to 1 Feb 43, issued by ASF; and Purchased Items and Purchasing Locations, 1 May 45, issued by ASF. All in Purchases Div, ASF.

[28] See ASF Man M–603, Procurement Office Procedures, Dec 44.

[29] ASF Man M–417, Depot Organization, 8 Dec 44.

brought about in any technical service field installation during the war. Yet the supervisory organization for depots continued to be a matter for each chief of a technical service to determine. Thus, at one time the Ordnance Department grouped depots into zones. This practice was abandoned a short time later as merely introducing an unnecessary supervisory echelon. But each technical service controlled its depots as it saw fit.

ASF headquarters did endeavor to encourage the chiefs of the technical services to discharge some of their functions through the service commands. This effort (described in the next chapter) circumscribed somewhat the freedom of action for the chiefs of the technical services in organizing their field activities. The desire of the ASF to strengthen the service commands became a factor which the chiefs of technical services constantly had to contend with. For the most part, they were less than enthusiastic about service commands as field organizations and were little disposed to work through them.

Technical Service Duties of Army-Wide Scope

The technical services had a kind of dual responsibility during World War II. First of all, each chief of a technical service was head of a major operating unit of the Army Service Forces with extensive duties in the procurement and distribution of supplies and in the performance of various central services. But second, the chiefs of technical services as heads of branches of the Army were expected to exercise technical supervision over their specialty wherever performed in the Army. In this second capacity it was never clear just what the responsibility of the ASF was, nor was it easy to draw a clear

distinction between what constituted a central War Department service rather than technical supervision. A few illustrations may help to indicate the difficulty.

There was never any doubt about the nature of the procurement and storage activities of the technical services. These were sizable operations indeed. Because there was a need for central direction to insure co-ordinated action among seven different procurement agencies, the ASF had been set up to give unity to Army supply operations. On all procurement, storage, and distribution activities the status of the offices of chiefs of the technical services as constituent operating units of the ASF was clear.

The technical services also performed certain centralized services for the War Department, as noted above. If the Ground Forces or the Air Forces wished to turn in trucks for extensive repairs or overhauling, the Chief of Ordnance provided the maintenance facilities. If the Ground Forces or the Air Forces wished to use the Chief Signal Officer's communications network for sending messages, they were free to do so. The Surgeon General, through service commands, directed a number of general hospitals to care for patients turned over by the Ground Forces, the Air Forces, or overseas theaters of operations. The Chief of Engineers had a construction service ready to build any structures wanted by the Ground Forces, the Air Forces, or the War Department General Staff. But this raised questions. Did the Chief of Engineers, for example, operate a maintenance service for structures, or exercise technical supervision of maintenance activities?

When it came to exercising their authority as heads of Army branches with Army-wide supervisory duties, the chiefs of the technical services ran into difficulties, primarily with the AAF, as already indicated.[30] Certain additional aspects deserve further comment here. To the Army Air Forces, the ASF was simply a coordinate command. How then could the chiefs of the technical services in the ASF exercise technical supervision over medical, engineering, communications, and other services in the AAF? The answer of the WDGS to such questions was to reaffirm the technical supervisory authority of the chiefs of technical services.

Thus in March 1945, War Department instructions were issued on responsibilities for the maintenance of ordnance matériel. The order began by asserting that maintenance of ordnance equipment was the responsibility of the commander concerned. The Chief of Ordnance, however, would communicate directly with and issue "necessary technical instructions and information" to the ordnance staffs of AGF and AAF headquarters. The Chief of Ordnance would provide qualified military personnel for maintenance duties, publish maintenance procedures and methods, provide technical guidance, and repair equipment returned from other commands. The order never once mentioned the existence of the Commanding General, Army Service Forces.[31] When the food service program started by the ASF was made Army-wide in scope, War Department instructions provided that the preparation of general policies and standards "of a technical nature which have an Army-wide application to food service activities" would be the responsibility of The Quartermaster General and The Surgeon General. Their respective duties were then detailed. The only mention of the commanding general of the ASF came later when he was authorized to gather "data

for establishment or revision of Army-wide" policies, procedures, standards, and methods of a technical nature.[32]

A different kind of statement of responsibility was prepared and issued to define the status of The Surgeon General. War Department orders in April 1945 began by asserting that The Surgeon General of the Army was the "chief medical officer of the Army and the chief medical adviser to the Chief of Staff and the War Department." As such, he was to make recommendations to the Chief of Staff and the War Department General and Special Staffs on matters pertaining to the health of the Army, and to prepare publications announcing general policies and "technical inspections" on health matters throughout the Army. This particular order went on to provide that The Surgeon General would address communications on the establishment of new policies and procedures to the Chief of Staff through the Commanding General, ASF. The Commanding General, ASF, might comment and make recommendations on these proposals but could not reject them. Furthermore, The Surgeon General was authorized to communicate directly with other commands on matters of a routine nature.[33] This order had the effect of giving The Surgeon General a special status on matters of medical policy and procedure. The Commanding General, ASF, could no longer disapprove recommendations of The Surgeon General; he had authority only to comment on them and to suggest alternatives for the consideration of the War Department General Staff.

---

[30] See above, Chs. VIII and XI.
[31] WD Cir 94, 26 Mar 45.
[32] WD Cir 149, 21 May 45.
[33] WD Cir 120, 18 Apr 45.

THE CHIEFS OF THE TECHNICAL SERVICES. *Top row, left to right: General Magee, The Surgeon General, June 1939–May 1943, General Kirk, The Surgeon General, June 1943–May 1947, General Campbell, Chief of Ordnance. Middle: General Reybold, Chief of Engineers, General Gross, Chief of Transportation, General Gregory, The Quartermaster General. Bottom: General Porter, Chief of Chemical Warfare Service, General Olmstead, Chief Signal Officer, October 1941–June 1943, General Ingles, Chief Signal Officer, July 1943–March 1947.*

There were two basic complications in orders of this sort. First, the War Department instructions seemed to suggest that on technical matters the chiefs of the technical services were not parts of the ASF but were members of the War Department staff. And second, they simply filled the chiefs of technical services with a sense of restiveness at being parts of the Army Service Forces for their other duties. The technical services were never enthusiastic about being units of the ASF. They never seemed to realize that to continue procurement and supply operations under seven different systems, with seven different sets of objectives, seven different ideas about urgency, and seven different instructions on shipment would have meant chaos and waste, not effective and economical supply of military operations. But the obstacles placed in the way of technical supervision by the chiefs of the technical services were real enough—obstacles which were not imposed by the Commanding General, ASF, but by the very nature of the Army Service Forces as a War Department command.

The technical services were large and essential elements of the ASF. They performed the actual work of calculating supply needs, procuring war equipment, and storing and issuing supplies to troops. They provided the medical, construction, communications, photographic, and transportation services for the War Department. As of 31 July 1943 the total operating strength of the seven technical services within the United States was 728,796 military and civilian personnel. This was 48 percent of total ASF operating strength. This personnel was divided among the technical services as follows: [34]

Chief of Transportation	149,121
Ordnance	261,118
Engineers*	90,493
Quartermaster	103,450
Signal	72,109
Chemical Warfare	35,569
Surgeon General	16,936

*Including civilian functions and MANHATTAN DISTRICT supervising development of the atomic bomb.

Of the total strength of technical services on 31 July 1943, 16,904 military and civilian personnel were located in the offices of the chiefs of the technical services in Washington. Another 13,787 were field employees in the District of Columbia area. The remainder were field employees in the United States or on special overseas missions.

[34] Section 5 of the ASF Monthly Progress Report, Personnel and Training, 31 July 1943, pp. 8, 10. These strength data pertained to ASF personnel only, not to ordnance personnel in the AGF, Air Forces, or overseas theaters.

CHAPTER XXI

The Service Commands

War Department Circular 59 of 1942 included in the list of War Department "offices and agencies" placed under the command of the ASF "all corps area commanders." There was no other reference to corps areas in the document. There was no indication of what the corps areas were to do or how they were to do it. The first ASF order on internal organization simply listed corps areas at the end of the description of the new command. The organization chart showed nine corps areas, along with the supply services and the administrative services, as "operating divisions." A footnote added: "field agents of the operating divisions on designated functions." This was the extent of the prescription of a role for the corps areas.[1]

The War Department history of field organization reached back to an early date. Territorial districts for the Army had first been created in 1813. In 1815 these had been renamed departments and grouped under two divisions. These territorial departments continued, with various modifications, until 1920. The amendments to the National Defense Act approved on 4 June 1920 provided for the creation of corps areas to replace the territorial departments. These corps areas were to be organized on the basis of potential military population. Originally it was intended to include in each corps area at least one division of the Regular Army, a division of the National Guard, and a division of the Organized Reserve. Each corps area had a threefold mission: tactical, training, and administrative.

The corps areas steadily diminished in importance throughout the 1920's and 1930's because of two developments. First, more and more field installations were exempted from the command of corps area commanders. This was particularly true of the field installations of the supply arms and services. Second, the corps areas were not satisfactory tactical commands. Because of curtailments in appropriations, the War Department was never able to effect the tactical organization in each corps area on the scale originally planned. Furthermore, the War Department found the fixed geographical boundaries a definite disadvantage in the training and deployment of troops. Maneuver areas available to the Army were mainly located in two of the corps areas—the Fourth and Eighth. In order to assemble large troop units for tactical training, the War Department in 1932 set up four armies embracing the nine corps areas. The final step in the separation of tactical and administrative duties in the field was taken with the creation of General Headquarters of the field forces in July 1940. Thereafter the corps areas were left with

---

[1] Ltr, CG SOS to Chiefs of all SAS, etc., 9 Mar 42, sub: Initial Dir for the Org of SOS, Ret files ASF, DRB AGO.

administrative and supply duties only.[2]

Because of this remaining supply and administrative mission of the corps area commands, the War Department decided to include them as a part of the newly created Army Service Forces. After 9 March 1942 the commanding generals of corps areas were told unofficially to continue to function as they had in the past, pending a study of function and organization of field installations. One of the first steps taken by the Control Division of General Somervell's office was to start two field surveys as a means of throwing light on organizational problems. The second of these field surveys was conducted in New York City in April. Some members of the survey staff visited the headquarters of the Second Corps Area at Governors Island. Their investigation immediately disclosed a great amount of confusion in the headquarters regarding its duties and responsibilities. The survey staff reported: "The corps area command is not geared into the SOS operating system to the maximum possible benefit of the organization. The directives which the corps area receives are not always in harmony with those received by the district supply officers." The report on the field survey proposed that "consideration should be given to reorganization of the corps area commands as regional administrative and supervisory centers for the Services of Supply."[3]

As a result of this recommendation, the director of the Control Division, ASF, initiated a full-scale survey of the organization and operation of corps areas. A group from the division visited the Third Corps Area headquarters in Baltimore in May and the Sixth Corps Area headquarters in Chicago in June.[4] Both emphasized the same findings and both agreed there was

much confusion. First, the corps area mission was confused. While tactical responsibilities had been removed, there was no clear understanding of the supply and administrative functions that remained. Second, the relations of the corps area to the many different Army installations within its geographical limits were confused. Within the Sixth Corps Area there were as many as forty-nine exempted installations. Yet the commanding general found himself called upon from time to time to render a wide variety of services to these military posts. Third, the internal organization of corps area headquarters was confused.

The two surveys recommended that all existing orders assigning duties to corps areas be replaced by a consolidated and complete statement of the mission, duties, responsibility, and authority of the corps areas and their role in the ASF organization. They recommended further that a standard organization plan applicable to all be prescribed. In addition to these general recommendations, a number of specific proposals were made for improvement in various operations being carried on by corps areas. After reviewing these proposals, General Somervell directed the Control Division to prepare a statement on the mission and to recommend an organizational plan for corps areas.

Accordingly, on 8 July 1942 the director of the Control Division transmitted a number of recommendations to the commanding general. These included a re-

---

[2] A fuller account of these developments will be found in History of Service Commands, Army Service Forces, a manuscript prepared in the Control Division, ASF, located in Historical Files, ASF.

[3] CD Rpt 6, New York Field Survey, May 42, CD, ASF, pp. 4, 7.

[4] CD Rpt 9, Third Corps Area Field Survey, May 42; CD Rpt 15, Report of Survey of Sixth Corps Area, Jun 42. Both in CD, ASF.

definition of the mission and functions of corps areas, a standard organization pattern for corps area headquarters, and a system of classification for all War Department field installations. In addition, he proposed that these recommendations, if approved, be followed by a conference of corps area commanders at Chicago to discuss the new organization.[5] The commanding general approved the proposals submitted.

The Service Command Reorganization

The first official step in the reorganization of the corps areas occurred on 22 July 1942 when War Department orders redesignated corps areas as service commands of the ASF and provided that the commanding generals of corps areas would henceforth be known as commanding generals, service commands, Army Service Forces.[6] This change in title emphasized the fact that corps areas had become entirely supply and administrative agencies of the ASF. The continued use of the designation "corps area" would have handicapped the ASF in establishing a new mission for these commands.

A conference of commanding generals of service commands was convened in Chicago on 30 July 1942. They received in advance a draft of the revised Army regulations which set forth a consolidated and simplified statement of the mission for service commands. This was accompanied by a mimeographed organization manual proposing a standard organizational pattern for each service command. General Somervell and his staff spent two days explaining the purpose of the reorganization. Somervell made it clear that he had two fundamental ideas in mind: geographical decentralization of the work of

the ASF and an increase in the responsibilities of service commands.[7]

The official statement of mission of the service commands was contained in revised Army regulations issued on 10 August 1942.[8] These regulations announced that the continental area of the United States was divided into nine service commands. The boundaries which had existed prior to the creation of the Army Service Forces were continued without change and the headquarters locations remained the same. The mission of each service command was to perform the various functions of the ASF in the field, with the exception of those relating to procurement, new construction, and the operation of depots, holding and reconsignment points, ports, and staging areas. These functions included the induction, classification, and assignment of military personnel; the training of all units and individuals assigned to service command control; the supervision of the housing and hospitalization of troops; the repair and maintenance of real property and the operation of utilities; the rendering of legal, financial, and administrative services to troops stationed within the limits of the service command; supervision of fixed signal communications; and the command of ASF training centers, except for the promulgation of training doctrine, the conduct and supervision of training, and the selection, assignment, and relief of training staff.[9]

All Army field installations in the zone of interior were classified into four cate-

---

[5] Memo, C. F. Robinson for CG SOS, 8 Jul 42, sub: Corps Area Reorg, CD, ASF.

[6] WD GO 35, 22 Jul 42.

[7] Min, Conf of CG's Sv Comds, Chicago, 30 Jul–1 Aug 42.

[8] AR 170–10, 10 Aug. 42.

[9] *Ibid.,* par. 4.

gories.[10] Class I installations were placed under the commanding generals of service commands. These included recruiting stations, induction centers, reception centers, internal security districts, motor repair shops, Ordnance and Signal Corps repair shops, enemy alien and prisoner of war camps, recreation camps, medical and dental laboratories, Reserve Officers' Training Corps (ROTC) units, State Guard affairs, general dispensaries except the General Dispensary in Washington, finance offices, disciplinary barracks, officer procurement boards, all named general hospitals except the Army Medical Center (Walter Reed General Hospital), and ASF training centers and schools. Class II installations were those where units of the Army Ground Forces were stationed; the authority of the commanding generals of the service commands in them was confined to control of administrative, housekeeping, and supply functions. It was emphasized that the commanding general of a service command had no control over or responsibility for the Ground Forces troops who were in training at the post. Class III installations were those utilized by the Army Air Forces. Here the duties of the commanding generals of service commands were limited to fourteen specified services which included supervision of the Army Exchange Service, fixed signal communications, ordnance maintenance, special services, disbursing activities, repair and utilities operations, and laundry operations. Finally, Class IV installations were those which "because of their technical nature" remained under the direct command of a chief of a supply or administrative service in the ASF. Here again the duties of the commanding generals of the service commands were limited to certain services

closely paralleling those provided stations of the AAF, plus additions which included medical service and public relations. Generally, these Class IV installations were government-owned manufacturing plants, proving grounds, procurement offices, storage depots, ports of embarkation, and certain specialized installations like the Signal Corps Photographic Center in New York, and the Army Medical Center in Washington.

This system of classification did much to clarify the duties of the commanding generals of the service commands. The new Army regulations transferred several field installations which had been under the direct control of offices in Washington to the jurisdiction of the commanding generals of service commands. The more important of these were prisoner of war camps previously under the direct control of the Provost Marshal General, the Army finance offices previously under the direct control of the Chief of Finance, the disciplinary barracks previously under the direct control of The Adjutant General, and all the named general hospitals (except Walter Reed General Hospital) formerly administered directly by The Surgeon General.

The new Army regulations were accompanied by an organization manual for service commands.[11] In a foreword General Somervell emphasized the importance of supply, administrative, and other service functions in the proper conduct of the war. He explained that the new plan of organization eliminated "the previous confusion arising from a large number of independent groups reporting separately to the service commander, most of which

---

[10] *Ibid.*, par. 6.
[11] Services of Supply Organization Manual, 10 Aug 42, Pt. IV, ASF files.

received instructions directly from autonomous offices in Washington." He also pointed out that one result of the reorganization must be the "maximum utilization of existing personnel" with a reduction in the number of military and civilian personnel required throughout service commands. On two types of work, commanding generals of service commands would continue to deal directly with the War Department staff without going through the Commanding General, ASF. Service command inspector generals might be utilized by The Inspector General of the War Department in making local inspections and investigations. The Inspector General was accordingly given authority to communicate directly with the service commands. Second, the Assistant Chief of Staff, G–2, remained responsible for military intelligence in the United States. Accordingly, the director of intelligence in a service command headquarters would follow policies fixed by G–2 and would report directly to G–2.

In several respects the organization prescribed for a service command headquarters differed from that in effect at ASF headquarters. In part, this can be explained by the lack of any procurement and storage responsibilities in service commands. Also, there was no provost marshal in a service command headquarters but only an internal security division. A supply division brought technical services officers in a service command under the immediate control of the division itself; thus instead of the old arrangement whereby a G–4 co-ordinated the work of supply officers, the officers of all seven technical services now became heads of branches in a supply division. The Army exchange branch was added to the supply division, although in ASF headquarters it was at

this time a separate administrative service. There was an administrative division in service command headquarters with three branches representing administrative services in Washington.

The service command organization realized one objective of the ASF organizational planners. There were seven divisions reporting to the commanding general of a service command, with only three branches in the commanding general's own personal office. This was regarded as a convenient number and was certainly a great improvement over the former arrangement whereby some thirty-six different officers had reported to a commanding general of a corps area.

As already mentioned, no change was made in the geographical boundaries of the old corps areas. The service commands inherited the boundaries as drawn in 1920 and as modified only slightly thereafter. With one exception, these boundaries were to remain unchanged throughout the history of the Army Service Forces. The exception resulted from the creation of a Military District of Washington (MDW) in May 1942.[12] It included the District of Columbia, Arlington County, and the water supply installations for the District of Columbia lying beyond the district line.[13] Army Regulations 170–10 issued in August 1942 provided that the geographical area of the MDW would be entirely removed from the Third Service Command.

Later an ASF order specified that the commanding general of the MDW would perform those services in the area which had heretofore been performed by the commanding general of the service com-

---

[12] WD GO 23, 5 May 42.
[13] WD Cir 236, 20 Jul 42.

mand.[14] The MDW was regarded as a tenth service command in the United States. It had three different functions. Until 1944 it had a tactical function for which it was responsible to the Eastern Defense Command. Second, its commanding general served as headquarters commandant for the War Department and as such, reported to the Deputy Chief of Staff of the War Department. Third, the MDW was a service command of the ASF in the administration of such activities as recreational camps, induction stations, and post operations at Fort Myer and later at Fort Washington and Fort Belvoir. In December 1942 the boundaries of the MDW were enlarged to include the last two posts.

Another service command was created in September 1942 as the Northwest Service Command with headquarters at Whitehorse, Yukon Territory.[15] This command took over the construction and operation of the Alaska Highway, the railway between Skagway and Whitehorse, and the construction work on the Canol project. In addition, it was the supply agency for the airfields in the area. Subsequent War Department general orders specified that the Northwest Service Command would have the same powers and authorities as service commands in the United States insofar as these applied to the activities of the Army in western Canada.[16] The Northwest Service Command came to an end on 30 June 1945 when its functions were transferred to the Sixth Service Command.[17] The liquidation of all U.S. military activities in the area followed.

Pressure for Decentralization

After the initial action had been taken to make service commands the field agencies of the Army Service Forces, it became necessary to keep the purpose of that arrangement constantly before all elements of the ASF. On 4 August 1942, immediately after the conference in Chicago, General Somervell called a staff conference in Washington to review the service command organization with the chiefs of the technical services. He explained that it was his intention to make the service commands the field units of the ASF for all activities except procurement and depot operations. The commanding generals of the service commands would be field general managers; the chiefs of technical services and ASF staff divisions would exercise staff supervision to insure that the work for which they were responsible was satisfactorily performed.[18]

To insure that service commands were performing as intended and that the reorganization was realizing its purpose, the Control Division kept one or two officers almost constantly in the field visiting service command headquarters and various posts. As a result, a small office was set up in Washington concerned with field relations,[19] and which cleared all matters affecting service commands.[20] This clearance procedure insured that no action was taken which impaired any of the fundamental objectives of the service command reorganization. Moreover, service commands now had a place to which they could refer any problem on which they were unable to obtain satisfaction through ordinary staff channels. General supervi-

---

[14] SOS Memo, 25 Aug 42.
[15] WD GO 44, 4 Sep 42.
[16] WD GO 15, 23 Mar 43.
[17] WD GO 50, 28 Jun 45.
[18] CD Rpt 22, Commanding General's Staff Conference on Reorganization of Service Commands, 4 Aug 42, CD, ASF.
[19] SOS Cir 79, 28 Aug 42.
[20] SOS Memo S170-1-43, 2 Jan 43.

sion of service commands through a single office in Washington continued throughout the war.

At the service command conference in July 1942 General Somervell asked each commander of a service command to submit a list of activities which he thought might be decentralized to service commands. Such lists were received during the summer and autumn of 1942. A final report of the action taken on these recommendations was transmitted to the service commanders in December 1942. For example, service commands had requested authority to appoint civilians to positions paying more than $4,600 per annum. This authority was granted by the Civilian Personnel Procedures Manual issued on 16 September 1942. Altogether some fifty suggestions were approved and another five were in the process of being carried out when the December report was made.[21] These covered 75 percent of all proposals. Another opportunity was given to service commands to suggest changes in field organization in 1943 through the Program for the More Effective Utilization of Personnel.[22]

An important administrative arrangement established after August 1942 was the use of a single channel for the allotment of funds and of personnel for field activities. Before the service command reorganization each technical service had allotted funds for its particular activities directly to corps areas. ASF headquarters had made personnel allotments but specified the type of work to be done. New channels for the allotment of personnel and funds to service commands were set forth in January 1943.[23] Thereafter, ASF headquarters made bulk allotments to service commands for all military personnel to perform all functions at Class I and II installations except training personnel at training installations. Enlisted personnel were allotted specifically to general hospitals, training activities, recruiting and induction stations, officer procurement service offices, reception centers, and to certain other activities such as prisoner of war camps. All funds were allotted directly to service commands for various projects, and the commanding generals of service commands in turn allocated these funds to commanders of Class I and II installations. While service commands made no personnel authorization to Class III installations, they did allot funds for the hiring of civilian personnel to perform ASF-type services at such installations. To Class IV installations the service commands allotted funds and military personnel for the same purposes as to Class I and II installations. Commanders at both Class III and IV installations directed the performance of all functions at their posts. They were responsible to their chiefs on some matters and to commanding generals of service commands for housekeeping operations. Subsequently, the commanders of the service commands were directed not to allot personnel to Class IV installations, but to allot funds instead and to exercise supervision over the performance of specified activities.[24] When a new method of authorizing and reporting personnel was set up in June 1943, both military and civilian personnel were brought under the authorization scheme.[25] Personnel control was entirely separated from budgetary controls.

---

[21] Decentralization to Service Commands, rpt by the Chief of Adm Svs to CG's Sv Comds, Dec 42, CD, ASF.
[22] See below, p. 381.
[23] SOS Cir 4, 6 Jan 43.
[24] ASF Cir 27, 10 May 43.
[25] ASF Cir 39, 11 Jun 43.

The intricacies of personnel and fund authorizations are not pertinent to the present discussion. Here the important point is simply to note that the ASF introduced a scheme of fund and personnel authorization which strengthened the position of the commanding general of a service command as general manager and made it clearly evident that he was responsible for the efficient operation of all the services assigned to him. Both types of authorization emphasized the administrative line of command: from Commanding General, ASF, to commanding general of each service command. This arrangement did much to change the old system which had encouraged chiefs of the technical services and of the administrative services to deal directly with their own counterparts in the corps areas and to ignore the co-ordinating authority of the corps area commander.

From time to time, as new functions were started by the ASF, a concerted effort was made to manage the program through a staff division in Washington with operating responsibility vested in service commands. Thus in October 1942, when five new depots were established to distribute printed publications, each was assigned to the service command in which it was located.[26] In April 1943 a new procedure was set up for the administrative settlement of claims against the government arising from military service.[27] The commanding generals of the service commands were directed to take all necessary action for investigating and reviewing tort claims, and to forward recommendations to the Judge Advocate General. In January 1943 labor branches were set up in service command headquarters.[28] Previously, the Industrial Personnel Division of ASF headquarters had had branch offices

scattered throughout the United States. Now, the service commands were made the field agencies for performing labor supply activities for the ASF. In February of the same year, Army specialized training branches were established in the headquarters of service commands.[29] The next month the field activities of the Officer Procurement Service were decentralized to service commands.[30] Later, the Food Service Program was established. It provided that the commanding generals of the service commands would be responsible for the operation of the program within their geographic limits.[31] When a Personal Affairs Division was created in ASF headquarters, a personal affairs division or branch in each service command was also provided for.[32] In October 1944 the laundry program was decentralized to the service commands.[33]

These examples illustrate the practice of turning things over to the service commands as new activities and programs were created. A staff division in ASF headquarters assumed supervision while service commands were directed to perform the actual operation in the field.

The Mission of the Service Commands

It may fairly be asked of the service command reorganization, and of the subsequent steps taken to make it effective: why was so much attention given to this whole effort? Why were the new arrangements regarded as so important by Gen-

---

[26] SOS Memo S15-1-42, 1 Oct 42.
[27] WD Cir 107, 23 Apr 43.
[28] SOS Cir 8, 26 Jan 43.
[29] SOS Cir 11, 18 Feb 43.
[30] SOS Memo S605-13-43, 8 Mar 43.
[31] ASF Cir 45, 3 Jul 43.
[32] ASF Cir 41, 7 Feb 43.
[33] ASF Cir 335, 6 Oct 44.

TYPICAL ASF INSTALLATIONS IN A CAMP

eral Somervell, and why was so much energy devoted to making the service commands essential and efficient parts of the ASF operating organization?

The answer is to be found in General Somervell's views on organization. He believed strongly in the efficiency of an integrated, or unified, field organization. He had come to this conviction from experience in a wide variety of administrative activities, and he was acquainted with some of the theoretical writings on the subject. Moreover, the concept of joining many specialties together under a single commander or general administrator in the field, was familiar to Army officers. A combat command such as a division or an army brings together under one leader elements from all major branches in the Army. These include combat elements such as the infantry, armored force, and the artillery; combined combat and service elements such as the signal, chemical warfare, and engineer troops; and service units such as the ordnance, quartermaster, medical, and transportation units, and miscellaneous units such as military police and administrative troops. An overseas theater of operations combined all these diverse elements in a still larger command organized on the basis of a geographical area.

Yet in 1941 this concept of an overseas command as an integrated geographical organization had not been applied to the functions of the Army in the United States. The departments, and later the corps areas into which the United States was divided, were never miniature War Departments. The Surgeon General ran his own field organization, the general hospitals. The Chief of Ordnance had his own procurement offices throughout the country, his own arsenals or manufacturing plants,

his own proving grounds and training centers, and his own depots for both ammunition and weapons. Other bureaus in Washington administered their own field installations.

At the time the Army Service Forces was created in 1942, it had become a firmly established tradition for each technical service to look upon its own work as being so highly specialized within the United States that it could accomplish its responsibilities only through a field organization over which it had complete administrative control and which was entirely separated from all other parts of the War Department. There were a number of "administrative services" with similar attitudes about field organization.[34]

The Army had for many years set up fixed or "command" installations all over the United States. These posts, camps, and stations were principally training centers. Yet each required extensive services to keep it in operation.[35] With the activation of General Headquarters in 1940 the command of a fixed installation and the command of the troops in training within them was separated. The operation of these installations was the first task which the ASF inherited when the corps areas were assigned to it on 9 March 1942. The service command reorganization was an attempt to strengthen the field organization for supervising army posts and to make this same organization an integrated field structure for many other ASF activities performed within the United States. But this effort ran into the strong separatist tradition of field administration in the various technical and administrative services making up the Army Service Forces. Thus it took constant effort by ASF head-

---

[34] This will be discussed in the next chapter.
[35] See above, p. 108.

COMMAND GENERALS OF THE SERVICE COMMANDS AND THE MDW. *Front row, left to right: Maj. Gens. James L. Collins, Fifth Service Command, John T. Lewis, MDW, Lt. Gen. B. B. Somervell, Commanding General, ASF, Maj. Gens. H. S. Aurand, Sixth Service Command, Sherman Miles, First Service Command, W. D. Styer, Chief of Staff, ASF. Back row: Maj. Gens. Philip Hayes, Third Service Command, Richard Donovan, Eighth Service Command, David McCoach, Ninth Service Command, Thomas A. Terry, Second Service Command, Clarence H. Danielson, Seventh Service Command, and Frederick E. Uhl, Fourth Service Command.*

quarters to maintain an integrated field organization.

General Somervell thought it expedient to exempt from service commands direction all the procurement and storage operations of the technical services. Then General Gross, the chief of the Transportation Corps, argued successfully that he needed direct control over the holding and reconsignment points, the staging areas, and the ports of embarkation if he was to ship men and supplies overseas efficiently and in balanced quantities. Therefore, a number of field installations were never placed under the "command" of the service commands. These became the Class IV installations of the service command reorganization. On the other hand, the administrative services retained few field installations under their direct control. For example, finance offices for the payment of Army bills became parts of service commands.

The ASF endeavored to strengthen the central management of the service commands and to lessen the centrifugal forces which always threaten to pull an integrated field organization apart. Washington offices were ordered to communicate instructions directly to service commanders, or at least through them. General Somervell made strenuous efforts to keep the commanders of the service command personally informed on all phases of ASF activities so that they would know what their specialists were expected to accomplish. One method was to hold important conferences every six months where all service commanders were brought together and where the discussion leaders were chiefs of the technical services and heads of staff offices in Washington. General Somervell himself missed only one of these conferences.[36]

It may well be asked again what the advantages of an integrated field organization were and why so much effort was expended to make it work. Why not let each specialty in Washington go its own way and have its own field organization? General Somervell believed that a varied or multiple field organization was wasteful of manpower and of other resources. In wartime especially, he felt that he had a major responsibility as commanding general of the ASF to conserve manpower and to operate an efficient organization. The service command reorganization was a full-scale endeavor to achieve economy in war administration.

He believed strongly that an integrated field organization, when carefully constructed and loyally and efficiently operated, could realize economy in three different ways: (1) by simplifying the supervisory organization and reducing supervisory personnel requirements; (2) by promoting close collaboration in the field among individuals with common objectives; and (3) by providing common local services for various field specialties. For instance, by placing the supervision of repair and utility operations at all Army installations under a service command engineer, a single staff became responsible for checking standards maintained at posts and for providing assistance in cases of trouble. By placing Army finance offices and legal offices under single direction in the field, common interests could be promoted and conflicts of jurisdiction could be settled locally on such problems as the investigation and payment of claims. Then, when many field offices were joined under single command they could utilize common personnel, mail, communications, transportation, and other housekeeping services. A consolidation of field offices under a single commander in one city alone during World War II realized a reduction of one third of the personnel involved in the performance of housekeeping duties.

The essence of an integrated field organization is a system of dual supervision.[37] Individual specialties, from head-

[36] Service Command Conferences were held in New Orleans, January 1943; Chicago, July 1943; Dallas, February 1944; Ft. Leonard Wood, July 1944; Gulfport, February 1945; and Camp Grant, June 1945. Minutes of each conference are in the files, Control Division, ASF.

[37] This "doctrine of dual supervision" as a basic concept in field organization was first presented in Macmahon, Millett, and Ogden, *The Administration of Federal Work Relief,* Ch. XI. This author has elaborated upon the theme in *New Horizons in Public Administration, a Symposium* (Tuscaloosa, Ala., University of Alabama Press, 1945), Ch. V.

quarters to the lowest level of field operation, continue to communicate freely on all technical questions of policy and procedure. Command supervision, on the other hand, is concerned with the most efficient utilization of all available resources in the realization of a common objective. This system of dual supervision was real enough in the Army Service Forces but never fully understood in the field; perhaps it would be more accurate to say that it was never explicitly expounded and that this failure contributed to misunderstanding. Yet it would be entirely unrealistic to suppose that constant explanation and patience would have solved the problem of ASF field organization. An official's concept of his prestige and of the conditions under which he is willing to work at his best is not a rational proposition; it is a compound of personal ambition and other more complex motivations.

The part of the service command reorganization which created the most controversy was the inclusion of general hospitals as field installations under the commanders of the service commands. During World War II there were some sixty general hospitals scattered throughout the United States. Before August 1942 they were all "exempted" field installations under the direct command of The Surgeon General in Washington. After the service command reorganization, The Surgeon General retained technical authority over the general hospitals but not administrative control. The Surgeon General was never happy about this arrangement. He and his office voiced various objections, although none of them was ever officially presented as a formal protest. They went along with the reorganization solely because they felt required to do so. At most it was a kind of reluctant compliance.

The organization planners of the ASF staff argued that a general hospital was a large military post. The buildings had to be repaired, the utilities operated, the patients and staff fed, entertainment provided, and other services rendered. In some cases there were even prisoners of war to guard, because many German and Italian prisoners were assigned to hospital duties. ASF headquarters said in effect: We want The Surgeon General's office to worry about medical care, but we don't want an engineer on his staff to supervise repairs and utilities, we don't want a provost marshal on his staff to supervise the care and guarding of prisoners of war. So as military posts, the general hospitals were placed under the commanders of service commands; but as centers of medical care, the general hospitals remained under The Surgeon General.

From the point of view of The Surgeon General, however, the organizational arrangement was never simple. The basic mission of the general hospital was medical care, not operating utilities, feeding people, or guarding prisoners of war. Why, he asked, should the primary task be subordinated in the organizational structure to the secondary or facilitative tasks? The Surgeon General naturally felt that the basic mission might be impaired if those directing its performance could not order all supplementary services to concentrate upon the medical task. It made no difference to him that the commanding officers of general hospitals continued to be medical corps officers, that surgeons on the staff of service commanders were in constant touch with general hospitals, and that the Washington office had direct communication with each general hospital. Command was command, and it was vested in the commanding generals of the service commands—not in The Surgeon General. The latter was on firmer ground when he pointed out that many essential field installations of other technical services remained under the direct control of chiefs of technical services; why should The Surgeon General be treated differently? And finally, the organizational prescription for a service command headquarters seemed to reduce the service command surgeon to the status of a supply officer, an action that was scarcely reassuring to The Surgeon General in Washington. There is no doubt that psychological factors in the matter had been given too little consideration, which in retrospect can be labeled a mistake on the part of the ASF organizational planners. It might have been more satisfactory to have designated general hospitals as Class IV installations.

This difference in point of view between ASF headquarters and The Surgeon General was never resolved during World War II. The general hospitals remained administratively under the service commanders. The Surgeon General was never satisfied with that arrangement. There is much to be said for The Surgeon General's point of view, although medical control of the hospitals was never weakened as much as was sometimes intimated. From the point of view of the ASF, the field administration of general hospitals must be set down as a noble ASF experiment. In the eyes of The Surgeon General it was a failure.

In reviewing the status of service command responsibilities in 1942, ASF headquarters planners were much impressed by how far the separatist tendencies of the various Army specialties or technicians had gone toward reducing the concept of integrated field command to impotency.

The ASF endeavored to dam the flow and turn it in new directions. This endeavor may have led General Somervell and his staff associates on occasion to overstate the responsibilities of the "general administrators," i. e., the commanders of the service commands. The problem was really one of balance between technical specialty and command. There was a tendency in ASF headquarters to redress a situation of autonomy run riot with a new one too heavily weighted on the command side. Yet there were times when General Somervell tried to restore the confidence of the technical supervisors. Officer procurement is an illustration of his effort in this direction. In March 1943 ASF headquarters issued an order creating a field organization for the Officer Procurement Service.[38] Each service command was directed to establish an officer procurement branch to handle applications in the field from civilians needed as officers. But the director of this work in a service command could be selected only with the approval of the head of the Officer Procurement Service in Washington. Subsequent transfer or reassignment of personnel engaged in officer procurement activities required Washington approval. This limitation upon the authority of the service commander as "general administrator" was imposed in order to reassure the specialist that his activity would be satisfactorily conducted in the field.

Three specific problems that arose during World War II will illustrate the ASF's continuing concern over field organization. These problems were the supervision of Class IV installations, the handling of labor shortages, and the prescription of a uniform internal organization for the service commands.

---

[38] SOS Memo S605-13-43, 8 Mar 43.

The Supervision of Class IV Installations

As noted earlier, an essential feature of the service command reorganization was the classification of all military installations within the United States into four major groups. To each of these the commanding general of a service command had a somewhat different relationship. Class I installations were the field installations carrying out the direct work of the service command, like a prisoner of war camp or an induction center. Here the service command supervisory authority was general, subject to the technical supervision of the staff offices of ASF headquarters. Class II installations were large military establishments where Army Ground Forces troops were in training. Here the service command supervised all the housekeeping operations. Class III installations were bases of the Air Forces. The controversy over the supervision of certain housekeeping activities within them has been related above. Class IV installations were field offices of the technical services of the ASF. In other words, these were separate field installations of operating units of the ASF. What relations were desirable between these installations and other parts of the Army Service Forces was the question.

It will be recalled that General Somervell in 1942 decided it was not expedient to create an integrated field organization for all ASF activities. Difficulties arose, however, when the ASF failed to distinguish between two very different types of field installations of the technical services. One type was the procurement offices and the storage centers. These operated principally with officer and civilian personnel. Only the large depots among them occasionally had to have enlisted personnel for operating duties. The second type was the training installation where technical service troops were trained.

Instead of drawing a clear distinction between these two types of installations, the ASF at first proposed to make all technical service training posts Class I installations. This proposal was opposed by chiefs of technical services. The result was a compromise. Replacement training centers and schools of the ASF were placed under service commands "except for promulgation of training doctrine, scheduling programs, the conduct and supervision of training, and the selection, assignment, and relief of training staff and faculty personnel assigned to the schools or the replacement training centers." This was an obviously bifurcated arrangement. Commanding generals had "command" of training centers, and yet the most important phases of training were immediately excepted from their command. Technical services and staff divisions with training responsibilities continued to prescribe the curriculum and prepare training programs. They determined training loads and assigned and relieved training personnel. There was little left for service commands to do other than manage the installation at which the training took place. In December 1942 an attempt was made to clarify training responsibilities.[39] This new statement enlarged service command authority to include inspection of training activities and recommendations for changes in training operations. Aside from this, chiefs of technical services and staff divisions continued to be responsible for training. The change was not particularly helpful.

Two types of training were operated

---

[39] AR 170-10, 24 Dec 42.

entirely by service commands. One of these was the Army Specialized Training Program. The other was Women's Army Corps training at three WAC training centers assigned to the commanding generals of the service commands in which they were located.[40] WAC basic training was supervised by the ASF Director of Military Training through service command channels. In other cases the supervision of training activities in the ASF was more complicated.

In May 1943 it was announced that thereafter training centers and schools would be designated as under the command of a chief of a technical service, an ASF staff division, or a service command.[41] When placed under a service command, ASF headquarters would continue to be responsible for the promulgation of training doctrine, the establishment of student quotas, and the preparation of training programs. In addition, the following schools were made Class IV stations: The School of Military Government under the Provost Marshal General; Edgewood Arsenal under the Chief of Chemical Warfare Service; Camp Lee under The Quartermaster General; Aberdeen Proving Ground under the Chief of Ordnance; Ft. Monmouth and Camp Murphy under the Chief Signal Officer; and Carlisle Barracks under The Surgeon General. These provisions were amplified in June 1943.[42] Chiefs of the technical services and ASF staff directors became responsible for all training activities at Class IV installations and at the posts just mentioned, except that commanding generals of service commands would supply or construct training aids, allot training ammunition, and allot and obligate special field exercise funds.

After the summer of 1943 training within the ASF was carried out according to the following general organizational pattern. Commanding generals of service commands were directly responsible for the training of special training units (illiterates), Army specialized training units, WAC units and detachments, station complements, and special schools such as those for cooks and bakers. ASF technical services and staff divisions were responsible for training troop units and individuals to be sent overseas to perform ordnance, quartermaster, medical, signal, engineer, transportation, chemical, fiscal, chaplain, special services, military police, military government, legal, adjutant general, and intelligence duties. Actually, the distinction was not as clear-cut as this. Camp Crowder in Missouri, for example, a Signal Corps training center, was a Class I installation. This meant it was under the commanding general of the Seventh Service Command except for training doctrine, training programs, supervision of training, and the selection of training staff. The same was true of Ft. Leonard Wood where Engineer troops were trained, of Ft. Warren where Quartermaster troops were trained, and of Camp Gordon Johnston where Transportation troops were trained. These were Class I training centers. Even Ft. Belvoir, the major training center of the Corps of Engineers, was a Class I installation of the Military District of Washington. Yet in reality, the commandant of each school or the commanding general of each training center was designated by the chief of a technical service, and all training activities were actually specified by the appropriate technical service.

---

[40] ASF Cir 106, 26 Oct 43.
[41] ASF Cir 28, 12 May 43; Changes 5 to AR 170-10, 12 May 43.
[42] ASF Cir 28, 4 Jun 43.

Personal observation convinced the author that service command responsibility at a Class I training installation where Engineer troops were trained was not essentially different from that at a Class II post where AGF troops were trained. It would have been simpler to make all technical service training centers Class II installations. This was never officially done. If these ASF training installations had been designated Class II installations, then their operation would have been under the supervision of a service command, but all training programs would have been supervised by ASF offices in Washington. Instead, the ASF tried to distinguish between the training and the supply work of the technical services by calling the first a Class I field office and the second a Class IV field office. As a result, a number of training posts later had to be transferred to Class IV to satisfy technical service wishes.

At a Class IV installation the service command was responsible for a designated list of duties. The last attempts to state these specific duties were made in 1945.[43] In general, the arrangement was that a technical service looked to a service command for supervision of those activities at a Class IV installation which did not fall within its own competence. Thus the service command supervised medical service, if there was any, at an Ordnance installation, and ordnance maintenance operations, if any, at a Quartermaster depot. Accordingly, there was just one supervisory force in the field for the varied work of the ASF in operating a training center, a depot or a staging area. The technical service named the field commander for its depot, its procurement office, or any other specialized (or Class IV) installation. But this officer looked to the service com-

mand—not to his superior in Washington—in providing internal services such as motion pictures for recreation, post exchanges, or utilities.

This was the best the ASF could do in trying to tie together the field offices of the technical services and the service commands. One other measure should be mentioned. The ASF asked the Chief of Engineers to set up "division" offices paralleling the service commands. The division engineer ran certain exempted activities for the Chief of Engineers in Washington, such as the letting and supervision of construction contracts. But the division engineer also worked for the service command in supervising the maintenance of physical properties and the operation of utility systems. A deputy division engineer for repairs and utilities was appointed by a division engineer and became in effect the service command engineer as well. Similarly, the Transportation Corps in 1943 set up zone transportation offices which were coterminous with service command boundaries. The zone transportation officer supervised some activities for the Chief of Transportation and on other matters was the transportation officer on the staff of the commander of a service command. This arrangement worked fairly well in practice.

But the ASF never fully settled the distinction between a Class I and a Class IV installation. The author has come to the conclusion that under the conditions prevailing during World War II, all technical service activities in the United States outside of Washington, except training, should have been classified as Class IV installations. Large Army installations utilized for training purposes by the technical services

---

[43] ASF Cir 265, 11 Jul 45; ASF Cir 312, 16 Aug 45.

and ASF staff divisions should have been designated Class II installations, with a post commander appointed by and responsible to a commanding general of a service command and a training center commander appointed by and responsible to a technical or administrative service chief in Washington. This conclusion seemed to be the prevailing one among ASF organizational planners as World War II came to an end.

The Handling of Labor Supply Problems in the Field

Originally, the ASF assigned manpower problems in the field arising out of technical service procurement activities to the service commands. Manpower difficulties were essentially an area problem. Labor shortages appeared in localities such as the Buffalo area or the Los Angeles area. Oftentimes the solution involved a number of adjustments within a particular community—better housing, recreational facilities, better transportation arrangements, an adjustment in shopping hours, and similar action. Since the technical services had separate field organizations and set up their local procurement offices in different cities, the ASF assigned labor relations and labor supply activities to the service commands. This did not prove a satisfactory arrangement.

In December 1943 new instructions were issued to define more precisely the labor functions of the various parts of the ASF and of the AAF.[44] In part, they were necessary in order to implement a memorandum from the Under Secretary dated 5 November 1943. In part, they dealt with an internal organization problem of the ASF. The circular specified that the technical services would give attention to the

labor situation in the placing of contracts, in following up on production performance, and in preparing estimates of labor requirements of contractors. Furthermore, technical services would "assist" service command labor branches in carrying out recommendations for solving labor problems. Moreover, they were to call upon service commands for assistance whenever necessary. When two or more technical services had an interest in a plant of a single contractor, they would work out with the service command a single labor responsibility for the plant.

Labor branches of the service commands were supposed to exercise general supervision over the labor activities of all War Department components in the field and provide assistance to any procurement office in meeting its labor problems. Furthermore, service commands were to keep the technical services and the procurement agencies of the Army Air Forces informed on labor market conditions and make recommendations for solving labor shortages. The service command labor branches were also designated as the official War Department agencies for liaison with local and regional offices of federal, state, and local government agencies concerned with manpower matters. This arrangement was intended to strengthen service command responsibility for handling labor problems in the field. At the same time, it recognized that the technical services could not be divorced from labor supply matters.

Manpower shortages grew more stringent as the war progressed. By early 1944 labor shortages appeared to be the single greatest obstacle to the realization of procurement schedules. The War Manpower Commission in March 1944 determined to

---

[44] WD Cir 317, 7 Dec 43.

establish manpower priorities committees in about one hundred areas of labor shortages. Previously, such committees had been used on the west coast and then in three other regions. At the same time, the War Production Board extended its production urgency committees into each labor area where a manpower priorities committee was established. This action on the part of the WMC and the WPB compelled the Army Service Forces to establish some organization for dealing with manpower and production problems in many different localities.

The director of matériel in ASF headquarters, General Clay, urged a new regional organization rather than the utilization of service commands for this function. His recommendations were accepted by General Somervell, and an ASF regional representative was designated for each of the thirteen regions in which the War Production Board had divided the United States.[45] The representative for each of these regions was a technical service officer in charge of an important activity in the area. Thus, for the Boston region the ASF regional representative was the commanding general of the Springfield Ordnance District. Other ASF regional representatives were as follows: New York, commanding officer of the New York Ordnance District; Philadelphia, commanding general of the Philadelphia Signal Depot; Atlanta, division engineer; Kansas City, commanding officer of the Kansas City Quartermaster Depot; Denver, commanding general of the Rocky Mountain Arsenal of the Chemical Warfare Service; Seattle, commanding officer of the Seattle ASF Depot.

A labor adviser was also named for each ASF regional representative. In six instances, this labor adviser was the head of a labor branch of a service command. In the other cases, the labor adviser came from the staff of a technical service. In one instance, he was named directly by the Industrial Personnel Division of ASF headquarters.

Each ASF regional representative was directed to organize an advisory committee representing the technical services, the Army Air Forces, and the service commands in the region. The regional representative was authorized to arrange for appropriate representation on all production urgency and manpower priorities committees set up in his region. The same representative was to serve on both committees and represent all Army contractors of the area on production urgency and manpower priorities matters. The area advisory committee assisted each area representative in fulfilling these responsibilities. Staff supervision of production problems in every region was vested in the Production Division under the ASF Director of Matériel, and staff supervision of all manpower problems was vested in the Industrial Personnel Division under the ASF Director of Personnel.

The establishment of these regional representatives introduced a whole new area organization into the ASF. There were now thirteen regional areas on production manpower problems, the areas following WPB regional boundaries. This coincided with no existing field boundary lines previously employed by the War Department. The ASF regional representative was potentially capable of exercising considerable authority in each region. On the other hand, he had an administrative responsibility which demanded his first allegiance. Often his reputation and his

---

[45] ASF Cir 85, 27 Mar 44; WD Cir 173, 4 May 44.

future depended upon how well he performed his job as head of an Ordnance district, of a Signal depot, of an Engineer division, or of a Chemical Warfare arsenal. His responsibilities as ASF regional representative were merely an added duty, which naturally tended to be of secondary interest. In fact, in many instances these individuals did almost nothing in their capacity as ASF regional representatives.

The labor advisers turned out to be the most important individuals in exercising supervision over local manpower priorities and production urgency committees. Where the labor adviser worked for both a service command and a regional representative, he found himself with divided loyalties. The head of the Labor Branch of the Third Service Command with headquarters in Baltimore, for example, was also regional labor adviser for the ASF third region with headquarters in Philadelphia. Thus he had two different headquarters and two regions with different boundaries. The situation was even worse on the west coast where the head of the regional branch of the Ninth Service Command with headquarters in Salt Lake City also served as labor adviser to the ASF regional representative with headquarters in San Francisco. Under such circumstances it was surprising that labor advisers accomplished as much as they did. In most instances it was at best a thankless task.

The entire setup was severely criticized by the commanding general of the Third Service Command at the Biloxi Service Command Conference in February 1945.[46] An investigation by General Somervell's Control Division after this conference revealed that the organizational difficulties were too deep-rooted to be adjusted in the closing weeks of the European war. The simple fact was that the technical services had first responsibility for procurement deliveries and were determined to handle their labor problems as a part of that responsibility. Never were they willing to turn labor supply administration over to service commands. The only completely satisfactory solution would have been an entirely new area organization for all procurement activities of the ASF. But this was out of the question at the time. It had once been proposed in 1943 and disapproved. There was no point in raising the issue again. Because it was expected that labor supply difficulties would ease greatly with the defeat of Germany, there was little disposition in ASF headquarters to change what was admittedly a bad situation.

It remains a fact that the Army Service Forces never solved the problem of a unified field structure for handling labor supply problems. On this subject the interests of the technical services and the service commands clashed. The technical services would not leave supervision of an important procurement matter, whether it pertained to manpower or supply, to the service commands. In consequence the ASF never had an effective field organization for labor supply questions. If the war had lasted longer, and labor matters had become more critical, the ASF probably would have had to devise a really effective field organization to handle manpower procurement problems. Whether this should have been a reaffirmation of the service command status as a field supervisory organization for general ASF work, or whether it should have been a new, integrated field organization for procurement operations, no one can say.

[46] See Min, 6th Conf of Sv Comdrs, 1–3 Feb 45, pp. 62–90.

Organization Within Service Commands

A fundamental element of administrative procedure which went into the service command organization was the establishment of a common internal organizational structure for all service commands. As noted above, the staff organization prescribed for service commanders introduced arrangements which differed from the organization of the ASF in Washington. The most notable of these was the creation in service command headquarters of a supply division with ordnance, quartermaster, engineer, signal, medical, and chemical warfare branches. This in effect made technical service officers not staff officers of a commander of a service command, but branch chiefs of a single staff officer in service command headquarters called a director of supply. The technical service chiefs in Washington were not enthusiastic about this arrangement, which may have been one reason why they sometimes resisted the transfer of any extensive technical supervisory authority of their own to service command channels.

A new organizational manual for service commands was issued in December 1942.[47] It modified the existing structure but made no important changes. Some new branches were created in service command headquarters, and the Army exchange branch was transferred from the supply division to the personnel branch. At the post level, intelligence work was separated from internal security.

A more radical change in post organization was made when in September 1943, by a War Department memorandum, posts were directed to integrate all maintenance activities in order to improve maintenance service.[48] This entailed a fiscal consolidation, a consolidation of administrative activities, a unification of command, and an interchange of skilled and unskilled personnel. Combined maintenance shops were set up at each post to perform third and fourth echelon maintenance along functional lines. Thus at each post there was a combined maintenance shop immediately under the director of supply and service. The shop was equipped to serve as an automotive shop, an armament and instrument shop, a clothing and equipment shop, an electrical equipment shop, a machine shop, and a paint shop. In addition, there were provisions for a single point of production control, a single shop supply unit, and a single shop salvage unit. This had the effect of breaking down technical service differentiations in maintenance activities in favor of a purely functional shop organization. In other words, no longer did the post signal officer run a signal maintenance shop or the post quartermaster a quartermaster shop. Instead, a combined maintenance shop handled all maintenance activities divided up into six functional groups.

This action was intended to improve maintenance work at posts, particularly through a better utilization of skilled labor. There had been much competition at posts for electricians, carpenters, painters, and other skilled workmen. The system of separate technical service shops made such competition inevitable, since all had an urgent need for competent mechanics. The combined maintenance shop was the answer to this situation.

When ASF headquarters in Washington was undergoing reorganization in October and November 1943, the ASF chief of

---

[47] Services of Supply Organization Manual, Dec 42, Pt. IV, ASF files.

[48] WD Memo W210-25-43, 7 Sep 43, sub: Integration of Maint Activities at Posts, Camps, and Stas.

staff, General Styer, decided to reorganize service command headquarters so that they would parallel ASF headquarters more closely. At the time, the chiefs of technical services were still unhappy about the service command organization which made technical service officers branch units under a director of supply. This was demonstrated at the Third Service Command Conference in Chicago in July 1943 when The Surgeon General recommended that the service command surgeon should report directly to the commanding general of a service command. He pointed out that the surgeon had personnel and training problems as well as medical service and supply problems.[49] In his closing remarks General Somervell disapproved this recommendation mainly on the ground that it would require a change in the status of each technical service officer in a service command headquarters. He added that he expected the commanding general of each service command to know his staff thoroughly and to be personally acquainted with the fiscal staff, the exchange staff, the judge advocate staff, and also with the technical staff. "Certainly you have got to talk to your doctor. You have to know what he has to say, and I expect you to do that."[50]

In November 1943 Styer had a letter dispatched to the commanding general of each service command which expressed the desire that the headquarters of each service command conform as closely as practicable to the organization of ASF headquarters.[51] This meant that each service command headquarters was to have organizational units including the technical services, corresponding in function to those in ASF headquarters. There followed a new organization chart and a new statement of functions. (*Chart 1*) The

quartermaster branch, the ordnance branch, and the other branches under the director of supply were abolished and replaced by a service command quartermaster, a service command ordnance officer, a service command signal officer, a service command surgeon, a service command transportation officer, and a service command chemical warfare officer—all reporting directly to the commanding general of the service command. The service command engineer already enjoyed this status. The organization chart and the statement of functions explained that technical service officers in service command headquarters would act as staff officers and advisers to the commanding general on their technical service functions.

The new organization increased the number of staff units reporting directly to a commanding general of a service command and at the same time, encouraged chiefs of the technical services in Washington to deal directly with technical service officers in service commands. This was the price of getting technical services in Washington to use service command channels in the field. Moreover, a type of organization in the field different from ASF organization in Washington simply did not prove feasible.

A further organizational revision was presented to service commands in a letter in December 1943.[52] Its purpose was to give effect to many recommendations

---

[49] Min, Conf of CG's Sv Comds, 22–24 Jul 43, p. 136.

[50] *Ibid.*, pp. 381–82.

[51] This letter had the file number SPX 323.3 (12 Nov 43) SPICY–MB–A, dated 12 Nov 43. Styer was commanding in Somervell's absence from the United States.

[52] Ltr, TAG to CG's Sv Comds, 8 Dec 43, SPX 323.3 (8 Dec 43) SPICY–MB–A.

CHART 1—ORGANIZATION OF SERVICE COMMAND HEADQUARTERS: 8 DECEMBER 1943

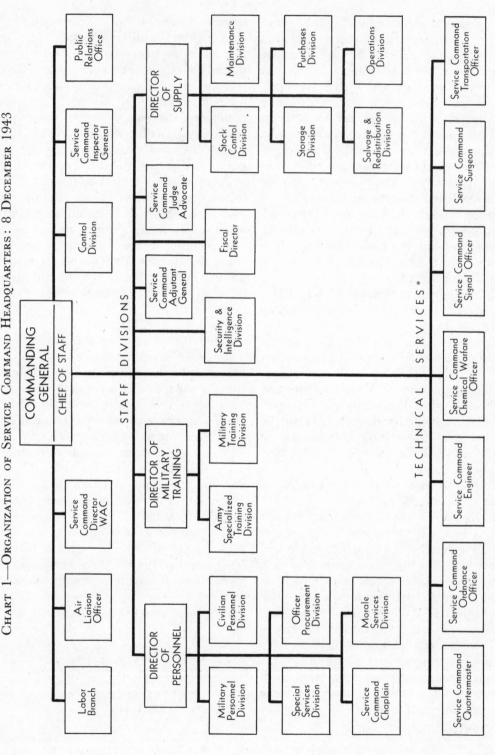

* Chiefs of Technical Services Act as Staff Officers and Advisors to the Commanding General on Their Technical Service Functions.

which had been received. The only structural change it set up was the addition of two new divisions under the director of supply. The statement of functions was somewhat more elaborate in order to provide more detailed instructions. An introduction said that a service command could not alter or transfer functions from one staff directorate to another without the prior approval of the Commanding General, ASF. The statement of functions also made it clear that the director of supply was expected to be the staff officer for co-ordinating storage, distribution, maintenance, and salvage activities. At the same time it was apparent that he would have to work through the technical service officers in service command headquarters. In the statement on technical service officers it was emphasized that these were likewise staff officers of the service command and would function as such. The letter also included an organization chart and statement of functions for posts. Their organization closely paralleled that provided for service command headquarters, including a post quartermaster, a post ordnance officer, a post surgeon, a post signal officer, a post chemical warfare officer, and a post transportation officer.[53] Despite the strong effort to establish a functional organization within posts, the system did not meet expectations.

In January 1945 ASF headquarters completed an important supply study pertaining to returns to stock.[54] Behind it was the fact that posts had not been obtaining prompt shipping instructions from depots on excess stocks at the posts. In turn, depots were failing to carry excess stocks as a supply asset with a possibly corresponding reduced need for procurement. The survey found that in large part the difficulty arose out of post maintenance work.

Depots were reluctant to accept supplies from posts for return to stock without inspecting them and oftentimes without further repair. One of the conclusions reached was that the combined shop operation at posts had tended to reduce technical service sense of responsibility for reporting property to depots. Thus technical service officers continued to be responsible for storage and issue of property at posts but were no longer responsible for its maintenance. This separation of responsibility had an adverse effect upon the prompt repair and return to stock of repairable items. As a result of the survey a new supply organization was directed for posts.[55] The combined maintenance shops might be continued at posts where its operation was proving satisfactory. Where it was not, the maintenance responsibility was to be returned to each technical service officer at a post. The post director of supply simply became a staff officer co-ordinating the maintenance activities of the various post technical service officers. With this experiment with combined shops, another attempt of the ASF to effect a functional organization came to an end. In only a few cases were combined shops retained.

One further major organizational change was introduced in service command headquarters in June 1945.[56] Many service commanders had complained that their director of personnel was overburdened. His six divisions (military personnel, civilian personnel, special services, personal affairs, chaplains, and informa-

---

[53] The new organization of service command headquarters and posts was republished in ASF Org Man M–301, 15 Dec 43, Pt. IV.

[54] Survey of Returns to Stock, CD, ASF.

[55] ASF Cir 228, 19 Jul 45.

[56] ASF Org Man M–301, 15 Jun 45, Pt. IV.

tion and education) made up one third of the total strength of a service command headquarters staff. The execution of various military and civilian personnel policies; the handling of strength control; and the supervision of separation center, reception station, and redistribution station activities had long since reached the point where they required the full attention of a director of personnel. Accordingly, service commands were permitted to establish a director of individual services supervising special services, information and education, personal affairs, and chaplains. This left the director of personnel in charge of direct military and civilian personnel. All service commands elected to make this change.

By 1945 the role of the service command in ASF organization was fairly well understood. The biggest contribution of the service command to ASF organization was as a supervisor of Army posts in the zone of interior. There were about one hundred large installations scattered throughout the United States where AGF troop units and replacements were trained. At each of these there was a post commanding officer responsible to the commanding general of a service command. The job of a post commander was to service the Ground Forces troops and activities located on the post. The service command provided the supervisory organization. In a sense the Ground Forces were in a position like that of guests at a hotel. The principle laid down was that the guests were always right, which meant that the post commander should comply with the wishes of Ground Forces units.

Only one important issue ever arose with the Ground Forces in connection with the operation of Class II installations.

With the growing manpower stringency in 1943, the ASF was pressed to find the available personnel to perform all station complement duties. As a result, the War Department issued a memorandum ordering Ground Forces troops to perform certain duties for themselves at posts.[57] These included the distribution of mail within units, the unloading of supplies at distribution points, the guarding and policing of areas assigned to AGF units, the maintenance of sanitary conditions in these areas, the operation of unit infirmaries, first and second echelon maintenance and third echelon maintenance when units and facilities for this were available, firing of small furnaces or stoves, the maintenance of unit records of all kinds, and the operation of target ranges and other training aids. In addition, Ground Forces troops were directed to assist the ASF in the policing of community areas adjacent to posts, in guarding garrison prisoners, and in meeting peak supply shipments or the reception of peak personnel loads at a post. In unusual circumstances the Ground Forces were also asked to assist the service commands in internal security duties. The AGF reluctantly agreed to render this assistance. It could hardly have done otherwise since its commander had long been critical of the growing number of specialized service units.

At large ASF training installations, service commands provided the same services. In a few instances the post commander was designated by the technical service or staff division responsible for the training. When this was done, however, the post commander was responsible to the service command for the internal management of his facility, rather than to

[57] WD Memo W600-69-43, 18 Aug 43.

the chief of a technical service or to a staff director.

The extent of service command supervision at arsenals, government-owned plants, procurement district offices, transportation offices, engineer division offices, and laboratories was more restricted. The important difference was the absence of any large number of enlisted personnel who had to be housed and cared for at these installations. The essential distinction between a Class II and Class IV should have been that one had the primary characteristics of a military post in the customary sense of that word, and the other resembled a manufacturing or great warehousing enterprise.

It was the concept of geographical unity, and the obvious need for single direction of the management of a military installation that gave the service commands vitality and which made them an essential element of the ASF operating organization.

As operating agencies of the ASF, the service commands, like the technical services, were large organizations. As of 31 July 1943 total operating civilian and military personnel of the nine service commands and the Military District of Washington (as far as ASF work was concerned) amounted to 751,911. This was 45 percent of the total ASF operating strength. The strength of the service commands varied as follows:[58]

First Service Command	31,246
Second Service Command	50,749
Third Service Command	60,548
Fourth Service Command	175,166
Fifth Service Command	42,600
Sixth Service Command	42,050
Seventh Service Command	76,530
Eighth Service Command	147,952
Ninth Service Command	106,991
Military District of Wash	18,079

Alongside the technical services, the service commands of the ASF were a second type of operating agency. Set up by geographical areas, the service commands were the regional organizations for most ASF activities other than procurement, supply, and certain other specialized tasks of the technical services. But the service commands never became complete and integrated replicas of ASF headquarters on a regional basis.

---

[58] ASF Monthly Progress Rpt, Personnel and Training, 31 Jul 43, Sec. 5.

CHAPTER XXII

The Evolution of ASF Headquarters

In addition to the six supply arms and services and the nine corps areas, the Army Service Forces absorbed eight administrative "bureaus," parts of the War Department General Staff, and the Office of the Under Secretary of War, as related earlier. These last three elements were eventually built into a single structure called Army Service Forces headquarters. The concept of such a headquarters emerged slowly; it was no overnight product. So complicated is the story that only the major organizational developments can be treated in this chapter.

The Merging of the OUSW and G–4

The first organizational challenge that faced General Somervell after 9 March 1942 was the need for some kind of integrated machinery above the level of the technical services to calculate supply requirements, to direct procurement operations, and to control the distribution of available weapons and equipment. The merging of the OUSW and the G–4 Division of the War Department General Staff, one of the principal advantages resulting from the creation of the ASF, provided such machinery. At the beginning of 1942 the Office of the Under Secretary of War numbered about 1,200 officers and civil-

ians. The Supply Division (G–4) of the General Staff had about 250 officers and civilians.

The OUSW consisted of a Resources Branch, a Procurement Branch, a Statistics Division, and an Administrative Branch. The Resources Branch was concerned with raw materials, machine tools, manpower, and labor matters. The Procurement Branch handled contract and legal questions, insurance, and production expediting. The Administrative Branch supervised tax amortization and accounting and finance services for contractors as well as general management services for the Office of the Under Secretary. The separate Statistics Division prepared monthly reports on procurement progress.

G–4, WDGS, had six branches—Planning, Supply, Construction, Transportation, Fiscal, and Development. The Planning Branch was generally concerned with planning the supply aspects of prospective military operations. The Supply Branch was responsible for estimating requirements and for distributing supplies and equipment. The Construction Branch handled construction requirements and supervised the purchase of real estate. The Transportation Branch exercised general supervision over transportation activities and for all practical purposes directed the operation of ports of embarkation. The Fiscal Branch was the General Staff agency for putting together the War Department budget. The Development Branch supervised the research programs of the supply arms and services.

In the Initial Directive for the Organization of the Services of Supply, General Somervell created two positions in his own office entitled Chief of Procurement and Distribution, and Deputy Chief of Staff for Requirements and Resources.[1] (*See Charts 2, 3, 4.*) Presumably the two posts were separate and neither subordinate to the other. The Deputy Chief of Staff was supposed to represent the commanding general on all matters involving the development of the Army Supply Program, the assignment of lend-lease military supplies, and raw material problems including relations with the War Production Board. The Director of Procurement and Distribution was responsible for questions involving the procurement and distribution of supplies. As might be expected, the line of demarcation between the two was by no means clear. The first position was filled by General Clay, formerly in G–4, while the second post was held by Col. Charles D. Young, who had been in the Under Secretary's office. This arrangement broadened Clay's concern with Army requirements to include raw material requirements, and enlarged Young's duties to include the distribution of supplies after they were procured. The initial directive also created the following "functional staff" divisions: Requirements, Resources, Procurement, Distribution, Defense Aid (lend-lease), Operations, Personnel, Training, and Budget and Financial Administration.

The Requirements Division directed the preparation of the Army Supply Program. It combined parts of three branches of G–4 and a part of the Procurement Branch of the OUSW. The Resources Division was a branch taken entirely from OUSW. The Procurement Division was made up of elements from both G–4 and OUSW; the same was true of the Distribution Division. The Defense Aid Division brought together personnel in a unit under the former Deputy Chief of the War Department General Staff, G–4, and OUSW. The Operations Division came entirely from G–4. The Personnel Division was composed mainly of officers from G–1 Division of the WDGS. The Training Division had to be built from scratch mainly with G–3 and technical service personnel. Finally, the Budget and Financial Administration Division combined units of both G–4 and OUSW. Thus the new functional staff of the ASF endeavored to draw together parts, especially of G–4 and OUSW, having common interests.[2]

This initial arrangement was purely experimental. For example, on 17 March, just eight days after the ASF was organized, the procurement and distribution units were combined into a single Procurement and Distribution Division with the former Chief of Procurement and Distribution as director, a post no longer on a par with the Deputy Chief of Staff for Requirements and Resources in the commanding general's office.[3] After one further abortive attempt to set up a Deputy Chief of Staff for Procurement and Distribution,[4] the status of procurement and distribution as a staff division

---

[1] Ltr, CG SOS to Chiefs of all SAS, etc., 9 Mar 42, sub: Initial Dir for the Org of SOS, Ret files ASF, DRB AGO.

[2] For the origins of each staff division, see ltr, cited in n. 1.

[3] SOS GO 2, 17 Mar 42.

[4] SOS GO 4, 9 Apr 42.

CHART 2—ORGANIZATION OF THE SERVICES OF SUPPLY: 20 FEBRUARY 1942

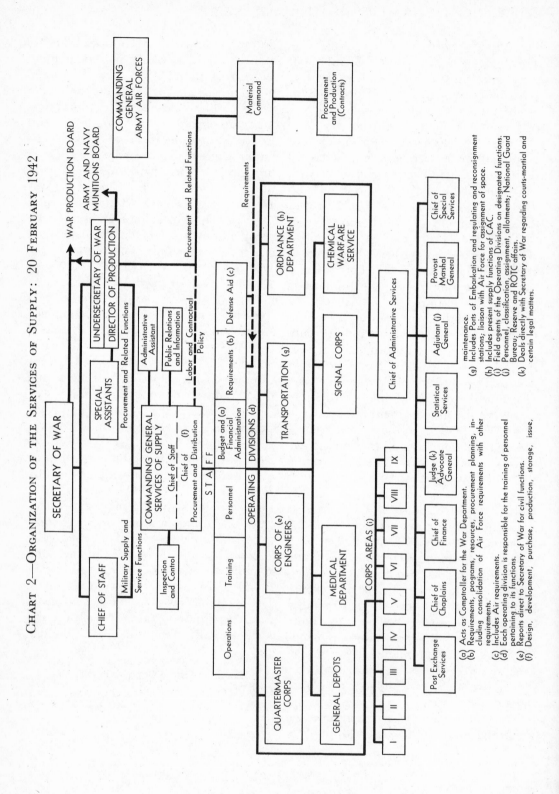

(a) Acts as Comptroller for the War Department.
(b) Requirements, programs, resources, procurement planning, including consolidation of Air Force requirements with other requirements.
(c) Includes Air requirements.
(d) Each operating division is responsible for the training of personnel pertaining to its functions.
(e) Reports direct to Secretary of War for civil functions.
(f) Design, development, purchase, production, storage, issue, maintenance.
(g) Includes Ports of Embarkation and regulating and reconsignment stations; liaison with Air Force for assignment of space.
(h) Includes present supply functions of CAC.
(i) Field agents of the Operating Divisions on designated functions.
(j) Personnel, classification, assignment, allotments; National Guard Bureau; Reserve and ROTC affairs.
(k) Deals directly with Secretary of War regarding courts-martial and certain legal matters.

CHART 3—ORGANIZATION OF THE SERVICES OF SUPPLY: 16 FEBRUARY 1943

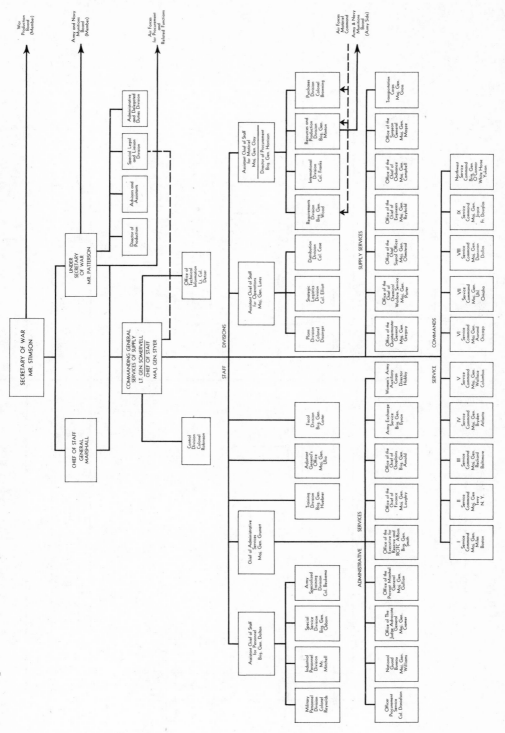

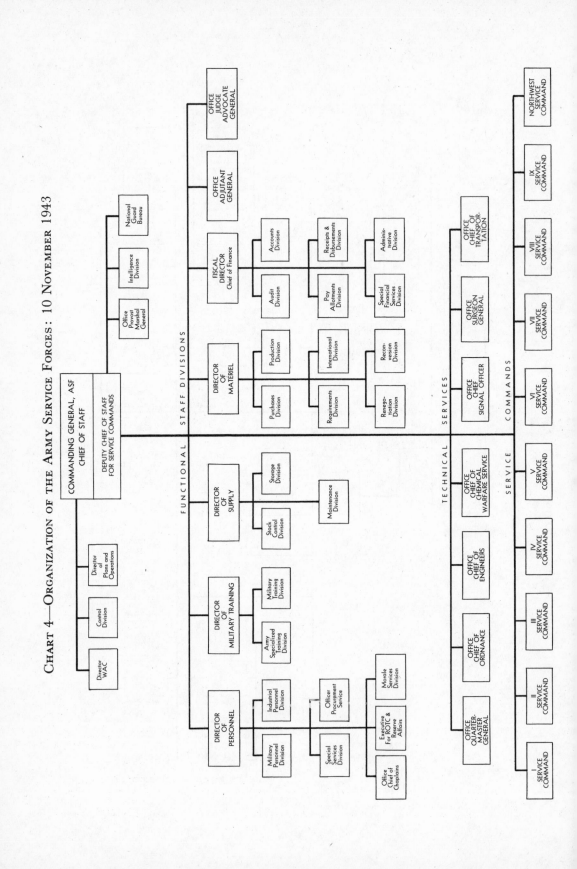

CHART 4—ORGANIZATION OF THE ARMY SERVICE FORCES: 10 NOVEMBER 1943

was confirmed.[5] The details of various subsequent staff organization changes are not as important here as an understanding of the basic organization problem in ASF headquarters pertaining to procurement and supply matters.

It must be remembered that ASF headquarters developed no new or improved weapons, let no contracts, operated no manufacturing plants, inspected no completed military articles, stored no supplies, and issued or shipped no military equipment. All these activities were performed by the technical services. ASF headquarters was a mechanism solely for insuring that all this work was performed according to plan. The organizational problem facing ASF headquarters was to determine what phases of military procurement and supply required central direction, emphasis, and follow-up. In other words, what interests shared in common by the technical services needed staff supervision?

Necessarily, changing circumstances produced new needs. For the duration of the war, however, ASF headquarters recognized certain definite functions common to all the technical services which demanded some degree of central direction. The first of these was research and development of new or improved weapons. Initially, this was a relatively small interest for ASF headquarters taken over from a unit in G–4 and combined with the supervision of procurement and distribution. Later supervision of development activities was lodged with the requirements division. It was not until May 1944 that a separate staff division for research and development was set up in ASF headquarters.[6] Thereafter, partly because of pressure from the War Department staff, ASF headquarters gave increasing attention to promoting research activity in the

technical services. But generally, the ASF staff role on development matters was a modest one.

The central control of purchasing policies and procedures was an important function of the ASF staff. As early as 17 March 1942 a Purchases Branch was established within the Procurement and Distribution Division.[7] Later, in July 1942, a separate Purchase Division was set up.[8] It was an extremely active staff office, developing and promulgating the procurement regulations which set forth standard purchasing policies to be observed by the technical services. It also watched over the prices paid for military equipment. Two parts of the Purchases Division's work became so important that new staff divisions were created to handle them. One of these was the supervision of the renegotiation of contracts where originally determined prices proved to be unduly high. A renegotiation division came into being in August 1943.[9] By November 1943 the work in preparing and supervising policies on the settlement of terminated contracts had become so important that a Reconversion Division was set up.[10] The designation was changed to Readjustment Division the same month.[11]

The control of procedures for calculating technical service needs for raw materials such as steel and copper, the presentation of these needs to the War Production Board, the allotment of raw materials supplies among Army procurement programs, and the conservation of materials had all been vital problems be-

---

[5] SOS GO 6, 15 Apr 42.
[6] ASF Cir 732, 9 May 44.
[7] SOS GO 2, 17 Mar 42.
[8] SOS GO 24, 20 Jul 42.
[9] ASF Adm Memo S–45, 16 Aug 43.
[10] ASF Cir 118, 12 Nov 43.
[11] ASF Adm Memo S–102, 29 Nov 43.

fore the ASF was created and were recognized as a major staff responsibility from the very beginning of the ASF. The Resources Division in charge of this work was taken over intact from the Office of the Under Secretary, as mentioned earlier. But as part of its work in determining new plant facility needs and in expediting production schedules, the Production and Distribution Division was also interested in the availability of raw materials. A separate Production Division was created in the ASF staff in July 1942 at the time that the Purchases Division was set up. Then in December, the Resources Division and the Production Division were combined into a single Resources and Production Division.[12] Eventually it was called just the Production Division.[13] Thus, production supervision became a major staff function.

Before examining the staff evolution of distribution activities, one peculiar function must be mentioned. The Defense Aid Division (renamed the International Division in April 1942) handled military lend-lease, a task which required special consideration throughout the war. In the beginning General Somervell was much concerned that lend-lease demands be fully included in the Army Supply Program and carefully adjusted to American Army needs as well as to production feasibility. Later, military lend-lease involved primarily the assignment of American Army supplies to other nations in accordance with broad strategic directives. It was such an important supply activity that it was directed by a separate staff agency throughout the war. Once supplies were assigned, someone had to follow the matter closely to make sure that they were actually shipped. From 1943 on, supplies to be used in the military government of conquered territories became an ASF problem handled by its International Division.

All of the staff functions just mentioned—the supervision of research and development, of purchasing policy, of renegotiation of contracts, of the termination and settlement of contracts, of raw material distribution and production expediting, and of lend-lease—were brought together under single direction within ASF headquarters. It took time to develop the concept of a number of staff divisions in ASF headquarters under a single director. But this idea was recognized by April 1942 when the Deputy Chief of Staff for Requirements and Resources was designated to direct three staff divisions: requirements, resources, and international.[14] The title of Assistant Chief of Staff for Matériel was introduced in July 1942,[15] and in turn gave way to the designation Director of Matériel in May 1943.[16]

The staff assignment for supervising procurement requirements had an interesting evolution. Before 9 March 1942, War Department instructions to the supply arms and services on procurement requirements originated in G–4. But all production aspects of the program, including control of raw materials, were supervised by the Under Secretary. It was the vital interrelationship of procurement programming and raw materials distribution which General Somervell sought to recognize when the position of Deputy Chief of Staff for Requirements and Resources was created in ASF headquarters.

---

[12] SOS Cir 96, 29 Dec 42.
[13] ASF Cir 32, 18 May 43.
[14] SOS GO 4, 9 Apr 42.
[15] SOS GO 24, 20 Jul 42.
[16] ASF Cir 30, 15 May 43.

As already mentioned, this post was at first assigned to General Clay, who remained in charge until June 1944.

This juxtaposition of procurement planning and production control was probably justified in 1942 when all equipment needs were in short supply and production limitations largely determined the supply program. In time these conditions changed. More and more procurement needs came to be calculated as a part of strategic and logistical planning. Moreover, when procurement requirements were too closely tied to production expediting, there was a marked tendency to overproduce some items and to permit shortages to arise in others. General Somervell eventually concluded that it was a mistake to assign staff supervision over procurement planning to the same person who had responsibility for production performance.

In 1942 control over the distribution of supplies, a former G–4 activity, had been joined in the staff with direction of production. This was the organizational answer to moving supplies from production lines to troops. But in constructing the original headquarters organization General Somervell also provided for an Operations Division. This division was to plan overseas troop and supply movements. Gen. LeRoy Lutes, who was placed in charge, had earlier while in G–4 developed the procedure for the supply of overseas theaters of operations, a procedure which endured with slight modification throughout World War II. Moreover, he was already emerging as the key figure in supply planning—not just within the ASF but within the entire War Department. General Lutes was not satisfied with the existing staff arrangements for supervising the distribution of supplies, since the

authority to issue orders to technical services on the actual movement of supplies was indispensable for the successful execution of his planning. As early as April 1942 an effort was made to define the respective responsibilities of the Procurement and Distribution Division and the Operations Division.[17] Among other duties, it was agreed, the Operations Division would henceforth issue orders to the technical services on the supply needs of overseas theaters and of troops on their way overseas. It would also plan the general system of supply distribution both overseas and within the zone of interior. The Distribution Branch within the Procurement and Distribution Division would supervise the actual physical storage of supplies within depots in the United States. This demarkation did not prove satisfactory and was scrapped entirely in July. The Procurement and Distribution Division as an experiment in staff organization thus lasted only four months, from March to July 1942.

A new staff organization was set up under General Lutes as Assistant Chief of Staff for Operations.[18] The Operations Division was now called the Plans Division, and the Distribution Branch became the Distribution Division under General Lutes. A strategic logistics unit was added in August for long-range overseas supply planning.[19]

Then in April 1943, following a study by General Somervell's control office, Lutes undertook a complete reorganization of his responsibilities.[20] A new ASF order called for five divisions under the

[17] SOS Cir 7, 25 Apr 42.
[18] SOS GO 24, 20 Jul 42.
[19] SOS Cir 53, 28 Aug 42.
[20] CD Rpt 92, Organization of the Office of Assistant Chief of Staff for Operations, Feb 43, CD, ASF.

Assistant Chief of Staff.[21] A Planning Division combined long-range strategic supply planning with the handling of immediate overseas supply needs. It was the connecting link between ASF headquarters and overseas theaters of operations. A Distribution Division supervised the machinery for maintaining inventory control records of all supplies and watched over general developments in the system for distributing supplies. For instance, it policed the new stock control system set up for military posts within the United States.[22] A Storage Division, under a reserve officer who was an experienced warehouseman, directed improvements in the physical handling of supplies, such as the introduction of fork lift machinery, and kept careful records of the utilization of storage space. A Mobilization Division, besides having responsibility for directing the movement of ASF troop units, also exercised important coordinating functions in the supply and transportation phases of the movement of other Army units. This division was also responsible for the organization of ASF troop units. Finally, a Maintenance Division checked upon the repair of troop equipment and its return to using units or to stock for re-issue. This new organization under the Assistant Chief of Staff for Operations recognized major supply functions of common concern along functional lines.

In the autumn of 1943 the Distribution Division (renamed Stock Control), the Storage Division, and the Maintenance Division, were grouped together under a Director of Supply, Maj. Gen. F. A. Heileman who had served as General Lutes' assistant since July 1942.[23] At the same time General Lutes was designated Director of Plans and Operations and along with his Planning Division and Mobilization Division was brought into the immediate office of the commanding general. This organizational change was intended to impress upon General Clay as director of matériel that Lutes would plan both the procurement and the distribution of supplies. But Clay was disposed to go his own way and Lutes was not inclined to raise a jurisdictional issue. Actually, the previous organization of ASF headquarters largely prevailed. General Heileman, while called Director of Supply, was still General Lutes' assistant. And Lutes went right on directing the overseas supply operations of the ASF with such assistance from General Clay's procurement activities as he could obtain.

A substantial organizational change was introduced in July 1944. By the spring of 1944 it had become apparent that procurement planning had moved into a new phase, making it possible to compare actual supply consumption with supply forecasts, and gear production demands to issue experience and stocks on hand. The answer was the evolution of the Army Supply Program into the Army Supply Control System, established in May 1944. In June the Requirements Division under General Clay and the stock control activities under General Heileman were merged into a single Requirements and Stock Control Division under General Lutes.[24] The former head of the Requirements Division became General Lutes' principal assistant in overseas supply planning. Procurement planning and supply distribution were joined in one staff division under an officer also responsible for logistical planning.

---

[21] ASF Cir 18, 13 Apr 43.

[22] WD TM 38–220, Stock Control at Posts, Camps, and Stations, 3 May 43.

[23] ASF Cir 118, 12 Nov 43.

[24] ASF Cir 175, 10 Jun 44.

Mention of some of the major problems facing the ASF staff on logistical planning will help illustrate why it was necessary to have a staff supervising the supply activities of the technical services. Some instances of ammunition shortages in Europe in 1944 were traced primarily to two factors. One was the failure to identify fully ammunition by calibers when it was shipped overseas in quantities by the Ordnance Department and the Transportation Corps. The other was the inadequate estimates of needs by overseas theaters. Moreover, the Ordnance Department felt that ammunition was being wasted, and in consequence had no strong incentive to raise production levels. This led General Lutes' office to put pressure on the production officials to increase output, on overseas theaters to increase their requisitions, and on the shipping personnel to manifest cargo more fully. Furthermore, it recognized that while the Transportation Corps was the shipping agent for all overseas supply, some central point had to provide instructions about the quantities of various supplies to be shipped to each theater. The development of a standard procedure for preparing troops for overseas movement (called POM) was of immense importance in determining the types of supplies needed, and in establishing definite supply schedules to maintain troops at overseas destinations. These are but a few examples of supply planning, which, all in all, attained a high level of performance during World War II.

The ASF staff structure in effect at the end of the war gave the Army Service Forces the best solution it could find to the problem of merging procurement planning and supply distribution. Organizationally, a Director of Plans and Operations, nominally a part of the commanding general's immediate office, was responsible for procurement planning and overseas supply planning; the essential feature of such planning was the supply control system. This office also supervised the determination of needs for service troop units overseas. It directed all troop movements. The staff activities concerned with depot operations, stock control procedures, and maintenance work were brought together under a Director of Supply. Research and development, purchasing policy (including renegotiation of contracts and the settlement of terminated contracts), production expediting including the distribution of raw materials, and lend-lease distribution, were organized under a Director of Matériel.

Yet it was General Somervell who personally effected such co-ordination of procurement and supply activities as was accomplished. His staff divisions were simply the institutional arrangements which made possible a personal direction of all phases of military supply.

The Administrative Services

The ASF as set up on 9 March included eight miscellaneous administrative "bureaus" of the War Department. These were the Offices of The Adjutant General, the Judge Advocate General, the Chief of Finance, the Chief of Chaplains, the National Guard Bureau, the Executive for Reserve and ROTC Affairs, the Provost Marshal General, and the Chief of Special Services. Each of these offices had functioned under the Chief of Staff, in actual practice dealing with various divisions of the War Department General Staff. Each performed miscellaneous duties, most of which were but slightly related. Most of the "bureaus" were of long standing, except the Special Services which had been set up during 1941 to direct certain morale, recreational, and welfare functions for soldiers.

When the ASF was created, General Somervell and his immediate advisers were uncertain how to handle these bureaus. At first they were labeled "administrative services" and were regarded as a third operating element, alongside the technical services and the service commands. Certain adjustments were made in their organization. The National Guard Bureau and the Executive for Reserve and ROTC Affairs were directed to report to The Adjutant General. By this time both agencies were mainly concerned with personnel records, since the National Guard had been federalized and most of the Reserve officers and men had been called to active duty. The Special Services as it had functioned before 9 March was split into two parts. One, still called Special Services, handled recreational and morale activities, while the other, renamed the Post Exchange Service, supervised the operation of Army post exchanges. Brig. Gen. Frederick H. Osborn, who had been commissioned from civilian life to direct these activities, was temporarily designated as chief of both services. Within a short time General Somervell obtained another officer from civilian life, Col. Joseph W. Byron, to direct the affairs of the Army Exchange Service. Finally, the Statistical Division of the OUSW was taken over and redesignated the Statistical Service. It remained under the direction of Brig. Gen. Leonard P. Ayres, who had been recalled to duty to make statistical studies similar to those on World War I— studies that had won widespread recognition. Of the eight administrative bureaus inherited on 9 March, the ASF merged

three into one, divided another into two parts, and added a new one. The end result was still eight administrative services.

Without endeavoring to follow the organizational vicissitudes of these administrative services in all their details, three important phases of subsequent developments may be noted. First, the concept of administrative services as operating units of the Army Service Forces was abandoned in favor of making these services integral parts of the ASF headquarters staff. Second, the idea of a Chief of Administrative Services to supervise the diverse activities of these various agencies proved impractical. Third, a number of subsequent adjustments were made in the composition of these agencies. None of these changes came suddenly. They evolved over the entire period of World War II.

In taking over this heterogeneous group of agencies, General Somervell was at first intent on imposing as little direct or personal burden of supervision upon himself as possible. Accordingly, the initial directive on ASF organization specified that there should be a "division, in charge of a Chief of Administrative Services . . ." to direct, supervise, and co-ordinate the functions and activities of the eight specified agencies. This seemed to suggest the creation of an "administrative service" within the ASF under a chief who was an operating, not a staff, officer. Actually, the language never had any real meaning. From the outset the Chief of Administrative Services found himself in an anomalous position. He was presumably a sort of commanding officer over a group of agencies which had almost nothing in common, which had numerous relations with many other parts of the ASF and of the War Department, and whose policy problems raised issues which General Somervell could not ignore. The first change came within a month, when a new order on general ASF organization provided that the Chief of Administrative Services was an ASF staff officer.[25] Yet he was still represented as having some sort of "line" authority over the administrative services. In July 1942, when the service command reorganization was in process, another reorganization of ASF headquarters took place. This began the process of absorbing administrative services into the ASF staff. The Office of the Chief of Special Services was moved into the personnel staff and renamed the Special Services Division. The Adjutant General became a separate staff officer for the commanding general. Although the Chief of Administrative Services remained, he had lost some of his responsibilities.[26]

By May 1943 it was apparent to General Somervell and his organization advisers that the concept of "administrative services" lacked reality. Most of these field activities had been transferred to the service commands in August 1942 and subsequently. Certainly the administrative services were not operating elements of the ASF in the same sense as the technical services or service commands. So the term "administrative service" was dropped and the offices were viewed as staff units of ASF headquarters. The position of Chief of Administrative Services was transformed into a Director of Administration, with certain staff offices assigned to his supervision; namely, The Adjutant General, the Judge Advocate General, the Army Exchange Service, the Provost Marshal General, the National Guard Bureau, and the Executive for Reserve and ROTC Affairs.[27]

The position of Director of Administration was abolished in November 1943.[28]

It was not revived during the remainder of the war. The staff units that had reported to the Director of Administration were assigned to other staff directors, and The Adjutant General and the Judge Advocate General reported directly to the commanding general.

The organizational fate of each of the original administrative services may be noted briefly. The positions of the Judge Advocate General, the Provost Marshal General, and the Chief of Chaplains were not substantially altered throughout the war. Their duties remained much the same, even though they functioned as staff agencies of the ASF. Other administrative services fared differently. The Statistical Service, created as a new administrative service on 9 March 1942, was abolished effective 1 July 1942.[29] Its statistical activities were divided among all staff agencies, each of which was expected to use statistical reporting and analytical techniques in its supervisory responsibilities. General oversight of all statistical reporting and of ASF performance as a whole was vested in the Control Division.

The most radical change in a long established War Department bureau was that involving the Chief of Finance. As previously noted, the ASF at the start set up a Fiscal Division as a part of its staff organization. This division combined certain budgetary and other fiscal duties previously vested in G–4 and OUSW. The Chief of Finance, on the other hand, became one of the administrative services. A demarkation line between the two offices proved difficult to draw, and so for a time

---

[25] SOS GO 4, 9 Apr 42.

[26] SOS GO 24, 20 Jul 42.

[27] ASF Cir 30, 15 May 43.

[28] ASF Cir 118, 12 Nov 43.

[29] SOS GO 14, 12 Jun 42. General Ayres retired from the Army as of 30 June 1942.

the ASF had in effect two staff offices concerned with fiscal matters.[30] The answer was an amalgamation of the two, the Chief of Finance becoming deputy fiscal director.[31] If personality factors had been different, the arrangement might have been reversed. The ASF Fiscal Director, Maj. Gen. A. H. Carter, enjoyed the complete confidence of Under Secretary Patterson; the Chief of Finance, Maj. Gen. Howard K. Loughry, a Regular Army officer, had not been especially aggressive in modernizing accounting practices to meet war circumstances.

As already noted, General Somervell divided the Office of the Chief of Special Services into two parts when the ASF was created. Later he decided this differentiation had not gone far enough. The designation "special services" then was used to refer to a combination of all recreational activities from the post exchange to athletic programs, from motion picture theaters to USO theatrical units. The original special services, or Special Services Division, became the Information and Education Division concerned exclusively with the transmission of general information to troops and the operation of education programs through the radio, newspapers and magazines, motion picture, correspondence courses, and other media.[32] The personnel and administrative requirements of the two services proved quite different in practice.

Finally, The Adjutant General's status was changed in two particulars. In addition to the central administrative services he rendered to the War Department as a whole, he also became the manager of internal housekeeping services for ASF headquarters. The other change was the loss of the National Guard Bureau and the Executive for Reserve and ROTC Affairs.

On 17 March 1942 the National Guard Association sent a resolution to the Secretary of War and to the Chief of Staff protesting that War Department Circular 59 "apparently emasculates and destroys the function and authority" of the National Guard Bureau. The association asked "that the Bureau be lifted from its obscure position in the Office of The Adjutant General of the Army to the status of an operating division of the Services of Supply." [33] When appearing before the House Committee on Appropriations on 21 March 1942 General Somervell was questioned on the National Guard Bureau. He bluntly stated: "No other branch of the Army feels that it has the authority to go out on its own to seek to nullify the decisions of the Chief of Staff and the Secretary of War." [34] Mr. Starnes of the committee expressed the opinion: "I think you should give consideration to the Committee's feelings and those of the National Guard Bureau." To this General Somervell replied, "The committee can be assured that we will give full consideration to anyone's feeling." [35]

General Somervell's reluctance to pledge an adjustment in the status of the National Guard Bureau is easily explained. He feared that pressure brought to bear on behalf of the National Guard Bureau might be an entering wedge for many other pressures intended to break down the War Department reorganization

---

[30] CD Rpt 46, Organization of Financial Activities, Oct 42; CD Rpt 59, Survey of the Office, Chief of Finance, Oct 42. Both in CD, ASF.

[31] WD Memo 35–10–43, 15 May 43.

[32] ASF Cir 118, 12 Nov 43.

[33] *Hearings before the Subcommittee of the Committee on Appropriations*, H.R., 77th Cong, 2d Sess, on Sixth Supplemental National Defense Appropriations Bill for 1942, Mar 42, Pt. 2, pp. 180–81.

[34] *Ibid.*, p. 35.

[35] *Ibid.*, p. 36.

of 9 March. Accordingly, he did not wish to acknowledge any justification for the criticisms voiced by the House Committee on Appropriations. By virtue of its close relations with state administrations, the National Guard Bureau was a special concern of many Congressmen. The opposition to this particular part of the 9 March reorganization came largely from officers in various states who had not been mobilized into the Army of the United States. Even though the National Guard itself was now a part of the Army, there were still many individuals who wished to maintain close relations between state military programs and the War Department. These groups looked with disfavor upon the assignment of the National Guard Bureau to The Adjutant General's office.

On 27 April 1942 General Somervell made the National Guard Bureau a separate administrative service under the Chief of Administrative Services.[36] On 27 June 1942 he made a similar change in the Office of the Executive for Reserve and ROTC Affairs.[37] Thus two new administrative services were added to the ASF. Both offices were quite small.

Other administrative services were created before the ASF decided to abandon the designation. One was the Women's Army Auxiliary Corps set up to train and assign units of women to assist the Army in its administrative work.[38] Another was the Officer Procurement Service set up in November 1942 to handle the recruitment of civilians as specialized officers in the Army.[39] Like all other administrative services, both became staff divisions of ASF headquarters after May 1943.

One other word must be added about the special duties of these administrative services. They performed two different types of work. First, they supervised the service commands in rendering various services. This was an internal ASF staff job. They also performed certain services directly for the War Department in Washington and watched over the technical performance of their specialty throughout the entire Army. For example, the Judge Advocate General was the legal adviser of the Army on all matters. The Adjutant General published and distributed official War Department orders. The Chief of Chaplains was the head of all religious activities in the Army. Such was the dual nature of the work of the ASF staff.

General Organization of the Staff

Thus far, two aspects of ASF headquarters have been noted: how G–4 and OUSW were merged and how certain administrative bureaus finally became integral parts of the ASF staff. It is time to take a quick glance at the problem of organizing the ASF staff as a whole. This problem also had two aspects: the recognition of various major duties which the ASF had to perform and the prevention of an undue proliferation of staff units. The reconciliation of these two somewhat opposing objectives was not easy.

The evolution of the office of the commanding general as a part of the staff can be briefly sketched. The ASF organizational planners envisioned the office of the commanding general as being a particular part, but not all, of the staff. It was characterized by the fact that it had a broad point of view covering the ASF as a whole, and that it was peculiarly the per-

[36] SOS GO 9, 27 Apr 42.
[37] SOS GO 16, 27 Jun 42.
[38] WD Cir 169, 1 Jun 42.
[39] WD Cir 367, 7 Nov 42.

sonal staff of General Somervell. The office consisted of General Somervell, his chief of staff, and their immediate aides, who never numbered more than five officers and three or four civilians, plus a mail unit. Originally, there was also a Deputy Chief of Staff for Requirements and Resources, but this office soon evolved into a particular segment of the ASF staff. A new Deputy Chief of Staff for Service Commands was created in May 1943.[40]

The office of the commanding general also had a number of more highly organized units. The Control Division was set up on 9 March 1942 and functioned throughout the war as an adviser on organizational, procedural, and statistical matters. An administrative office to handle ASF headquarters personnel, space, transportation, and similar matters was abolished and the work assigned to other offices, principally to The Adjutant General.[41] A Public Relations Division was abolished when the Secretary of War directed that most of its work be transferred to the War Department Bureau of Public Relations.[42] A successor Technical Information Division lasted until the end of 1943. After that General Somervell had only a single officer to assist him on public relations matters. The principal addition to the office of the commanding general was the Director of Plans and Operations in November 1943.[43] This action placed a planning unit in General Somervell's immediate office with fairly wide interests covering most ASF activities. But primarily, this office was concerned with overseas supply operations.

The tendency of the functional staff toward reproduction by fission was early revealed. On 21 March 1942 the Personnel Division was split into a Military Personnel Division and a Civilian Personnel Division.[44] A possible solution to this kind of expansion was suggested in April when the then Deputy Chief of Staff for Requirements and Resources was designated to direct three staff divisions.[45] This had the effect of combining three staff divisions into one unit, as far as the commanding general was concerned. The idea of a level of supervision intervening between the commanding general and the functional staff divisions was then given general application in July 1942. Three assistant chiefs of staff were set up, one for matériel, one for operations, and one for personnel.[46] To each of these assistant chiefs of staff two or more staff divisions were assigned. After 20 July there were sixteen staff divisions in ASF headquarters but only nine staff officers reporting directly to the commanding general.

As new activities came into being, new staff units were created. These new divisions were assigned to the jurisdiction of one of the assistant chiefs of staff. Thus, for example, when the Army Specialized Training Division was set up, it was placed under the Assistant Chief of Staff for Personnel.[47]

The label "assistant chief of staff" gave way to "director" in May 1943. At the same time, the entire functional staff was placed under six directors: Personnel, Military Training, Operations, Matériel, Fiscal, and Administration.[48] (See Chart

---

[40] ASF Cir 30, 15 May 43.
[41] SOS GO 24, 20 Jul 42. Civilian personnel matters in ASF headquarters were assigned to The Adjutant General by SOS Cir 78, 26 Oct 42.
[42] SOS Cir 54, 29 Aug 42.
[43] ASF Cir 118, 12 Nov 43.
[44] SOS GO 3, 21 Mar 42.
[45] SOS GO 4, 9 Apr 42. See above, p. 344.
[46] SOS GO 24, 20 Jul 42.
[47] SOS Cir 95, 18 Dec 42.
[48] ASF Cir 30, 15 May 43.

CHART 5—ORGANIZATION OF THE ARMY SERVICE FORCES: 20 JULY 1943

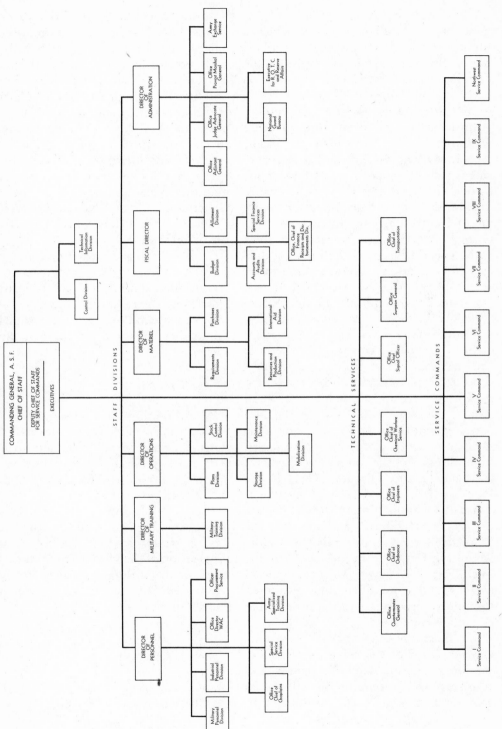

5.) This was the most symmetrical, the most "orderly" staff organization achieved during the war. It looked "good" on paper. But there is more to organization than just an attractive chart. The creation of the various "directors" worked well in some cases; in the case of the Director of Administration it did not, and the office was abolished in November 1943. The Adjutant General and the Judge Advocate General were positions with too much importance and prestige to be thus subordinated. The staff organization thereafter became more complicated, more extensive. Certain staff units—a new Intelligence Division,[49] the Provost Marshal General and the National Guard Bureau—were directed to report to the commanding general through the Deputy Chief of Staff for Service Commands. This was only a partly successful arrangement.

But the staff organization worked out in November 1943 continued with minor modifications until the end of the war.[50] New units were added, such as a Personal Affairs Division[51] and a Research and Development Division. The director of the Women's Army Corps was transferred from the office of the commanding general to the Personnel Division (G–1) of the War Department General Staff on 10 February 1944. Immediately after V-E Day, the National Guard Bureau and the Executive for Reserve and ROTC Affairs were transferred from the ASF to the WDGS.[52] The Provost Marshal General and the Intelligence Division were ordered to report directly to the commanding general in June 1945.[53]

By the end of the war ASF headquarters consisted of the office of the commanding general, five staff directors, and four staff units reporting directly to the commanding general. (*See Chart 6.*) In addition to a Chief of Staff and a Deputy Chief of Staff for Service Commands, the office of the commanding general included a Director of Plans and Operations (requirements and stock control, planning, and mobilization divisions) and a Control Division. The five staff directors were for personnel, military training, matériel, supply and fiscal matters. They had a total of twenty-two staff divisions under them. Reporting separately to the commanding general were The Adjutant General, the Judge Advocate General, the Provost Marshal General, and the Intelligence Division.

This staff organization was not very simple, it didn't look symmetrical on an organization chart. But it had the virtue of expressing the realities of administrative relationships and procedures as they had finally been worked out in ASF headquarters.

The Technical Services as Staff Divisions

Attention thus far has been directed to what the ASF called functional staff divisions. This picture is incomplete without reference to the staff responsibilities vested in the chiefs of the technical services. After the service command reorganization in August 1942 many operating functions previously exercised by the technical services were transferred to the administrative supervision of the service command. The chiefs of the technical services however, retained staff or technical supervision over these activities.

---

[49] Created by ASF Cir 36, 30 May 43, from a unit developed under the Chief of Administrative Services.

[50] ASF Cir 118, 12 Nov 43, set forth the new organization.

[51] ASF Cir 41, 7 Feb 44.

[52] WD GO 31, 17 May 45.

[53] ASF Cir 238, 25 Jun 45; ASF Cir 240, 26 Jun 45.

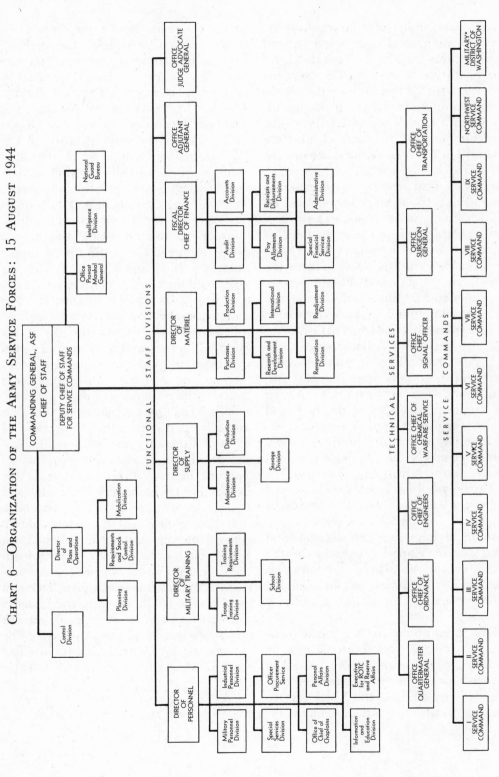

CHART 6—ORGANIZATION OF THE ARMY SERVICE FORCES: 15 AUGUST 1944

COMMANDING GENERAL, ASF
CHIEF OF STAFF

DEPUTY CHIEF OF STAFF
FOR SERVICE COMMANDS

Control Division

Director of Plans and Operations
— Planning Division
— Requirements and Stock Control Division
— Mobilization Division

Office Provost Marshal General

Intelligence Division

National Guard Bureau

FUNCTIONAL STAFF DIVISIONS

Director of Personnel
— Military Personnel Division
— Industrial Personnel Division
— Special Services Division
— Officer Procurement Service
— Office of Chief of Chaplains
— Personal Affairs Division
— Information and Education Division
— Executive for ROTC and Reserve Affairs

Director of Military Training
— Troop Training Division
— Training Requirements Division
— School Division

Director of Supply
— Maintenance Division
— Distribution Division
— Storage Division

Director of Materiel
— Purchases Division
— Production Division
— Research and Development Division
— International Division
— Renegotiation Division
— Readjustment Division

Fiscal Director Chief of Finance
— Audit Division
— Accounts Division
— Pay Allotments Division
— Receipts and Disbursements Division
— Special Financial Services Division
— Administrative Division

Office Adjutant General

Office Judge Advocate General

TECHNICAL SERVICES

Office Quartermaster General

Office Chief of Ordnance

Office Chief of Engineers

Office Chief of Chemical Warfare Service

Office Chief Signal Officer

Office Surgeon General

Office Chief of Transportation

SERVICE COMMANDS

I Service Command

II Service Command

III Service Command

IV Service Command

V Service Command

VI Service Command

VII Service Command

VIII Service Command

IX Service Command

Northwest Service Command

Military* District of Washington

*Under Army Service Forces for Administrative and Supply Functions.

An outstanding example was hospital administration. As already noted, general hospitals were transferred from the direct administrative control of The Surgeon General to that of the commanders of the service commands. This step was not intended to diminish the authority of The Surgeon General in medical matters. Rather, The Surgeon General became the staff officer of the commanding general, ASF, on medical activities at general hospitals. The responsibility for repairs and utilities functions at posts, camps, and stations was transferred from the Chief of Engineers to service commands. Thereupon the Chief of Engineers became the staff officer for repair and utility functions. The Chief Signal Officer became the staff officer on communications activity within service commands. The Chief of Ordnance supervised automotive maintenance activities. The Chief of Transportation supervised transportation activities at posts, camps, and stations. From time to time the staff responsibilities of the technical services were increased. Whenever it became apparent that an activity fell solely within the jurisdiction of a single technical service, that technical service became the staff agency insofar as service command supervision was concerned. The ASF functional staff confined its interests to programs involving more than one technical service or developed programs for the service commands where there was no technical service interest, as, for example, the induction and separation of military personnel.

This expansion of the role of the technical services as staff divisions can be illustrated by two examples involving The Quartermaster General. Mention has already been made of the Food Service Program in the ASF which brought to-gether the training of mess supervisors, cooks, and bakers; mess management; and the food conservation program. This Food Service Program was operated by each service command. The staff officer in ASF headquarters for this program was The Quartermaster General.[54] Similarly, in May 1943 the responsibility of The Quartermaster General for the procurement, storage, and distribution of fuels and lubricants was greatly increased.[55] The Planning Division in ASF headquarters screened requirements and requisitions for fuel and lubricants from theaters of operations just as it did for all supply questions. The Stock Control Division supervised the arrangements made for distributing fuels and lubricants; the Requirements Division incorporated fuel and lubricant requirements into the Army Supply Program, and the Purchases Division exercised the same supervision over the purchase of fuels and lubricants that it did over the purchase of other commodities. But The Quartermaster General was made "responsible for the performance of all staff functions necessary to the discharge of the operating responsibilities assigned herein." Prior to this time the Production Division, ASF, had included a Petroleum Section whose chief had been the representative of the commanding general on the Army-Navy Petroleum Board. He had handled most petroleum questions. While there were some petroleum activities under the jurisdiction of the Chief of Ordnance and the Chief of Transportation, most of the procurement operations were actually handled by The Quartermaster General. Thus, in effect the ASF had a situation where a staff offi-

---

[54] ASF Cir 45, 3 Jul 43.
[55] ASF Cir 33, 26 May 43.

cer in the Production Division was direct-ing work done almost exclusively by The Quartermaster General. This arrangement was recognized as faulty and so The Quartermaster General became the staff officer on all petroleum matters. He was designated as the War Department Liaison Officer for Petroleum and was ordered to assign a representative to act as deputy to the commanding general in his capacity as a member of the Army-Navy Petroleum Board. Moreover, The Quartermaster General was given staff supervision over the petroleum activities of the Chief of Ordnance and the Chief of Transportation and for all other parts of the ASF.[56] Thereafter, The Quartermaster General, through a Fuels and Lubricants Division, was the staff officer on all petroleum matters. On various matters, then, the chiefs of technical services were drawn into close personal relations with the Commanding General, ASF, and served as staff officers in their special fields.

Interstaff Relations

The creation, abolition, and amalgamation of staff divisions was not the only type of staff adjustment that took place from 1942 to 1945. On occasion a staff responsibility assigned to one unit was transferred to another. For example, in February 1943 supervision of activities pertaining to claims against the government was transferred from the Chief of Finance to the Judge Advocate General.[57] This step was taken in an effort to centralize in one office all action on claims matters. Previously the work had been divided between the Chief of Finance and the Judge Advocate General.

From time to time new activities were added to the work of the ASF staff. These were often absorbed within an existing staff division. Sometimes the activity was one which had only been partially recognized in past staff work, as, for example, when experience indicated the need for careful co-ordination of all troop movements. Accordingly, the Movements Branch in the Mobilization Division was designated the "Troop Movement Co-ordinating Center" for ASF headquarters.[58] The branch was directed to develop procedures and policies on troop movements, to issue alert orders to ASF units, to prepare orders for the movement of ASF units, and to report the status of units being moved.

Still another type of staff adjustment was required in handling specific problems. The ASF staff, as already indicated, was a functional staff. On occasion this meant that some particular subject might be of interest to several different staff divisions. Two examples will suffice. A major problem which emerged during 1943 was that of proper packing and packaging of equipment for overseas shipment.[59] In an effort to clarify responsibility for proper packaging and packing of supplies, an ASF order assigned staff supervision of packing and packaging at production points to the Director of Matériel, the staff

---

[56] It should be noted that at the same time, Somervell and The Quartermaster General agreed upon a former Engineer officer in whom Somervell had great confidence as head of the Fuels and Lubricants Division in the Office of The Quartermaster General. The commanding general had great confidence in the man heading petroleum activities in The Quartermaster General's office.

[57] SOS Cir 9, 10 Feb 43.

[58] ASF Cir 23, 28 Apr 43.

[59] The term "packaging" meant that the product itself was put in a container; this process was performed at the place of production. "Packing" was the process of preparing items for shipment; it might be performed at the production point or at a depot.

supervision over packing and packaging at depots and of organization equipment at posts to the Director of Operations, while marking-policy was the responsibility of the War Department Code Marking Committee.[60] The Director of Matériel and the Director of Operations were instructed to get together and standardize their policies on packaging. In actual practice, the Director of Matériel assumed the leadership in developing packaging and packing specifications while the Director of Operations, and later the Director of Supply, carried out these policies at depots.

A similar problem which cut across a number of functional fields was that of spare parts. The assurance of an adequate supply of spare parts became increasingly difficult after 1943 as larger quantities of matériel came into the hands of troops. Staff responsibility for developing spare parts requirements was assigned to the Requirements Division.[61] The Production Division was made responsible for supervising production policies and scheduling spare parts production. The Maintenance Division was made responsible for preparing spare parts lists, for developing policies to determine the basis of issue of these parts, and for supervising their utilization at shops. The Storage Division was responsible for the proper warehousing of spare parts, the Stock Control Division for developing appropriate records on their supply, and the Training Division for the proper training of military personnel in depots and maintenance units in the efficient handling of these items.

These are but a few examples of the constant adjustment that had to be made in staff responsibilities. Since no organization was possible which would entirely prevent overlapping responsibility among staff divisions, the Army Service Forces relied on each staff division to co-operate with other staff divisions whenever they had mutual interests. Where difficulty arose which could not be resolved amicably and directly between the staff divisions, the ASF chief of staff might make some adjustment or the Control Division might be asked to make recommendations.

A case in point was the continual difficulty in drawing a line of demarcation between the Intelligence Division and the Office of the Provost Marshal General on internal security and counterintelligence functions. War Department orders provided that the functions of the Counter Intelligence Corps (CIC) within the zone of interior would become the responsibility of the Commanding General, ASF, effective 1 January 1944.[62] The supervision of investigative functions was then vested in the Provost Marshal General.[63] At the same time, the Intelligence Division in ASF headquarters looked upon itself as the direct liaison with G–2 on all investigative matters. The Intelligence Division trained CIC personnel for overseas duty while the Provost Marshal General directed the training of personnel for investigative work in the zone of interior. There remained some duplication in the handling of investigation of suspected subversives. Partly because of personality factors, this conflict was not resolved at any time during 1944. Finally, under a circular issued in August 1945, all counterintelligence activities were transferred from the Provost Marshal General to the Director of Intelligence.[64] This circular made the

---

[60] ASF Cir 29, 13 May 43.
[61] ASF Cir 31, 15 May 43.
[62] WD Cir 324, 14 Dec 43.
[63] ASF Cir 149, 1943.
[64] ASF Cir 314, 18 Aug 45.

Provost Marshal General responsible for criminal investigations and loyalty checks of civilians employed in industrial establishments having contracts with the War Department. Otherwise, the Director of Intelligence exercised all supervision of investigative activities into military and War Department civilian personnel. The circular pointed out, however, that it was necessary for a high degree of co-operation to continue between the Intelligence Division and the Provost Marshal General's office in handling domestic disturbances.

Organizational adjustments were not always possible as a means of eliminating conflict between staff agencies. Sometimes the only possible answer to conflict was an insistence upon closer co-operation between staff officers. Thus the Director of Matériel was responsible for fixing general purchasing policy for the ASF, including control of the provisions of procurement contracts. These contracts necessarily had to conform with general federal statutes governing purchasing operations by the government, had to be enforceable in courts of law, and had to meet the special fiscal requirements surrounding government contracts. This last requirement meant that contracts had to be satisfactory to the General Accounting Office (GAO) so that the disbursements made thereunder would not subsequently be suspended or even disallowed in the GAO audit.

The ASF Fiscal Director was responsible for financial administration, including supervision of all disbursement operations. To carry out this responsibility, the Fiscal Director was designated as the liaison officer between the ASF and the GAO. The legal adviser to the Director of Matériel found that 50 percent of his time was involved in negotiating various questions with the Fiscal Law and Regulations Branch in the Office of the Fiscal Director. Yet the Fiscal Director insisted that only his officers should discuss any questions with the GAO. The legal assistant to the Director of Matériel felt that this insistence prevented him from explaining purchasing problems to the General Accounting Office and strongly expressed the belief that many rulings of the GAO might have been different if that office had been given a clearer understanding of the procurement problems confronting the War Department. The legal assistant accordingly wanted the authority to negotiate with the GAO transferred from the Fiscal Director to the Director of Matériel. The only solution to this type of conflict was closer working relationships within the staff. For example, in the instance cited, the merits of both sides should have been acknowledged. A great many of the questions arising between the Fiscal Director and the GAO dealt with details of governmental accounting or other issues not involving procurement contracts. At the same time, the special interest of the Director of Matériel in contracting arrangements should have been acknowledged by the Fiscal Director.

Enough has been said here to indicate the types of interstaff issues which arose during the war. There was a continuing need for co-ordinating the work of the staff and for settling conflicts. In short, organizational problems did not end when new organization charts were drawn and issued.

A Functional Staff

From the beginning the ASF referred to its staff as a functional staff. The customary staff designations in the Army—G–1, G–2, G–3, and G–4—were never employed. In fact, the labels Assistant Chief of Staff for Matériel, Assistant Chief of Staff for Personnel, and Assistant Chief of Staff for Operations gave way, as already indicated, to the designation of Director of Matériel, Director of Personnel, and Director of Operations. The commanding General wanted a staff on functional lines in order to avoid the old conflict between the duties of a "general" and a "special" staff. The designations were changed also to avoid confusion with the War Department General Staff and to emphasize that staff officers were expected to perform the responsibilities assigned to them and not simply to co-ordinate other staff officers. For example, any past tradition that a G–1 was a planning agency and a means of co-ordinating other staff officers was broken by designating the personnel officer in the ASF as Director of Personnel, and by placing other units directly and fully under his responsibility. Thus, the Chief of Chaplains and the Executive for Reserve and ROTC Affairs were also under the Director of Personnel.

The staff was functional in another sense. It was concerned with those major purposes which the operating units—the technical services and the service commands—shared in common. Thus in the procurement and storage field, although operating responsibilities were divided by the type of commodity purchased, the functional staff was concerned with those activities common to all procurement operations. The Director of Matériel was concerned with pricing policy regardless of the type of commodity procured. The ASF developed standard procurement contracts as a means of preventing competition between the technical services in offering attractive contract provisions to suppliers. Standard contracts also meant that any company having contracts with several different procuring agencies of the War Department could be sure that all its contracts contained the same provisions on such matters as contract termination, price readjustment, and legal liabilities.

The Storage Division well illustrated the need for a central co-ordinating staff. Each technical service operated its own warehouses and other storage facilities. Each determined its own special storage needs. The job of the Storage Division as a staff agency was to see that all followed the most modern warehousing practices, that storage facilities were located in close proximity to the places where supplies were needed, and that unnecessary facilities were not built. In fact, there were frequent shifts of storage space from one service to another to meet peak loads or other special needs. Without such a staff agency many more storage facilities would probably have been constructed by the technical services.

To perform administrative services, the ASF was set up organizationally along geographical lines, by service commands. Thus there was a need for functional staff units to insure that various activities were performed in a uniform manner by all service commands.

Admittedly the ASF functional staff was large. On 31 July 1943 it numbered 45,186 military and civilian personnel, not including the technical services.[65] On 31 August 1945 its strength had dropped to 34,138 military and civilian personnel. Of this total strength, 16,305 were located in ASF headquarters and the remainder were outside of Washington. The division

---

[65] ASF Monthly Progress Rpt, Personnel and Training, 31 Jul 43.

of this strength among the various parts of the staff was as follows: [66]

Office of the Commanding General	723
Director of Personnel	2,675
Director of Military Training	205
Director of Supply	523
Director of Matériel	913
Director of Intelligence	136
Judge Advocate General	815
Provost Marshal General	856
Fiscal Director	14,718
Adjutant General	12,574
	34,138

Of the 16,000 personnel in Washington, over 9,000 were in the Office of The Adjutant General. This included personnel operating reproduction facilities, running the mail center, maintaining central records, and providing other services for the entire War Department.

More than half of the ASF staff, it will be noted, was located outside the District of Columbia. This in itself might seem odd. The ASF at one time hoped that all the work done outside Washington would come under the direct control of either a service command or a technical service. Actually this did not prove feasible. Of the 17,500 staff personnel located outside the District of Columbia on 31 August 1945, 12,466 were in the Office of Dependency Benefits located in Newark and in four regional accounting offices, all under the Fiscal Director. When the Office of Dependency Benefits was established in Newark, it was decided that it would be preferable administratively to keep it under the control of a staff officer in Washington. The four regional accounting offices handled work which had previously been centralized in Washington.

There were other situations where field offices continued under staff control. In a sense, these were not field offices but rather branch offices located outside of Washington in order to prevent the concentration of all staff work in the Capital. Thus, the Special Services Division kept only a small group in Washington and had its main offices in New York City directing the activity of the post exchanges and the athletic and recreation program. The Information and Education Division had a publishing office in New York City as the central headquarters for *Yank* and for distributing releases to post and division newspapers throughout the Army. The correspondence school for the Army had its office in Madison, Wisconsin; the Armed Forces Radio Service had its principal offices in Los Angeles and New York. These were branch offices of the Information and Education Division. Where some large central service had to be performed for the War Department as a whole, the ASF followed the practice of having the staff division retain control over the branch offices outside Washington.

At an early date General Somervell endeavored to give his staff a clear conception of what it was expected to do. The first published organization manual in 1942 explained the desired role of staff agencies. This was elaborated somewhat more fully in the organization manual published in February 1943.[67] Section 103.03 of this manual pointed out: "The nature of staff responsibilities include: (a) *pure staff activities,* (b) *activities performed for headquarters,* (c) *supervision of certain field activities.*"

It defined "pure staff activities" as advising the commanding general in its field of responsibility; formulating plans, poli-

---

[66] ASF Monthly Progress Rpt, Personnel and Training, 31 Aug 45, Sec. 5.
[67] Services of Supply Organization Manual, 15 Feb 43.

cies, and procedures for the performance of a function throughout the ASF; advising and assisting subordinate operating units; and following-up on performance to insure that policies, plans, and procedures were carried out as specified. In essence this meant that staff work was planning and supervising. The manual emphasized the point that staff agencies did not perform a job. Rather, the staff divisions were to state the objectives and establish policies to guide performance and then to follow up in order to determine that performance met these objectives and policies.

The manual's mention of "activities performed for headquarters" referred to another type of duty necessarily performed by the staff divisions of the ASF. Actually, some offices had to render a central service for the War Department, and since the ASF was a central service these offices were lodged in it. Thus the publications work of The Adjutant General's office was in reality a large operating job. But the work was also a central service rendered for the War Department. As far as the distribution of publications in the field was concerned, The Adjutant General's was a "pure staff" agency, since the distribution depots were under the command of service commands. The central legal service rendered by the Judge Advocate General was another illustration of a central War Department service performed by an ASF staff division. The Transportation Corps also operated a central transportation service for ASF personnel and one for War Department personnel stationed in Washington as well. The Military Personnel Division of ASF handled the personnel problems of ASF headquarters. In short, several ASF staff divisions and technical services provided a

central service, either for the War Department or for ASF headquarters, which was functionally related to the staff responsibility of that agency. As has already been explained staff divisions also exercised direct control over a number of field agencies.

The most important single aspect of the staff concept of the ASF was simply this: staff agencies planned and supervised. For example, the Readjustment Division outlined the major policies and procedures to be followed in settling terminated contracts, but the actual conduct of the negotiations to reach an agreement with a contractor remained in the hands of the technical services. The Readjustment Division then kept records to determine how well each technical service was performing its responsibility and checked up from time to time to make sure that the work was going satisfactorily and that obstacles were being overcome. This same arrangement was true in every functional field.

There were occasions when staff divisions tried to argue that they could only advise and suggest, that they could not be held responsible for results. General Somervell refused to accept this point of view. A staff division was expected to insure that results were obtained by the operational agencies of the ASF. Staff officers and chiefs of the technical services or commanding generals of service commands were held equally responsible for getting the job of the ASF done.

Finally, one other aspect of the ASF staff should be noted. Even after the originally designated administrative services had been absorbed into the ASF staff, for reasons of convenience they were still often referred to as administrative services. This was primarily true of those parts of the ASF staff whose head was also the chief of a branch of a service in the Army. The Adjutant General was head of The Adjutant General's Department, the Judge Advocate General the head of the Judge Advocate General's Department, the Chief of Chaplains head of the Corps of Chaplains, the Chief of Finance head of the Finance Department, and the Provost Marshal General was head of the Corps of Military Police. Each of these were branches of the military service with personnel assigned to various commands of the Army throughout the world. For this reason it was convenient to continue to refer to their offices as administrative services, since their heads were responsible for the development of technical standards and procedures to be observed in the Army as a whole.

This, then, was the ASF staff, a large organization required to insure that appropriate service was given the Army. The supply problem itself was indivisible. Units in the United States and overseas commands were not considered properly supplied unless they had all of their ordnance equipment, their quartermaster equipment, their signal equipment, and their medical supplies. It took a great amount of work to insure balance in procurement programs, to maintain satisfactory distribution procedures in all technical services, and to keep the right types of supplies flowing out of ports of embarkation to overseas commands. Administration of a military post was geographically indivisible, but again it took a great amount of work to insure that posts inducted military personnel, ran their hospitals, stored and issued supplies, provided recreational facilities, and performed all their housekeeping duties proficiently. The ASF staff was always busy.

CHAPTER XXIII

The Management of the Army Service Forces

In a headquarters as large as that of the ASF, top direction was necessarily a collective enterprise. Yet General Somervell was able to impress the force of his own personality upon his staff and throughout the command to a remarkable degree. To be sure, there was no uniform response to that personality. There were individuals who were resentful of or even hostile to General Somervell's leadership. Yet most of his staff were intensely loyal to him, and faithful communicants of his purposes. In between these two groups were the great bulk of ASF personnel who in various ways received some indication of the drive of Somervell's personality and were, perhaps unknowingly, affected by it.

General Somervell's basic beliefs about management were summarized in an article published in 1944:

Successful management depends on five factors. The first factor is a precise understanding of the job to be done. The second is qualified and capable men in key positions. The third is a workable organization properly adapted to the job to be done. The fourth is a simple, direct system for carrying on the activities involved in the job. The fifth is a positive method of checking on results. Given any three of these five, a business or an agency can probably function with fair success. Four of them operating together will result in much better than average efficiency. However, it requires all five to create the best management obtainable.[1]

General Somervell ended his brief statement on a characteristic note. While acknowledging that in two years the ASF had much to show for its efforts, he concluded: "We are not satisfied. If the day ever comes when we are satisfied, we shall know that we have started to fail."[2]

The foundation stone of management, Somervell constantly emphasized, was planning. General Somervell was above all else a man of action. He wanted things done now. But he was no advocate of a hand-to-mouth administrative existence. He insisted that action be purposeful, in other words, that action be planned to accomplish desired objectives. This probably stemmed from his engineering training and experience. But his concern about planning was more than an accident of background; it was a profound administrative conviction. Somervell's interest was that of an "operational" planner, rather than that of one concerned with broad questions of policy. He was happy indeed to take basic direction from Under Secretary Patterson on such matters as price policy and the utilization of small plants

---

[1] Gen Brehon Somervell, "Management," *Public Administration Review*, IV (autumn 1944), 257. This and other articles in a symposium about the ASF were reprinted as a separate booklet entitled *Administrative Management in the Army Service Forces* (Chicago, Public Administration Service, 1944).

[2] Somervell, "Management," p. 259, cited in n. 1.

in war production. On the other hand, as already noted, when the Operations Division of the War Department General Staff seemed to lag somewhat in providing strategic guideposts to the ASF, Somervell was by no means averse to providing the missing direction for himself.

When Somervell became G–4 in 1941, he immediately encountered criticism by the Office of Production Management that the War Department was not doing a satisfactory job in determining its long-run supply needs. He acknowledged the inadequacies of the then so-called equipment expenditure programs which were no more than broad statements of budgetary needs. To remedy this situation, he wanted a program which would show supply needs in detail based upon the contemplated mobilization of men, overseas operations, and lend-lease requirements, and he wanted these needs projected ahead for about two years. This insistence helped to produce the Army Supply Program which first appeared in April 1942 and which was periodically revised thereafter.[3]

Supply planning for overseas operations was of a high order throughout World War II. This was not only the most important single interest of General Somervell but also undoubtedly the major contribution of the Army Service Forces to the conduct of the war. Perhaps the most thorough planning effort of the ASF was the preparation for redeployment after the defeat of Germany, and for demobilization after the defeat of Japan. The War Department officially began to think about redeployment and demobilization in May 1943, when General Somervell was instructed by the Chief of Staff to set up a small unit to start preliminary planning for redeployment. When this unit was moved to the War Department Special Staff in July 1943 as the Special Planning Division, General Somervell assigned ASF responsibility in this field to the Director of Plans and Operations.[4] This arrangement was formalized in April 1944 by the creation of the position of Deputy Director for Demobilization.[5] From this time on, redeployment planning received major attention throughout the Army Service Forces. A special report was devised on a monthly basis to indicate the kinds of demobilization plans being prepared, the staff agencies primarily responsible for preparation of these plans, and the status in the preparation of a fully approved plan for each activity.

Demobilization planning was undoubtedly helped by the fact that while the war continued, various adjustments were made in Army activities. Procurement programs, for example, had to be changed during the war; this brought experience in the termination and settlement of contracts long before V-E Day. Thus during the single year ending 30 June 1944, the technical services terminated 20,052 contracts, even though the total volume of procurement activity was greater than in the preceding fiscal year.[6] The decline in the number of troops in training in the United States during early 1944 made it necessary to put twenty-eight posts and camps on an inactive status and to prepare for further curtailment in the months thereafter.[7] The extent of active ASF planning for redeployment and demobilization was indicated in the ASF annual report

[3] There is a history of the Army Supply Program in the historical files of the ASF. For a summary of the program's purposes and primary features see Maj. Gen. Lucius D. Clay, "The Army Supply Program," *Fortune*, February 1943.

[4] Ltr, TAG to CG ASF, by order of SW, 22 Jul 43.

[5] ASF Cir 106, 18 Apr 44.

[6] Annual Rpt of ASF, 1944, pp. 108, 336.

[7] *Ibid.*, p. 348.

for the fiscal year 1944. It ranged from the preparation of modernized separation procedures, to a program for modernization of industrial plants to be used after the war; from transportation schedules to move three million men to the Pacific, to a point scheme for determining eligibility for individual release from the Army; from a large-scale program for general and vocational education for soldiers in Europe awaiting transportation home, to proposals for postwar organization of the Army.

In June 1945 General Somervell remarked:

It has been the greatest satisfaction to me, and I know it has been to all of you who have had to do with these things, to see how smoothly these redeployment plans have worked. In the first place, in checking the movement of men and supplies to Europe, diverting them to the Pacific where we could, or bringing them back, checking the flow of requisitions which are no longer needed, we have an accomplishment which went by throughout the country, and to a large extent throughout the Army, practically unnoticed—and if there could be any higher praise for an operation than that, I do not know what it could be.[8]

Urgency

Closely allied to his faith in advanced planning of operations was General Somervell's abiding sense of urgency. Much as he disliked improvisation, even more was he intolerant of hesitancy and complacency. Wartime, of course, was a period of crisis. A nation which began its military mobilization late and had immense obligations to fulfill could not afford the luxury of leisure. General Somervell's natural temperament was admirably attuned to the needs of the time. Early in the war Somervell gave his whole command a

slogan: "In an emergency any intelligent quick action is better than a delay in search of the ideal." These words were printed on a card and widely distributed. They were often invoked as an exhortation to desirable behavior. On one occasion, Somervell told a meeting it seemed to him that too many Army officers were still living in a "muzzle-loading era" and failed to realize that modern warfare was a "fast-moving job."

Somervell's constant onslaught against red tape was prompted by his own sense of urgency. His definition of red tape was not a narrow one of administrative procedures; as he expressed it:

Red tape generally is defined as customs, rules and procedures that cause unnecessary delay and its use is considered to be a prerogative of government. But red tape is everywhere—it is a state of mind as well as a method of procedure. Red tape is the act of postponing decisions, taking your time, playing safe, following routine, stifling initiative, quitting when the whistle blows, business as usual, politics, picnics, and golf as usual.[9]

At a conference of service commanders in Chicago in July 1943, General Somervell emphasized his criticism of red tape by reading a letter which became famous in the War Department.

Above all, we must maintain a sense of balance, of proportion, and I may add, of humor. We can't afford the luxury of red tape and channeling that makes issues like that of the medical supply officer who had trouble with his ants. Whether they are outside under Engineer control or inside ants under Quartermaster control for orderly issue of the same ant-killing carbon disulphide is not the point. Ants inside, outside or

---

[8] Min, Sv Comd Conf, ASF, 28–30 Jun 45, Camp Grant, Ill. (mimeographed), p. 2.

[9] Gen Brehon Somervell, "Red Tape Must Go," *American Magazine* (December 1942), p. 30.

commuting, are still ants and they need exterminating. Some of you undoubtedly are familiar with this story but for the benefit of those who aren't, I will read you this communication as it was actually written:

1st Wrapper Ind.

Medical Inspector's Office, Sta. Hosp., Robins Field, Warner Robins, Ga., June 12, 1943.

To: Medical Supply Officer, Sta. Hosp., Robins Field, Warner Robins, Ga.

1. Following telephone information from your office that you were unable to issue carbon disulphide for use in this office in ant control, and following receipt of your letter listing insect repellents furnished by your office, request was made of Quartermaster for carbon disulphide for use by this office in ant control. We were informed by Quartermaster that they could issue such preparation if the ant to be exterminated was in the building. If it was outside of the building, the issue of such preparation properly should come from Engineering. It is difficult to determine the intentions of the ants we are attempting to exterminate—some live inside and wander outside for food, while some live outside and forage inside for food. It is a rather difficult problem to determine which ant comes from without and is what might be called an Engineering ant, and which ant comes from within and is what would be a Quartermaster ant. Some of our ants appear to be going in circles and others are apparently wandering at random with no thought of destination—such ant tactics are very confusing and could result in a Quartermaster ant being exterminated by an Engineering poison or an Engineering ant being exterminated by a Quartermaster poison which would be contrary to the letter of regulations and would probably lead to extensive investigation and lengthy letters of explanation.

2. In view of the fact that Quartermaster issued poison has been found to kill an ant just as dead as an Engineering issued poison—and vice versa, request is made that your office draw identical poisons for issue to this office from both Engineering and Quartermaster and to mix same so that there will be no way of knowing which poison killed the ant—the assumption being that no well-bred G. I. ant would eat other than poison issued through proper channels to final destination, which destination being aforementioned dead or dying ant.[10]

General Somervell's invariable prescription for cutting red tape was common sense. He told commanding generals of service commands at the very first meeting in 1942: "Use common sense. In other words, I am just not going to have the issue of necessary supplies and equipment delayed because some fellow somewhere has not signed some piece of paper. We must get these supplies in the hands of the troops when they are wanted, and you must see that that is done."[11] Somervell liked to express a sense of urgency by setting deadlines. If a job was important enough to start, it was important enough to finish on some kind of schedule. In a memorandum to General Clay in August 1942, Somervell cautioned that additional personnel, even of high quality, would not solve the production problems which constituted "the present major effort" of the Army Service Forces. He urged General Clay to do two things: (1) to review assignments of functions and redefine them where necessary, and (2) to give "a series of definite directives to your division directors, outlining the objectives which you expect them to attain. Wherever possible, I should like to have deadlines fixed for each of these objectives."[12] This was not an isolated kind of instruction. It was a general practice. Deadlines constantly urged key individuals in the ASF to keep moving and to get their work done as soon as, or sooner than, possible.

[10] Min, Conf of CG's Sv Comds, Chicago, 22–24 Jul 43, pp. 4–5.
[11] Min, Conf of CG's SOS, 2d Sess, 30 Jul 42, p. 63.
[12] Memo, Somervell for Clay, 15 Aug 42, CG ASF.

General Somervell sought other ways of emphasizing urgency. At the beginning of 1944 he asked each staff division head and each chief of a technical service to send him a brief statement of the most important problems each office was working on. This was consolidated and edited by the Control Division into a Check List of Current Problems. The check list was reproduced and distributed to each office. It numbered fifty-nine items. Thereafter, for about three months, each office was required to submit a monthly report showing progress in completing the handling of each item shown on the check list. The mechanism was certainly imperfect, but it helped to spread a sense of urgency. It was tried again in January 1945.[13]

In the summer of 1944 General Somervell was greatly concerned about what he sensed to be a growing national complacency based on the feeling that the war was practically over. Mr. Nelson of the WPB, as has been noted, was talking about reconversion. ASF deliveries were declining and manufacturers were reporting increased difficulty in obtaining and retaining the necessary labor force. How could the continuing needs of the day be dramatized, how could a sense of urgency once more be instilled, first throughout the ASF and then throughout the nation? General Somervell worried about the problem for several days, and then personally wrote out a brief order. The workday throughout the command was to be lengthened by one hour.[14] Officially, the War Department at this time had an eight-hour day, and a forty-eight-hour week. In practice many, if not all, offices used considerable overtime. But the order was nonetheless greeted by some grumbling, and a good deal of adjustment in working arrangements and transportation

schedules followed.[15] On 1 August 1944 General Somervell issued a public statement explaining the need for the increased working day.[16] He spoke of "serious concern during the last few months over the lack of progress in disposing of a number of pressing problems." He mentioned shortages in the deliveries of 320 vital categories of munitions and pointed out that monthly procurement deliveries had declined since November 1943. He also referred to a growing backlog of equipment to be repaired, and the need to speed up the settlement of terminated contracts and to increase work efficiency. He concluded: "The Army Service Forces have discharged their duties in exemplary fashion. They now face the task of meeting these additional and heavy burdens, and the accompanying exacting requirements for speed and accuracy, with the same determination, vigor and freshness with which lesser tasks were met and disposed of during the earlier months of the war. This is the homestretch in our race to defeat Germany and speed and stamina are demanded on every hand."

The incident was noted throughout the United States. Certainly, the cost to one million workers directly affected was a small one compared with the sacrifices of combatants overseas in Europe and in the Pacific. In September General Somervell rescinded the order, leaving hours of work to be determined by the chiefs of the technical services, commanding generals of service commands, and directors of staff

---

[13] The two check-lists of current problems and the monthly reports on each item were bound and filed in Hq ASF, Check-Lists.

[14] ASF Cir 233, 26 Jul 44.

[15] See ASF Cir 240, 29 Jul 44.

[16] WD press release, BPR, "Statement by Lieutenant General Brehon Somervell on Order Increasing Hours of Work of ASF Personnel," 1 Aug 44.

divisions.[17] Urgency had been dramatized.

No doubt there were times when to some this sense of urgency seemed closely akin to ruthlessness. There were times when Somervell seemed insensitive to considerations of personal prestige or dignity Mr. Nelson of the WPB no doubt felt so on occasion. So probably did chiefs of the technical services within the ASF. Yet the fact remains that, to a remarkable degree, General Somervell, through the driving force of his personality, succeeded in transmitting a sense of urgency throughout the management and the operations of the Army Service Forces. It was one of his major accomplishments.

Chief Lieutenants

General Somervell enjoyed the advantage of able assistants. The work of the ASF would never have been done otherwise. His chief of staff during most of the war was Lt. Gen. W. D. Styer, a fellow Engineer officer who had graduated from the U.S. Military Academy a year after Somervell. General Styer came from an old Army family, and his father had been an outstanding officer. In personal appearance and in temperament, Styer was the antithesis of General Somervell. The commanding general was of medium build, wiry, quick-moving, full of nervous energy, incisive, at times, impulsive. His chief of staff was taller and heavy-set, rather slow-moving, somewhat easy-going in disposition, always even-tempered, calm. He was a born negotiator and never believed in extreme positions on any subject. In some ways the two must have seemed a peculiar team, so different were they in appearance and disposition. But they made a perfect combination. Each had the greatest respect for the other.

Somervell knew and appreciated General Styer's abilities. He learned to rely upon his skill in calming troubled waters. In turn, General Styer was loyal to his chief and sought faithfully to carry out his orders.

As ASF chief of staff, General Styer was conversant with all matters which came to Somervell's attention. When Somervell was out of the country or on an inspection trip in the United States, Styer commanded in his absence. Many items coming to the commanding general's office were handled directly by General Styer. Thus, when the Office of Price Administration complained to the Under Secretary of War about excess Army issue of rationed gasoline, General Styer looked into the matter and arranged a mutually satisfactory adjustment for the two agencies. Many matters involving research and development, and especially relations with the Office of Scientific Research and Development, were handled by Styer without prior consultation with Somervell. The commanding general also asked his chief of staff to take care of other matters. When Mayor LaGuardia, remembering the Black Tom explosion in World War II, raised the question of the threat to downtown Manhattan through Army loading of ammunition at Caven Point on the Jersey side of the port, General Styer took up the matter with all interested groups and arranged to shift some of the loading to Navy facilities in the lower harbor.

When General Styer left to take a command in the Pacific in the spring of 1945, Lt. Gen. LeRoy Lutes became ASF chief of staff. General Lutes throughout most of the war was chief planner and director of supply operations for the ASF. He came into the Army during World War I

---

[17] ASF Cir 317, 22 Sep 44.

through the National Guard, and remained in the Regular Army as an Artillery officer. He came to the War Department General Staff after the Louisiana maneuvers in 1941. Always diffident in manner, hard-working, reliable, General Lutes was the "ideal staff officer" in Somervell's judgment.

General Clay was another Engineer officer whom Somervell had known since West Point days. General Somervell brought him into G–4 from construction activities, and selected him to direct procurement activities for the ASF. Clay was another hard-working officer, and like General Somervell, intense, quick, full of nervous energy.

When Clay went to the Office of War Mobilization and Reconversion in the autumn of 1944, his successor was Mr. Howard Bruce, Baltimore businessman and chairman of the board of the Worthington Pump Company. Mr. Bruce had been a leading figure in the ASF since the beginning, one of a number of businessmen brought in by General Somervell. Other prominent staff officers on procurement matters were Maj. Gen. W. H. Harrison, formerly vice-president of the American Telephone and Telegraph Company; Brig. Gen. Frank R. Denton, a Pittsburgh businessman; Brig. Gen. A. J. Browning, formerly president of the United Wall Paper Factories, Inc.; Col. Fred C. Foy, of a large New York advertising firm; Mr. W. C. Marbury, a prominent Baltimore lawyer; Mr. Joseph M. Dodge, president of a Detroit bank; and Col. Maurice Hirsch, prominent Houston lawyer. Every one of these men was a civilian, serving as such or as an officer commissioned in the Army of the United States. Indeed, there were more temporarily commissioned than Regular

Army officers in the key positions of the ASF staff. These included Maj. Gen. F. H. Osborn, of a prominent New York family, who headed the Information and Education Division; Mr. James P. Mitchell and Col. Ralph F. Gow of the Industrial Personnel Division; and Col. A. B. Drake of the Storage Division; not to mention the many immediate associates of various division heads.

In a few cases, graduates of the U.S. Military Academy who had left the Army for private enterprise returned to important positions in the ASF. One of these was Maj. Gen. J. W. Byron, who became head of the Special Services Division running the Army's recreation and athletic program and the post exchanges. General Somervell felt that General Byron uniquely combined the qualities of a soldier and businessman and that his performance was exemplary. Others with a similar background were Maj. Gen. A. H. Carter, senior partner of Haskens and Sells, who became the ASF Fiscal Director, and Brig. Gen. C. E. Dissinger.

Among the Regular Army officers whose performance on the ASF staff Somervell regarded as outstanding were Maj. Gen. C. F. Robinson; Maj. Gen. W. A. Wood, Jr.; Col. C. B. Magruder; Maj. Gen. Glen E. Edgerton; Maj. Gen. Myron C. Cramer; Maj. Gen. F. A. Heileman; Brig. Gen. Theodore M. Osborne; Brig. Gen. D. N. Houseman; Brig. Gen. Hugh C. Minton; and Maj. Gen. W. L. Weible. This list by no means exhausts all of the individuals who played a key role in ASF staff activities and who in various ways contributed so much to ASF performance. General Somervell took great pride in his associates, from staff directors and division heads to their many field grade and company grade subordinates.

The chiefs of the technical services were all Regular Army officers, mainly men who had spent long years in their particular branch of service. Three of the seven were serving as chiefs when the ASF was created and remained until the end of the war: The Quartermaster General, Lt. Gen. Edmund B. Gregory; the Chief of Engineers, Lt. Gen. Eugene Reybold; and the Chief of Chemical Warfare Service, Maj. Gen. William N. Porter. Three replacements were made during the war: Maj. Gen. Charles M. Wesson, Chief of Ordnance for four years, retired in June 1942 and was succeeded by Lt. Gen. L. H. Campbell, Jr. Maj. Gen. James C. Magee retired as The Surgeon General in 1943 and was followed by Maj. Gen. Norman T. Kirk. Maj. Gen. Harry C. Ingles became Chief Signal Officer in 1943, succeeding Maj. Gen. Dawson Olmstead. General Somervell and General Marshall jointly selected the new chiefs of technical services, although considerable external pressure had to be met in the selection of a Surgeon General. The chief of the seventh technical service, Maj. Gen. C. P. Gross, head of the newly created Transportation Corps, was General Somervell's personal selection.

As the war progressed, there was a big turnover in commanders of the service commands. A few of these were General Somervell's personal selection: Maj. Gen. Philip Hayes in the third; Maj. Gen. James L. Collins in the fifth; Maj. Gen. H. S. Aurand and later Maj. Gen. Russel B. Reynolds in the sixth; Maj. Gen. Clarence H. Danielson in the seventh; and Maj. Gen. David McCoach in the ninth. Two of the men whom the ASF inherited turned in especially outstanding performances—Maj. Gen. Richard Donovan in the eighth and Maj. Gen. Frederick E. Uhl

who served first in the seventh and then in the fourth. The service of Maj. Gen. Sherman Miles in the first and Maj. Gen. Thomas A. Terry in the second was also exemplary.

The service commands tended to be the dumping ground for all the field grade officers whom the Army Ground Forces found unsatisfactory. This produced a difficult personnel situation and helped to explain why some of the technical services and perhaps even the Army Air Forces distrusted the service commands. General Somervell and the commanders of the service commands could only make the best of a troublesome situation.

Sense of Organization

A cardinal element of General Somervell's conception of effective management was "good organization." While he was not a slavish adherent to some overly simplified, mechanistic idea about organization, he nevertheless was a firm believer in a few essentials governing group relationships. One of his basic organizational propositions was expressed in 1943 in connection with a possible reorganization of the War Department and of a standard organization for overseas commands.[18] During a discussion of the subject Somervell had suggested that the supply commander should also be the staff adviser to a commanding general on supply matters. Another officer objected on the grounds that such an arrangement would place too much authority in a single person. To this General Somervell countered:

All military and industrial experience compels the conclusion that best results are secured by selecting an individual in whose

---

[18] See above, p. 145.

judgment one has confidence, placing him in charge of the work and giving him the necessary authority to carry it out. Checks and balances and the "counter-poise" theory are tools for use when one questions the integrity, loyalty, or judgment of the agent entrusted with the mission. They only serve to delay matters and introduce a feeling of bewilderment, confusion, and frustration in the minds and hearts of those who are honest and loyal, and a conviction that there is a lack of faith in their good judgment and that something is wrong with them. They destroy the prestige and power of accomplishment of the leader and if carried far they destroy the very qualities which one strives to develop in one's subordinates. If this theory were carried to a logical conclusion, there would be a counter-poise for our commanders in the field and a counter-poise for their chiefs of staff and all subordinate commanders. Trust and confidence must be the keystone of whatever plan is adopted.[19]

As regards the ASF he summarized his organizational thinking in these words:

There are many ways to divide a job organizationally; functional division, division by clientele, division by geographic areas, division by professions. Some organizations combine two or even more types. There are so-called "vertical" organizations, "staff-line" organizations. The theoretical relative merits of various types of organizations are not the important consideration. What is important is that the organization adopted for performing a mission be the most suitable for that specific mission. It should be as direct and simple as possible. It should contain the fewest possible levels of supervision—echelons of command, in Army language. It should be easily understood. It should not lead to questions of duplication, overlapping in duties, jurisdiction of authority, division of responsibility. Every man should know exactly where he fits into the organizational structure, what his responsibilities are, what his authority is. These considerations become doubly important when it is necessary, as in the case of the ASF, to build a large organization in a very short period of time.[20]

In presenting the service command organization in July 1942 General Somervell explained ASF intentions in this way:

The basic principles underlying the whole scheme are to put more responsibility and authority in the field, and in the hands of the Service Command; to eliminate, insofar as possible, duplications which may exist between the work that is being done by you and by other agencies. We want to get away, as far as we can, from this motherly or fatherly attitude that has been adopted by Washington and to put not only these responsibilities squarely on your shoulders, but let you alone and let you do them.

So that is the basic fundamental that is underneath this reorganization:

1. Decentralization
2. An increase in the responsibilities that are to be placed on you, and,
3. To let you do it.[21]

It was not enough to have decentralization from the center to the next level in the hierarchy; decentralization of authority should go all the way down the administrative ladder. A year after the service commands were created, General Somervell told a conference of their commanding generals:

Whereas we have made tremendous strides in decentralizing to the service commanders I am not so sure that that same decentralization has been passed to post commanders. Most of you assure me that it has. I would just like for you to check on that a little bit and find out to what extent this has been done. It is only human to feel that one should be given certain authority, but once it is given to him there is always a tendency to believe that: Well, I can handle this a little better than so-and-so, and I had better handle it. We do not want to get ourselves into that fix. So I wish you would look into that.[22]

---

[19] Memo, Somervell for Marshall, 31 Jul 43, CG ASF.

[20] Somervell, "Management," p. 258, cited in n. 1.

[21] Min, Conf of CG's SOS, 1st Sess, 30 Jul 42, p. 3.

[22] Min, Conf of CG's Sv Comds, Chicago, 22–24 Jul 43, p. 382.

At another conference of commanding generals of service commands General Somervell remarked:

Next, we must not be satisfied until we have the best organization that there ever has been. The job is so big and so difficult and so tremendous and so widespread that nothing short of the best organization that has ever been on the face of this globe will do this job and do it right. Now, we have just got to get it and we will get it. I say what I say in all seriousness. I have no illusions about the size of the job that is ahead of us or the difficulty of getting the type of organization I am talking about. But this is not just talk. We will have to have it and we are going to get it.

Our organization must be such that it can respond instantly and effectively to any demand that is put on it. I do not care whether it is a big, important task that is thrown at us, like setting up, equipping, moving a whole Army corps from some place in the United States to India and supplying it over there, or whether it is some very inconsequential thing like catching a deserter out in the mountains of Arizona. We have got to be able to do either one of those things and do it instantly, effectively, all the way down the line. Furthermore, we have to be able to do it with a proper emphasis on the amount of effort involved in doing that job. It is a big job to move an Army corps and it requires a certain amount of effort, but we ought to be so organized that for this other little job we do not require very much effort to do it. In other words, we want emphasis on the right thing.[23]

In summary, there were these elements in General Somervell's organizational thinking: (1) clear responsibility should be vested in individuals with authority to perform the assigned task; (2) decentralization of operations on a geographical basis with a general administrator in the field; (3) a functional "staff" with full supervisory responsibility for results in its specialized field of effort; (4) shifts in organization to meet changing circumstances of workload and importance; and

(5) constant assurance that the organizational arrangements in effect at any one time were producing results with the least possible expenditure of manpower and other resources.

In one important respect Somervell's organizational thinking was formalistic; he made few allowances for the personality factors in group operations. He was inclined to believe that men work together in whatever patterns of work assignment are necessary to achieve maximum operating results. He was apt to ignore, or underestimate, the importance to many persons of tradition, prestige, need for recognition, and other such considerations. Circumstances compelled Somervell in 1943 to give more attention to the personal aspects of his relations with the chiefs of the technical services.[24] In many informal ways he was able to build more co-operative relationships with these officers, but he could not help but regret that others did not share his own concept of organization as a formal rather than personal arrangement.

The Quest for Unity

Perhaps no challenge to the management of the ASF was greater than that of building unity in its operations. It was not an easy task. In an organization as large and loosely jointed as the ASF, with many different component parts and widely divergent duties, it was difficult to identify and emphasize the common elements making for unity. War Department Circular 59 in 1942 defined the mission of the ASF as being "to provide services and supplies to meet military requirements." This

---

[23] Min, Conf of CG's SOS, 5th Sess, 1 Aug 42, pp. 259–60.
[24] See the following chapter for an account of these circumstances.

definition of purpose was too broad to be very helpful. But there was little else about which to build a concept of common purpose. There was an essential element of unity in the supply mission of the ASF; there was an essential element of unity in post management. But the ASF also had many other duties.[25]

Somervell endeavored continually to stress that the common element in the ASF was service, service to the overseas theater of operations and service to the AGF and AAF in the United States. To the individual units, such as the Office of the Chief of Ordnance, or the Office of the Chief of Finance, or Information and Education Division, service meant certain specific activities. To the Army Service Forces as a whole, service was everything necessary to support the combat commands of the Army everywhere.

In various ways General Somervell sought to emphasize the unity of the ASF. Immediately after its creation he initiated periodic conferences of his chief staff officers, and early in 1943 he brought into them the chiefs of technical services. These conferences continued on a twice-a-month basis until the autumn of 1945. Agenda were prepared in advance, and summary minutes were reproduced and distributed within twenty-four hours. On these occasions various officers were requested to present problems of general interest, and each conference ended with a call around the table for any items of importance. Semiannual conferences were held for all commanding generals of service commands and their principal staff assistants. General Somervell missed only one of these and then because of absence from the country.

In November of 1942 he inaugurated a brief series of orientation lectures for all important personnel in his organization in Washington. About one thousand persons were gathered together for these talks in the departmental auditorium on Constitution Avenue. In his opening remarks the commanding general stressed the importance of knowing "what we're all trying to do together." [26] On 9 March 1943 General Somervell called together three hundred of the important ASF people in Washington. They met in the small Pentagon auditorium to mark the first anniversary of the Army Service Forces. Here he reviewed the major accomplishments of the first year and then outlined the main problems to be anticipated in the year ahead.[27] This pattern was repeated at similar gatherings on 9 March 1944 and 9 March 1945.[28]

At Ft. Belvoir, Virginia, on the occasion of the second birthday of the organization, Somervell used the facilities of the National Broadcasting Company to address ASF employees throughout the United States. On 9 March 1945, through the facilities of the Columbia Broadcasting System, he spoke to "the men and women of the Army Service Forces." [29]

In his talk in the Pentagon on 9 March 1944, General Somervell said:

We must never forget that the ASF is *one* organization. All parts must act as a team. No *one* service can do the job alone. No one

---

[25] For a list of the duties of the ASF as developed by the Control Division in 1945, see Appendix I.

[26] This opening statement on 30 November 1942 was mimeographed and distributed to every ASF officer and key civilian in Washington.

[27] This talk was reproduced as a press release by the War Department, Bureau of Public Relations, 10 March 1943.

[28] The 1944 and 1945 talks were reproduced by The Adjutant General's office and distributed over a personal letter from General Somervell to all military and civilian personnel in the ASF.

[29] Both the 1944 and 1945 radio addresses were reproduced and released by the War Department, Bureau of Public Relations.

WEEKLY STAFF CONFERENCE, *Hq, SOS, June 1942. Seated left to right: Mr. A. R. Glancy, Chief of Production Br, Brig. Gens. James E. Wharton, Dir of MPD, H. S. Aurand, Dir of Intn Div, Charles Hines, Dir of Resources Div, C. D. Young, Dir of Production and Distribution Div, Maj. Gen. John P. Smith, Chief of Adm Svs, Brig. Gen. L. D. Clay, DCofS, Requirements and Resources, Hon. Robert P. Patterson, USW, Lt. Gen. B. B. Somervell, CG, ASF, Brig. Gens. W. D. Styer, CofS, ASF, L. Lutes, Dir of OPD, Clarence R. Huebner, Dir of Tng Div, C. P. Gross, Chief of Trans Div, Mr. J. P. Mitchell, Dir of Civilian Pers Div, Cols. F. A. Heileman, Chief of Distribution Br, A. Robert Ginsburgh, Chief of Public Relations Br, A. J. Browning, Chief of Purchases Br. Standing left to right: Cols. C. F. Robinson, Dir of CD, W. A. Wood, Jr., Dir of Requirements Div, Robinson E. Duff, Chief of Gen Depots Sv, Brig. Gen. A. H. Carter, Dir of Fiscal Div, Col. J. N. Dalton, Chief of Adm Br, Capt. Harold K. Hastings, Aide to CG.*

can eat without the Quartermaster. The Ordnance Department cannot deliver ammunition to Italy without the Transportation Corps. No technical service or service command can secure men to train for overseas without The Adjutant General. We depend upon each other. We must pull together. In many activities, unified direction and uniform systems and methods are essential. Occasions demand that for the common good we bury honest differences of opinion, pride of sub-organization, of methods or systems, natural resentment against central direction. We must be loyal to each other, must move on a united front. Such an attitude must underlie all our thinking, all our actions.

This particular talk was a kind of peace offering after the conflict of the preceding October over the internal organization of the ASF. The existing pattern of duties had been established. But unity of purpose and effort was still essential. It now became the major theme within the ASF. Some progress in this direction had been made by the time the war ended, eighteen months later. But behind this quest for a sense of unity there was not the same urgency which marked the actual performance of the work of the ASF. Unity remained a continuing but elusive aim for ASF management.

Management Improvement

General Somervell introduced a new kind of staff office in the War Department. This was the Control Division.[30] Somervell in 1942 explained his concept of the office in these words:

It may help you a little bit if I made just a few observations. Colonel Johnston said in a small command the job of the Control Division would be done by the Commander himself. In a little larger command it might be shared by the Commander and the Chief of Staff. But when your show gets as big as the one you have here, you have to bring an additional person into the picture who does nothing but devote his whole time to keeping the elements before the Commander in such a way that he can keep his show under control.

This idea of handling the thing came to me a number of years ago, and I tried it out in an organization where we had a lot of people who weren't too well instructed in executive duties or in handling a big organization, the type of organization where you could not by your own personal contact with the people, impress your own ideas on them of how things ought to work. Gradually this idea evolved. I found in discussing it with people on the outside, that there are not very many people who had this same concept of what a

control section is for, not very many people in the world had it. When you talk about control you talk of things that Colonel Johnston mentioned. But there are a few people who have made a study of the conduct of big organizations, who have come to the conclusion that you have to have some kind of organism like this if you are going to put the thing over, something that is always on the job and always following through.[31]

The Control Division had a number of assignments. First, it made various organizational surveys and prepared recommendations on organizational questions for General Somervell. Second, the Control Division gave continuing attention to the promotion of a management improvement program. The subjects which received primary attention were:

1. Work Simplification (a formalized process for analyzing and simplifying both the processing of large-scale paper work and work-gang operations as in loading and storing supplies).
2. Work Measurement (a device for comparing workloads and manpower utilization among field offices performing a comparable task, such as supply depots).
3. Procedures Standardization (the development of simplified, standard, basic procedures for various types of work such as letting procurement contracts, the handling of supply requisitions from overseas theaters of operations, sales from post commissaries, classification of military personnel, maintaining depot inventory records, preparing bills of lading for supply shipment, and the separation of military personnel from service).
4. Forms Standardization (the careful design of simplified forms to be used for various procedures; perhaps the best illustration of this work was the redesign of the old, tradi-

---

[30] The best available general account is *Administrative Management in the Army Service Forces,* cited in n. 1. A longer, more detailed account, written by Richard M. Leighton, History of Control Division, ASF, 1942–1945 (mimeographed), is available in OCMH.

[31] Min, Conf of CG's Sv Comds, Chicago, 30 Jul–1 Aug 42, pp. 213–14.

tional "Service Record," the basic piece of paper showing an enlisted man's military career).

5. Centralization and Control of Publications (the number of Army field printing plants was reduced from seventy to thirty-five and costs of operation reduced 17 percent even in the face of a 20 percent increase in volume).

In the third place, the Control Division directed the statistics system for the ASF. An elaborate system of monthly reports covered practically all essential ASF activities susceptible of quantitative measurement. Eventually there were some twenty sections of the Monthly Progress Report on such subjects as procurement deliveries, storage operations, distribution of supplies, transportation, construction, health, military training, administrative services, fiscal operations, personnel. The preparation of these reports was assigned to the appropriate staff agency. The Control Division itself prepared a monthly Analysis Section which summarized the data in the individual reports and called attention to the problems and difficulties indicated by the data. General Somervell read the report carefully and regularly used it as the subject of a staff conference each month. In addition, no new recurring report could be introduced within the Army Service Forces without the prior approval of the Control Division. All existing reports were carefully scrutinized and approved or discontinued. Within one year from the time when this work was begun in the ASF, some 2,900 reports and records were discontinued.[32]

The Control Division was organizationally and personally close to General Somervell. Its point of view was the ASF as a whole. It had no purpose except to help make Somervell's direction effective. The division helped other staff units do their work but never took over their jobs. It also tried in many ways to encourage the technical services and the service commands to develop control programs of their own.

It would be an exaggeration to suggest that the Control Division was ever a popular or universally accepted part of the Army Service Forces. An agency for exercising the administrator's critical faculties is not likely to be highly regarded by those who get criticized. Then, too, there were times when the Control Division was probably in too big a hurry. And sometimes, no doubt, its ideas were not entirely reasonable, or it overlooked essential elements of a situation. Yet the management improvements introduced by the ASF were noteworthy. According to such standards of measurement as the Control Division could devise, the volume of work done by the ASF steadily increased during the war, while the number of persons performing it declined. With the workload and total operating personnel of March 1942 used as an index number of 100, the ASF workload on 30 June 1945 had risen to 350, while the number of operating personnel had increased to only 170. Moreover, from 1 July 1943 to 30 June 1945, while the workload was rising from about 230 to 350, operating personnel was declining from about 200 to 170.[33] The final annual report of the Army Service Forces listed the major management improvements achieved within the ASF from March 1942 through June 1945. A list of 116 items ranged from the Supply Control System and the Food Service Program to the general hospital system and the service command reorganization.[34]

---

[32] Annual Rpt of ASF, 1943, p. 252.
[33] Annual Rpt of ASF, 1945, pp. 302–03.
[34] *Ibid.*, pp. 325–39.

After the war had ended, the U.S. Bureau of the Budget began to advocate throughout the entire federal administrative structure just the kind of work which the Control Division did within the ASF. The work of the Control Division managed to survive in various parts of the Department of the Army and the national Military Establishment as well, which justifies the conclusion that the promotion of the concept of management improvement was not the least of General Somervell's wartime contributions. Admittedly, he was not alone in his thinking and action on this score but, of all contemporary administrators in the federal government, he probably made the most use of an institutionalized effort to achieve increased administrative efficiency in the performance of essential government operations.

Personnel Management

The internal personnel problems of the Army Service Forces during the war were not unique. But in two or three respects, the ASF did explore new phases of personnel management. A basic concern of the ASF throughout the war was effective utilization of personnel. There was no way for the ASF to escape the general manpower shortage within the United States during the war years. It had to compete with other employers, both military and civilian. Only by reducing its requirements, therefore, could it find enough persons to do its work.

The top management of the Army Service Forces turned to manpower problems with a new urgency in the autumn of 1942. One influence was the known intention of Chairman Robert P. Ramspeck of the House Committee on the Civil Service to investigate the rapidly increasing employment of civilians in all government agencies, an inquiry which was eventually held in the spring of 1943. Another factor was growing external criticism about the projected size of the Army. It became clearly apparent that with all its substantive problems of production, raw materials control, transportation, supply distribution, and the like, the ASF could not afford to be indifferent to its own personnel management problem.

ASF headquarters had begun an extensive personnel recruitment and training program soon after its creation.[35] A second important step was the preparation of a statement on personnel policies. This statement was drawn up by a prominent labor relations adviser brought in by the Civilian Personnel Division, was personally approved by General Somervell, and was printed as a pamphlet in August 1942 for widespread distribution. It began:

1. The establishment and maintenance of proper and mutually satisfactory working relationships among all employees and between employees and management is a fundamental requirement of successful operation. This is a prime responsibility of the chief executive and his subordinate supervisors in each organization.

2. It is the primary objective of personnel management to build up, develop, and maintain an adequate and effective employee work force which will completely fulfill the mission of the organization. This means specifically that action is directed toward placing each individual in that particular job for which he or she is best suited and providing a total work environment which will enable all employees to utilize their skills and abilities to the maximum and find sufficient satisfactions in their daily jobs to make them want to stay in the organization.

3. From the management point of view, this involves matters of selection, placement,

---

[35] See New York Field Survey, Contl Br, SOS, May 42 (mimeographed), CD, ASF, p. 149.

remuneration, supervision, training and development of employees, and the maintenance of proper working conditions.

4. From the viewpoint of employees, good personnel management includes the right of employees to obtain and hold a job on the basis of ability and performance without discrimination of prejudicial action, opportunity for advancement both in money and position, adequate pay for services rendered, recognition as individuals, respect for their rights and interests, and fair treatment from supervisors.[36]

The statement set forth a clear determination that "all employees will be fairly treated at all times and that those who believe they have been unfairly treated will be given the right and opportunity to discuss such matters with higher supervisors and executives." It then set forth general practices in presenting and adjusting employee grievances. On the subject of employee organization, the statement declared: "Employees are considered free to join or refrain from joining employee organizations or associations without interference, coercion, restraint, or fears of discrimination or reprisal because of such membership or nonmembership." The right of employees to present matters for consideration individually or through representatives was recognized. These "principles and policies" remained the guiding canons of personnel management within the Army Service Forces throughout the war. They placed the ASF in the front ranks of government agencies with an "enlightened" personnel program.

But important as these actions were, they were by no means the final solution to the central problems of personnel management in wartime. The basic issue continued to be numbers and utilization of manpower. A first need was for accurate, useful data on personnel strength. War Department military personnel reporting

practices simply indicated the total military personnel under the jurisdiction of the ASF as of the date of a report. Total military personnel included men at induction stations and reception centers in the process of assignment, troops in staging areas and en route overseas, individuals and troop units being trained by the ASF for duty with the ground forces of the AAF or an overseas command, and patients in hospitals. Immediately the ASF divided its military strength into two categories—nonoperating personnel and operating personnel. ASF internal management was concerned only with the second group, those who performed the activities of the ASF. On 1 July 1942, for example, the total military strength of the ASF was 540,000, of whom only 252,000 officers and enlisted men were operating personnel. As of 31 July 1943 total military strength was 1,364,342, of whom 554,287 officers and enlisted men were operating personnel.[37] The nonoperating personnel were individuals in process of classification and assignment, receiving medical treatment, being transported overseas, or similarly under temporary ASF jurisdiction.

The use of troops for the operating work of the Army Service Forces became the first concern in personnel utilization. The War Department General Staff began in the winter of 1942–43 to place increasing pressure upon the command to cut its use of enlisted men. As a matter of policy, they were not assigned to any duties in ASF headquarters or in the Washington offices of the technical services. Neither were enlisted men used to any important extent in

---

[36] Principles and Policies of Personnel Management, WD, SOS, signed by Somervell.

[37] Annual Rpt of ASF, 1943, p. 231; ASF Monthly Progress Rpt, Personnel and Training, 31 Jul 43, Sec. 5.

the procurement and storage operations of the technical services. For this work the general practice was to use officers, mostly Reserve officers or individuals commissioned directly from civilian life, and civilians. Officers and enlisted men, however, were used extensively in the operation of military posts throughout the United States.

As of 30 June 1943 the military complement in ASF headquarters numbered 5,400, of whom 5,260 were officers. The technical services outside their Washington headquarters used about 28,750 officers and 120,000 enlisted personnel. Service commands employed 43,500 officers and nearly 408,000 enlisted personnel.[38] The first drive was aimed at reducing the "general service" group in the ASF. Whereas in December 1942 about 60 percent of all enlisted men in operating jobs of the ASF were classified as "general service" by 30 June 1943, the proportion had been reduced to 47 percent.[39] By 30 June 1945, of the 383,056 enlisted operating personnel of the ASF, 76 percent were either men who were not physically qualified or had returned from overseas service, or members of the WAC; another 13 percent were on ASF operating missions. The remaining 42,696, or 11 percent, were physically qualified for overseas service, but of these, 421 had an Adjusted Rating score of 85 or above which precluded overseas shipment, and 24,770 were specifically exempted by War Department orders as critically needed specialists. This left but 17,505 available for overseas duty.[40]

The second great drive was aimed at reducing the number in operating jobs. In July 1943 there were 554,000 officers and enlisted men in ASF operating jobs. The number was reduced to 426,000 by July 1944. Thereafter the number gradually

rose again to 484,000 in June 1945 as enlisted men became available on return from overseas duties.[41] Enlisted men were prohibited from employment in many types of jobs, such as national cemeteries, operation of depots and arsenals, salvage and reclamation facilities, government-owned manufacturing plants and proving grounds, construction projects, repairs and utilities work, and operation of laundries. Exceptions to the rule for these activities might be granted by commanding generals of service commands. General Somervell insisted that he alone would pass on the use of enlisted personnel in post exchanges, officers' messes, and officers' clubs.[42]

The number of civilians in ASF operating jobs reached a peak of 1,023,000 in June 1943. Thereafter, the numbers steadily declined to 748,000 on 30 June 1945, a reduction of 25 percent.[43] This reduction was not entirely voluntary on the part of the ASF. It was occasioned by growing manpower shortages throughout the United States and the preference of many workers for employment at other than military installations. Many posts were geographically removed from centers of population and provided few attractions for civilian employees. Wages in private industry, moreover, were frequently higher than pay rates on military posts. The ASF could have gone farther in replacing military personnel with civilians if the latter had been available at the places where needed.

As early as November 1942 the ASF top

---

[38] ASF Monthly Progress Rpt, Personnel and Training, 31 Jul 43, Sec. 5.
[39] *Ibid.*, p. 233.
[40] *Ibid.*, pp. 38–45.
[41] CD, ASF, *Statistical Review, World War II,* p. 213.
[42] ASF Cir 44, 27 Jun 43.
[43] *Ibid.*

command realized that large-scale efforts would have to be launched to improve personnel efficiency. The Chief of Ordnance, on 3 November 1942, had issued a pamphlet for the guidance of his field installations entitled Program for the More Effective Utilization of Personnel. When this came to the attention of General Somervell, he had copies sent to the chiefs of the other technical services with the request that they develop comparable efforts. This was a beginning, but the methods were general and exhortative. Something more specific and more authoritative was required.

On 1 March 1943, under the leadership of the ASF chief of staff, a formal program was launched for the more effective utilization of personnel. This program had eight basic objectives:[44]

1. To develop and utilize adequate personnel data.

2. To establish an effective control over the numbers of personnel.

3. To replace certain types of personnel.

4. To expand, refine, and speed up the program for personnel management.

5. To eliminate all nonessential activities.

6. To improve the organizational structure.

7. To decentralize activities and authority to act to the greatest extent possible.

8. To increase the efficiency with which essential activities were performed.

General Styer issued a series of directives to accomplish these purposes and an intensive drive began throughout the ASF to improve the utilization of personnel.[45] With varying degrees of intensity this drive continued throughout the war under the general oversight of the Control Division.

In December 1942 the ASF began a system of allotting military personnel to its

major component parts in accordance with instructions from G–1 of the War Department General Staff. This was intended to limit the categories of military personnel which the ASF might employ. Then on 7 May 1943 the President approved increased pay legislation which at the same time required the Bureau of the Budget to approve civilian personnel ceilings for all government installations. With this as an added incentive, the ASF developed its own method for authorizing, reporting, and controlling personnel.[46] The new system, announced on 11 June 1943, covered both military and civilian personnel. It set up a total authorization and then subtotals for various military categories. The difference between the authorized military employment and the total authorization was the available civilian employment. In addition, the authorization covered all types of civilians, thus going beyond the requirements of Public Law 49 which did not include employees on transport vessels or persons paid on an hourly wage basis. Second, the system made "bulk" authorizations to the major units of the ASF: the technical services, the service commands, and the staff agencies. No longer did ASF headquarters try to specify where personnel was to be used; the distribution by type and place of employment was left to the discretion of each

---

[44] This effort was described by Somervell in *Hearings before the Committee on the Civil Service*, H.R., 78th Cong, 1st Sess, on Investigation of Civilian Employment, 15 Jun 43, pp. 557ff. See also Constance McL. Green, Harry C. Thomson, and Peter Roots, The Ordnance Department: Organization and Research and Development, a volume in preparation for the series UNITED STATES ARMY IN WORLD WAR II, Chs. V. and VI.

[45] These instructions are reproduced in Report on the Program for More Effective Utilization of Personnel, prepared by CD, ASF, and reproduced by TAGO, CD, ASF.

[46] ASF Cir 39, 11 Jun 43.

major unit of the ASF. Third, a single form was used to report personnel strength monthly, and to authorize personnel on a quarterly basis.

At the beginning authorizations of personnel reflected the existing personnel strength, except that General Somervell insisted upon a total reduction of 105,000 persons which was distributed among all units in the authorization for the first quarter ending 30 August 1943. Thereafter, only in unusual circumstances were requests for increased strength approved.

One other item should be noted in passing. When the Control Division and the Industrial Personnel Division began to worry about utilization of civilian employees in the ASF, they found no adequate information on what they did. To be sure there were records by classification grade, but only about one half of ASF civilians were actually classified. The others were paid the wage rates prevailing in the area where employed as fixed by wage boards. The records also showed *where* civilians were employed, but not the *type* of work performed. Obviously, these employees were not all government clerks, shuffling papers. Accordingly, a sample survey was made to determine just what kinds of work they performed. As of 1 May 1943 the distribution of civilian employees by major categories of work performed in the ASF was as follows:[47]

Kind of Work	Percent of Total
Departmental Service	3.6
Service Command Hq and Misc	4.4
Manufacturing (in arsenals)	18.0
Operation of Camps and Posts	24.5
Operation of Storage Facilities	15.1
Maintenance and Utilities	12.2
Construction	7.6
Procurement (operation of purchasing offices)	6.7
Transportation	4.9
Proving Grounds and Laboratories	3.0

Thus, of one million civilians employed at this time, just 8 percent were engaged in general administration overhead, including service commands. Another 6.7 percent were in procurement offices, where there was a considerable volume of paper work. The great bulk, 85 percent, were employed as workers in arsenals and other manufacturing establishments, in the loading and storage of supplies at depots, in handling supplies at ports, in operating military posts (especially the storage, repair, utilities, and maintenance activities), and on construction projects. While this kind of reporting was never placed on a systematic basis in the ASF, it served to reveal the kind of work the bulk of ASF employees performed and where the largest savings in personnel might be realized. It was one reason why so much attention was given to improving all storage and warehouse activities.

It is impossible here to cover all aspects of personnel management in the Army Service Forces. Considerable attention was given to officer classification and assignment, for instance. Great improvements were introduced in wage administration for civilian employees, and particular attention was given to employee training, and especially to the training of supervisors, all of which were important to ASF personnel management.

The ASF did succeed in drawing a distinction between internal personnel management—the utilization of personnel performing the work of the ASF—and general personnel services performed by the ASF for the Army as a whole. The first involved the persons employed; the second was the substance of work done, such as inducting and assigning men into the Army. It was an important distinction

[47] Annual Rpt of ASF, 1943, p. 239.

Budget Administration

The process of budget preparation within the ASF during World War II never served as an important technique of management for three reasons. In the first place, after Pearl Harbor, budget estimates were prepared upon the basis of planning documents fixing the size and organization of the Army, its prospective deployment, and the requirements of the Army Supply Program. Budget preparation consisted mainly in translating these decisions into cost estimates. Budgeting therefore tended to be a secondary and somewhat mechanical activity.

In the second place, the appropriation structure for the War Department in World War II by no means reflected the administrative realities of war operations. Budget preparation was intended primarily to give the House Committee on Appropriations estimates in the form to which the committee was accustomed. The emphasis then was on the committee's attitude and not upon the management needs or possibilities of the Army Service Forces. There was no appropriation estimate for the ASF as such or for any of the broad phases of ASF activity such as procurement, storage and distribution of supplies, transportation, training, administrative services, or management expenses. These items entered into the preparation of appropriation estimates, to be sure, but they were not submitted separately. Instead, the estimate for Ordnance Service and Supplies, for example, included not just procurement and storage activities by the Chief of Ordnance in the United States, but estimates of local procurement and other local activities in overseas theaters which might be charged to this particular appropria-

tion. Eight major appropriation titles (Finance Service, Ordnance Service and Supplies, Signal Service, Quartermaster Service, Transportation Service, Engineer Service, Medical and Hospital Department, and Chemical Warfare Service) in the War Department appropriation acts included not just ASF operating expenditures but Army-wide operating expenditures, although these estimates were presented by the ASF. But wartime appropriation estimates were not ASF management estimates, and so could not be used systematically to review the adequacy of internal ASF operations.

In the third place, there were personality factors within the ASF fiscal machinery and in the War Department budget office which did little to encourage General Somervell to make extensive use of budget preparation as a tool of management information and direction. On one occasion General Somervell asked his own budget office to explore the possibility of an ASF budget estimate which could be used for both internal management and appropriation purposes. He was subsequently informed that the budget officer of the War Department had made inquiries and reported general hostility to the idea on the part of the House Appropriations Committee. Thus rebuffed, and busy with other more pressing matters, Somervell let the matter drop.

In 1944 Somervell set a precedent in his appearance before the House Appropriations Committee. Regularly after 9 March 1942 he appeared briefly before the committee to describe the nature and activities of the Army Service Forces. The committee thus had an opportunity to see him and to ask questions. But the main burden of justifying War Department estimates fell upon the ASF Fiscal Director, the Chief of Finance, and the chiefs of technical services. General Somervell personally played no part in this process. When a general statement was prepared for him to present to the Appropriations Committee in the spring of 1944, he rejected it as inadequate. Instead he called upon staff aides to prepare a summary of ASF accomplishments and problems in the style of his own statistical reports. Consequently, when he appeared before the committee on 10 May 1944, he was able to give to each member a book of facts and figures with charts and graphs showing just what the ASF had done and was doing. He then read through the explanatory text, with the congressmen able to follow each word and chart in the material before him. The entire text and all the graphic materials were reproduced eventually in the printed hearings, with certain eliminations for security reasons.[48]

When he finished, the chairman of the subcommittee, Mr. J. Buell Snyder of Pennsylvania, remarked:

General Somervell, I have been a member of the Committee on Appropriations for 10 years and for 8 years I have been chairman of the subcommittee, and am also a member of the subcommittee on Deficiencies, which hears the representatives of practically all Government agencies.

This is one of the most outstanding, splendid, detailed, and understandable presentations which I have heard during the 10 years. I want to commend you and your group for the perfectly splendid way in which, what I conceive to be the biggest job in history, has been performed.[49]

In a way, Somervell was endeavoring to suggest a program or "performance" budget such as was to be advocated by the (Hoover) Commission on Organization of the Executive Branch of the Government in 1949 and which was actually started on

a general scale in the federal government with the budget estimates for the fiscal year 1951. He was relating workload, past and future, to budget requests. But the actual development of systematic program budgeting was not undertaken by the ASF.

In spending its funds, the ASF did make use of fiscal control techniques for management purposes. Funds to be spent for printing and reproduction were limited in order to curtail activity. In addition, local purchasing funds to be used by posts, camps, and stations were carefully controlled, as were expenditures for repair of structures and for recreational activities for enlisted men. Accounting records were constantly used, moreover, to check the fidelity with which all financial transactions of the ASF were conducted. Indeed, the accounting improvements introduced by the ASF were numerous and extensive.

Public Relations

In one phase of management, public relations, General Somervell was never especially interested. He had no flair for personal publicity and no disposition to cultivate those who commanded the media of mass communication. To be sure, he was not indifferent to a good reputation, but he believed that performance, not words, should be its basis. Moreover, there was a real question in his mind whether a subordinate command of the War Department should have its own public relations program. The War Department Bureau of Public Relations was

---

[48] *Hearings before the Subcommittee of the Committee on Appropriations*, H.R.; 78th Cong, 2d Sess, on Military Establishment Appropriation Bill for 1945, pp. 62–122.

[49] *Ibid.*, p. 122.

the only authorized agency for handling Army publicity, and its efforts were concerned with the Army as a whole.

Somervell believed that the bureau should give more attention to the supply aspects of the war. For a time an "Army Service Forces Hour" was broadcast over a national radio network on Saturday nights. In these programs attention focused on the work of individual parts of the ASF, such as the chaplains, the medical service, communications, and construction. General Somervell was not personally "played-up" on any of these occasions. In the spring of 1945 he suggested publication of a book which would do for the rest of the Army what pictorial books then appearing were doing for the Army Air Forces and the Navy.[50] With General Marshall's approval, Somervell asked his aide, in civilian life a roving editor of *Reader's Digest,* to prepare a readable story about the Army for popular consumption. This was done. The resulting product explained in general terms what the ASF did, but gave much more attention to combat achievements.[51]

Because of his position, General Somervell had to make numerous personal appearances at various gatherings. A few talks were made before business groups to whom Somervell invariably spoke on the importance of America's productive capacity in the conduct of the war.[52] Occasionally there were talks to labor groups; the most notable of which was a great labor luncheon in Detroit on 4 July 1942. Personal appearances were also made on Memorial Day (Arlington National Cemetery, 30 May 1943), at an Army Day celebration (Mayflower Hotel, Washington, 6 April 1942), and at an Armistice Day observation (Pittsburgh, 11 November 1942). He often spoke at

American Legion conventions, graduating exercises of officer candidates in ASF schools, and general hospitals. To the Women's National Advisory Council set up by the War Department Bureau of Public Relations, General Somervell appealed on 25 June 1943 for assistance in Army nurse and WAC recruiting. He also addressed the semiannual meeting of the Academy of Political Science in New York on 10 November 1942 (the request to appear coming from Lewis Douglas, then deputy administrator of War Shipping), and the *New York Herald Tribune* Forum on 16 October 1944. These public relations activities were in "the line of duty," and can be considered as required by his job as a top administrator of the War Department. He accepted them as such, without either particular enthusiasm or dislike. It was not the kind of activity which most interested him.

An apparent tendency to ease up on the home front during the last half of 1944 filled Somervell with the deepest concern over the Army's wartime public relations. This concern was expressed in a personal memorandum to General Marshall in which he protested against the prevailing tone of optimism in War Department press releases, and particularly the dispo-

---

[50] See, for example, *Target: Germany;* the AAF official story of the VIII Bomber Command's first year over Europe (New York, Simon & Schuster, Inc., 1943); Oliver Jensen, *Carrier War* (New York, Simon & Schuster, Inc., 1945).

[51] Detzer, *The Mightiest Army.* This book was printed on paper taken from the *Reader's Digest* quota, published without profit, distributed at cost, with royalties going to the Army Emergency Relief Fund.

[52] For example, Somervell spoke before the National Industrial Conference Board 24 September 1942; U.S. Chamber of Commerce 27 April 1943; Dallas Chamber of Commerce 18 February 1944; Atlanta Chamber of Commerce 12 June 1944; Indianapolis Chamber of Commerce 4 July 1944; and the National Association of Manufacturers 6 December 1944.

sition, then current, to call the German counterattack in the Ardennes a serious German error. General Somervell commented:

We need more workers in our critical war programs and we need more production per man per hour from those workers already in our plants. We are losing thousands of war workers each month because they have come to the conclusion that it is time to move to a more permanent peacetime job before the collapse of our enemies. We know that in certain critical items such as tires we could get an immediate and significant production relief if the workers in the tire plants felt that the urgency of the situation was greater than their distaste for establishing high production records which might be used as a peacetime basis for negotiating labor rates.

The basis of this public opinion is the fact that since Guadalcanal the daily news has been an almost constant repetition of good news, victories, spectacular bombings, enemy fleet losses and ground advances. And now a serious German thrust into our lines is keyed to the comparison of their last thrust in 1918 and is a "disastrous throw of the dice" for the Germans.

All this is fine if we believe that there is little probability that we still face a tough bitter struggle with Germany of an unknown number of months of duration, followed by a longer and in some ways tougher struggle with Japan.

Our people are more prosperous than ever before in their history. They have responded to the call for war production by longer hours, shift work, living in uncomfortable temporary housing and with numerous other sacrifices. They have never been bombed, they have little appreciation of the horrors of war and only in a small percentage of instances do they have enough hate, for that alone to act as a driving force.

You hold me responsible for production. Our material requirements for ETO have been increased since last September. I have no mandatory authority by which I can command people to produce more. I can only get that production through leadership and a common understanding of our problems.

It is recommended that beginning at once all press conferences, theater news releases and official statements on the war be pitched to a tone more conducive to a public appreciation of a long tough war.[53]

As required General Somervell had his office prepare an annual report for each year of the war. The reports for the fiscal years 1944 and 1945 were summarized and distributed to the press. The annual report is a traditional government communications device, and the annual reports of the ASF were written to provide a broad survey of activity for the use of those who might be interested in the general problems encountered.

In essence General Somervell's attitude toward public relations was quite clear. He fulfilled as best he could the "legitimate" public relations activities inherent in his job and scrupulously avoided all purely social gatherings, parties, and other such affairs throughout the war. He felt that he had one, or at most two, public messages to emphasize. First, he wanted workers, managers, and the public at large to understand the importance of supply in the military operations of World War II. Second, he wanted "efficiency" constantly held up as the goal of ASF operating methods; he hoped that the efficiency of Army Service Forces efforts would be "news." In this he was disappointed, and when it was all over he wondered what more might have been done to have made both aims more popular.

Legislative Relations

While Somervell's relations with the members of the military affairs and appropriations committees of Congress were

---

[53] Memo, Somervell for Marshall, 30 Dec 44, CG ASF.

friendly, they were not particularly close. On Congressional matters generally, it was the Secretary of War and the Chief of Staff who spoke for the War Department. The Legislative and Liaison Division, which maintained close relations with Congressional committees, was an instrument of the Department's chiefs. When the Army Service Forces was created, General Somervell inherited one type of Congressional relationship from the Office of the Under Secretary. As the head of statistical activities, Brig. Gen. L. P. Ayres began the practice of meeting periodically with the Senate and House Committees on Military Affairs to present data on procurement progress and certain other activities. For a time after June 1942 General Somervell continued the practice. The last such meeting was held in June 1944 when Somervell himself appeared to explain the supply details of the invasion of France to the Senate Committee on Military Affairs.

There were various factors which tended to discourage these meetings. The two military affairs committees would not meet jointly, and so an appearance before one had to be counterbalanced with an appearance before the other. Moreover, Senators and Representatives were too busy with other activities to take much interest in the general administrative arrangements of the ASF as long as the desired results were forthcoming. Since the initiative for arranging these meetings came from within the War Department rather than from the committees, no complaints were received from the committee when the practice died out.

From time to time the ASF did arrange for members of important committees to visit near-by installations such as Ft. Belvoir and Aberdeen Proving Grounds.

General Somervell twice directed a showing of new weapons at Ft. Myer for the information of the Secretary of War, the Chief of Staff, and Congressional leaders.

General Somervell's formal appearance at Congressional hearings were infrequent during the war. Each year he appeared before the Subcommittee of the House Committee on Appropriations handling War Department appropriations.[54] He testified before the Senate Special Committee to Study and Survey Problems of Small Business Enterprise on 7 December 1942. He was asked to testify before the House Committee on the Civil Service in June 1943. In 1944 he appeared before the House Committee on Military Affairs to testify on the postwar organization of

---

[54] Appropriations Committee members were especially complimentary when Somervell appeared. On 26 February 1941, at a hearing of the House Committee on Military Affairs, Representative Matthew J. Merritt of New York remarked: "Just one question I had in mind, General, and before I ask you that, I just want to tell you that New York has had a loss and Washington had a gain because of the fact that you left New York and came down to Washington. We were very much enthused over your work up there and appreciated all of your help." *Hearings before the Committee on Military Affairs,* H.R., 77th Cong, 1st Sess, on Inquiry as to National Defense Construction, p. 177.

Some two months later, the chairman of the House Committee on Appropriations, Clifton A. Woodrum of Virginia, remarked: "I do not know how other members of the Committee feel about it, but I think the Committee has a lot of confidence in General Somervell." To which Mr. Snyder replied: "So do the members of the War Department Subcommittee." *Hearings before the Subcommittee of the Committee on Appropriations,* H.R., 77th Cong, 1st Sess, on Military Establishment Appropriation Bill for 1942, 7 May 41, p. 414.

A year later, on 11 June 1942, Mr. Snyder amplified his sentiments when General Somervell appeared to defend the War Department budget requests for the fiscal year 1943. Mr. Snyder, the chairman of the War Department subcommittee said: "General, at the outset may I express to you the great pleasure it is to each of us to get most complimentary reports from many different sources of the magnificent job

the Army.[55] On 17 December 1945 he urged defense unification before the Senate Committee on Military Affairs. Occasions such as these were rare. Formal legislative relations were neither an important or burdensome part of the work of the commanding general of the Army Service Forces. This suited General Somervell.

One annoying criticism of Somervell came from a member of the House Committee on Appropriations, Representative Albert J. Engel of Michigan. On 1 October 1942 Mr. Engel, on the floor of the House, accused the War Department in general, and General Somervell in particular, of concealing the full cost of the Pentagon Building from the House Committee on Appropriations and of spending more money for the structure than Congress appropriated for that purpose.[56] This accusation was repeated on subsequent occasions.[57] In his official reply to these charges in a letter on 2 October 1942 to the chairman of the House Committee on Appropriations, Representative Clifton A. Woodrum of Virginia, General Somervell declared:

I cannot agree, however, that the War Department failed to keep faith with the Congress of the United States with respect to the construction of this building.

In the House hearings of July 22, 1941, I stated that the building could be built, on the then contemplated site, for $35,000,000 (exclusive of parking facilities). I pointed out that the Bureau of Public Roads had already prepared a general plan for the highway development from the south and west to the city of Washington and that the proposed building site would fit into that layout without difficulty. None of the costs of this general highway system was therefore included in the estimate.

In the Senate hearings of August 8, 1941, I stated, with reference to the proposed change in location, "it is impossible for me to give you any accurate figures on the southern site." I further added that the costs would be considerably increased due to the additional roads and expensive foundation and grading requirements. You are, of course, aware that this change in site was made.

The comparative figures as to building costs are extremely misleading if those costs are not based on comparable facilities, as was the case in Mr. Engel's discussion. The Pentagon Building is entirely self-contained, including its own sewage-disposal plant, heating plant, etc. In any event, it is hardly fair to charge the general road development of the Washington approaches against the

---

you are doing. It is very gratifying and reassuring to us to know that, as representatives of the people and the taxpayers of the nation, we have such capable hands to entrust with such tremendous responsibilities." *Hearings before the Subcommittee of the Committee on Appropriations,* H.R., 77th Cong, 2d Sess, on Military Establishment Appropriation Bill for 1943, 11 Jun 42, p. 31.

On the same occasion Mr. D. Lane Powers, Republican from New Jersey, declared: "General Somervell, I say this absolutely from the heart: I think you are doing a magnificent job. I think you have one of the most difficult jobs any military man ever had in the history of the world, and I think every member of this committee agrees with me; and I certainly hope that the people of the United States some day will show their appreciation of you for the work that you have done, that you are doing, and that you will do. I think it is grand." *Ibid.,* p. 47.

On 26 May 1943, when General Somervell appeared again before the House Committee on Appropriations, one of its members, Mr. Joseph Starnes of Alabama, had this to say: "General Somervell, I think the high point in the history of this World War II will be the operations of the Services of Supply . . . it will provide the most fascinating chapter in the history of man. Under your superb leadership we have improved the science of logistics. Time and space have been a challenge met with spirit and incomparable results." *Hearings before the Subcommittee of the Committee on Appropriations,* H.R., 77th Cong, 2d Sess, on Military Establishment Appropriation Bill for 1944, p. 36.

[55] See above, p. 383.

[56] *Congressional Record,* October 1, 1942, pp. 7939–45.

[57] *Congressional Record,* February 29, 1944, p. 2124, and March 6, 1944, p. 2315.

per square-foot costs of the Pentagon Building. If we compare the cost of the building proper, $49,194,000, we find that that cost per square-foot gross is only $8.52, a figure comparable to that of other government buildings. Comparing the net costs, it is found that the Pentagon Building drops well below others.

The attack on Pearl Harbor on December 7, 1941, changed the requirements of the War Department, both as to the needs for space and speedy construction. Changes in the building necessarily followed. On May 7, 1942, I informed the House Appropriations Committee, through its chairman, of all the developments in connection with the size and cost of the building.[58]

Representative Engel never succeeded in persuading any of his colleagues to join him in his charges; the Truman Committee later explored the project but soon dropped it.[59] The House Committee on Appropriations never questioned the War Department's action, but the charges of wrong-doing were nevertheless repeated from time to time and were taken up by radio commentators generally hostile to the administration. For this reason, General Somervell had a complete brief prepared on the Pentagon project and left this in his official files as a statement of exactly what happened.[60] It seems evident from this record that the House Appropriations Committee was kept fully informed by the War Department on Pentagon costs, that the intention to use funds from general construction appropriations was clearly indicated to the committee, and that the committee never questioned or objected to the procedure. Moreover, the continuing usefulness of the building during and after the war, and the advantages derived from its location outside the congested central area of Washington, were too apparent to arouse any real criticism.

The Congressional agency which continually kept various War Department activities under surveillance was the Senate Special Committee Investigating the National Defense Program, originally created by a Senate resolution in 1941, and popularly known as the Truman Committee, mentioned earlier. From the summer of 1944 to 1946, its chairman was Senator James M. Mead of New York. Many different phases of ASF activity were privately investigated by the Truman Committee. A special assistant to the Secretary of War, working under the supervision of Under Secretary Patterson, was assigned on a full-time basis to keep in touch with the committee and provide it with requested information. Formal hearings were held on only a few activities of the ASF.[61]

There were three relatively minor matters on which the Truman Committee criticized the ASF. One was the manner in which the leasing of large, luxury hotels was handled. The committee declared that the Army's "entire hotel acquisition program which basically contained much merit, was hastily conceived."[62] It disclosed that the Army acquired properties on short notice, used them only a short time, and conducted a program that "re-

---

[58] *Congressional Record,* Vol. 88, Pt. 10, Appen., p. A3568.

[59] Ltr, Julius H. Amberg, Spec Asst to SW, to the Truman Com, USW files, 13 Jul 43.

[60] When this brief was prepared it was thought that the Truman Committee would hold a hearing on the Pentagon. This was never done. The brief, entitled The Pentagon Project, was prepared by the Control Division, and the original is in the files of the Commanding General, ASF.

[61] See *Hearings before a Special Committee Investigating the National Defense Program,* Senate, 78th Cong, 2d Sess, Pt. 21.

[62] *Third Annual Report of the Special Committee Investigating the National Defense Program,* Senate, 78th Cong, 2d Sess, 3 Mar 44, Senate Rpt 10, Pt. 6, p. 131.

sulted in many injustices which the War Department has shown little inclination to correct." [63] To add insult to injury, the committee concluded: "The Navy showed greater efficiency and care than the Army, both in formulating its original program and in carrying it out with the fairness and courtesy that citizens are entitled to expect from the military." [64]

General Somervell was inclined to dismiss this matter as of little importance. Behind the charge was the fact that the Army had driven some hard bargains with real estate owners, and the owners were disgruntled by a failure to obtain larger sums of money. Originally, the owners had been eager to have their properties used by the Army because of the wartime curtailment of vacation travel. Later, they wanted more money or a return of their facilities. In any event, the committee did not charge that the War Department, through the ASF, had wasted funds or that Army officers had been engaged in collusion with hotel owners.

Second, the Truman Committee looked somewhat askance upon the Alaska Highway project, and in a postwar report referred to that project as "in itself a dubious undertaking." [65] No formal hearings were ever held on the project, although one was threatened. General Somervell had a complete account of the entire undertaking prepared for use in case of an investigation. [66] The role of the ASF, through the Chief of Engineers, was one of carrying out instructions which came from the War Department General Staff; the basic decision was made in the War Plans Division before 9 March 1942 and was approved by President Roosevelt. There was no indication that the performance of the ASF in carrying out this task had been less than exemplary.

In the autumn of 1944 an intermediary arranged for General Somervell to have lunch with one of the members of the Mead Committee in the course of which he learned that the committee intended shortly to release a highly critical report on Army accumulation of surplus supplies. General Somervell naturally was concerned and obtained a preliminary copy of the report. This was carefully studied by ASF staff agencies and was made the subject of a special conference. Somervell took the stand that where criticisms in the report were warranted, they should be faced, and when unwarranted, the committee should be asked to modify its report. As eventually released, the committee's original draft contained a few modifications. For example, it reported a situation in which the ASF disposed of five-gallon gasoline containers in the summer of 1944 and then had to re-order nearly four million cans in September of the same year. The committee was willing to add that this situation "resulted from the unexpectedly rapid advance of combat forces and the inability to establish an adequate supply of petroleum products through pipelines and other forms of conveyance." The committee concluded: "The instance is mentioned to illustrate the difficulties

---

[63] *Ibid.*, pp. 131–32.

[64] *Ibid.*, p. 132.

[65] *Fifth Annual Report of the Special Committee Investigating the National Defense Program*, Senate, 79th Cong, 2d Sess, 2 Aug 46, Senate Rpt 110, Pt. 7, p. 23. For a more detailed treatment of the Alcan Highway see Bykofsky and Larson. Activities in the Oversea Commands; Jesse A. Remington, Blanche D. Coll, Lenure Fine, ZI Construction, II, one of the Engineer volumes in the series, UNITED STATES ARMY IN WORLD WAR II. See also Stetson Conn and Byron Fairchild, The Framework of Hemisphere Defense, a volume in preparation for the series UNITED STATES ARMY IN WORLD WAR II. Ch. XIII.

[66] CD Rpt 175, The Alaska Highway, 1 Jun 45, CD, ASF.

involved in declaring surpluses, which, after all, must be subject to the vagaries and uncertainties of the progress of military campaigns." [67]

For the most part, the report of the Mead Committee on "Accumulation of Surpluses" commented on situations which were well known in ASF headquarters and to which continuing attention was being given. The committee found failures, "both avoidable and unavoidable," to forecast requirements correctly, failure to standardize specifications "more universally," duplication of procurement programs, inadequate inventory control, and establishment of stock levels that were too high. But it made no recommendations which had not already been considered by the ASF. The committee criticized the Army for "being very loathe to declare surpluses," but then commented, as noted above, about having to recall five-gallon gasoline cans previously declared surplus. When the committee declared: "A great deal more could be done, however, in centralizing control of procurement between branches within the War Department and bureaus within the Navy Department and more could be done toward centralizing procurement as between the War and Navy Departments," [68] General Somervell could only ruefully recall the reception given his 1943 plan to centralize ASF procurement and his unremitting effort to collaborate with the Navy. The committee did at least pat the ASF on the back for "greater uniformity" in storage operations than obtained in the Navy, and for employing "modern warehousing equipment and modern warehousing methods." [69] But the committee was critical because the ASF measured efficiency in terms of tons handled per man-hour instead of dollar costs, and strongly criticized

the management of the Engineer Section of the ASF general depot at Columbus, Ohio. Admitting that the ASF had become aware of the situation before the committee did and had taken steps to change it, the committee argued that "good controls would have disclosed the inefficiency of operations earlier, and less drastic action to correct it would have been required." [70] In conclusion, the committee acknowledged that the Army and Navy were making some efforts to improve supply practices but urged "intensification." [71] General Somervell felt that the report was deficient in ignoring the complexities of the problems discussed and misleading in omitting adequate reference to the unceasing administrative attention being given to them.

The one strongly personal attack upon General Somervell by the Truman Committee was the criticism of the Canol project. The committee held extensive public hearings on this undertaking in the autumn of 1943 while General Somervell was outside the United States. On 20 December 1943 he was given an opportunity to present his side of the matter.[72] The Canol project was a fourfold endeavor: (1) the construction of an oil refinery at Whitehorse, Yukon Territory, Canada; (2) the construction of distribution pipelines from Skagway, Alaska, to Whitehorse and up and down the Alaska

---

[67] *Additional Report of the Special Committee Investigating the National Defense Program*, Senate, 78th Cong, 2d Sess, 19 Dec 44, Senate Rpt 10, Pt. 20, p. 29.

[68] *Ibid.*, p. 17.

[69] *Ibid.*, p. 21.

[70] *Ibid.*, p. 23.

[71] *Ibid.*, p. 33.

[72] *Hearings before the Special Committee Investigating the National Defense Program*, Senate, 78th Cong, 1st Sess, on the Canol Project, Pt. 22. Somervell's testimony begins on p. 9655.

Highway; (3) petroleum extraction from the Norman Wells fields in Northwest Territory, Canada, and pipeline connection to the refinery at Whitehorse; and (4) exploration for additional petroleum reserves in the Canadian Northwest.

General Somervell explained that he made the decision to exploit local oil resources in Canada in April 1942 in an atmosphere of general gloom and military setback. Alaska was vital to American defense; an air route to Alaska had been started which needed oil supplies, and a highway had been authorized, principally to service the chain of airfields. The nation was short of tankers and the German submarine campaign was destroying American shipping off the American coast. The Navy said it could not guarantee to keep shipping lanes open. He reported the consideration given the matter, the various persons who advised him, and how he in turn had discussed the matter with General Marshall and the Operations Division of the War Department General Staff. He pointed out that he then had the matter presented to a War Council Meeting (where both Secretary Stimson and Under Secretary Patterson were present) on 11 May 1942. He added that, at this same time, he had approved a project to explore for oil in New Zealand.[73] Second, General Somervell defended the feasibility of the project. He mentioned the various fears— inadequate supply, failure of oil to flow through pipes at low temperatures, paraffin content, construction obstacles—and how all of them had failed to materialize.[74] Third, he insisted that the job had been done competently.[75] The fourth question was whether the project should have been continued in the light of changed circumstances. Here General Somervell simply rested his case on the argument that the

Joint Chiefs of Staff had reviewed the project and had decided "to continue the project as essential to the war effort." [76] He went on to comment about the national concern for petroleum supply as one element behind that decision. To halt the project would save the expenditure of about $10,000,000. General Somervell then turned to an explanation of the agreements with the oil companies, the contractors, and the Canadian Government.[77] In answer to questions on the subject, General Somervell stated that had he known in 1942 that the project could not be finished until 1944, he "doubted" if he would have approved it. The project had not been pushed as hard as it might have been because the urgent need for it had diminished.[78] Many of the essential papers on the project were published at the conclusion of the hearings.

General Somervell's testimony was not convincing to the committee. On 8 January 1944, the report of the Truman Committee on the Canol project was presented to the Senate by Senator Kilgore.[79] The committee declared that the project "was undertaken without adequate consideration or study," that General Somervell's "continued insistence upon the project," in the face of these repeated warnings about the project's unsoundness and excessive cost, "is inexcusable," that the project failed to provide a local source of oil products for the defense of Alaska in 1942 and 1943, that the Petroleum Ad-

---

[73] Ibid., p. 9655–62.
[74] Ibid., pp. 9662–64.
[75] Ibid., pp. 9664–65.
[76] Ibid., p. 9665.
[77] Ibid., p. 9670–72.
[78] Ibid., p. 9688.
[79] Additional Report of the Special Committee Investigating the National Defense Program, Senate, 78th Cong, 1st Sess, Senate Rpt 10, Pt. 14.

ministrator for War should have been consulted before the Canol project was undertaken, that the contracts with the Imperial Oil Company and the Canadian Government "were improvidently drawn," and that the War Department should review the project to decide whether it was worthwhile to complete it.[80] The committee concluded "that the Canol project should not have been undertaken, and that it should have been abandoned when the difficulties were called to the attention of the War Department."[81] The committee declared that it believed in prompt action, even when subsequent events proved it unwise, but that in this instance, General Somervell acted "on the basis of a faulty and unnecessarily incomplete consideration of the project by himself and his subordinates and without consulting other governmental agencies and private concerns with oil experience."[82] Some newspaper and radio commentators repeated these criticisms widely for a protracted period of time.

The Senate committee returned to its criticism of the Canol project in filing a Fifth Annual Report on 3 September 1946.[83] The project was referred to as "a glaring example of this type of waste."[84] The committee declared that General Somervell had "stubbornly refused" to admit a mistake in authorizing the program and that the whole project had in fact turned out to be unnecessary. It further criticized Admiral King, Chief of Naval Operations, because he had signed a letter on behalf of the Joint Chiefs of Staff stating the opinion that the project should be continued.[85] The committee concluded that: "This action constitutes a blot upon the record of two otherwise capable officers, which it is the duty of the committee to report and comment on to the end that

there shall be in the future no recurrence of a similar type of action."[86]

In judging General Somervell's position on the Canol project, two aspects of the matter should be noted. He firmly believed that in the light of the circumstances of 1942 he was justified in making the decision to undertake the project. Oil was scarce, ocean-going tankers were in short supply, and any assistance to the operation of the line of communication between the United States and Alaska was worthwhile. Even the Truman Committee in 1944 had been willing to admit that there might be "some slight excuse" for this original decision.[87] In the second place, when the project was criticized by Secretary Ickes, the Bureau of the Budget, and others in 1943, the entire matter was reviewed by the Operations Division of the WDGS, by General McNarney, and by agencies of the JCS. Upon the basis of this review, the Joint Chiefs of Staff agreed on 26 October 1943 to continue the project. To be sure, General Somervell had strongly urged this approval.[88] Nonetheless, other elements of the high command had associated themselves with General Somervell's point of view. From this point on General Somervell felt that he was car-

---

[80] *Ibid.*, pp. 6–7.

[81] *Ibid.*, p. 7.

[82] *Ibid.*, p. 7.

[83] *Fifth Annual Report of the Special Committee Investigating the National Defense Program*, Senate, 79th Cong, 2d Sess, 3 Sep 46, Senate Rpt 110, Pt. 7.

[84] *Ibid.*, p. 23.

[85] Admiral King subsequently protested vigorously the implication of the committee that he had acted as an individual rather than simply as spokesman of the views of the Joint Chiefs of Staff collectively. See *Hearings before a Special Committee Investigating the National Defense Program*, Senate, 79th Cong, 2d Sess, Pt. 39, p. 22983.

[86] Fifth Annual Report, p. 25, cited in n. 83.

[87] *Additional Report*, p. 6, cited in n. 79.

[88] See for example, Memo, Somervell for ACofS OPD, 20 Jul 43, CG ASF.

rying out not "his" project but one directed by higher authority.

Perhaps the last word on the Canol project was provided in October 1946. The explanation was that the real motive of the JCS in approving the continuation of the Canol project was a strategic one. As long as the project was continued, the Japanese were uncertain whether the United States intended to make an attack upon the Japanese Islands from the North. To have abandoned the project would have been an indication to the Japanese that a northern attack was no longer planned.[89]

Somervell reacted to these criticisms with mixed sentiments. On the one hand he felt that the attack upon the Canol project was personal, inspired by some imagined affront to certain individual Senators.[90] On the other, he felt relieved that this was the only important decision the committee could find to criticize in an activity as gigantic and complicated as the supply and service of the American Army in World War II.

The Truman Committee was disposed also to be critical of another project, the Pan American Highway. Extensive hearings on this project were held between 13 July and 26 July 1945 and between 3 and 28 September 1946. The documents in the case showed that General Somervell on 30 March 1942 asked his Chief of Transportation to study and report on the desirability of the Army undertaking the completion of the Pan American Highway to the Panama Canal Zone. General Gross endorsed the project on 9 May 1942 and General Styer sent a memorandum to the Chief of Staff on 25 May 1942 recommending the construction of an all-weather road. On 6 June General McNarney authorized the Army Service Forces to make

a preliminary survey while deferring final decision. On 17 June General Styer forwarded to the Chief of Staff a memorandum from the Chief of Engineers in which the latter recommended immediate construction. This was approved by General Handy for General Eisenhower, then Assistant Chief of Staff, OPD. Thus the decision to go on with the Pan American Highway was a collective decision. The Secretary of War informed the Secretary of State on 10 September 1943 that "changes in the strategic situation have eliminated the war necessity" for the Pan American Highway and that the "War Department participation in this project must, therefore, be terminated."[91]

Legislative oversight and criticism is an essential part of the administration of public activities. Somervell was inclined to welcome the existence of an investigating committee for its salutary effect in keeping administrative officials on their toes. But he felt that, as far as the Truman Committee itself was concerned, its inquiries into the Army Service Forces were largely motivated by a desire to embarrass him personally, as indicated above. Thus he believed the committee dropped its criticism of the Pan American Highway because it discovered that a number of others had participated in the decision, especially the Chief of Engineers. The committee, Somervell suspected, was in-

---

[89] JCS 528/1, Joint Production Survey Com Rpt, 23 Oct 43, ABC 463.7 Canol (11 Oct 43) Sec. 1-A; JCS 528/7, JLC Rpt, 23 Oct 46, ABC 463.7 Canol (11 Oct 43) Sec. 1-B.

[90] A complete history of the Canol project was prepared by the Office of the Chief of Engineers in 1945 at the request of General Somervell. See files, CD, ASF.

[91] These documents are contained in Report on the Pan American Highway, a typed report prepared by the Construction Planning Branch, Requirements Division, ASF, 12 January 1944, CG ASF.

terested primarily in finding something to "pin" on him, and was not interested in criticizing other officials within the ASF. It is, of course, difficult to determine the exact motivation of Congressional committee members, and those newspaper writers and radio commentators who exploit their inquiries. Whatever the motive Somervell believed much of the personal criticism arose because he had alienated an influential member of the Truman Committee by refusing to do him a favor when he was in direct charge of construction work.

Undoubtedly Somervell was regarded by some congressmen as imperious, headstrong, and little inclined to consult or cooperate with them in the fulfillment of their duties. Indeed, he was disposed to stay as far away from Congress as possible. This attitude did not make for harmonious legislative relations, and it may have contributed to the vigorous criticism heaped on him, criticism which may have had some justification but which was certainly unrestrained in tone and greatly exaggerated in both press and radio. The experience left Somervell with a feeling of considerable bitterness. He was not the kind of person who could by temperament be philosophical about the price the public administrator pays for high office in our democracy.

In evaluating the work of the ASF from 1942 to 1945, Somervell concluded that its major accomplishments were five in number. In the first place, the Army had been better supported than any previous American Army in history. Certainly the supply accomplishments of World War II contrasted vividly with the failures in the Civil War, the Spanish-American War, and World War I. As American production facilities reached a peak in turning out military items, and as shipping became increasingly available, military operations overseas were almost never seriously handicapped by a lack of supply. In the second place, the quality of weapons and of other equipment had not been sacrificed in order to obtain quantity. In the last half of 1942, for example, the medium tank model was completely changed even though some production loss was necessarily entailed. Heavier tanks and heavier tank weapons were also introduced. Combat clothing was almost completely redesigned as a result of experience gained in North Africa. Wherever improvements became possible or experience demonstrated new needs, the ASF went to work. In the third place, no substantiated charges of dishonesty were ever brought against any of the top staff of the ASF. This was a tribute to the integrity of the thousands of men engaged in the supply task, and to the administrative machinery which provided a constant check on possible dishonesty. The few individuals who were detected profiting from war contracts were promptly prosecuted. In the fourth place, the Army Service Forces constantly strived for and attained increased efficiency in the performance of its work. Finally, the volume of ASF activity told its own story. An almost unheard-of expansion had to be undertaken in the supply and support operations of the American Army in World War II. Yet it was done, and done in a short period of time. This, after all is said and done, must stand as the real tribute to ASF management.

In so far as the failures were concerned, Somervell believed that they all involved deficiencies in his personal relations with others. He decided in retrospect that if he had the job to do over again, he would first of all have consulted more frequently with the G–4 Division of the WDGS, and would have used its influence in the General Staff to assist the ASF in the performance of its work. Second, he would have preferred more friendly relations with the WPB and with Mr. Nelson in particular. If the press of events had permitted more personal contact, Somervell believed that the bitter disputes that developed might have been avoided. Third, he felt that more attention should have been given to the attitudes and aspirations of the chiefs of the technical services. Finally, Somervell believed he should have worked more closely with various Congressional leaders. These were the principal management failures of the Army Service Forces, failures that were destined to influence the postwar organization of the Army. Somervell in the end discovered that vigorous internal leadership was not enough. External reputation was equally vital.

CHAPTER XXIV

The Proposed ASF Reorganization of 1943

In the summer and autumn of 1943 General Somervell and his chief advisers on organization gave careful attention to the possibility of a far-reaching and general reorganization of the entire Army Service Forces. Out of this consideration came four proposals which were submitted to Secretary of War Stimson for approval. This they failed to receive, and so the suggested reorganization of the ASF was never effected.

The entire story might perhaps be passed over without any mention or dismissed in a few words as an abortive effort. Indeed, the whole experience was a painful one for all participants. Yet there are at least three compelling reasons why the story should be told. In the first place, allusions to the incident have already been made in two widely read wartime biographies, those of Secretary Stimson and of Mr. Harry L. Hopkins. As these accounts stand they fail to reveal what actually happened. It therefore seems appropriate and even obligatory to give the matter fuller treatment. In the second place, the episode may provide useful information for future planners in the Department of the Army who will have to struggle with organizational problems. Third, the experience provided a number of lessons for the participants. If the immediate results

were negative, the incident was nonetheless instructive.

The ASF Organization Situation in 1943

The orders on headquarters organization on 15 May 1943 marked the end of a distinct period in ASF history.[1] After a year of deliberation and experimentation, a structural pattern for the ASF had finally emerged. This pattern, as already noted, consisted of three major parts. There were the seven technical services, with headquarters in Washington and various field installations to perform procurement, storage, and specialized operations. There were nine service commands, organized geographically, that were primarily responsible for supervising post management throughout the United States. Third, there was the ASF headquarters staff which, after May 1943, combined various so-called administrative services and other staff offices into a single command directing and supervising the work of the two types of operating agencies, as well as performing central services for the War Department as a whole.

This was a complex organization structure. It had numerous defects. Yet it had

---

[1] ASF Cir 30, 15 May 43.

certain virtues, too. The structure provided elements of unity and working relationships, which although they did some violence to the status and prestige of various prewar War Department offices, retained the identity and much of the substance of each. It was a cumbersome organization in many respects, but it was also a workable one, as the war experience demonstrated.

The basic question after May 1943 was whether General Somervell and his organization planners, mostly located in his Control Division, should accept this general pattern as permanent, adjusting and perfecting some of its parts, but retaining its essential features as fixed for the duration of the war; or should they consider other organizational arrangements for performing the task of the Army Service Forces. General Somervell had no hesitancy in answering this question. Organizational exploration and thinking was to continue.

There were a number of reasons for dissatisfaction with the existing ASF organization structure. One of these was the criticism of the size of the ASF headquarters in Washington. ASF staff divisions and the offices of chiefs of the technical services numbered about 32,000 soldiers and civilians during the war. This was a large force, one which could not be housed in the Pentagon alone, and so was scattered in various permanent and temporary structures all over the nation's capital. From time to time the Deputy Chief of Staff, General McNarney, pressed General Somervell to decrease this force. General McNair of the Army Ground Forces on occasion also pointed to ASF headquarters as a conspicuous example of the "overstuffed headquarters" which was absorbing the strength of the Army. Such criticisms led to numerous studies to determine what activities performed by staff divisions and chiefs of the technical services might be moved away from Washington and where other savings in manpower might be achieved. All of these studies came to one conclusion. The existing organizational structure of the ASF made a large headquarters staff inevitable.

ASF staff divisions performed their procurement, distribution, and training responsibilities through the offices of chiefs of the technical services in Washington. Thus, there was a large staff office under the Director of Matériel in ASF headquarters and large procurement staffs in the office of each chief of the technical service directing the field procurement operations of each individual service. There was a large staff in ASF headquarters supervising storage, distribution, and maintenance operations, again working through the offices of chiefs of the technical services handling these activities in each particular service. The training personnel in ASF headquarters was not very numerous, but there were training divisions in turn in the office of each chief of the technical service directing the training programs carried out in the field. In short, for many different functions there were dual staffs in Washington, one in the office of the commanding general, and one in the office of the chief of a technical service. As long as the technical services were organized along commodity and specialist lines, no remedy could be effected. On the other hand, since the functional co-ordinating burden of the Commanding General, ASF, was a large one it could be reduced only by a fundamental shift in organizational structure.

Studies by the Control Division clearly emphasized other structural defects in the existing organization. The New York Field Survey of May 1942 had called attention to the fact that there were five separate procurement offices in New York City alone with resulting duplication in personnel, fiscal, clerical, and other administrative operations. The survey pointed further to duplication in the maintenance of facilities records and in inspection activities and plant protection. The report suggested that a district commanding officer of the ASF be set up in the New York area to centralize and furnish administrative services for the various procurement offices. It would make the local supply sections responsible administratively to the district commanding officer, but technically responsible to the various technical service offices in Washington. This survey also recommended that the primary organizational arrangement for purchasing operations in the field should be based on a geographical division of duties.[2] As has been noted, General Somervell did not act immediately on these recommendations at the time the report was submitted.

Other weaknesses in ASF organization also existed. There were duplications in personnel work between the ASF Director of Personnel and The Adjutant General. The Army Exchange Service had procurement responsibilities. The Special Services Division was producing motion pictures and publishing books and pamphlets, types of work that were also being performed elsewhere. Often the lack of a uniform pattern of organization throughout the ASF impeded the establishment of simplified and uniform procedures and the prompt interchange of information and instructions between various echelons.

Another grave difficulty in the ASF organization was the wide variety of field units employed by the technical services.

Each service had its own system of field offices and in some cases had more than one set of field offices doing different jobs throughout the United States. This lack of uniformity made field co-ordination extremely difficult. Even the service commands themselves followed different practices within their own boundaries. Each one, for example, had district offices at this time, but apart from internal security activities these offices had little in common. One service command had placed all of its field functions except those located at Class I and Class II posts under district offices. Six gave certain training responsibilities and military police troops to district commanding officers, while the others did not. Only one service command delegated officer-procurement activities to its district commanders. Seven of the service commands followed state boundary lines in setting up districts and two did not.[3]

Another major problem in field organization was revealed by workload studies prepared in the Control Division in February and March 1943. These studies found a great disparity in the workload carried by the nine service commands. Three service commands, the Fourth, Eighth, and Ninth, performed 46 percent of the work of all service commands. Four other service commands, the First, Second, Fifth, and Sixth, accounted for 24 percent of the service command workload. Such a variation was inevitable under the circumstances, largely because the original

---

[2] New York Field Survey, Contl Br, SOS, May 42 (mimeographed), CD, ASF, pp. 1, 5.

[3] These facts are taken from a memorandum prepared within the Control Division on 21 August 1943, summarizing data received from each service command in response to a questionnaire on the subject of district organization and responsibilities. Files, CD, ASF.

boundary lines for service commands had been determined on the basis of potential military population in the United States. Accordingly, those service commands with the smallest geographical areas were located within highly urbanized and highly industrialized sections of the United States. These were the areas with the smallest number of military training posts, particularly posts for training AGF units, which in 1943 was the major portion of the service command workload. In other words, service command boundary lines that had been drawn for a particular purpose in 1920 no longer had any reality for the tasks to be performed by the ASF in 1943.

The disparities in workload meant waste in overhead personnel since the larger service commands had a lower proportion of operating personnel to workload than the smaller service commands. It was estimated that the amalgamation of the smaller service command headquarters and the lifting of all operating standards to the level of that of the most efficient service command would result in a savings of at least 45,000 military and civilian personnel.[4]

All of these deficiencies were clearly recognized by General Somervell. They were inherent in the existing organizational structure of the Army Service Forces. They arose essentially out of the long-time and separate existence of such technical services as the Office of the Chief of Ordnance and the Office of The Quartermaster General, and of such administrative bureaus as the Office of The Adjutant General. The War Department reorganization of March 1942 had not touched the separate existence of the various agencies; it had simply gathered them all together in one command which General Somervell was told to direct as best he could.

General McNair in the Army Ground Forces had fared quite differently. The 1942 reorganization had abolished the Offices of the Chief of Infantry, the Chief of Cavalry, the Chief of Field Artillery, and the Chief of Coast Artillery. But in creating the Army Service Forces, the War Department reorganization had not abolished the Offices of the Chief of Ordnance, The Surgeon General, or The Adjutant General. The Deputy Chief of Staff of the War Department, after the event, remarked to a key ASF officer that failure to abolish these offices had been the biggest single mistake of the 1942 reorganization. Perhaps it was. But General Somervell knew that in 1942 neither he nor anyone else at the center of the War Department was prepared to devise an organization which would have abolished these old and time-honored agencies in favor of something else. It was not until the summer of 1943 that General Somervell felt he had had sufficient experience to prepare an organizational structure for the ASF different from that evolved out of the immediate needs apparent in 1942.

The Preparation of an Alternative Organization for the ASF

From the outset a few fundamental concepts guided all organizational planning in 1943. The first of these was to build a single field organization to perform all the work of the Army Service Forces. This meant enlarging the service command arrangement to include all the activities directly performed in the field by the chiefs of technical services. The second

---

[4] CD Rpt 95, Operating Personnel and Workload in Service Commands, Mar 43, CD, ASF, pp. 3–5.

idea was to merge the Washington offices of chiefs of the technical services with ASF headquarters. A third idea was that the primary basis of specialization in ASF headquarters would be functional. Among other things this meant that old traditional designations would give way to new names indicating solely the type of work done.

There were, of course, various specific questions to be answered in attempting to apply these fundamental concepts to the existing ASF range of duties. For example, what should be done about a specialized field agency like the Tank-Automotive Center in Detroit? Was it to be made a part of one service command or to be treated as a special field agency with certain nationwide responsibilities? The same kind of question had to be answered for a field unit like the Office of Dependency Benefits in Newark. In the end, it was proposed that certain service commands might be designated through a special installation to handle a nationwide job, calling upon other service commands for assistance as needed. Another question was whether state boundary lines should be followed in organizing service commands and the technical service districts within service commands. Some technical services, such as the Ordnance Department and the Corps of Engineers, did not follow them in their field organization. The decision was made to adopt state boundary lines for both types of areas. Since the ASF had to maintain certain relationships with state and local governments it was believed that such an arrangement would create less confusion.

A complete list of sixty-eight different types of field installations within the ASF was drawn up and the place of each under the proposed scheme of organization was determined. These were assigned to service districts under service commands or to service commands as special field installations.

A memorandum on the proposed transfer of all field activities to the service commands, drawn up and presented to General Somervell in July 1943 by the director of the Control Division, suggested three "guiding principles" for the transfer.[5] The first was the need for carefully worked out plans in the form of detailed instructions so that the transfer could be made without any disruption of operations. The second was the organization of the field activities of the technical services into regions corresponding to service command areas with a competent officer in charge of each region. The third proposition was the establishment of a standard organization for ASF headquarters, the technical services, and the service commands which would facilitate a change at a later date to an organization based upon "functional staff and a regional line."

In commenting upon these principles in handwritten marginal notations, General Somervell indicated that it might be desirable to keep a minimum number of development and experimental stations under the direct control of ASF headquarters. There then followed some recommendations for further adjustments in the reorganization of ASF headquarters. Somervell pointed out that he was uncertain about combining training and personnel

---

[5] Since the 1943 reorganization plan was never adopted or put into effect, and because of the antagonisms aroused by it, none of the final papers on this subject were officially filed. The author, who was one of the organizational planners involved, preserved some working papers (not final papers) in his possession. This chapter has been prepared primarily from these papers.

functions and that he definitely wanted fiscal activities separated from other administrative tasks. He also questioned the desirability of transferring all security activities from the Intelligence Division to the Provost Marshal General and expressed doubt about transferring certain field offices of staff divisions to the supervision of the service commands. Finally, he directed that in the preparation of new procedures, careful attention should be given to experimentation before they were given general effect.

A new organizational plan for the ASF was finally prepared in August 1943 and presented in the form of six large charts. The first page set forth four major steps in the realization of the long-range organizational plan. These four steps were as follows:

1. *Effective October 1943*—Modifications in ASF headquarters organization, with reorganization of technical services and of headquarters, service commands, to parallel organization of headquarters, ASF.

2. *Effective October 1943*—Reduction of number of service commands from nine to six, with more equal workloads, the use of the same boundaries for the major geographic areas of technical services, and the appointment of zone administrators for field activities of technical services.

3. *Effective December 1943*—Transfer zone administrators of technical services to the staff of service commanders.

4. *Effective Spring 1944*—Final step: adopt organization in headquarters as shown on Chart 4 with same structure in service commands, and create service districts with similar organization.

The second page pictured a new organization for staff divisions within ASF headquarters. This chart involved certain changes in the organization that had been put into effect on 15 May 1943. The Director of Operations was renamed Di-

rector of Supply with only three divisions under his supervision. The Plans Division and the Mobilization Division were merged in a new Planning Division to be established in the office of the commanding general and the former Requirements Division and the International Division were eliminated as separate agencies and transferred from the Director of Matériel to this new division. A note at the bottom of the chart also explained that the Planning Division would handle all programming matters that cut across more than one staff directorate. The divisions under the Director of Military Training were increased to six, including an Information and Education Division which took over the existing orientation work performed by the then Special Services Division. All training functions of chiefs of the technical services and of staff divisions were to be transferred to the Director of Military Training in ASF headquarters. Several new divisions were also created and placed under a Director of Personnel. These were a Headquarters Personnel Division, a Personnel Control Division, and a Special Services Division which was to include the Army Exchange Service then under the Director of Administration. All personnel functions and records in The Adjutant General's office were to be consolidated under the Director of Personnel. In other respects ASF headquarters was to continue along the lines then actually in effect.

Chart 3 showed the proposed changes in the boundaries of the service commands. The existing nine were to be replaced by six service commands. (*Table 3*)

The new service command boundaries meant a consolidation of the existing First and Second Service Commands into one command, the consolidation of the Third

TABLE 3—PROPOSED SERVICE COMMAND
REALIGNMENT

Service Command	States	Headquarters
1st	Maine	New York City
	New Hampshire	
	Vermont	
	Massachusetts	
	Rhode Island	
	Connecticut	
	New York	
	New Jersey	
	Delaware	
2d	Pennsylvania	Pittsburgh
	Maryland	
	Virginia	
	West Virginia	
	Ohio	
	Kentucky	
3d	N. Carolina	Atlanta
	S. Carolina	
	Georgia	
	Florida	
	Alabama	
	Mississippi	
	Tennessee	
4th	Michigan	Chicago
	Indiana	
	Wisconsin	
	Illinois	
	Minnesota	
	Iowa	
	Missouri	
	N. Dakota	
	S. Dakota	
	Kansas	
	Wyoming	
	Colorado	
5th	Arkansas	Dallas
	Louisiana	
	Oklahoma	
	Texas	
	New Mexico	
6th	Montana	San Francisco
	Idaho	
	Utah	
	Arizona	
	Nevada	
	Washington	
	Oregon	
	California	

and Fifth Service Commands with the exception of the State of Indiana, and the consolidation of the existing Sixth and Seventh Service Commands. The Fourth, Eighth, and Ninth Service Commands would be left undisturbed but would be renumbered. The new boundaries provided a more equal workload than the one then in effect. It was estimated that it would be as follows:

1st Service Command...................	19.2%
2d Service Command....................	20.0%
3d Service Command....................	16.3%
4th Service Command...................	14.6%
5th Service Command..................	12.0%
6th Service Command.................	17.9%
	100.0%

Under the proposed arrangement, it should be noted, the existing service command headquarters in Boston, Baltimore, Columbus, and Omaha would be abandoned; the headquarters in Salt Lake City would be moved to San Francisco and a new headquarters would be established in Pittsburgh.

The next two charts were maps indicating the adjustments in the Ordnance and Engineer procurement districts that would be necessary in order to conform to the new boundary lines specified for the six service commands.

Finally, Chart 6 diagrammatically presented the long-range organizational plan for the ASF. Under the proposed plan, the staff of the commanding general would consist of a Surgeon General, a Director of Utilities, a Director of Communications, a Director of Transportation, a Director of Procurement, a Director of Supply, a Director of Personnel, a Director of Administration, and a Fiscal Director. The old chiefs of technical services disappeared as such. This represented a basic change.

Under the Director of Procurement were three functional divisions (Design and Development, Purchases, and Production) and ten commodity divisions (Guns and Ammunitions, Automotive, Communications Equipment, Subsistence, Clothing and Equipage, Construction Supplies and Equipment, Medical Supplies and Equipment, Ship and Rail Equipment, Petroleum Products, and General Supplies). Under the Director of Supply were five functional divisions (Distribution, Overseas Supply, Storage, Maintenance, Salvage and Surplus Property) and ten commodity divisions paralleling those created under the Director of Procurement. A Pictorial Division to handle Army motion picture activity and a Remount Division for the purchase and distribution of horses and mules were created and placed under the Director of Supply. All training activity was centralized in a Military Training Division under the Director of Personnel. The Director of Administration had four divisions under his office (Legal, Security, Postal, and Office Service).

The long-range organizational plan then showed the six service commands performing all of these functions in the field. Their headquarters were to parallel ASF headquarters in organization. Below the service command there would be service districts, but the exact number of these was not specified. Actually the basic planning called for twenty-five service districts—three in the First Service Command, four in the Second, five in the Third, six in the Fourth, three in the Fifth, and four in the Sixth Service Command. In addition to the districts, two types of installations were to report directly to the commanding general of a service command. These were ports of embarkation

and proving grounds. Service district organization was expected to follow the same pattern established for the headquarters of service commands and the ASF.

This series of six charts and maps was prepared as a summary of the proposals for Army Service Forces reorganization. They were shown to Under Secretary Patterson, General Marshall, General McNarney, and Secretary Stimson. In addition to this summary, the Control Division prepared more detailed supplementary data and draft orders to carry out all the contemplated changes, should the reorganization be approved. For example, additional charts were drawn up to show the branches which would be established under each division of ASF headquarters. Other charts showed the field offices that would be absorbed into ASF headquarters such as the Army Map Service, the Medical Library, the Arlington National Cemetery, the General Dispensary, and the U.S. Finance Office—all in or near Washington. All other field installations were assigned to an appropriate service district and service. One of the draft orders changed the boundaries of service commands. Other orders drafted required the chief of each technical service to establish a single geographic pattern of zone headquarters to be put into effect by the end of September. Installations to be excluded from the jurisdiction of the commander of a zone were Ft. Monmouth, Carlisle Barracks, Aberdeen Proving Ground, Edgewood Arsenal, Ft. Belvoir, Camp Lee, The Tank-Automotive Center, all ports of embarkation, and staging areas. Draft orders also were prepared to transfer field offices of staff divisions to service commands. Additional draft orders made changes in ASF headquarters and provided a standard organization to be followed in the headquarters of chiefs of the technical services. Finally, draft orders were prepared which would have amalgamated technical services zones and service commands. (No draft orders were actually prepared which would have abolished chiefs of technical services or chiefs of administrative services.)

A memorandum to accompany the summary charts listed the following ten advantages in the new plan of organization. All staff activities would be combined into functional groups. Those activities duplicated by the staff of the commanding general and the staff of the chief of a technical service would be brought together and performed in a single staff unit. All operating responsibility would be vested in field commanders and no person would have more than one "boss." All field activities would be brought under service commanders, thus eliminating the distinction between Class I and Class IV installations and permitting greater field co-ordination. The workload of service commands would be more nearly equalized, and the number of separate administrative regions reduced with corresponding savings in overhead personnel. A single geographical pattern would be established for all field activities of the ASF. The immediate subordinates of the commanding general would be reduced to nine staff directors and six field commanders. All responsibilities would be clearly and carefully defined. The common staff pattern would facilitate intercommunication and the development of uniform, simplified procedures. Finally, the new organization pattern would reduce the structure to a functional and geographical arrangement which would make it easier to understand

how the ASF was organized and expected to operate.

At the same time the memorandum acknowledged that there would be certain disadvantages in the proposed plan. It would involve a basic change in ASF organization in the middle of the war and would disrupt existing working relationships. It would take time to develop new procedures essential for the work of the new organization. It was uncertain whether procurement operations would be greatly improved by the new organization during the remainder of the war. It was also uncertain whether supply operations would be greatly improved. Finally, the morale of many individuals throughout the ASF might be adversely affected by so fundamental a change in organization. Yet, in spite of these difficulties, the director of the Control Division recommended that the changes be put into effect in the course of the next six to nine months.

General Somervell was disposed to accept the recommendations of his organizational planners. He had kept General Marshall and General McNarney informed on the thinking going on within the ASF, and their favorable attitude encouraged him to submit the new plan for approval to the Under Secretary of War and to the Chief of Staff.

Consideration of the 1943 Plan

In August 1943, about the time that the long-range organization plan for the Army Service Forces was finished, General Somervell left Washington to attend the meeting of the Combined Chiefs of Staff and of the President and the Prime Minister at Quebec. At the same time, arrangements were completed for General Somervell's world-wide inspection trip, which he made immediately after the conference. The director of the Control Division was included in the party accompanying the commanding general overseas. Thus at the time that General Somervell was ready to recommend a far-reaching reorganization of his command, he was also preparing to leave on an extensive overseas mission.

Before he departed overseas, Somervell presented his proposals to General Marshall and Secretary Stimson for consideration. Assistant Secretary McCloy attended a conference on the subject in Stimson's office. The entire matter was taken under advisement, partly awaiting the reaction of Under Secretary Patterson, who was absent during much of July and all of August on a trip to the South Pacific. Accordingly, General Somervell had his first opportunity to place the recommendations before the Under Secretary when the two met in Hawaii early in September. In a memorandum to General Marshall, dispatched from Hawaii on 12 September 1943, Somervell reported that he had spent his entire first day there talking with the Under Secretary of War, first, acquainting him with the principal matters which would require his attention upon his return to Washington, and second, attempting "to secure his approval of the proposed reorganization of the Army Service Forces." The second paragraph of General Somervell's memorandum read:

With regard to the second phase of our discussion, the reorganization of the Army Service Forces, he indicated his approval of steps one and two, but reserved an opinion on steps three and four. He stated that he thought an extraordinarily good job was being done and he hated to be a party to making a change at this time, when matters were moving so smoothly. I explained to him that although I also believed this to be the case, I felt we can do a better job with the reorganization and that it would have far-reaching effects, extending to the next war. He seemed to be concerned about the sentimental side of the change, stating that he, as an Infantry Officer, had a strong sentimental attachment for the infantry and that he was afraid that if there were to be any suppression of the existing services we would lose an asset in the esprit in those services, which had been built up in the past hundred years. I explained the various steps which were to be taken, and indicated my opinion that they could all be carried out without any dislocation of production or interference with our operation. As to the sentimental angle, I told him that this was probably stronger in my own Corps than in any other in the Army, and though there would be some adverse reaction to it, that I felt that the clean-cut logic of the arrangement would dispose of those sentimental objections. He stated that Mr. McCloy had indicated that he wished to discuss the matter with him prior to his taking action. I told him that Mr. McCloy had sat in at the Secretary's conference on the matter, and it was my impression that Mr. McCloy was in favor of the scheme although he, McCloy, had some reservations along the lines of those voiced by Mr. Patterson, and had some additional qualms about political repercussions on the removal of the Service Command Headquarters. Mr. Patterson stated that he would discuss these matters with you on his arrival, and I hope that by the time this reaches you he has become convinced of the wisdom of the proposed move. In any event, I believe we should go through with steps one and two. I am sure that with the completion of step two, step three will sell itself and that will leave us only with the problem of step four.[6]

General Somervell then proceeded south from Hawaii. From this time on, the decision on ASF reorganization rested with his superiors in the War Department. His chief of staff, General Styer, had to carry the burden of the argument for the

[6] Memo, Hq USAFICPA (signed by Somervell) for Marshall, 12 Sep 43, CG ASF.

change. Somervell realized afterward that once he sensed Under Secretary Patterson's reluctance, he should have postponed all further consideration of the proposals until his own return. He did not do so because General Marshall had indicated a favorable attitude toward the plan, and he had assumed that General Marshall would handle the final consideration by the War Department.

General Styer and the acting director of the Control Division took up the reorganization issue with Under Secretary Patterson upon the latter's return. The Under Secretary again indicated his willingness to approve steps one and two. These, the first two recommendations on the summary chart, proposed (1) to reorganize ASF headquarters and to create parallel organizations (with certain modifications) in the office of each chief of a technical service and in the service commands; and (2) to reduce the number of service commands from nine to six and have each chief of a technical service set up a unified field structure utilizing the same boundary lines as those of the service commands. He still indicated opposition to the other two steps which would have transferred the field activities of the technical services to the service commands and merged the offices of chiefs of the technical services in Washington with ASF headquarters.

With the Under Secretary opposed to part of the plan and General Marshall favorably disposed toward all its proposals, the final decision on ASF reorganization fell to Secretary Stimson. According to Mr. Stimson's memoirs, the Secretary of War was prepared to accept General Somervell's judgment that the proposed reorganization would increase the efficiency of the Army Service Forces, but he questioned whether the improvement

would outweigh "its concomitant disadvantages in the creation of bad feeling."[7] According to the record of conversations on ASF reorganization with Under Secretary Patterson and Assistant Secretary McCloy on 21 September, as found in his personal diary, Mr. Stimson had begun to feel that the reorganization was "ill-advised." He adds that he had learned only too well in 1911 and 1912 how deeply imbedded in sentiment were the memories of all the people who had ever served in the Ordnance Department, the Quartermaster Corps, or the Corps of Engineers. He was sure that a "tremendous uproar" would arise if the War Department tried to wipe out the distinctions between these services. Since Under Secretary Patterson had advised that the work of procurement and production was proceeding satisfactorily, he was, for that reason alone, against stirring up a "hornets' nest" in the middle of the war. Mr. Stimson ended his diary record with the notation that both the Under Secretary and the Assistant Secretary "shared" his views.[8] The Stimson memoirs indicate that on 22 September the Secretary held another and larger conference (presumably including General Marshall and General McNarney among others) where the "proposal was killed":

Remembering his experiences in supporting Leonard Wood, "who was not unlike General Somervell in his temperament and other characteristics," Stimson saw no reason to create bitterness which could be avoided. Nor was it as if the service branches, like General Ainsworth in the olden time, had shown themselves insubordinate or un-co-operative. There had been slow and unim-

---

[7] Stimson and Bundy, *On Active Service in Peace and War*, p. 451.
[8] *Ibid.*, pp. 451–52.

aginative work in the early days of the emergency, but Stimson had observed with satisfaction the high quality of the work done by such men as Campbell in Ordnance, and the Chief of Engineers and Quartermaster General were men of whom Somervell himself thought well enough to intend giving them new and enlarged responsibilities in his organization. General Somervell's driving energy was an enormous asset to the Army, but in this case it seemed better that it should be curbed.[9]

The Public Controversy

About the time that Secretary Stimson was deciding that the ASF reorganization was "ill-advised," the "tremendous uproar" he feared did in fact break out. On 22 September 1943, Mr. Paul W. Shafer, Republican Representative from Michigan, asked and obtained permission from the House of Representatives to extend his remarks in the *Congressional Record*. The next day, the following statement appeared in the printed edition of the *Record:*

Mr. Speaker, I am deeply disturbed. With the lives of millions of our boys at stake in this global war there are those in Government today who would play politics with the War Department.

I have seen a blueprint of a plan which would presumably streamline the War Department, but in reality its intent is to convert that great department into a New Deal political organization. In my opinion the activities of the men behind this plan are nothing less than treasonous.

I know nothing about what authority General George C. Marshall will have as global Chief of Staff. All I know is that he has built up a General Staff that has functioned well and on its record should, with one or two exceptions, remain intact. I feel that General Marshall is a great leader and I do not believe that he is the type of man who will permit himself to be jockeyed into a phoney position.

Congress cannot and should not attempt to interfere with the proposal to make General Marshall the global Chief of Staff. Such a move should not be criticized until it is shown at least that he is not to have full authority in that position. I prefer to think that his promotion is a fine recognition of his ability.

Congress, however, is in a position to prevent the conversion of the War Department into a New Deal political general to succeed General Marshall as Chief of Staff and thus thwart the carefully laid plans of the administration's fourth term strategists.

Congress should see to it that those generals who have so ably served under General Marshall are retained and that the new Chief of Staff shall be one of those best qualified to serve in that important position.

I make this statement merely to serve notice as a Member of Congress and of the House Committee on Military Affairs that I do not intend to sit idly by and permit the Hopkins-Niles-Rosenman regime to turn the War Department into a global political organization.[10]

This item was immediately picked up and published on Friday morning, 24 September, in the Washington *Times-Herald,* the *Chicago Daily Tribune,* and the New York *Daily News.* The story implied that General Marshall was to become Supreme Allied Commander and that General Somervell was to replace him as Chief of Staff in the War Department. The following day, 25 September 1943, more sensational charges were made in the three newspapers. Representative Shafer was reported to have informed the newspapers that five ranking Army officers were slated for dismissal if General Somervell replaced General Marshall as Chief of Staff. Mr. Shafer was then supposed to have said that four members of the White House "palace

---

[9] *Ibid.,* p. 452.

[10] *Congressional Record*, September 22, 1943, p. A4286.

guard"—Justice Frankfurter, Mr. Harry Hopkins, Mr. Samuel I Rosenman, and Mr. David K. Niles—were planning "to replace veteran, conservative generals with brain trusters." The newspaper article also reported Mr. Shafer as saying that he had received a blueprint of the White House palace guard "plans to streamline the War Department into a global political organization." He identified as the officers who were "slated to go" the following: the Chief of Ordnance, General Campbell; The Quartermaster General, General Gregory; the Chief of Chemical Warfare Service, General Porter; the Chief of Transportation, General Gross; and the Chief of Engineers, General Reybold. Mr. Shafer, according to the newspaper article, added that "brain trusters" would replace the generals and listed, among those being considered for top appointment, Dr. Eli Ginzberg and James P. Mitchell. At least one other member of Congress, Shafer's account continued, was present in the office of "a high government official" when he was given the information on which his charges were based. He refused to identify the person with whom he had talked. The article then went on to quote the *Army and Navy Register* as saying that General Eisenhower was most likely to succeed General Marshall as Chief of Staff but added that Mr. Hopkins was understood to prefer General Somervell, "a New Deal favorite."[11]

These charges were elaborated in an even more sensational article which appeared in a later edition on the same day. It began by claiming that a group of influential "White House advisers" was planning to give General Somervell personal control of the expenditure of twenty-two billion dollars by a complete reorganiza-

tion of the Army production front. This move was made a part of a larger campaign "to oust General Marshall from his post as Chief of Staff." The third paragraph declared: "Informed sources say the motive is to use the Army's vast production program, excepting aircraft, as a political weapon in the 1944 presidential campaign." A subsequent paragraph added: "Some observers believe the cabal also intend to build up Somervell as an Army running mate for Mr. Roosevelt on a fourth term ticket to offset the possible Republican nomination of General Douglas MacArthur."[12]

Another paragraph in the news story admitted that there was no evidence that either President Roosevelt or General Marshall were aware of the purpose or potential effect of the "plot." At the same time, the article declared: "Knowledge of it, however, has spread terror through the highest ranks of the War Department." Mr. Hutchinson went on to say that the plot could be stopped by the President's refusing to oust General Marshall, or it could be stopped by Congress.

The newspaper article then provided some of the details of the so-called plot. All production activity of the seven "technical supply services" would be transferred to the ASF under General Somer-

[11] Washington *Times-Herald*, September 25, 1943, first edition, front page article under by-line of Walter Trohan. Mr. James P. Mitchell was director of the Industrial Personnel Division in ASF headquarters. He was at no time consulted about the preparation of ASF organization plans and was completely unaware of their existence. Dr. Eli Ginzberg was a statistician in the ASF Control Division who had made the original workload studies of service commands. Other than this, he had played no part in the development of the long-range organization plans.

[12] Washington *Times-Herald*, September 25, 1943, second edition, front page article under by-line of William K. Hutchinson and copyrighted by the International News Service.

vell. While these services were grouped under Somervell, Hutchinson stated, he had no "control over their expenditures, contract negotiations, or production schedules." The article further stated that actual regulation of production would be turned over to the Army service commands but added that the existing nine service commands were to be abolished and six new ones created, "with six political generals named to command the new areas." It then went on to state that the present chiefs of supply services would become armchair generals handling routine paper work. "Leaders of the cabal" would defend their plot by contending that they proposed to streamline antiquated War Department production organization. The present commodity organization would be eliminated in favor of a functional organization. The article then proceeded to declare that "prominent industrialists" were certain that a commodity organization could out-produce a functional organization. It asserted that the Army's commodity organization was patterned after the successful production practices of Sears-Roebuck, Ford, General Motors, and duPont. The failures of War Department production in World War I were attributed to a functional organization. The present practice of letting contracts locally through regional offices would be eliminated under the new scheme in favor of centering procurement authority in Washington. At the same time the account acknowledged that the six service commands would be responsible for production in their own areas. The apparent contradiction was ignored. To clinch the argument against reorganization an anonymous "nationally known industrialist" was introduced and quoted as saying that any shift from com-

modity to functional procurement would lose the war and be the most "monumental mistake in the history of our country."

On 28 September 1943, Mr. Andrew J. May, Democratic Representative from Kentucky and chairman of the House Military Affairs Committee, told the House of Representatives that he had had a conference that morning with General Marshall. He added that Marshall had authorized him to say that: ". . . there was complete harmony among the high officials of the War Department and the Administration." [13] Mr. R. Ewing Thomason, Democratic Representative from Texas, reported that General Marshall had called him on the telephone at his residence to express "regret and deep concern at some of the statements that have appeared in local papers and also on the floor of this House." Mr. Thomason went on to say that General Marshall had expressed "the greatest confidence in General Somervell and also stated that there is complete harmony and cooperation between him and General Somervell and all the other high-ranking generals who have been mentioned on this floor and in the newspapers during the last few days." Mr. Walter G. Andrews, Republican Representative from New York, added:

I want to quote General Marshall as of this morning in saying that he greatly resents all references that have been made to his keyman, General Somervell, on the floor of this House, and in the newspapers, and that he considers it harmful to Army morale and grossly unfair to a truly great American officer.[14]

The majority floor leader in the House of Representatives, Mr. John W. McCor-

[13] *Congressional Record*, September 28, 1943, p. 7883.
[14] *Ibid.*, p. 7883.

mack, of Massachusetts, arose to read an authorized statement from Secretary Stimson:

The President has absolutely refrained from interfering in any way with the War Department and in the choice of any generals of the United States Army, and in their assignment to duty. The President has followed the advice of his military advisers in the consideration of all questions of strategy which have governed the war, and so far as his intrusion in any political or personal way it has been absolutely non-existent.[15]

The furor was sufficient to warrant comment by President Roosevelt at his news conference on 28 September 1943. A reporter asked the President if he had anything to say about General Marshall whereupon the President picked up a copy of the Washington *Times-Herald* and read from the front-page article written by the head of the Washington office of the International News Service. In reply to it, Mr. Roosevelt chose to read from two editorials in the *New York Herald-Tribune* published on 22 and 23 September. One of these editorials accused "The Patterson press" of "sleepless efforts to spread disunion among the Allies and confusion in their war planning." It was obvious that these words reflected the President's own sentiments.[16]

The Plan Dropped

General Styer reported this sequence of events in a personal letter to General Somervell. His story is best conveyed in his own words:

The reorganization is temporarily stymied, if not permanently so. Mr. Patterson came back and exhibited no enthusiasm for the reorganization in his conferences with me, or with the Secretary, at which General Marshall, General McNarney, Mr. McCloy, and I were present. We had two such sessions with the Secretary. Mr. Patterson indicated to me that he was willing to go along with steps 1 and 2, but stated that he thought we were doing a pretty good job under our present organization, and that there was no need for reorganization. However, he said that if you desire steps 1 and 2, he would not object.

General Marshall, General McNarney, Mr. McCloy and I have all been advocating the adoption of the reorganization, but the Secretary is as yet undecided. The whole matter was complicated by a leak, the source of which I have been unable to determine, and the story of the consolidation of the 6th and 7th Service Commands broke in the Omaha papers. This, of course, was taken up immediately by the Senators and Congressmen from that area. They were not at all belligerent about it, but of course, argued against making the change. Senators Wherry and Butler, and Congressman Buffett, came in to see me and later came in to see Judge Patterson and myself. They indicated their desire to keep the headquarters at Omaha, but stated that if it was in the interests of the war effort, they, of course, would not interpose strong objections. The Secretary of War did not seem to be disturbed by this activity because he said we had the same thing every time we tried to make a change in any Army installation.

The reorganization was further complicated by many rumors in the paper concerning the future of General Marshall. This was blown up by the chief of the News Bureau Service of I.N.S. in Washington, who had an article in the paper concerning the mystery surrounding General Marshall's future status, and intimating that a plot was on foot to kick General Marshall upstairs to make room for you as Chief of Staff, and that there was a political clique close to the White House which was planning to reorganize the War Department to put all of the procurement under you so that the twenty billion dollar program could be used for political purposes. This, of course, upset everybody,

---

[15] *Ibid.*, p. 7884.
[16] *The New York Times*, September 29, 1943.

and General Marshall talked to influential Senators and Congressmen, who came out in speeches on the floor of the House and Senate reiterating their confidence in General Marshall, and stated that General Marshall had confidence in you and resented the implications concerning one of his key men. He further stated that there was perfect harmony among the high officials of the War Department, and that these newspaper rumors were unfounded.

The Secretary of War also came forward with a statement to the effect that the White House had never interfered in the selection of key officials of the War Department, and the operations of the War Department.

Mr. Patterson and Mr. Stimson, I think, both felt it would be unwise to attempt to put into effect the reorganization until this furor had died down.

At his last press conference, the President pinned back the ears of the chief of the I.N.S. News Bureau Service here in Washington, and refused to make any statement concerning the future status of General Marshall.

Mr. Stimson indicated to General Marshall that he was not going ahead with the reorganization, as a result of which General Marshall directed that we do not bother him for a few days until he has a chance to get over the confusion which I have indicated above.

Mr. McCloy told me he talked with the Secretary the night before last, and the Secretary indicated that he would give consideration to step No. 1, but he was concerned about the consolidation of training activities in the Headquarters, A.S.F., and he would like to talk the matter over with two or three of the chiefs of Technical Services. I told Mr. McCloy the chiefs of Technical Services would be cold as they were not informed of the details of the reorganization provided for in step No. 1, and he therefore directed me to talk with Generals Campbell, Reybold and Ingles in regard to step No. 1, but to base it solely on going ahead with step No. 1, and possibly step No. 2, but with no reference to any further changes.

General Campbell has been out of town on an inspection trip, and will not return until next Tuesday, so I have not talked the mat-

ter over with him. However, I have talked the matter over with Generals Reybold and Ingles, and while they think training activities should stay with them, I do not think they will indicate any strong opposition to the suggested move. The other changes in organization for their offices can be effected without much trouble.

I regret to give you this long tale of woe, but I assure you we have been doing everything we could to push this matter but have been stymied for reasons indicated above. While the reorganization picture does not look too rosy of accomplishment at the present time, I still have hopes that we can go ahead with step No. 1, if we proceed cautiously.

I think Mr. Patterson's feeling that we are doing pretty well at the present time with our present organization, and that we should not invite antagonism from an already antagonistic Congress, has caused the Secretary of War to hesitate to make the move. Also, Mr. Patterson feels that the sentiment and tradition which will be affected by the later steps of the plan have not been given full consideration. At one of our meetings with the Secretary he appeared to share this feeling.[17]

On 14 October 1943, General Styer sent General Somervell an account of the latest developments in the consideration of ASF reorganization:

The reorganization matter has been one of our great worries as we have not been able to accomplish what you desired. I wrote you some of the details of our troubles, and they are still continuing.

Mr. Stimson has sent the Chief of Staff a memorandum disapproving steps 3 and 4, and stating that for the present, he was not ready to approve steps in paragraphs 1 and 2. However, he left a small loophole for reopening steps 1 and 2, and we had a meeting with him yesterday morning. He is particularly undecided about the advisability of consolidating the training activities of the Technical Services under the Director of Training, Headquarters, ASF. He wanted to discuss

---

[17] Ltr, Styer to Somervell, 2 Oct 43, CG ASF.

this matter with some of the principal chiefs of Technical Services. In accordance with his instructions, I assembled Generals Campbell, Reybold and Ingles, and General Weible, and we all discussed the matter before discussing it with the Secretary. We had a meeting with the Secretary yesterday morning on this step, at which Mr. McCloy, Generals Campbell, Reybold, Ingles, Weible and myself were present.

Naturally, the Chiefs of Technical Services prefer not to lose their training activities, although a large percentage of the training of their units is done at present in the Service Commands.

The Secretary stated he was not ready to make up his mind on this training matter, so I asked him if we could put the rest of step No. 1 in effect. He said he was not going to approve anything he did not understand, so I outlined the whole step No. 1 to him again, and he told me we could go ahead with the changes in Osborn's and Byron's organizations, and with the WACs. The principal one of these changes, however, which we desired to effect as soon as practicable was the consolidation of all personnel activities under the Director of Personnel. He told me he did not hold the same sentimental feeling about breaking up The Adjutant General's office that he had about making changes that would effect the long established Technical Services, but that he would reserve that for a decision after he had thought over the matter some more. Sentiment and branch esprit de corps appear to be worrying him, and he said he did not want to do anything to disturb this.

This reorganization problem has been a long, drawn out, uphill battle, and it appears that we will accomplish it only by taking a small bite here and there from time to time. I hate to give you this very discouraging report on this matter, which I know you wished to have accomplished, but it has been a tough one.[18]

General Styer's letters reached Somervell in Chungking. There was nothing to be done about the situation from that distance. And furthermore, General Somervell then had his hands full with the Stilwell situation. He commented on the matter only briefly in a letter to General Marshall. He expressed his "disgust" with the "unfavorable publicity which was given to the rumor of your appointment as supreme commander." He added that he was "distressed that my name was mixed up in it in any way, and that you had this stupid thing to contend with in addition to all your other burdens."[19]

On 5 October 1943 the Secretary of War officially disapproved of Proposals 3 and 4 for ASF reorganization in a memorandum to the Chief of Staff. In a memorandum for record dated 13 October, the Secretary noted that he had disapproved Steps 1 and 2 except for certain modifications in ASF headquarters itself.[20] Thus the basic organization pattern of the Army Service Forces as worked out by May 1943 survived all attempts at revision.

General Somervell did not return to the United States until the middle of November. Then he once more had to prepare to leave the country, this time to attend the meeting of the Combined Chiefs of Staff in Cairo in December and to go on to Tehran. Not until the end of December 1943 was General Somervell back at his desk in the Pentagon to give attention to the internal affairs of the Army Service Forces. He had been out of the United States almost four months. He chose to forget the reorganization episode—there was no alternative. At the same time, he tried gradually to build closer and more friendly relationships between his own office and the chiefs of the technical services.

---

[18] Ltr, Styer to Somervell, 14 Oct 43, CG ASF.
[19] Ltr, Somervell to Marshall (written in New Delhi), 24 Oct 43, CG ASF.
[20] These papers are in the files of the Secretary of War.

Lessons of the Episode

There are no objective data by which it is possible to judge whether the proposed reorganization of the Army Service Forces would have accomplished what its advocates claimed or whether it would have brought great confusion and even chaos into the supply and service activities of the War Department. General Somervell and his advisers approached the whole question of reorganization as a technical problem. They conceived of the working relationships between the various parts of the ASF as more or less mechanically contrived, and subject to the same kind of rearrangement that an industrial engineer might make in the array of machine tools in a production plant.

Organization is far from being a purely technical matter. Technical considerations undoubtedly exist in organizational arrangements, but of equal or more importance are the political and psychological factors. Organization is people working together. The reactions of the people involved to proposed changes should therefore be a major concern for any organizational planner. This consideration was largely ignored in the 1943 reorganization plan for the Army Service Forces.

There is probably a correct strategy in achieving any far-reaching reorganization of a public agency of long standing. The only time that extensive change is likely to prove feasible is when there is a shift in the political control of government, as between a Democratic and Republican administration, or during a major crisis. Pearl Harbor brought such a crisis. With the advent of war, it proved possible to make basic changes in the structure of the War Department without arousing immediate and politically effective opposition. But in 1943, there was no similar crisis which would make possible an important alteration in the structure of the ASF. The only arguments on which its advocates would rest their case were economy and efficiency. They learned to their distress that few persons in government are especially impressed by or favorably disposed toward efficiency at a time when no serious criticism is being voiced against existing conditions.

The ASF reorganization plan was developed in considerable secrecy. The organizational planners were a small, cohesive group, staunchly loyal to General Somervell and without any prior attachment to the constituent parts of the ASF. With the exception of the director and deputy director of the Control Division, who were Regular Army officers, these planners were all civilians in peacetime, although most of them were in uniform. All but one had had experience in private business before World War II began. The planners did not consult any of the offices to be affected by the proposals. They simply assumed that these offices would be opposed, and that their opposition was not as important a consideration as an efficiently run war effort. No attempt was made to "sell" the plan by developing a sense of participation and direct interest on the part of those concerned.

Moreover, no official explanation of the plan or the considerations motivating it was provided the chiefs of the technical services. In short there was no attempt to make the plan attractive or even palatable to them. Later the planners conceded that it had been a mistake to employ designations like Director of Procurement and Director of Utilities in their plan. It would have been just as easy, and perhaps more satisfactory to those affected by the plan, if the designations Chief of Ordnance and Chief of Engineers had been retained.

Without doubt it was the newspaper and Congressional criticism that strengthened Under Secretary Patterson and Secretary Stimson in their belief that ASF reorganization on a major scale was "ill-advised" at the time. The "leak" to Congress and the newspapers probably came from within the ASF, from individuals who felt that the proposals would be harmful to their operations. The motivation may have been sincerely prompted by a desire not to disrupt procurement and supply operations which seemed to be proceeding satisfactorily. On the other hand it may have been largely personal, prompted by a concern for considerations of prestige, status, recognition, and tradition. General Somervell never learned the identity of the particular individual or individuals who prompted the newspaper and Congressional attack. He had his suspicions but they remained only that.

The "leak" is of course a familiar device for influencing action in public administration. General Somervell was by no means the first person in government service to feel the effects of such a technique. It made no difference that the actual newspaper stories were almost complete fabrication. Truth is not an essential element in the "leak." Familiar charges were employed for the attack—such stereotypes as turning the War Department into a "global WPA," appointing "political generals," "brain trusters" and sinister "palace guards," and plotting a fourth term campaign. Such tactics are commonly used by individuals endeavoring to prevent administrative action which concerns them and which they firmly believe to be undesirable.

A military establishment is generally believed to be one that operates on a "command" relationship, a hierarchy of individuals who have command authority over their subordinates. But even in the military agencies of the government, command is not as simple as this traditional concept would suggest. Command authority does not remove the psychological factors motivating persons working together. Somervell and his organizational planners made the mistake of believing that the concept of command could effect a far-reaching alteration in the customary working relationships of an enterprise having the vast scope of the ASF. It was unfortunate that ASF reorganization plans came to a head at the time when various rumors were circulating about the future military status of General Marshall. We know now that both Mr. Roosevelt and Mr. Churchill had tentatively decided at Quebec to make General Marshall commander-in-chief of the invasion of France. We know that Secretary Stimson was one of the strongest advocates of this step. Had General Marshall assumed this command, however, he was to have been replaced by General Eisenhower and not Somervell. Then at Cairo, President Roosevelt decided to retain General Marshall as Chief of Staff and to give the allied command to General Eisenhower. As between the two assignments Marshall himself refused to express a preference, although many, including Secretary Stimson, thought he would have liked the field command. President Roosevelt finally decided that Marshall was more valuable as Chief of Staff. There are few today who would want to question the wisdom of that decision.[21]

One can appreciate the astonished reaction of Mr. Harry Hopkins to the news-

[21] The events of this story are now fully available in Harry C. Butcher, *My Three Years With Eisenhower* (New York, Simon & Schuster, Inc., 1945); Eisenhower, *Crusade in Europe*; Stimson and Bundy, *On Active Service in Peace and War*; and Sherwood, *Roosevelt and Hopkins*.

paper stories. At least it is possible to assert here positively that he was never consulted on the reorganization of the ASF and knew nothing about the proposals. General Somervell had for four years been an administrative subordinate of Mr. Hopkins in the WPA, and Somervell saw him periodically during the war on official business. But reorganization of the ASF was a matter for General Somervell to recommend to Under Secretary Patterson, General Marshall, and Secretary Stimson. And it was these superiors of General Somervell who decided the issue.

Mr. Hopkins could only record that it was "amazing" that the story involving him and General Somervell should have been "cooked up."[22]

At all events, the Army Service Forces was not reorganized along the lines proposed by the organizational planners in 1943. On the contrary, the basic structure described in the preceding chapters was confirmed as the wartime organization of the ASF for performing the mission entrusted to it.

---

[22] Sherwood, *Roosevelt and Hopkins*, p. 761.

Epilogue

The Army Service Forces was an experiment in War Department organization for handling wartime supply for, and service to, the Army of the United States. It was set up in response to various weaknesses in prewar organization. These were recognized early. There were too many separate bureaus and commands, requiring in turn a large top staff for planning and co-ordinating the various units; duplications and uncertain spheres of responsibilities among some of the bureaus and commands; and separate top supervisory staffs for procurement and supply duties. Therefore one result of the simplification of the general top command reorganization which followed was the creation of the Army Service Forces.

In large part the organizational purposes posed in the winter of 1941–42 were realized. All supply and service activities, with a few exceptions, were concentrated under the jurisdiction of the commanding general of the Army Service Forces. He became the one person whom the Chief of Staff could hold responsible for the performance of essential and diverse duties. While the many individual parts of the ASF were largely responsible for the high degree of achievement that resulted, the command as a whole insured that a wide variety of duties were done promptly, on a balanced schedule, and with a minimum of waste.

There were questions that were left unanswered in the organizational rearrangement of March 1942. Did the Army Service Forces top command function as staff on supply and service matters as well as an operating command for the War Department? General Somervell maintained that it did. Some persons in the War Department General Staff were not so certain. The fact that it proved difficult in practice to draw hard and fast lines between strategic planning and logistical planning further complicated the arrangement. But in effect there can be no doubt that Somervell combined the duties of top logistical planner for the Army with command of the various agencies charged with carrying out the logistical mission.

Was the ASF co-ordinate in authority and responsibility with the AGF and the AAF? Somervell maintained that it was not. In his view the ASF was a centralized supply and service agency for the War Department, with duties entirely different from those assigned to the Ground Forces, the Air Forces, and overseas theaters of operations. The ASF was a central service agency existing for the purpose of helping the other two commands perform their operating duties successfully. The Army Air Forces in particular was not enthusiastic about this definition of the ASF mission. It desired to handle supply and service as incidental to its operating activities. Here was a direct conflict in organizational thinking, a conflict between the concept of centralized supply and service and decentralized supply and service. Related as it was to Air Forces aspirations for a separate military status coequal with that of the Army and Navy, this issue could not be resolved within the Army during World War II.

In the third place, the many and varied component parts of the Army Service Forces were restive because of their subordinate position under the commanding general of the ASF and resentful because of the strong central direction provided by the ASF staff. To overcome this and build a sense of loyalty and unity to a common purpose of supply and service was not easy to achieve in a short period of time.

There was external criticism of the ASF as well. Some of this criticism came from elements in agencies having central control over the nation's economic resources, especially the War Production Board. Other criticism came from legislative groups, perhaps prompted in turn by dissidents within the War Department.

Much of the criticism of the Army Service Forces centered upon the person of its commanding general. As already stated, it was difficult to distinguish between the ASF and General Somervell. The two were virtually synonymous during World War II. A different kind of personality might have aroused different reactions, but he would have commanded a very different kind of agency from that which the ASF proved to be. Somervell was Somervell, and his energy, his drive, his penchant for efficiency, his seeming indifference to the personal prestige and status of others made the Army Service Forces what it was.

One of the criticisms which arose out of the difficulties mentioned above was that Somervell was an "empire builder." This charge is perhaps best answered by a sympathetic observer of the ASF during the war:

In the jurisdictional wrangles that developed there was one argument *ad hominem* that was constantly used, to wit: that the A.S.F.

and its dynamic Commanding General were constantly seeking as 'Empire Builders' to enlarge their job by encroaching on that of others. By dint of repetition it got considerable acceptance inside the Department and out. There was something in the drive of the Commanding General of the A.S.F., his quickness on the mental trigger, his adroitness and his evident ambition to tackle tough jobs that in itself lent some support to this feeling of impending encroachment among those of a more deliberate pace. I should be surprised if the Chief of Staff ever had any such feeling though he must have been well aware of the feelings of others in his organization in this respect.

As a matter of fact, if the feeling was well founded, then Somervell, no matter how efficient he was in other respects, showed himself to be a very poor 'encroacher.' During the whole four years he held the job I cannot think of a single direction in which he enlarged the scope of the S.O.S. and the A.S.F. beyond the initial scope of the function that the terms of the Reorganization Plan of 1942 assigned to it in Circular 59 or the scope of the War Department supply function beyond that defined in the joint circular of the Chairman of the W.P.B. and the Under-Secretary on March 12, 1942. On the other hand, by interpretation or formal change from the terms of Circular 59, the scope of A.S.F., as pointed out above, was narrowed in a number of respects.

Perhaps I should record as bearing on this an incident of my first talk with Somervell when I came down to Washington on January 7, 1942. He showed me with evident pride a draft of an executive order he had just prepared on the functions of the War Shipping Administration. This draft as he pointed out would subordinate certain functions relating to shipping, which he had been exercising as head of G–4, to the Shipping Administration. Such subordination he felt essential to a proper overall handling of the shipping situation. That it meant a contraction of his 'empire' had not dulled his instinct for efficiency and his drive for what he felt would help win the war.[1]

---

[1] Dorr, Memorandum Notes, pp. 60–62.

Somervell's Departure

All day on 14 August 1945 General Somervell waited in his office for the official announcement that the Japanese had surrendered. The decision was known in the War Department in the morning, but the official announcement did not come from President Truman until seven o'clock that evening. When it came, General Somervell signed the order on his desk for the Army Service Forces to put its demobilization plans into effect. He signed another piece of paper that day: a short memorandum written in longhand to the Chief of Staff. It was an official request for voluntary retirement from the Army to be effective on the same day that General Marshall retired from the post of Chief of Staff. Because he had completed more than thirty-one years of active service since his graduation from the U.S. Military Academy in 1914, Somervell was eligible for retirement on his own request.

Several reasons motivated General Somervell's determination to leave the ASF. In the first place, he felt that his task had been completed. True, demobilization meant heavy tasks for the ASF, ranging from the return of troops to the United States and their separation, to the settlement of terminated contracts. Plans for these activities had been prepared, reviewed and revised over a considerable period of time. All that one man at the head of a great organization could do to anticipate this task had been done. Others could now direct actual performance. In the second place, Somervell had not been indifferent to or unaffected by the criticisms of his wartime conduct. He was ready and willing to step aside, to let others continue the work. Moreover, since the Army Service Forces had been so

peculiarly the creation of the Chief of Staff, Somervell thought it particularly fitting that his own retirement should coincide with that of General Marshall. Somervell received no official acknowledgment of his request. Marshall indicated only that he believed Somervell's usefulness was by no means ended, and that in any event he preferred to have his own successor act on the request.

On 2 September, coincident with the formal capitulation of the Japanese Government in Tokyo Bay, General Somervell issued a memorandum of appreciation to all members of the Army Service Forces. In the next few weeks he gave special attention to expressing in various ways his awareness of the loyalty and hard work of his associates. At a military review at Ft. Belvoir he presented Distinguished Service Medals to each of the technical service chiefs and to other heads of army branches such as The Adjutant General, the Judge Advocate General, and the Provost Marshal General. Awards to his staff assistants were presented in a series of ceremonies in his own office.

On 14 October 1945 he entered an Army general hospital and later underwent two surgical operations. He returned to his office briefly on 17 December to prepare testimony on postwar military organization for presentation to the Senate Committee on Military Affairs. In the meantime, General Eisenhower had become Army Chief of Staff. On 26 December Somervell's retirement was announced, to go into effect on the expiration of his terminal leave at the end of April 1946.

Secretary of War Patterson issued the following statement to the press:

It is with extreme regret that I announce the retirement of General Somervell as Commanding General, Army Service Forces. In

SECRETARY OF WAR ROBERT P. PATTERSON *decorating General Somervell for distinguished service, October 1945.*

organizing and directing the world-wide supply lines on which our troops depended for their offensive power, General Somervell performed a service without parallel in military history. He was completely dedicated to the task of winning the war in the shortest possible time and with the smallest cost in American lives, and the energy and ability he applied to his task contributed in great measure to the force of our attack and the speed of our victory. My own work in the field of procurement would have been impossible of accomplishment without his help and counsel. He has been an inspiration to all who worked with him. He will be sorely missed, but he has earned his relief. He carries with him the eternal gratitude of the Army he served so unselfishly and so well.[2]

Of the many expressions of appreciation which came to him, one that expressed the sentiments of many officers came from the then supply commander in China, a man who had served both as an ASF staff officer and as a service commander:

To return to the subject of your retirement, I feel sure that all of us who have been under your command since the SOS was established in March 1942 regret very much that you will no longer have the directing hand in it. As I remember these Service Command conferences with your key staff people in attendance, I was always impressed by the fact that most of those close to you were of the

[2] WD press release, BPR, 26 Dec 45.

high-spirited, imaginative and forceful type. The job of controlling so many adventurous souls always appealed to me as insurmountable, yet you turned all of the best qualities of these people in the right direction to achieve a common end, and as long as we stayed headed that way, you let us run.

Through your kindness, I have gotten around the world quite a bit and I can say truly that I have not found a single commander with whom I worked or under whom I served who displayed the qualities of leadership that you have as head of this great organization.

What is more, I was fairly familiar with the mess the War Department was in in March 1942. I knew of the conflict between those who would prefer to go into procurement on a small scale rather than the all-out procurement which the emergency indicated. I know of the difficulties and dangers attendant upon the course which you took. Those of us who served under you well remember the many courageous decisions you made during those early days when the war's outlook was the blackest. No one can challenge the fact that the war would probably have lasted a great deal longer had you not, at that time, made the courageous decisions of which I speak.

It has been a great privilege to be a subordinate of yours, not only in those days, but in the more outwardly successful ones which followed. All of us will long remember the great loyalty to your subordinates which you displayed even at a sacrifice to your own prestige. When you do leave the Army, we will continue to admire you for the unsurpassable job which you have done for your country.[3]

Somervell's chief of staff, General Lutes, succeeded him as commanding general of the Army Service Forces. For all practical purposes he had already been in command continuously since 15 October 1945.

In the meantime the ASF was performing its burdensome responsibilities in demobilizing the Army, terminating war contracts, and disposing of property. There were numerous problems to decide, such as what equipment to leave in Europe and what to return to the United States, what property to preserve and store for possible future use and what to declare surplus, and what procurement and research to continue.[4] The Army Service Forces still had much to do.

The key organizational problem for the future, of course, was whether the ASF was to continue as a War Department agency. It was to a consideration of this question that the War Department had turned immediately after the conclusion of hostilities.

The Dissolution of the ASF

On 30 August 1945 General Marshall created a Board of Officers on Reorganization of the War Department. The head of the board was Lt. Gen. Alexander M. Patch, who had commanded a division in the Pacific in the early days of the war and an army in the European Theater of Operations later. There were five other members, all general officers. One came from the Operations Division of the War Department General Staff, one from the Office of The Inspector General, and one from the Special Planning Division of the WDGS; the others were the Chief Signal Officer and the commanding general of the Aberdeen Proving Ground of the Ordnance Department. There was no one on the board from the ASF staff but rather two officers from technical services. Somervell had urged General Handy, the deputy chief of staff of the War Department and former head of OPD, to include

---

[3] Ltr, Aurand to Somervell, 24 Sep 46, CG ASF.

[4] Dept of the Army Pam 20–210, John C. Sparrow, History of Personnel Demobilization in the United States Army, Jul 52.

General Robinson of the ASF as a board member. This was not done, with the result, as just indicated, that there was no one on the Patch Board who had been active in the central direction of the ASF.

The Patch Board held extensive hearings on the question of War Department organization during September. Somervell was among those invited to testify. As early as the summer of 1944 he had his Control Division prepare a plan on postwar organization.[5] These ideas became the basis of his proposals to the Patch Board. He argued first of all for the continuance of the Army Service Forces as a central supply and service agency of the War Department. Second, he urged that the commanding general of the ASF should be the logistical planner for the Chief of Staff. Third, he proposed a simple "staff-line type of organization" for the ASF. These proposals closely paralleled those which had been developed for ASF reorganization in 1943. The principal change was that the staff of the Commanding General, ASF, would consist of twelve officers, all but one of whom was a head of a traditional branch of the Army. Six chiefs of technical services would be joined on the staff by the Judge Advocate General, the Chief of Finance, The Adjutant General, and the Provost Marshal General. The two staff titles would be Chief of Military Training and Inspector General, ASF. One technical service would be dropped, the Chemical Warfare Service, with its duties transferred to the Ordnance Department. Each of these staff officers would have functional rather than commodity specializations. Thus the Chief of Ordnance would become the procurement officer of the Army; The Quartermaster General, the supply officer; The Surgeon General, the medical officer; the

Chief of Engineers, the construction and maintenance officer; and the Chief of Transportation, the movements officer. Most field activities would come under the general administrative direction of service commands. (*See Chart 7.*)

By September 1945 Somervell had modified his 1943 organizational thinking somewhat, partly at the suggestion of Under Secretary Patterson. He now proposed that there be commodity procurement divisions under the Chief of Ordnance located outside Washington and administered directly by the Chief of Ordnance, not by the service commands. These procurement divisions would let some contracts centrally. Others would be let, administered, and inspected by ordnance officers under the commanders of the service commands. The same type of system was recommended to function under The Quartermaster General in the storage and distribution of supplies. There would be commodity supply divisions under The Quartermaster General which would be located at commodity reserve depots outside of Washington. These reserve depots, in fact, would be located near the commodity procurement divisions which purchased the item and operate under the direct authority of The Quartermaster General. Distribution depots would be under the service commands. The reserve depots would be the central point of record keeping for the entire military supply of a particular commodity. They would handle such central bulk storage as was desirable and issue shipping instructions for the delivery of supplies to other reserve depots or on fast-moving items directly to the various distribution depots. The Quar-

[5] Memo, Dir CD for Somervell, 15 Jul 44, sub: Org of ASF in the Postwar Military Establishment, CD, ASF.

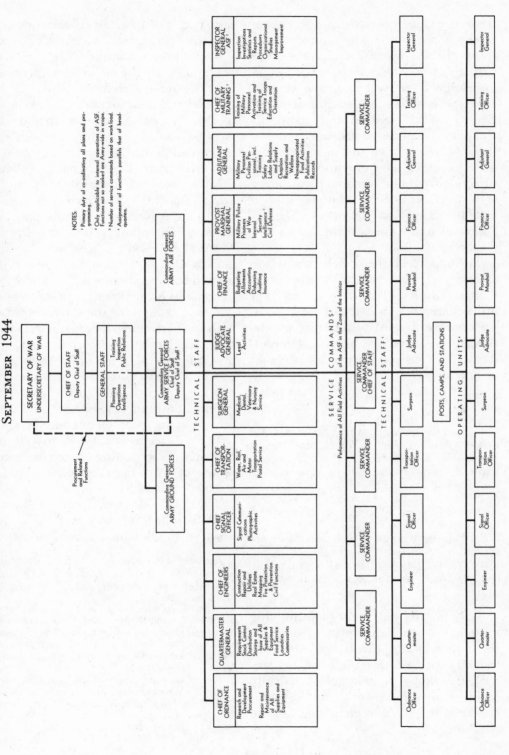

CHART 7—POSTWAR LOGISTIC ORGANIZATION WITHIN THE WAR DEPARTMENT, PROPOSED TO PATCH BOARD: SEPTEMBER 1944

termaster General would also have commodity maintenance shops for the major (fifth echelon) repair of equipment for return to reserve depots for distribution. Otherwise Somervell proposed that all ASF field installations—staging areas and ports, hospitals, field printing plants, disciplinary barracks, posts, and others—should come under the administrative direction of service commands; technical direction would be retained by the chiefs of the services in ASF headquarters. These were the basic ideas put forth by General Somervell and his organizational adviser, General Robinson.[6]

The report of the Patch Board was transmitted to the Chief of Staff by a memorandum on 18 October 1945.[7] The instructions to the board had been to consider the War Department proper, its relationship with overseas bases and departments, the arms and services, and the zone of interior. The board declared that its problem had resolved itself into four major issues:

1. Shall the major commands—Army Air Forces, Army Ground Forces, and Army Service Forces—be retained as now constituted or with modifications as to responsibilities and functions?
2. What shall be the scope of the War Department General Staff responsibilities and functions?
3. Shall the arms and services as now constituted be retained?
4. What type of territorial organization shall be used for the continental United States?

Without any statement of underlying reasons, the board then presented twelve recommendations, the first of which was that the postwar organization be prescribed as shown in an attached chart. By omitting any reference to the ASF, this chart implied that the command was to be dissolved. The Patch Board recommended that the existing technical services be continued as then constituted, that the Transportation Corps be made permanent, and that the service commands be "discontinued" and their functions be taken over by four Army areas to be set up under the Army Ground Forces. What had been ASF headquarters was now to be divided into three parts. The designation "administrative services" was revived, to be applied to The Adjutant General's office, the Judge Advocate General's office, the Chief of Chaplain's office, the Provost Marshal General's office, and the Civil Affairs Division. Second, these services were to be supervised by a Director of Personnel and Administration of the WDGS, who was to combine the activities of G–1 with the personnel work taken over from the ASF. Third, the procurement and supply duties of ASF headquarters were to be combined with G–4 under a Director of Service, Supply, and Procurement. Procurement and supply supervision were to remain under common military·direction, with the Director of Service, Supply, and Procurement reporting to the Under Secretary of War on procurement policy matters.

The basis for staff operation by the WDGS in the future was put forth in these words in Tab B to the Patch Board report:

The Staff must operate, in order to direct and supervise. The old theory that a staff must limit itself to broad policy and planning ac-

---

[6] These ideas were worked out in considerable detail by the Control Division, ASF, for General Somervell to be published in a final report. The report was never issued as prepared. Eventually a factual record was published over General Lutes' signature entitled, *Logistics in World War II.*

[7] The report was reproduced and transmitted under a covering memorandum by the Assistant Deputy Chief of Staff to all parts of the War Department on 19 October 1945.

tivities has been proved unsound in this war. This was clearly demonstrated as a result of the 9 March 1942 reorganization of the War Department. In that reorganization, G–1, G–3, and G–4 were stripped of all "operating" functions and personnel assigned was reduced in the case of G–4 from 211 officers and 275 civilians to 8 officers and 31 civilians. This reduction rendered the office ineffective and did not even permit membership on the important logistical committees of the Combined and Joint Chiefs of Staff. Under such circumstances, G–4 (and G–1 and G–3) could be of no real assistance to the Chief of Staff as an adviser in Army-wide, world-wide logistical matters. Nor could he adequately assist the Chief of Staff in his exercise of command of supervision of the Army program. Unless a staff officer is able to assist his commander in getting things done, in addition to co-ordinating, planning and policy making, he is not serving his full usefulness. In short, a staff is a commander's principal means for determining that his orders, instructions, and directions are being carried out as he intended.

This was in a sense a reply to General Somervell. He wanted the commanding general of the Army Service Forces to be both staff adviser to the Chief of Staff and a subordinate commander. The Patch Board preferred to strengthen the War Department General Staff and to eliminate ASF headquarters as an unnecessary echelon. The seven technical services were still to be designated as such, together with an eighth, the Chief of Finance. These and the administrative services were to become a separate level of War Department organization, operating under the direction and supervision of five WDGS directors.

The recommendations of the Patch Board were transmitted to the commanding general of the ASF, among others, for comment. In General Somervell's absence, General Lutes was responsible for the reply. There was no question of concurrence, but only one of how strong a protest to record. An analysis of testimony before the Patch Board revealed that only one chief of a technical service favored the continuation of the ASF—General Gross of the Transportation Corps. Others who had favored its continuation included Under Secretary Patterson, Assistant Secretary Lovett, General McNarney, and Maj. Gen. Russell L. Maxwell, the G–4. Among those opposed were General Eisenhower and his chief of staff, General Walter Bedell Smith.[8] It was unofficially learned that objections to the Patch Board report would be in vain since it had already been approved in principle and only minor modifications would be considered. Lutes knowing this nevertheless dissented. A new board headed by Lt. Gen. William H. Simpson considered the various adjustments suggested and recommended only minor changes to the Chief of Staff on 28 December 1945.

The demise of the ASF became official on 14 May 1946 with the issuance of a new organization plan for the War Department, effective 11 June 1946.[9] The War Department order establishing it stated: "Headquarters, Army Service Forces is abolished." The various major functions of the ASF were transferred as shown in table on next page.

In another section the order declared: "The command functions of Headquarters, Army Service Forces with respect to service, supply, and procurement activities are abolished." The Director of Service, Supply, and Procurement of the WDGS assumed "general staff responsibility" in these fields. His office absorbed

---

[8] This analysis made for General Lutes is in the files of the Commanding General, ASF.

[9] WD Cir 138, 14 May 46.

ASF Staff Divisions	*New Location*
Military Personnel Division	Personnel and Administration Division, WDGS
Personal Affairs Division	The Adjutant General
Director of Military Training	Organization and Training Division, WDGS
Intelligence Division	Intelligence Division, WDGS
Labor supply and industrial relations activities of Industrial Personnel Division	Service, Supply, and Procurement Division, WDGS
Civilian personnel functions, Industrial Personnel Division	Civilian Personnel Division, Office, Secretary of War
Research and Development Division	Research and Development Division, WDGS
Office of Fiscal Director	Chief of Finance
Special Services Division	Special Services Division, a new administrative service of the Army

most of ASF headquarters, including all duties performed by the ASF Director of Plans and Operations, the Director of Matériel, and the Director of Supply. In addition, it took over both the former G–4 Division of the WDGS and the Logistics Group of the Operations Division.

Finally, the nine service commands of the ASF were abolished and their duties assigned to the headquarters of six armies set up under the Army Ground Forces. For general administrative purposes the continental United States was divided into six Army areas. While Ground Forces commanders were to operate the six Army areas, on all supply, service, and administrative matters (that is, all matters affecting the operation of Army posts as installations and not troop organization and training matters), the Army areas were to receive orders and instructions directly from the War Department General Staff.

The new War Department order provided for six administrative services: The Adjutant General's Department, the Judge Advocate General's Department, the Corps of Chaplains, the Office of the Provost Marshal General, and the Special Services Division. The technical services of the War Department provided for were eight in number: the Ordnance Department, the Signal Corps, the Quartermaster Corps, the Corps of Engineers, the Transportation Corps, the Medical Department, the Chemical Warfare Service, and the Finance Department. The heads of administrative staff services were recognized as administrative staff officers of the War Department while the chiefs of the technical services became technical staff officers of the War Department. The new orders declared: "These two separate functions of staff and command, although vested in a single individual, are separate and distinct in that each involves different responsibilities and duties, and the exercise of one is not to be confused with nor permitted to interfere with the exercise of the other." [10]

The May 1946 reorganization of the War Department profited somewhat from the experience gained in World War II. First of all, it officially combined ASF headquarters and the Logistics Group of OPD under G–4, WDGS. The head of the division was no longer termed a "commanding general," but was labeled the Director of Service, Supply, and Procurement for the War Department General Staff. As already noted, the first officer appointed to fill this post was General Lutes, successor to General Somervell in

---

[10] *Ibid.*, Sec. 29.

the command of the ASF and his close associate throughout the war.[11] The concept for which Somervell had stood, of one individual combining the functions of adviser to the Chief of Staff on the interrelationship of supply and strategy and director of all procurement activity, was not accepted officially in the sense that it had been practiced in World War II. Second, the vital interrelationship of procurement and supply was acknowledged. No longer was there to be a G–4 Division of the General Staff and a separate Office of the Assistant Secretary of War giving instructions to the supply arms and services, as was the case from 1921 to 1941. Rather, there was to be one staff office, whose director reported separately to the Under Secretary of War "on procurement and related matters." Third, the Department-wide responsibilities of chiefs of the administrative and technical services were reaffirmed and, if anything, somewhat strengthened by the new arrangements. The service commands reverted to the status of serving the Army Ground Forces, but the chiefs of technical services now were in a position to supervise equally the work done at air bases and ground installations. This arrangement, however, became less significant after 1947 when the National Security Act created a new executive department: the Department of

the Air Forces. In the fourth place, all the management improvement accomplishments were by no means thrown away; in fact most of the procedures and methods of doing business within the ASF were carried over almost intact into the War Department General Staff.[12]

The Army Service Forces as an experiment in centralized command of War Department supply and service activities had come to an end. But its experiences and accomplishments continued to influence the postwar thinking and activities of the Army. No institutional effort so widespread and so vital as that of the ASF could be eliminated overnight. The Army Service Forces had written a memorable chapter in the history of the Army on the organization and methods required to meet the tremendous supply and service needs of global warfare.

---

[11] Lutes' successors from 1947 to 1950 had also had experience with the ASF: Lt. Gens. H. S. Aurand and T. B. Larkin.

[12] The organizational history of the Army underwent a major change with the passage of the National Security Act of 26 July 1947, and later a change was to be made in the status of the technical and administrative services. See, Department of the Army Circular 342, 1 November 1948, which placed the "Technical Staffs and Services" *under* the Director of Logistics (changed from Service, Supply, and Procurement), and placed the "Administrative Staffs and Services" *under* the Director of Personnel and Administration. This was a return to the *command* arrangement which characterized the ASF.

Appendix A

Key Personnel of the ASF
9 March 1942—31 December 1945*

Commanding General . . . . General Brehon Somervell
Chief of Staff . . . . Lt. Gen. W. D. Styer (to 18 Apr 45);
Lt. Gen. LeRoy Lutes

OFFICE OF THE COMMANDING GENERAL

Deputy Chief of Staff for Service Commands.
Maj. Gen. George Grunert (from 15 May 43 to 15 Aug 43); Brig. Gen. Philip Hayes, Acting (15 Aug to 1 Dec 43); Brig. Gen. C. H. Danielson (to 6 Jan 44); Brig. Gen. J. F. Battley (to 15 Jun 45); Maj. Gen. Richard Donovan

Director of Plans and Operations . . . .
Maj. Gen. LeRoy Lutes (from Oct 43 to Oct 43 to 18 Apr 45); Maj. Gen. W. A. Wood, Jr. (to May 45); Maj. Gen. Daniel Noce

Deputy Director . . . .
Maj. Gen. W. A. Wood, Jr. (to 19 Apr 45); Maj. Gen. Stanley L. Scott (from 27 Jun 45)

Deputy Director for Demobilization . . .
Brig. Gen. Stanley L. Scott (from Jan 44 to Nov 44)

Planning Division . . . .
Col. C. B. Magruder (to Nov 44); Maj. Gen. Stanley L. Scott (Nov 44 to 27 Jun 45); Brig. Gen. Henry C. Wolfe

Requirements and Stock Control Division.
Col. H. M. Reedall (from Mar 44 to 1 Nov 44); Brig. Gen. T. M. Osborne

Mobilization Division . . . .
Brig. Gen. C. E. Dissinger

*Highest rank held while serving in the position has been used in each instance.

Chief of Administrative Services or Director of Administration.	Maj. Gen. John P. Smith (to Sep 42); Maj. Gen. George Grunert (to May 43); Maj. Gen. James L. Collins (to Nov 43 when position was abolished)
Control Division	Maj. Gen. C. F. Robinson
Intelligence Division	Col. J. A. Roamer
Technical Information Division	Lt. Col. Karl Detzer (from Jul 42 to Feb 43); Col. Kilbourne Johnston, Acting (to Jun 43); Mr. Harry M. Shackleford (to Dec 43); Col. Karl Detzer

TECHNICAL SERVICES

The Quartermaster General	Lt. Gen. E. B. Gregory
The Chief of Ordnance	Maj. Gen. C. M. Wesson (to 1 Jun 42); Lt. Gen. L. H. Campbell, Jr.
The Chief of Engineers	Lt. Gen. Eugene Reybold
The Surgeon General	Maj. Gen. James C. Magee (to 1 Jun 43); Maj. Gen. Norman T. Kirk
The Chief Signal Officer	Maj. Gen. Dawson Olmstead (to 30 Jun 43); Maj. Gen. Harry C. Ingles
The Chief of Chemical Warfare Service .	Maj. Gen. William N. Porter
The Chief of Transportation	Maj. Gen. C. P. Gross

SERVICE COMMANDS

First	Maj. Gen. Sherman Miles
Second	Maj. Gen. T. A. Terry
Third	Maj. Gen. M. C. Reckord (to Dec 43); Maj. Gen. Philip Hayes
Fourth	Maj. Gen. William Bryden (to 15 Jan 44); Maj. Gen. Frederick E. Uhl (to 10 Jun 45); Maj. Gen. E. H. Brooks

Fifth . . . . Maj. Gen. D. L. Van Voorhis (to 2 Jul 43); Maj. Gen. F. C. Wallace (to 2 Dec 43); Maj. Gen. James L. Collins

Sixth . . . . Maj. Gen. George Grunert (to 4 Sep 42); Maj. Gen. Henry S. Aurand (to 22 Nov 44); Maj. Gen. R. B. Reynolds (to 23 May 45); Maj. Gen. David McCoach, Jr.

Seventh . . . . Maj. Gen. Frederick E. Uhl (to 10 Jan 44); Maj. Gen. C. H. Danielson

Eighth . . . . Maj. Gen. Richard Donovan (to 15 Jun 45); Lt. Gen. Walton H. Walker

Ninth . . . . Maj. Gen. K. A. Joyce (to 11 Oct 43); Maj. Gen. David McCoach, Jr. (to 1 Sep 44); Maj. Gen. W. E. Shedd

Military District of Washington . . . . . Maj. Gen. John T. Lewis (to 6 Sep 44); Maj. Gen. C. F. Thompson

Northwest Service Command . . . . . . Brig. Gen. J. A. O'Connor (to 20 Feb 44); Brig. Gen. K. D. Worsham (to 6 May 44); Col. F. S. Strong

STAFF DIVISIONS

The Adjutant General . . . . Maj. Gen. J. A. Ulio (to Aug 45); Maj. Gen. E. F. Witsell, Acting

The Judge Advocate General . . . . . Maj. Gen. M. C. Cramer

The Provost Marshal General . . . . . Maj. Gen. A. W. Gullion (to 21 Jun 44); Maj. Gen. A. L. Lerch

The National Guard Bureau . . . . . . Maj. Gen. J. F. Williams (to May 1945)

Director of Matériel . . . . Maj. Gen. L. D. Clay (to 27 Nov 44); (Assistant Chief of Staff for Require-   Mr. Howard Bruce (to 1 Sep 45); Maj. ments and Resources, Assistant   Gen. G. E. Edgerton Chief of Staff for Matériel)

Research and Development Division . . . Col. R. M. Osborne (to 11 Jan 45); Col.
  (from May 1944)   P. R. Faymonville (to 27 Jun 45); Brig.
                                        Gen. E. A. Regnier

Requirements Division . . . . Brig. Gen. W. A. Wood, Jr.
  (to June 1944)

Production Division . . . . Brig. Gen. Charles Hines (to Sep 42);
  (to September 1945)   Brig. Gen. H. C. Minton (to Sep 45)

Purchases Division . . . . Brig. Gen. A. J. Browning (to 11 Sep
  (to September 1945)   44); Col F. C. Foy (to 1 Aug 45); Mr.
                                        W. C. Foster (to 1 Sep 45)

Production and Purchases Division . . . Brig. Gen. G. H. Drewry (to 5 Dec 45);
  (from September to December 1945)   Col. P. W. Smith

International Division . . . . Brig. Gen. H. S. Aurand (to Jul 42);
                                        Col. J. B. Franks, Acting (to Mar 43);
                                        Brig. Gen. Boykin C. Wright (to 31 May
                                        43); Maj. Gen. G. E. Edgerton (to 19
                                        Apr 45); Brig. Gen. D. G. Shingler

Renegotiation Division . . . . Mr. Maurice M. Karker (to 15 Sep 43);
  (from August 1943)   Mr. Joseph M. Dodge (to 1 Sep 44);
                                        Col. Maurice Hirsch

Readjustment Division . . . . Brig. Gen. D. N. Houseman
  (from September 1944)

Director of Supply . . . . Maj. Gen. F. A. Heileman (to 10 Jul
  (from October 1943)   45); Brig. Gen. N. H. McKay

Distribution Division . . . . Col. R. A. Case (to 21 Jul 45); Col.
                                        H. A. Markle (to 24 Aug 45); Brig. Gen.
                                        F. A. Henning

Storage Division . . . . Col. A. B. Drake (to 28 Apr 45); Brig.
                                        Gen. H. W. Bayette (to 4 Aug 45); Col.
                                        W. C. Crosby

Maintenance Division . . . . Col. W. S. Conrow (to 17 Jan 45); Col.
                                        M. K. Barroll, Jr.

Fiscal Director . . . . Maj. Gen. A. H. Carter (to 1 Dec 45);
  (from May 1943)   Maj. Gen. W. H. Kasten

Chief of Finance . . . . Maj. Gen. H. K. Loughry (to Jul 45); Maj. Gen. W. H. Kasten

Director of Military Training. . . . . . Brig. Gen. C. R. Huebner (to 31 Mar 43); Maj. Gen. W. L. Weible (to 6 Jun 45); Brig. Gen. A. G. Trudeau (7 Jul 45); Maj. Gen. F. L. Walker

Director of Personnel . . . . Maj. Gen. J. N. Dalton (to 6 Jun 45); Maj. Gen. V. L. Peterson (to 14 Sep 45); Maj. Gen. J. N. Dalton

Chief of Chaplains . . . . Maj. Gen. W. R. Arnold (to 15 Apr 45); Brig. Gen. L. D. Miller

Executive for Reserve and ROTC Affairs . Brig. Gen. E. W. Smith
  (until May 1945)

Military Personnel Division . . . . . . Brig. Gen. J. E. Wharton (to 19 Sep 42); Brig. Gen. R. B. Reynolds (to 22 Nov 44); Col. C. E. Hixon

Industrial Personnel Division . . . . . . Mr. James P. Mitchell (to 17 Apr 44); Mr. W. A. Hughes (to 4 Sep 44); Col. R. F. Gow (to 15 Sep 45); Col. F. L. Furphy

Information and Education Division . . Maj. Gen. F. H. Osborn
  (until September 1945)

Special Service Division . . . . Maj. Gen. J. W. Byron
  (Army Exchange Division until October 1943)

Personal Affairs Division . . . . Col. F. G. Munson
  (after August 1943)

Appendix B

Documents on the Relations With the AAF:
Position of ASF in the War Department

Army Service Forces
Office of the Commanding General
Washington 25, D. C.

6 August 1945

MEMORANDUM FOR THE CHIEF OF STAFF

SUBJECT: Position of ASF in the War Department

1. The purpose of this memorandum is to invite attention to certain aspects of the current relationship between the War Department General Staff, the Army Air Forces, and the Army Service Forces, which place the ASF in an undesirable position.

2. The current problems in relationship go back to Change 13 to AR 170–10 (Tab A) which transferred supervision of certain Army-wide service activities at Class III installations from service commands to Army Air Forces. This transfer resulted from an investigation ordered by the Secretary of War into the complexity of the flow of funds in the Army; the *ad hoc* committee directed that funds for the performance of repairs and utilities, fixed signal communications, etc., at Class III stations should flow through Air Forces channels and, since responsibility and funds had to flow together, directed the change in responsibility.

3. Because of the uncertainty of respective ASF and AAF responsibility and authority, on 28 December 1944, the Deputy Chief of Staff addressed a letter to the three major commands, subject: Service Responsibilities (Tab B). Despite this letter, differences of opinion between Air Forces and Service Forces have continued.

4. Even prior to Change 13 to AR 170–10, the lines of authority of The Surgeon General over the Air Surgeon and medical activities of AAF were not clear. Early this year, this Headquarters proposed a War Department circular which would clarify the responsibility of The Surgeon General, acting under the Commanding General, ASF, over all medical activities of the Army. Considerable difficulty was encountered with this circular. It finally appeared as War Department Circular 120 (Tab C). Paragraph 3 of that circular for the first time established the rule that The Surgeon General could communicate directly with the Chief of Staff and that such communications would be merely "forwarded through" the Commanding General, ASF, who, in turn, would forward the communications "with such remarks and recommendations" as he might desire. In other words, the Commanding General, ASF, was no longer fully responsible for nor had full authority over the activities of The Surgeon General.

5. As a result of Change 13 to AR 170–10, War Department Circular 388, 1944, was

published, which required Headquarters, ASF, to prepare and, after co-ordination with AAF, to forward to the War Department General Staff necessary revisions in Army regulations and War Department circulars. In compliance with that responsibility, this Headquarters has had continuous difficulty in reaching agreements with AAF and on several occasions has been forced to submit directives to the General Staff for determination of opposing ASF and AAF views.

6. One of these problems was the insistence by AAF that War Department Circular 388, in referring to "commanding generals of service commands, ASF (division engineers)", required all ASF–AAF contacts on repairs and utilities to be through division engineer offices. This matter was submitted to G–4 and, it is understood, subsequently submitted to the Chief of Staff. Determination was made on 24 April 1945 (Tab D). It is believed that this determination was a satisfactory answer to the current problem of relationships between ASF agencies and other agencies of the War Department outside ASF.

7. Subsequently, the Commanding General, AAF, submitted to the General Staff a staff study alleging that War Department Circular 388 in providing technical inspections by ASF elements of the technical sufficiency of operations at Class III stations was intended to be only temporary in nature, and requesting transfer of authority of all technical inspections at Class III stations to AAF. Determination on this issue was made on 17 July (see Tab E). It is to be noted that this determination picked up bodily certain language from Circular 120 on the position of The Surgeon General.

8. This Headquarters since 1944 has been attempting to obtain a republication of AR 100–80, Repairs and Utilities. Draft of this regulation was completed just prior to Change

13 to AR 170–10 which necessitated its complete revision. Then followed all the discussions with AAF indicated above, further delaying publication of the draft. Following the determination of 17 July with reference to technical inspections, this Headquarters on 18 July received a further directive from G–4 with reference to publication of this regulation (see Tab F). Paragraph 2b of this directive goes further than any of the previous directives in attempting to distinguish between functions of ASF elements. It is stated that the Chief of Engineers has "technical supervisory responsibility to the Chief of Staff" (apparently without reference to the Commanding General, ASF) and has "supply and service responsibilities" under the Commanding General, ASF. In the minutes of the General Council meeting of 23 July 1944, this language was changed to provide that "the chiefs of technical services, in addition to their other duties, will act as chief technical advisers to the Chief of Staff and the War Department." The General Council Minutes omitted recognition of the "supply and service responsibilities of technical services under the direction of the Commanding General, Army Service Forces." This attempt to separate technical from service activities is not clear and in practical application has little meaning. This directive further modifies the organizational principle established in paragraph 2a of directive of 24 April 1945.

9. The same position was taken by the General Staff in a further directive (Tab G) with reference to publication of AR 105–5 and AR 105–20 setting forth responsibilities of the Chief Signal Officer.

10. It appears to this Headquarters that the War Department General Staff is attempting to view its mission as not merely dealing with the ASF as a whole but as dealing with the separate elements of the ASF independently of the authority of this Head-

quarters. Under this new concept, a chief of a technical service is apparently being viewed as being an adjunct of the War Department General Staff independent of the Commanding General, ASF, for certain responsibilities, while for other responsibilities he is under the command of the Commanding General, ASF. This Headquarters is unable to distinguish clearly between the respective areas of responsibility for which a chief of a technical service is under the command of ASF or independent of ASF.

11. The above developments have reached a stage at which their continuation threatens the stability of the ASF. Clarifying action is urgently needed. It has always been the understanding of this Headquarters that the reorganization of the Army in 1942 made this Headquarters responsible for those supply and service activities, common to the Army as a whole. The accomplishment of the ASF mission is hindered by steps which have the tendency to raise a question as to the extent of the authority of the Commanding General, either over his own subordinate units or with respect to the Army-wide supply and service activities with which he is charged. If this tendency is continued, it can only result in three independent self-sufficient commands—each with its own supply and service functions, each duplicating the overhead of the other. Such a development would result in lack of cohesion and nonuniformity unless a very large and cumbersome General Staff is created to co-ordinate and standardize policies and certain related supply and administrative procedures of the major commands. Such an organization might be subject to criticism for being unnecessary.

12. It is accordingly recommended that:

   a. The attached draft of a statement of War Department policy to clarify the organizational position of the ASF (Tab H)

be sent to the three major commands and be published in the Minutes of the General Council.

   b. The directives of 17 and 18 July 1945 (Tabs E and F) be withdrawn and rewritten in accordance with the policy statement attached.

8 Incls.   BREHON SOMERVELL
   Tabs A–H, incl.   General, Commanding

Proposed Statement To Be Sent to the Three Major Commands and for Insertion in Minutes of the General Council

1. It is the purpose of this statement to clarify relationships within the War Department among the three major commands and between those commands and the War Department General Staff. This statement does not modify, but rather reinforces, the principles governing the organization of the War Department as outlined in Circular 59, 2 March 1942.

2. The following excerpts from WD Circular 59 are pertinent:

   a. The WDGS "is specifically charged with the duties of providing such broad basic plans as will enable the commanding generals of the Army Ground Forces, Army Air Forces and Services of Supply (now Army Service Forces), defense commands, task forces, and theaters of operations to prepare and execute detailed programs."

   b. "The mission of Army Ground Forces is to provide ground force units properly organized, trained and equipped for combat operations."

   c. "The mission of Army Air Forces is to procure and maintain equipment peculiar to the AAF and to provide air force units properly organized, trained and equipped for combat operations."

   d. "The mission of the Services of Supply

is to provide services and supplies to meet military requirements except those peculiar to the AAF."

e. "Supply arms and services and War Department offices and agencies will come under the direct command of the Commanding General, SOS, as indicated below;" (there follows a list of agencies now under Army Service Forces).

3. A common supply and service organization is essential. Except with respect to materiel peculiar to Army Air Forces, the Commanding General, ASF, is responsible for supplies and services common to the Army and will act as the chief technical adviser to the Chief of Staff and the War Department. The Commanding General, ASF, is responsible for preparing, and after co-ordination with the other major commands, submitting to the Chief of Staff for publication policies, procedures, methods and standards affecting such common supply and service functions. The Commanding General, ASF, is fully responsible for and has command over the various organizational units of that command including all of the Army-wide functions of the technical and administrative services (other than civil work of the Chief of Engineers).

4. At all types of installations, the Commanding General, ASF, through the appropriate subordinate agencies of that command, will inspect the technical sufficiency of the operation and performance of the common supply and service functions for which that command is responsible.

5. Agencies of the WDGS have responsibility for co-ordinating and approving War Department-wide policies and directives initiated by any one of the three major commands. However, in accordance with AR 10–15, no War Department General Staff agency will engage in duties or operations for the performance of which an agency exists within one of the major commands. Subordinate organizational units of the major commands are neither instrumentalities nor adjuncts of the War Department General Staff but are a part of the major command to which they are subordinate.

6. Communications.

a. Communications on major policy matters will be:

(1) Directly among the three major commands.

(2) Between the General Staff agencies and the commanding generals of the three major commands.

b. Communications on matters of a routine technical nature are authorized between agencies of the General Staff and subordinate agencies of the three major commands.

7. Paragraph 4 of Minutes of General Council Meeting, 23 July 1944, is rescinded.

Appendix C

Documents on the Relations With the AAF:
Relation of Supply and Service Agencies to Combat Forces

War Department
Washington 25, D. C.

27 November 1944

MEMORANDUM FOR THE CHIEF OF STAFF:

SUBJECT: Relation of Supply and Service Agencies to Combat Forces.

1. Pursuant to your Memorandum dated 26 October 1944, the Commanding Generals, Army Air Forces, Army Ground Forces, and Army Service Forces have met and considered "the over-all question of service and supply functions and responsibilities together with their relation to command." Throughout our examination of the subject, the necessity of demonstrating within the Army unity of purpose and action within itself and a satisfactory relation of service agencies and combat forces, as well as between combat forces themselves, was considered desirable for securing the acceptance of a single Department of National Defense. The Army Air Forces, however, have felt that no relation can be satisfactory that prevents either combat force from operating at maximum efficiency, and also that if the desired objective of a single Department is to be realized, the over-all organization must be designed to fit the not dissimilar problems of the third combat force, the Navy. The commanding generals have been unable to resolve certain fundamental differences of view as to functions which should be performed for the Army as a whole by a common service agency, and those which should be performed for itself by the combat force.

2. It is the view of the Commanding General, Army Air Forces, that the basic command responsibility of the air combat force is and must be to maintain quantitative and qualitative superiority in the air; that this responsibility extends far beyond employment of aircraft in combat and training of personnel to fly and maintain aircraft; and that successful performance of this responsibility requires ability to maintain most continuous operations from bases both in the zone of interior and the theater of operations. The administrative, supply and service functions related to maintenance of air superiority are and must be so completely integrated with combat and training operations of the Air Forces that their performance by a distinct command produces fatal divided responsibility. Such a relationship transfers from the Commanding General, Army Air Forces, duties and responsibilities, with accompanying command authority, which are essential

to effective operations of the Air Forces. The Commanding General, Army Air Forces, recognizes, however, that there are certain supply and service activities, common to the Army as a whole, which in the interest of economy and uniformity must be performed by a central service agency.

3. The Commanding General, Army Ground Forces and Army Service Forces, believe that the primary purpose of the War Department and the components thereof should be to maintain quantitative and qualitative superiority over the forces of the enemy and that the decision with regard to the role which the Air Forces are to play should be a War Department decision and not the responsibility of the commanding general of the Army Air Forces. They believe further that the system proposed by the commanding general of the Army Air Forces would, to all intents and purposes, create a separate Air Force within the framework of the War Department with direct command over its activities extending into the theaters of operations. The original paper on this subject submitted by the Commanding General, Army Service Forces, was submitted to secure a decision whether this is indeed the policy of the War Department. Commanding Generals, Army Ground Forces and Army Service Forces, are further of the opinion that:

a. The system adopted for the organization of supply and services should be such as to most effectively promote the maximum combat effectiveness, the efficiency and welfare of the Army as a whole, as distinguished from that of any individual component.

b. The establishment of a single agency within the Army to provide supplies and render common services is vital to avoid duplication and in the interest of economy.

c. Uniformity in the supply and service system of the Army is highly desirable and the relationship between the Ground and Service Forces and between the Air and Service Forces can and should be made substantially identical.

d. The combat forces should be relieved to the maximum extent possible from supply and service functions to permit them to devote their time to training and combat; combat units should be organized to perform only those supply and service functions essential to their internal operations to meet their combat missions; all supply and service functions not so organic to combat units should be performed by a common service agency; unity of command and authority commensurate with responsibility within the combat forces is assured when a combat commander has authority over his unit and the supply and service functions organic thereto.

4. Proper definition of the functions and responsibilities which should be performed by a service agency on an Army-wide basis is not a simple matter. The Commanding General, Army Air Forces, believes the definition of paragraph 3d to be so uncertain as to be impossible of practical application and to beg the question. The Commanding Generals, Army Ground Forces and Army Service Forces, believe that this definition is based on the same principle of "economy of force" historically and properly used in the Army in the organization of tactical units, provides a satisfactory basis for assignment of responsibilities and authority for supply and services, and will result in a system which will tend to weld the Army into one force and promote the efficiency and welfare of the Army as a whole, whereas the system proposed by the Air Forces will tend to separate the combat forces of the Army. The basic

differences, described above, are best illustrated by the main specific differences set forth in Tab A. Consideration and resolution of these specific differences in relation to the command responsibilities of the respective combat forces should pave the way for a sound determination of the Army-wide functions of the common service agency.

5. There are attached as Tab B and Tab C respectively, statements submitted by the Commanding General, Army Air Forces, and by the Commanding Generals, Army Ground Forces and Army Service Forces, in further development of the views set forth in the foregoing and in Tab A.

H. H. ARNOLD
General, U.S. Army
Commanding General, Army Air Forces.

BEN LEAR
Lieutenant General, U.S. Army
Commanding General, Army Ground Forces.

BREHON B. SOMERVELL
Lieutenant General, U.S. Army
Commanding General, Army Service Forces.

AGF and ASF are of the opinion that

1. Development, design and procurement of all matériel (to requirements of the combat forces) should be performed by the ASF, except that during this war procurement of aircraft and spare parts therefore should be done by the AAF.

2. Maintenance, salvage and disposal of matériel, except that performable by personnel and facilities organic to tactical units of AGF or AAF, should be performed by the ASF, except that during this war maintenance, salvage and disposal of aircraft and spare parts therefore should be done by the AAF.

3. Storage and distribution of all matériel, except that performable by personnel organic to tactical units of AGF or AAF, should be performed by the ASF, except that during this war storage and distribution of aircraft and spare parts therefore should be done by the AAF.

AAF is of the opinion that

1. Development, design and procurement of matériel of a type of peculiar utility to AAF or in which its interest is predominant should (as at present) be the responsibility and under command control of AAF. ASF's function in this regard must be correspondingly limited as at present.

2. All maintenance of matériel utilized by AAF which is of peculiar utility to AAF, or of a type in which its interest is predominant and all maintenance of all matériel performable at AAF stations should (as at present) be the responsibility and under command control of AAF. ASF's function in this regard must be correspondingly limited as at present.

3. All distribution of all matériel utilized by AAF of peculiar utility to AAF or of a type in which its interest is predominant, and distribution at AAF stations, whether by personnel organic to AAF tactical units or not, of all matériel should (as at present) be the responsibility and under command control of AAF. ASF's function in this regard must be correspondingly limited as at present.

AGF and ASF are of the opinion that

4. On posts utilized by the combat forces in the zone of interior, the Service Force should perform supply and service activities not organic to tactical units utilizing the post. This can take the form of:

a. A service commander on the post responsible for such activities and under the supervision of the commanding general of the ASF Service Command. This method relieves the tactical command of direct responsibility and provides the maximum amount of time and freedom for the command and training of his combat unit.

b. A tactical commander being responsible to the commanding general of an ASF Service Command for the performance of these activities. For this method the tactical commander would be furnished the necessary station complement. Such an arrangement provides full command supervision over supply and services at the station level and will permit tactical troops to leave a station without disturbing station activities.

5. Establishment of Army-wide technical standards, techniques and procedures for all phases of supply and service activities not directly connected with training and preparation for combat of troops organic in AGF or AAF should be the responsibility of the ASF.

6. Except for that "organic to tactical units of the combat forces at various echelons, and to the requirements of the combat forces as approved by the War Department," the ASF should perform the following service functions for the Army. Transportation of troops and supplies by rail, water, air and motor vehicles; operation of fixed signal communications; procurement and disposal of real estate; construction, maintenance of structures, and fire protection; care of the sick and wounded, hospitalization, sanitation, and veterinary services; fiscal services; accounting, disbursing, auditing; personnel services, procurement, classification, assignment, discharge, recreation, and welfare; legal services, litigation, claims, contract law, military justice; and other service activities such as exchanges, laundries, publications and blank forms, insurance, mapping, military police, prisoners of war, files and records.

AAF is of the opinion that

4. Administration of all AAF stations and of all services and facilities thereon should (as at present) be the responsibility and under command control of AAF. Full command control of AAF stations and of all facilities and administrative, supply and service activities continuously required thereon is essential to effective operation of AAF units. Because of the inherent nature of Air Force operations, these activities are all interdependent and must be fully available and integrated under one command.

5. Establishment of technical standards, techniques and procedures for supply and service activities of peculiar utility to AAF or in which its interest is predominant should (as at present) be the responsibility and under command control of AAF, ASF's function in this regard being limited to establishment of technical standards, techniques and procedures for certain supplies and services of Army-wide utility.

6. Performance, as at present, of all administrative, supply and service functions continuously required either at AAF stations or by AAF organizations, and control of personnel and funds required therefore should be the responsibility and under command control of AAF, recognizing, however, that certain administrative, supply and service functions which are of Army-wide utility and are not continuously required at AAF stations or by AAF organizations (such as construction of fixed facilities, storage of matériel of Army-wide utility prior to distribution, factory overhaul or quantity repair of such matériel, review of court martial proceedings, establishment of procurement regulations in co-ordination with AAF and others of like nature) should be the responsibility of ASF, and should be so designated from time to time by the Under Secretary of War or the Chief of Staff.

AGF and ASF are of the opinion that

7. In order to secure maximum economy and efficiency of the Army, the degree of dependency of the combat forces (AGF and AAF) on the service agency (ASF) for administration, supplies and services should be substantially identical on whatever basis established.

8. ASF should act as the staff agency of the Chief of Staff and the Under Secretary of War for supply and service activities throughout the entire Army; i. e., there should be only one Surgeon General who should act as *The* Surgeon General of the Army.

9. No direct command responsibilities below the Chief of Staff should be exercised by any agency in the zone of interior over any supply and service activities in overseas theaters. The theater commander must have command over and be responsible for all Army activities in his theater. Each theater of operations should have a service force for the performance of supply and service functions not organic to the combat elements in the theater. In theaters of operations, all supply and service activities are the responsibility of the theater commander. The air and ground forces should have organic units to perform supply and service functions back to the same tactical level—army for ground, and air forces for air. In the rear of this level a theater service force should support ground and air alike.

10. AGF and ASF believe that the principles advanced by it, and illustrated by the above examples, afford a satisfactory and practical basis for the creation of a single agency for a Department of National Defense.

AAF is of the opinion that

7. AAF, while recognizing the value of uniformity within appropriate limits, is of the opinion that uniformity is not an end in itself, and should be applied only to the extent that it promotes the effectiveness of the combat forces; and that the relationship advocated by AGF and ASF, if conducive to the effectiveness of AGF, is detrimental to AAF effectiveness and should not be applicable as between AAF and ASF.

8. The AAF believes that all of the activities of the ASF should be subject to general policies laid down by the General Staff as now constituted, that the requirements of the combat forces should be determined and adjudicated by a General Staff in no respect subject to one of the major commands, and further that many staff functions now performed for the Army by ASF should be restored to General Staff level, ASF to retain necessary operating functions subject to General Staff direction. The AAF disagrees with the view that a service agency under independent command should act as a staff agency for the Chief of Staff and Under Secretary of War for administrative, supply or service activities.

9. Except as to supply and service functions and activities which are of a world-wide or intertheater nature (such as weather service, airways communications air transport including delivery of aircraft), no direct command responsibilities below the Chief of Staff should be exercised by an agency in the zone of interior over such functions and activities in overseas theater. Subject to the above exceptions, the theater commander must have a service agency for performance for the theater ground force and theater air force of all supply and service functions other than (*a*) those of peculiar utility to the air force, (*b*) those continuously required at air force stations and (*c*) those in which its interest is predominant. These functions should be performed by and under command control of the air force, subject to the theater commander. A relationship apparently considered appropriate as between the ground force and service agency has no applications to the air force and would be detrimental to the effectiveness of theater air operations.

10. The AAF is convinced that it will be completely impossible to organize a single Department of National Defense if the position taken by AGF and ASF prevails within the Army, but on the other hand, believes that if the Army organization follows the lines advocated by the AAF it can be adapted without great difficulty to a single department.

Appendix D

ASF Relations With WPB

12 March 1942

TO: Officers and Employees: Services of Supply and Material Command of the Army Air Forces, War Department, and War Production Board.

FROM: Chairman, War Production Board; Under Secretary of War.

SUBJECT: Relationships Between the War Production Board and the War Department.

GENERAL

1. The following statement is made for the purpose of facilitating the effort now in process to perfect the governing relationships between the War Production Board and the War Department in effectuating the war supply program.

2. The Chairman of the War Production Board is charged with the duty and given the power to "exercise general direction over the war procurement and production program," to "determine the policies, plans, procedures, and methods of the several Federal departments, establishments, and agencies in respect to war procurement and production, including purchasing, contracting, specifications, and construction; and including conversion, requestioning, plant expansion and the financing thereof; and issue such directives in respect thereto as he may deem necessary or appropriate;" to organize and direct the mobilization of industry and to maintain a civilian economy consistent with war necessity.

3. The war supply organizations should be viewed by all participants as a single integrated system operating under the general direction of the Chairman of the War Production Board in a unified effort to win the war and not as a group of autonomous or semiautonomous organizations acting in mere liaison with one another.

4. Although the immediate responsibility, initiative, and decision for a particular function is placed in one part of the organization, the assistance of the other parts is expected and directed.

DUTIES OF THE WAR PRODUCTION BOARD

5. In broad terms, the War Production Board gives general direction and supervision to the war supply system, formulates broad policies with respect to that system, makes the basic decisions on the allocation of resources to the various parts of the supply system in accordance with strategic directives and plans, makes provision for materials, services, tools, and facilities needed for the military effort and the civilian economy, and organizes industry for war production. Therefore, specifically, the War Production Board will—

a. Co-operate with the War Department in the formulation and review of supply programs, and in the light of military needs as expressed by the War Department, determine the resources that will be applied to war production and to the civilian economy consistent with war necessity and aid the War Department in adjusting its programs to such determinations.

b. Supervise the over-all utilization of the economic resources of the nation.

c. Develop raw material sources and increase production of raw materials.

d. Develop services, including transportation, power and communications.

e. Stock pile materials and certain end products for which a future shortage is indicated.

f. Expedite the production of raw materials, machine tools and industrial supplies and also expedite production of other items where effective expediting by the War Department cannot be carried on without conflict with other agencies.

g. Eliminate by curtailment, conservation, and otherwise less essential uses of materials, facilities, services, and manpower essential to the accomplishment of the munitions program.

h. Expand available skilled manpower for war production through training, transfer from nonessential activities, and reduction in the loss of man-hours through stoppages resulting from all causes.

i. Direct the provision of facilities needed to produce raw materials, equipment, tools, and services.

j. Determine the plants or industries which should be converted to the production of supply for the War Department and assist the War Department in such conversion.

k. Assure preservation and production of the necessary facilities auxiliary to the production and distribution of military supply.

l. Enlist the participation of industry by organizing industry committees, by promoting cooperation between industrial units and by securing from the Department of Justice clearance for such co-operative action.

m. Assure the maintenance of a virile civilian economy consistent with war necessity.

n. Distribute the available supply of materials and equipment by priorities, allocations, and otherwise, with particular reference to apportioning in a major way of scarce materials between principal users. (Much of the detail assignment of ratings will continue to be made by the Army and Navy Munitions Board operating under policies and procedures approved by the Chairman of the War Production Board.)

o. Adjudicate and make decisions on matters pertaining to priorities, allocations, requisitioning, and to placement of orders in existing facilities, as between the military and other needs.

DUTIES OF THE WAR DEPARTMENT IN THE SUPPLY PROGRAM

6. In broad terms, the War Department, through the Services of Supply and the Matériel Command of the Army Air Forces, in accordance and compliance with the policies and directives of the War Production Board, carries on its supply functions of research, design, development, programming, purchase, production, storage, distribution, issue, maintenance, and salvage. Therefore, specifically, the War Department will—

a. Determine military needs and compile requirements for supplies, new facilities, transportation, and communication as to quantity, types, and time, and translate these into requirements for resources, including raw materials, tools, and labor, and keep the War Production Board continually informed of these requirements.

b. Receive from the War Production Board descriptions of plans or industries available for conversion, and convert these with the assistance and under the direction of the War Production Board.

c. Purchase, including the negotiation, placement and administration of contracts.

d. Produce, including preparation of schedules, inspection and acceptance of product, issuance of shipping instructions, and distribution (including arrangements for storage, receipt, issue, inspection of use, transportation, and maintenance).

e. Expedite production in facilities producing finished items, parts, components, and subassemblies where there is no conflict with other agencies.

f. Construct and expand plants for production of finished items.

g. Conduct research and development and set specifications.

h. Conserve materials, facilities, and manpower used in war supply by substitution of more available materials in place of scarcer materials by elimination, by development, by simplification, and by standardization of types of equipment and supplies. (While equipment and supplies must have the essential military characteristics, their specifications should also be such as to permit rapid mass production. On the other hand, ease of production should not entirely control design of articles. Moreover, the real necessity for military characteristics must be constantly challenged and reanalyzed with reference to the practical life of the product.)

CONTACTS BETWEEN THE WAR PRODUCTION BOARD AND THE WAR DEPARTMENT

7. Relationships will include frequent contacts by the Chairman of the War Production Board, the Under Secretary of War, the Director of Production of the War Department, the Commanding General of the Services of Supply, the general in charge of the Matériel Command of the Army Air Forces, and their key subordinates; directives issued by the War Production Board; membership on the War Production Board; the Army and Navy Munitions Board; representatives on committees and units; and constant co-operation between the Chief of the Control Division of the Services of Supply and the Office of the Chairman of the War Production Board for the purpose of continuous survey of working relationships between the two agencies.

8. Members of both organizations are alike engaged in the mission of obtaining maximum balanced supply in the most expeditious manner possible. Obstacles to this end must and will be removed. One such obstacle is an organizational practice known as "layering." This means that a subordinate charged with a task in one organization or subdivision thereof must go *up* through the layers of his superiors, across from the top of his agency to the top of the other agency and then *down* through the layers of the other organization to the subordinate responsible for decision or other action. Such action may then have to go back through the layers again.

9. From this time forward there is to be no layering within or between the War Production Board and the War Department. Any officer of either agency is not only free, but is hereby directed to make direct contact with his opposite or any person from whom he needs advice, assistance, or decision by personal interview, telephone, or written communication. Wherever possible, missions should be accomplished *first* and thereafter may be confirmed, where necessary for routine, "through channels." Personal interview or telephone communication is to be

used in preference to written communications in handling urgent matters.

10. Finally, the war supply system shall be operated in accordance with the basic principle of effective organization that immediate responsibility, authority, and scope for initiative shall be placed as far down in the operating organizations and as close to the actual doing of the various procurement tasks as possible.

[s]   D. M. Nelson

D. M. NELSON
Chairman, War Production Board

[s]   Robert P. Patterson

ROBERT P. PATTERSON
Under Secretary of War

Appendix E

Nelson-Somervell Correspondence in 1942

War Department
Headquarters, Services of Supply
Washington, D. C.

15 May 1942

Dear Mr. Nelson:

I am inclosing for your consideration the proposal which we discussed informally after our Tuesday morning meeting. Before this transmittal of the detailed proposal to you, I asked Dr. Gulick, Mr. Baruch, Judge Patterson, Mr. Eberstadt, and Mr. Forrestal to criticize it. All of us are agreed that the reorganization proposed will do much to streamline present procedure and make for effective action.

Our war munitions program has reached at this time an industrial rate comparable in dollar value to peak production in time of peace. Nevertheless, in many items, it would appear that this rate represents a war production peak due to shortage in critical materials. For instance, the copper supply allocated to the Army barely suffices now to maintain ammunition lines which are far from adequate to meet requirements. It is believed that this condition has resulted in large part due to (1) the absence of any strategic control or direction in the allocation of raw and basic industrial materials among the United Nations, other nations, and essential civilian requirements including indirect military requirements; and (2) inade-

quate control over the supply of critical materials available for allocation to United States production. No one can be sure that a specific allocation reaches the desired end product.

The allocation of raw and basic industrial materials is the responsibility of a combined raw materials board composed of Mr. Batt representing the United States and Sir Clive Baillieu, the United Kingdom. This Board does not operate on a formal basis. It reports directly to the President and to the Prime Minister and is in touch with the combined Chiefs of Staff only through a liaison agency established by the Munitions Assignments Board. Requirements submitted to this board by other nations are not subject to the same detailed review which United States requirements receive in the Requirements Committee, War Production Board. This board allocates materials to areas where the Munitions Assignments Board has refused to assign finished munitions.

It is proposed that the Raw Materials Allocations Board be made a Combined Resources Board operating directly under the Combined Chiefs of Staff and under the same chairmanship as the Munitions Assignments Board. Its composition should be extended to include not only representation of War Production Board and the British Supply Ministry but also of the Armed Services of both countries. The board should consider all available resources and requirements in the light of known strategical objectives with a view to matching resources against requirements so as to best meet these objectives. It would follow the pattern established by the Munitions Assignments Board, utilizing the Requirements Committee, War Production Board as its working committee.

Weaknesses in the existing system are described in more detail in pages 6 to 10 inclusive, of the attached detailed report, remedial measures are discussed in pages 25 and 26, and an organizational chart is given in Exhibit I.

The Requirements Committee, War Production Board, in becoming the working committee of the Combined Resources Board, would be designated as a Resources Committee under a chairman appointed by War Production Board. Its membership would include representatives of our Armed Services Civilian Supply, Lend-Lease, and of the United Kingdom when requirements and resources pertaining to the latter are under consideration. This committee would examine all requirements for critical materials and recommend an appropriate allocation of available resources. Its recommendations would become final unless appealed immediately to the Combined Resources Board.

In order that this Committee could function effectively, major organizational changes would be required within the War Production Board. The Commodity Branches of the War Production Board do not adequately concern themselves with all of the raw materials and facilities resources which are already in a critical stage. Moreover, other Government agencies including the Army and Navy Munitions Board also are concerned with these problems. Consequently, there is no central clearing house for the correlation of all such data. In order that the Resources Committee may function more intelligently,

it should create a Commodity Committee for each critical material. The Commodity Committee thus formed would be headed by a permanent chairman, also from the War Production Board, with permanent representation from Civilian Supply and for the Armed Services from the Army and Navy Munitions Board. A committee staff would include the best known experts available for the commodity in question and it would maintain constant liaison with selected representatives of the industry, also permanently located in Washington. The Army-Navy representation on the committee would reconcile any service differences prior to the action of the Commodity Committee as a whole. The Commodity Committee would be responsible for the analysis and forecasting of requirements, the determination and allocation of available resources, the scheduling of deliveries, and the enforcement of compliance. Each commodity presents a special problem, and the present system of priority control and enforcement under separate divisions with allocations on a hit-or-miss basis is falling down. Positive control over a commodity can be obtained only through the establishment of a Commodity Committee representative of all users including the Armed Services with a Chairman who is fully responsible for the administration and execution of approved decision.

Weaknesses in the present system are covered in detail in pages 16 to 24 of the detailed report, remedial measures are proposed in detail in pages 26 to 32 inclusive, and a proposed organization chart is given in Exhibit L.

Immediate and positive steps must be taken to control raw and basic industrial materials if production lines are to be maintained. Present control has proved definitely inadequate to insure the delivery of requisite materials on schedule with a consequent lag in production. Remedial measures are essential. The priority system has functioned to preclude lower priority end products receiving any critical materials and balanced production cannot be maintained. The measures proposed herein can be undertaken within the existing framework with a minimum of change and delay and without destruction of public confidence in the existing organization.

I shall be out of town today, but hope that you will be able to give me some time either Saturday afternoon or Sunday to discuss the matter.

Sincerely,
BREHON SOMERVELL
Lieutenant General, Commanding.

1–Incl.
Report dated 5 May 1942

War Production Board
Washington, D. C.

May 21, 1942

Office of
DONALD M. NELSON
Chairman

Lt. Gen. Brehon Somervell
Commanding General, Services of Supply
War Department
Washington, D. C.

Dear General Somervell:

This will acknowledge and thank you for your letter of May 15, 1942, together with an accompanying "Report on Certain Features of the Organizational Problems Involved in Developing Resources To Meet Strategic Requirements," setting forth certain proposals relating to the control of materials and to the correlation of strategic organization with

production organization. Broadly stated, the proposals embody four principal elements, which I should like to discuss separately. All are important, but one has especial significance. I refer to the suggested over-all arrangement for the coordination of strategy and production. I should like to consider this at some length, after first dealing more briefly with other factors.

1. *The Inadequacy of the Present Machinery for Controlling the Distribution of Materials.*

The letter and the accompanying report describe certain weaknesses which have developed in the mechanism for controlling the distribution of materials. These weaknesses are real, and have been foreseeable for some time. (Your analysis overlooks certain of the contributing causes, such as the loose issuance and extension of PD–3A preference rating certificates by the procurement officers of the Army and Navy, and the failure of the Services to present accurate statements of their requirements.) For several months the War Production Board has recognized that, following substantial completion of the vital curtailment program and the effective launching of the program of conversion, it would be necessary to shift the primary emphasis of the entire organization to the development and operation of a new and uniform basis for guiding the distribution of materials. In the light of extensive analysis and developmental work, in consultation with the staff of the Army and Navy Munitions Board, and after preliminary testing of new devices, we have tentatively adopted a new system for administering the distribution of materials, to take effect July 1st of this year. The system will substitute for the present multiplication of devices, which have grown up more or less independently of one another, a single system for the distribution of materials based upon the importance to the war of the products of the various applicants, accurate estimates of the material actually needed by them to make the products, knowledge of their inventories, and the scarcity of the particular materials and the possibilities of increasing the supply, or reducing the demand by substitution and conservation. By letter of May 13, 1942, I advised the Under Secretary of War and the Under Secretary of the Navy of the prospective institution of the new system; solicited their further advice and criticism; and indicated that we desired to be able to announce our decision at the earliest possible date, preferably not later than May 24th. A copy of the letter to Mr. Patterson, together with the enclosures, is enclosed for your information.

There is another aspect of the matter which must be emphasized. The control of the distribution of materials is not merely a matter of mechanism. It depends also upon the determination of the uses to which materials are to be put. Unless these uses are soundly determined, no mechanism will work, for the mechanism must be guided by the established purposes. It is with this in mind (and related considerations affecting management, labor and machine tools) that we have so drastically curtailed the production of consumers durable goods and other goods for civilian use, and that we are pushing our programs for the conservation and substitution of materials. But the determination of uses has more than a civilian aspect. It has the all-important military side. That is why I have pressed during the past weeks for the earliest possible determination of the production program. It also explains why, in the development of a comprehensive program, adjustments must be made in the light of production factors, as well as the strategic direction of the war. As you know, the War Production Board has been acting upon a recognition of these facts. I have in mind,

among other things, the Committee on Facilities and Construction which I recently constituted with your collaboration and the collaboration of the Navy, in order to screen out all new facilities not really needed for the accomplishment of the munitions program. I think I may also appropriately mention at this point our difficulties with the stated requirements of the services for nonmilitary items. You will recall, for example, that the Army's original stated requirement for additional new typewriters for the year 1942 was more than twice the total calculated to be adequate for the entire civilian economy during the same period.

2. *The Situation With Respect to Civilian Supply.*

There is another fundamental which I believe your suggested plan of organization violates. The War Production Board not only has responsibility for production of material for war, but also for the production of the necessary material for the essential civilian economy. It is a fact that no war program can go forward with the required speed unless the essential civilian services are maintained at the same time. Transportation and communication systems must be sound; the health, police and fire services of our municipalities must be maintained and the minimum needs for the economy must be met; otherwise no war program can be carried forward in any country. In my opinion, it would be a fundamental mistake to put the apportionment of materials for the essential civilian economy under the military.

3. *Organizational Changes Within the War Production Board.*

The War Production Board has recognized that the substantial completion of the curtailment program, and the adoption of the new system for controlling the distribution of materials, will require a radical reorientation of the work of the War Production Board, and corresponding changes in its organization. Related changes will be necessary in the procedure of the Army and Navy Munitions Board and the procurement arms of the Services. Your suggestion for the reorganization of the Requirements Committee, and for the formation of commodity committees, is helpful, and corresponds in certain aspects to plans which we have under consideration. I have asked Mr. Knowlson, the Director of Industry Operations for the War Production Board, and Mr. Batt, the Chairman of the Requirements Committee, to discuss this aspect of the matter further with you and Mr. Eberstadt.

4. *Proposed Over-all Arrangement for Correlation of Strategy and Production.*

As I have indicated, this phase of the proposal seems to me the most far-reaching and fundamental. With the need for perfecting the mutual co-ordination of strategy and production, I emphatically agree. For the rest, however, your proposal seems to me to be basically in error.

The report on page 2 refers to the "co-ordination of strategy and the utilization of available industrial resources." On page 6 it refers to the "formulation of strategic decisions on the basis of availability of industrial resources." At the foot of page 6 and on page 7, it states that the Combined Chiefs of Staff must "take into account not only purely military questions but also economic factors," and that the "responsibility for establishing policies to govern the mobilization, use and apportionment of resources is essential to the fulfillment of their primary mission." In my judgment, these statements, and other similar statements in the letter and report, taken together, reveal two fundamental misconceptions. They misconceive the nature of the "materials problem"; and

they misconceive the relationship of strategy to production.

First, the letter and the report seem to proceed on the assumption that the management of "raw and basic industrial materials" can be ripped out of the process of managing production, segregated and handled separately. This overlooks the simple fact that the management of materials is one phase of the process of guiding production. The materials problem, the facilities problem, the management problem, the labor problem, all are inextricably intertwined. As a matter of fact, most of the acute "material shortages" are not shortages in raw materials, but in processed materials with respect to which the limiting factor is the amount of facilities. For instance, the limiting factor in aircraft production today is aluminum forgings; and increasing the supply of aluminum forgings depends not on finding more aluminum, but tools and dies and labor in the forging shops. Similarly, the limiting factor in shipbuilding at this time is steel plate; and the supply of plate is limited not by the availability of steel but by the availability of rolling facilities.

The report seeks to draw a parallel between the work of the Munitions Assignments Board and the work of a proposed Combined Resources Board which would occupy a corresponding position in the structure of the Combined Chiefs of Staff. In all candor, I must say that the attempted parallel seems to me to miss the point. The work of the so-called Combined Resources Board must be an integral part of the whole vast process of production, and must be subject to the direction of those charged with ultimate responsibility for production. The munitions assignment operation, on the other hand, is essentially a scheduling operation, dealing with specific completed military end products, and based upon military needs as of the time of the assignment.

Second, as I have said, I fully agree that strategy and production must be mutually co-ordinated. But it is strategy and *production goals* which must be correlated, not strategy and the apportionment of raw and basic industrial materials. The concepts of strategy govern, not the use of resources, *but the determination of the production program.* When the program has been determined, responsibility for utilizing all resources—raw materials, basic industrial materials, machine tools, fabricating machinery, plants, management and labor—to achieve this program rests not with the Chiefs of Staff, but with the chiefs of production. The President of the United States has placed upon the Chairman of the War Production Board the duty of exercising direction over the entire war procurement and production program. The battle of production is the primary responsibility of the Chairman of the War Production Board in much the same sense that the military battles are the primary responsibility of the military chiefs.

As the report recognizes, the reciprocal adjustment of strategy and production, to be effective, implies the integration of the American and British production programs, just as it implies the integration of American and British strategic decisions. I have been discussing the need for such an integration of production programs with Mr. Hopkins for some time. By a letter dated April 22d to the Chairman of the British Supply Council in North America (copies of which were sent to the Secretary of War and the Secretary of the Navy), I arranged for the preliminary phases of the work. I have recently asked Mr. Lyttleton, the British production chief, to come to America to carry the work forward with me, with particular emphasis upon 1942 and the early part of 1943, in order that the combined production program, together with a statement of adjustments therein required by production factors, may then be placed before the Combined Chiefs of Staff for final determination in the light of strategic decisions. Mr. Lyttleton has agreed to come.

The Combined Chiefs of Staff cannot determine their plans without a picture of the current facts and the future practical possibilities of production. The chiefs of production cannot achieve the best possible results without accurate and up-to-date knowledge of the material requirements of the Services. It is only through close and continuous relations between the Combined Chiefs of Staff and those charged with ultimate responsibility for production that we can bring about a situation in which equipment will be ready for military action—in the right amount, of the right kind, in proper balance, and at the right time.

Sincerely yours,

[s]   DONALD M. NELSON
Chairman
War Production Board

Appendix F

Stimson Letter to Senator Reynolds on Organization of an Office of War Mobilization and Civilian Versus Military Responsibility for Procurement

March 13, 1943

Honorable Robert R. Reynolds,
  Chairman, Committee on Military Affairs,
  United States Senate.

Dear Senator Reynolds:

You have asked the views of the War Department concerning S.607, a bill "To Establish an Office of War Mobilization and for other purposes." The War Department is opposed to the enactment of this bill.

The bill would establish an Office of War Mobilization under a Director of War Mobilization. Section 3 of the Bill creates a Committee on Requirements and Program of nine members, four of whom represent the Armed Services. This Committee is authorized to develop, subject to the approval of the President, a comprehensive national program for maximum use of resources for military and essential civilian needs. The Section provides: "This program shall be based on schedules of military requirements furnished by the War and Navy Departments and determinations as to minimum essential civilian needs and available resources by the Office of War Mobilization."

I.

One of the constituent offices of the proposed Office of War Mobilization is the Office of Production and Supply (Section 6). This office, in addition to other duties, is to translate the production program into a detailed time schedule of end and intermediate military and civilian production by plants. It is given the function to "procure, through contracts or otherwise, the requirements of the Departments of War and Navy and of the Maritime Commission, and all foreign requirements, including Lend-Lease." Likewise, it reviews progress on all outstanding contracts and renegotiates such contracts where necessary so as to conform to the schedule. In addition, it is to check on the use of facilities, materials and other production factors through plant inspection.

By section 7 (a) of the bill, there would be transferred to the Office of Production and Supply, the functions and personnel of, among others, those subdivisions of the War and Navy Departments as shall be determined by the Director, subject to the approval of the President, "as being related to, engaged in, or concerned with the procurement, manufacture or other provision of war material."

Section 7 (e) provides: "All persons attached to the military services who are transferred to the Office of War Mobilization by this act, or who are subsequently so transferred, shall be relieved from service for such lengths of time as shall be requested by the Director."

By Section 9 (a) of the bill, all appropriations for any agency available for use in connection with any function transferred to the Office of War Mobilization are transferred and made available to the Office of War Mobilization.

The bill is based on the assumption that it will be advantageous to the prosecution of the war for the armed forces to state what they need for victory, while another agency, separate and independent of the Army and Navy, reviews the stated needs and attends to their fulfillment to the extent that it approves. However, it is impossible thus to separate the military program into parts, introducing dualism and divided responsibility, without disruption of the Army in its military operations.

The task of providing the Army with weapons and other equipment is a continuous process, from strategic and tactical planning through production and distribution to use on the field of battle, including maintenance, salvage and rehabilitation. Research is required to develop new and improved weapons and their design, specifications and drawings. Pilot models must be produced. Requirements must be established. Spare parts and tools for maintenance in the field must be determined. Facilities must be examined for capacity to produce, and the needed capacity assured. Part of the production must be placed in Army arsenals. Contracts must be placed with industrial concerns and performance expedited. Inspection, testing and proof-firing are required. Shipping orders must be given. Transportation, here and abroad, must be provided. Finally, we have the phases of field maintenance, repair and salvage.

In actual practice there is no chronological sequence whereby some of these functions may be culled out and given to a separate agency. Strategic and tactical planning continue throughout the process and are, in turn, affected by the progress of munitions manufacture. Research and preparation of specifications change the course of production, as to military testing and inspection which occur simultaneously with production. Battle experience must be translated into production changes forthwith. Weapons already completed must be modified or changed in light of such experience or the requirements of the particular area in which combat operations are taking place. Production schedules and whole programs must be immediately changed by direct contact with manufacturers to meet the varying needs of task forces overseas.

None of these things can be accomplished through the complexities of a dual organization as proposed in the bill. The submission by the armed services of schedules for thousands of weapons and tens of thousands of components for approval and placement by another agency would present insurmountable difficulties, particularly when revisions in quantities and specifications are constantly required as the result of strategic and tactical changes. Duplication of labor, red tape and jurisdictional disputes would cause disastrous delay.

A dual arrangement and the interruption of the flow of production of weapons can be avoided only by continuing the entire process in the armed forces. Modern warfare is largely a war of logistics. Our strategy depends upon the control of military procurement and supply. It is the basic mission of the War Department, under the direction of our Commander-in-Chief, to organize, equip, dispose and direct our Army so as to defeat the enemy completely and without delay. This mission can be accomplished only by placing complete responsibility and authority in a single chain of command for the design, procurement, storage, distribution, use, maintenance and salvage of weapons. Strategy and production of weapons are inseparable.

Divided responsibility could cause the loss of the war.

The impossibility of dividing planning, supply and use into separate compartments is demonstrated by an attempt to determine what subdivisions and personnel of the War Department may be transferred to the Office of War Mobilization under the provisions of the bill. The Chief of Staff, the General Staff and the Staffs of the Ground Forces, Air Forces and Services of Supply are all "concerned" with the provision of war materiel. They are engaged at some point in the continuous flow of munitions to the troops. Which ones should be transferred to the civilian agency? The Chief of Ordnance, for example, as the best qualified officer in ordnance matters, now is charged with responsibility for planning and procuring weapons and also for supplying and maintaining them in the field. If he is transferred to a civilian agency, his training and skill will be lost to the field service. If, on the other hand, he is retained in the Army because of his field responsibilities, his experience will be lost in the procurement of munitions.

The Army and Navy would no longer control government-owned arsenals and shipyards. Modification Centers also are maintained by the Army, where planes, tanks and other weapons, after their original manufacture, are changed to meet the particular needs of battle in the desert, the Arctic, the mountains or the jungle. This is "related to" the "provision of war materiel," and hence would no doubt be transferred to the civilian agency and, if so, how can military requirements just developed from battle experience be immediately translated into modified weapons required at once for delivery to troops?

Even if it were theoretically advisable to split into parts the organization of the Army as a machine both for combat and supply, such disruption would be disastrous in the midst of war. Contracts have been placed and are being administered by the Army. Contractors and subcontractors have learned to meet military requirements, specifications and procedures. A procurement organization has been established throughout the country and overseas. Relieving Army officers from active duty in time of war would ruin the morale of the experienced personnel upon which we must depend. It would mean the destructions of a going organization in favor of one untried and inexperienced. If it were physically possible to make the transfer without delay of six months or a year, there is no assurance that the new agency could do the job. The civilian agencies have been changed repeatedly both in organization and personnel. A transfer of procurement to another such agency might result in further reorganizations and new transfers.

The War Department has a remarkable record of accomplishment in military production during this war. No case is made for a change from a method which made successful the most difficult logistic operation of all times, the recent invasion of North Africa. Our troops are being supplied in quantity with weapons of high quality, superior to those of our enemies. Our allies have likewise been supplied. In spite of the lack of a munitions industry in the United States and a constantly changing control of the flow of materials by other agencies, the War Department has directed the production of $20,000,000,000 of military supplies during 1942, increasing such production from less than $1,000,000,000 in 1940. The performance of our aircraft, tanks and other weapons is praised by all who have used them in action.

The production achieved by the War Department and the greater production on the way for the present year have not been accomplished without dislocation of the peacetime economy. But it is a forlorn hope that some other agency could accomplish the task without the same dislocations. We had no munitions industry. Our facilities for aircraft production were inadequate. Only a portion of our industrial establishments was equipped with the facilities and skills that could be converted to the manufacture of weapons. A number of plants had to be erected. Others had to be enlarged and converted. Employees had to be trained and placed. Congestion and housing difficulties were unavoidable. The demands of total war reduced the supply of critical materials for use in commercial manufacture. Plants unable to manufacture military items were, therefore, often in distress. These pains are inherent in a transfer from a civilian to a war economy. The Armed Services have done everything reasonably possible to minimize the necessary dislocations. They have endeavored to use all industrial plants which can be used. Thousands of small businesses have been brought into the program. Subcontracting has been insisted upon. Every attempt is made to place contracts and facilities where possible in areas of sufficient labor supply. The War Department has also used the large mass production industries which existed in America and were usable for our task. Any civilian agency, desirous of winning the war, would of necessity do the same thing.

II.

I desire to comment on some other phases of the bill. Section 6 (c) creates an Office of Scientific and Technical Mobilization. By Section 8 (c) the Director of War Mobilization is authorized and directed, through this office, to review all proposals for development of improved processes, products and materials or for other scientific research and development, including developments of models and pilot plants, and to promote proposals deemed in aid of war mobilization through the establishment of research facilities and pilot plants. He is given access to all production facilities and all information bearing on processes, products, materials or other factors of production.

Research with respect to weapons and their development has always been the function of the armed services. They are practically alone in such activities in time of peace. During the war the services of civilians have been mobilized to aid the Army and Navy under organizations heretofore created. The Army and Navy must continue to be responsible for military research and development as part of the flow of munitions to the troops. Much of this development is of a highly secret nature. All of it has a direct bearing upon military strategy and tactics and is an inseparable part thereof. Control of such development and research by an independent civilian agency reviewing all proposals and promoting only those which the agency approves (Army and Navy Appropriations having been transferred to the Office of War Mobilization) would disrupt the military organization as much as the transfer of other phases of procurement. Personnel would be shifted and forced into new activities. Men who for reasons of competent administration and control should be on the active list of the armed services would be forced into inactive status.

III.

Section 6 (b) of the bill gives to the Office of Manpower Supply, among other things, the power to allocate manpower as between combat and other essential needs. This apparently would give to the civilian agency the power to determine the size of the armed forces and the qualifications of the men to be inducted into service. The War Department could not be held responsible for its task of defeating the enemy if it is intended that such control be given to a separate and independent agency.

In summary, under this bill, if enacted, nonmilitary control will be substituted for military control over the procurement of the basic weapons with which the war must be waged. The modification and adaptation of these weapons in accordance with the lessons of field experience, and their replacement, will be put into nonmilitary hands. Nonmilitary judgment will supersede military judgment as to the most profitable aims and ends of research and development in regard to current armament. Vital technological and military secrets will become subject to exposure to civilian personnel not under military control. A civil agency, instead of the Staffs, will determine the optimum size of the armed forces, the times and rates of their mobilization and availability for use, and the nature and qualifications of their personnel. Taken together, the result of these several provisions of the bill would be that strategy and the control of strategic decisions would in effect be transferred from the military establishments.

In conclusion, I state that the nation's task at this time is to make every aspect of our effort contribute to winning the war. Success in arms is the first condition of the completion of that task. Every step and every device that is proposed must, for the duration of the war, be evaluated in terms of its value as a weapon for winning success in arms. The primary responsibility for defeating the enemy rests upon the military establishments. They should not be deprived of the necessary tools therefore. These tools are men and material. Assurance of the necessary tools for the military establishments must be the first consideration in judging any proposal,—not in the interest of the armed forces, but in the paramount national interest.

S.607 will not, in my opinion, further the paramount national interest, but will do irreparable injury to it.

Inasmuch as the Committee has requested that this report be expedited, the Bureau of the Budget has authorized its submission without a determination by the Bureau as to whether it conforms to the program of the President.

Sincerely yours,

(s) HENRY L. STIMSON
Secretary of War

Appendix G

Stimson-Knox Agreement on Organization and Functions of the Production
Executive Committee of the WPB

(1) The Production Executive Committee of the War Production Board consists of the following:

General Brehon B. Somervell
Admiral S. M. Robinson
General Oliver P. Echols
Admiral R. A. Davison
Admiral Howard L. Vickery
Mr. Ferdinand Eberstadt
Mr. C. E. Wilson, Chairman

The Chairman, acting upon the advice and with the assistance of this Committee, shall determine whether the war production program, as scheduled by the services, is within the capacity of the country to produce it. If it shall be determined that the capacity of the country is insufficient to fulfill the war production program or any part of it, the Chairman shall so advise, either directly or through the respective services, the Joint Chiefs of Staff of such fact and it shall become the duty of the Joint Chiefs of Staff to take such steps as shall be necessary to bring such program within the limits of the capacity of the country. In any such determination of capacity, there will be co-ordination with the Controlled Materials Plan.

(2) Mr. Wilson as Chairman of the Production Executive Committee and with the advice and assistance of such Committee shall be charged with the particular duty of investigating and supervising, through the supply and procurement branches of the armed services and the Maritime Commission, the programs for the production of radar equipment and escort vessels to the end that the production of these items shall be increased and expedited.

(3) There shall also be constituted an aircraft production board, of which Mr. C. E. Wilson will also act as Chairman. The other members will be General Knudsen, General Echols, Admiral Davison and T. P. Wright, Mr. Wright to act as recorder. As Chairman of this Committee, Mr. Wilson will have the duty of giving general direction, through the respective supply branches of the armed forces, to the aircraft production program of the armed forces.

(4) The foregoing constitutes the general objectives and authority of the Production Executive Committee and the aircraft production board. In order to clarify further the position of these agencies with relation to the functions of the respective supply services, it is understood:

(a) That Mr. Wilson shall have authority to inquire into any feature of the war production program, including its scheduling and may consult freely on production matters (1) with the heads of the armed services or any of their various subordinates who are charged with the preparation and maintenance of the program or any parts thereof, and (2) with any supplier or group of suppliers.

(b) That Mr. Wilson shall issue his directions through and by means of the respective supply services. Responsibility for the quality and quantity of weapons or munitions remains with the armed services, within the limits of the capacity of the country to produce.

(Signed) HENRY L. STIMSON

(Signed) FRANK KNOX

Appendix H

Statement by Under Secretary Robert P. Patterson on Responsibility for Military Procurement Before the Senate Special Committee Investigating the National Defense Program, 77th Congress, 2d Session, 16 December 1942

What I have said raises a second point—the control of production of weapons by the armed forces. There has been confusion in the minds of many people on this subject. It is incorrectly assumed that the armed forces are not now engaged in the procurement of weapons and that they want to take this function away from other agencies. There is also the absurd belief on the part of some that the armed forces desire to control and regiment the American economy. How that story started I do not know.

Since the American Revolution, the Army and the Navy have been in charge of production of their weapons. The War Production Board is mobilizing the resources, facilities and materials (raw and semi-finished) necessary to such production and necessary also to civilian activities. It likewise allocates and controls the flow of materials so as to resolve conflicting demands of the Army, Navy, Maritime Commission, and other agencies and to adjust the program to available resources. A similar arrangement worked well in the last war. The Army and Navy have now experienced two years of successful operation under the arrangement. I believe in its continuance. We are not seeking new fields of endeavor.

The functions of the War Department and Navy Department on production of weapons cover the entire range of production and distribution. They include strategic and tactical planning, experiment, design, selection of types to be produced, obtaining funds from Congress, procurement (partly by orders to Government plants and partly by contracts to private industry), scheduling follow-up of production inspection, delivery, provision of spare parts, distribution, and field maintenance. I could add to that, and finally, salvage. These are phases in a continuous operation from drafting board to scrap pile. Changes dictated by demands from the fighting forces are constantly made. Programs are readjusted while manufacture is in process. Research and preparation of specifications overlap production and change the course of production. Military testing and inspection occur simultaneously with manufacture. Battle experience must reach the production line with minimum delay.

Tactical developments in the Aleutians created an urgent necessity for a change in bomb fuses. The fuses, while satisfactory for high altitude or dive bombing, were not adapted to the new type of bombing required. An ordnance officer was flown to the Aleutians and participated in bombing attacks. He flew back to Picatinny Arsenal and designed a new fuse for this particular requirement. He supervised production-line changes, flew back with the first units produced, and there supervised the trials and the instruction of others in the use of fuses in battle. This is one instance out of a great many, which indicates that production of weapons is not a process that can be broken up into separate compartments for separate control by separate agencies.

For maximum effectiveness the stages of production must be under direction of the same agency as to each type of weapon. Experience has shown that where successive stages or production are under control of separate agencies the results are not the best. It does not work well to place procurement (making of contracts) in another agency. The operation is a single continuous one. Duality of control will not work.

The officers of the armed forces are the persons best fitted by experience to direct the production of weapons. They have spent years in turning out rifles, artillery, cruisers, and so forth. They know by direct contact with troops on the fighting fronts what weapons are needed by the troops. They have the background to decide where manufacture can best be carried on, whether in Army arsenals, Navy shipyards, or private industrial plants. They have been engaged for years in surveying industrial plants and in instructing them in military production needed in the event of war. They know what steps must be taken to make sure that the weapons when manufactured will function as intended. They know from experience that the lives of American soldiers depend upon the accuracy of a rifle and the correct timing of a shell.

Many civilians with technical skills and industrial backgrounds have been taken into the armed services to assist the Regular officers in solving the many problems presented. But it would have been impossible to create and continue in efficient action our Army without the framework of Regular Army officers especially trained in the production

of weapons. No civilian agency of the Government has had experience in meeting the infinite variety of problems involved in production of weapons. No man who was not trained through years for the work could go to Libya, as did an ordnance officer, and participate in battle with our tanks being used by the British against Rommel. As a result of his experience, he not only changed the system for supply and maintenance of armored forces, but also went to work designing and supervising production of our newer tanks.

On the other hand, control of materials is properly placed in a civilian agency, the War Production Board. In the first place, the officers of the armed services are not as well qualified to handle production and distribution of steel, copper, and other materials as men from these industries. Their experience in time of peace, while ample in directing production of weapons, does not extend to directing production of materials. In peace the Army and Navy requirements for steel and copper are so modest that the supply of such requirements raises no difficulty. In the second place, the Army and Navy demands for materials such as copper, steel, and aluminum, while of great importance, are not the sole demands for these materials. The railroads, the mining industry, the machine-tool industry, and other industrial activities essential to the war effort also need these materials. Control of the supply of these materials is properly placed under a civilian agency.

The function of the civilian agencies who are called in to aid the Army and Navy in time of war, as I see it, is to provide an increased supply of critical materials, the facilities for the production of semi-finished products required for military end-items, the administrative control of the flow of materials and the elimination of these materials for nonessential purposes. They can be of assistance to the services in other ways as well. They are also charged with the duty of continuing civilian supply necessary to support the war effort. Among the duties of such agencies are priority and price control, allocation of facilities, control of raw materials and other commodities, control of labor supply, power and fuel, transportation, finance, and foreign trade.

There is no thought that the military departments should control American economy. It is essential merely that the armed forces procure munitions which they alone are able to procure, while civilian agencies direct the economy of the country to assist and make possible such procurement.

Appendix I

The Duties of the Army Service Forces

I. ARMY-WIDE TECHNICAL SUPERVISION OVER CERTAIN ACTIVITIES

1. Supply procedures (requisitioning, distribution stock control, disposition)
2. Storage
3. Maintenance and repair
4. Construction
5. Acquisition and disposal of real estate
6. Port operations
7. Railway operations
8. Medical care and hospitalization
9. Army physical standards
10. Military Police activities
11. Special Service activities
12. Chaplain activities
13. Legal activities
14. AG activities
15. Financial activities
16. Signal communications
17. Photography and cryptography
18. Signal security
19. Food preparation
20. Laundry operations

II. PARTICIPATION IN PREPARATION OF WAR PLANS

(With respect to activities over which ASF possesses Army-wide technical supervision as listed under I)

III. PERFORMANCE OF SERVICES FOR THE ARMY

A. Supply Services
1. Procures all supplies for the Army (except those peculiar to the AAF)
2. Storage in the zone of interior
3. Issues to troops in the zone of interior and to overseas theaters

B. General Services
1. Hospital service

251863 O—54——31

   2. Transportation service (for supplies and personnel)
   3. Construction service
   4. Communications service
   5. Photographic service

C. Personnel Services
   1. Operation of induction stations and reception centers
   2. Operation of reception stations
   3. Operation of Ground and Service Forces redistribution stations
   4. Operation of separation centers
   5. Orientation and information programs
   6. Supply of athletic and recreational supplies and equipment
   7. Supply of Army Exchange merchandise
   8. Operates disciplinary barracks and rehabilitation centers

D. Administrative Services
   1. Maintains accounting records for the War Department
   2. Pays War Department bills in the U. S.
   3. Pays family allowances and allotments to beneficiaries
   4. Reviews courts martial cases and records
   5. Operates the Army Postal Service
   6. Publishes Army documents
   7. Maintains central personnel records
   8. Operation of PW camps
   9. Casualty records and notifications
  10. Legal service for War Department
  11. Security of production installations
  12. Criminal investigations of military personnel
  13. Military policing in cities and on trains
  14. Maintains War Department records

E. Management of Stations Used for Ground Force Training
   1. Buildings, roads and utilities (operation and maintenance)
   2. Supply warehouses and dumps
   3. Maintenance shops
   4. Hospitals and dispensaries
   5. Internal transportation
   6. Security
   7. Communication centers
   8. PX
   9. Theaters
  10. Service clubs
  11. Field houses
  12. Post offices
  13. Religious services

14. Disbursing offices
15. Laundries
16. Stockades
17. Photographic laboratories
18. Film exchanges
19. Civilian housing

IV. TRAINING OF SERVICE TROOPS AND ORGANIZATION OF SERVICE UNITS

1. Organization and training of ASF units for theater communications zones (ASF's or SOS's)
2. Training of fillers for Ground and Air Force service units
3. Training of specialists for Ground and Air Force service units
4. Training and providing replacements for all types of service units
5. Special training activities: Military Government, Students, Army Specialized Training Program

Glossary

AAF	Army Air Forces
ABC	American-British Conversations
ACofS	Assistant Chief of Staff
Adm	Administrative, administration, Admiral
Adm O	Administrative Order
AEF	American Expeditionary Forces (1917–18)
AG	Adjutant General
AGF	Army Ground Forces
AGWAR	Adjutant General, War Department
ANEPA	Army-Navy Electronics Production Agency
ANMB	Army and Navy Munitions Board
Appen	Appendix
AR	Army Regulations
ARGONAUT	International conference held at Malta and Yalta, 30 January–9 February 1945
ASF	Army Service Forces
Asst	Assistant
ASW	Assistant Secretary of War
Atchd	Attached
Bd	Board
BOLERO	The build-up of troops and supplies in the United Kingdom in preparation for a cross-Channel attack.
BPR	Bureau of Public Relations, War Department
Br	Branch
Bull	Bulletin
CBI	China, Burma, and India
CCS	Combined Chiefs of Staff
CD	Control Division, Army Service Forces
CG	Commanding General
Chm	Chairman
CIC	Counter Intelligence Corps
CINC	Commander in Chief
Cir	Circular
CMP	Controlled Materials Plan
CO	Commanding Officer
CofS	Chief of Staff
Com	Committee
Comd	Command

Comdr	Commander
Conf	Conference
Cong	Congress
Contl	Control
Corresp	Correspondence
COS	British Chiefs of Staff
CPRB	Combined Production and Resources Board
DAD	Defense Aid Division
DCofS	Deputy Chief of Staff
Dept	Department
Dir	Director, directive
Div	Division
Doc	Document, documentary
DRB	Departmental Records Branch, The Adjutant General's Office
Env	Envelope
EO	Executive Order
Equip	Equipment
ETO	European Theater of Operations
EUREKA	International conference at Tehran, 28–30 November 1943
FEA	Foreign Economic Administration
G–1	Personnel Section of divisional or higher headquarters
G–2	Military Intelligence Section
G–3	Operations Section
G–4	Supply Section
GAO	General Accounting Office
GO	General Orders
GOGO	Government-owned, government-operated
GOPO	Government-owned, privately operated
GS	General Staff
HB	Historical Branch
Hist	Historical
Hosp	Hospital
Hq	Headquarters
H&R	Holding and reconsignment
H.R.	House of Representatives, U.S. Congress
HUSKY	Allied invasion of Sicily in July 1943
ICC	Interstate Commerce Commission
Ind	Indorsement
Info	Information
Interv	Interview
Intn	International
JAC	Joint Administrative Committee

JAG	Judge Advocate General
JB	Joint Board (Army and Navy)
JCS	Joint Chiefs of Staff
JLC	Joint Logistics Committee
JLPC	Joint Logistics Plans Committee
JPC	Joint Planning Committee
JPS	Joint Staff Planners
LL	Lend-Lease
MAB	Munitions Assignments Board
MAC(G)	Munitions Assignments Committee (Ground)
Maint	Maintenance
Man	Manual
MANHATTAN DISTRICT	Atomic bomb project
MBW	Munitions Assignments Board, Washington
MDW	Military District of Washington
Med	Medical
Min	Minutes
MP	Military Police
MPD	Military Personnel Division
MS	Manuscript
Mtg	Meeting
NAM	National Association of Manufacturers
NDAC	Advisory Commission to the Council of National Defense
NDRC	National Defense Research Committee
NYPE	New York Port of Embarkation
OCD	Office of Civilian Defense
OCMH	Office of the Chief of Military History
OCofS	Office of the Chief of Staff
OCT	Office of the Chief of Transportation
OCTAGON	International conference at Quebec, 12–16 September 1944
ODCofS	Office of the Deputy Chief of Staff
ODT	Office of Defense Transportation
Off	Officer
OLLA	Office of Lend-Lease Administration
OPA	Office of Price Administration
OPD	Operations Division, War Department General Staff
OPM	Office of Production Management
Opn	Operation
OQMG	Office of The Quartermaster General
Org	Organization, organizational
OSRD	Office of Scientific Research and Development
OUSW	Office of the Under Secretary of War

OVERLORD	Plan for the invasion of northwest Europe in the spring of 1944
OWMR	Office of War Mobilization and Reconversion
Pam	Pamphlet
Pers	Personnel
PRP	Production Requirements Plan
Pub	Publication
PW	Prisoner of War
QUADRANT	International conference at Quebec, 14–24 August 1943
Rad	Radio, radiogram
RAINBOW	Name for various prewar plans of military action to meet situations created by Axis aggression
Rec	Record
Reorg	Reorganization
Rep	Repair
Ret	Retired
RFC	Reconstruction Finance Corporation
ROTC	Reserve Officers' Training Corps
Rpt	Report
SAS	Supply Arms and Services
Sec	Section
Sess	Session
SEXTANT	International conference at Cairo, 22–26 November and 3–7 December 1943
SG	Surgeon General
Shipmt	Shipment
SigC	Signal Corps
SN	Secretary of the Navy
SO	Special Orders
SOS	Services of Supply
SPAB	Supply Priorities and Allocation Board
Spec	Special
Sta	Station
Stat	Statistics, statistical
Sup	Supply
Sv	Service
SW	Secretary of War
SWPA	Southwest Pacific Area
TAG	The Adjutant General
Tech	Technical
Tel	Telephone
TERMINAL	International conference near Potsdam, 16–26 July 1945

TM	Technical Manual
Tng	Training
T of Opns	Theater of Operations
TORCH	Allied invasion of North and Northwest Africa, November 1942
Trans	Transportation
Trf	Transfer
TRIDENT	International conference at Washington, 12–25 May 1943
USAFICPA	United States Army Forces in the Central Pacific Area
USASOS	United States Army Services of Supply
USN	Under Secretary of the Navy
USSR	Union of Soviet Socialist Republics
USW	Under Secretary of War
Vice CNO	Vice Chief of Naval Operations
WAC	Women's Army Corps
Wash	Washington
WD	War Department
WDGS	War Department General Staff
WMC	War Manpower Commission
WPA	Works Progress Administration
WPB	War Production Board
WPD	War Plans Division, War Department General Staff
WSA	War Shipping Administration

Bibliographical Note

The narrative in this volume has been prepared primarily upon the basis of personal observations and recorded interviews. The author participated in the initial planning which preceded the creation of the Army Service Forces on 9 March 1942, and served in the Control Division, Headquarters, Army Service Forces from 5 July 1942 until the start of his terminal leave on 15 January 1946. During this period, the author had in mind that some day he would prepare a record of the organizational experience of the Army Service Forces, and collected numerous papers bearing on this subject during the course of his regular duties. Interview notes and other papers were accumulated, all of which were collected in an historical file of the Army Service Forces deposited with the Office of the Chief of Military History, Department of the Army.

General Somervell kept intact a personal file of correspondence and memoranda prepared during the course of service as Commanding General, Army Service Forces. These personal files, amounting to about five file cabinets, were turned over to The Adjutant General of the Army in January 1946 when General Somervell went on terminal leave. These files have been kept intact and have been consulted freely by the author in the course of preparing this narrative. Considerable file material from the Office of the Secretary of War, the Office of the Under Secretary of War, and from the Chief of Staff has been used. This material has been deposited with the Departmental Records Branch, Adjutant General's Office, Department of the Army.

Each of the major staff divisions in Headquarters, Army Service Forces, was required to prepare a narrative history of its activities immediately after the conclusion of hostilities in August 1945. These narratives, along with an account of the organizational history of the Army Service Forces as a whole, prepared by the author, were deposited with the Office of the Chief of Military History, Department of the Army, and have been freely consulted in the course of preparation of the present volume.

The Army Service Forces prepared a large number of documents for internal use which are extremely helpful to anyone inquiring into the organization of the agency. The ASF had an elaborate monthly statistical reporting system which eventually numbered some twenty different sections. The most useful report for the general student is the Monthly Analysis Report which was a summary of all the individual reports and called attention to the major developments in the work of the command. In addition, beginning in July 1942 and terminating in July 1945, the ASF held semiannual service command conferences, the minutes of which were reproduced in mimeograph form. These minutes contain papers prepared by leading officers of the command as well as floor discussions of major administrative problems. General Somervell also held biweekly staff conferences of headquarters personnel, the minutes of which were reproduced in similar form and then distributed to staff directors and chiefs of technical services. From time to time also, reports were prepared such as documents on the Canol project, the Pentagon, and the Inter-American Highway. These documents have been preserved in the historical file of the Army Service Forces.

An annual report of the work of the Army Service Forces was prepared for each fiscal year from 1942 to 1945. In both 1944 and 1945, these were released in summary form and given out for general distribution. A longer and more detailed printed copy was deposited in the Pentagon Library and also in about one hundred depository libraries throughout the United States. These reports contain extensive information about the Army Service Forces and are available to any person who might wish to consult them.

Much of the history of the Army Service Forces in World War II will of necessity appear in other volumes in this series. The author has consulted many volumes, published and in manuscript form, prepared in the Office of the Chief of Military History. Among the volumes and manuscripts most frequently consulted were the following:

Richard M. Leighton and Robert W. Coakley, Logistics of Global Warfare, 1941–1943

R. Elberton Smith, Army Procurement and Economic Mobilization

Jonathan Grossman, Industrial Manpower Problems and Policies of the War Department

Charles F. Romanus and Riley Sunderland, *Stilwell's Mission to China*

Maurice Matloff and Edwin M. Snell, *Strategic Planning for Coalition Warfare: 1941–1942*

Chester A. Wardlow, *The Transportation Corps: Responsibilities, Organization, and Operations*

Chester A. Wardlow, The Transportation Corps: Movements, Training, and Supply

Joseph Bykofsky and Harold Larson, The Transportation Corps: Activities in the Oversea Commands

Erna Risch, *The Quartermaster Corps: Organization, Supply, and Services,* Vol. I

Chester L. Kieffer and Erna Risch, The Quartermaster Corps: Organization, Supply and Services, Vol. II

Constance McL. Green, Harry C. Thomson, and Peter Roots, *The Ordnance Department: Organization and Research and Development*

Clarence McK. Smith, Hospitalization and Evacuation: ZI

Dulany Terrett, The Signal Corps: The Test to Mid-1943

Dulany Terrett, The Signal Corps: Outcome Through 1945

Blanche B. Armfield, The Medical Department: Organization and Administration

Blanche D. Coll and Herbert H. Rosenthal, Corps of Engineers: Troops and Supply

Jesse A. Remington, Blanche D. Coll, and Lenure Fine, Corps of Engineers: ZI Construction

Troyer Anderson, Introduction to the History of the Under Secretary of War's Office, MS, OCMH

While most of the material has been derived from War Department sources, the author has also utilized some of the more important records of the War Shipping Board (Lewis Douglas files) and of the War Production Board (monographs and reports).

UNITED STATES ARMY IN WORLD WAR II

The multivolume series, UNITED STATES ARMY IN WORLD WAR II, consists of a number of subseries which are tentatively planned as follows: The War Department, The Army Air Forces, The Army Ground Forces, The Army Service Forces, The Defense of the Western Hemisphere, The War in the Pacific, The European Theater of Operations, The War in the Mediterranean, The Middle East Theater, the China-Burma-India Theater, Civil Affairs, The Technical Services, Special Studies, and Pictorial Record.

The following volumes have been published or are in press: *

The War Department
  Chief of Staff: Prewar Plans and Preparations
  Washington Command Post: The Operations Division
  Strategic Planning for Coalition Warfare: 1941–1942
The Army Ground Forces
  The Organization of Ground Combat Troops
  The Procurement and Training of Ground Combat Troops
The Army Service Forces
  The Organization and Role of the Army Service Forces
The War in the Pacific
  Okinawa: The Last Battle
  Guadalcanal: The First Offensive
  The Approach to the Philippines
  The Fall of the Philippines
  Leyte: Return to the Philippines
The European Theater of Operations
  The Lorraine Campaign
  Cross-Channel Attack
  Logistical Support of the Armies (Volume I)
  The Supreme Command
The Middle East Theater
  The Persian Corridor and Aid to Russia
The China-Burma-India Theater
  Stilwell's Mission to China
The Technical Services
  Transportation Corps: Responsibilities, Organization, and Operations
  The Quartermaster Corps: Organization, Supply, and Services, Volume I
  The Ordnance Department: Organization and Research and Development
Special Studies
  Three Battles: Arnaville, Altuzzo, and Schmidt
  The Women's Army Corps
Pictorial Record
  The War Against Germany and Italy: Mediterranean and Adjacent Areas
  The War Against Germany: Europe and Adjacent Areas
  The War Against Japan

---

* The volumes on the Army Air Forces are not included in this list.

Index